HOMERIC GREEK

HOMER, ideal bust

National Museum, Naples

καὶ γάρ κ᾽ εἰς ἐνιαυτὸν ἐγὼ παρὰ σοί γ᾽ ἀνεχοίμην. — δ, 595.

For I would fain tarry with thee throughout the year.—Od. 4, 595.

HOMERIC GREEK

A BOOK FOR BEGINNERS

by Clyde Pharr

Revised by John Wright

To love Homer, as Steele said about loving
a fair lady of quality, "is a liberal education."
—Andrew Lang

UNIVERSITY OF OKLAHOMA PRESS : NORMAN

By John Wright

The Play of Antichrist (Rome, 1968)
Dancing in Chains: The Stylistic Unity of the Comoedia Palliafa (Rome, 1974)
The Life of Cola di Rieuzo (Rome, 1975)
(editor) *Essays on the Iliad* (Bloomington, Ind., 1978)
(editor) *Plautus: Curculio* (Chico, Calif., 1981)
(revised edition, with Clyde Pharr) *Homeric Greek: A Book for Beginners* (Norman, 1985)

Library of Congress Catalog Card Number: 84–40698

ISBN: 0–8061–1937–3

7   8   9   10   11   12   13   14   15   16   17   18   19

CONTENTS

vii

CONTENTS

ix

SUGGESTIONS TO INEXPERIENCED TEACHERS

The wise teacher knows what to omit. Try once making all students learn thoroughly *one* form for each declension and conjugation, using the adjective κᾱλός, ή, όν, as a model for the first two declensions, ἄναξ for the third, and as λύω the model verb. Hold them strictly to these and use all other forms for reference, teaching them so far as practicable, without overloading, as they occur in reading. Lay special emphasis on infinitives and participles, including their meanings, and the declension of the latter. The full grammar of Homeric Greek in this book is given primarily for reference. Reserve a lot of it for second year work and see how much better progress your students make. Have the students recite their model forms, κᾱλός, ή, όν, ἄναξ, λύω, a great deal in concert. At the beginning of each lesson send everybody to the board. The teacher may underline errors as they are made, may make students change places and mark each other's work, or may require them to be seated and go over two or three typical exercises, calling on the class to indicate from their seats the various mistakes. Vary the method. When marking errors in written work that has been handed in, never write out the corrections. Underline the errors and require each student to correct his own mistakes. If he must have help, remember that hints are usually more valuable than direct information. Ordinarily spend not less than one third of the time of each recitation on the lesson following. Require the students to look over the vocabulary of the advance lesson, or even to memorize it before coming to class. Then look over with them in class the forms for the next lesson. After that, have them translate at sight the Greek sentences, giving them hints when necessary, particularly reminding them of forms which have not yet been studied, but do not translate for them. They will enjoy this, and it will greatly lighten their burden of preparation. Vary the work continually, giving drills in different ways, occasionally talking informally on Homeric and Greek ideas of various kinds, and particularly giving them some insight into the historical and cultural background of the Homeric poems. A theme of some length from each student at the end of the year often arouses considerable enthusiasm. A great variety of topics for themes can be found in Jebb's *Introduction to Homer*, Ginn & Co. For drill on vocabularies use Owen and Goodspeed's *Homeric Vocabularies*, University of Chicago Press. Cheap texts of the first book of the *Iliad*, for use in recitation and examinations, are published by Longmans, Green & Co., Macmillan, and several others.

PREFACE TO THE REVISED EDITION

Producing Greek books these days is an extraordinarily difficult and expensive operation. Therefore, when I was given the opportunity by the University of Oklahoma Press to revise the late Clyde Pharr's *Homeric Greek*—a book I have used with great pleasure in my classes for many years now—I determined to handle the job with as light a hand as possible. *Pietas* was in part the reason, but *pietas* joined by harsh economic necessity.

I have tried to do two things. First, in those lessons where it seemed necessary, I have added in square brackets short explanations of traditional grammatical terminology (no explanations were needed in previous editions, when the author could assume that anyone who planned to study Greek had already been exposed to Latin). Second, where possible, I have shortened Pharr's notes to the first book of the *Iliad*, removing only the material that, in my experience, tended to obscure the essential grammatical information contained in the notes. No other changes have been made in the format or contents of the book.

I support without reservation Pharr's enthusiastic arguments for the Homeric method of introducing students to ancient Greek. *Homeric Greek* has always been an excellent book; I only hope that my revisions have made it even more useful.

John Wright

Evanston, Illinois

PREFACE TO THE NEW EDITION

IT IS WITH unusual pleasure and satisfaction that I greet the appearance of this new edition of *Homeric Greek*. At a time when general publishers for the most part are curtailing and even abandoning the publication of Greek books and especially of Greek language books, on the ground that they are not sufficiently profitable financially, the University of Oklahoma Press shows its unshaken belief in the fundamental and permanent values inherent in Hellenic civilization and in their significance for our own troubled times, for the present as well as for the future.

In 1914, in another period of world travail and dismay, I first proposed this new approach to the study of Greek and prepared mimeographed lessons for the purpose. In 1920 appeared the first printed edition of *Homeric Greek,* which has now been taught for nearly forty years with marked success and enthusiasm in many of our leading schools, colleges, and universities, to many of the leading classical scholars of the English speaking world. My experience with it in the classroom has been so encouraging and decisive that I have found beginning Greek the most stimulating course in my teaching experience. I have been amply rewarded by the fact that the classes were much larger and the percentage of students continuing the study of Greek much greater than had ever been the case under the old system. I take this opportunity to express the profound gratitude of a host of classical scholars to the Uni-

versity of Oklahoma Press for making possible the success-
ful continuation of this program.

Clyde Pharr

Austin, Texas
September 21, 1959

PREFACE

This book, now offered to the public, is the fruit of seven years of experimentation and of much counsel with those interested in the plan which it embodies.

It has already gone through four mimeographed editions, and has been used for several years: in Ohio Wesleyan University, in Oberlin College, and in Southwestern Presbyterian University. In all these cases it has had marked success in creating and sustaining interest in beginning Greek, where the crux of the whole problem of the future of Hellenic studies lies.

The reasons which have convinced the author of the necessity for basing the work of beginners on Homeric instead of on Attic Greek will be found in a paper, entitled "A Year — or more — of Greek," published in the *Classical Journal* for February, 1918, and in a second paper, "Homer and the Study of Greek," which is printed in this book, following the table of contents. To all who may be interested in the subject, from the standpoint of humanistic studies, the author would heartily commend the reading of Andrew Lang's delightful little essay, "Homer and the Study of Greek," published in his collection of *Essays in Little*.

It is hardly to be hoped that a book of this kind, which seeks to establish a new path to our common goal, will be so free from minor errors as would one along the old established lines. Hence the author will be profoundly grateful to those who will be generous enough to make suggestions looking toward the betterment of the work as well as to those who will be kind enough to point out any errors. Naturally, in a work of this nature, there is the constantly recurring problem of how to reconcile most successfully effective pedagogy and scientific accuracy of statement.

The book does not pretend to be a text where the advanced Homeric scholar will find catalogued every stray Homeric form, or supposedly Homeric form, but its first object is to teach beginners to read Greek intelligently and with pleasure.

It is not intended that the ordinary student shall master all the grammar found in this text : much of it is for reference only. But certainly every teacher should have at least this much Homeric grammar thoroughly at command and be overflowing with it, not, however, to the extent of attempting to teach all of it. The prime object of first year work, as so admirably stated by Prof. Gilder-sleeve, is "a maximum of forms, a minimum of syntax, and early acquaintance with Greek in the mass." To gain this object, it is necessary to read, *read*, READ Greek.

In the paradigms and vocabularies, both simple and compound forms of verbs are used to supplement each other, and a free use of analogy is employed, as is commonly done in books of this kind. In the verbal forms, the augment is regularly supplied when missing.

Those opposed to the employment of prose sentences in Homeric language will find it easy to omit these ; but the author is convinced that a better grasp of Homeric forms can be secured by their use.

After this book is completed successfully, any one of several roads is open for a continuation of the Greek course :

(1) Probably the most satisfactory method is to continue for some time with Homer, reading copious extracts from the Iliad and Odyssey. The student is now well prepared to handle successfully the standard school editions of these.

(2) The passage from Homer to the Attic Drama is an easy one, and is the most satisfactory introduction to the Attic dialect. This is the course which the author would strongly recommend, as most likely to be of the greatest value and as having probably the strongest appeal to the most students. Euripides furnishes the easiest reading, and several of his plays have been published in convenient form with vocabularies (Longmans, Green & Co.), and with both vocabularies and notes (Macmillan & Co.). This could be followed by any one of several possibilities, some more drama, Plato, or the New Testament.

(3) Some Herodotus could now be read with not much difficulty, and his work would admirably supplement the Homeric stories.

(4) It is quite possible to read some Plato now, using a good edition of one of the dialogues, with vocabulary and notes, such as that of Seymour and Dyer.

(5) Many will find a strong appeal in the Lyric Poets, which are very easy after a fair amount of Homer and contain some of the choicest gems in all Greek literature.

(6) Some may want to read Hesiod, who is the easiest of all authors after Homer. His importance has not always been recognized, and he has been entirely too much neglected in our colleges.

(7) The New Testament could be studied to good advantage after Homer, and is recommended to those intending to enter the ministry.

(8) Those who are wedded to Xenophon, who teach him with success, and who feel that he *must* come early in the course, will find Homer a much better preparation for Xenophon than Xenophon is for Homer. There are a number of good school editions, and students can now read rapidly considerable quantities of the *Anabasis*, or of any of the other works of Xenophon.

Other things being equal, the teacher should of course select the author in which he has the greatest interest and for which he has the most enthusiasm. He will find the work not only much easier, but more successful as well.

To all who have assisted, directly or indirectly, in the production of the present book, the author would here express his sincerest appreciation and gratitude. Lack of space prevents giving a complete list of names, but the author feels that special mention is due to Prof. Francis G. Allinson of Brown University, for generously reading the whole of the manuscript and for making many helpful suggestions; to Prof. Samuel E. Bassett of the University of Vermont, and to Prof. Edward Fitch of Hamilton College, who also went over the manuscript and made many valuable criticisms; to Prof. Walter Petersen of Bethany College, whose help on a number of grammatical problems has been invaluable; to Miss Mabel

Drennan of the Swanton, Ohio, High School, for making the whole of the two general vocabularies; to Miss Shirley Smith and to Mr. Charles J. Adameç, graduate students at Yale, for checking up the general vocabularies; to Mr. W. J. Millard, student at Southwestern Presbyterian University, for verifying the Biblical quotations; to Prof. Wilmot Haines Thompson of Acadia University, for reading the manuscript, making a number of valuable suggestions, and for much valuable assistance in reading proof; to Prof. Leigh Alexander of Oberlin College, who has generously placed at the disposal of the author the results of two years of experience with the book in his classes, who has read all the proof and has saved the book from a number of errors; to the Boston Museum of Fine Arts, for the loan of some unusually fine photographs for illustrations; to D. C. Heath & Co., for the use of illustrations from Webster's *Ancient History*, one of their texts; to Prof. Frank E. Robbins of the University of Michigan, and to the *Classical Journal*, for permission to use Prof. Robbins's valuable statistics on Greek verb forms, which appeared in the *Classical Journal*, 15, 2; to Dr. Alice Braunlich of the Davenport High School, to Prof. G. B. Waldrop of the Westminster School, and to Dr. D. W. Abercrombie, recently of Worcester Academy, for help in reading the proof; and to the J. S. Cushing Company (The Norwood Press) for their very careful and painstaking typographical work.

If this book will contribute to the value and interest of the study of beginning Greek, the author will feel that his seven years of work upon it have not been spent in vain. The time has come when lovers of the humanities everywhere must join hands in the promotion of the common cause. If anything seems to be of mutual advantage, we must first test it carefully and then hold fast to it if we find it good. Then, to all teachers of Greek and every true friend of humanistic studies and of culture in its best sense, the author would say in conclusion:

> "Vive, vale. Si quid novisti rectius istis,
> Candidus imperti; si non, his utere mecum."

HOMER AND THE STUDY OF GREEK

IN an article entitled "A Year — or more — of Greek," contributed to the February, 1918, number of the *Classical Journal,* the author sets forth a few of the more important reasons why the present system of teaching beginners in Greek should be revised to meet modern conditions. The sum and substance of the article was a plea for the abandonment of Xenophon for beginning work, something which should have been done years ago, and the substitution of Homer in his place. The paper embodied the results of several years of experimentation; and the primary reason urged for the change was based on the comparative literary value of the two authors and their appeal to beginning students. As we view the situation to-day, we are compelled to confess that in the hands of the average teacher, when applied to the average student, Xenophon and all his works are all too often found to be tedious and dreary. This leaves out of count the exceptional teacher, who has large and enthusiastic classes in the Anabasis year after year, for such teachers could make any subject fascinating. Homer on the other hand possesses those qualities which make him especially interesting, as well as of permanent value, to the majority of students who still take Greek.

In this connection the author may be permitted to quote from the article just mentioned: [1] "The reasons which make Homer so desirable are apparent when once the question is seriously considered. His work is homogeneous in vocabulary, in literary style and idioms employed, and in metrical form; so that when students once get a fair start in him, further progress becomes easier and more accelerated. He employs all three persons, with all modes and tenses of the verb, so that all forms that are learned

---

[1] *C. J.* 13, 5.

are used enough to be kept fresh in the students' mind and do not have to be learned again when they begin anything which is in dialogue form. His vocabulary is fairly limited, enough so in fact that it does not present any special difficulty to the beginner. His sentences are short, simple, and clear-cut, having none of the involved structure which makes so much of Xenophon really too difficult for first-year work. The verse, which has been considered a bar, is an actual help, as it is quite easily learned and is a marked aid in memorizing considerable portions of Greek, which is important at this stage. Furthermore, the rules of quantity are a considerable help in simplifying and illustrating the principles of accent. As he uses only one type of verse, and that the simplest — the dactylic hexameter — the ordinary student usually becomes quite adept at reading this before the end of the first year's work.

"The prose composition for the first year's work may be based upon Homer, the students using Homeric forms and constructions, without knowing of the existence of any other kind. This may be done without the slightest fear of blunting their sense of discrimination between poetic and prose diction and style, a sense which cannot possibly be developed until they have had several years' work and have read a considerable amount of Greek in both prose and poetry. Homer is so straightforward and simple in what he has to say, with nothing obscure, mystical, or far-fetched in any way, that he is quite intelligible to the average high-school freshman; and at the same time he possesses the qualities of high literary art in such a marked degree that he appeals strongly to the oldest and most advanced members of any college class.

"Furthermore, Homer is the best possible preparation for all later Greek literature, much of which is unintelligible without a fair knowledge of him. He was to Greek literature what the Bible has been to English, and a great deal more as well. He leads us somewhere, not merely into a blind alley as does Xenophon, both with reference to later Greek literature and to much of the best in later European literature as well, where his influence has been incalculable and perhaps greater than that of any other single writer. In him are the germs of so many things. We have the narrative highly developed, the beginning of the drama, oratory, statecraft, seamanship, war, adventure, and religion — in fact, life as it was to the old Greeks in its manifold aspects.

"Then the student who has taken only a very little of beginning Greek, even if he has progressed no farther than the end of the first book of the *Iliad*, has come into vital contact with the magic and the music of the Greek language, used in one of the most beautiful, one of the most varied, and one of the most influential literary compositions of all ages; and though he may have devoted considerable labor to mining the gold, he cannot truthfully say, and probably will not want to say, that Greek for him has been a waste of time."

To begin the study of Greek with Homer, it would be necessary to substitute Homeric for Attic Greek for the work of the first year : the student would be taught Homeric forms and constructions as a basis for future work, and would devote to the study of Homer the time which is now occupied by Xenophon. It is the purpose of the present paper to develop more in detail some of the most important reasons which make such a change not only desirable but imperative if Greek is to be saved as a vital factor in our educational system.

The idea of such a plan first suggested itself to the writer several years ago, when, full of boundless enthusiasm for his subject and for all things Greek, he was attempting to teach first-year work and Xenophon, and was compelled to admit to himself that his efforts were not meeting with what might be called success. Too many good students refused to take Greek in the first place, and of those who did enlist, too many, even of the better ones, were discouraged by the unending round of grammatical forms, leading up to an author whose works are not of a nature to fire the imagination and stir the hearts in the breasts of our youth, as can be, and is, done by the great masterpieces of Hellas such as the *Iliad* and the *Odyssey*.

The writer would like to make it plain that he is not a hater of Xenophon, but that he greatly enjoyed his first year of Greek, taken in the old way, as well as his Xenophon, later. The same is probably true of most classical scholars. This goes a long way toward explaining why they are now teaching Greek and Latin instead of sociology or mechanical engineering. It would be distinctly misleading however for those who have a special taste for linguistic work and who enjoyed reading the production of such authors as Caesar and Xenophon to infer therefrom that their case is at all typical of the mass of students who take these subjects. Although the description in Andrew Lang's essay, "Homer and the Study of Greek," is probably too highly colored, the account that he gives of his own experience and that of his fellows in the study of beginning Greek and Xenophon ought to have a lesson and a warning for every one who is still a friend of the classics. He makes it quite plain that they found Xenophon anything but inspiring, and that most of them thoroughly hated him, an experience of many good students, which is too common to be ignored.

It is only fair to state that although this idea of beginning Greek with the reading of Homer is original with the writer, it is not new. This was the regular method employed by the old Romans in teaching their boys Greek, and it was highly commended by that capable and judicious old schoolmaster, Quintilian, as the best possible plan. Since that time it has been used now and then by some of the world's ablest educators and scholars. It was thus that Joseph Scaliger (de la Scala), one of the most brilliant names in the whole history of classical scholarship, taught himself Greek at Paris; and many more of the great scholars of the past learned their Greek through Homer. It was tried also by Herbart, who began a series of experiments in Switzerland, in 1797, where he employed this method with marked success in private tutoring. Later he continued his experiments on a larger scale in the teachers' training college at Koenigsberg, with such good results that he was thoroughly convinced that this was the only suitable method of teaching beginning Greek. At his suggestion it was tried by Dissen, by Ferdinand Ranke, and by Hummel, all of whom were hearty in its praise; and, most important of all, by Ahrens, at Hanover, where it was used for thirty years (1850–1881), with great success, but was finally abandoned because of the lack of suitable text books and because of the opposition of other Gymnasia which refused to adopt such a revolutionary plan. It has also been recommended occasionally, but without success, by other scholars and humanists, notably by Goethe, by Andrew Lang, and by Wilamowitz, in Europe; while in America it has been advocated in one form or another by Seymour, Bolling, Shorey, Lane Cooper, and others. But hitherto no systematic series of text books has been issued which are so well adapted to carry the students through Homer and introduce them to Attic Greek as the ones which have been worked out in connection with Xenophon. It has become highly important that this lack be supplied, if possible, in order that this plan, which has been tried by several with such good success, may be tested on a wider scale, so that we may see whether or no it will succeed in the hands of the average teacher of beginning Greek. Thus students should be prepared to strike immediately into the heart of Greek literature, instead of having to go a long way around, as at present.

As to the superiority of Homer over Xenophon, from the standpoint of literary values, and of interest for the average student, there can be no quarrel. It remains for us to investigate the relative advantages and demerits of each as mediums for teaching the language.

In the first place it is essential that we disabuse our minds of the once prevalent notion, long since exploded, but still more or less consciously held by many, that the Attic dialect is the norm by which all other Greek is to be judged. The language of Homer is earlier and naturally differs from it in many essentials; therefore it was long maintained that Homeric Greek is irregular, crude and unfinished. Hellenistic Greek, which represents a later development of the language, has its differences; therefore Hellenistic Greek must be degenerate. Such an idea is utterly unscientific and ignores completely the modern historical point of view of the development and growth of languages. Any period which has given birth to literary productions of surpassing merit and artistic excellence is justified by its own works; it contains its own lin-

guistic standards, and will richly repay those who take the trouble
to study it. To call Homeric Greek anomalous and irregular,
because it differs in some particulars from the Attic dialect, is as
misleading as it would be to say that the language of Shakespeare
is immature and eccentric because he does not write the same type
of English as does George Ade or Stephen Leacock. As a matter
of fact, the language of the Homeric poems is quite as finished, has
quite as many virtues, and is quite as much of a norm for its
period and style of composition as Xenophon is for his; and the
different forms in Homer are no more aberrations on his part than
those of Xenophon are marks of degeneracy for him. And Attic
Greek, after all, is but one of a number of dialects, coming at neither
end but in the middle of the development of the Greek language.
It is rarely found pure in any of the great authors, and in none
which are suitable for beginners.

According to our present system, students are taught a smatter-
ing of Attic Greek. Then they are given a smattering of Homer,
who represents a period several centuries earlier. Then again
comes some more Attic Greek, and if the student continues in his
work he usually gets some Doric, with sometimes a little Lesbian,
and the Ionic of Herodotus, to which is commonly added a dash
of the Koinè for further confusing variety. All of this comes at
such times and at such points in his development that it is practi-
cally impossible for the ordinary student to obtain a clear concep-
tion of what the Greek language is like and what are the funda-
mental processes of its development. As a result grammar becomes
a nightmare to be dreaded instead of an opportunity to study the
structure of one of the most interesting and instructive languages
in existence. This has reference to the linguistic features, apart
from its literary value. If on the other hand we begin with Homer
and obtain a good grounding in his language, the transition from
that to later Greek is simple and natural and in accordance with
well-established laws, so that a student who once gets a grasp
of the processes involved not only has acquired a valuable scientific
point of view, but he might be untrue enough to the traditions of
countless students of the past to find Greek grammar interesting.

Furthermore, since most of us learned our Attic Greek first, when we came to Homeric Greek and found so many different forms, the feeling very naturally arose with many that Homer has many more forms than Attic Greek, and that they are more difficult. On the contrary, the Homeric forms are not only simpler and more transparent than the Attic and as a consequence more easily learned — many Attic forms have to be explained by a reference to the Homeric ones — but the Homeric forms are considerably fewer in number. This is best seen by a reference to the declensional endings, as exemplified in the two tables, 479, 649.

From these tables we see that there are, all told, 86 Homeric forms of the noun and adjective to be learned as against 108 Attic forms. But this is not all. Many forms in both Attic and Homeric Greek are so rare that it would be manifestly absurd to compel first-year students to memorize them. For our purposes, then, we must omit the unusually rare forms from both tables. In the first table (479) we shall omit a number of forms which many would include, and count only those not inclosed in brackets which are regularly included as essential by the standard beginners' books based on the Attic dialect. We shall not count the very rare Homeric forms, but shall be liberal enough to include a few which are too rare to be learned in reading Homer but are important for students intending to read Attic Greek later. We find then that students who begin with Homeric Greek need to learn only 55 forms as against 80 (88 according to some) of the Attic. This means that it is necessary to memorize about fifty per cent more forms in order to be able to read the first four books of the *Anabasis* than it would be to read the first six books of the *Iliad*. Furthermore, in the pronouns, by not compelling the student to memorize any form which does not occur on an average of at least once every two or three thousand verses, there would be fewer Homeric forms to be learned here also. The same is true of the verbs. The reflexive pronoun, for example, and the future passive and future optative of verbs are not found in Homer; the middle voice regularly retains the uncontracted forms of the endings and not in a part only as in Attic

Greek; and in many other ways the forms are simpler and more easily learned. In fact many books for beginners find it easier to teach Attic Greek by a constant reference to the earlier forms, which in many cases are the Homeric.

The occasional irregular forms, which are omitted from the ones to be learned, should be grouped in some convenient way for reference, but need not be memorized, as they are regularly given in their alphabetical place in the vocabulary of any good school edition and in the ordinary lexicons. Thus the student need not be required to memorize the five forms of the present infinitive of εἰμί, or the five forms of the genitive of ἐγώ, e.g., but could learn one of each and not burden his memory with forms which are found in every vocabulary.

Many Atticists have maintained that the great number of irregularities in Homeric Greek would be an added difficulty to the beginner. It is true that they are troublesome, but not so troublesome as the considerably greater number of irregularities in Attic Greek. Any one who will take the trouble to count them will find that the irregular formations in Attic Greek considerably outnumber those in Homer. There is not space here to catalogue the various irregularities, heteroclites, metaplastic forms, etc., of Attic Greek, but the lists given in Kuehner-Blass, or any other of the more elaborate Greek grammars, are enough to convince the most skeptical.

If we leave aside the irregularities and look at a few regular formations which must be memorized, the evidence is none the less conclusive. For example, the "regular" declensions of such words as πόλις, βασιλεύς, ναῦς, πῆχυς, ἄστυ, comparatives in -ιων, and other forms which will readily occur to any one who has studied Attic Greek, are so complicated that they are not ordinarily mastered by students of beginning Greek, and it would be rather remarkable if they were. Or let us consider a single class, such as typical words of the third declension in υς, as πῆχυς, δίπηχυς, ἡδύς, ἔγχελυς, ἰχθύς. If the student learned the declension of any one of these, and attempted to decline the rest accordingly, he would go far astray; for of these five words, all of the third declension, and all ending in υς in the nominative, no two are declined alike throughout. A comparison of the declensions of ἔγχελυς (eel) with that of ἰχθύς (fish) will illustrate the point. It seems that the old Athenians were never able to decide definitely whether an eel was a fish or a serpent. Accordingly, we find that they declined ἔγχελυς the first half of the way like ἰχθύς, while the other half was different. What a pity that there are not a few more such convenient mnemonic devices to help the student keep his bearings on his way through the maze of Greek morphology! If a student finally learned to decline such a word as ναῦς, he would not know how to begin the declension of another word formed in the same way, such as γραῦς; nor would a student who had learned the declension of βοῦς in Attic Greek know the declension of the next word like it, χοῦς, and he might be led very far astray by such a simple and common word as νοῦς. All of these forms, and many more which could be cited, are highly interesting to philologists, as they illustrate so beautifully certain abstruse principles in Greek phonology and morphology. Unfortunately they do not usually have the same strong appeal to the beginner who is trying very hard to learn how to read Greek.

The whole system of contraction, which is regular at times, and the variations caused by it in the general rules of accent and quantity, all of which are so confusing and so difficult to the ordinary beginner, are so little used in Homer that they can very profitably be omitted, or else touched quite lightly, and the time saved can be invested elsewhere to much greater advantage.

In the field of syntax Homer is so much simpler than Xenophon that students ordinarily find him a great deal easier. Thus Homer lacks the articular infinitive; long and involved passages in indirect discourse never occur, as well as many other strange and foreign characteristics of Attic Greek and Xenophon, all of which give a great deal of trouble to the ordinary beginner.

These elements all contribute to a quicker and an easier learning of Greek through Homer, as has been abundantly proved by experiments also. Thus students who begin with Homer regularly read more Greek in the time devoted to him than do those who begin with Xenophon and spend this time on the *Anabasis*.

It has long been a commonly accepted myth that Homer has such an enormous vocabulary that students would have more than ordinary trouble with it. In fact the vocabulary of the first six books of the *Iliad* is no larger than that required for reading the *Anabasis*, and one can read the whole of the Homeric poems, including the hymns, without having to learn many more words than to read Xenophon, and without having to learn so many words as are necessary for the reading of Plato.

There are, it is true, a great number of words in Homer which are used only once (ἅπαξ λεγόμενα).[1] The *Iliad* has 1097 of these, while the *Odyssey* has 868, making a total of 1965. However, this is not nearly so large as the number used by Xenophon, who has 3021 ἅπαξ λεγόμενα,[2] of which 433 are in the *Anabasis*, as compared with 266 (238 if we omit the *Catalogue of Ships*) in the first six books of the *Iliad*.

It is highly important too in gaining a vocabulary to learn words which will be used in other authors read later in the course, and to acquire so far as possible the more fundamental meanings of words from which their later uses are derived. Ahrens, who made a careful study of this problem, gives the palm to Homer here without question. According to him, the words in Homer are much nearer their fundamental meanings, and take on different shades of significance in the various later authors. If one wishes to obtain a clear grasp of Greek onomatology and semasiology, he should begin with Homer by all means and would thus be prepared to see more readily the later turns in the meanings of words and phrases, which in many cases vary considerably in authors of the same period, and sometimes even in the same author. Thus there are over 400 words in the Anabasis which either do not occur at all in Xenophon's other works, or else with a different signification. Rutherford (*The New Phryn.*, 160 ff.) says : "It did not

---

[1] L. Friedländer, *Zwei hom. Wörterverzeichnisse.*

[2] G. Sauppe, *Xen. Op. V, 298.*

escape the notice of later Greeks that Xenophon's diction was very different from that of pure Attic writers, and there are still extant several remarks upon this point. . . . A busy man, living almost wholly abroad, devoted to country pursuits and the life of the camp, attached to the Lacedaemonian system of government, and detesting the Athenian, Xenophon must have lost much of the refined Atticism with which he was conversant in his youth. It is not only in the forms of words that he differs from Attic writers, but he also uses many terms — the ὀνόματα γλωσσηματικά of Galen — altogether unknown to Attic prose, and often assigns to Attic words a meaning not actually attached to them in the leading dialect."

When it comes to the actual number of words of Xenophon and Homer which enter into the vocabulary of other Greek writers, the following tables will show their relation to some of the most important authors read in college.

The following table indicates the authors whose vocabularies have more words in common with Homer than with Xenophon, the figures showing the excess.

AUTHOR	WORDS	PAGES	AUTHOR	WORDS	PAGES
Hesiod . . .	904	87	Aeschylus .	524	309
Pindar . . .	485	236	Sophocles .	400	365
Bacchylides . .	347	73	Euripides .	428	916
Elegiac and Iambic Poets . .	514	160	Aristophanes	148	612
			Theocritus .	466	93

The following table indicates the authors whose vocabularies have more words in common with Xenophon than with Homer, the figures showing the excess.

AUTHOR	WORDS	PAGES	AUTHOR	WORDS	PAGES
Herodotus .	100	799	Isocrates . . .	371	514
Thucydides .	371	645	Lucian . . .	119	1301
Plato . . .	90	2442	Plutarch . . .	19	5639
Demosthenes	366	1379	Menander . .	176	102
Lysias . . .	362	246	New Testament	209	543

The vocabularies of Xenophon and Homer, which are compared in these lists, are: Xenophon's *Anabasis* entire, and Homer's *Iliad*, books I–VI. The pages as given above are according to the Teubner texts. The number of words in Xenophon's *Anabasis* is approximately the same as that of Homer's *Iliad*, books I–VI.

In these lists, words which are closely enough related to others that ordinary students who know the meaning of one may infer the other are counted but once, as θάνατος, ἀθάνατος; βαίνω, ἐκβαίνω, καταβαίνω, ἀναβαίνω, etc. Proper names are also omitted.

From this table it will be seen that Homer is a much better preparation for the Greek drama, Hesiod, the elegiac and iambic poets, than is Xenophon, and it is along these lines that the course should be developed. For Plato the difference is so exceedingly slight that in the matter of vocabulary one is practically as good a preparation as the other, and a few of his easier dialogues should find a place after some of the best poetry has been read. After that the Greek course ought to be able to take care of itself. Herodotus might come at any point. There is a slight advantage here on the side of Xenophon in the matter of vocabulary, but his language is so much closer to that of Homer, as well as his general style and imaginative genius, that he would be very easy and stimulating to those who had read any considerable amount of Homeric Greek. Those who wished to read Thucydides and the orators would find Xenophon's vocabulary somewhat better for their purpose, and the same is true if they wished to read the New Testament and Menander; but in all these the advantage is relatively slight, and in most cases the difference would probably not be noticeable. In the case of the New Testament, for example, the difference is less than one word in two Teubner pages of Greek text.

It is generally recognized that for the best results in the study of the New Testament, students should read a considerable amount of other Greek first. In the whole circle of Greek literature the two authors most important for the student of the New Testament are Homer and Plato. Herodotus informs us that Homer and Hesiod were the chief sources of the Greek popular religion; and certainly one cannot obtain a clear grasp of the forces opposed to Christianity without a good knowledge of Homer and of the hold that Homer had upon the popular mind. If one is to read intelligently the works of the early church fathers, he must be well acquainted at first hand with Homer. It is Homer, Homer's religion, and Homer's gods which recur constantly in their works and which are attacked over and over again as being the bulwarks of the heathen faith which they are striving to supplant. Homer and the ideas he represents are infinitely more important for the student of the New Testament and of the early church than is Xenophon; and if one can study not more than a year or so of Greek before taking up the New Testament, he should by all means have some Homer followed by Plato. Experience has shown that after a year of Homer, students can and do pass with little difficulty into the New Testament. The passage from Homer to Attic, or to Hellenistic, Greek is of course a great deal easier than *vice versa,* and occupies very little time and effort.

Some have urged that since the bulk of the work in the ordinary college course in Greek is in the Attic dialect, students who begin with this would get a firmer grasp of it than if they began with Homer. Some even feel that a student who did his beginning work in Homeric forms would never be able to feel thoroughly at home in Attic Greek. Yet few teachers would be rash enough to suggest that because a student has had a thorough training in Attic Greek he is thereby disqualified from doing first-class work in the language of the Hellenistic period, nor would many teachers of New Testament Greek, *e.g.,* object to a student who wished to specialize in their subject, or even in Patristic Greek, if he came to them with a good knowledge of Plato. Students who wish to specialize in Pliny and Tacitus, or even in Mediaeval Latin, do not find themselves handicapped because they did their earlier work in such authors as Caesar, Cicero, Vergil, Horace, and Catullus. Teachers of the Romance languages also universally recognize that a thorough course in Latin is a prerequisite for the highest type of scholarship in their field, and no student could hope to do advanced linguistic work in any of these languages without a thorough training in Latin. In the same way Homer offers an unexcelled preparation not only for all later Greek literature but for the later language as well; and instead of the present system of confusion in the teaching of Greek grammar, particularly with reference to the various dialects, some attempt should be made to develop the subject in a more scientific fashion.

Some feel that Homer is too beautiful and too exquisite to be used as a *corpus vile* for the teaching of Greek grammar. But the very fact that he is so beautiful and so exquisite is the very reason why he should be used at this early stage, that the students may have an added incentive for learning their grammar, and may not come to hate and despise the whole subject. Thus they may see, even from the beginning, that Greek is something worth working at, and they may have material interesting enough that the necessary grammatical drill will not seem so much useless drudgery.

A highly important consideration in placing Homer before Xenophon in the curriculum is the fact that as matters now stand such a large per cent of our students never reach Homer. The problem before us with regard to these students is whether we are to give them Xenophon *or* Homer. Since they represent a very large element, not all of whom are loafers either, we owe it to ourselves and to the cause of Greek, as well as to them, to give them that which will be of most lasting value to them.

Furthermore, Homer is interesting not only to older students, but is particularly adapted to the youngest who now take Greek, as the earliest experiments, made with boys from nine to fourteen years of age, have amply demonstrated. He serves the double purpose of introducing them adequately to the language and of furnishing them with reading material as interesting as can be found in any literature, something too of permanent value; and he should come by all means as early as possible in the course, that he may serve as a suitable basis for the development of those qualities of taste and appreciation, without which the study of all art is in vain. And after we have begun with him, we find his treasures inexhaustible. In Herbart's expressive phrase, "Homer elevates the student without depressing the teacher." To quote further from his lectures on education, he says (VI, 283): "The reasons for giving the preference to Homer's *Odyssey* in early instruction are well known. Any one who reads the *Odyssey* carefully, with an eye to the various main classes of interest which are to be aroused by education, can discover the reasons. The point, however, to be gained here is not merely to produce a direct effect, but beyond that to get points of connection for progressive instruction. There can be no better preparation for ancient history than gaining interest for ancient Greece by the Homeric stories. The ground is prepared for both the cultivation of taste and the study of languages at the same time.

"Philologists will be obliged sooner or later to listen to reasons of this kind, which are actually derived from the chief aim of all instruction, and are only opposed by tradition (the conventional study of Latin). This they must do, unless they desire that now, with the growth of history and science, and the pressure of material interests, Greek should be restricted in schools as Hebrew is at present.

"The *Odyssey*, it is true, possesses no magic power to animate those who are entirely unsuccessful in languages, or who do not work at them seriously; nevertheless it surpasses in definite educative influence, as is proved by the experience of many years, every other work of classic times that could be chosen."

In conclusion the writer would earnestly suggest that it is high time that Xenophon be omitted completely from at least the first three years of Greek study. The time and labor now devoted to both Xenophon and Homer should be spent on Homer alone, and for the three books of the *Iliad* and the four books of the *Anabasis* usually read should be substituted a course in Homer which would be extensive enough to give the students a real insight into his poetry, that they may learn to wander for themselves in the realms of gold, that they may be allowed to become so familiar with his language and his style that reading from him will be a pleasure and not a lot of hard work to be waded through, that they may become so filled with his spirit that they may catch a glimpse of what it means to be Homeric, and in later years, if they have gone out into other fields and would like to turn back to Greek literature, it would be a comparatively simple matter for them to bring out their old book and enter again with delight into his world of song. In the secondary schools we should have a course in Homer comprehensive enough to enable the students to obtain a firm grounding in his language and ideas, instead of the present smattering of both Xenophon and Homer, neither of which the average student knows well enough for it to serve as a stable and satisfactory basis for future work. It would be a real step forward on the part of the colleges, and should largely increase the number of those now offering Greek for admission, if the requirements in Greek should be made a requirement in Homer only, due attention being paid to composition and grammar, of course. Thus the secondary schools could intensify their efforts on one dialect and on one homogeneous mass of literature, which would materially simplify their problems, and ought to produce a much higher grade of work than is possible at present. If colleges would admit students on one, two, and three years, respectively, of Homer, with due credit for each, and reserve all work in the Attic dialect for the college course proper, the secondary teachers would have their burdens greatly lightened, with a corresponding increase in effectiveness. In no other language do the secondary schools undertake to prepare a student in two separate dialects. To do so in Greek is a pedagogical blunder which should be perpetuated no longer.

HOMERIC GREEK

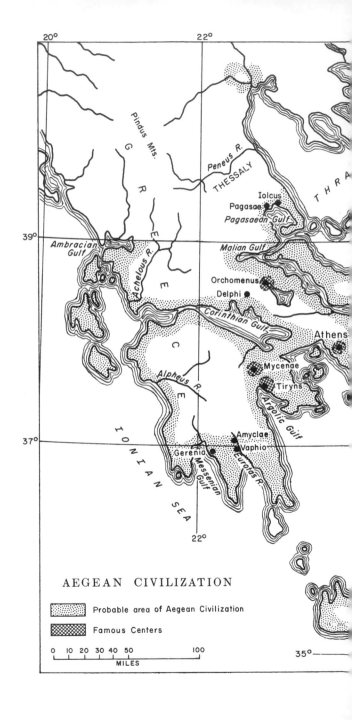

AEGEAN CIVILIZATION

Probable area of Aegean Civilization

Famous Centers

0 10 20 30 40 50   100
MILES

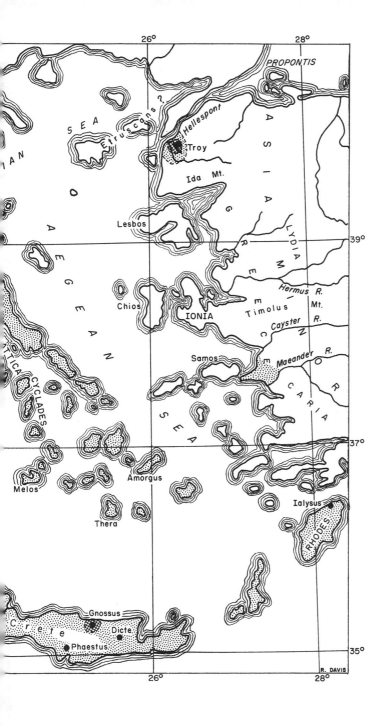

PROPONTIS

SEA

Etruscans ?

Hellespont

Troy

Ida Mt.

A
S
I
A

Lesbos

O

A
E
G
E
A
N

39°

Chios

IONIA

L
Y
D
I
A

G
R
E
M

Hermus R.

T
I
m
o
l
u
s Mt.

Timolus

Cayster R.

Samos

Maeander R.

CARIA

M
I
N
O
R

ATTICA

CYCLADES

SEA

37°

Melos

Amorgus

Ialysus

Thera

RHODES

Crete

Gnossus

Dicte.

Phaestus

35°

INTRODUCTION

I

THE *Iliad* and the *Odyssey*, the two great Greek epics, and the greatest of all epic poems, belong to the earliest Greek literature that has been preserved.

Their action and stories are legendary and are grouped around the incidents concerning the long siege of Troy by the Greeks, its final capture and destruction, and the return of the Greeks home. No attempt is made to give a systematic account of those events, but certain leading features of the legends are developed.

The *Iliad* has for its central theme and as the thread upon which it strings its various events the *Menis*, the mad anger of Achilles, and its dire consequences to the Greeks.

According to the story, Paris, son of King Priam of Troy (Ilios) in Asia Minor, eloped with Helen, the most beautiful woman in the world, wife of King Menelaus of Sparta, in southern Greece. The Greeks united under the command of King Agamemnon of Mycenae, brother of Menelaus, and the most powerful of the Greek chieftains, to avenge this wrong, capture Troy, and bring back Helen. After ten years of preparation they gathered their forces, sailed across the Aegean to the shores of the Hellespont (Dardanelles), landed, and drew up their ships, out of the water, in long lines on the shore. For ten years the siege continued before the Greeks were able to capture the city.

The *Iliad* opens, in the ninth year of the siege, with the deadly quarrel of Agamemnon and Achilles. Before all the assembled Greeks, Agamemnon disgraces and humiliates Achilles, and robs him of his prize of honor which had been previously bestowed upon him by the army. In rage and disgust, Achilles retires from

the conflict and sulks in his tent.   As he had been their stoutest
warrior, his absence is keenly felt by the Greeks, who suffer many
defeats and heavy losses at the hands of the Trojans, now that
Achilles has withdrawn.   It is only the death of his bosom friend,
Patroclus, in battle, which furnishes a motive sufficiently powerful
to induce him to take a further part in the war.   To avenge his
death, Achilles enters the conflict once more, and kills Hector,
who had slain Patroclus.   Shortly thereafter he was himself killed
by an arrow shot by Paris with the help of Apollo.   Finally, in the
tenth year of the siege, Troy was captured by the Greeks, by
means of the well-known stratagem of the Wooden Horse.   The
city was plundered and burned ; the men were killed and the women
taken as slaves.   Helen was recovered ; and after many adventures
and losses by shipwreck and other misfortunes the Greeks returned
home.

The traditional date of the fall of Troy was 1184 B.C.   The date
of the Homeric poems is not at all certain.   Some think they are
as early as 850 B.C., while others would date them as late as the
latter part of the seventh century B.C.   Many scholars have
thought that the poems represent a gradual growth of a long period
of time, that they were composed by a number of different bards,
and have been worked over, edited and re-edited, till they gradually
acquired their present form.   Many of these scholars would deny
that any one by the name of Homer ever lived.   Others think that
Homer was one of the editors, perhaps the most important of the
editors, of the poems, that he may have composed a considerable
amount of material in them, but that his chief function consisted
in combining and working over the various lays handed down by
his predecessors.   Still others are of the opinion that the whole
of the poems, or practically all of them, as we have them, were
composed outright by a single poet, who was a real historical
character, and whose name was Homer.   Most are agreed that
there must have been some great, master mind, whose influence is
felt throughout the poems, but who made free use of the work
of other poets who had preceded him and who had sung of various
events connected with the same theme.   As Kipling would say :

xl

INTRODUCTION

W'en 'Omer smote 'is bloomin' lyre,
'E'd 'eard men sing by land and sea,
And wot 'e thought 'e might require,
'E went and took, the same as me.

The old Greeks were practically unanimous in believing that the poems were composed by a bard, named Homer, and that he traveled about, in various parts of Greece, a poor, old, blind beggar, eking out an existence by singing his poems. After his death, we are told that: "Seven cities claimed the Homer dead, through which the living Homer begged his bread." The chief contestants for the honor of his birthplace were Smyrna and Chios, and the evidence of the poems would seem to point to that region.

The poems represent a very unsettled condition of society in the Greek world, corresponding in many ways to the Middle Ages in Europe. Preceding this period, there had been a brilliant civilization in the Greek world in the Aegean basin. This civilization is generally called the *Minoan* or *Aegean* civilization. Its flourishing period extended from about 2500 B.C. to about 1500 B.C., but it was not completely overthrown till about

CRETAN WRITING

A large tablet with linear script found in the palace at Gnossus, Crete. There are eight lines of writing with a total of about twenty words. Notice the upright lines which appear to mark the termination of each group of signs.

1000 B.C. Its chief center in early times was Crete, where recent excavations have revealed the existence of the seat of a great island empire. Its commerce and its influence touched all the shores of the Mediterranean, and it seems to have been in vital touch with the early Babylonian and Egyptian cultures. Other centers were Mycenae,

xli

Argos, Athens, Pylus, and Sparta, in Europe, and Troy in Asia Minor.

It was finally destroyed by invasions of barbarians from the North, much as the Roman Empire finally succumbed to the Germanic invasions. These invaders were the early Greeks, and this period is usually called the Homeric Age, because so many of its features are reflected in the Homeric poems, the *Iliad* and the *Odyssey*.

The times were rude, and social life was primitive. War and piracy were ordinary pursuits. The people grouped themselves around powerful chieftains for protection, but marauding bands were common, which killed, burned, and plundered. Personal valor and prowess in battle were of supreme importance, not only for one's own safety, but for the safety and freedom of his friends and family as well. Accordingly, the greatest virtue, and the one held in highest esteem, was bravery in war.

For our picture of the culture of this period we are dependent upon the Homeric poems. In them we see how expeditions were made by the Greeks against their enemies, whom they considered at all times as legitimate objects of plunder. Usually such expeditions were under one of the many petty Homeric "kings." Of these there were a great number; and there was no unity and no central authority in Homeric Greece any more than there were in the later historical period.

According to the tradition, the expedition against Troy was undertaken by the whole of Greece, united under the leadership of Agamemnon. Some think that this tradition rests upon an ultimate basis of fact; but this may be merely an idealistic touch, expressing an earnest hope of the poet, that the various Greek tribes may reconcile their differences and stop warring on each other long enough to make war upon the common foe, the barbarians, as represented by the non-Greek inhabitants of Asia Minor. In the Homeric poems we find that although Agamemnon was commander in chief of the allied Greek military expedition, the various contingents were led by their own commanders, most of whom were their kings, apparently quite independent of Aga-

xlii

memnon when at home, and semi-independent of him during the expedition. The most important of these secondary leaders were: Nestor of Pylus, the oldest man in the world; Agamemnon's brother, Menelaus, the wronged husband of Helen; the young, daring, generous, and impetuous Achilles of Phthia; the mighty Diomedes of Argos, who fought with the very gods themselves; the wily Odysseus (Ulysses) of Ithaca, who wandered for ten years after the fall of Troy before he arrived safe at home and saw once more his wife, the faithful Penelope; the huge and brutal Telamonian Ajax of Salamis; the lesser Ajax, son of Oïleus of Locris;

GALLERY AT TIRYNS

The gallery roof is formed by pushing the successive courses of stone farther and farther inward from both sides until they meet. The result is, in form, a vault, but the principle of the keystone arch is not employed.

Teucer, the Archer, brother of Telamonian Ajax; and Idomeneus of Crete, the far-famed isle of a hundred cities.

On the Trojan side the most important characters are: Hector, eldest son of Priam and commander-in-chief of the Trojan forces; the aged Priam, King of Troy; Hecuba, his wife; Andromache, wife of Hector; Paris, brother of Hector and the one who had brought on the war by stealing Helen; Glaucus and Sarpedon, princes of Lycia, whose beautiful and unselfish friendship is only matched by that of Achilles and Patroclus on the Greek side.

The divinities take an active part in the conflict, some siding with the Greeks, the others with the Trojans. Zeus, who stands at the head of the gods, as father and king of gods and men, seems inclined to be neutral. Hera his wife, queen of the gods, cherishes an implacable hatred against the Trojans, as does Athena, his daughter, goddess of war, wisdom, and the arts. Poseidon, brother of Zeus, the mighty god of the sea, is also on the side of the Greeks, and loses no opportunity to help them. On the Trojan side were Apollo, god of light, who wards off darkness and evil, patron of music, poetry and healing; Artemis, his sister, a divinity of the moonlight, goddess of the woods and wild animals, and patroness of the chase; Leto, their mother; Aphrodite, born of the white sea-foam, goddess of love and beauty, who had assisted Paris in obtaining Helen; Hephaestus, the lame god of fire, patron of all useful mechanical arts and the working of metals; and the river-god Scamander, a stream near Troy.

The gods are distinctly human in their characteristics and attributes, with human appetites and passions. They differ from men primarily in being more powerful and in being immortal. They enjoy a good dinner, where they feast on nectar and ambrosia; they love and hate, are envious and jealous, but on the whole live a happier and serener life than mortals.

In translating Homer, it would be well to hold in mind the four essential characteristics of his poetry as enumerated by Matthew Arnold: "Homer is rapid in his movement, Homer is plain in his words and style, Homer is simple in his ideas, Homer is noble in his manner."

For a good characterization of the Homeric poems, from the point of view of literary art, one should by all means read Andrew Lang's Essay, "Homer and the Study of Greek," from which the following is taken. "Homer is a poet for all ages, all races, and all moods. To the Greeks the epics were not only the best of romances, the richest of poetry; not only their oldest documents about their own history — they were also their Bible, their treasury of religious traditions and moral teaching. With the Bible and Shakespeare, the Homeric poems are the best training for life. There is no good quality that they lack: manliness, courage, reverence for old age and the hospitable hearth; justice, piety, pity, a brave attitude toward life and death, are all conspicuous in Homer. He has to write of battles; and he delights in the joy of battle, and in all the movements of war. Yet he delights not less, but more, in peace: in prosperous cities, hearths secure, in the tender beauty of children, in the love of wedded wives, in the frank nobility of maidens, in the beauty of earth and sky and sea and seaward murmuring river, in sun and snow, frost and mist and rain, in the whispered talk of boy and girl beneath oak and pine tree.

"Living in an age when every man was a warrior, where every city might know the worst of sack and fire, where the noblest ladies

STOREROOM IN THE PALACE AT GNOSSUS

might be led away for slaves, to light the fire and make the bed of a foreign master, Homer inevitably regards life as a battle. To each man on earth comes 'the wicked day of destiny,' as Malory unconsciously translates it, and each man must face it hardily as he may.

"Homer encourages them by all the maxims of chivalry and honor. His heart is with the brave of either side — with Glaucus and Sarpedon of Lycia no less than with Achilles and Patroclus. 'Ah friend,' cries Sarpedon, 'if once escaped from this battle we were for ever to be ageless and immortal, neither would I myself fight

xlv

now in the foremost ranks, nor would I urge thee into the wars that give renown; but now — for assuredly ten thousand fates of death on every side beset us, and these may no man shun, nor avoid — forward let us go, whether we are to give glory or to win it.' And forth they go, to give and take renown and death, all the shields and helmets of Lycia shining behind them, through the dust of battle, the singing of arrows, the hurtling of spears, the rain of stones from the Locrian slings. And shields are smitten, and chariot-horses run wild, with no man to drive them, and Sarpedon drags down a portion of the Achaean battlement, and Aias leaps into the trench with his deadly spear, and the whole battle shifts and shines beneath the sun. Yet he who sings of the war, and sees it with his sightless eyes, sees also the Trojan women working at the loom, cheating their anxious hearts with broidery work of gold and scarlet, or raising the song to Athena, or heating the bath for Hector, who never again may pass within the gates of Troy. He sees the poor weaving woman, weighing the wool, that she may not cheat her employers, and yet may win bread for her children. He sees the children, the golden head of Astyanax, his shrinking from the splendor of the hero's helm. He sees the child Odysseus, going with his father through the orchard, and choosing out some apple trees 'for his very own.' It is in the mouth of the ruthless Achilles, the fatal, the fated, the swift-footed hero of the hands of death, that Homer places the tenderest of his similes. 'Wherefore weepest thou, Patroclus, like a fond little maid that runs by her mother's side, praying her mother to take her up, snatching at her gown, and hindering her as she walks, and tearfully looking at her till her mother takes her up? — Like her, Patroclus, dost thou fondly weep.' . . . Such are the moods of Homer, so full of love of life and all things living, so rich in all human sympathies, so readily moved when the great hound Argus welcomes his master, whom none knew after twenty years, but the hound knew him, and died in that welcome. With all this love of the real, which makes him dwell so fondly on every detail of armor, of implement of art; on the divers-colored gold work of the shield, on the making of tires for chariot-wheels, on the forging of iron, on the rose-tinted ivory of the Sidonians, on cooking and eating and sacrificing, on pet dogs, on wasps and their ways, on fishing, on the boar hunt, on scenes in baths where fair maidens lave water over the heroes, on undiscovered isles with good harbors and rich land, on plowing, mowing, and sowing, on the furniture of houses, on the golden vases wherein the white dust of the dead is laid, — with all this delight in the real, Homer is the most romantic of poets. He walks with the surest foot in the darkling realm of dread Persephone, beneath the poplars of the last beach of Ocean. He has heard the siren's music, and the song of Circe, chanting as she walks to and fro, casting the golden shuttle through the loom of gold. He enters the cave of the man-eater; he knows the unsunned land of the Cimmerians; in the summer of the North he has looked, from the fiord of the Laestrygons, on the midnight sun. He has dwelt on the floating isle of Aeolus, with its wall of bronze unbroken, and has sailed on those Phaeacian barks that need no help of helm or oar, that fear no stress either of wind or tide, that come and go and return, obedient to a thought and silent as a dream. He has seen the four maidens of Circe, daughters of wells and woods, and of sacred streams. He is the second-sighted man, and beholds the

AEGEAN SNAKE
GODDESS

shroud that wraps the living who are doomed, and the mystic dripping from the walls of blood yet unshed. He has walked in the garden closes of Phaeacia and looked on the face of gods who fare thither and watch the weaving of the dance. He has eaten the honey-sweet fruit of the Lotus, and from the hand of Helen he brings us that Egyptian Nepenthe which puts all sorrow out of the mind. His real world is as real as that of *Henry V.*, his enchanted isles are charmed with the magic of the *Tempest*. His young wooers are as insolent as Claudio, as flushed with youth; his beggar-men are brethren of Edie Ochiltree; his Nausicaa is

xlvii

sister to Rosalind, with a different charm of stately purity in love. His enchantresses hold us yet with their sorceries; his Helen is very beauty; she has all the sweetness of ideal womanhood, and her repentance is without remorse. His Achilles is youth itself, glorious, cruel, pitiful, splendid, and sad, ardent and loving, and conscious of its doom. Homer, in truth, is to be matched only by Shakespeare, and of Shakespeare he has not the occasional willfulness, freakishness, and modish obscurity. He is a poet all of gold, universal as humanity, simple as childhood, musical now as the flow of his own rivers, now as the heavy plunging wave of his own ocean. . . .

"Such then, as far as weak words can speak of him, is the first and greatest of poets."

II

Vocabulary. — One of the things most important in learning any language so as to be able to read it with profit and pleasure is to acquire a fair-sized vocabulary. In doing this, one should learn thoroughly the words that are used most. For this purpose there is a highly practical little book, *Homeric Vocabularies*, Owen and Goodspeed, published by the University of Chicago Press. The most common Homeric words are arranged in it in groups, according to frequency of occurrence. A copy of this book should be in the hands of every student who wishes to lighten his work in learning to read and enjoy Homer.

Forms of the Greek Verb. — In learning the Greek verb, the most difficult part of Greek grammar, it is highly important to know which forms are most essential. The following material, with the two tables, compiled by Professor Robbins, will indicate where the stress of work should come. These tables will be found valuable, not only for Homeric Greek, but for other Greek as well. By emphasizing strongly the forms which are most common, it will be found that the work will be materially lightened, and the Greek verb will not be found at all formidable.

"Table I tabulates the result of counting the verb forms found on ten pages each of Homer, Euripides, Herodotus, Demosthenes, and Plato, and on twenty of Xenophon (ten each from the *Anabasis* and the *Memorabilia*). In most cases the pages of the Oxford Classical Texts or the Bibliotheca Teubneriana have been made the unit, and for the present purpose the variation in the amount of Greek on the page need cause no concern. It may be remarked, also, that first and second perfects have been counted together because they are best taught together, and that the present participle of εἰμί has been included among the thematic present participles.[1]

"The revelations of Table I make clear a few points that have a definite bearing on the teaching of Greek. In the first place, it shows that a large majority of the verbs one meets in reading Greek are confined to a small group of forms. Table II will make this clearer; it will then appear that nine or ten forms make up over a half, and twenty-four forms three-quarters, of the verbs in average Greek. Is it not right that we should first concern ourselves with teaching these forms? Of course, one must not guide himself entirely by these, or any similar, statistics; often it is advantageous to teach a whole group together, even though this involves the introduction of certain rather rare forms together with others that are commoner. On the other hand, here we have a definite, practical ground for demanding that certain forms be introduced very early.

"Among these the present active participle deserves special mention. The statistics show the high frequency of its occurrence, and indeed few sentences, save the most elementary, can be mastered without a knowledge of it. Furthermore, its inflection can easily be made an introduction to both the first and third declensions, and one should not readily pass by an opportunity to kill three birds with one stone.

"The apparently high frequency of the present and imperfect indicative and the present infinitive of -μι verbs is due not so much to ἵστημι, τίθημι, δίδωμι, and δείκνυμι as to the constant

---

[1] "Another liberty which I have taken is to disregard perfects of the -μι form, reckoning all perfects together. Aorists like ἔβην are counted as -μι forms."

TABLE I

The Greek Verb Forms, with the Number of Occurrences and Percentage of Occurrence of Each

| | Number of Occurrences | | | | | | | | Percentages of Occurrence | | | | | | | |
| | ω-verb Forms | | | | μι-verb Forms | | | Total All Forms | ω-verb Forms | | | | μι-verb Forms | | | Total All Forms |
	Active	Middle Passive	Passive	Total ω-verb Forms	Active	Middle Passive	Total μι-verb Forms	Total All Forms	Active	Middle Passive	Passive	Total ω-verb Forms	Active	Middle Passive	Total μι-verb Forms	Total All Forms
Indicative:																
Present	282	136		418	122	18	140	558	8.18	3.94		12.1	3.54	.52	4.07	16.2
Imperfect	150	91		241	146	22	168	409	4.35	2.64		7.00	4.23	.63	4.8	11.8
Future	58	49	3	110				110	1.68	1.42	.086	3.2				3.2
First aorist	139	29	37	205				205	4.03	.84	1.07	5.9				5.9
Second aorist	87	33	6	126	23	4	27	153	2.55	.957	.17	3.6	.66	.12	.78	4.4
Perfect	67	24		91				91	1.94	.69		2.6				2.6
Pluperfect	12	7	1[1]	20				20	.35	.20	.03	.5				.5
Totals	795	369	47	1211	291	44	335	1546	23.1	10.7	1.3	35.2	8.4	1.2	9.7	44.9
Subjunctive:																
Present	38	19	4	57	13	4	17	74	1.1	.55	.12	1.68	.38	.12	.49	2.1
First aorist	20	5	0	29				29	.58	.14		.8				.8
Second aorist	21	15		36	8	0	8	44	.61	.43	0	1.00	.23	0	.23	1.23
Perfect	1	1		2				2	.03	.03		.06				.06
Totals	80	40	4	124	21	4	25	149	2.3	1.1	.1	3.6	.6	.1	.7	4.3
Optative:																
Present	43	14		57	27	7	34	91	1.24	.41		1.68	.78	.20	.96	2.64
Future	1	0	0	1				1	.03	0	0	.03				.03
First aorist	13	4	4	21				21	.38	.12	.12	.61				.61
Second aorist	16	11	1	28	4	1	5	33	.46	.32	.03	.8	.12	.03	.15	.9
Perfect	0	0		0				0	0	0		0				0
Totals	73	29	5	107	31	8	39	146	2.1	.8	.1	3.1	.9	.2	1.1	4.2
Imperative:																
Present	39	12		51	3	1	4	55	1.13	.35		1.5	.09	.03	.12	1.6
First aorist	13	10	0	23				23	.38	.29	0	.66				.66
Second aorist	7	3	0	10	6	0	6	16	.28	.09	0	.29	.17	0	.17	.46
Perfect	2	0		2				2	.06	0		.06				.06
Totals	61	25	0	86	9	1	10	96	1.7	.7	0	2.5	.2	.02	.2	2.7

[1] Future perfect, placed here for convenience.

Infinitive:																
Present	216	70	......	286	69	12	81	367	6.26	2.03	......	8.3	2.00	.35	2.2	10.6
Future	16	13	2	31	......	......	......	31	.46	.38	.06	.9	......	......	......	.9
First aorist	69	20	7	96	......	......	......	96	2.00	.58	.20	2.8	......	......	......	2.8
Second aorist	52	26	5	83	16	1	17	100	1.51	.75	.14	2.4	.46	.03	.49	2.9
Perfect	17	7	......	24	......	......	......	24	.49	.20	......	.69	......	......	......	.69
Totals	370	136	14	520	85	13	98	618	10.7	3.9	.4	15.4	2.5	.3	2.8	17.9
Participles:																
Present	357	133	......	490	8	22	30	520	10.35	3.86	......	14.2	.23	.64	.8	15.1
Future	9	3	0	12	......	......	......	12	.26	.09	0	.35	......	......	......	.35
First aorist	84	32	29	145	......	......	......	145	2.43	.92	.84	4.2	......	......	......	4.2
Second aorist	61	22	7	90	27	4	31	121	1.77	.64	.20	2.6	.78	.12	.9	3.5
Perfect	32	53	......	85	......	......	......	85	.92	1.53	......	2.5	......	......	......	2.5
Totals	543	243	36	822	35	26	61	883	15.7	7.00	1.00	23.9	1.00	.7	1.7	25.6
Totals of all moods	1922	842	106	2870	472	96	568	3438	55.9	24.4	3.00	83.4	13.7	2.8	16.5	100
Summary by tenses:																
Present	975	384	......	1359	242	64	306	1665	28.3	11.1	......	39.5	7.00	1.8	8.8	48.4
Imperfect	150	91	......	241	146	22	168	409	4.3	2.6	......	7.00	4.2	.6	4.8	11.8
Future	84	65	5	154	......	......	......	154	2.5	1.8	.1	4.4	......	......	......	4.4
First aorist	338	100	81	519	......	......	......	519	9.8	2.9	2.3	15.00	......	......	......	15.00
Second aorist	244	110	19	373	84	10	94	467	7.00	3.2	.5	10.8	2.5	.2	2.7	13.5
Perfect	119	85	......	204	......	......	......	204	3.4	2.5	......	5.9	......	......	......	5.9
Pluperfect	12	7	1	20	......	......	......	20	.3	.2	.02	.5	......	......	......	.5
Totals	1922	842	106	2870	472	96	568	3438	55.9	24.4	3.00	83.4	13.7	2.8	16.5	100

occurrence of forms of εἰμί and φημί (ἐστί, εἰσί, ἦν, ἦσαν, εἶναι, ἔφη). These particular forms are entitled to an early hearing in the classroom and are probably best taught separately, as indeed they usually are, the other athematic verbs being postponed.

" In Table II there have been set down the twenty-four forms which occur most frequently, with the percentage of their occurrence in ordinary Greek.

" From Table II, which is based upon Table I and is really a summary of the most important facts to be gleaned from Table I, one might conclude that the student should as soon as possible be put in command of the present, imperfect, first and second aorist, perfect, and future indicative, the present and first and second aorist, infinitive and participle, at least the active present optative, subjunctive, and imperative, εἰμί in full, and some forms of φημί; with these mastered, he will have to depend on the teacher or notes in the textbook for only a quarter of the verb forms he sees, and of course this proportion will be cut down as he progresses."

TABLE II

The Twenty-four Commonest Verb Forms

Rank and Form	Percentage of Occurrence	Rank and Form	Percentage of Occurrence
1. Them. pres. ppl. act. . .	10.35	13. Them. pres. inf. mid. . .	2.03
2. Them. pres. ind. act. . .	8.18	14. Athem. pres. inf. act. . .	2.00
3. Them. pres. inf. act. . .	6.26	15. Perf. ind. act.	1.94
4. Them. impf. ind. act. . .	4.35	16. Them. 2d aor. ppl. act. .	1.77
5. Athem. impf. ind. act. . .	4.23	17. Fut. ind. act.	1.68
6. 1st aor. ind. act. . . .	4.03	18. Perf. ppl. mid.	1.53
7. Them. pres. ind. mid. . .	3.94	19. Them. 2d aor. inf. act. .	1.51
8. Them. pres. ppl. mid. . .	3.86	20. Fut. ind. mid.	1.42
9. Athem. pres. ind. act. . .	3.54	21. Them. pres. opt. act. . .	1.24
10. Them. impf. ind. mid. . .	2.64	22. Them. pres. imper. act. .	1.13
11. Them. 2d aor. ind. mid. .	2.55	23. Them. pres. sub. act. . .	1.10
12. 1st aor. ppl. act. . . .	2.43	24. 1st aor. ind. pass. . . .	1.07
		Total	76.78

HOMERIC GREEK

AN ATHENIAN SCHOOL

Royal Museum, Berlin

A painting by Duris on a drinking-cup, or cylix. The picture is divided by the two handles. In the upper half, beginning at the left: a youth playing the double flute as a lesson to the boy before him; a teacher holding a tablet and stylus and correcting a composition; a slave (*pæda-gogus*), who accompanied the children to and from school. In the lower half: a master teaching his pupil to play the lyre; a teacher holding a half-opened roll, listening to a recitation by the student before him; a bearded *pædagogus*. The inner picture, badly damaged, represents a youth in a bath.

HOMERIC GREEK

LESSON I

INTRODUCTORY

[The pronunciation equivalents given in 501 and 504[1] are only approximate and represent the received American pronunciation of classical Greek. For a full account of the pronunciation of ancient Greek, incorporating all the available evidence, see W. Sidney Allen, *Vox Graeca* (2d ed., London: Cambridge University Press, 1974).]

1. Learn the alphabet and sounds of the letters, breathings, and quantity, 501–508, 519–520, 527–533.

2. *Optional:* [2]

3. The easiest and simplest way to learn the sounds of the letters is to use the two right-hand columns of 501 for practice, covering with a card the English transliteration (the column to the extreme right).

4. WORD LIST FOR PRACTICE IN PRONUNCIATION

Spell and pronounce : [3]

μῆνις wrath, fury, madness, rage.	θεά goddess.
ἀείδω sing (of), hymn.	Πηληιάδης son of Peleus, *Achilles*.

---

[1] The figures refer to sections in this book.

[2] Sections to be assigned at the discretion of the instructor.

[3] In spelling these words it is not necessary to have memorized the *names* of the Greek letters, but the *sounds* should be familiar. Thus, for the present, α may be called *a*, β may be called *b*, γ may be called *g*, etc.

3

'Αχιλλεύς Achilles.

οὐλόμενος accursed, destructive.

ὅς who, which, what.

μυρίοι countless, innumerable.

'Αχαιός Achaean, *Greek.*

ἄλγος grief, pain, woe, trouble.

τίθημι put, place, cause.

πολλός much, many, numerous.

δέ but, and, for, so.

ἴφθιμος valiant, mighty.

ψῡχή soul, spirit, breath, life.

"Αις (nominative not used), Hades, *god of the lower world.*

προϊάπτω hurl forward, send forth.

ἥρως hero, mighty warrior, protector, savior.

αὐτός self, same.

ἐλώριον booty, prey, spoils.

τεύχω make, fashion, cause.

κύων dog.

οἰωνός bird (of prey), vulture, omen.

τέ and, also.

δαίς portion, feast, banquet.

Ζεύς Zeus, *father and king of gods and men.*

τελείω accomplish, fulfill.

βουλή will, wish, plan, purpose, counsel, council.

Derivatives:[1] mania(c-al) 621; ode(um), melody, palinode; myriad; neur-, nost-algia; psychology; hero(ic); automaton, -cracy; cynic(al); teleology.

LESSON II

SYLLABLES, ACCENTS, ELISION, PUNCTUATION, AND TRANSLITERATION

5. Learn the principles of accentuation, the formation of syllables, elision, punctuation, etc.: 534–551, 553, 560, 575, 622–625.

6. Review the previous lesson.

7. *Optional:*

---

[1] Connect these with the Greek words, consulting a *good* English dictionary when in doubt. A few cognates are included, as 87, 101, etc.

LESSON III

NOUNS OF THE FIRST DECLENSION

[Greek nouns change their endings, known as *case endings*, to indicate their function in a sentence. The *nominative* case is used for the subject of a sentence and for the predicate nominative (sometimes called the subject complement). The *genitive* indicates possession ("of") or origin ("from") The *dative* is used for the indirect object ("to," "for"). The *accusative* is used for the direct object of a verb. The *vocative* is used for direct address. (For fuller accounts of these uses see 978ff.) These functions are generally indicated in English by word order; contrast "The player hit the ball" and "The ball hit the player." Greek word order, however, is relatively free; therefore, it is essential to learn and recognize the case endings to determine the meaning of a Greek sentence.]

8. Learn : 1) the principles of the formation of **nouns of the first declension**: 626–658.

2) the declension of βουλή, and κᾱλὴ βουλή (659–662).

3) the rules of syntax : 970, 1011, 1025.

9. *For classroom recitation, give only the first form of each case. Never memorize forms in parentheses or brackets.*[1]

10. **VOCABULARY**

βουλή, ῆς, ἡ[2] plan, will, wish, purpose, counsel, council.

δεινή fearful, terrible, awful, dread-(ful).

ἐν(ί), εἰν adv., *and prep. with dat.*, in, among, there(in, -on).

ἔχει (he, she, it) has, holds.

ἔχουσι(ν)[3] (they) have, hold.

---

[1] This applies to *all* paradigms.

[2] The form of the noun found in the Vocabulary is regularly the nominative singular, followed by the ending of the genitive singular, to indicate the declension, and by the pronoun ὁ, ἡ, or τό, to indicate the gender, 637–638.

[3] Nu-movable, 561.

5

ἦν (he, she, it) was, there was.

ἦσαν (they) were, there were.

καί and, also, even.

κακή bad, poor, ugly, mean, cowardly, evil, wicked.

κᾱλή good(ly), noble, handsome, brave, fair, beautiful.

κλαγγή, ῆς, ἡ CLANG, (up)roar, roar, noise.

τίς (m., f.), who? which? what?

τί (neut.), which? what? why?

Χρύση, ης, ἡ Chrysa, *a town in the Troad.*

φίλη dear, darling, lovely, beloved.

Derivatives: dino-saur, din-ichthys, -ornis; caco-graphy, -phony; calli-graphy, -ope; clang; Phil-adelphia, -anthropy.

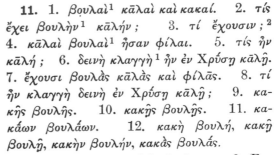

Translate:

11. 1. βουλαὶ[1] κᾱλαὶ καὶ κακαί.   2. τίς ἔχει βουλὴν[1] κᾱλήν ;   3. τί ἔχουσιν ;[2] 4. κᾱλαὶ βουλαὶ[1] ἦσαν φίλαι.   5. τίς ἦν κᾱλή ;   6. δεινὴ κλαγγὴ[1] ἦν ἐν Χρύσῃ κᾱλῇ. 7. ἔχουσι βουλὰς κᾱλὰς καὶ φίλᾱς.   8. τί ἦν κλαγγὴ δεινὴ ἐν Χρύσῃ κᾱλῇ ;   9. κακῆς βουλῆς.   10. κακῆς βουλῆς.   11. κακάων βουλάων.   12. κακὴ βουλή, κακῇ βουλῇ, κακὴν βουλήν, κακὰς βουλάς.

12. 1. Of good and bad plans.   2. For the[1] noble plan.   3. Who has the[1] evil plan?   4. There was a[1] terrible uproar in beautiful Chrysa.   5. Was the[1] plan good?   6. The[1] plans were cowardly.

GRAVESTONE OF ARISTION

National Museum, Athens

Found near Marathon in 1838. Belongs to the late sixth century B.C. Incorrectly called the "Warrior of Marathon."

LESSON IV

NOUNS OF THE FIRST DECLENSION
(*Continued*)

13. Learn the declension of θεά, *goddess,* and θάλασσα, *sea* (663), and review the paradigms of βουλή and κᾱλὴ βουλή, 659–662.

14. See 9.

---

[1] 660.   [2] Nu-movable, 561.

15.   VOCABULARY

γάρ *post.*[1] *conj.*, for, in fact.

δέ, *post. conj.* but, and, so, for.

εἰσί(ν)[2] (they) are, there are.

ἐστί(ν)[2] (he, she, it) is, there is.

ἐκ (ἐξ)[3] *adv.*, *and prep. with gen.* from, out of.

ἐπί *adv.*, *and prep. with gen.*, *dat.*, *and acc.* to, at, (up)on, against, over, for; *adv.*, (up)on, thereon; *with gen.*, (up)on, over, during; *with dat.*, (up)on, in, for, about, against, at, beside, by; *with acc.*, to, up to, over, (up)on.

θάλασσα, ης, ἡ sea.

θεά, ᾶς, ἡ goddess.

Κίλλα, ης, ἡ Cilla, a town in the Troad.

οὐ (οὐκ, οὐχ)[4] not, no.

πάτρη, ης, ἡ fatherland, native land.

πολλή much, many, numerous.

πυρή, ῆς, ἡ (funeral) PYRE.

ψῡχή, ῆς, ἡ soul, breath, life, spirit.

Derivatives: thalasso-cracy; patriotic; pyro-latry, -technic(al), -graphy; psycho-logy, -therapy, psychic(al).

Translate:

16. 1. ἔχει κᾱλὴ θεὰ βουλὴν κᾱλήν; 2. κᾱλαὶ θεαί[5] εἰσι[5] φίλαι ψῡχῇ θεᾶς θαλάσσης δεινῆς. 3. Κίλλα καὶ Χρύση εἰσὶ[6] κᾱλαὶ καὶ φίλαι θεῇσι θαλασσάων. 4. κᾱλὴ θεὰ οὐκ ἔχει ψῡχὴν κακήν. 5. κᾱλή[5] ἐστι[5] θεά, ἔχει δὲ ψῡχὴν κακήν. 6. δεινὴ κλαγγή[5] ἐστιν[5] ἐκ θαλάσσης. 7. Κίλλα καὶ Χρύση ἦσαν ἐπὶ θαλάσσῃ. 8. θεαὶ θαλάσσης εἰσὶ[6] φίλαι ψῡχῆς πολλῆς, φίλαι γάρ[5] εἰσιν.[5] 9. πάτρη κᾱλή[5] ἐστι[5] φίλη πολλῆς ψῡχῆς κᾱλῆς. 10. ἐκ πάτρης κακῆς ἦν. 11. ἦσαν πυραὶ πολλαὶ ἐν φίλῃ πάτρῃ ἐπὶ δεινῇ θαλάσσῃ. 12. τίς οὐκ ἔχει κᾱλὴν ψῡχήν;

---

[1] A postpositive word never comes first in its sentence, but usually second.

[2] These words are enclitics, 553-554.

[3] ἐκ before consonants, ἐξ before vowels.

[4] οὐ before consonants, οὐκ before the smooth breathing, οὐχ before the rough breathing, 527-530.

[5] 553-554.   [6] 555.

17. 1. Are the good plans dear to the souls of the goddesses? 2. They have many plans, but (they are) cowardly (ones). 3. The plans are dear to the soul of the beautiful goddess, for they are noble. 4. The lovely goddess of the sea was not in Cilla. 5. There are many funeral pyres by the sea in (our) beloved fatherland. 6. Who was in Cilla by the sea?

NOTE. — Do not translate words in parentheses.

LESSON V

THE PRESENT ACTIVE INDICATIVE OF VERBS IN -ω

[Like Greek nouns, Greek verbs change their forms to indicate their function in a sentence. To a certain extent English verbs do so as well; for example, we say, "I go" and "he goes." The Greek verb employs different endings for the *first person* (the speaker: "I," "we"), the *second person* (the one addressed: "you"), and the *third person* (the one spoken about: "he," "she," "it," "they"), in the singular, dual, and plural. The personal pronouns ("I," "you," etc.) are seldom employed unless special emphasis is desired; hence, the verb endings must be thoroughly memorized in order to understand a Greek sentence.

The *present tense* is used to describe action taking place in the present time. The meaning of the terms *active* and *indicative* will be explained in later lessons.]

18. 1) Read carefully the sections regarding the verb : 789–806.

2) Learn the present active indicative of λύω, 904.

19. See **9.**

8

20.   VOCABULARY

ἀείδω[1] sing (of), hymn, chant.
ἀν-[2] (ἀ- *before consonants*), *an inseparable prefix*, not, un-, dis-, -less, without.
ἀνδάνω please (*with dat.*, 996).
ἀ-τῑμάζω dishonor, slight, insult.
βαίνω come, go, walk.
εἰς (ἐς) *adv.*, *and prep. with acc.*, to, into, until, therein.

ἔχω have, hold, keep.
καίω burn, consume.
λύω loose, free, break up, destroy.
ὀλέκω kill, destroy, ruin.
πέμπω send, escort, conduct.
τελείω accomplish, fulfill, complete.
τεύχω make, do, fashion, perform, cause, prepare.
φέρω bear, carry, bring.

Derivatives : ode(-um), mel-ody, palin-ode ; a-theist, anarchy ; caustic, cauterize, holo-caust ; ana-lysis ; pomp (593) ; teleo-logy ; peri-phery, phos-phor-us (593).

Translate :

21. 1. ἀείδομεν βουλὰς θεάων πολλάων. 2. κλαγγὴ δεινὴ κακῆς θαλάσσης οὐχ ἀνδάνει ψῡχῇ θεᾶς. 3. τίς ἀτῑμάζει κᾱλὰς θεᾱς; 4. οὐκ ἀτῑμάζομεν πάτρην, φίλη γάρ ἐστιν. 5. βαίνουσιν ἐκ Κίλλης εἰς Χρύσην. 6. καίουσι πυρὰς πολλὰς ἐν Χρύσῃ ἐπὶ θαλάσσῃ; 7. ἔχομεν πολλὰς καὶ κᾱλὰς βουλάς. 8. καίετε πυρὰς ἐν πάτρῃ; 9. λύετον, λύεις, λύομεν, λύουσιν, λύετε. 10. ὀλέκομεν ψῡχὰς πολλὰς καὶ κακὰς ἐν πάτρῃ φίλῃ. 11. τίς πέμπει θεὰς ἐς Χρύσην; 12. τελείετε βουλὰς κᾱλὰς πάτρῃ φίλῃ. 13. τελείομεν βουλὴν φίλης θεᾶς. 14. τεύχομεν πυρήν. 15. τί φέρετε; τί φέρουσιν;

22.[3] 1. Who is singing the evil plans of the fair goddesses ?
2. The roar of the sea is pleasing to the soul of the goddess

---

[1] The form of the verb (if not defective) appearing in the Vocabulary is the first person singular of the present active indicative.
[2] Sometimes called "alpha privative."
[3] The English sentences to be translated into Greek are given in considerable number, so that the teacher may have a wider range of choice. Most will find three or four of the more representative of these quite sufficient for their purposes; some may give less, others may wish to use all of them.

9

in Cilla.   3. We do not dishonor the goddesses of (our)
dear fatherland.   4. Are you going from Chrysa to Cilla
by the sea ?   5. The two goddesses come from the sea into
Cilla.   6. They are burning two funeral pyres in (their)
fatherland.   7. They have many fair plans.   8. We loose,
you loose, they (two) loose, he is loosing.   9. The goddess
destroys many wicked souls.   10. We escort the goddesses
into (our) dear fatherland.   11. They accomplish the will
of (their) fatherland.   12. He is making a funeral pyre.
13. What does he bring ?

LESSON VI

THE SECOND DECLENSION

[Up to this point all nouns given in the Vocabularies have been
feminine nouns of the *first declension*. The *declension*—a group
of nouns having similar case endings—to which a noun belongs
is indicated by its genitive singular form, which should be
learned along with the nominative in the Vocabulary. This
lesson introduces the *second declension*, which has a new group of
case endings (678, 679).

Nouns of the second declension can be in the masculine,
feminine, or neuter *gender*. Although the names of men, gods,
and male animals are always in the masculine gender, and those
of women, goddesses, and female animals always in the feminine,
as a rule grammatical gender has nothing to do with sex. With
a few exceptions (see 635) the gender of each noun, indicated by
the demonstrative pronoun (637), must be learned along with
the nominative and genitive forms of the noun in the vocabulary.

The neuter nouns of the second declension employ the same
endings as the masculine nouns, with two exceptions which
apply to *all* neuter nouns: (1) the nominative and accusative
forms of a neuter noun are always identical; (2) the nominative
and accusative *plural* of a neuter noun always end in -α.

10

An adjective always agrees with the noun it modifies in gender, number (singular, dual, or plural), and case. This does not mean that the actual *ending* will necessarily be identical; for example, a feminine noun of the second declension, such as νοῦσος in this lesson, may be modified by an adjective employing the feminine, *first*-declension endings: νοῦσος κακή. In the vocabulary list the masculine form of an adjective is followed by the feminine and neuter endings, which must be learned along with the masculine form: καλός, ή, όν. The adjective μυρίοι in this lesson is used only in the plural; consequently, the feminine and neuter endings are plural: μυρίοι, αι, α.]

23. 1) Learn the declension of θῡμός *heart, spirit,* ἔργον *deed, work,* 678-679, and the adjectives κᾱλός, ή, όν, *good,* and φίλος, η, ον *dear, darling, lovely, beloved,* 717-721.

2) Learn 1025.

Note. — Observe that the masculine of these adjectives is declined like a masculine noun of the second declension (θῡμός, for example), the neuter like a neuter noun of the second declension (ἔργον, for example), and the feminine like a feminine noun of the first declension (βουλή).

24. *Optional : Henceforth use only three sentences of the Greek prose composition in each lesson.*

25. VOCABULARY

ἀγλαός, ή, όν bright, shining, splendid, glorious.

ἀνά, ἄν adv., *and prep. with gen., dat., and acc.,* up(on), along, up through; *adv.,* (up)on, thereon; *with dat.,* (up)on, along; *with acc.,* through(out), up through.

ἀ-περείσιος, η, ον boundless, countless, immeasurable (1168).

ἄποινα, ων, τά ransom(s).

Ἀχαιός, οῦ, ὁ Achaean, *Greek.*

δεινός, ή, όν terrible, awful, dread(ful), fearful.

ἐλώριον, ου, τό booty, spoils, prey.

θεός, οῦ, ὁ god, divinity.

θῡμός, οῦ, ὁ heart, soul, spirit, courage, passion.

κακός, ή, όν bad, poor, ugly, mean, cowardly, evil, wicked.

κᾱλός, ή, όν good(ly), noble, handsome, brave, fair, beautiful.

λᾱός, οῦ, ὁ people, host, soldiery.

μῡρίοι, αι, α countless, innumerable.

νοῦσος, ου, ἡ plague, disease, pest(ilence).

οἰωνός, οῦ, ὁ bird (of prey), vulture, omen.

πολλός, ή, όν much, many, numerous.

11

στρατός, οὗ, ὁ army, encampment, host.   φίλος, η, ον dear, darling, lovely, beloved.

Derivatives: ana-tomy; pena-lty; theo-logy, -cracy, a-theism, poly-, mono-, heno-, pan-theism; laity, lay-man; hoi polloi; strat-egy, -egic(al).

NOTE. — Observe that adjectives are given in the nominative singular (plural, when the singular is not used) of all genders.

Translate:

26. 1. ἀγλαὰ ἄποινα φέρουσιν Ἀχαιοὶ εἰς στρατόν. 2. φέρομεν ἀπερείσι᾽ (575) ἄποινα ἀνὰ στρατὸν Ἀχαιῶν. 3. θεὸς τεύχει πολλοὺς Ἀχαιοὺς ἑλώρια οἰωνοῖσιν. 4. ἦσαν Ἀχαιοὶ κακοί; 5. οὐκ ἦσαν κακοί, κᾶλοὶ δέ. νοῦσος κακὴ ὀλέκει λᾶὸν κᾶλόν. 6. Ἀχαιοὶ πέμπουσιν ἄποινα μῦρί᾽ (575) εἰς πάτρην. 7. θεὸς βαίνει ἐς στρατόν, ὀλέκει δὲ λᾶὸν Ἀχαιῶν. 8. τίς ἀτιμάζει θεοὺς κᾶλούς; 9. κακοὶ λᾶοὶ ἀτιμάζουσι θεοὺς πάτρης. 10. θεὸς πέμπει νοῦσον κακὴν ἀνὰ στρατὸν Ἀχαιῶν, οὐ γὰρ τελείουσι βουλὴν θεῶν πάτρης. 11. βαίνει ἐπὶ θάλασσαν δεινὴν καὶ τεύχει πυρὰς πολλὰς ἀνὰ στρατὸν Ἀχαιῶν. 12. ἔχουσιν ἀπερείσι᾽ (575) ἄποινα Ἀχαιῶν ἐνὶ στρατῷ. 13. βουλὴ στρατοῦ οὐχ ἁνδάνει θυμῷ (996) θεοῦ. 14. λᾶὸς Κίλλης φίλος ἦν ψυχῇ θεᾶς θαλάσσης. 15. οὐκ ἀείδομεν κᾶλὰς βουλὰς θεῶν στρατῷ, οὐ γὰρ ἁνδάνει Ἀχαιοῖσι (996) θυμῷ (1009).

27. 1. The terrible roar of the sea is pleasing to the goddess (996) in (her) soul (1009). 2. We bring many splendid ransoms to the army of the Achaeans. 3. The god does not destroy the host of the Achaeans, for they do not dishonor the gods of (their) fatherland. 4. The evil plague makes countless Achaeans a booty (*use plural*) for many birds. 5. The people of the Achaeans send countless shining ransoms to the goddess of the sea in Cilla. 6. The Achaeans go to the sea and sing, but the noise is not

12

pleasing to the goddess (996) in (her) soul (1009). 7. The plague destroys the people, for they dishonor the god of Chrysa. *See 24.*

LESSON VII

REVIEW

[The Vocabulary in this lesson includes all the words assigned thus far. For most students homemade flash cards are the best device for memorizing vocabulary. They are efficient because the student who uses them will not waste time studying words that have already been learned, and they make rapid review very easy.]

28. Review carefully everything studied thus far.

29. *Optional:* review all the optional sections studied thus far.

30.   VOCABULARY

ἀγλαός, ή, όν bright, shining, splendid, glorious.

ἀείδω sing (of), hymn, chant.

ἀν- (ἀ- *before consonants*), *an inseparable prefix* ("*alpha privative*"), not, un-, dis-, -less, without.

ἀνά, ἄν, *adv., and prep. with gen., dat., and acc.,* up(on), along, up through, thereon, high on; *adv.,* (up)on, thereon; *with dat.,* (up)on, along; *with acc.,* through(out), up through.

ἀνδάνω please (*with dat.* 996).

ἀ-περείσιος, η, ον boundless, immeasurable, countless (1168).

ἄποινα, ων, τά ransom(s).

ἀ-τῑμάζω dishonor, slight, insult.

Ἀχαιός, οῦ, ὁ Achaean, *Greek.*

βαίνω come, go, walk.

βουλή, ῆς, ἡ plan, will, wish, purpose, council, counsel.

γάρ (*postpositive*) for, in fact.

δέ (*postpositive*) but, and, so, for.

δεινός, ή, όν terrible, awful, dread-(ful), fearful.

εἰς (ἐς) *adv., and prep. with acc.,* into, to, until, therein.

εἰσί(ν) are. ἐστί(ν) is.

ἐκ (ἐξ), *adv., and prep. with gen.,* out of, from, away (from).

ἐλώριον, ου, τό booty, spoil(s), prey.

ἐν(ί), εἰν *adv., and prep with dat.,* in, among, on, there(in, -on).

ἐπί *adv., and prep. with gen., dat., and acc.,* to (up)on, against, by; *adv.,* (up)on, thereon; *with gen.,* (up)on, over, during; *with dat.,* (up)on, in, for, about, against,

13

at, beside, by; *with acc.*, to, up
to, over, (up)on.
ἐστί(ν) is.
ἔχω have, hold, keep.
ἦν was. ἦσαν were.
θάλασσα, ης, ἡ sea.
θεά, ᾶς, ἡ goddess.
θεός, οῦ, ὁ god, divinity.
θῡμός, οῦ, ὁ heart, spirit, soul, courage, passion.
καί and, also, even; καί . . . καί
both . . . and.
καίω burn, consume.
κακός, ή, όν bad, poor, ugly, mean, cowardly, wicked, evil.
κᾱλός, ή, όν good(ly), brave, noble, handsome, fair, beautiful.
Κίλλα, ης, ἡ Cilla, *a town.*
κλαγγή, ῆς, ἡ CLANG, noise, (up)-roar.
λᾱός, οῦ, ὁ people, host, soldiery.
λύω loose, free, destroy, break up.
μῡρίοι, αι, α countless, innumer-

able.
νοῦσος, ου, ἡ disease, plague, pest-(ilence).
οἰωνός, οῦ, ὁ bird, vulture, omen.
ὀλέκω kill, destroy, ruin.
οὐ (οὐκ, οὐχ) not, no.
πάτρη, ης, ἡ fatherland, native land.
πέμπω send, escort, conduct.
πολλός, ή, όν much, many, numerous.
πυρή, ῆς, ἡ (funeral) pyre.
στρατός, οῦ, ὁ army, encampment, host.
τελείω accomplish, fulfill, complete.
τεύχω do, make, perform, fashion, cause, prepare.
τίς, τί who? which? what? (τί why?)
φέρω bear, bring, carry.
φίλος, η, ον dear, darling, lovely, beloved.
Χρύση, ης, ἡ Chrysa, *a town.*
ψῡχή, ῆς, ἡ soul, breath, life, spirit.

NOTE. — No word will be found in any reading lesson which has not first been given in a special vocabulary. If the student will memorize accurately all the words in each special vocabulary, it will not be necessary to consult the general vocabulary at the end of the book.

Translate :

31. 1. ἀείδομεν θεὰν θαλάσσης δεινῆς κλαγγῇ πολλῇ.
2. οὐκ ἀτῑμάζουσι θεούς. 3. βουλαὶ Ἀχαιῶν οὐχ ἀνδάνουσι
θεᾷ κᾱλῇ θῡμῷ. 4. βαίνει ἐκ στρατοῦ Ἀχαιῶν εἰς Κίλλαν καὶ
φέρει ἀπερείσι᾽ ἄποινα θεῷ. 5. νοῦσος κακὴ βαίνει ἀνὰ στρα-
τὸν καὶ τεύχει πολλοὺς Ἀχαιοὺς ἑλώρια οἰωνοῖσιν. 6. καὶ θεοὶ
καὶ θεαὶ ὀλέκουσι λᾱὸν Ἀχαιῶν. 7. τίς Ἀχαιῶν ἔχει θῡμὸν
κακόν; 8. ἦσαν πολλαὶ θεαὶ ἐνὶ θαλάσσῃ; 9. καίει πυρὰς
ἐπὶ θαλάσσῃ. 10. λύετε στρατὸν Ἀχαιῶν. 11. πάτρη ἐστὶ
φίλη ψῡχῇ μῡρίων Ἀχαιῶν. 12. τίς πέμπει στρατὸν ἐκ

14

Κίλλης εἰς Χρύσην;   13.   βουλὴ κακή ἐστιν, ἀνδάνει δὲ θεᾷ
θῡμῷ.   14.   τί ἀείδετε ;

32. 1. The Achaeans sing the beautiful goddess of the ter-
rible sea.   2. We do not dishonor the gods, for they are dear
to (our) souls.   3. The plans of the army are pleasing to
the goddess in (her) noble soul.   4. Many Achaeans are
going from the encampment and are bringing countless
glorious ransoms to the gods.   5. The evil plague destroys
the people and makes the army a booty for countless birds.
6. We do not sing, for it is not pleasing to the soul of the
goddess. *See 24.*

LESSON VIII

SECOND DECLENSION (*Continued*)

[The terminology in 34 (below) is apt to be very confusing to a
student who has not been exposed to traditional grammar. This
difficulty can be overcome by studying very carefully the English
meanings of the pronouns listed here and by paying particularly
close attention to their use in the Greek sentences given in 38.]

33. Several words (all of them pronouns except ἄλλος, η,
ο) are declined like κᾱλός, ή, όν (721), with the exception
that the neuter nominative, accusative, and vocative singular
ends in -o instead of in -ον.

34. These words are :

ὅs, ἥ, ὅ *relative pronoun,* who, which, what.

ὁ, ἡ, τό *demonstrative, personal, and relative pronoun,* this, that; he,
she, it; who, which, what.

(ἐ)κεῖνος, η, ο *demonstr. pron.,* that (one), he, she, it.

αὐτός, ή, ό, *intensive pron.,* self, him(self), her(self), it(self), same.

ἄλλος, η, ο other, another.

35. Learn the declension of these words (765–766, 773–774).

36. *Optional. See 24.*

37.　　　　　　　VOCABULARY

ἀλλά but, moreover.

ἄλλος, η, ο other, another.

αὐτός, ή, ό self, him(self), her(self), it(self), same.

δῖος, α,[1] ον DIVINE, heavenly, glorious.

(ἐ)κεῖνος, η, ο = κεῖνος, η, ο that (one), he, she, it.

ἑκη-βόλος, ου, ὁ free-shooter, sharpshooter, *epithet of Apollo*. *As an adjective*: shooting, hitting, according to will (desire, inclination, pleasure); *as subst.:* freeshooter, sure-shooter, sharp-shooter, a dead shot.

κακῶς evilly, wickedly, harshly, with evil consequences.

κεῖνος, η, ο = ἐκεῖνος, η, ο.

ὁ, ἡ, τό this, that; he, she, it; who, which, what.

ὅς, ἥ, ὅ who, which, what.

οὕνεκα (οὗ-ἕνεκα) because.

σκῆπτρον, ου, τό SCEPTRE, staff.

τέ (*enclitic, postpositive*) and, also; τέ . . . τέ (or τέ . . . καί, or καὶ . . . τέ) both . . . and, not only . . . but also.

χρύσεος, η, ον gold(en), of gold.

Derivatives : allo-pathy; auto-maton, -cracy, -graph, -nomy; chrys-anthemum, -alis, -olite.

Translate :

38. 1. δῖος ἑκηβόλος αὐτὸς ἀείδει, ἀλλ᾽ οὐχ ἀνδάνει ἄλλοισι θεοῖσι θυμῷ (996, 1009). 2. κεῖνοι Ἀχαιοὶ ἀτῑμάζουσι τοὺς θεούς. 3. ὁ ἑκηβόλος πέμπει νοῦσον κακὴν ἀνὰ στρατὸν Ἀχαιῶν καὶ κακῶς ὀλέκει κεῖνον λᾱόν, οὕνεκα τὸν ἀτῑμάζουσιν. 4. οὐκ ἀτῑμάζομεν τοὺς θεούς, οἳ ἔχουσι σκῆπτρα χρύσεα. 5. ὁ ἑκηβόλος τε καὶ οἱ ἄλλοι θεοὶ φέρουσι χρύσεα σκῆπτρα κᾱλά. 6. τίς τεύχει τὰ σκῆπτρα χρύσεα τοῖσι θεοῖς θαλάσσης; 7. ἀείδει ἑκηβόλος αὐτὸς βουλὰς ἄλλων θεῶν τοῖσιν Ἀχαιοῖσιν; 8. εἰσὶν οἱ Ἀχαιοὶ κᾱλοί, οἳ ὀλέκουσι τὸν στρατὸν καίουσί τε τὰς πυράς; 9. ἡ θεὰ τῆς δεινῆς θαλάσσης ἔχει τὸ σκῆπτρον χρύσεον. 10. ἐνὶ τῇ πάτρῃ εἰσὶν αἱ πυραί. 11. τίς τεύχει τὸν στρατὸν ἑλώρια τοῖσιν οἰωνοῖσιν;

39. 1. Does the divine free-shooter himself sing these noble plans of the gods? 2. Why is it not pleasing to these

---

[1] Declined like θάλασσα.

16

other gods who are in the sea? 3. That Achaean dishonors those gods of (his) fatherland who have these golden sceptres. 4. This free-shooter sends many evil plagues up through that camp of the Achaeans and destroys countless people (plural), because they dishonor him. 5. Who is burning those funeral pyres of the Achaeans by the terrible sea? 6. This free-shooter makes countless Achaeans a booty for the birds, because they dishonor these beautiful goddesses of the sea.

LESSON IX

THE IMPERFECT OF VERBS IN -ω

[The *imperfect tense* describes incomplete or continuous action taking place in the past. Its approximate English equivalent is the past progressive tense (ἔλυον, "I was loosing"), but a simple past tense is often more appropriate in the English translation.]

40. Learn : 1) the principles of the formation of the imperfect, 830–840.

2) the imperfect active indicative of λύω, 904.

41. *Optional :*

42.   **VOCABULARY**

ἄλλη elsewhere.

'Αργεῖος, ου, ὁ Argive, *Greek.*

-δε *with acc.* 788, 4, to.

διά *adv., and prep. with gen. and acc.,* through, on account of, by means of; *adv.,* between, among; *with gen.,* through; *with acc.,* through, by means of, on account of, during.

δι-φιλος, η, ον dear to Zeus (1168).

εἴρω speak, say, tell.

ἐμός, ή, όν my, mine.

ἔργον, ου, τό (Ϝεργον) WORK, deed, accomplishment.

-θεν *gen. ending* 788, 3, from.

Κλυταιμ(ν)ήστρη, ης, ἡ Clytaem(n)estra, *wife of Agamemnon, leader of the Greeks before Troy. She proved unfaithful to her husband in his absence, and murdered him on his return home.*

μαντοσύνη, ης, ἡ gift of prophecy.

οἶκος, ου, ὁ house, home.

'Ολύμπιος, η, ον Olympian.

"Ολυμπος, ου, ὁ Olympus.

Πρίαμος, ου, ὁ Priam, *king of Troy.*

σός, σή, σόν your, yours.

17

Derivatives: dia-meter; erg, en-ergy; mantic, mantis; necro-mancy; eco-nomy, -logy.

Translate:

43. 1. ὁ ἑκηβόλος διὰ μαντοσύνην εἴρει βουλὰς τῶν θεῶν Ἀργείοισιν. 2. οἱ Ὀλύμπιοι θεοὶ εἶχον (836) οἴκους ἐν Ὀλύμπῳ. 3. ὁ ἑκηβόλος διίφιλος ἔτευχε τοὺς Ἀργείους Ἀχαιούς τε ἑλώρια οἰωνοῖσιν. 4. Ἀχαιοὶ Ἀργεῖοί τ᾽ ἔτευχον ἔργα κακὰ διὰ βουλὴν θεᾶς. 5. Κλυταιμ(ν)ήστρη διὰ τὸν θῡμὸν ἔτευχεν τὰ ἔργα δεινά. 6. Πρίαμος λᾱός τε Πριάμου ὤλεκον πολλοὺς Ἀργείους. 7. τίς εἴρει τὰ σὰ ἔργα κακὰ Πριάμῳ; 8. τὰ ἔργα ἐμά ἐστι (973, 1) κᾱλά, οὕνεκα ἔτευχον βουλὰς θεῶν καὶ θεάων διὰ τὴν μαντοσύνην. 9. ἐπέμπομεν τὰ χρύσεα σκῆπτρα εἰς οἶκον Πριάμῳ. 10. ἐκαίετε τὰς πυρὰς δεινῇ κλαγγῇ; 11. οὐχ ἥνδανε ἡ βουλὴ θεᾷ θαλάσσης θῡμῷ; 12. αἱ θεαὶ ἀείδουσι τὰ κᾱλὰ ἔργα τῶν θεῶν, ἑκηβόλος δὲ βαίνει ἄλλῃ. 13. εἶχε (836) Πρίαμος ἀγλαὸν καὶ κᾱλὸν οἶκον.

44. 1. Who brought these countless shining ransoms to the beautiful home of Priam? 2. The Achaeans and the Argives burned many funeral pyres in your beloved fatherland. 3. Clytaem(n)estra was wicked and performed many dreadful deeds. 4. Through the gift of prophecy we tell many glorious deeds of the gods and goddesses who have Olympian homes. 5. My deeds are noble but yours are cowardly. 6. The gods sent an evil plague up through the camp and destroyed many Achaeans, because they dishonored the free-shooter. 7. It was not pleasing to Clytaem(n)estra in (her) wicked soul.

YOUTH READING A PAPY-
RUS ROLL

Relief on a sarcophagus

LESSON X

THE FUTURE AND AORIST OF VERBS IN -ω

[The *future tense* describes action taking place in the future: λύσω, "I shall loose."

There is no precise English equivalent of the *aorist tense* (from ἀόριστος, "without boundaries, indefinite"). It expresses not so much the *time* of action as its type or *aspect*: momentary or instantaneous action as opposed to the continuous action described by the present and imperfect (1078–1081). It can also be used to express general truths (1082). It is usually best translated by a simple English past: ἔλυσα, "I loosed." Occasionally, however, the present tense must be used in translation.

Note that a substantial number of important verbs employ an alternate form of aorist known as the *second aorist* (see 46 below). Generally these differ only in form, not in meaning, from first aorists (cf. 864), and very few verbs employ both.

The future first singular and the aorist first singular form the second and third *principal parts* of the verb, and should be learned along with the present first singular. If a verb employs a second aorist as well as a first, it appears in parentheses after the first aorist among the principal parts.]

45. Learn: 1) the principles of the formation of the future and the aorist of verbs, 841–857.

2) The future and aorist active indicative of λύω, 904.

46. Learn 863–866 and the first column of 933.

47.   **VOCABULARY**

ἄγ-ω, ἄξω, ἤγαγον, 863; 865, 1, 4, lead, drive, conduct, bring, carry, take.

ἀνάσσω (Ϝανακ-), ἀνάξω, ἤναξα, *with gen.*, 985, rule (over), guard, protect.

ἄριστος, η, ον best, noblest, bravest, fairest, *superl. of* ἀγαθός, ή, όν good.

αὖτις (back) again, anew.

Δαναός, οῦ, ὁ Danaan, *Greek.*

ἑκατόμ-βη, ης, ἡ HECATOMB, sacri-

19

fice, *a number of animals (origi-*
nally one hundred cattle) offered
in sacrifice.
θάνατος, ου, ὁ death.
ῖλιος, ου, ἡ Ilium, Troy; 2) the
Troad, *i.e.* the region around
Troy.

μεγά-θῡμος, η, ον great-souled, brave.
ὄχα (by) far, much, considerably.
πείθω (πειθ-, ποιθ-, πιθ-), πείσω,
ἔπεισα (πέπιθον) persuade, win
over, mislead.
φιλέ-ω, φιλήσω, ἐφίλησα love, cher-
ish, entertain hospitably.

Derivatives : ped-, dem-, syn-agogue ; aristo-cracy ;
thanat-opsis, eu-thanasia 610, 9.

NOTE. — *Henceforth the first three forms of all complete verbs, as found
in the vocabulary, will be the first person singular of the present, future, and
aorist active indicative. These should be mastered absolutely.*

Translate :

48. 1. τίς ἦν ὄχ᾽ ἄριστος Δαναῶν; 2. Πρίαμος μεγάθῡμος
ἤνασσεν Ἰλίου (985). 3. οὐκ αὖτις ἄξουσι Δαναοὶ μεγάθῡμοι
ἑκατόμβᾱς πολλὰς εἰς Χρύσην. 4. οὐκ ἔπεισαν ἑκηβόλον
πολλῇς ἑκατόμβῃσι κᾱλῇσιν. 5. οὐ φιλήσομεν θεούς, οὕνεκα
κᾱλοί εἰσιν; 6. Δαναοὶ τεύξουσι θάνατον Πριάμῳ ἐν Ἰλίῳ.
7. ἐφίλησα θεὰν θαλάσσης, ἀλλ᾽ οὐχ ἥνδανε ἑκηβόλῳ θῡμῷ.
8. ἀείσομεν καὶ πείσομεν θεούς. 9. ὄχ᾽ ἄριστοι ἐν Ἰλίῳ τὰ
εἶπον [εἴρω 57] Πριάμῳ, ἀλλὰ τοὺς ἠτίμασεν. 10. Πρίαμος
ἔπεμψε τὸν στρατὸν ἄριστον ἐπ᾽ Ἀργείοισιν. 11. ἔβησαν
[βαίνω 57] αὖτις Δαναοὶ εἰς Ἰλιον, ἀλλ᾽ οὐκ ἔπεισαν Πρίαμον.
12. ἀείσομεν ἑκηβόλον ὄχ᾽ ἄριστον θεῶν, οὕνεκ᾽ ἤγαγε [ἄγω]
Δαναοὺς εἰς Ἰλιον.

49. 1. The great-souled Achaeans will not persuade the
free-shooter with goodly hecatombs, but he will prepare evil
death for the people. 2. The noblest of the Achaeans
went to Ilium, but they did not persuade the soul of Priam.
3. We shall sing, because the gods have led (*aor.*) the peo-
ple into Troy. 4. We shall have many shining golden
sceptres. 5. Did you not love the gods who have Olympian
homes? 6. Priam shall not rule Ilium again, for the

Achaeans will prepare evil death for him. 7. Did he speak to the beautiful goddess of the sea? 8. They will persuade the souls of the gods with many hecatombs.

LESSON XI

MASCULINE NOUNS OF THE FIRST DECLENSION. COMPOUND VERBS

[The endings of first-declension masculine nouns differ from those of first-declension feminine nouns in the nominative and genitive singular only: αἰχμητής, ᾱο but βουλή, ῆς.]

50. Learn : 1) the declension of 'Ατρεΐδης and αἰχμητής, 664–675.

2) The principles of the formation of compound verbs, 838–839.

51. *Optional :*

52. VOCABULARY

ἀνα-βαίνω (βαν-, βα-), ἀναβήσω (ἀνα-βήσομαι), ἀνέβησα (ἀνέβην) go up, ascend, embark.

ἀπο-λύ-ω, ἀπολύσω, ἀπέλῡσα loose, set free, release.

Ατρείδης, ᾱο (εω), ὁ son of Atreus, *usually refers to Agamemnon.*

κατα-καίω (καυ-, καϝ-, και-), κατα-καύσω*, κατέκηα burn, consume.

*κλεύω (κλευ-, κλεϝ-, κλυ-), —, ἔκλυον *with* gen. 984, hear, hearken to.

μετ-έειπον or μετεῖπον = μετὰ-εῖπον

(Fεπ-), *2d* aor. *of* εἴρω spoke among, addressed, *with dat.*

ὅτε when(ever).

Πηληιάδης, ᾱο (εω), ὁ son of Peleus, *Achilles.*

προσ-έειπον or προσεῖπον *2d* aor. *of* εἴρω (Fεπ-) addressed, spoke to.

τότε then, at that time.

χολό-ω, χολώσω, ἐχόλωσα anger, enrage, vex.

Χρῦσης, ᾱο (εω), ὁ Chryses, *a priest of the god, Apollo, from the town Chrysa.*

Translate :

53. 1. κᾱλοὶ θεοὶ ἔτευξαν θάνατον κακὸν δίῳ Πηληιάδῃ, ὁ δ' ἀνέβη πυρήν. 2. ἐκηβόλος ὤλεκε λᾱὸν 'Αχαιῶν, οὕνεκα

21

δῖος Ἀτρείδης ἠτίμασε Χρύσην. 3. κατέκηα ἑκατόμβας πολ-
λάς. 4. ἐκηβόλος οὐκ ἔκλυεν Ἀτρείδαο, οὕνεκα ἠτίμασε
Χρύσην. 5. Χρύσης μετέειπεν Ἀχαιοῖσιν, ἀλλ᾽ οὐκ Ἀτρείδῃ
ἥνδανε θυμῷ. 6. ὅτε κακῶς προσέειπεν Ἀτρείδης Χρύσην,
τότε ἐχόλωσεν ἐκηβόλον. 7. ἀπελύσαμεν Χρύσην, οὕνεκα τὸν
ἐφιλήσαμεν. 8. Χρύσης ἤνεικεν [φέρω, 57] ἀπερείσι᾽ ἀγλά᾽
ἄποινα Ἀτρείδῃ. 9. οἴσομεν [φέρω, 57] ἄποινα πολλὰ καὶ
ἀπολύσομεν Χρύσην, οὕνεκα τὸν ἐφιλήσαμεν, καὶ φίλος ἐστὶν
ἐκηβόλῳ. 10. τίς φέρει ἄποινα Χρύσᾱο Ἀτρείδῃ; 11. δῖος
Πηληιάδης ἐχόλωσεν Ἀτρείδην. 12. ὅτε κατεκήαμεν πολλὰς
ἑκατόμβας κᾱλάς, τότε ἐπείσαμεν θῡμοὺς θεῶν. 13. διὰ μαν-
τοσύνην Χρύσης εἶπε βουλὰς θεῶν Ἀτρείδῃ Πηληιάδῃ τε.

54. 1. The Achaeans ascended into Troy and killed the
noble Priam. 2. We burned many goodly hecatombs to the
Olympian gods. 3. Chryses spoke among the Achaeans
(*dat.*), but the son of Atreus did not hearken to him (*gen.*,
984). 4. The Achaeans addressed the son of Atreus, but
he did not free Chryses. 5. The son of Atreus will bring
many ransoms into the camp of the Achaeans. 6. Who
will persuade the gods with many goodly hecatombs?

LESSON XII

REVIEW

[Once again (and for the last time) the Vocabulary in this lesson
includes all the words assigned thus far. Note particularly the
principal parts of the verbs.]

55. Memorize the names and order of the letters in the
Greek alphabet, 501.

56. Review all the forms that have been given in the pre-
ceding lessons, and learn the following vocabulary absolutely.

57.   VOCABULARY

ἀγλαός, ή, όν bright, shining, splendid, glorious.

ἄγ-ω, ἄξω, ἤγαγον lead, drive, conduct, bring.

ἀείδ-ω, ἀείσω, ἤεισα sing (of), hymn, chant.

ἀλλά but, moreover.

ἄλλη elsewhere.

ἄλλος, η, ο other, another.

ἀν- (ἀ- before consonants), an inseparable prefix ("alpha privative"), not, un-, dis-, -less, without.

ἀνά, ἄν adv., and prep. with gen., dat., and acc., up(on), along, up through, thereon, high on; adv., (up)on, thereon; with dat., (up) on, along; with acc., through (out), up through.

ἀνα-βαίνω (βαν-, βα-), ἀναβήσω (ἀναβήσομαι), ἀνέβησα (ἀνέβην) go up, ascend.

ἀνάσσω (Ϝανακ-), ἀνάξω, ἤναξα (with gen. 985) rule (over), guard, protect.

ἀνδάνω (σϝαδ(ε)), ἁδήσω†, ἴαδον (εὔαδον), (with dat. 996) please.

ἀ-περείσιος, η, ον boundless, countless, immeasurable (571, 1168).

ἄποινα, ων, τά ransom(s).

ἀπο-λύ-ω, ἀπολύσω, ἀπέλῦσα loose, set free.

Ἀργεῖος, ον, ὁ Argive, Greek.

ἄριστος, η, ον best, noblest, bravest, fairest (superl. of ἀγαθός).

ἀ-τῑμάζω (τῑμαδ-), ἀτῑμάσω*, ἠτίμασα dishonor, slight, insult.

Ἀτρείδης, āο (εω), ὁ son of Atreus, usually refers to Agamemnon.

αὖτις (back) again, anew.

αὐτός, ή, ό self, him(self), her(self), it(self), same.

Ἀχαιός, οῦ, ὁ Achaean, Greek.

βαίνω (βαν-, βα-), βήσω (βήσομαι), ἔβησα (ἔβην) come, go, walk.

βουλή, ῆς, ἡ plan, will, wish, purpose, counsel, council.

γάρ (postpositive) for, in fact.

Δαναός, οῦ, ὁ Danaan, Greek.

δέ (postpositive) and, but, for, so.

-δε, with acc. (788, 4) to.

δεινός, ή, όν terrible, awful, dread (ful), fearful.

διά, adv., and prep. with gen. and acc. through, by means of, on account of; adv., between, among; with gen., through; with acc., through, by means of, on account of, during.

διΐ-φιλος, η, ον dear to Zeus, beloved of Zeus (1168).

δῖος, a, ον divine, godlike, glorious, heavenly.

εἴρω (Ϝερ-, Ϝρη-, Ϝεπ-), ἐρέω, εἶπον (ἔειπον) speak, say, tell.

εἰς (ἐς) adv., and prep. with acc. into, to; until, therein.

εἰσί(ν) are.

ἐκ (ἐξ), adv., and prep. with gen. out of, (away) from.

ἑκατόμ-βη, ης, ἡ hecatomb, sacrifice.

(ἐ)κεῖνος, η, ο that (one), he, she, it.

ἑκη-βόλος, ον, ὁ free-shooter, epithet of Apollo.

ἐλώριον, ον, τό booty, spoil(s), prey.

ἐμός, ή, όν my, mine.

ἐν(ί), εἰν adv., and prep. with dat. in, among, at, on, there(in, -on).

ἐπί, adv., and prep. with gen., dat., and acc. to, (up)on, against, by; adv., (up)on, thereon; with gen., (up)on, over, during; with dat., up(on), in, for, about, against, at, beside, by; with acc., to, up to, over, (up)on.

ἔργον, ου, τό (ϝεργον) WORK, deed, accomplishment, feat.

ἔς = εἰς.

ἐστί(ν) is.

ἔχω (σεχ-, σχ-, σχε-, 603, 619) ἔξω (σχήσω), ἔσχον have, hold, keep.

ἦν was. ἦσαν were.

θάλασσα, ης, ἡ sea.

θάνατος, ου, ὁ death.

θεά, ᾶς, ἡ goddess.

-θεν gen. ending (712), from.

θεός, οῦ, ὁ god, divinity.

θῡμός, οῦ, ὁ heart, soul, spirit, courage, passion.

Ἴλιος, ου, ἡ Ilium, Troy, the Troad.

καί and, also, even, furthermore.

καί . . . καί both . . . and, not only . . . but also.

καίω (καυ-, καϝ-, και-), καύσω*, ἔκηα burn, consume.

κακός, ή, όν bad, poor, ugly, mean, cowardly, wicked, evil.

κᾱλός, ή, όν good(ly), noble, brave, fair, righteous, beautiful, handsome.

κατα-καίω (καυ-, καϝ-, και-), κατακαύσω*, κατέκηα burn (down), consume.

κεῖνος, η, ο = ἐκεῖνος, η, ο.

Κίλλα, ης, ἡ Cilla, a town in the Troad.

κλαγγή, ῆς, ἡ CLANG, noise, shriek, (up)roar.

Κλυταιμ(ν)ήστρη, ης, ἡ Clytaem-(n)estra.

*κλεύω (κλευ-, κλεϝ-, κλυ-), —, ἔκλυον (with gen., 984) hear, hearken to.

λᾱός, οῦ, ὁ people, host, soldiery.

λύ-ω, λύσω, ἔλῡσα loose, free, break up, destroy.

μαντοσύνη, ης, ἡ gift of prophecy.

μεγά-θῡμος, η, ον great-souled.

μετ-έειπον (2d aor.), (ϝεπ-), spoke among, addressed (with dat.).

μῡρίοι, αι, α countless, innumerable.

νοῦσος, ου, ἡ plague, pest(ilence), disease.

ὁ, ἡ, τό this, that; he, she, it; who, which, what.

οἶκος, ου, ὁ house, home.

οἰωνός, οῦ, ὁ bird (of prey), vulture, omen.

ὀλέκ-ω kill, destroy, ruin.

Ὀλύμπιος, η, ον Olympian.

Ὄλυμπος, ου, ὁ Olympus.

ὅς, ἥ, ὅ who, which, what.

ὅτε when(ever).

οὐ (οὐκ, οὐχ) not, no.

οὕνεκα (οὗ-ἕνεκα) because.

ὄχα far, by far, much, considerably.

πάτρη, ης, ἡ fatherland, native land.

πείθω (πειθ-, ποιθ-, πιθ-), πείσω, ἔπεισα (πέπιθον) persuade, win over, mislead.

πέμπω (πεμπ-, πομπ-), πέμψω, ἔπεμψα send, escort, conduct.

Πηληιάδης, αο (εω), ὁ son of Peleus, Achilles.

πολλός, ή, όν much, many, numerous.

24

Πρίαμος, ου, ὁ Priam, *king of Troy.*
προσ-έειπον *(2d aor.)* (ϝεπ-) spoke to, addressed.
πυρή, ῆς, ἡ (funeral) pyre.
σκῆπτρον, ου, τό SCEPTRE, staff.
σός, σή, σόν your, yours.
στρατός, οῦ, ὁ army, encampment, host.
τέ *(postpositive enclitic)*, and, also; τέ . . . τέ (or τέ . . . καί) both . . . and, not only . . . but also.
τελείω (τελεσ-), τελέω (τελέσ(σ)ω), ἐτέλεσ(σ)α accomplish, fulfill, perform.
τεύχω (τευχ-, τυχ-, τυκ-), τεύξω, ἔτευξα (τέτυκον) do, make, perform, cause, fashion, prepare.

τίς, τί who? which? what? τί why? (780–781).
τότε then, at that time.
φέρω (φερ-, οἰ-, ἐνεκ-), οἴσω, ἤνεικα bear, bring, carry.
φιλέω, φιλήσω, ἐφίλησα love, cherish, entertain hospitably.
φίλος, η, ον dear, darling, lovely, beloved.
χολό-ω, χολώσω, ἐχόλωσα anger, enrage, vex.
χρύσεος, η, ον gold(en), of gold.
Χρύση, ης, ἡ Chrysa, *a town in the Troad.*
Χρύσης, āο (εω), ὁ Chryses, *a priest.*
ψῡχή, ῆς, ἡ soul, life, breath, spirit.

NOTE. — Throughout this book, words preceded by an asterisk (*) are assumed forms; those followed by an asterisk are Attic, analogous to known Homeric forms, but not found in Homer; those followed by a double asterisk (**) are Attic, not analogous to Homeric forms; those followed by a dagger (†) are not Epic or Attic, but are Ionic or Lyric; those followed by a hyphen (-) are stems (628–630).

LESSON XIII

NOUNS OF THE THIRD DECLENSION

ILIAD, 1–5

[The *third declension* completes the Greek noun system. It includes adjectives and masculine, feminine, and neuter nouns. With the exception of the accusative singular (685), the case endings (other than the nominative singular) of all third-declension nouns are identical in the epic dialect. Of course, the basic rule about neuters (656) still applies, as in the declension of ἔπος (707). It is particularly important to learn the genitive singular of third-declension nouns, since this provides the stem to which the other case endings are attached.

25

Reading of the *Iliad* begins with this lesson. This is the standard text of the poem; it is not abridged or modified in any way. It is advisable to study the prose sentences (61) with great care first; the poetical text will then be much easier to understand. Be sure to check all the cross-references in the notes; they often point the way to very important grammatical information.]

58. 1) Learn the principles of formation of nouns of the third declension, 680–692.

2) Learn the declension of βασιλεύς *king*, ἥρως *hero*, πόλις *city*, and ἔπος *word*, 701–709.

3) Read the Introduction, pp. xxxix--lii.

4) Memorize thoroughly the word list, 4, which has all the words used in this lesson.

59. *Optional:*

60. **VOCABULARY**

*"Ἀις, "Ἀιδος, ὁ (*nom. not used*) Hades, *god of the lower world.*

ἄλγος, εος, τό grief, pain, woe, trouble.

'Ἀχιλλεύς, ῆος, ὁ Achilles.

δαίς, δαιτός, ἡ feast, banquet, portion.

Ζεύς, Διός, ὁ Zeus, *father and king of gods and men.*

ἥρως, ἥρωος, ὁ HERO, mighty warrior, protector, savior.

ἴφθιμος, (η), ον mighty, valiant, stout-hearted, brave; 723–724.

κύων, κυνός, ὁ, ἡ dog.

μῆνις, ιος, ἡ wrath, fury, madness, rage.

οὐλόμενος, η, ον accursed, destructive, deadly (= ὀλόμενος, 1168).

προ-ϊάπ-τω, προϊάψω, προΐαψα hurl forward, send forth.

τί-θημι,[1] (θη-, θε-), θήσω, ἔθηκα[1] put, place, cause.

Derivatives: see 4, and find some new ones in the dictionary.

---

[1] Verbs (if not deponent, 897) as they appear in the Vocabulary (in the first person singular, present active indicative) ordinarily end in -ω, but some end in -μι. Several of those ending in -μι reduplicate (874, 886) the present with ι, as τίθημι (τι–θημι) = θι–θημι (619) *put, place, cause,* δίδωμι (δι–δωμι) *give, grant.* Of these verbs ἵημι, δίδωμι, and τίθημι have -κα as the ending of the aorist instead of -σα, 841–843.

Translate:

61. 1. μῆνις Πηληιάδεω Ἀχιλῆος ἦν οὐλομένη, ἔθηκε γὰρ μυρί' ἄλγεα τοῖσιν Ἀχαιοῖσιν, προΐαψε δὲ πολλὰς ψῡχὰς ἰφθίμους ἡρώων Ἄιδι, ἔτευχε δ' αὐτοὺς ἑλώρια καὶ δαῖτα κύνεσσιν οἰωνοῖσί τε, ἐτέλεσε δὲ βουλὴν Διός. 2. θεὰ ἀείδει μῆνιν οὐλομένην Ἀχιλῆος, ἣ ἔθηκεν μυρί' ἄλγε' Ἀχαιοῖσιν. 3. θεοὶ ὀλέκουσι τὸν στρατόν, καὶ προϊάπτουσι πολλὰς ψῡχὰς ἡρώων Ἄιδι. 4. τεύξομεν μῡρίους Ἀχαιοὺς ἑλώρια κύνεσσιν καὶ δαῖτα τοῖσιν οἰωνοῖσιν, οὕνεκα ἠτίμασαν Χρύσην. 5. κᾱλὴ ἦν ἡ βουλὴ Διός.

GREEK SOLDIERS IN ARMS

From a Greek vase of about the time of the battle of Marathon.

62. *Iliad, 1–5.*

Μῆνιν ἄειδε, θεά, Πηληιάδεω Ἀχιλῆος   1
οὐλομένην, ἣ μυρί' Ἀχαιοῖς ἄλγε' ἔθηκεν,
πολλὰς δ' ἰφθίμους ψυχὰς Ἄιδι προΐαψεν
ἡρώων, αὐτοὺς δὲ ἑλώρια τεῦχε κύνεσσιν
οἰωνοῖσί τε δαῖτα, Διὸς δ' ἐτελείετο βουλή,   5

NOTE. — Observe that the long doubtful vowels (519) are not marked in the Homeric passages (520), as their length must be learned from the metre.

63. 1. **Μῆνιν** is emphatic, by position, as the central theme of the *Iliad*. It is the mad *wrath* of Achilles, and its terrible consequences to the Greeks, which the poet uses as a thread for his plot. — **ἄειδε** [ἀείδω]: pres. act. imperat., 2d sing., *sing, i.e.* inspire me with thy gift of song,

27

1069. — θεά (the muse of song) is vocative. — Πηληιάδεω = Πηληιάδᾱο, 573 (probably Πηληιάδᾱ᾽ Ἀχιλῆος stood here originally).

2. οὐλομένην is emphatic as being at the head of the verse, and at the end of its clause, and out of the natural order. It is in a kind of apposition with μῆνιν, as though it were an afterthought, and is expanded and amplified by the following clause. — ἥ [ὅς, ἥ, ὅ 773] refers to μῆνιν. — μῡρί᾽ Ἀχαιοῖς: for the hiatus see 576; 1178, 3.

3. Merely a picturesque way of saying "killed." — προΐαψεν: 830–831, 837. — Ἄιδι = Ἄϝιδι. To the ancient Greeks the realm of Hades was not primarily a place of punishment, of tortures, and of horrors, as the Christian Hell, but was a faint and cheerless copy of the upper world, and was the abode of *all* departed spirits of the dead. Consequently no one, no matter how good and pious, was anxious to die. — ἰφθ-: 724.

4. ἡρώων is emphatic, as coming at the beginning of the verse, and out of its natural order. — δὲ ἑλώρια = δὲ ϝελώρια (580). — αὐτούς: *themselves*, *i.e.* their bodies, as contrasted with their shadows, or souls. — τεῦχε = ἔτευχε: 837. In order for the soul of the deceased to obtain rest, it was necessary that the body be buried, or cremated, with the proper funeral rites. If the enemy gained possession of his foe's body, as a mark of the worst he could do, he might give it over to the dogs and birds to devour. This heightened the pathos of the poet's theme.

5. ἐτελείετο [τελείω]: imperf. pass. indic., 3d sing., *was being accomplished*.

These verses, together with the two following, form the prooemium, or introduction to the *Iliad*. The subject is announced in the very first word (μῆνις). It is the wrath of Achilles and its disastrous consequences to the Greeks, but all in accordance with the will of Zeus, which form the principal theme of the poem.

64. Translate :

1. The valiant Achaeans are singing the accursed wrath of Achilles. 2. The wrath of Achilles caused many woes to the Achaeans and sent many valiant souls of heroes to the god Hades. 3. We shall make the army of the Achaeans a booty for the dogs and a banquet for the birds. 4. We are accomplishing the will of the goddess.

LESSON XIV

PROSODY. THE GREEK HEXAMETER

ILIAD, 1-5

65. 1) Read carefully the sections on quantity and prosody, 519–526 and 1159–1192.

2) Copy and mark the scansion of the first five verses of the *Iliad*.

66. Remember that the only vowels the quantity of which is not known are *a, ι, υ* and that their length is indicated in the vocabulary. As soon as possible the student should master the rules for the length of vowels of the inflectional endings, so as to be free from the vocabulary in this particular.

67. In marking the scansion of these verses, use the sign (⁻) to indicate a long syllable, and the sign (˘) for a short syllable, separating the feet from each other by the perpendicular line (|).

68. The written word-accent must be disregarded in reading the verse.

69. *Iliad 1–5*

Μῆνιν ἄειδε, θεά, Πηληϊάδεω ᾿Αχιλῆος   1
οὐλομένην, ἣ μυρί᾽ ᾿Αχαιοῖς ἄλγε᾽ ἔθηκεν,
πολλὰς δ᾽ ἰφθίμους ψυχὰς ῎Αϊδι προΐαψεν
ἡρώων, αὐτοὺς δὲ ἑλώρια τεῦχε κύνεσσιν
οἰωνοῖσί τε δαῖτα, Διὸς δ᾽ ἐτελείετο βουλή,   5

70. The first syllable of *μῆνιν* must be long, having a long vowel, 522. The accent shows that the second syllable must be short, 545, 1160. Then, having one long and one short, the next syllable (*ἄ-*) must be short, as when there is one long followed by a short, there must be another short to complete the foot, 1169.

The next syllable (*-ει-*) is long, being a diphthong, 521–522.

29

The next syllable (-δε) is short, having a short vowel followed by a single consonant.

The next syllable (θε-) is short also, having a short vowel followed by another vowel.

As this completes this foot, the final syllable (-ά) of θεά must be long, as it is the first syllable of the next foot, 1171.

The next syllable (Πη-) is long, having a long vowel, 522.

The next syllable (-λη-) is long, having a long vowel, 522.

The next vowel (-ι-) is short. See the vocabulary.

Then the next syllable (-ά-) must be short to complete the foot.

The next vowel (-ε-) is short, but as the first syllable of a foot must be long, 1171, the -δεω is pronounced as one long syllable, by synizesis, 586.

The next vowel ('Α-) is short. See the vocabulary.

Then the next syllable (-χι-) must be short to complete the foot.

The next syllable (-λῆ-) is long, having a long vowel.

The final syllable (-ος) is short, having a short vowel, but must be marked long here, as the final syllable is always long, owing to the pause in the verse, 1184.

Therefore the metrical scheme of this verse is:

$$-\cup\cup \mid -\cup\cup \mid -- \mid -\cup\cup \mid -\cup\cup \mid --$$

Now mark the next verse : οὐλομένην, ἣ μυρί᾽ Ἀχαιοῖς ἄλγε᾽ ἔθηκεν,

The first syllable (οὐ-) is long, being a diphthong.

The second syllable (-λο-) is short, having a short vowel.

The next (-μέ-) is short, having a short vowel.

The next (-νην) is long, having a long vowel.

The next (ἣ) is long, having a long vowel.

As this completes the second foot, the next syllable (μυ-) must be long, as it is the first syllable of the next foot.

The next syllable (-ρί᾽) is short, as is indicated by the accent, since only short vowels are elided, 575, 1162.

Then the next syllable ('A-) must be short, to complete the foot.

The next syllable (-χαι-) is long, having a diphthong.

The next syllable (-οῖς) is long, having a diphthong.

The next syllable (ἀλ-) is long, followed by two consonants.

The next syllable (-γε᾽) is short, having a short vowel.

The next syllable (ἔ-) is short, having a short vowel.

The next syllable (-θη-) is long, having a long vowel.

The next syllable (-κεν) is short, but is long here, owing to its place in the verse, 1184.

Therefore this verse should be scanned as follows:

71. Using these principles, and the rules given, 1159–1192, mark the scansion of the first five verses, and do not attempt any further work in Homer till the first three have been memorized and can be repeated rhythmically with ease.

72. A good plan to follow at first is to mark only the syllables of which the quantity is certain, without having to consult the vocabulary. When this is done, the quantity of the remaining syllables can usually be determined from their position in the verse.

73. Before attempting to memorize a verse, it should always be translated several times, till the student is quite familiar with the exact meaning of every word and understands accurately every construction in it.

74. First the teacher may repeat these verses a few times for the students, then with them, till they have the movement mastered, but after that the students should be able to recite them alone.

75. Let each student recite these separately, then let them be repeated by small groups, and finally in concert by the entire class.

76. In repeating these verses orally, the words must of course be kept distinct and no break must be made between the separate feet, unless there is a pause in sense, caesura, 1185, or diaeresis, 1188.

77. Careful attention must be paid to the meaning of the passage, and the various pauses should be indicated by the voice. Of course the voice must not be allowed to drop at the end of a verse unless there is a distinct pause there.

LESSON XV

THIRD DECLENSION (*Continued*)

ILIAD, 1–10

[The third-declension nouns assigned in this and succeeding lessons follow the principles outlined in Lesson XIII. Once their genitive singulars are learned, the student should have no difficulty in predicting their remaining forms. As Pharr suggests, ἄναξ (693) can be used as a paradigm for the entire third declension.

Pharr's suggestion (in the note to 78 below) about memorization may seem a bit old-fashioned to the modern reader, but in fact such memorization is one of the very best ways of learning the language and appreciating the unique qualities of Homeric poetry.]

78. 1) Learn the declension of ἄναξ *king*, παῖς *child*, and ἀνήρ *man*, 693–694, 697–700.

2) Memorize the first five verses of the *Iliad*, 82.

NOTE. — Henceforth always copy and scan each lesson from Homer, and memorize not less than one verse per day till the first twenty-one are covered. In copying these verses, the accents and breathings must not be omitted.

79. *Optional:*

80.   **VOCABULARY**

ἄναξ, ἄνακτος, ὁ king, lord, protector.
ἀνήρ, ἀνέρος (ἀνδρός), ὁ (real) man, warrior, hero (571, 1168).

ἄρ(α), (ῥά) naturally, of course, as you know, as you might expect, that is, in effect. *It is not always*

32

translatable into English, which has for it no exact equivalent.

βασιλεύς, ῆος, ὁ king, ruler.

δή indeed, truly, forsooth, now.

δι-ί-στημι (στη-, στα-), διαστήσω, διέστησα (διέστην) STAND apart, separate.

ἐρίζω (ἐριδ-), —, ἥρισ(σ)α quarrel, strive.

ἔρις, ιδος, ἡ strife, quarrel.

Λητώ, Λητόος (Λητοῦς 584–585) ἡ Leto, *mother of Apollo.*

μάχ-ομαι,[1] fight, battle.

ξυν-ί-ημι (= σι-σημι 603–604; ἡ-, ἑ-), ξυνήσω, ξυνῆκα[2] (ξυνέηκα),[2] bring together, throw together, hearken, heed.

ὄρ-νυμι, ὄρσω, ὦρσα (ὤρορον) stir up, kindle, incite, excite, arouse.

πρῶτος, η, ον first, foremost, chief; τὸ πρῶτον, τὰ πρῶτα, *as adverb,* 780–781, at first, firstly, first.

υἱός, οῦ (ἑος, ος), ὁ son.

Derivatives: poly-andry, phil-anderer, Andrew, andro gynous; basil-isk, -ica; stay, static, stand; eristic; logo-, theo-machy; proto-plasm, -zoön, -type.

81. Translate.

1. θεὰ ἀείσει μῆνιν Ἀχιλῆος, ἐξ οὗ (*from the time when,* i.e. beginning at the point in the story) δὴ τὰ πρῶτα δῖος Ἀχιλλεὺς καὶ Ἀτρεΐδης ἄναξ ἀνδρῶν ἠρισάτην [ἐρίζω] καὶ διεστήτην [διίστημι]. 2. τίς θεῶν ξυνέηκε [ξυνίημι] δῖον Ἀχιλῆά τε καὶ Ἀτρεΐδην ἔριδι (1009) μάχεσθαι (*to fight*); 3. υἱὸς Λητόος καὶ Διός, ἑκηβόλος, ξυνέηκέ σφωε (*these two*) ἔριδι μάχεσθαι, τὸν γὰρ βασιλεὺς Ἀτρεΐδης ἐχόλωσεν, ὁ δ᾽ ὦρσε κακὴν νοῦσον ἀνὰ στρατὸν Ἀχαιῶν, ὤλεκε δὲ λαούς.

82. Copy, scan, and translate:

Iliad, 1–10.

Μῆνιν ἄειδε, θεά, Πηληιάδεω Ἀχιλῆος
οὐλομένην, ἣ μυρί᾽ Ἀχαιοῖς ἄλγε᾽ ἔθηκεν,
πολλὰς δ᾽ ἰφθίμους ψυχὰς Ἄιδι προΐαψεν
ἡρώων, αὐτοὺς δὲ ἑλώρια τεῦχε κύνεσσιν
οἰωνοῖσί τε δαῖτα, Διὸς δ᾽ ἐτελείετο βουλή,   5

[1] 87, Note.   [2] 60, footnote.

ἐξ οὗ δὴ τὰ πρῶτα διαστήτην ἐρίσαντε
'Ατρεΐδης τε ἄναξ ἀνδρῶν καὶ δῖος 'Αχιλλεύς.
τίς τ' ἄρ σφωε θεῶν ἔριδι ξυνέηκε μάχεσθαι;
Λητοῦς καὶ Διὸς υἱός. ὁ γὰρ βασιλῆι χολωθεὶς
νοῦσον ἀνὰ στρατὸν ὦρσε κακήν, ὀλέκοντο δὲ λαοί,   10

83. 6. οὗ [ὅς, ἥ, ὅ, 773], **ἐξ οὗ,** referring back to **ἄειδε** *from the time when,*
literally, *from what* [*time*]. — **τὰ πρῶτα:** 780–781. — **διαστήτην** = διεστή-
την, 837 [διίστημι]. — **ἐρίσαντε** [ἐρίζω] : aor. active participle, nom., dual,
masc., (*they two) having quarreled.*
7 is in apposition with the subject of **διαστήτην.** The son of Atreus is
Agamemnon, commander-in-chief of the allied Greek military expedition
against Troy, undertaken to bring back Helen, wife of Menelaus, brother
of Agamemnon : she had been stolen away from her home in Greece by
Paris, son of Priam, and was now in Troy. — **τε ἄναξ** = τε ϝάναξ, 580.
The son of Atreus was so well known to Homer's hearers, it was not
necessary to give his name, Agamemnon.
8. This verse is a rhetorical question, addressed by the poet to his
audience, to arouse attention and curiosity, and which he then answers
himself : a common device of public speakers. — **σφωε** [ἕο] : 3d pers.
pron., acc. dual, *these two.* — **ἔριδι:** 1009. — **μάχεσθαι** [μάχομαι] : pres. act.
infinitive, deponent, *to fight.*
9. **βασιλῆι:** 996. — **χολωθεὶς** [χολόω] : aor. pass. particip., nom. sing.
masc. (modifies ὁ), *having been enraged.* — **Λητοῦς** = Λητόος, 584–585. —
βασιλῆι = 'Αγαμέμνονι. — **Λητοῦς καὶ Διὸς υἱός** = 'Απόλλων, who was me-
diately the cause of the quarrel, since he brought a plague upon the
Greeks, which gave occasion for the strife between Achilles and Aga-
memnon.
10. **νοῦσον** is emphatic by position, as is **κακήν,** which is further ex-
plained and expanded by the following clause. — **ὀλέκοντο** = ὠλέκοντο,
837 [ὀλέκω], imperf. pass. indic., 3d plur., *were being destroyed, kept per-
ishing.* — **λᾱοί:** the soldiers in the Greek army.

84. Translate :

1. We were singing the accursed wrath of Achilles, from
the time when first the son of Atreus, king of men, and
divine Achilles quarreled and separated.   2. Which (one)
of the gods brought together the Achaeans and the people
of Priam in strife to fight?   3. Did the son of Leto and of

Zeus, the free-shooter, bring these two together in strife to fight? 4. The son of Atreus, king of the Achaeans, and the divine Achilles enraged the lord, the free-shooter, and he kindled many evil plagues up through the camp of the Achaeans and kept destroying the brave people evilly.

LESSON XVI

PRESENT AND FUTURE, MIDDLE AND PASSIVE OF VERBS. DEPONENT VERBS

ILIAD, 11–16

[Up to this point all the verb forms studied have been in the *active* voice, found in both Greek and English, in which the subject performs the action (λύω, "I loose"). Both Greek and English also possess a *passive* voice, in which the subject is acted upon ("I am loosed"). The Greek language, however, has in addition a *middle* voice, which indicates roughly that the subject has a special interest in the action being performed (λύομαι, "I loose for myself"—but a simple active will often do for translation; see 1067). Except for the aorist (and, in later Greek, the future), there are no separate passive endings; the middle endings are used with either a middle or passive meaning, and therefore might be called "medio-passive" endings. The reader must decide from the context whether a middle or passive meaning is indicated by these forms.

Some verbs employ only the medio-passive endings in all or most of their tenses and are known as *deponent* verbs.]

85. 1) Learn the principles of the formation of the middle and passive verbs, and of deponent verbs : 887–897.

2) Learn the present and future, middle and passive, of λύω, 910.

3) Read 1065–1068.

4) Memorize the first seven verses of the *Iliad*.

5) Henceforth always copy and scan each lesson from Homer, and memorize not less than one verse per day till the first twenty-one are learned. The first hundred verses, or more, should be copied and scanned. In copying these verses the word accents and breathings must not be omitted.

6) Learn the declension of θυγάτηρ *daughter*, νηῦς *ship*, δῶμα *house*, and πᾶς, πᾶσα, πᾶν *all, every*, 697–703, 707, 710, 732.

86. *Optional:*

87.　　　　　　　　VOCABULARY

Ἀπόλλων (᾿Απόλλων 571), ωνος, ὁ Apollo (1168).

ἀρητήρ, ῆρος, ὁ priest, pray-er.

δύο (δύω) two.

ἔρχομαι (ἐρχ-, ἐλθ-, ἐλευθ-, ἐλυθ-), ἐλεύσομαι, ἦλθον (ἤλυθον) come, go.

θοός, ή, όν swift, speedy.

θυγάτηρ, τέρος (τρός), ἡ daughter.

κοσμήτωρ, ορος, ὁ commander, marshaller.

λίσσομαι (λιτ-), —, ἐλ(λ)ισάμην (ἐλιτόμην) beg, entreat.

μάλιστα most, especially, by all means.

νηῦς, νηός (νεός), ἡ ship (572).

πᾶς, πᾶσα, πᾶν all, every, (the) whole.

στέμμα, ματος, τό fillet, wreath.

χείρ, χειρός, ἡ hand, arm.

NOTE. — The first form of a regular verb which appears in the vocabulary (pres. act. indic., first sing.) usually ends in -ω, as ἀείδω, λύω, ἔχω, but some end in -μι, as ἴστημι, τίθημι, δίδωμι, ἵημι. The corresponding form for all deponents ends of course in -μαι, as μάχομαι, ἔρχομαι, λίσσομαι.

Derivatives: dual, dy-ad; cosm-etics, -ic, -o-gony (logy); naval, nautical; pan-theism, -demonium, -oply, -orama; chir-o-graphy, -urgeon = surgeon.

88. Translate:

1. ᾿Απόλλων ἑκηβόλος χολοῦται (584–585, 943) βασιλῆι ᾿Ατρείδῃ καὶ πέμπει νοῦσον κακὴν ἀνὰ στρατὸν ᾿Αχαιῶν, ὀλέκονται δὲ λαοί, οὕνεκα δῖος ᾿Ατρείδης ἠτίμασε Χρύσην ἀρητῆρα. 2. Χρύσης γὰρ ἀρητὴρ ἑκηβόλου ἔρχεται ἐπὶ θοὰς νῆας ᾿Αχαιῶν, φέρει δ᾿ ἀπερείσι᾿ ἄποινα θυγατρός, ἣν [ὅς, ἥ, ὅ,

773] Ἀτρείδης ἔχει ἐν στρατῷ. 3. ὁ δ' ἀρητὴρ ἔχει στέμματα ἑκηβόλου Ἀπόλλωνος ἐν χερσὶν ἀνὰ χρῡσέῳ σκήπτρῳ καὶ λίσσεται πάντας Ἀχαιούς, μάλιστα δ' Ἀτρεΐδᾱ δύω κοσμήτορε λᾱῶν. 4. Ἀπόλλων χολώσεται βασιλῆι καὶ ὄρσει νοῦσον κακὴν ἀνὰ στρατόν. 5. ἐλεύσονται ἐπὶ θοὰς νῆας Ἀχαιῶν καὶ οἴσουσι [φέρω] ἀπερείσι' ἄποινα βασιλῆι. 6. λίσσονται πάντας Ἀχαιούς. 7. Ἀτρείδης ἠτίμασεν ἀρητῆρα καὶ οὐκ ἀπέλῡσε θύγατρα.

89. Copy, scan, and translate :

Iliad, 11–16.

οὕνεκα τὸν Χρύσην ἠτίμασεν ἀρητῆρα   11
Ἀτρεΐδης. ὁ γὰρ ἦλθε θοὰς ἐπὶ νῆας Ἀχαιῶν
λῡσόμενός τε θύγατρα φέρων τ' ἀπερείσι' ἄποινα,
στέμματ' ἔχων ἐν χερσὶν ἑκηβόλου Ἀπόλλωνος
χρῡσέῳ ἀνὰ σκήπτρῳ, καὶ ἐλίσσετο πάντας Ἀχαιούς, 15
Ἀτρεΐδα δὲ μάλιστα δύω, κοσμήτορε λᾱῶν ·

90. 11. τόν = (illum): *that well-known*, since the circle of legends is familiar to the hearers of the bard. — **ἠτίμασεν** [ἀτῑμάζω]. **ἀρητῆρα** : 1182. Observe that this verse ends in two spondees, making it a "spondaic" verse. This, together with the position of the final word, throws special emphasis upon it, making it practically equivalent to "although he was a priest," which would of course make him an object of more than ordinary reverence.

12. **Ἀτρεΐδης** is made distinctly emphatic by position. It is he who must bear the burden of responsibility in slighting the priest. — **ἐπὶ νῆας,** *i.e.* to the Greek camp on the shore, where they had drawn up their ships, out of the water.

13. **λῡσόμενος** [λύω]: fut. mid. particip., nom. sing. masc. (modifying ὁ, which refers to the priest) *being about (desiring) to ransom, to ransom,* 1109, 5. — **φέρων** [φέρω]: pres. act. part., nom. sing. masc. (also modifies ὁ), *bearing, bringing.*

14. **ἔχων** [ἔχω]: pres. act. part., nom. sing. masc. (modifies ὁ), *having, holding.* — **χερσὶν ϝεκηβόλου**: explained in 526. — **ἑκηβόλου Ἀπόλλωνος** : 571, 1173.

15. **χρῡσέῳ**: synizesis, 586. — **χρῡσέῳ ἀνά**: 1173. — **καὶ ἐλίσσετο**: 1173.

The latter part of this verse would imply that the scene takes place at a meeting of the assembly of the Greeks.

The sceptre was a symbol of authority. Of course it was of gold if it is to appear decently in epic. The whole atmosphere of a poem of this kind is supramundane. Its leading characters are divine or semi-divine, and their equipment must all be of more precious material than that which suffices for ordinary mortals. Thus Apollo has a golden sword. Several of the warriors before Troy have golden armor, and the gods sit on golden thrones which rest upon the golden pavements of their palaces in Olympus. In the same way the new Jerusalem has streets of gold and gates of pearl. — ἐλίσσετο [λίσσομαι]: imperf. act. ind. 3d sing. deponent verb. Observe the force of the imperfect, the old priest *kept* entreating Agamemnon and his brother Menelaus, but Agamemnon, in spite of these repeated opportunities to avail himself of the mercy of the god, chose deliberately to slight his holy ambassador.

16. ᾽Ατρεΐδᾱ = Menelaus and Agamemnon.

The priest is a native of Chrysa, a small town near Troy, which has been plundered by the invading Greeks. His daughter has been taken prisoner of war, and he now comes to the Greek camp, where the ships have been drawn up on the shore, to ransom her.

91. Translate :

1. Chryses, the priest of Apollo, is dishonored by (dative) the son of Atreus. 2. The Achaeans will go from (their) swift ships to Troy and ransom the beloved daughter of the priest. 3. We shall bring many ransoms and shall hold in (our) hands the fillets of Apollo. 4. We do not have a golden sceptre, but we entreat Priam and all the people of Troy. 5. The two sons of Atreus, marshallers of the people(s), are entreating Priam, but he will slight them. 6. The son of Atreus, king of men, slighted the priest and did not release (his) daughter.

LESSON XVII

THE IMPERFECT, MIDDLE AND PASSIVE, AND THE AORIST MIDDLE OF VERBS

ILIAD, 17–21

[The μέν . . . δέ combination which appears in this lesson's Vocabulary is perhaps the most important pair of particles in the Greek language. These two words make comparison and contrast—essential to logical thought—very easy and natural. Translating them fully ("on the one hand . . . on the other") can be a little awkward. Even if they are not expressed in translation, however, the reader must always be aware of their implications. When the word μέν appears in a line, it means, in effect, "Wait a minute; this is only half the story; the other half will be coming up shortly" (cf. note to line 18). In Homer ἀλλά occasionally takes the place of δέ.]

92. 1) Learn the imperfect middle and passive, and the aorist middle of λύω, 910.

2) Learn the table of endings of the three declensions, 648–658.

93. *Optional:*

94. VOCABULARY

ἅζομαι (ἀγ-) *defect.* reverence.
δέχ-ομαι, δέξομαι, ἐδεξάμην (ἐδέγμην) accept, receive.
δί-δωμι (δω-, δο-), (δι)δώσω, ἔδωκα give, grant.
δῶμα, ατος, τό house, home.
ἐγώ(ν), μέο (μεῦ 584–585), 760, I.
ἐκ-πέρθω (περθ-, πραθ-), ἐκπέρσω, ἐξέπερσα (ἐξέπραθον) sack (utterly).
ἐύ, εὖ well, happily, successfully.
ἐυ-κνήμις, ῖδος well-greaved.
ἱκ-νέομαι, ἵξομαι, ἱκόμην arrive, reach (one's destination).

μέν (*correlative with* δέ) on the one hand, truly. μὲν . . . δέ on the one hand . . . on the other, partly . . . partly, the one . . . the other, etc.
οἴκα-δε 788, 4 home(ward), to home, home.
παῖς, παιδός, ὁ, ἡ child, son, daughter.
π(τ)όλις, ιος, (ηος), ἡ city, state.
σύ, σέο (σεῦ 584–585), 760, you.

39

Derivatives : dose, anti-dote ; dome ; ego-(t)istic(al) ;
eu-phony, -logy, -phemism ; ped-agogue, -o-baptism ; acro-,
necro-, metro-polis, cosmo-politan, politic(s, al).

95. Translate :

1. θεοὶ ἔχουσιν Ὀλύμπια δώματα, ἔδωκαν δ᾽ Ἀτρεΐδης καὶ
ἄλλοισιν ἐϋκνημῖδεσσιν Ἀχαιοῖσιν ἐκπέρσαι (to sack utterly)
πόλιν Πριάμου, τότε δ᾽ ἵκοντο ἐὺ οἴκαδε, οὕνεκα παῖδα φίλην
ἀρητῆρος ἔλυσαν. 2. ἀπέλυσαν ἐϋκνήμῖδες Ἀχαιοὶ θύγατρα
φίλην ἀρητῆρος, ἐδέξαντο δ᾽ ἀγλαὰ ἄποινα, οὕνεκα ἐκηβόλον
Ἀπόλλωνα Διὸς υἱὸν ἅζοντο. 3. ἅζεται ἐκηβόλον. 4. Ἀτρεΐ-
δης οὐκ ἐδέξατο τὰ ἀγλά᾽ ἄποινα. 5. Χρύσης ἀρητὴρ ἔδωκεν
ἄποινα πολλὰ βασιλῆι Ἀτρεΐδη. 6. πάντες θεοὶ καὶ πᾶσαι
θεαὶ εἶχον [ἔχω] Ὀλύμπια δώματα. 7. Ἀχαιοὶ ἐϋκνήμῖδες
ἐκπέρσουσι Πριάμοιο πόλιν, ἵξονται δ᾽ ἐὺ οἴκαδε. 8. παῖς
φίλη ἀρητῆρος ἐλύσατο, ἵκετο δ᾽ ἐὺ οἴκαδε.

96. Copy, scan, and translate :

Iliad, 17–21.

" Ἀτρεΐδαι τε καὶ ἄλλοι ἐϋκνήμῖδες Ἀχαιοί,　　　　17
ὑμῖν μὲν θεοὶ δοῖεν Ὀλύμπια δώματ᾽ ἔχοντες
ἐκπέρσαι Πριάμοιο πόλιν, ἐὺ δ᾽ οἴκαδ᾽ ἱκέσθαι·
παῖδα δ᾽ ἐμοὶ λῦσαί τε φίλην, τά τ᾽ ἄποινα δέχεσθαι　20
ἀζόμενοι Διὸς υἱὸν ἐκηβόλον Ἀπόλλωνα."

97. 17. Ἀτρεΐδαι, etc., vocatives.—καὶ ἄλλοι ἐϋκνήμῖδες: 1173. Greaves
were a kind of leggings, serving as shin guards, for protection against
weapons and to prevent chafing from the long shield of the wearer.
18. ὑμῖν [σύ]: dat. plur., *to you.* — θεοί: one syllable by synizesis, 586.
μέν: correlative with δέ, vs. 20. — δοῖεν [δίδωμι]: aor. act. optative, 3d plur.
(its subject is θεοί), *may they grant.* — ἔχοντες [ἔχω]: pres. act. part.,
nom. plur. masc. (modifies θεοί), *having, possessing,* i.e. inhabiting. The
gods lived in palaces on the top of Olympus, a high mountain in
northern Thessaly. See note on vs. 44, § 138.
19. ἐκπέρσαι [ἐκπέρθω]: aor. act. inf., *to sack utterly.* — ἱκέσθαι [ἱκνέο-
μαι]: aor. act. inf., *to arrive.* — πόλιν: 1167, 1. — δ᾽ϝοίκαδ᾽: 580–1, 1174.

20. From its position in the verse παῖδα is emphatic. " It is my child for whom I make my entreaties." Observe how the addition of φίλην heightens the pathos of the old man's plea. — λῦσαι, δέχεσθαι : aor., and pres. act. inff., used as imperatives, 1107, 11, *free and accept.* 18 ff. ὑμῖν θεοὶ δοῖεν, etc. : " may you get your wish, I mine." 21. ἁζόμενοι [ἄζομαι]: pres. act. part., nom. plur. masc. (modifying the implied subjects of λῦσαι and δέχεσθαι), *reverencing.* 21 is a spondaic verse, 1182. — υἱὸν ϝεκη-, 526.

98. Translate :

1. The gods who have (ἔχοντες) Olympian homes will grant to the sons of Atreus and to the other well-greaved Achaeans to sack utterly (ἐκπέρσαι) the city of Priam. 2. When they sacked the city of Priam, they returned happily home. 3. They accepted the shining ransoms and freed the darling daughter of the priest Chryses. 4. We reverenced the free-shooter Apollo, son of Leto and Zeus, and escaped death. 5. Will the son of Atreus accept the shining ransoms ? 6. The child of the priest was freed, when he gave many shining ransoms, which the two sons of Atreus accepted.

LESSON XVIII

THE PERFECT AND PLUPERFECT ACTIVE OF VERBS

[The *perfect tense* describes action that is complete (Latin *perfectum*): λέλυκα, "I have loosed." Since the action is complete in the present time, the English present is occasionally used to translate this tense; cf. the note on ἀμφιβέβηκας, line 37 (123).

The *pluperfect tense* describes action that has been completed in the past: ἐλελύκη, "I had loosed."

The perfect active first singular is the fourth principal part of the verb. The Tables of verb forms following the Introduction are useful guides to the most efficient use of time and effort in the memorization of forms.]

41

99. 1) Learn the perfect and pluperfect indicative active of λύω 904, and of βαίνω 922, and read 867–886.

2) Learn the declension of γέρων *old man*, αἴξ *goat*, and παῖς *child*, 693–695.

100. *Optional:*

101.   VOCABULARY

ἀγορή, ῆς, ἡ, assembly, meeting place, gathering, harangue.
αἴξ, αἰγός, ὁ, ἡ goat
Ἄργος, εος, τό Argos, *a country and city in Greece.*
γέρων, οντος, ὁ old man.
γῆρας, αος, τό old age, eld.
δέκατος, η, ον tenth.
ἡμέτερος, η, ον our, ours.
θνήσκω (θνη-, θαν), θανέομαι, ἔθανον, τέθνηκα die, perish.
ἱερεύς, ῆος, ὁ priest, holy man.

κοῖλος, η, ον hollow.
μηρίον, ου, τό thigh-piece, thigh-bone.
πούς, ποδός, ὁ foot.
ταῦρος, ου, ὁ bull.
φεύγω (φευγ-, φυγ-), φεύξομαι, ἔφυγον, πέφευγα flee, fly, escape, run (off, away, along).
φρήν, φρενός, ἡ diaphragm, mind, heart, soul, spirit, disposition.
ὠκύς, ὠκεῖα, ὠκύ swift, speedy.

Derivatives: gray 597–598, gero-comy, -cracy; deca-logue, -gon; hier-archy, -o-glyphic(al); anti-podes, tri-pod, poly-p(ous); phreno-logy, frenzy.

102. Translate:

1. Ἀτρείδης οὐκ ἀπολέλυκεν ἱερῆος παῖδα φίλην. 2. βέβαμεν [βαίνω] ἐξ ἀγορῆς. 3. κατέκηε γέρων Ἀπόλλωνι ἄνακτι πολλὰ μηρία ταύρων καὶ αἰγῶν. 4. γῆρας ἔσχεν [ἔχω] ἱερῆα. 5. γῆρας οὐχ ἵκετο βασιλῆι Ἀτρείδῃ, ἔθανε δὲ κακῶς ἐνὶ οἴκῳ ἐν Ἄργει, οὕνεκα τὸν ὤλεκε Κλυταιμ(ν)ήστρη. 6. πόδας ὠκὺς [1014] Ἀχιλλεὺς τέθνηκεν ἐν Ἰλίῳ. 7. ὁ γέρων πέφευγεν εἰς τὴν ἀγορήν.

103. Translate.

1. We have freed the beloved daughter of the priest, because we reverence the free-shooter Apollo. 2. All the Achaeans have gone from the assembly to the hollow ships.

3. The priest burned many thigh-pieces of bulls and of goats to the gods who had Olympian homes. 4. That old man has died in our home. 5. The swift-footed Achilles has gone. 6. The old man has not persuaded the mind of the son of Atreus. 7. Apollo had loved the beautiful goddess of the sea. 8. Shall we flee with swift feet into the city of Priam?

LESSON XIX

THE INFINITIVE

ILIAD, 22–27

[The *infinitive* is a verbal noun. It has no personal endings and hence is not "finite," but it does appear in all tenses and voices: λύειν, "to loose"; λύσειν, "to be about to loose"; etc. In the Homeric text the infinitive has been used in several ways already; in line 8 (Lesson XV) the infinitive complements a verb: ξυνέηκε μάχεσθαι, "brought (them) together to fight" (similar examples appear in lines 18 and 19 in Lesson XVII and in line 23 in this lesson). In line 20 (Lesson XVII) two infinitives are used as imperatives: λῦσαι, δέχεσθαι: "free," "accept." The infinitive can be the subject of a verb; cf. 110, sentence 3 (below). Another important use of the infinitive will be discussed in Lesson XXVI.]

104. Learn all the forms, the meanings, and uses of the infinitives, 908, 914, 920, 1107.

105. *Optional:*

106.   **VOCABULARY**

Ἀγαμέμνων, ονος, ὁ Agamemnon, *king of Mycenae, brother of Helen's husband, Menelaus, and commander-in-chief of the allied Greek military expedition against Troy.*

αἰδέομαι (αἰδεσ-) αἰδέσ(σ)ομαι, ᾐδεσ-(σ)άμην reverence.

ἀφ-ί-ημι (ἡ-, ἑ-), ἀφήσω, ἀφῆκα (ἀφέηκα) send away, dismiss, hurl, drive off.

43

δηθύ-νω (def.), loiter, tarry, delay.
εἶμι (εἰ-. ἰ-) εἴσομαι come, go; pres. often with fut. meaning, shall come, shall go (965).
ἔνθα then, there(upon), here.
ἐπ-ευ-φημέ-ω, ἐπευφημήσω, ἐπευφήμησα shout assent, approve.
ἤ (ἠέ) or, than, whether.
ἤ ... ἤ either ... or, whether ... or.
κιχάνω (κιχ-, κιχε-), κιχήσομαι, ἐκιχησάμην (ἔκιχον, ἐκίχην) come upon, overtake, arrive (at).
κρατερός, ή, όν strong, harsh, powerful, stern, mighty.
μή not, lest, that not.
μῦθος, ου, ὁ word, command, story.
νῦν now, at this time, as matters

now are, as it is. Commonly implies a contrast.
παρά, πάρ, παραί adv., and prep. with gen., dat. and acc., from the side of, by the side of, to the side of, beside, along; adv., beside, near by; with gen., from (the side of, beside); with dat., by (the side of), near, beside; with acc., to the side of, along (by), beside, stretched along.
τέλλω (τελ-, ταλ-), ἔτειλα, τέταλμαι command, enjoin (upon), accomplish, rise.
ὕστερος, η, ον behind, later, at another time, further(more).

Derivatives: eu-phemis(m, tic); mytho-logy, myth-ical; para-graph, par-allel; hysteron proteron.

107. Translate.

1. ὅτε γέρων ἐλίσσετο πάντας Ἀχαιοὺς καὶ Ἀτρεΐδα μάλιστα, ἄλλοι μὲν πάντες Ἀχαιοὶ εἶπον αἰδεῖσθαι τὸν ἱερῆα καὶ δέχθαι ἀγλά' ἄποινα, ἀλλ' οὐχ ἥνδανεν Ἀτρεΐδῃ Ἀγαμέμνονι θυμῷ, ἀλλ' ἀφίει γέροντα κακῶς, ἔτελλε δὲ κρατερὸν μῦθον. 2. Ἀγαμέμνων οὐ κιχήσεται γέροντα παρὰ κοίλῃσι νηυσίν, οὐ γὰρ δηθύνει ἐν στρατῷ Ἀχαιῶν. 3. δηθύνειν, αἰδεῖσθαι, ἰέναι, ἴμεναι, ἰέναι, ἐπευφημέειν, ἐπευφημῆσαι, ἐπευφημήσειν, τέλλειν, τέλλεσθαι, κιχάνειν, κιχάνεσθαι, κιχήσεσθαι, κιχήσασθαι, μάχεσθαι, ἐκπέρθειν, ἐκπέρσειν, ἐκπέρσαι, ἐκπέρσασθαι, ἱκέσθαι, δέχεσθαι, δέξασθαι, ἄζεσθαι.

108. Copy, scan, and translate.

Iliad 22–27

ἔνθ' ἄλλοι μὲν πάντες ἐπευφήμησαν Ἀχαιοὶ
αἰδεῖσθαί θ' ἱερῆα καὶ ἀγλαὰ δέχθαι ἄποινα·

44

ἀλλ' οὐκ Ἀτρείδῃ Ἀγαμέμνονι ἥνδανε θυμῷ,
ἀλλὰ κακῶς ἀφίει, κρατερὸν δ' ἐπὶ μῦθον ἔτελλεν·   25
" μή σε, γέρον, κοίλῃσιν ἐγὼ παρὰ νηυσὶ κιχήω
ἢ νῦν δηθύνοντ' ἢ ὕστερον αὖτις ἰόντα,

109. **22.** **μέν**: corrrelative with **ἀλλ'**, vs. 24, whereby **ἄλλοι πάντες** Ἀχαιοί is contrasted with Ἀτρείδης. **23.** **αἰδεῖσθαι** = αἰδέεσθαι, 584–585. — **θ'** = τε, 575, 582. — **καὶ ἀγλαὰ δέχθαι ἄποινα**: 1173. **24.** **ἀλλ' οὐκ** brings the action of Agamemnon into sharp contrast with that of all the other Achaeans (**ἄλλοι μὲν πάντες**). — Ἀτρείδῃ: 996, 1176. — **ἥνδανε** = ἑάνδανε = ἐσϝανδανε, 835–836, 603–604. — **θυμῷ**: 1009. **25.** **ἐπὶ** . . . **ἔτελλεν**: "tmesis," 1048–1049. — **κακῶς**: harshly (also perhaps with evil, i.e. disastrous consequences). **26.** "Let me not come upon you." — **κιχήω** [κιχάνω]: aor. act. sub_ junctive, 1st sing., with **μή**, may I not come, let me not come upon. — **σέ** [σύ]; acc. sing., you (thee). — **ἐγώ** is always emphatic, 761. **27.** **δηθύνοντ'** = δηθύνοντα [δηθύνω] and **ἰόντα** [εἶμι] are pres. act. participles, acc. sing. masc. (modifying σε), loitering, tarrying. — **αὖτις ἰόντα**: coming back, returning. — **ὕστερον**: adv., 781. — **ἢ ὕστερον** = ἦϝ' ὕστερον.

110. Translate:

1. All the other Achaeans will not shout assent, to reverence the priest and to accept the shining ransoms. 2. We shouted assent, to free the beloved daughter of the priest. 3. To free the daughter of that old man was not pleasing to Agamemnon in his soul. 4. The king sent away that old man harshly, and enjoined a stern command upon (him). 5. Agamemnon did not find the old man beside the hollow ships of the Achaeans, for he did not loiter. 6. To reverence, to fight, to loiter, to send, to have sent, to shout assent, to come upon, to command, to sack utterly, to accept, to be accepted, to be sacked utterly.

LESSON XX

PARTICIPLES, ACTIVE

ILIAD, 28–32

[The *participle* is a verbal adjective: λύων, "loosing." It appears
in all tenses and voices: λύσων, "being about to loose"; λύσας,
"having loosed"; etc. Since it is an adjective, it has different
endings for gender (masculine, feminine, and neuter) and for
number (singular, dual, and plural). The endings for active
participles follow the pattern of ἄναξ (693) in the masculine and
neuter and of θάλασσα (663) in the feminine. Special attention
should be paid to the shorter forms of the masculine and neuter
dative plural.

The participle is used very frequently in Greek; in fact, the
present active participle is the most common verb form in
Greek. For examples of its use review the following participles
from the Homeric text (all of which are translated and identified
in the notes), noting carefully the tense, case and number, full
context, etc.: Lesson XV, line 6, ἐρίσαντε; line 9, χολωθείς;
Lesson XVI, line 13, λυσόμενος and φέρων; line 14, ἔχων; Lesson
XVII, line 18, ἔχοντες; line 21, ἀζόμενοι; Lesson XIX, line 27,
δηθύνοντα and ἰόντα.

Two ambiguities in English can lead to difficulties in trans-
lating from English into Greek. In the sentence "He was freeing
his daughter," "freeing" would not be translated with a Greek
participle; rather, "was freeing" is the way of expressing in
English the meaning of the Greek imperfect tense. In the sen-
tence "Freeing captives was expensive," "freeing" is the subject
of "was" and functions as a noun, not as an adjective; hence, it
would be translated with a Greek infinitive (a verbal noun) and
not with a participle (a verbal adjective).]

111. Learn all the forms of the active participles of λύω,
736 ff., 909.

112. *Optional :*

113. VOCABULARY

ἀντιά-ω, ἀντιάσω (ἀντιόω = ἀντιάω,
945–948,603), ἤντίασα approach,
prepare, partake, share, go
(come) to meet.

ἔπ-ειμι (εἰ-, ἰ-), ἐπείσομαι, come upon,
come on, approach.

ἐπ-οίχομαι (οἰχ-, οἰχε-, οἰχο-), ἐποι-
χήσομαι*, ἐπῴχωκα go to, go
against, attack, ply.

ἐρεθίζω, ἐρεθίσω, ἠρέθισα vex.

ἰστός, οῦ, ὁ loom, mast.

κέ(ν), ἄν (1085–1091) haply, per-
chance, perhaps.

λέχος, εος, τό bed, couch.

μίν acc. only, enclitic, him, her, it.

νέομαι (νεσ-) usually in fut. sense,
come, go, return.

νύ encl. now, indeed, surely, then.

πρίν sooner, until, before, formerly.

σαώτερος, η, ον, comparative of σαός,
ή, όν 747–748, safer.

τηλόθι far (from, away), at a dis-
tance, with gen., 992.

*χραισμέω (χραισμε-, χραισ-), χραι-
σμήσω, ἐχραίσμησα (ἔχραισμον)
with dative, 996, help, assist,
benefit, avail.

ὡς so, how, so that, in order that,
since, like (as), as, when.

Derivatives: soterio-logy, 584–585; tele-graph, -phone,
-pathy, -scope.

114. Translate :

1. σκῆπτρον καὶ στέμμα θεοῖο οὐ χραισμήσουσι τῷ γέροντι,
θανέεται γὰρ παρὰ νηυσὶν Ἀχαιῶν ἢ νῦν δηθύνων ἢ ὕστερον
αὖτις ἰών. 2. οὐ λύσει παῖδα φίλην, πρὶν δὲ γῆρας ἔπεισί
μιν ἐν οἴκῳ Ἀγαμέμνονος ἐν Ἄργεϊ τηλόθι πάτρης γέ-
ροντος. 3. ἔνθα δ᾽ ἀντιάει λέχος Ἀγαμέμνονος καὶ ἐποίχεται
ἱστόν. 4. ἐρεθίσᾱς Ἀγαμέμνονα γέρων οὐ νέεται σαώτερος.
5. Ἀτρεΐδης τε ἄναξ ἀνδρῶν καὶ δῖος Ἀχιλλεὺς ἐρίσαντε διεστή-
την [διίστημι]. 6. γέρων ἦλθε θοὰς ἐπὶ νῆας Ἀχαιῶν φέρων
ἀπερείσι᾽ ἄποινα, ἔχων δὲ στέμματα ἐκηβόλου Ἀπόλλωνος ἐν
χερσίν. 7. θεοὶ ἔχοντες Ὀλύμπια δώματα δώσουσιν [δίδωμι]
Ἀχαιοῖσιν ἐκπέρσαι Πριάμοιο πόλιν, εὖ δ᾽ οἴκαδ᾽ ἱκέσθαι.

115. Copy, scan, and translate :

Iliad, 28–32.

μή νύ τοι οὐ χραίσμῃ σκῆπτρον καὶ στέμμα θεοῖο.

τὴν δ᾽ ἐγὼ οὐ λύσω· πρίν μιν καὶ γῆρας ἔπεισιν

ἡμετέρῳ ἐνὶ οἴκῳ ἐν Ἄργεϊ, τηλόθι πάτρης,

30

47

ἱστὸν ἐποιχομένην καὶ ἐμὸν λέχος ἀντιόωσαν.
ἀλλ᾽ ἴθι, μή μ᾽ ἐρέθιζε, σαώτερος ὥς κε νέηαι."

116. 28. τοι [σύ]: 760, 996. — χραίσμῃ [χραισμέω]: 2d aor. act. subjunct., 3d sing., *may help, avail.* Although singular, this verb has a plural subject. It agrees, however, with the nearest σκῆπτρον, 973, 2.

29. τήν is emphatic, and is said with haughty brevity, and perhaps with a contemptuous gesture or jerk of his thumb over his shoulder toward the tent where the girl was. — ἐγώ is placed in emphatic contrast to the other Greeks. " Even though the others do agree with you, *I* have something to say here." — καί : *even.*

LIONS' GATE, MYCENÆ

The stone relief of triangular shape represents two lions (or lionesses) facing each other on opposite sides of a pillar. The heads of the animals have been lost.

30 ff., said with the definite intention of insulting the father and wounding his feelings as deeply as possible. — ἡμετέρῳ: emphatic; she shall never be returned to *you* and *yours.*

31. ἐποιχομένην [ἐποίχομαι]: pres. act. (deponent) part., acc. sing. fem. (modifies μιν, *her*), *plying.* — ἀντιόωσαν: an "assimilated" form, 945–948.

32. ἴθι [εἶμι]: pres. act. imperat., 2d sing., *go, begone.* — ἐρέθιζε [ἐρεθίζω]: pres. act. imperat., 2d sing., *vex, anger.* — νέηαι [νέομαι], pres. act. (deponent) subjunct., 2d sing., *you may return.* — σαώτερος (emphatic by position) : *more safe(ly),* i.e. than if you should attempt to remain. — νέηαι (οἴκαδε).

117. Translate:

1. The sceptre and the fillets of the god will not avail the old man (*dat.*) if he tarries (*particip.*) beside the hollow ships of the great-souled Achaeans, or if he returns later, for Agamemnon will attack him and send (his) soul to Hades. 2. He will not free his darling daughter, but old age will come upon her in the home of Agamemnon and Clytaem(n)estra, far from (her) native land. 3. Vexing, having vexed, quarreling, having quarreled, bearing, having borne, having, sacking, having sacked, helping, having helped, sharing, having shared, going, tarrying.

LESSON XXI

MIDDLE AND PASSIVE PARTICIPLES

ILIAD, 33-37

[The declension of middle participles follows the pattern of καλός, ή, όν; the aorist passive participle follows the pattern of active participles.

The future middle participle λυσόμενος in line 13, Lesson XVI, is an excellent example of the effect of the middle voice on the meaning of a verb. The future active participle λύσων means "being about to loose" or "free"; the future middle means "being about to free *for himself*"; hence, "being about to *ransom*."]

118. 1) Learn all the forms of the middle and passive participles of λύω, 735–746, 915, 921.

2) Review the active participles, 909, and memorize all eleven forms of the participles, so as to be able to give the nominative singular (all genders) of all of these, together with the meaning.

119. *Optional:*

120.   VOCABULARY

ἀκέων, ουσα, ον silent, quiet, being silent.

ἀμφι-βαίνω (βαν-, βα-), ἀμφιβήσω, (ἀμφιβήσομαι), ἀμφέβησα, (ἀμφέβην), ἀμφιβέβηκα surround, go round, protect.

ἀπ-άνευθε(ν) apart, away.

ἀρά-ομαι, ἀρήσομαι, ἠρησάμην pray, curse, invoke.

ἀργυρό-τοξος, η, ον of a silver bow, equipped with a silver bow, silver-bowed one. Apollo.

γεραιός, ή, όν old; masc. as substantive, old man.

δείδω (δϜι-, δϜει-, δϜοι-), δείσομαι, ἔδεισα, δείδοικα (δείδια) fear, be afraid.

ἔπειτα then, thereupon.

ἠύ-κομος, ον fair-haired, well-haired, beautiful-tressed, well-tressed, having a rich harvest of long, flowing hair (ἐύ-, 571, 1168).

θίς, θῖνός, ἡ beach, shore, strand.

κί-ω (def.) come, go, depart.

πολύ-φλοισβος, ον loud-roaring, heavy-thundering.

τίκτω (= τι-τεκω; τεκ-, τοκ-) τέξω, ἔτεκον, τέτοκα* bear, produce, give birth to.

φημί (φη-, φα-), φήσω, ἔφησα*, imperf. act. ἔφην, mid. ἐφάμην speak, say, tell.

ὥς (ὣς, ὡς) thus, so, in this way; ὡς . . . ὥς as . . . so.

Derivatives : tox-ic(ology), -ine, anti-tox-ine, in-tox-icate ; gray (597–598); comet; poly-gamy, -gyny, -andry, -theism, -technic; pro-phet, -phecy.

121. Translate :

1. Ἀγαμέμνων ὣς ἔφατο, ὁ δὲ γέρων δείσᾱς ἐπείθετο μύθῳ κρατερῷ (996), ἀκέων δ᾽ ἔβη παρὰ θῖνα πολυφλοίσβοιο θαλάσσης, ἔπειτα δὲ κιὼν ἀπάνευθεν ὁ γεραιὸς ἠράετο πολλὰ (780–781) ἄνακτι Ἀπόλλωνι, τὸν ἠύκομος Λητὼ ἔτεκεν. 2. Ἀπόλλων ἄναξ ἔκλυε ἱερῆς ἀραομένου (984), τὸν γὰρ ἐφίλησε. 3. ἑκηβόλος θεὸς ἀμφιβαίνει Χρύσην φίλην. 4. μήνιος (1111) Ἀχιλῆος προϊαψάσης πολλὰς ψυχὰς ἡρώων Ἄιδι τευξάσης δ᾽ αὐτοὺς ἑλώρια κύνεσσιν οἰωνοῖσί τε δαῖτα βουλὴ Διὸς ἐτελείετο. 5. τευχόμενος, τευξόμενος, τευξάμενοι, μαχομένης. 6. γέρων ἦλθε θοὰς ἐπὶ νῆας Ἀχαιῶν λῡσόμενος θύγατρα. 7. πάντες Ἀχαιοὶ λύσουσι παῖδα φίλην γέροντος, ἁζόμενοι υἱὸν Διὸς ἑκηβόλον Ἀπόλλωνα. 8. γῆρας ἔπεισι τὴν ἐνὶ οἴκῳ Ἀγαμέμνονος Κλυταιμ(ν)ήστρης τε ἐποιχομένην ἱστόν.

122. Copy, scan, and translate :

Iliad, 33–37

ὣς ἔφατ᾽, ἔδεισεν δ᾽ ὁ γέρων καὶ ἐπείθετο μύθῳ.
βῆ δ᾽ ἀκέων παρὰ θῖνα πολυφλοίσβοιο θαλάσσης.
πολλὰ δ᾽ ἔπειτ᾽ ἀπάνευθε κιὼν ἠρᾶθ᾽ ὁ γεραιὸς   35
Ἀπόλλωνι ἄνακτι, τὸν ἠύκομος τέκε Λητώ ·
" κλῦθί μευ, ἀργυρότοξ᾽, ὃς Χρύσην ἀμφιβέβηκας

123. 33. ἔδεισεν = ἔδϝεισεν. — ὁ: demonstrative, as in vs. 35 below, *that old man.* — μύθῳ : 996.
34. βῆ = ἔβη.

35. πολλά : 780–781. — ἠρᾶθ᾽ = ἠρᾶτο = ἠράετο [ἀράομαι], 575, 582, 584–585.
36. τέκε = ἔτεκε. — ϝάνακτι : *protecting lord, protector.* — τόν : relative, may have been thought of as demonstrative, 1028, 3, Note.
37. κλῦθι [*κλεύω]: aor. act. imperat., 2d sing., *hear!* — μευ [ἐγώ]: gen. sing., 984. — ἀργυρότοξ᾽(ε) is of course vocative. The use of this epithet instead of the name indicates how intimate the priest was with the god whom he served. "Come, O Lord, with thy silver bow!" By calling upon him in his capacity as archer god, the priest already has in mind the kind of answer he desires to his prayer. He would have the god slay the Greeks with his arrows. Naturally the bow of Apollo must be of precious metal, as befits the dignity of a god. Read again the note on vs. 15, § 90. — ἀμφιβέβηκας : the perfect is to be translated as a present, *dost protect.* It is the figure of a warrior bestriding a fallen comrade, or of an animal bestriding its young, in the face of danger, for protection.

124. Translate:

1. Thus spoke Agamemnon, and the old man obeyed the stern command, because he feared (*use the aor. particip.*). 2. They went in silence along the strand of the loud-roaring sea, and going apart they prayed much to (their) lord Apollo, whom fair-haired Leto bore to Zeus. 3. Apollo of the silver bow heard the Greeks praying, for they were dear to (his) soul. 4. Many aged men came from Troy to the camp of the Achaeans to ransom (their) beloved sons.

5. The Achaeans will free the two sons of the priest and accept the shining ransoms, because they reverence the gods who have Olympian homes. 6. Old age will come upon the daughters of Priam while they are plying the loom in the homes of the sons of the Achaeans.

LESSON XXII

THE PERFECT, PLUPERFECT, AND FUTURE PERFECT OF VERBS

Iliad, 38–42

[Note that the middle voice is included in this lesson. The perfect middle first singular is the fifth principal part of the verb.

The instrumental case which survives in ἶφι (see Vocabulary) was practically extinct in Greek by the time the *Iliad* was composed; its function was taken over by the dative.]

125. 1) Read the sections dealing with the formation of these tenses, 867–892.

2) Learn the perfect, pluperfect, and future perfect indicative, active, middle and passive of λύω, 904, 910.

126. *Optional:*

127.   VOCABULARY

βέλος, εος, τό dart, arrow, shaft, missile. (*Cf.* βάλλω.)

δάκρυ, υος, τό tear.

ἐέλδωρ (*indecl.*) τό desire, wish.

εἰ (αἰ) if, whether.

ἐρέφ-ω*, ἐρέψω*, ἤρεψα ROOF (over), cover, build.

ζά-θεος, η, ον very sacred, holy, sacrosanct.

ἠδέ and, also.

ἶφι mightily, with might: *an old instrumental of* Ϝἶς, *might, cf. Lat. vis.*

κραιαίνω (κραν-), ἐκρήηνα accomplish, perform, fulfill.

νηός, οῦ, ὁ temple, shrine.

ὅ-δε, ἥ-δε, τό-δε this, that.

πίων, πίειρα, πῖον fat, rich.

ποτέ (*encl.*) ever, at any (some) time, once.

Σμινθεύς, ῆος, ὁ Smintheus, *mouse god, an epithet of Apollo.*

Τένεδος, ου, ἡ Tenedos, *an island near Troy.*

τίνω (τει-, τι-, τινϝ-), τίσω, ἔτῑσα,

τέτῑκα*, τέτῑσμαι* requite, atone for, pay the penalty.

χαρίεις, εσσα, εν pleasing, grateful, graceful, agreeable.

Derivatives : charity, eu-charist.

128. Translate :

1. Ἀπόλλων ἄναξ ἀμφιβέβηκε Χρύσην Κίλλαν τε ζαθέην.
2. Σμινθεὺς ἀνάσσει ἶφι Τενέδου φίλης. 3. ἤρεψαν Σμινθῆι νηὸν χαρίεντα κατέκηαν δὲ πίονα μηρία ταύρων αἰγῶν τε. 4. εἴ ποτε κραιαίνει ἄναξ ἐέλδωρ ἱερῆι, Δαναοὶ τίσουσι δάκρυα γέροντος βέλεσσιν θεοῦ.

129. Copy, scan, and translate.   *Review the preceding lesson to get the connection.*

Iliad, 38–42

Κίλλαν τε ζαθέην, Τενέδοιό τε ἶφι ἀνάσσεις,
Σμινθεῦ, εἴ ποτέ τοι χαρίεντ' ἐπὶ νηὸν ἔρεψα,
ἢ εἰ δή ποτέ τοι κατὰ πίονα μηρί' ἔκηα
ταύρων ἠδ' αἰγῶν, τόδε μοι κρήηνον ἐέλδωρ·
τίσειαν Δαναοὶ ἐμὰ δάκρυα σοῖσι βέλεσσιν."

40

130. 38. Τενέδοιο : 985. — ἀνάσσεις : *art protecting lord.* — τε ϝίφι ϝανάσσεις.

39. ἐπί . . . ἔρεψα : 1049. The part the old priest took in building the temple may have involved no more work than the superintending of the job, while ordinary people performed the labor. — τοι [σύ] : dat. sing., *for thee.* — Σμινθεῦ : as in vs. 37 the priest calls upon the god by his title of ἀργυρότοξος, thereby intimating that he should bring along his bow, so here he evidently has a purpose in mind by calling upon him by his title of Smintheus, *mouse god.* For the old Greeks, probably without knowing the scientific basis, recognized the connection of mice with plagues. (Compare the spread of the bubonic plague by means of rats.) Thus Apollo with his mice could bring a deadly plague upon whomsoever he chose.

40. τοι [σύ] : dat. sing., *for thee.* — κατὰ . . . ἔκηα : 1049.

41. **μοι** [ἐγώ]: dat. sing., *for me.* — **κρήηνον** [κραιαίνω]: aor. act. imperat., 2d sing., *accomplish!*

42. **τίσειαν** [τίνω]: aor. act. optative, 3d plur., *may they atone for!* **βέλεσσιν**: 1005. — **Δαναοί** seems to be used as a name for the Greeks in Homer, with no particular distinction in meaning from Ἀχαιοί or Ἀργεῖοι.

131. Translate:

1. All the gods who have Olympian homes protect very sacred Chrysa and Cilla.   2. Apollo Smintheus will rule Tenedos by his might.   3. We roofed many pleasing temples to the Olympian gods and burned for them the fat thigh-pieces of bulls and goats.   4. If we accomplish the will of the god, he will destroy the wicked Danaans with his darts.   5. Agamemnon will atone for the tears of the old man.

LESSON XXIII

THE SUBJUNCTIVE MODE OF VERBS

Iliad, 43–47

[The *subjunctive mode* is almost extinct in English (in the expression "if this be true," "be" is a subjunctive). The translations of the subjunctive given with the paradigms (905, 911) are, as Pharr notes, approximate and incomplete. For the uses and various translations of the subjunctive see 1098–1101 and 1115–1117.]

132. The subjunctive has only the present, aorist, and perfect tenses.   The perfect is seldom found.   In all tenses the subjunctive has the primary (816) endings.

133. Learn the conjugation of the active, middle and passive, subjunctive of λύω, 905, 911, observing that the thematic vowel (796) sometimes called the *mode vowel,* which is short in the indicative, regularly becomes long in the subjunctive. That is, ε and ο in the indicative regularly become η and ω in the subjunctive. Thus λύομεν, λύετε, λύομαι, λύεαι, λύεται, λυόμεθα, etc., of the indicative regularly become λύωμεν, λύητε, λύωμαι, λύηαι, λύηται, λυώμεθα, etc., in the subjunctive, 799–800.

134. *Optional:*

135. VOCABULARY

ἀμφ-ηρεφής, ές (731) covered at both ends.

εἴκω (ϝεικ-, ϝοικ-, ϝικ-), εἴξω, ἔοικα be like, resemble, be fitting, seem (likely), appear (suitable).

εὔχ-ομαι, εὔξομαι, εὐξάμην, εὖγμαι* pray, talk loud, boast, exult.

κάρηνον, ου, τό peak, summit, headland, citadel.

κατά *adv.*, *and prep. with gen. and acc.*, down (from), down over, down through; *adv.*, down, below; *with gen.*, down (over, from, below); *with acc.*, down (along, through), according to, on.

κῆρ, κῆρος, τό heart, soul.

κῑνέ-ω*, κῑνήσω*, ἐκίνησα, κεκίνημαι* move, stir; *middle and pass.*, move self, bestir, go, come.

κλάζω (κλαγγ-, κλαγ-), κλάγξω*, ἔκλαγξα (ἔκλαγον), κέκληγα CLANG, roar, shriek, resound.

νύξ, νυκτός, ἡ night, darkness.

ὀϊστός, οῦ, ὁ arrow, shaft.

τόξον, ου, τό bow.

φαρέτρη, ης, ἡ quiver.

Φοῖβος, ου, ὁ Phoebus, = clear, bright, shining, *surname of Apollo.*

χώ-ομαι, χώσομαι, ἐχωσάμην be angry, be enraged, be irritated.

ὦμος, ου, ὁ shoulder.

Derivatives: cranium (597–598); kinetic(al), cinema (tograph).

136. Translate:

1. εὔχετο πολλὰ ὁ γέρων, τοῦ δ᾽ ἔκλυε Φοῖβος Ἀπόλλων.
2. θεοὶ δ᾽ ἔκλυον Ἀχαιῶν εὐχομένων. 3. βαίνουσι θεοὶ πάντες κατὰ καρήνων Ὀλύμπου χωόμενοι κῆρ (1014). 4. ἔχουσι τόξα καὶ φαρέτρᾱς ἀμφηρεφέας ὤμοισιν. 5. κλάζουσιν ὀϊστοὶ ἐπ᾽ ὤμων Ἀπόλλωνος χωομένου. 6. χωόμενος θεὸς ᾔε [εἶμι] ἐοικὼς νυκτὶ κατὰ καρήνων Οὐλύμπου (Ὀλύμπου, 571). 7. μή σε κοίλῃσιν ἐγὼ παρὰ νηυσὶν κιχήω, μή νύ τοι οὐ χραίσμῃ σκῆπτρον. 8. γέρων ἐρεθίσᾱς Ἀγαμέμνονα μὴ σαώτερος νέηται. 9. σαώτερος ὥς κε νέηαι.

55

137. Copy, scan, and translate:

Iliad, 43-47

ὣς ἔφατ᾽ εὐχόμενος, τοῦ δ᾽ ἔκλυε Φοῖβος Ἀπόλλων,
βῆ δὲ κατ᾽ Οὐλύμποιο καρήνων χωόμενος κῆρ,
τόξ᾽ ὤμοισιν ἔχων ἀμφηρεφέα τε φαρέτρην.   45
ἔκλαγξαν δ᾽ ἄρ᾽ ὀιστοὶ ἐπ᾽ ὤμων χωομένοιο,
αὐτοῦ κινηθέντος · ὁ δ᾽ ἤιε νυκτὶ ἐοικώς.

138. 43. ἔφατ᾽ [φημί]. — τοῦ: 984. — Φοῖβος : *bright, shining;* Apollo
was god of light.

44. βῆ = ἔβη [βαίνω], set out. — Οὐλύμποιο, 1168, 571. — κῆρ: 1014.

45. τόξα : only one bow; the use of the plural visualizes its various
parts. — ὤμοισιν : 1009. — ἀμφηρεφέα has its final vowel long here,
although it is short by nature. See 1168 for explanation.

46. ἔκλαγξαν : like πολυφλοίσβοιο (vs. 34) is an onomatopoetic word,
by the use of which we are made to *hear* the rattle of the arrows of the
god in his rage. — χωομένοιο is used substantively, *of him enraged.*

47. αὐτοῦ κῑνηθέντος : 1111. — νυκτί : 1007. — ϝεϝοικώς. — αὐτοῦ is em-
phatic by position. It is none less than the mighty god himself who is
now before us. νυκτὶ ἐοικώς : *like unto night*, both in swiftness of com-
ing and in the awful gloom and dread which night brings to primitive
peoples who have no adequate lighting facilities. This expression visu-
alizes his appearance for the eye, as ἔκλαγξαν presents his coming to the
ear.

139. Translate:

1. Apollo heard the Achaeans as they prayed.   2. The
gods went down from the summits of Olympus.   3. Let us
carry bows and quivers on (our) shoulders.   4. The arrows
may clang upon the shoulders of the angry gods.   5. May
we not come upon the children, beside the hollow ships.
6. They may return more safely home when they have
sacked utterly the city of Priam.

LESSON XXIV

IMPERATIVE VERBS, ACTIVE

ILIAD, 48-52

[The *imperative* is used for commands: λύε, "loose." Although the imperative appears in the aorist tense as well as in the present, it is very difficult to indicate the difference between the two tenses in translation; as Pharr suggests (907, and notes to 905), the present λύε means approximately "continue to loose" or "keep loosing," while the aorist λῦσον means "loose (once and for all)." One way to remember the aorist second singular imperative (λῦσον) is to recall the phrase *Kyrie eleison* ("Lord, have mercy") from the Roman Catholic Mass.]

140. Learn all the active imperative forms of λύω, 907.

141. Spend the next two lessons in a careful review of all forms and vocabularies that have been covered. Then read again Homer's *Iliad*, 1–52, with special attention to each form, and more particularly the imperatives.

142. VOCABULARY

αἰεί, αἰέν (= αἰϝεί) always, EVER, continually, eternally.

ἀργός, ή, όν bright, swift, flashing.

ἀργύρεος, η, ον silver(y), of silver.

αὐτάρ (ἀτάρ 571) but, moreover, on the other hand.

βάλλω (βαλ-, βλη-) βαλέω, ἔβαλον, βέβληκα, βέβλημαι throw, hurl, shoot, dash.

βιός, οῦ, ὁ bow.

γί-γνομαι (γεν-, γενε-, γον-) γενήσομαι*, ἐγενόμην, γέγονα, γεγένημαι* become, be, arise.

ἔζομαι (σεδ- 603), ἕσσομαι, εἷσα, ἑ(ε)σσάμην SIT down, seat.

ἐφ-ί-ημι (σι-σημι 603, ση-, σε- = ἡ-, ἑ-), ἐφήσω, ἐφῆκα (ἐφέηκα), ἐφεῖκα*, ἐφεῖμαι*, *with dat.*, 1004, shoot against, hurl upon, send upon.

ἐχε-πευκής, ές sharp, biting.

θαμέες, ειαί, έα thick, crowded.

ἵ-ημι (= σι-σημι 603-4, ση-, σε- = ἡ-, ἑ-) ἥσω, ἧκα (ἕηκα), εἷκα*, εἷμαι* throw, hurl, shoot, send.

ἰός, οῦ, ὁ arrow.

μετά, adv., and prep. *with gen., dat.,*

57

and acc., with, in, among, amid, into the midst of, after, next to; adv., among, after(ward), around, about, in the direction, in pursuit; *with gen.*, with; *with*

dat., among, in the midst of; *with acc.*, among, into the midst of, after, in pursuit of, to.

νέκῡς, νέκυος, ὁ dead body, corpse.

οὐρεύς, ῆος, ὁ mule.

Derivatives: hyper-bole, -bolic(al), para-bola, -ble, 593–597; gen-esis, hydro-, oxy-gen, theo-, cosmo-gony; sedentary; nec(ro)-polis, -logy, -mancy, -sis.

143. Translate:

1. κιὼν κατ᾽ Οὐλύμποιο καρήνων Ἀπόλλων ἔζετ᾽ ἀπάνευθε νηῶν Ἀχαιῶν καὶ ἕηκεν ἰὸν μετὰ στρατόν. 2. κλαγγὴ δ᾽ ἀργυρέου βιοῦ ἦν δεινή. 3. Ἀπόλλων ἔχει βιὸν ἀργύρεον. 4. ἑκηβόλος ἐποίχεται πρῶτον οὐρῆας καὶ κύνας ἀργούς. 5. ὀλέκονται οὐρῆες καὶ κύνες ἀργοί. 6. ὁ θεὸς ἐφιεὶς ἐχεπευκέα βέλεα αὐτοῖσιν (Ἀχαιοῖσιν) ἔβαλλεν. 7. πολλαὶ δὲ πυραὶ νεκύων ἐκαίοντο θαμειαί. 8. μῆνιν ἄειδε, θεά, Πηληϊάδεω Ἀχιλῆος. 9. ἀλλ᾽ ἴθι, μή μ᾽ ἐρέθιζε, σαώτερος ὥς κε νέηαι. 10. κλῦθί μευ, ἀργυρότοξε. 11. τόδε μοι κρήηνον ἐέλδωρ.

144. Copy, scan, and translate:

Iliad, 48–52

ἕζετ᾽ ἔπειτ᾽ ἀπάνευθε νεῶν, μετὰ δ᾽ ἰὸν ἕηκεν·
δεινὴ δὲ κλαγγὴ γένετ᾽ ἀργυρέοιο βιοῖο.
οὐρῆας μὲν πρῶτον ἐπῴχετο καὶ κύνας ἀργούς,		50
αὐτὰρ ἔπειτ᾽ αὐτοῖσι βέλος ἐχεπευκὲς ἐφιεὶς
βάλλ᾽· αἰεὶ δὲ πυραὶ νεκύων καίοντο θαμειαί.

145. 48. νεῶν [νηῦς] = νηῶν, 572, 992. — μετά: 1049. — ἰόν: the first arrow. The poet thus makes definite and clear the picture he is seeking to paint.
49. δεινή: *terrifying.* — κλαγγή: onomatopoetic. We thus *hear* the clang of the bow. The rhythm of the verse, especially toward the end, helps in producing this effect. — βιοῖο: gen. of source, 987.
50. πρῶτον: 780–781. — ἐπῴχετο [ἐποίχομαι] ἀργούς: swift as a sil-

very flash, a highly picturesque way of presenting the effect upon the eye of the swift glancing motion of the feet of dogs as they run.

This passage gives accurately the ordinary course of such plagues, where the poet, perhaps without realizing it, follows closely the results of modern medical science, in establishing the fact that such pestilences usually attack animals first, and from these the contagion would spread among human beings.

51. **αὐτοῖσι**: 1004, the men (their masters), as contrasted with the animals, 1041, 6. — **βέλος ἐχεπευκές**: for the metre, see 1168; 619. — **αὐτοῖσι** refers of course to the Greeks, and brings them into sharp prominence.

52. **βάλλ'** is emphatic by position, by the following pause, by the prolonged sound of the trilled λλ (making it onomatopoetic), and by meaning (imperfect). The imperfect represents a series of repeated actions. Observe how vividly the poet presents to the eye the great number of deaths due to the arrows of the god. We can see the funeral pyres, with their heaps of corpses, burning on every side.

On this whole passage, compare what Lessing says in the Laocoön, when discussing some of the fundamental differences between the art of the painter and that of the poet. "The picture of the plague. What do we see on the canvas? Dead bodies, the flame of funeral pyres, the dying busied with the dead, the angry god upon a cloud discharging his arrows. The profuse wealth of the picture becomes poverty in the poet. Now let us turn to Homer himself. The poet here is as far beyond the painter as life is better than a picture. Wrathful, with bow and quiver, Apollo descends from the Olympian towers. I not only see him, but hear him. At every step the arrows rattle on the shoulders of the angry god. He enters among the host like the night. Now he seats himself over against the ships, and with a terrible clang of the silver bow sends his first shaft against the mules and dogs. Next he turns his poisoned (deadly) darts upon the warriors themselves, and unceasing blaze on every side the corpse-laden pyres. It is impossible to translate into any other language the musical painting heard in the poet's words."

The stage is now all set for the introduction of the hero, the divine Achilles, who henceforth plays a prominent part, and is never wholly lost sight of for the rest of the poem.

146. Translate:

1. When the gods had come down from the summits of Olympus, they seated themselves apart from the ships and

shot arrows among them, and a terrible clang arose from their silver bows. 2. All the gods have bows and quivers covered at both ends. 3. The bow of Apollo is of silver. 4. First let us attack the mules and swift dogs, and then hurling biting darts upon themselves, let us shoot (them). 5. Let many funeral pyres be burned. 6. Burn the pyres of dead bodies. 7. Shoot your sharp arrows, and sit down. 8. Attack the army of the Achaeans, for they insulted Chryses, the beloved priest of the great god, Apollo.

LESSON XXV

MIDDLE AND PASSIVE IMPERATIVE OF VERBS

ILIAD, 53–58

147. Review all the active forms of the imperative of λύω, 907, and learn the middle and passive forms, 913.

148. *Optional :*

149.   VOCABULARY

ἀγείρω (ἀγερ-) ἤγειρα, ἀγήγερμαι col-
lect, assemble, gather.

ἀν-ί-στημι (στη-, στα-), ἀναστήσω,
ἀνέστησα (ἀνέστην), ἀνέστηκα,
ἀνέσταμαι* stand up, set up, raise,
(a)rise.

ἐννῆμαρ nine days.

ἐπεί when, since, for.

Ἥρη, ης, ἡ Hera, *consort of Zeus
and queen of the gods.*

καλέω (καλε-, κλη-), καλέω, ἐκά-
λεσ(σ)α, κέκληκα*, κέκλημαι call,
summon, convoke.

κήδω (κηδ-, κηδε-, καδ-), κηδήσω,
ἐκήδησα*, κέκηδα* (*with gen.* 984),
grieve, distress, hurt, afflict.

κῆλον, ου, τό arrow, shaft, dart.

λευκ-ώλενος, ον white-armed.

μετά-φημι (φη-, φα-), μεταφήσω, μετ-
έφησα* speak among, address,
converse with.

οἴχομαι (οἰχ-, οἰχε-, οἰχο-), οἰχή-
σομαι*, ᾤχωκα come, go, de-
part.

ὀμη-γερής, ές collected, assembled,
gathered together.

ὁράω (ϝορ-, ϝιδ, ὀπ-), ὄψομαι, εἶδον,
ὄπωπα see, behold, look, ob-
serve.

ὅτ(τ)ι that, because.

οὖν therefore, hence, now, then, in
fact.

Derivatives : pan-orama, optic(al), syn-opsis, aut-opsy.

150. Translate :

1. οἴχεο ἀνὰ στρατὸν Ἀχαιῶν. 2. οἰχέσθω ἀνὰ στρατόν.
3. κῆλα θεοῦ Ἀπόλλωνος οἴχονται ἀνὰ στρατὸν Ἀχαιῶν.
4. πόδας ὠκὺς (1014) Ἀχιλλεὺς ἐκαλέσατο λᾶὸν Ἀχαιῶν
ἀγορήνδε. 5. θεὰ λευκώλενος Ἥρη ἐπὶ φρεσὶν ἔθηκε τὴν
βουλὴν Ἀχιλῆι. 6. Ἥρη ἐκήδετο Δαναῶν (984) ὅτι τοὺς
θνήσκοντας ὡράετο. 7. ἠγέροντο οἱ Ἀχαιοί, ἐγένοντο δ᾽
ὁμηγερέες. 8. ἀνέστη [ἀνίστημι] πόδας ὠκὺς (1014) Ἀχιλλεὺς
τοῖσιν Ἀχαιοῖσιν, μετέφη τε.

151. Copy, scan, and translate :

Iliad, 53-58

ἐννῆμαρ μὲν ἀνὰ στρατὸν ᾤχετο κῆλα θεοῖο,
τῇ δεκάτῃ δ᾽ ἀγορήνδε καλέσσατο λαὸν Ἀχιλλεύς·
τῷ γὰρ ἐπὶ φρεσὶ θῆκε θεά, λευκώλενος Ἥρη· 55
κήδετο γὰρ Δαναῶν ὅτι ῥα θνήσκοντας ὁράτο.
οἱ δ᾽ ἐπεὶ οὖν ἤγερθεν ὁμηγερέες τε γένοντο,
τοῖσι δ᾽ ἀνιστάμενος μετέφη πόδας ὠκὺς Ἀχιλλεύς·

152. 53. ᾤχετο [οἴχομαι] : 973, 1.
54. τῇ δεκάτῃ (ἡμέρῃ) : 1009, illa die decima, *on that (never-to-be-forgotten) tenth (day)*. — τῇ is emphatic, and of importance for the further development of the plot. Read again the note on τόν (vs. 11), 90. — (ἐ)καλέσ(σ)ατο : causative, 1069. — ἀγορήν-δε : 788, 4 ; 558.
55. τῷ : 997. — ἐπὶ φρεσὶ θῆκε Ἥρη : Achilles has an idea, which is represented by the poet as an inspiration from heaven.
56. Δαναῶν : 984. — ὁράτο = ὡράετο, 584-585 ; 837 ; middle of interest, 1067, 2-3. Hera has a special affection for the Greeks : "She kept seeing her own Danaans dying." Observe the force of the imperfects : she had no opportunity to assuage her grief, because she had to keep watching her beloved Danaans perishing.
57. ἤγερθεν = ἠγέρθησαν [ἀγείρω] : aor. passive ind., 3d plur., *they were assembled*. This with the following phrase is a good example of epic fullness of expression.
58. τοῖσι : 997, or 1009. — πόδας : 1014.

153. Translate :

1. Nine days we shoot many arrows up through the camp of the well-greaved Achaeans.   2. Who summoned those people to the assembly?   3. The swift-footed Achilles called all these Achaeans to the assembly, because he was grieved for them in (his) heart.   4. We see many of the Achaeans dying, and we are grieved for them.   5. I suggest a noble plan to the son of Peleus in (his) heart. 6. We were assembled and became gathered together beside the swift ships of the Achaeans.   7. I arise and address these Danaans, who are gathered together.

LESSON XXVI

THE OPTATIVE MODE

ILIAD, 59–63

[The *optative mode* may be said to express the *wish* of the speaker, whereas the subjunctive expresses the *will* of the speaker. Hence, the optative is further removed from reality. Pharr translates the subjunctive "I may loose" and the optative "May I loose."

This lesson's reading introduces a very important grammatical construction: the infinitive in indirect discourse. Direct discourse is straight quotation: "I said, 'They are going.'" Indirect discourse reports rather than quotes: "I said that they are going." One way this is expressed in Greek is by putting the verb of the indirect statement in the infinitive and its subject in the accusative; if this were done in English we would have "I said *them to go.*" Because this is not real English, in translating a Greek indirect statement we must supply "that" and turn the infinitive into an appropriate finite verb form. For example, sentence 1 in 158 (below), translated into literal (non-)English, would read, "Achilles thinks those Achaeans to-be-about-to-return home." In proper English, "Achilles thinks that those Achaeans will return home."]

154. In the optative mode occur the present, aorist, perfect, and future perfect. The tenses have the same relation to time expressed as in the subjunctive, 905 note.

155. Learn the conjugation of the optative, active, and middle of λύω, 906, 912, and learn the declension of μέγας great, mighty, large, 733.

156. Optional :

157. VOCABULARY

ἄγε, ἄγετε [ἄγω] strictly imperative, but used as an interj., up, come, go, go to.

ἀπο-νοστέ-ω*, ἀπονοστήσω, ἀπενόστησα return (home), go home, come, go.

ἄψ back (again), backward(s).

γέ postpos. encl., emphasizing the preceding word or clause, at least, indeed, at any rate.

δαμάζω (δαμαδ-), δαμά(σ)ω (603–604) ἐδάμασ(σ)α, subdue, overcome, crush, DOMINATE.

ἐρέω (ἐρεϝ-) (def.) ask, inquire, seek.

λοιμός, οῦ, ὁ plague, pest(ilence).

μάντις, ιος, ὁ seer, prophet, soothsayer; literally, MANIAC.

οἴω (ὀίω) (οἰ-, οἰε-), οἰήσομαι*, ὠϊσά-μην think, suppose, imagine, expect, believe.

ὁμοῦ together, at the same time.

ὄναρ (indecl.) τό dream.

ὀνειρο-πόλος, ου, ὁ dream interpreter, dreamer of dreams.

πάλιν back, backward(s), again, anew.

πλάζω (πλαγγ-), πλάγξομαι, ἔπλαγξα, beat (back), baffle, (cause to) wander.

π(τ)όλεμος, ου, ὁ war, battle, fray.

τὶς, τὶ (encl.) some (one), something, any (one), any(thing) ; τὶ as adv. (780–781) at all.

Derivatives : nost-algia ; dame ; oneiro-mancy, -scopy, critic ; palin-genesis, -ode, -drome ; Planctae ; polem-ic(al).

158. Translate :

1. οἴει Ἀχιλλεὺς τοὺς Ἀχαιοὺς ἀπονοστήσειν οἴκαδε.
2. Ἀχαιοὶ οὐκ ἔφυγον θάνατον, τοὺς γὰρ πόλεμος ἐδάμασε καὶ λοιμὸς ὁμοῦ. 3. ἐρείωμεν τοῦτον μάντιν, ὁ γὰρ φίλος ἐστὶν

'Απόλλωνι. 4. ἐκηβόλος βάλλοι ὀιστοὺς πολλοὺς ἀνὰ στρατὸν 'Αχαιῶν. 5. βουλὴν Διὸς τελείωμεν. 6. πόλεμος κακὸς ὀλέκοι κακῶς Δαναούς, οὕνεκ' ἠτίμασαν 'Απόλλωνα. 7. πῦρ μέγα καίοι ἑκατόμβᾱς ταύρων ἠδ' αἰγῶν. 8. τελέσειε βουλὴν ἐκηβόλος ἄναξ. 9. ὑμῖν μὲν θεοὶ δοῖεν 'Ολύμπια δώματ' ἔχοντες ἐκπέρσαι Πριάμοιο πόλιν, ἐὺ δ' οἴκαδ' ἱκέσθαι, παῖδα δ' ἐμοὶ λύσαιτε φίλην. 10. τίσειαν Δαναοὶ ἐμὰ δάκρυα σοῖσι βέλεσσιν.

159. Copy, scan, and translate :

Iliad, 59–63

" 'Ατρείδη, νῦν ἄμμε πάλιν πλαγχθέντας ὀίω
ἂψ ἀπονοστήσειν, εἴ κεν θάνατόν γε φύγοιμεν,   60
εἰ δὴ ὁμοῦ πόλεμός τε δαμᾷ καὶ λοιμὸς 'Αχαιούς.
ἀλλ' ἄγε δή τινα μάντιν ἐρείομεν ἢ ἱερῆα
ἢ καὶ ὀνειροπόλον, καὶ γάρ τ' ὄναρ ἐκ Διός ἐστιν,

160. 59. ὀίω is trisyllabic; observe its accent and breathing. — ἄμμε [ἐγώ] 971, acc. plur., *us.* — πάλιν πλαγχθέντας: *i.e.* without having captured Troy, the object of the expedition.

60–61. φύγοιμεν . . . δαμᾷ = δαμάει = δαμασει [δαμάζω], 603–604 ; 584–585, 973, 2 : by the use of the optative in the first clause and the future indicative in the second, Achilles would imply that he felt it more probable that they would all die there rather than escape.

62. τινα [τὶς, τὶ]: acc. sing. masc. — μάντιν ἐρείομεν : when an insoluble difficulty of any kind arose among uncivilized peoples, it was customary to consult a specialist in theology, a priest, a prophet, or any one to whom the lord had revealed his will directly or indirectly, as through dreams. The true significance of dreams could be known only by those to whom the god had given the faculty of interpreting them, as to Joseph and to Daniel. Read 1 Sam. ix, 3–10, and 2 Kings i, 2–3. — ἐρείομεν = ἐρεύομεν = ἐρεύωμεν, 800, 1098. — ἢ καί : *or even.* — καὶ γάρ τ' ὄναρ : *for the dream also,* as well as other signs and portents.

161. Translate :

1. All these Achaeans are driven back, and they will return homeward, if haply they may escape evil death. 2. They will not escape death, for war and pestilence will

crush them at the same time. 3. May the fire burn the
hecatombs of bulls and of goats beside the swift ships of
the Achaeans. 4. May the great gods shoot many arrows
up through the camp of the Danaans. 5. May all the
Danaans fulfill the plans of Zeus and escape evil death.
6. May the war and pestilence at the same time crush these
wicked people, because they dishonored Chryses, priest of
Apollo the free-shooter.

LESSON XXVII

THE PASSIVE VOICE

ILIAD, 64–69

[The aorist passive first singular is the sixth and last principal
part of the verb.]

162. Learn the principles of formation and the conjuga-
tion of the passive of λύω and of τρέφω, all modes, 888–896,
916–921, 935, read 810–812, and review the preceding lesson
in Homer for the connection of thought.

163. Review 863–866 and learn 930–935.

164.   VOCABULARY

αἱ (= εἱ 127), if, whether.
ἀμῡνω (ἀμυν-), ἀμυνέω*, ἤμῡνα ward
  off, defend, protect, avert.
ἀπό adv., and prep. with gen., off,
  from, away, back.
ἀρήν, ἀρνός, ὁ, ἡ lamb.
βούλομαι (βουλ-, βουλε-), βουλήσο-
  μαι*, βέβουλα, βεβούλημαι*, ἐβουλή-
  θην* wish, desire, be willing,
  prefer.
εἴ τε (εἴτε) . . . εἴ τε (εἴτε) whether
  . . . or.

ἐπι-μέμφ-ομαι, ἐπιμέμψομαι*, ἐπεμεμ-
  ψάμην*, ἐπεμέμφθην* blame, find
  fault (with), reproach.
εὐχωλή, ῆς, ἡ vow, boast, prayer.
ἦ (τοι) (ἦτοι) surely, indeed, truly,
  certainly, for a fact.
Θεστορίδης, āo, ὁ son of Thestor,
  Calchas.
Κάλχᾱς, αντος, ὁ Calchas.
κνίση, ης, ἡ fat, savor, odor of
  roast meat.
λοιγός, οῦ, ὁ destruction, ruin,

65

death, curse.

ὅ γε, ἥ γε, τό γε (ὅγε, ἥγε, τόγε) this, that; he, she, it.

οἰωνο-πόλος, ου, ὁ bird-interpreter, augur, soothsayer, seer.

ὅ(σ)-τις, ἥ-τις, ὅ(τ)-τι who(so)ever, whichever, what(so)ever; who, which, what; ὅ(τ)τι as adv., 780–

781, why.

πώς encl., (in) some way, somehow, (in) any way, perhaps.

τέλειος, η, ον complete, finished, full-grown, unblemished, perfect.

τόσ(σ)ος, η, ον so much, so great, so large, so many, so long.

165. Translate :

1. ὀνειροπόλος εἴποι ὅτι τόσσον ἐχώσατο Φοῖβος Ἀπόλλων. 2. οὐκ ἐλύθη θυγάτηρ ἱερῆος. 3. παῖδες Ἀχαιῶν ἐλύθησαν Ἀγαμέμνονι. 4. ἐλύθητε, Δαναοί, γέροντι. 5. ἤγερθεν Ἀχαιοί. ἠγέρθησαν Ἀχαιοί. 6. ἐδάμησαν Ἀχαιοὶ πολέμῳ τε καὶ λοιμῷ ὁμοῦ. 7. πάντες ἥρωες ἐπλάγχθησαν πάλιν. 8. θεοὶ ἐπιμέμψονται Ἀχαιούς, οὕνεκα τὰς εὐχωλὰς οὐκ ἐτέλεσαν καὶ τὰς ἑκατόμβᾱς ἀρνῶν αἰγῶν τε τελείων οὐκ ἔκηαν. 9. Ἀπόλλων βούλεται ἀντιάειν κνίσης (982) ἀρνῶν αἰγῶν τε τελείων καὶ λοιγὸν ἀμῦναι ἡμῖν. 10. Κάλχᾱς Θεστορίδης οἰωνοπόλων ὄχ᾽ ἄριστος εἴποι μῆνιν Ἀπόλλωνος.

166. Copy, scan, and translate:

Iliad, 64–69

ὅς κ᾽ εἴποι, ὅτι τόσσον ἐχώσατο Φοῖβος Ἀπόλλων,
εἴ τ᾽ ἄρ᾽ ὅ γ᾽ εὐχωλῆς ἐπιμέμφεται εἴ θ᾽ ἑκατόμβης,　　65
αἴ κέν πως ἀρνῶν κνίσης αἰγῶν τε τελείων
βούλεται ἀντιάσᾱς ἡμῖν ἀπὸ λοιγὸν ἀμῦναι."
ἦ τοι ὅ γ᾽ ὣς εἰπὼν κατ᾽ ἄρ᾽ ἕζετο, τοῖσι δ᾽ ἀνέστη
Κάλχᾱς Θεστορίδης, οἰωνοπόλων ὄχ᾽ ἄριστος,

167. 64. εἴποι: 1145. — ὅτι: 780–781, 1014. — τόσσον: 780–781. Apollo, as god of health and disease, would be the first one thought of in the present emergency. — ὅς κ᾽ Ϝείποι: 580, 581, 1174.

65. εὐχωλῆς, ἑκατόμβης: 970, 6 : *on account of a vow* (unfulfilled), *or on account of a hecatomb* (unoffered).

66. κνίσης: 982. — τελείων goes with both nouns.

67. βούλεται : 800. — ἡμῖν [ἐγώ] : dat. plur., 997. — ἀπὸ . . . ἀμῦναι
1048–1049.

68. κατ᾽ . . . ἵετο: 1049.

168. Translate :

1. Calchas, son of Thestor, is the seer who may tell the
Danaans why Phoebus Apollo is so greatly enraged.
2. Did Apollo blame the Achaeans on account of a vow, or
on account of a goodly hecatomb of unblemished lambs and
goats ? 3. Apollo the free-shooter did not wish to partake
of the fat of unblemished lambs and goats, but he warded
off evil destruction for the Danaans. 4. When the swift-
footed Achilles had spoken thus he sat down, and the
good(ly) seer, Calchas, son of Thestor, arose and spoke
among the Achaeans in the assembly. 5. May Calchas,
son of Thestor, far the best of seers, speak the will of Zeus.

169. *Optional. At this point a thorough review of all the
preceding Homer should be taken ; all the paradigms of all the
nouns should be memorized ; the irregular adjectives should now
be learned, and a review taken of all the others ; and the verb
λύω in all its forms, including infinitives and participles, should
be mastered before attempting to read further. A good plan to
fix both forms and vocabulary is to take each word of the* Iliad
*as it appears in the text, locate the form, and give the meaning
of the word according to the model found in the vocabulary at
the end of this book. This should be done orally for these
verses, and this should be followed by a comprehensive written
examination. A good drill on these will materially lighten the
following work.*

LESSON XXVIII

ADJECTIVES OF THE THIRD DECLENSION

ILIAD, 70–75

170. Only the masculine and neuter of these adjectives have separate forms in the third declension. When the feminine differs from the masculine, it is of the first declension.

171. 1) Learn the declension of all the regular adjectives of the third declension (725–732). The feminine of these adjectives ending in -ᾰ is declined like θάλασσα *sea*, 663.

2) Review the paradigms of all the third declension nouns, 680–710.

172. *Optional:*

173. VOCABULARY

ἀγορά-ομαι, ἠγορησάμην harangue, address an assembly.

*εἴδω (εἴδομαι) (ϝειδ-, ϝοιδ-, ϝιδ-), εἰδήσω (εἴσομαι), εἶδον, οἶδα, *plu-perf.* ᾔδεα; *in act., aor.,* see; *fut. and perf.,* know; *mid.,* seem, appear.

εἴσω *often with acc.,* into, to, within.

ἑκατη-βελέτης, ᾱο, ὁ free-shooter, free-shooting, sharp-shooter.

ἑο *gen.* 760, οἱ *dat.* (*encl.*), (of) him, her, it.

ἡγέ-ομαι, ἡγήσομαι, ἡγησάμην, ἥγημαι* *with dat.,* 1001, lead, guide, lead the way; *with gen.,* 985, command, rule.

κέλομαι (κελ-, κελε-, κλ-), κελήσομαι,

ἐκελησάμην* (ἐκεκλόμην) urge, command, bid, request.

μῡθέ-ομαι, μῡθήσομαι, ἐμῡθησάμην speak, tell, declare.

ὅς, ἥ, ὅν (ἑός, ἑή, ἑόν), his, her(s), its (own).

πόρον (πορ-, πρω-) (= ἔπορον, 837), (*2d aor., no pres.*); give, grant, furnish, bestow; *perf.* πέπρωται it is fated.

πρό *adv., and prep. with gen.,* before, in front, forth, forward.

φρονέ-ω, φρονήσω*, ἐφρόνησα*, think, consider, plan; εὖ φρονέω be well (kindly) disposed, be wise, think carefully.

ὦ *interj.,* O!

Derivatives: hegemony; wit, wot, wise, witch, wizard, idol, kaleido-scope, idea(1); sage, presage, 603, 604, 621.

174. 1. Ἀχιλεὺς πόδας ὠκὺς ὣς εἶπε καὶ ἕζετο, τοῖσιν δ' Ἀχαιοῖσιν ἀνέστη Κάλχᾱς, οὕνεκ' ἦν ὅχ' ἄριστος οἰωνοπόλων

68

καὶ ἤδη [*εἴδω] πάντα, μάλιστα δὲ πάσας βουλὰς θεῶν.
2. Κάλχας ἡγήσατο νήεσσι θοῆς Ἀχαιῶν εἰς Ἴλιον. 3. θεοὶ
ἔπορον Κάλχαντι μαντοσύνην, διὰ τὴν ἡγήσατο νήεσσιν Ἀχαιῶν
Ἴλιον εἴσω. 4. μάντις Ἀχαιοῖσιν ἐὺ φρονέων ἡγορήσατο καὶ
μετέειπεν.

175. Copy, scan, and translate :

Iliad, 70–75

ὃς ἤδη τά τ᾽ ἐόντα τά τ᾽ ἐσσόμενα πρό τ᾽ ἐόντα,　　70
καὶ νήεσσ᾽ ἡγήσατ᾽ Ἀχαιῶν Ἴλιον εἴσω
ἣν διὰ μαντοσύνην, τήν οἱ πόρε Φοῖβος Ἀπόλλων·
ὅ σφιν ἐὺ φρονέων ἀγορήσατο καὶ μετέειπεν·
" ὦ Ἀχιλεῦ, κέλεαί με, διίφιλε, μυθήσασθαι
μῆνιν Ἀπόλλωνος, ἑκατηβελέταο ἄνακτος ·　　75

176. 70. ὅς ϝῄδη [*εἴδω 966].—τά τ᾽ ἐόντα τά τ᾽ ἐσσόμενα πρό τ᾽ ἐόντα
participles of εἰμί, 964, used substantively with the "article," 1034, *both
what is and shall be and was before*, that is, he knew everything.
71. νήεσσ᾽ (ι) 1001.
72. ἥν [ὅς, ἥ, ὅν] *his own.* — τήν rel. pron. — οἱ [ἑο] 760.
73. σφιν [ἑο] : 760.
75. Ἀπόλλωνος ϝεκετηβελέτᾱο ϝάνακτος.

177. Translate :

1. I spoke thus and sat down. 2. Calchas the son of
Thestor who arose was far the best of seers, but he did not
know everything. 3. Who knows what is, what was, and
what shall be ? 4. We do not know the will of all the gods
who have Olympian homes. 5. Calchas the seer, who was
far the best of soothsayers, guided the ships of the Achaeans
into Ilium by his gift of prophecy which the gods gave to
him. 6. Phoebus Apollo granted to many Achaeans the
gift of prophecy. 7. Since we are well disposed toward the
Danaans, we addressed them and spoke among them.

LESSON XXIX

DEMONSTRATIVE PRONOUNS

ILIAD, 76–80

178. Learn the declension of all the demonstrative pronouns, and of αὐτός, 765–766, 771–772, 774–775, together with their uses, 1028–1041.

179. *Optional:*

180. VOCABULARY

ἀρήγ-ω, ἀρήξω, ἤρηξα (with dat., 996), help, assist, succor.

ἔπος, εος, τό word, saying, command, speech.

ἦ surely, indeed, truly, for a fact.

κρατέω (κρατεσ-), with gen., 985, rule, bear sway.

κρείσσων, ον, comparative of κρατύς, mightier, more powerful, better.

μέγας, μεγάλη, μέγα great, large, tall, mighty.

ὅ-δε, ἥ-δε, τό-δε this (here).

ὄμνῡμι (ὀμ-, ὀμο-, ὀμε-), ὀμοῦμαι (= ὀμό(σ)ομαι = ὀμόομαι 603, 584–

585), ὤμοσ(σ)α, ὀμώμοκα*, ὀμώμο(σ)μαι*, ὠμό(σ)θην* swear, pledge with an oath, swear by as witness, swear to.

οὗτος, αὕτη, τοῦτο that.

πρό-φρων, ον eager, zealous, glad, joyful, kindly.

συν-τί-θημι (θη-, θε-), συνθήσω, συνέθηκα, συντέθεικα*, συντέθειμαι*, συνετέθην put together, unite, perceive, comprehend, heed.

τοι-γάρ therefore.

χέρης, ες (dat. χέρηι), worse, inferior, underling, subject, meaner.

Derivatives: epic, ortho-epy; demo-, aristo-, auto-, pluto-, theo-cracy; mega-phone, -cephalous, megalo-mania, -polis, -saurus; syn-thesis.

181. Translate:

1. Ἀγαμέμνων διίφιλος ἐκέλετο τόνδε μάντιν μυθήσασθαι τὰς βουλὰς θεῶν πάντων. 2. μυθήσομαι μῆνιν Ἀπόλλωνος Ἀχαιοῖσιν. 3. μῆνις Ἀπόλλωνος ἑκατηβελέταο ἄνακτος ἦν οὐλομένη Ἀχαιοῖσιν, ἔτευχε γὰρ αὐτοὺς ἑλώρια κύνεσσι πᾶσι. 4. ἐγὼ ἐρέω, εἰ συνθήσεις καί μοι ἀρήξεις πρόφρων ἔπεσι χερσί τε. 5. εἰ Κάλχας ἐρέει, χολώσει Ἀγαμέμνονα, ὃς μέγα κρατέει πάντων Ἀργείων. 6. οὗτοι Ἀχαιοὶ πείθονται Ἀγαμέμνονι.

7. βασιλεύς ἐστιν κρείσσων ἀνδρὸς ἄλλου (993), ὅτε δὲ χώσηται ἀνδρὶ χέρηι, τὸν ὀλέκει κακῶς. 8. Ἀγαμέμνων βασιλεὺς ἐχώσατο Κάλχαντι χέρηι ἀνδρί, οὕνεκα ἐμύθήσατο μῆνιν Ἀπόλλωνος.

182. Copy, scan, and translate:

Iliad, 76–80

τοιγὰρ ἐγὼν ἐρέω, σὺ δὲ σύνθεο καί μοι ὄμοσσον   76
ἦ μέν μοι πρόφρων ἔπεσιν καὶ χερσὶν ἀρήξειν.
ἦ γὰρ ὀίομαι ἄνδρα χολωσέμεν, ὃς μέγα πάντων
Ἀργείων κρατέει καί οἱ πείθονται Ἀχαιοί.
κρείσσων γὰρ βασιλεύς, ὅτε χώσεται ἀνδρὶ χέρηι·   80

183. 76. ἐγὼ ϝερέω. — σύνθεο [συντίθημι] : imperat., 960.
77. μοι : 996. — πρόφρων : observe that the Greek uses the adjective where the English idiom would ordinarily prefer the adverb. — ἔπεσιν καὶ χερσὶν : 1005.
78. χολωσέμεν = χολώσειν, 908; observe its accent, 902, 2. — ὅϊω Κάλχαντα χολώσειν ἄνδρα, ὃς μέγα κρατέει πάντων Ἀργείων. μέγα : 780–781.
79. Ἀργείων (another name for the Greeks before Troy), 985. — οἱ can be only the dat. of ἑο, 760, since it is an enclitic (as can be seen from the accent of καί, 550, and formerly had ϝ before it (ϝοι) as is seen from the meter, 1173, 1175. It is a dative with a special verb, 996.
80. κρείσσων (ἐστίν) βασιλεύς : that is, when a king and a man of the common people become at odds, the king is the mightier, and naturally will punish the ordinary man for his presumption. — ἀνδρί : 996.

184. Translate:

1. The seer will speak if Achilles will hearken and swear to defend him zealous(ly) with words and hands. 2. I think Calchas will enrage Agamemnon, who rules all the Argives, and the Achaeans obey him. 3. Agamemnon is king and is mightier than the seer or any other inferior man. 4. When the king is enraged at an inferior man, he will destroy him, for he is mightier.

71

LESSON XXX

PERSONAL AND POSSESSIVE PRONOUNS

ILIAD, 81–85

185. Learn the declension of the personal and possessive pronouns, 760–764.

186. See 9.

187. VOCABULARY

ἀπ-αμείβ-ω, ἀπαμείψω*, ἀπήμειψα, ἀπημείφθην* (ex)change; middle, reply, answer.

αὐτ-ῆμαρ the (self)same day.

ἑός, ἑή, ἑόν (= ὅς, ἥ, ὅν), his, her(s), its, his own, her own, its own.

θαρσέ-ω, θαρσήσω*, ἐθάρσησα, τεθάρσηκα take heart, take courage, be bold, dare, be resolute.

θεο-πρόπιον, ου, τό oracle, prophecy

κατα-πέσσω (πεκ-, πεπ-), καταπέψω*, κατέπεψα, καταπέπεμμαι*, κατεπέφθην* digest, repress, cook.

κότος, ου, ὁ grudge, rancor, hate.

μάλα very, exceedingly, even, by all means, much, enough.

μετ-όπισθε(ν) afterward(s), later, hereafter.

ὄφρα until, in order that, while.

πέρ encl., exceedingly, very, even (if), although.

πρόσ-φημι (φη-, φα-), προσφήσω, προσέφησα* speak to, address.

σαό-ω, σαώσω, ἐσάωσα, ἐσαώθην, save, protect, rescue, preserve.

στῆθος, εος, τό breast, chest.

φράζω* (φραδ-), φράσω*, ἔφρασα ((ἐ)πέφραδον), πέφρακα*, πέφρασμαι*, ἐφράσθην tell, point out, declare; mid. consider, plan, think.

χόλος, ου, ὁ hot, furious wrath, blind anger, CHOLER.

Derivatives : amoeba, amoebean (593–595); pep-sin, -tic, eu-, dys-pep-sia, -tic ; opistho-dome, -graphy ; stetho-scope; phrase-o-logy, peri-phrasis, para-phrase.

188. Translate :

1. Ἀγαμέμνων ἄναξ ἀνδρῶν καταπέψει χόλον αὐτῆμαρ, ἀλλὰ μετόπισθεν ἕξει [ἔχω] κότον ἐν οἶσι στήθεσσιν, ὄφρα τελέσσῃ. 2. πόδας ὠκὺς Ἀχιλλεὺς φράσεται εἰ σαώσει Κάλχαντα μάντιν ὄχ᾽ ἄριστον. 3. Κάλχας θαρσήσει καὶ ἐρέει θεοπρόπιον Ἀπόλλωνος. 4. μάντις οἶδε θεοπρόπια πάντα.

72

LESSON XXX   [189–191

189. Copy, scan, and translate:

Iliad 81–85

εἴ περ γάρ τε χόλον γε καὶ αὐτῆμαρ καταπέψῃ,   81
ἀλλά τε καὶ μετόπισθεν ἔχει κότον, ὄφρα τελέσσῃ,
ἐν στήθεσσιν ἑοῖσι. σὺ δὲ φράσαι, εἴ με σαώσεις."
τὸν δ' ἀπαμειβόμενος προσέφη πόδας ὠκὺς Ἀχιλλεύς·
" θαρσήσας μάλα εἰπὲ θεοπρόπιον, ὅτι οἶσθα·   85

190. 81. εἴ περ γάρ τε *for even if.*
82. τε καί *also.* — ὄφρα τελέσσῃ (parenthetical): *i.e.,* till he obtains his revenge.
81–82. χόλος, κότος : the first of hot resentment, which may pass, the second of a deepseated grudge, which calculates upon revenge.
83. ἐν στήθεσσιν ἑοῖσι : the possessive pronoun is emphatic, to indicate that he keeps it absolutely secret and bides his time for revenge.
— στήθεσσι : plural, to individualize the various parts of the chest. — σύ : everything now depends upon *you.* — φράσαι : imperative.
85. εἰπέ : imperative, observe accent, 902, 1.

A SILVER COIN OF
SYRACUSE

The profile of the nymph
Arethusa has been styled
the most exquisite Greek
head known to us.

191. Translate:

1. The very mighty king was enraged at an inferior man, but on that selfsame day he digested his wrath. 2. Many men have evil grudges in their own breasts until they accomplish (them). 3. Let us consider if we will save the king of men Agamemnon. 4. The seer will take courage and speak the oracles of the gods, for he knows them all.

LESSON XXXI

RELATIVE, INTERROGATIVE, AND INDEFINITE PRONOUNS

ILIAD, 86-92

192. Learn the declension of the relative, interrogative, and indefinite pronouns, 767-773, 776-777.

193. *Optional :*

194. VOCABULARY

ἀ-μύμων, ον blameless, noble.

ἀνα-φαίνω (φαν-), ἀναφανέω, ἀνέφηνα, ἀναπέφηνα*, ἀναπέφασμαι, ἀνεφάνην reveal, show (up), manifest.

αὐδά-ω, αὐδήσω*, ηὔδησα speak, say, declare, shout, cry out.

βαρύς, εῖα, ύ heavy, weighty, violent, severe, grave, serious.

δέρκομαι (δερκ-, δορκ-, δρακ-), —, ἔδρακον, δέδορκα, ἐδέρχθην* (ἐδράκην)* see, look, behold.

ἐπι-φέρω (φερ-, οἰ-, ἐνεκ-), ἐποίσω,

ἐπήνεικα (ἐπήνεικον), ἐπενήνοχα*, ἐπενήνεγμαι*, ἐπηνέχθην* bear upon, bear against.

ζώ-ω live.

ἤν (= ἄν) if.

θεο-προπίη, ης, ἡ oracle, prophecy.

μά adv. of swearing, surely, verily.

ὅς τε, ἥ τε, ὅ τε (ὅστε, ἥτε, ὅτε) who, which, what(ever).

οὐ-δέ not even, and not, nor, but not.

σύμ-πᾶς, σύμ-πᾶσα, σύμ-παν all (together).

χθών, χθονός, ἡ earth, land, country.

Derivatives : phenomenon, dia-phanous, phan-tasm, -tom, fan-tasy, -cy ; bar-o-meter, -y-tone ; Dorcas, drag-on, -oon ; epi-zoötic, zoö-logy, -chemistry, -morphism, proto-, palaeo-, meso-, ceno-, eo-, a-zoic ; chthon-ic, -o-phagy.

195. Translate :

1. πόδας ὠκὺς Ἀχιλλεὺς εἶπε μάντει ἀμύμονι · "ὄμνυμι μὰ θεὸν Ἀπόλλωνα διΐφιλον, Ἀγαμέμνων ἄριστος Ἀχαιῶν οὐκ ἐποίσει βαρείᾱς χεῖράς σοι κοίλης παρὰ νηυσίν." 2. Κάλχᾱς μάντις ἀμύμων εὐχόμενος Ἀπόλλωνι ἀναφαίνει θεοπροπίᾱς Δαναοῖσιν. 3. Ἀχιλῆος ζῶντος καὶ δερκομένοιο (1111) ἐπὶ χθονί, οὔ τις συμπάντων Δαναῶν ἐποίσει βαρείᾱς χεῖρας Κάλ-

74

χαντι μάντει. 4. δῖος 'Αχιλλεὺς σαώσει Κάλχαντα μάντιν, ἣν εἴπῃ 'Αγαμέμνονα, ὃς εὔχεται εἶναι πολλὸν ἄριστος 'Αχαιῶν. 5. ἢν 'Αχιλλεὺς σαώσει μάντιν, θαρσήσει καὶ αὐδήσει θεοπροπίας ἑκατηβελέταο ἄνακτος. 6. 'Απόλλων ἐστὶ θεὸς ᾧ τε [ὅς τε, ἥ τε, ὅ τε] Κάλχας εὔχεται.

196. Copy, scan, and translate :

Iliad, 86–92

οὐ μὰ γὰρ 'Απόλλωνα διίφιλον, ᾧ τε σύ, Κάλχαν,   86
εὐχόμενος Δαναοῖσι θεοπροπίας ἀναφαίνεις,
οὔ τις ἐμεῦ ζῶντος καὶ ἐπὶ χθονὶ δερκομένοιο
σοὶ κοίλης παρὰ νηυσὶ βαρείας χεῖρας ἐποίσει
συμπάντων Δαναῶν, οὐδ' ἢν 'Αγαμέμνονα εἴπῃς,   90
ὃς νῦν πολλὸν ἄριστος 'Αχαιῶν εὔχεται εἶναι."
καὶ τότε δὴ θάρσησε καὶ ηὔδα μάντις ἀμύμων ·

197. 86. οὐ μὰ γὰρ 'Απόλλωνα (ὄμνυμι) : this is the answer of Achilles to the demand of Calchas that he *swear* (ὄμοσσον, vs. 76) to protect him. He meets the issue fairly and promises frankly. — ᾧ τε [ὅς τε, ἥ τε, ὅ τε].

88 : 994.

89. σοί : 1004.

92. θάρσησε : *took courage :* inceptive aorist, 1081. — ηὔδα = ηὔδαε [αὐδάω], 584–585.

198. Translate :

1. Take courage and speak the oracles of Apollo the free-shooter. 2. By Apollo, son of Zeus, the Achaeans shall not lay heavy hands upon you beside the hollow ships. 3. The blameless seer prays to Apollo the free-shooter and reveals the oracles of God to the Danaans. 4. While the Achaeans live and look out upon the earth Agamemnon shall not lay heavy hands upon the old priest of Apollo beside the hollow ships. 5. Who boast that they are far the best of the Danaans ?

LESSON XXXII

REGULAR VERBS IN -μι

ILIAD, 93–100

199. Learn the conjugation of the present, and the first and second aorist, active of ἵστημι, τίθημι, ἵημι, and δίδωμι, 949–956.

200. *Optional:*

201.   VOCABULARY

ἀ-εικής, ές unseemly, grievous, shameful, unfitting.

ἀν-ά-ποινος, ον unransomed, without a ransom paid.

ἀπο-δέχ-ομαι, ἀποδέξομαι, ἀπεδεξάμην (ἀπεδέγμην), ἀποδέδεγμαι, ἀπεδέχθην* receive, accept.

ἀ-πρίατος, η, ον unbought, without price.

ἀπ-ωθέω (ὠθ-, ὠθε- = Ϝωθ-, Ϝωθε-), ἀπώσω, ἀπέωσα, ἀπέωσμαι*, ἀπεώσθην* shove away, push off, drive off.

ἀ-τῑμά-ω, ἀτῑμήσω, ἠτίμησα, dishonor, insult, slight, despise.

ἑλίκ-ωψ, ωπος *m.*, ἑλικ-ῶπις, ιδος *f.*, bright-eyed, flashing-eyed.

ἕνεκα (εἵνεκα, 571) *with gen.*, *usually postpos.*, on account, because of, for the sake of.

ἔτι yet, still, in addition, further.

ἱερός, ή, όν sacred, holy.

ἱλά-σκομαι, ἱλάσ(σ)ομαι, ἱλασ(σ)άμην, ἱλάσθην* propitiate, appease.

κούρη, ης, ἡ girl, maiden, young woman.

οὔ-τε and not, nor.   οὔτε . . . οὔτε neither . . . nor.

πατήρ, πατέρος (πατρός), ὁ father, sire.

τοὔνεκα (= τοῦ ἕνεκα) on account of this, for this reason, therefore, consequently.

Derivatives : pan-dect ; helix, op-tic(al), syn-opsis, autopsy ; hiero-glyphics, hier-archy ; patri-arch(al, -ate).

202. Translate :

1. Ἀπόλλων ἐπιμέμφεται ἡμᾶς εὐχωλῆς καὶ ἑκατόμβης (979, 6).   2. θεοὶ ἐπιμέμφονται Ἀχαιοὺς ἕνεκ' ἀρητῆρος φίλου Ἀπόλλωνι, τὸν γὰρ ἠτίμησαν.   3. Ἀπόλλων ἔδωκεν ἄλγεα τοῖσιν Ἀχαιοῖσιν ἠδὲ δώσει ἔτι, οὕνεκ' Ἀγαμέμνων ἠτίμησεν ἀρητῆρα, οὐδ' ἐβούλετο λύειν θύγατρα καὶ ἀγλαὰ δέχθαι ἄποινα.   4. εἰ ἑκηβόλος ἀπώσει λοιγὸν ἀεικέα Δαναοῖ-

76

σιν, δώσουσι ἑλικώπιδα κούρην φίλῳ πατρὶ ἀπριάτην ἀνάποινον,
ἄξουσι δ᾽ ἱερὴν ἑκατόμβην ἐς Χρύσην · τότε θεὸν ἱλασσάμενοι
πείσουσιν.

203. Copy, scan, and translate :

Iliad, 93-100

" οὔτ᾽ ἄρ᾽ ὅ γ᾽ εὐχωλῆς ἐπιμέμφεται οὔθ᾽ ἑκατόμβης,   93
ἀλλ᾽ ἕνεκ᾽ ἀρητῆρος, ὃν ἠτίμησ᾽ Ἀγαμέμνων,
οὐδ᾽ ἀπέλυσε θύγατρα καὶ οὐκ ἀπεδέξατ᾽ ἄποινα,   95
τούνεκ᾽ ἄρ᾽ ἄλγε᾽ ἔδωκεν ἑκηβόλος ἠδ᾽ ἔτι δώσει.
οὐδ᾽ ὅ γε πρὶν Δαναοῖσιν ἀεικέα λοιγὸν ἀπώσει,
πρίν γ᾽ ἀπὸ πατρὶ φίλῳ δόμεναι ἑλικώπιδα κούρην
ἀπριάτην ἀνάποινον, ἄγειν θ᾽ ἱερὴν ἑκατόμβην
ἐς Χρύσην · τότε κέν μιν ἱλασσάμενοι πεπίθοιμεν."   100

204. 93. εὐχωλῆς, ἑκατόμβης : 979, 6.

94. ἀρητῆρος : emphatic by position, and placed in strict contrast
with εὐχωλῆς, as both occupy the same position in the verse.

96. τούνεκ'(α) sums up the preceding and brings it out prominently,
so that there can be no mistaking what the real cause of the trouble is.

97. Δαναοῖσιν : 997. —ὅ γε resumes the subject, Apollo, with empha-
sis.

98. The subject of δόμεναι may be the Greeks, but more likely it is
intended to refer to Agamemnon, and would thus be omitted on purpose
by the priest, who is afraid of his anger, in spite of the assurance of
Achilles.

97-98. πρὶν . . . πρίν : *he will not sooner drive off pestilence* . . . *till*
(we) *give back* . . . . —ἀπριάτην ἀνάποινον : "without money and with-
out price." Tautology for the sake of emphasis.

100. ἐς Χρύσην : *into Chrysa*, the town, not to Chryses, the priest.
— πεπίθοιμεν : 1105.

205. Translate :

1. Do the gods blame the Achaeans on account of a vow,
or of a hecatomb, or on account of Chryses the priest, whom
Agamemnon dishonored ? 2. If Agamemnon will not re-
lease the dear daughter of the aged priest and receive the

shining ransoms, the free-shooter will still give many woes to
the Danaans, nor will he ward off unseemly destruction for
them until they give back to her own father the white-armed
maiden, unbought, and unransomed, and lead a sacred heca-
tomb into Chrysa ; then perhaps they may appease the god
and persuade his soul.

LESSON XXXIII

REGULAR VERBS IN -μι (*Continued*)

ILIAD, 101–108

206. Learn the conjugation of the present, and the first
and second aorist, middle and passive of ἵστημι, τίθημι, ἵημι,
and δίδωμι, 957–962.

207. *Optional. Discontinue written scansion.*

208.   VOCABULARY

ἀμφι-μέλᾱς, αινα, αν   black all
around, very black.

ἄχ-νυμαι be grieved, be vexed, be
enraged.

ἐσθλός, ή, όν good, noble, brave,
true, helpful, kindly, virile.

εὐρύς, εῖα, ύ broad, wide, large.

κρείων, ουσα, ον ruling, prince,
ruler.

κρήγυος, η, ον good, helpful, favor-
able, honest, true, truthful, use-
ful.

λαμπετά-ω shine, gleam, blaze,
flame.

μαντεύ-ομαι, μαντεύσομαι, ἐμαντευσά-
μην predict, prophesy, divine,
literally, be crazy.

μένος, εος, τό rage, anger, might,
courage, fury, power, spirit.

ὄσσε (*dual only*), eyes.

ὄσσομαι (ὀκ-) eye, look upon, look,
glare at.

πίμ-πλημι (πλη-, πλα-), πλήσω,
ἔπλησα (ἐπλήμην), πέπληκα*, πέ-
πλησμαι*, ἐπλήσθην, *with gen. of
material*, 986, fill, sate, stuff.

πρώτιστος, η, ον *a double superlative*,
first, chiefest, the very first.

πῦρ, πυρός, τό fire, flame.

πώ (*enclit.*) in some way, any way,
ever, yet, at some time, at any
time.

Derivatives: melan-choly; lamp-a-drome; mant-ic, -is (42); oc-u-lar, -list; ple-thora, -onasm; proto- (80); pyr(e)- (15).

209. Translate:

1. τοῖσι δ' ἀνιστάμενος μετέφη εὐρὺ κρείων 'Αγαμέμνων.
2. βασιλεὺς 'Αγαμέμνων ἄχνυται μέγα, πίμπλανται δ' ἀμφιμέλαιναι φρένες μένεος κακοῦ. 3. ὄσσε ἄνακτος πυρὶ λαμπετόωντι ἐίκτην [*εἴκω]. 4. 'Αχαιοὶ δ' ὄσσονται μάντιν κακά. 5. Κάλχᾱς μάντις κακῶν οὐ πώ ποτε κρήγυα εἶπεν 'Αγαμέμνονι ἄνακτι. 6. τὰ κακὰ μάντει αἰεὶ φίλ' ἐστὶν μαντεύεσθαι. 7. 'Αχιλλεὺς εἶπεν ἐσθλὰ ἔπεα πολλὰ καὶ τὰ ἐτέλεσσεν.

210. Read and translate:

Iliad, 101–108

ἦ τοι ὅ γ' ὣς εἰπὼν κατ' ἄρ' ἕζετο, τοῖσι δ' ἀνέστη   101
ἥρως 'Ατρεΐδης εὐρὺ κρείων 'Αγαμέμνων
ἀχνύμενος· μένεος δὲ μέγα φρένες ἀμφιμέλαιναι
πίμπλαντ', ὄσσε δέ οἱ πυρὶ λαμπετόωντι ἐίκτην.
Κάλχαντα πρώτιστα κάκ' ὀσσόμενος προσέειπεν·   105
" μάντι κακῶν, οὐ πώ ποτέ μοι τὸ κρήγυον εἶπας·
αἰεί τοι τὰ κάκ' ἐστὶ φίλα φρεσὶ μαντεύεσθαι,
ἐσθλὸν δ' οὔτε τί πω εἶπας ἔπος οὔτε τέλεσσας.

211. 102. εὐρύ: adverbial, 780–781.— εὐρὺ κρείων: *widely ruling.*
103. μένεος: 986.— μέγα: adverbial, 780–781.
104. οἱ [ἕο]: dat. of interest or reference (or possibly of possession).
— πυρί: 1003. — ἐίκτην [*εἴκω]. — λαμπετόωντι (945–948): to contrast with ἀμφιμέλαιναι, verse 103.

103 f. The diaphragm was thought of as the seat of the emotions and evil passions, just as the word "heart" is still used in English.

105. πρώτιστα: 780–781. — κάκ': 780–781, 1012. — κάκ' ὀσσόμενος: "with evil look" (literally "looking evil things"), *i.e.* a look that boded trouble for Calchas. — πρώτιστα: a double superlative, as "most unkindest, most highest, chiefest," etc.

106. τὸ κρήγυον Ϝεῖπας corresponds to the rule in the latter part of 526. — εἶπας: 865, 3.

107. τοι echoes the μοι of the preceding verse, with which it is contrasted. — τὰ κάκ' ἐστί: 973, 1.

212. Translate:

1. The swift-footed Achilles arose and spake among the Achaeans. 2. When he is vexed, his heart, black all around, is mightily filled with anger, and his eyes are like unto blazing fire. 3. Agamemnon eyed Calchas evilly and addressed him. 4. Because you are a prophet of evils you have never spoken or accomplished anything good for me, but it is always dear to your heart to prophesy evil. 5. "Prophet," said I, "bird of evil!"

LESSON XXXIV

REVIEW OF REGULAR -μι VERBS

ILIAD, 109–117

213. Learn all the forms, active, middle, and passive of ἵστημι, τίθημι, δίδωμι, and ἵημι 949–963, 924.

214. *Optional :*

215.   VOCABULARY

ἀ- (ἀ-) *inseparable prefix* ("*alpha copulative*"), *denoting likeness, union, association with, intensification.*

ἀγορεύ-ω, ἀγορεύσω, ἠγόρευσα speak, say, tell, harangue, address an assembly.

ἄ-λοχος, ου, ἡ (cf. λέχος) wife, spouse.

ἀμείνων, ον better, braver, superior, preferable; *compar. of* ἀγαθός 754.

ἀπ-όλλῡμι (ὀλ-, ὀλε-, ὀλο-), ἀπολέσ(σ)ω, ἀπώλεσ(σ)α, ἀπόλωλα, destroy, kill, ruin.

δέμας, αος, τό build, stature, size, form, body, structure.

(ἐ)θέλω (ἐθελ-, ἐθελε-) ἐθελήσω, ἠθέλησα, ἠθέληκα* wish, desire, be willing.

εἰμί (ἐσ-), ἔσ(σ)ομαι be.

θεο-προπέ-ω prophesy, foretell, declare an oracle, inquire of a god, interpret the divine will.

κουρίδιος, η, ον lawfully wedded, legally married, wedded in youth.

οἴκοι [οἶκος loc. 657, 714], at home.

προ-βούλομαι (βουλ-, βουλε-), προβου-
λήσομαι*, προβέβουλα, προβεβού-
λημαι*, προεβουλήθην* prefer,
wish rather.

σόος, η, ον (= σάος = σάϝος) safe,
sound, unhurt, unharmed, well.

φυή, ῆς, ἡ form, nature, beauty,
growth, appearance, character.

χερείων, ον worse, inferior (754, 3).

Χρῡσηΐς, ΐδος, ἡ Chryseïs, daughter
of Chryses.

Derivatives : Apollyon ; am, is, ontology (584–585).

216. Translate :

1. θεοπροπέοντες ἐν ᾿Αχαιοῖσι μάντιες ἀγορεύουσιν, ὡς (how)
δὴ ᾿Αγαμέμνονος ἕνεκα ἑκηβόλος τεύχει ἄλγεα, οὕνεκ᾿ οὐκ ἤθελε
δέξασθαι ἀγλά᾿ ἄποινα κούρης Χρῡσηΐδος. 2. ᾿Αγαμέμνων
οὐκ ἤθελε δέξασθαι ἄποινα, ἐπεὶ πολὺ βούλεται ἔχειν τὴν κούρην
αὐτὴν οἴκοι. 3. προβουλήσεται ᾿Αγαμέμνων Χρῡσηΐδα Κλυ-
ταιμ(ν)ήστρης κουριδίης ἀλόχου ; (988). 4. Χρῡσηΐς οὐκ
ἐστι χερείων Κλυταιμ(ν)ήστρης (988), οὐ δέμας οὐδὲ φυὴν οὔτ᾿
ἂρ φρένας οὔτε τι ἔργα (1014). 5. ἐθέλουσιν ᾿Αχαιοὶ δόμεναι
πάλιν ἑλικώπιδα κούρην, εἰ τό γ᾿ ἐστὶν ἄμεινον, ἐπεὶ βούλονται
λᾱὸν εἶναι σόον ἢ (rather than) ἀπολέσθαι. 6. δοθείη ἡ κούρη
πατρὶ φίλῳ. 7. ἔστη ἱερεὺς Χρύσης ἐν στρατῷ ᾿Αχαιῶν καὶ
ἑλίσσετ᾿ ᾿Αγαμέμνονα, ἀλλ᾿ οὐδ᾿ ὣς παῖς φίλη ἐτέθη πατρὶ ἐν
χερσίν.

217. Read and translate :

Iliad, 109–117

καὶ νῦν ἐν Δαναοῖσι θεοπροπέων ἀγορεύεις,
ὡς δὴ τοῦδ᾿ ἕνεκά σφιν ἑκηβόλος ἄλγεα τεύχει,   110
οὕνεκ᾿ ἐγὼ κούρης Χρυσηΐδος ἀγλά᾿ ἄποινα
οὐκ ἔθελον δέξασθαι, — ἐπεὶ πολὺ βούλομαι αὐτὴν
οἴκοι ἔχειν. καὶ γάρ ῥα Κλυταιμνήστρης προβέβουλα,
κουριδίης ἀλόχου, ἐπεὶ οὔ ἑθέν ἐστι χερείων,
οὐ δέμας οὐδὲ φυὴν οὔτ᾿ ἂρ φρένας οὔτε τι ἔργα.   115
ἀλλὰ καὶ ὣς ἐθέλω δόμεναι πάλιν, εἰ τό γ᾿ ἄμεινον·
βούλομ᾿ ἐγὼ λᾱὸν σόον ἔμμεναι ἢ ἀπολέσθαι.

218. **109.** In vss. 106 ff. Agamemnon makes sweeping general charges against Calchas; in vs. 109 he proceeds to the particular, καὶ νῦν, as proof of his assertions. — ἀγορεύεις : contemptuously, *you play the demagogue.*

110. ὡς : 1154, 1.

111. κούρης : 979, 5.

112. αὐτήν : the girl's own self, as contrasted with the ransom. — βούλομαι : *prefer.* — πολύ : 780–781.

113. ῥα Κλυταιμ(ν)ήστρης : 524, 988. The correct spelling of this name is Κλυταιμήστρη, although practically all modern texts have Κλυταιμνήστρη, and we ordinarily have " Clytaemnestra " in English.

114. ἑθέν [ἑο] : 993.

115. δέμας, φυήν, φρένας, ἔργα (ϝέργα) : 1014. — τι : 780–781.

116. καί : *even.*

117. ἤ : *rather than.*

219. Translate :

1. You prophesy to the Danaans and harangue them, saying that it is on account of me that the free-shooter is causing them countless woes. 2. For this (reason) the free-shooter has caused many woes to the Achaeans, and he will still cause them, because Agamemnon was not willing to accept the splendid ransoms for (of) the bright-eyed maiden Chryseïs. 3. Agamemnon wished to have her at home, since he greatly preferred her to Clytaem(n)estra his lawful wife. 4. Chryseïs is not inferior to Clytaem(n)estra, either in build, in beauty, or in accomplishments. 5. If that is better, Agamemnon will be willing to give back the bright-eyed maiden to her dear father. 6. We wished the people to be safe rather than to perish.

LESSON XXXV

IRREGULAR VERBS IN -μι, εἰμί, AND ENCLITICS

ILIAD, 118-125

220. Learn the conjugation of εἰμί complete, 964, and read 553-559.

221. *Optional. See 9.*

222.   **VOCABULARY**

ἀ-γέραστος, η, ον without a prize of honor (γέρας).

ἀμείβ-ω, ἀμείψω*, ἤμειψα, ἠμείφθην* (ex)change; (*mid.*), answer, reply.

αὐτίκα immediately, forthwith.

γέρας, αος, τό prize (of honor).

δατέομαι (δατ-, δατε-), δάσ(σ)ομαι, ἐδασ(σ)άμην, δέδασμαι divide, distribute, allot.

ἑτοιμάζω* (ἑτοιμαδ-), ἑτοιμάσω*, ἡτοίμασα prepare, make ready.

κεῖ-μαι, κείσομαι lie, recline, repose.

κύδιστος, η, ον most glorious,

superl.

λεύσσω (λευκ-) see, behold, observe, LOOK.

ξυνήιος, η, ον common (stock, possessions).

οἶος, η, ον alone, sole, only.

ποδ-άρκης, ες swift-footed, able-footed.

πού (*encl.*), any way, anywhere, some way, somewhere, somehow, perhaps.

πῶς how? in what way?

φιλο-κτεανώτατος, η, ον *superl.* most avaricious, most greedy of gain.

Derivatives : amoeba, amoebean (593-595), pod- (101).

223. Translate :

1. ἑτοιμάσομεν αὐτίκα γέρας Ἀγαμέμνονι, ὄφρα μὴ οἶος Ἀχαιῶν ἔῃ ἀγέραστος, τό γε γὰρ οὐδὲ ἔοικεν. 2. πάντες Ἀχαιοὶ λεύσσουσιν ὅτι γέρας Ἀγαμέμνονος ἔρχεται ἄλλῃ. 3. ἠμειψάμεθα ἄνακτα καὶ εἴπομεν. 4. ποδάρκης δῖος Ἀχιλλεὺς εἶπε μῦθον κρατερὸν Ἀγαμέμνονι κυδίστῳ, φιλοκτεανωτάτῳ δὲ πάντων ἀνδρῶν. 5. Ἀχαιοὶ ἐκπέρσουσι πολλὰ ἐκ λάων πολίων καὶ δάσονται πάντα λᾱῷ. 6. οὐ δώσομεν γέρας Ἀγαμέμνονι, οὐ γὰρ ἔχομέν που ξυνήια κείμενα (1027).

224. Read and translate :

Iliad, 118–125

αὐτὰρ ἐμοὶ γέρας αὐτίχ᾽ ἑτοιμάσατ᾽, ὄφρα μὴ οἶος
'Αργείων ἀγέραστος ἔω, ἐπεὶ οὐδὲ ἔοικεν ·
λεύσσετε γὰρ τό γε πάντες, ὅ μοι γέρας ἔρχεται ἄλλῃ.''	120
τὸν δ᾽ ἠμείβετ᾽ ἔπειτα ποδάρκης δῖος 'Αχιλλεύς ·
''Ατρεΐδη, κύδιστε, φιλοκτεανώτατε πάντων,
πῶς γάρ τοι δώσουσι γέρας μεγάθυμοι 'Αχαιοί;
οὐδέ τί που ἴδμεν ξυνήια κείμενα πολλά,
ἀλλὰ τὰ μὲν πολίων ἐξεπράθομεν, τὰ δέδασται,	125

225. 118. ἐμοί : 997.

119. "Even if I should not demand a **γέρας** as justly due to me in
return for my giving back mine, common decency would require that
the king should have one, and thus not be lacking in this matter of
honor, while all the other chieftains have prizes." The possession of
the **γέρας** was looked upon as a mark of honor due to royal station;
to give one was to honor the king and exalt his station; to take it away
without due recompense was felt as a keen disgrace. This the army
must prevent by giving him an equivalent for the prize he is about
to surrender. Thus Agamemnon's demand is prompted by his feeling
of wounded honor, and by his inherent sense of the prerogatives due to
his exalted station, and not by avarice as Achilles thinks (vs. 122).
The injustice in his claim consists in his demand for immediate
(αὐτίχ᾽) recompense, which Achilles clearly shows to be impracticable,
without committing an injustice to the others. But Achilles unfortu-
nately goes entirely too far in insulting the king and accusing him of
avarice beyond all other men.

120. ὅ = ὅτι : *that.* — μοι : dat. of interest, or possibly of disadvan-
tage, 997–998.

124 : litotes, with a touch of the sarcastic in πολλά. — τί : 780–781. —
ξυνήια : used substantively, 1027, *common stores.*

125. τά, τά : the first of these should be translated as a relative, the
second as a demonstrative used substantively : *Whatsoever we took as
plunder . . . these have been divided.* — δέδασται : this tense would
indicate that the matter is settled, and not to be reconsidered. The
Greeks had already captured and plundered many cities of the Troad,
but had not yet been able to take Troy. This verse would indicate that

they had already met with considerable successes, and that a goodly amount of spoil had been taken and distributed among the soldiers.

226. Translate :

1. The Achaeans will prepare another gift of honor immediately for Agamemnon, in order that not alone of all the Argives he may be without a prize of honor ; for it is not seemly so. 2. They all see that the prize of the king is going elsewhere. 3. Thereupon all the Achaeans answered the swift-footed, god-like Achilles. 4. The son of Atreus was the most glorious, but the most avaricious of all men, for he was not willing to give his own prize of honor back to her beloved father, because he did not see many common (stores) lying about, and what the great-souled Achaeans had sacked from the cities had been divided.

227. *Optional. At this point another review, similar to the one at the end of Lesson XXVII, should be taken. Before going further the student should make a clean sweep of all the forms of all the nouns, pronouns, and adjectives, and the verbs λύω, τρέφω, ἵστημι, τίθημι, δίδωμι, ἵημι, and εἰμί, in all voices, modes, and tenses, with special attention to the participles and infinitives. Repeat the drill for the first hundred and twenty-five verses in the location of forms, as at the end of Lesson XXVII.*

LESSON XXXVI

IRREGULAR VERBS

ILIAD, 126-132

228. Some verbs are formed the same as regular verbs in -μι in the present and first aorist systems, but are more or less irregular in certain respects. Some of these do not

85

have the second aorist. So far as they have other forms they follow the analogy of λύω.

229. Certain verbs have second perfects and pluperfects without the tense suffix, the same as verbs in -μι. Their personal endings are added directly to the verb stem.

230. In this class is the irregular verb οἶδα (2d perf. of *εἴδω, with pres. meaning) *know*, which is not reduplicated. The pluperfect (with imperfect meaning) is ἤδεα *knew*.

231. Learn the conjugation of εἰμί *come, go*, φημί *say, speak*, ἧμαι *sit, be seated*, κεῖμαι *lie, recline*, the perfect οἶδα *know*, and the second perfect (without tense suffix) of ἵστημι *set, stand*, 924, 965-969.

232. *Optional:*

233. VOCABULARY

ἀπο-τίνω (τει-, τι-, τινϝ-), ἀποτίσω, ἀπέτῑσα, ἀποτέτῑκα*, ἀποτέτῑσμαι*, ἀπετίσθην* repay, requite, recompense, atone for.

ἐξ-αλαπάζω (ἀλαπαγ-), ἐξαλαπάξω, ἐξηλάπαξα sack utterly, destroy utterly.

ἐπ-αγείρω (ἀγερ-), ἐπήγειρα, ἐπαγήγερμαι, ἐπηγέρθην collect, gather (together).

*ἐπείκω (ϝεικ-, ϝοικ-, ϝικ-), ἐπ-έοικα, *perf. as pres.* be seemly, be fitting (either, also, in addition).

ἐυ-τείχεος, ον well-walled.

θεο-είκελος, η, ον godlike.

κλέπτω (κλεπ-, κλοπ-, κλαπ-), κλέψω*, ἔκλεψα, κέκλοφα**, κέκλεμμαι*, ἐκλέφθην† (ἐκλάπην)* steal, be stealthy, deceive, hide.

νόος, ου, ὁ mind, plan, purpose.

ὅ-δε, ἥ-δε, τό-δε this, that; he, she, it.

οὕτω(s) thus, so, in this way.

παλίλ-λογος, η, ον gathered together again, re-collected, re-assembled.

παρ-έρχομαι (ἐρχ-, ἐλθ-, ἐλυθ-, ἐλευθ-), παρελεύσομαι, παρῆλθον (παρήλυθον), παρελήλυθα (παρειλήλουθα) evade, pass by, outwit, elude, circumvent.

ποθί (*encl.*) ever, at any time.

προ-ΐ-ημι (ση-, σε- = ἡ-, ἑ-), προήσω, προέηκα (προῆκα), προεῖκα*, προεῖμαι*, προείθην send forward, send forth, give up.

τετρα-πλῆ fourfold, quadruply.

τρι-πλῆ threefold, triply.

Τροίη, ης, ἡ Troy, *the city, a famous ancient city in Asia Minor, commanding the Hellespont (Dardanelles). According to the legend it was sacked by the ancient Greeks, under Agamemnon, after a siege of, ten years.*

Derivatives: klepto-mania(c), cleps-ydra; tetra-gon, -hedron, -meter; tri-ple(t), -ply, -gono-metry, -meter, -pod; ply.

234. Translate:

1. ἐπέοικεν Ἀχαιοὺς γέρα παλίλλογα βασιλῆι ἐπαγείρειν; 2. νῦν μὲν Ἀγαμέμνων προήσει Χρυσηίδα κούρην ἑλικώπιδα θεῷ ἐκηβόλῳ, ὕστερον δ' Ἀχαιοὶ τὸν ἀποτίσουσιν. 3. δώσει Ζεὺς Ἀχαιοῖσίν ποθι ἐξαλαπάξαι Τροίην πόλιν ἐντείχεον. 4. Ἀχαιοὶ προσέφασαν Ἀχιλῆα ποδάρκεα. 5. ἀγαθὸς μέν ἐστι θεοείκελος Ἀχιλλεύς, κλέπτει δὲ νόῳ καὶ ἐθέλει παρελθεῖν Ἀγαμέμνονα ἄνακτα ἀνδρῶν.

235. Read and translate:

Iliad, 126–132

λαοὺς δ' οὐκ ἐπέοικε παλίλλογα ταῦτ' ἐπαγείρειν.   126
ἀλλὰ σὺ μὲν νῦν τήνδε θεῷ πρόες, αὐτὰρ Ἀχαιοὶ
τριπλῇ τετραπλῇ τ' ἀποτίσομεν, αἴ κέ ποθι Ζεὺς
δῷσι πόλιν Τροίην ἐντείχεον ἐξαλαπάξαι."
τὸν δ' ἀπαμειβόμενος προσέφη κρείων Ἀγαμέμνων ·   130
" μὴ δὴ οὕτως, ἀγαθός περ ἐών, θεοείκελ' Ἀχιλλεῦ,
κλέπτε νόῳ, ἐπεὶ οὐ παρελεύσεαι οὐδέ με πείσεις.

236. 126. λᾱούς: 971.
127. πρόες [προίημι].
128. τριπλῇ τετραπλῇ τ': threefold, yea, even fourfold.
129. δῷ(σι) (ἡμῖν). — πόλιν: object of ἐξαλαπάξαι.
131. δὴ οὕτως: synizesis, 586. — ἀγαθός περ ἐών (concessive): although you are brave.
132. νόῳ: 1009. — παρελεύσεαι is a figure taken from the race course: you shall not pass (me). Agamemnon begins his speech as did Achilles (vs. 122) by addressing his opponent with a highly honorable title, which is immediately followed by an abusive term.

237. Translate:

1. What the Achaeans had sacked from the well-walled

cities had been divided, and Agamemnon was not willing to gather this together again from the people. 2. If Agamemnon will give up his prize of honor to the gods, the Achaeans will recompense him threefold, yea fourfold, if ever the gods who have Olympian homes should grant to them to sack utterly the well-walled city of Priam. 3. The Achaeans answered the ruling Agamemnon and said, "Though you are very brave in war, divine son of Atreus, do not be stealthy in mind, for it is not fitting for a very mighty king to outwit the people and persuade them evilly."

LESSON XXXVII

PREPOSITIONS

Iliad, 133–141

238. Read carefully 1048–1061.

239. *Optional:*

240.   VOCABULARY

Αἴας, αντος, ὁ Ajax.

αἱρέω (αἱρε-, ἑλ-), αἱρήσω, ἕελον (εἷλον, 584–585), ᾕρηκα*, ᾕρημαι*, ᾑρέθην* take, seize, deprive, (*mid.*) choose.

ἅλς, ἁλός, ὁ, ἡ sea, brine.

ἀντ-άξιος, η, ον equivalent, of equal value.

ἀπο-δί-δωμι (δω-, δο-), ἀποδώσω, ἀπέδωκα, ἀποδέδωκα*, ἀποδέδομαι, ἀπεδόθην give back, return, give away, pay.

ἀρ-αρ-ίσκω (ἀρ-), ἦρσα (ἤραρον), ἄρηρα, ἤρθην join, fit, suit, adapt, adjust.

αὔτως in the same way, thus, so, as matters now are.

δεύομαι (δευ-, δενε-), δευήσομαι, ἐδεύησα lack, need, be in want.

ἐρύω (ϝερυ-, ϝρυ-), ἐρύω, εἴρυσ(σ)α, εἴρυσ(σ)μαι draw, drag, launch.

ἧμαι (ἡσ-) (*pres. only*) sit, be seated.

μέλᾱς, αινα, αν black, dark, dusky.

μετα-φράζω* (φραδ-), μεταφράσω*, μετέφρασα (μετεπέφραδον), μετα-πέφρακα**, μεταπέφρασμαι*, μετε-φράσθην tell, point out, declare; *mid.*, consider later, plan hereafter, reflect on later.

Ὀδυσ(σ)εύς, ῆος, ὁ Odysseus (Ulysses).

ὅπ(π)ως in order that, that, how (that).

τεός, ή, όν thy, thine, your(s).

88

Derivatives : sal-t, -ine (603–604), hali-eutic(s), -o-graphy, halite ; axiom(atic) ; dose, dowry ; mela(n)- (208).

241. Translate :

1. οὐκ ἐθέλει 'Αχιλλεὺς 'Αγαμέμνονα δευόμενον ἧσθαι, ὄφρ' αὐτὸς ἔχῃ γέρας. 2. 'Αγαμέμνων ἧσται αὔτως δευόμενος, κέλεται δ' 'Αχιλῆα γέρας ἀποδοῦναι. 3. μεγάθυμος 'Αχιλλεὺς οὐ δώσει 'Αγαμέμνονι πολλὰ γέρα, ἄρσᾱς τὰ κατὰ θῡμόν, ὅπως ἔσονται ἀντάξια. 4. εἰ δέ κε μὴ δώωσιν 'Αχαιοὶ μεγάθῡμοι γέρας 'Αγαμέμνονι, ἄρσαντες τὸ κατὰ θῡμόν, ὅπως ἔσται ἀντάξιον, αὐτός κεν ἕληται ἢ γέρας 'Αχιλῆος ἢ Αἴαντος ἢ 'Οδυσῆος. 5. 'Αγαμέμνων ἰὼν ἕληται γέρας, ἑλὼν δὲ τὸ ἄξῃ, 'Αχιλλεὺς δέ κε κεχολώσεται, τόν κεν 'Αγαμέμνων ἵκηται. 6. πάντες 'Αχαιοὶ μετεφράζοντο ταῦτα καὶ αὖτις. 7. εἴρυσαν νῆας μελαίνᾱς εἰς ἅλα δῖαν.

242. Read and translate :

Iliad, 133–141

ἢ ἐθέλεις, ὄφρ' αὐτὸς ἔχῃς γέρας, αὐτὰρ ἔμ' αὔτως
ἧσθαι δευόμενον, κέλεαι δέ με τήνδ' ἀποδοῦναι;
ἀλλ' εἰ μὲν δώσουσι γέρας μεγάθυμοι 'Αχαιοί,   135
ἄρσαντες κατὰ θῡμόν, ὅπως ἀντάξιον ἔσται —
εἰ δέ κε μὴ δώωσιν, ἐγὼ δέ κεν αὐτὸς ἕλωμαι
ἢ τεὸν ἢ Αἴαντος ἰὼν γέρας, ἢ 'Οδυσῆος
ἄξω ἑλών · ὁ δέ κεν κεχολώσεται, ὅν κεν ἵκωμαι.
ἀλλ' ἦ τοι μὲν ταῦτα μεταφρασόμεσθα καὶ αὖτις,   140
νῦν δ' ἄγε νῆα μέλαιναν ἐρύσσομεν εἰς ἅλα δῖαν,

243. 133. ἔχῃς : keep, 1115–1116. — ὄφρ' αὐτὸς ἔχῃς γέρας : parenthetical.

137. ἕλωμαι : 1146.

138. Observe how the addition of ἰών makes the picture definite and adds a touch of the dramatic.

137–139. ἵκωμαι : 1146.

141. ἐρύσσομεν [ἐρύσωμεν] : 800, 1098. — μέλαιναν ϝερύσσομεν, 526.

244. Translate :

1. Surely we do not wish that the son of Atreus should sit (*inf.*) thus lacking, in order that we ourselves may have prizes of honor; and we do not order him to give back the flashing-eyed maiden to her dear father.   2. We shall give the great-souled Achaeans many prizes of honor, adapting them to their desire, so that they may be equivalent.   3. If we do not give (it), the son of Atreus himself will seize either your prize, or (that) of Ajax, or of Odysseus, and when he has seized (it), he will lead (it) to the broad camp of the Achaeans.   4. If Agamemnon should come upon Achilles, he would perchance be enraged.   5. But he considered this also afterward.   6. We shall now drag many swift black ships into the divine sea.

LESSON XXXVIII

COMPARISON OF ADJECTIVES

ILIAD, 142–151

245. Read the sections treating of the comparison of adjectives, 747–756.

246. *Optional :*

247.   VOCABULARY

ἀν-αιδείη, ης, ἡ shamelessness.

ἀρχός, οῦ, ὁ leader, commander, ruler, pilot, guide, chief.

βουλη-φόρος, ον counsel-bearing, full of counsel, discreet.

εἷς, μία, ἕν (758) one, only, sole.

ἑκά-εργος, ου, ὁ free-worker, working his will, *Apollo.*

ἔκ-παγλος, ον terrible, awful, dread (ful), frightful, fearful.

ἐπι-έννυμι (ἐφ-έννῡμι) (ϝεσ-), ἐφέσ(σ)ω, ἔφεσ(σ)α, ἐφεῖμαι (ἐφέσμαι) (*both with and without elision of the prep.*) clothe, invest.

ἐπι-τηδές sufficiently, in sufficient numbers, appropriately, suitably.

ἐρέτης, āο, ὁ oarsman, rower, sailor.

Ἰδομενεύς, ῆος, ὁ Idomeneus.

ἱερόν, οῦ, τό sacrifice, sacred rite, victim for sacrifice (1168).

καλλι-πάρῃος, ον beautiful-cheeked, fair-cheeked.

κερδαλεό-φρων, ον crafty-minded, cunning-(minded), sly, mindful of gain.

ὁδός, οῦ, ἡ road, way, path, journey, expedition.

ῥέζω (ϝρεγ-), ῥέξω, ἔρ(ρ)εξα, ἐρέχθην work, accomplish, do, perform, make, sacrifice.

ὑπό-δρα scowlingly, askance, looking at darkly, *from beneath* (ὑπό) *the brows drawn down.*

ὤ μοι alas! ah me! good gracious!

Derivatives: an-, hier-, mon-, olig-, patri-arch(y, ic(al)), arch-angel, -bishop, -duke, -i-tect, arch- (as arch-fiend, etc.); phos-, zoö-phorus; work (593–595); vest-ment; hier- (101); calli-graphy, -ope, cali-sthenics; syn-, meth-od(ist), hodometer; drag(o)on.

248. Translate:

1. Ἀχαιοὶ μεγάθυμοι ἤγειραν ἐρέτᾱς ἐπιτηδὲς εἰς νῆα μέλαιναν. 2. εἰς νῆας Ἀγαμέμνων ἔθηκεν ἑκατόμβην ἱερὴν θεῷ. 3. ἀνὰ τὴν θοὴν νῆα μέλαιναν Ἀγαμέμνων ἔβησεν (1069) αὐτὴν Χρῡσηΐδα καλλιπάρῃον. 4. εἰς τις ἀνὴρ βουληφόρος ἔσται ἀρχὸς τῶν νηῶν Ἀχαιῶν. 5. Πηλειάδης ἐκπαγλότατος ἀνδρῶν ἔσται ἀρχὸς τῆς νηός. 6. Ἀχιλλεὺς ῥέξει ἱερὰ καὶ ἱλάσεται ἑκάεργον Ἀπόλλωνα τοῖσιν Ἀχαιοῖσιν. 7. οὔ τις Ἀχαιῶν πρόφρων πείσεται ἔπεσιν Ἀγαμέμνονι ἀναιδείην ἐπιειμένῳ (1020, 1; 1071) καὶ κερδαλεόφρονι. 8. οὔ τις ἐθέλει ὁδὸν ἐλθεῖν ἢ ἀνδράσιν μάχεσθαι ἶφι.

249. Read and translate:

Iliad, 142–151

ἐς δ' ἐρέτας ἐπιτηδὲς ἀγείρομεν, ἐς δ' ἑκατόμβας
θήομεν, ἂν δ' αὐτὴν Χρυσηΐδα καλλιπάρῃον
βήσομεν. εἰς δέ τις ἀρχὸς ἀνὴρ βουληφόρος ἔστω,
ἢ Αἴας ἢ Ἰδομενεὺς ἢ δῖος Ὀδυσσεὺς   145
ἠὲ σύ, Πηλεΐδη, πάντων ἐκπαγλότατ' ἀνδρῶν,
ὄφρ' ἡμῖν ἑκάεργον ἱλάσσεαι, ἱερὰ ῥέξας."
τὸν δ' ἄρ' ὑπόδρα ἰδὼν προσέφη πόδας ὠκὺς Ἀχιλλεύς·

" ὦ μοι, ἀναιδείην ἐπιειμένε, κερδαλεόφρον,
πῶς τίς τοι πρόφρων ἔπεσιν πείθηται 'Αχαιῶν   150
ἢ ὁδὸν ἐλθέμεναι ἢ ἀνδράσιν ἶφι μάχεσθαι ;

250. 142. ἐς, ἐς: 1048–1049. — ἀγείρομεν: 800, 1098.
143. θήομεν [τίθημι]: 800, 1098. — ἀν = ἀνά: 1048–1049, 567.
144. βήσομεν: 1049, 800, 1069, 1098.
146–147. ἐλάσσεαι: 800, 1115–1116. — ἱερὰ ῥέξᾱς: (by) performing
sacrifices.
149. ἀναιδείην ἐπιειμένε: 1020, 1; 1071.
150. τοι: 997. — ἔπεσιν: 996. — πείθηται: 1100.
151. ὁδόν: 1012. — ἀνδράσιν: 1007.

251. Translate :

1. But come, drag the swift black ships into the divine sea, collect oarsmen in sufficient numbers therein, place in them many sacred hecatombs, and cause to go on board many beautiful-cheeked maidens.   2. Some counsel-bearing man shall be commander.   3. Neither Ajax nor Idomeneus nor the divine Odysseus was cowardly, but they feared the son of Peleus, most terrible of men.   4. Will you perform sacrifices and appease the free-worker for us?   5. We looked askance at the swift-footed Achilles and addressed him.   6. Alas ! how many of the great-souled Achaeans will zealously obey a crafty-minded man clothed in shamelessness, either to go on an expedition or to fight mightily with men?

LESSON XXXIX

FORMATION AND COMPARISON OF ADVERBS

ILIAD, 152-157

252. Read carefully 780–788.

253. *Optional :*

254. VOCABULARY

αἴτιος, η, ον blamable, to blame, guilty, accountable, responsible.

αἰχμητής, ᾶο, ὁ spearman, warrior.

βοῦς, βοός, ὁ, ἡ ox, cow, bull.

βωτι-άνειρα *fem.*, man-nourishing, nurturing heroes; *subst.* nurse of heroes.

δεῦρο hither, to this place, here.

δηλέ-ομαι*, δηλήσομαι, ἐδηλησάμην, δεδήλημαι* harm, hurt, destroy, damage, wrong, ruin.

ἐλά-ω, ἐλά(σ)(σ)ω, ἤλασ(σ)α, ἐλήλακα*, ἐλήλαμαι, ἠλάθην* drive, strike, carry on, push, press.

ἐρι-βῶλαξ, ακος rich-clodded, heavy-clodded, fertile.

ἠχήεις, εσσα, εν *onomatopoetic,* (re)echoing, roaring, (re)sounding, thundering.

ἵππος, ου, ὁ, ἡ horse, mare.

καρπός, οῦ, ὁ fruit, crop, produce, harvest.

μαχέ-ομαι (**μάχομαι**), **μαχήσομαι** (**-έσσομαι?**) (**μαχέομαι**), **ἐμαχεσ(σ)άμην** fight, battle.

μεταξύ between, intervening.

οὖρος (**ὄρος, 571**), **εος, τό** mountain.

σκιόεις, εσσα, εν shady, shadowy.

Τρῶες, ων, οἱ Trojans.

Φθίη, ης, ἡ Phthia, *a town and district in northern Greece, home of Achilles.*

Derivatives : (a)etio-logy, -logic(al) ; bu-colic, -cranium, bovine ; elas-tic(ity) ; echo-ing, -meter, -scope ; hippo-potamus, -drome, -crene, -crates, Phil-ip ; carp-el, carpo-genic, -lite, -phore, Poly-carp ; or-ead, oro-logy, -graphy, -hippus ; squi-rrel, scio-graph(y), -machy, -mancy, sci-optic(al).

255. Translate:

1. ἦλθον Ἀχαιοὶ δεῦρο μαχησόμενοι ἕνεκα Τρώων αἰχμητάων.

2. εἰσὶ Τρῶες αἴτιοι Ἀχαιοῖσιν; 3. ἠλάσαμεν βοῦς (= βόας) τε καὶ ἵππους Ἀχιλῆος, καρπὸν δ᾽ ἐδηλησάμεθ᾽ ἐν Φθίῃ ἐριβώλακι. 4. Τρῶές εἰσιν τηλόθι Φθίης βωτιανείρης, ἐστὶ δὲ μάλα πολλὰ σκιόεντ᾽ οὔρεα καὶ ἠχήεσσα θάλασσα μεταξύ.

93

256. Read and translate :

Iliad, 152–157

οὐ γὰρ ἐγὼ Τρώων ἕνεκ᾿ ἤλυθον αἰχμητάων
δεῦρο μαχησόμενος, ἐπεὶ οὔ τί μοι αἴτιοί εἰσιν ·
οὐ γάρ πώ ποτ᾿ ἐμὰς βοῦς ἤλασαν οὐδὲ μὲν ἵππους,
οὐδέ ποτ᾿ ἐν Φθίῃ ἐριβώλακι βωτιανείρῃ   155
καρπὸν ἐδηλήσαντ᾿, ἐπεὶ ἦ μάλα πολλὰ μεταξύ,
οὔρεά τε σκιόεντα θάλασσά τε ἠχήεσσα ·

257. 152. ἐγώ: emphatic (1039), as contrasted with Agamemnon and his brother Menelaus, who had a strong personal interest in the success of the expedition.

153. μαχησόμενος : 1109, 5. — τι : 780–781.

154. βοῦς = βόας.

157. ἠχήεσσα : onomatopoetic, to represent the sound of the roaring sea. — σκιόεντα refers to the long shadows which high mountains throw. This verse is in apposition with πολλά (used substantively) of the preceding verse.

Observe the heaping up of the first personal pronouns in this passage, to indicate that Achilles had no personal interest, as did Agamemnon, in the expedition. Achilles emphasizes his own generous motives and self-sacrificing spirit in joining the undertaking, thereby throwing into high relief the ingratitude of Agamemnon and the deep injustice of his selfishness. " The Trojans have never done me the slightest harm, that I should have gone to all this trouble in making this expedition against them."

258. Translate :

1. We came hither to fight with the Trojan warriors ; for they are blamable to us.   2. Once the Achaeans drove away our cattle and horses, and destroyed our crops in fertile, man-nourishing Phthia.   3. Phthia is far from Troy, and there are very many shadowy mountains and the roaring sea between.

LESSON XL

NUMERALS

ILIAD, 158–164

259. Study the table of cardinals, ordinals, and numeral adverbs, 757. Commit the first twelve of each to memory, and learn the declension of εἷς, μία, ἕν one ; δύο (δύω) two ; τρεῖς, τρία three ; and τέσσαρες, τέσσαρα four, 758–759.

260. Optional :

261. VOCABULARY

ἀλεγίζω (ἀλεγιδ-), with gen., 984 care, reck, consider, regard, worry.

ἅμα with dat., at the same time, together (with).

ἀν-αιδής, ές shameless, unfeeling.

ἀπειλέ-ω, ἀπειλήσω, ἠπείλησα threaten, boast, menace.

ἄρ-νυμαι, ἀρέομαι*, ἠρόμην acquire, win, save, preserve.

ἀφ-αιρέω (αἰρε-, ἑλ-), ἀφαιρήσω, ἀφέελον (ἀφεῖλον), ἀφῄρηκα*, ἀφῄρημαι*, ἀφῃρέθην* take away, rob, deprive.

ἕπω (σεπ-, σπ-), ἕψω, ἕσπον be busy, perform; mid., follow, accompany, attend.

ἴσος, η (ἴση), ον equal, equivalent, well-balanced, symmetrical.

κυν-ώπης (voc. κυνῶπα) dog-faced, dog-eyed, shameless.

Μενέλαος, ου, ὁ Menelaus, brother of Agamemnon, and husband of Helen.

μετα-τρέπω (τρεπ-, τροπ-, τραπ-), μετα-

τρέψω, μετέτρεψα, (μετέτραπον), μετατέτροφα**, μετατέτραμμαι, μετετράφθην (μετετράπην*) turn (around) ; mid. turn oneself toward, heed.

μογέ-ω, ἐμόγησα toil, struggle.

ναίω (νασ-), ἔνασσα, ἐνάσθην dwell, inhabit; mid. be situated.

ὁπ(π)ότε when(ever).

πρός (π(ρ)οτί) adv., and prep. with gen., dat., and acc., to, toward, also, at, on, from, on behalf of ; with gen., from, before, at the bidding, in the sight; with dat., on, at, by ; with acc., to, toward, (up)on, against.

πτολίεθρον (= π(τ)όλις), ου, τό city.

τῑμή, ῆς, ἡ honor, satisfaction, recompense, retribution, value.

χαίρω (χαρ-, χαρε-, χαιρε-), χαιρήσω, κεχάρη(κ)α, κεχάρη(η)μαι*, ἐχάρην rejoice, be glad, hail ! welcome !

262. Translate :

1. Ἀχιλλεὺς ἕσπετο ἄνακτι ἀνδρῶν Ἀγαμέμνονι μέγ'

95

ἀναιδέι, ὄφρα χαίρῃ. 2. Ἀχαιοὶ ἔσποντ' Ἀγαμέμνονι ἅμα,
τῖμὴν ἀρνύμενοι (1070) τῷ καὶ Μενελάῳ. 3. ἦν Ἀγαμέ-
μνων κυνώπης; 4. ἀρνύμεθα τῖμὴν πρὸς Τρώων Μενελάῳ.
5. Ἀγαμέμνων οὐ μετατρέπεται οὐδ' ἀλεγίζει τῶν. 6. βασι-
λεὺς αὐτὸς ἠπείλησεν ἀφαιρήσεσθαι γέρας Ἀχιλῆι. 7. Ἀχιλ-
λεὺς ἐμόγησε πολλὰ τῷ γέραϊ. 8. γέρα πάντες ἔξομεν ἴσα
βασιλῆι, ὁππότε ἐκπερσώμεθα πτολίεθρα Τρώων.

263. Read and translate :

Iliad, 158–164

ἀλλὰ σοί, ὦ μέγ' ἀναιδές, ἅμ' ἑσπόμεθ', ὄφρα σὺ χαίρῃς,
τῖμὴν ἀρνύμενοι Μενελάῳ σοί τε, κυνῶπα,
πρὸς Τρώων. τῶν οὔ τι μετατρέπῃ οὐδ' ἀλεγίζεις ·   160
καὶ δή μοι γέρας αὐτὸς ἀφαιρήσεσθαι ἀπειλεῖς,
ᾧ ἔπι πολλὰ μόγησα, δόσαν δέ μοι υἷες Ἀχαιῶν.
οὐ μέν σοί ποτε ἶσον ἔχω γέρας, ὁππότ' Ἀχαιοὶ
Τρώων ἐκπέρσωσ' ἐὺ ναιόμενον πτολίεθρον ·

264. 158. σοί : 1007, emphatic, as may be seen from the accent, 762.
— μέγ'(α) : 780–781. — χαίρῃς : 1115–1116. — σύ : very emphatic, as con-
trasted with Achilles (1039).
159. ἀρνύμενοι : 1070. — Μενελάῳ σοί τε : 997.
160. τῶν (used substantively) : 984. — τι : 780–781.
161. μοι : 997. — αὐτός : *yourself*, i.e. " arbitrarily," without the con-
sent of the army or the other chieftains.
162. ἔπι : 1050. — πολλά : 780–781.
163. σοί : a brachylogical comparison, as in English, " what is good
for a cold," *i.e.* " what is good for a man who has a cold." This thought
intensifies the injustice of Agamemnon's action.
Observe the emphasis and contrast so effectively obtained by the use
of the personal pronouns in this passage, and the rhyming effect of σοί,
σύ, σοί, μοί μοί, σοί.

265. Translate :

1. They followed the very shameless Agamemnon and
Menelaus, that they might win recompense for them from

the Trojans. 2. But the two kings did not regard or consider these things at all. 3. The king of men, Agamemnon, threatened to take away the prize of Achilles, for which he had struggled much, and which had been given to him by the sons of the Achaeans. 4. We never had a prize of honor equal to Agamemnon('s), whenever we sacked a well-situated city of the Trojans.

LESSON XLI

PRESENT, FUTURE, AND FIRST AORIST SYSTEM OF VERBS

ILIAD, 165-172

266. 1) Review carefully all the forms of λύω in the present, future, and first aorist, all voices, modes, and tenses, 904–921, and read 789–809.

2) Learn the conjugation of φαίνω in the first aorist system, 931–932.

267. *Optional:*

268. VOCABULARY

ἀτάρ (= αὐτάρ 571) but, moreover.

ἄ-τῑμος, η, ον dishonored, unhonored.

ἄφενος, εος, τό wealth, riches.

ἀφύσσω (ἀφυγ-), ἀφύξω dip up, draw (out), collect, heap up.

δασμός, οῦ, ὁ division (of spoils).

δι-έπω (σεπ-, σπ-), διέψω, διέσπον accomplish, perform, go through, be engaged (in).

ἐνθά-δε here, hither, there, thither.

κάμνω (καμ-, κμη-), καμέομαι, ἔκαμον, κέκμη(κ)α do, make, toil, be weary, suffer, accomplish with pain.

κορωνίς, ίδος curved, bent.

ὀλίγος, η, ον little, few, small, of slight value, cheap.

πλοῦτος, ου, ὁ wealth, riches, abundance.

π(τ)ολεμίζω (cf. π(τ)όλεμος), π(τ)ο-λεμίξω war, battle, fight.

πολυ-άϊξ, ῑκος impetuous, onrushing.

σύν adv., and prep. with dat., with, together (with), along with.

φέρτερος, η, ον (comparat. 754, 2), mightier, better, braver, stronger, more powerful, more productive, more profitable.

Derivatives: corona-tion, crown; olig-archy; pluto-crat, -cracy; polem-ic(al); syn-agogue, syn-.

269. Translate:

1. διέπομεν πόλεμον πολυάϊκα χείρεσσιν.   2. ποτὲ δασμὸς ἵκηται, Ἀγαμέμνων ἔχει τὸ γέρας πολὺ μεῖζον, Ἀχιλλεὺς δ' ἔχει (γέρας) ὀλίγον μὲν φίλον δέ.   3. Ἀχιλλεὺς ἔχων γέρας ὀλίγον τε φίλον τ' ἔρχεται ἐπὶ νῆας, ἐπεί κε κάμῃ πολεμίζων.   4. νῦν Ἀχιλλεὺς εἰσι Φθίηνδε.   5. ἦ πολὺ φέρτερόν ἐστιν ἴμεν οἴκαδε σὺν νηυσὶν κορωνίσιν.   6. Ἀχιλλεὺς ἐὼν ἄτιμος, οὐκ ἀφύξει ἄφενος καὶ πλοῦτον Ἀγαμέμνονι ἐνθάδε.

270. Read and translate:

Iliad, 165–172

ἀλλὰ τὸ μὲν πλεῖον πολυάϊκος πολέμοιο   165
χεῖρες ἐμαὶ διέπουσ', ἀτὰρ ἤν ποτε δασμὸς ἵκηται,
σοὶ τὸ γέρας πολὺ μεῖζον, ἐγὼ δ' ὀλίγον τε φίλον τε
ἔρχομ' ἔχων ἐπὶ νῆας, ἐπεί κε κάμω πολεμίζων.
νῦν δ' εἶμι Φθίηνδ', ἐπεὶ ἦ πολὺ φέρτερόν ἐστιν
οἴκαδ' ἴμεν σὺν νηυσὶ κορωνίσιν, οὐδέ σ' ὀίω   170
ἐνθάδ' ἄτιμος ἐὼν ἄφενος καὶ πλοῦτον ἀφύξειν."
τὸν δ' ἠμείβετ' ἔπειτα ἄναξ ἀνδρῶν Ἀγαμέμνων·

271. 165. τὸ πλεῖον: comparat. of πολύς, 754, 9, *the greater* (part).
166. χεῖρες ἐμαί: *my hands*, a more effectual and picturesque way of saying " I did it."
167. τό: *the well-known, usual* (gift of honor). — πολύ: 780–781. —
μεῖζον: comparat. of μέγας, 754. — ὀλίγον: *of slight value* (not *petite*).
— ὀλίγον τε φίλον τε: *of slight value, yet dear* (to me).   Cf. Shakespere:
" a poor virgin, an ill-favoured thing, but mine own."
168. ἔρχομ'(αι). — *when I am weary (of) fighting.*
170. σ'(οι): 997. — ὀίω: ironically, as often. — κορωνίσιν: this word
visualizes the curved line of the Greek ship, with its high prow and stern.

272. Translate:

1. Although the greater (part) of this impetuous war was

98

accomplished by our hands, you always have much the greater prize, whenever a division of spoil(s) comes.   2. When they grew weary (of) fighting, they went to their ships with (having) prizes, small yet dear to their hearts.   3. It was much better to go to Phthia; nor did they think that since they had been dishonored here they would collect wealth and riches for Agamemnon.

LESSON XLII

THE SECOND AORIST, AND THE FIRST AND SECOND PERFECT SYSTEMS OF VERBS

Iliad, 173–181

273. 1) Learn the conjugation of the perfect and second aorist systems of λύω and of βαίνω, 904–915, 922, 930.

2) Read carefully 810–818.

274. *Optional:*

275.   **VOCABULARY**

διο-τρεφής, ές Zeus-nourished.

εἵνεκα (= ἕνεκα, 571) on account of.

ἐπι-σσεύω (σευ-, συ-), —, ἐπέσσευα, ἐπέσσυμαι, ἐπεσ(σ)ύθην drive on, hurry on, urge.

ἕταρος (ἑταῖρος, 571), ου, ὁ companion, comrade, follower, friend.

ἐχθρός, ή, όν (*compar.* ἐχθίων, ον; *superl.* ἔχθιστος, η, ον) hateful, hated, enemy, hostile, odious.

καρτερός, ή, όν (= κρατερός) (597–598), strong, mighty, severe, harsh, stern.

κοτέω, ἐκότεσ(σ)α, κεκότη(κ)α hold a grudge, be angry, be vindictive.

μάλιστα (*superlat. of* μάλα) most

of all, especially, by all means, decidedly.

μάχη, ης, ἡ battle, fight, fray.

μένω (μεν-, μενε-) μενέω, ἔμεινα, μεμένηκα** remain, await.

μητίετα, ᾱο, ὁ counsellor, (prudent) adviser.

Μυρμιδών, όνος, ὁ Myrmidon, *Greek.*

ὄθ-ομαι *with gen.* 984, reck, care, consider, regard, worry.

τῑμά-ω, τῑμήσω, ἐτῑμησα, τετῑμηκα*, τετῑμημαι, ἐτῑμήθην* honor, gain honor; *mid.* avenge, exact recompense.

ὧδε thus, so, in this way, as follows.

Derivatives: Dino-mache, logo-, scio-, theo-machy; timocracy.

276. Translate:

1. φεύξομαι μάλα, ἐπεί μοι θυμὸς ἐπέσσυται τόδε. 2. λισσόμεθα Πηληιάδην μένειν εἵνεκ' 'Αγαμέμνονος. 3. παρ' 'Αγαμέμνονί γε ἄλλοι εἰσίν, οἵ κε τὸν τιμήσουσι, μάλιστα δὲ μητίετα Ζεύς. 4. 'Αχιλλεύς ἐστιν ἔχθιστος πάντων διοτρεφέων βασιλήων 'Αγαμέμνονι. 5. ἔρις τε φίλη 'Αχιλῆί ἐστιν αἰεὶ πόλεμοί τε μάχαι τε. 6. 'Αχιλλεὺς μάλα καρτερός ἐστιν, ἀλλά που θεός οἱ τό γ' ἔδωκεν. 7. 'Αχιλλεὺς εἶσι οἴκαδε σὺν νηυσί τε καὶ ἑτάροισιν, ἀνάξει δὲ Μυρμιδόνεσσιν. 8. 'Αγαμέμνων οὐκ ἀλεγίζει οὐδ' ὄθεται 'Αχιλῆος κοτέοντος.

277. Read and translate:

Iliad, 173–181

" φεῦγε μάλ', εἴ τοι θυμὸς ἐπέσσυται, οὐδέ σ' ἐγώ γε
λίσσομαι εἵνεκ' ἐμεῖο μένειν · παρ' ἐμοί γε καὶ ἄλλοι,
οἵ κέ με τιμήσουσι, μάλιστα δὲ μητίετα Ζεύς.   175
ἔχθιστος δέ μοί ἐσσι διοτρεφέων βασιλήων ·
αἰεὶ γάρ τοι ἔρις τε φίλη πόλεμοί τε μάχαι τε.
εἰ μάλα καρτερός ἐσσι, θεός που σοὶ τό γ' ἔδωκεν.
οἴκαδ' ἰὼν σὺν νηυσί τε σῆς καὶ σοῖς ἑτάροισιν
Μυρμιδόνεσσιν ἄνασσε, σέθεν δ' ἐγὼ οὐκ ἀλεγίζω   180
οὐδ' ὄθομαι κοτέοντος · ἀπειλήσω δέ τοι ὧδε ·

278. 173. **τοι**: 998. — **φεῦγε**: *flee, desert*. It is this insinuation which helps Achilles decide to stay.
173–174. "Run along home, by all means; don't stay on my account."
Ironical, of course. — **ἄλλοι** (εἰσίν).
175. A reply to the assertion of Achilles in vs. 159. This is a good example of the subtle irony of the poet; for it is Zeus and no other who *dis*honors Agamemnon in the sequel. The king's proud speech here and his haughty presumption upon the favor of Zeus, the natural protector of kings, thus make his later discomfiture all the more striking and humiliating. — **τιμήσουσι**: 1144.

177. ἔρις τε φίλη (ἐστίν). φίλη agrees with ἔρις, but is to be taken with πόλεμοί τε μάχαι τε also.
180. Μυρμιδόνεσσιν: 1001, but in the mouth of Agamemnon may be considered a dative of disadvantage, 997. — Μυρμιδόνεσσιν Ϝάνασσε: see 526. — σέθεν: 984.
181. κοτέοντος (σέο): 984.

279. Translate:

1. Agamemnon, king of men, said to Achilles, "Fly by all means, if your soul urges you." 2. The Achaeans entreated us greatly to remain with them, that we might honor them especially. 3. Zeus, the counselor, will especially honor all the kings. 4. Agamemnon and Menelaus were to Achilles the most hateful of all the Zeus-nourished kings; for always strife and wars and battles were dear to their hearts. 5. Although they were very strong, some god had given that to them. 6. Let us go home with our ships and our comrades, and rule the Myrmidons. 7. We do not regard Achilles, nor do we care when he holds a grudge; since we are much mightier.

LESSON XLIII

THE PERFECT MIDDLE SYSTEM OF VERBS

ILIAD, 182-192

280. 1) Learn the perfect middle system of λύω, 910-915, τρέπω, τεύχω, and πεύθομαι, 925-929.

2) Study the table of personal endings of verbs, 819-829.

281. *Optional:*

282.   VOCABULARY

ἄντην openly, before the face.
ἄχος, εος, τό woe, pain, grief.
Βρῑσηΐς, ίδος, ἡ Briseïs, daughter of Briseus, *prize of Achilles.*

δι-άν-διχα in two ways, differently.
ἐναρίζω (ἐναριγ-), ἐναρίξω, ἠνάριξα strip of armor, spoil, slay.
ἐρητύ-ω, ἠρήτῡσα, ἠρητύθην check,

restrain, control, contain, hold back, curb.

ἦτορ, ορος, τό heart, soul, spirit.

κλισίη, ης, ἡ hut, barrack, tent.

λάσιος, η, ον hairy, shaggy, rough, bushy.

μερ-μηρίζω (μηριγ-), ἐμερμήριξα ponder, consider.

μηρός, οῦ, ὁ thigh.

ὁμοιό-ω*, ὁμοιώσω*, ὡμοιώθην liken, make like, compare, make equal.

ὀξύς, εῖα, ύ sharp, biting, cutting, keen, acid.

ὅσ(σ)ος, η, ον how much, how great, how many, how large, how long.

παύ-ω, παύσω, ἔπαυσα, πέπαυκα*, πέπαυμαι, ἐπαύθην* cease, stop, PAUSE, check, restrain, hold off.

Πηλεΐων, ωνος, ὁ son of Peleus, Achilles.

στυγέω (στυγ-, στυγε-), ἔστυξα (ἔστυγον), ἐστυγήθην† hate, loathe, dislike, make hateful, hold in horror, fear.

φάσγανον, ου, τό sword, sabre.

Derivatives: hom(o)e-o-pathy, homo-logous, -geneous; Stygian.

283. Translate:

1. ἀφαιρεόμεθα βασιλῆα Χρυσηίδα τὸ γέρας κᾱλόν. 2. Ἀγαμέμνων πέμψει Χρυσηίδα ἐς Χρύσην σὺν νηὶ καὶ ἑτάροισιν ἐοῖσιν. 3. ἄναξ αὐτὸς ἰὼν κλισίηνδε ἄξει Βρισηίδα καλλιπάρῃον τὸ γέρας Ἀχιλλῆος, ὄφρ' Ἀχιλλεὺς ἐὺ εἴδη ὅσσον φέρτερός ἐστιν Ἀγαμέμνων. 4. ἄλλοι στυγέουσι φάσθαι σφέας αὐτοὺς εἶναι ἴσους Ἀγαμέμνονι καὶ ὁμοιωθήμεναι ἄντην. 5. ἦτορ Πηλεΐωνος ἐμερμήριξε διάνδιχα, ἢ ὅ γε ἐρυσσάμενος φάσγανον ὀξὺ παρὰ μήρου ἀναστήσειε μὲν τοὺς Ἀχαιούς, ἐναρίζοι δ' Ἀτρεΐδην, ἠὲ παύσειε χόλον ἐρητύσειέ τε θῡμόν. 6. ἄχος μέγα ἐγένετο τοῖσιν Ἀχαιοῖσιν, οὕνεκα Ἀγαμέμνων ἀφείλετο Βρισηίδα καλλιπάρῃον Ἀχιλῆα.

284. Read and translate:

Iliad, 182–192

ὡς ἔμ' ἀφαιρεῖται Χρυσηίδα Φοῖβος Ἀπόλλων,
τὴν μὲν ἐγὼ σὺν νηί τ' ἐμῇ καὶ ἐμοῖς ἑτάροισιν
πέμψω, ἐγὼ δέ κ' ἄγω Βρισηίδα καλλιπάρῃον

αὐτὸς ἰὼν κλισίηνδε, τὸ σὸν γέρας, ὄφρ' ἐὺ εἴδῃς   185
ὅσσον φέρτερός εἰμι σέθεν, στυγέῃ δὲ καὶ ἄλλος
ἶσον ἐμοὶ φάσθαι καὶ ὁμοιωθήμεναι ἄντην."
ὣς φάτο· Πηλείωνι δ' ἄχος γένετ', ἐν δέ οἱ ἦτορ
στήθεσσιν λασίοισι διάνδιχα μερμήριξεν,
ἢ ὅ γε φάσγανον ὀξὺ ἐρυσσάμενος παρὰ μηροῦ   190
τοὺς μὲν ἀναστήσειεν, ὁ δ' Ἀτρείδην ἐναρίζοι,
ἦε χόλον παύσειεν ἐρητύσειέ τε θυμόν.

285. 182. ἔμ'(ε), Χρῦσηίδα : 1020, 1. —ἀφαιρεῖται = ἀφαιρέεται : 584–
585. — ὡς : *as, since.*

184. πέμψω, ἄγω : observe the variation due to the use of the indicative and subjunctive. Agamemnon is more sure of the first than of the second. — ἄγω : 1101.

185. " To prove my superior power, I shall go myself." — τὸ σὸν γέρας : in apposition with Βρῑσηίδα. The addition of the demonstrative pronoun (τό) makes the expression more vivid. — εἴδῃς : 1115–1116.

186. ὅσσον : 564, 3. — σέθεν : 993. — στυγέῃ : 1115–1116. — καί : *also,* even (as well as yourself).

187. ἐμοί (εἶναι) : 1003. — φάσθαι [φημί]. — ὁμοιωθήμεναι : *liken himself,* 890.

188. Πηλείωνι : 998. — ἐν δέ οἱ . . . στήθεσσιν : 998, 1009.

190. ἤ : *whether.*

191. τοὺς (ἄλλους Ἀχαιούς) : evidently Agamemnon was sitting down in the assembly, with the other chieftains seated around him. Achilles would need to make these start up in order to get at Agamemnon. — ἀναστήσειεν, ἐναρίζοι : 1153.

192. ἦε : *or.* — παύσειεν, ἐρητύσειέ τε : 1153.

286. Translate :

1. Since the gods thus take away our prize, we shall send it to Chrysa, with a sacred hecatomb for the god, but we shall go in person (αὐτοί) to the tent of Achilles and lead away his prize, the beauteous-cheeked Briseïs, that he may well know how much stronger we are than he, and all others may hate to say they are equal to us and compare themselves with us openly.   2. When he had thus spoken, grief arose

for the sons of the Achaeans, and within their hairy chests they pondered in two ways. 3. We shall draw our sharp swords from our thighs, and rouse the sons of the Achaeans, but slay the two sons of Atreus, or we shall check our wrath and curb our spirit.

LESSON XLIV

FIRST AND SECOND PASSIVE SYSTEM OF VERBS

ILIAD, 193–200

287. Read 830–859, and review the first passive system of λύω, 916–921, and of τρέφω, 935.

288. *Optional:*

289.   VOCABULARY

Ἀθηναίη (Ἀθήνη), ης, ἡ Athena, *goddess of war, wisdom, and the arts.*

ἄμφω, ἄμφοιιν, both.

γι-γνώσκω (γνω-, γνο-), γνώσομαι, ἔγνων, ἔγνωκα*, ἔγνωσμαι*, ἐγνώσθην* KNOW, recognize, learn, perceive.

ἕλκω (ἑλκ- = σελκ-, 603–604), draw, drag, pull, tug.

ἦος while, until.

θαμβέ-ω, θαμβήσω*, ἐθάμβησα wonder, be amazed, be frightened, stand aghast.

ἵ-στημι (στη-, στα-), στήσω, ἔστησα (ἔστην), ἔστηκα, ἔσταμαι*, ἐστάθην set (up), STAND, make stand, take one's stand, STATION.

κολεόν (κουλεόν, 571), οὗ, τό sheath, scabbard (1168).

κόμη, ης, ἡ hair, locks, tresses.

ξανθός, ή, όν tawny, yellow, blond.

ξίφος, εος, τό sword.

ὁμῶς equally, alike, together, at the same time.

ὄπι(σ)θε(ν) behind, from behind, later, latter.

ὁρμαίνω (ὁρμαν-), —, ὥρμηνα toss about (turn over) in mind, ponder, consider, plan.

οὐρανός, οὗ, ὁ heaven, sky.

Παλλάς, άδος, ἡ Pallas (Athena).

τρέπω (τρεπ-, τροπ-, τραπ-), τρέψω, ἔτρεψα (ἔτραπον), τέτροφα**, τέτραμμαι, ἐτράφθην turn (around), rout, put to flight; *mid.*, turn oneself, flee.

φαείνω (φαεν-); *aor. pass.* ἐφαάνθην shine, gleam, glare, flash.

φαίνω (φαν-), φανέω, ἔφηνα, πέφηνα*, πέφασμαι, ἐφάν(θ*)ην show, shine; *(mid.)* appear.

Derivatives : a-gnostic(ism), pro-gnosticate ; STAY, system, static ; comet; trope, *etc.*, 261 ; dia-phanous, *etc.*, 194.

290. Translate:

1. οἱ Ἀχαιοὶ ὥρμαινον ταῦτα κατὰ φρένα καὶ κατὰ θῦμόν.
2. ἔλκωμεν ἐκ κολεῶν μεγάλα ξίφεα καὶ ἐναρίζωμεν Ἀγαμέμνονα. 3. Ἀθήνη ἦλθεν οὐρανόθεν, τὴν γὰρ ἔηκεν Ἥρη λευκώλενος. 4. Ἥρη λευκώλενος φιλέει Ἀχιλῆά τε καὶ Ἀγαμέμνονα ὁμῶς θῦμῷ, κήδεται δέ τοῖιν ἄμφοιιν. 5. Ἀθήνη ἦλθεν οὐρανόθεν, ἔστη δ' ὄπιθεν, εἷλε δ' Ἀχιλῆα ξανθῆς κόμης (983). 6. Ἀθήνη ἐφαίνετ' Ἀχιλῆι οἴῳ, οὐ γάρ τις τῶν ἄλλων Ἀχαιῶν ὡράετο τὴν θεάν. 7. ἐπεὶ θεὰ εἷλεν Ἀχιλῆα κόμης, ἐθάμβησε, μετατρεψάμενος δ' ἔγνω αὐτίκα Παλλάδ' Ἀθηναίην. 8. ὄσσε Ἀθηναίης ἐφαάνθησαν δεινὼ Ἀχιλῆι.

291. Read and translate :

Iliad, 193-200

ἧος ὁ ταῦθ' ὥρμαινε κατὰ φρένα καὶ κατὰ θῦμόν,
ἕλκετο δ' ἐκ κολεοῖο μέγα ξίφος, ἦλθε δ' Ἀθήνη
οὐρανόθεν· πρὸ γὰρ ἧκε θεά, λευκώλενος Ἥρη,   195
ἄμφω ὁμῶς θῦμῷ φιλέουσά τε κηδομένη τε.
στῆ δ' ὄπιθεν, ξανθῆς δὲ κόμης ἕλε Πηλεΐωνα,
οἴῳ φαινομένη, τῶν δ' ἄλλων οὔ τις ὁρᾶτο.
θάμβησεν δ' Ἀχιλεύς, μετὰ δ' ἐτράπετ', αὐτίκα δ' ἔγνω
Παλλάδ' Ἀθηναίην · δεινὼ δέ οἱ ὄσσε φάανθεν.   200

292. 194. ἕλκετο: *was drawing.* — **ἦλθε δ Ἀθήνη** : coördinate, instead of subordinate construction, 1114.

196. ἄμφω = Ἀγαμέμνονα Ἀχιλῆά τε : Hera did not want to see either of them get hurt. — **θῦμῷ** : 1009. — **φιλέουσα, κηδομένη** : 1109, 2.

The situation has now reached the point where Achilles feels constrained to act, as he would rather die than endure such deep insults and humiliation at the hands of his most despised enemy. The imperfects in the first two verses make the description strikingly vivid and picturesque, while the hurried action of the two following aorists are well adapted to introduce Athena suddenly and dramatically.

197. κόμης: 983.

198. οἴῳ (Ἀχιλῆι). — ὁράτο = ὡράετο, 584–585, 837.

200. οἱ refers to Athena. — φάανθεν = ἐφαένθησαν, 973, 3; 945–948.

293. Translate :

1. While they were thus pondering in their hearts, but were drawing from their scabbards their great swords, the gods came from heaven, together with white-armed Hera who loves and cares for all men equally in her soul. 2. They stood behind the ships of the Achaeans. 3. Athena appeared to Achilles alone, and seized him by his tawny locks. 4. None of us saw the goddess, but we stood amazed. 5. When they turned around, they immediately recognized the goddess, for her (two) eyes gleamed terribly.

LESSON XLV

PRESENT, FUTURE, AND AORIST SYSTEM OF -μι VERBS
Iliad, 201–211

294. 1) Verbs ending in -μι differ from -ω verbs, by having no tense suffix (except in the subjunctive) in the present and imperfect active, middle, and passive, in the second aorist active and middle, and in the second perfect and pluperfect active.

2) Learn the inflection of the present, future, and both aorist systems of ἵστημι, τίθημι, ἵημι, and δίδωμι, 949–962.

295. *Optional:*

296.   **VOCABULARY**

ἄν = κέ(ν) (1085–1091).

αἰγί-οχος, η, ον aegis-holding.

αὖτε again, in turn, but, however, further(more), anew.

γλαυκ-ῶπις, ιδος gleaming-eyed, flashing-eyed (" owl-eyed ").

ἵνα in order that, (so) that, where.

λήγ-ω, λήξω, ἔληξα cease (from), retrain, SLACK(EN), weaken.

μη-δέ and not, but not, nor, not even; μηδὲ ... μηδέ neither ... nor.

ὄλλῡμι (ὀλ-, ὀλε-, ὀλο-), ὀλέσ(σ)ω, ὤλεσ(σ)α, ὄλωλα destroy, kill, ruin, lose; (mid.) perish, die.

ὀνειδίζω (ὀνειδιδ-), ὠνείδισα revile, reproach, abuse.

προσ-αυδά-ω, προσαυδήσω*, προσηύδησα address, speak to, say to.

πτερόεις, εσσα, εν winged, flying.

τάχα (ταχύς, 780–781) quickly, swiftly, soon.

τέκος, εος, τό child, descendant, offspring, young.

τί-πτε (τί ποτε, 592) why (in the world)?

ὕβρις, ιος, ἡ insolence, wantonness, frowardness, HYBRIS.

ὑπερ-οπλίη, ης, ἡ arrogance, insulting conduct (deed), 1168.

φωνέ-ω, φωνήσω*, ἐφώνησα speak, lift up the voice.

Derivatives : op-, 261 ; slack(en) ; ptero-pod, -dactyl ; tachy-graphy ; phono-logy, anti-, caco-, eu-, sym-, taut-o-phony, tele-, mega-, micro-phone.

297. Translate :

1. Ἀχιλλεὺς φωνήσᾱς προσηύδᾱ γλαυκώπιδα Ἀθήνην ἔπεα πτερόεντα. 2. τίπτ᾽ ἦλθεν αὖτε Παλλὰς Ἀθήνη τέκος αἰγιόχοιο Διός; 3. γλαυκῶπις Ἀθήνη ἦλθεν ἵνα ἴδῃ ὕβριν Ἀγαμέμνονος Ἀτρεΐδᾱο. 4. Ἀχιλλεὺς ἐρέει Ἀθήνῃ, τὸ δὲ τετελεσμένον ἔσται. οἴω ταῦτα τελέεσθαι. 5. τάχ᾽ ἄν ποτε Ἀγαμέμνων ὀλέσσῃ θῡμὸν ᾗς ὑπεροπλίῃσιν. 6. γλαυκῶπις Ἀθήνη ἦλθε παύσουσα τὸ μένος Ἀχιλῆος, αἵ κε πίθηται. 7. ἔληγεν Ἀχιλλεὺς ἔριδος, οὐδὲ ἕλκετο ξίφος χειρί; 8. ὀνειδίζει Ἀγαμέμνονα ἔπεσιν, ὡς ἔσεταί περ.

298. Read and translate :

Iliad, 201–211

καί μιν φωνήσας ἔπεα πτερόεντα προσηύδα ·   201
"τίπτ᾽ αὖτ᾽, αἰγιόχοιο Διὸς τέκος, εἰλήλουθας ;
ἦ ἵνα ὕβριν ἴδῃ Ἀγαμέμνονος Ἀτρεΐδαο ;
ἀλλ᾽ ἔκ τοι ἐρέω, τὸ δὲ καὶ τελέεσθαι ὀίω ·
ᾗς ὑπεροπλίῃσι τάχ᾽ ἄν ποτε θῡμὸν ὀλέσσῃ."   205
τὸν δ᾽ αὖτε προσέειπε θεά, γλαυκῶπις Ἀθήνη ·
" ἦλθον ἐγὼ παύσουσα τὸ σὸν μένος, αἵ κε πίθηαι,

οὐρανόθεν· πρὸ δέ μ' ἧκε θεὰ λευκώλενος Ἥρη,
ἄμφω ὁμῶς θυμῷ φιλέουσά τε κηδομένη τε.
ἀλλ' ἄγε λῆγ' ἔριδος, μηδὲ ξίφος ἕλκεο χειρί·   210
ἀλλ' ἦ τοι ἔπεσιν μὲν ὀνείδισον, ὡς ἔσεταί περ.

299. 201. μιν: object of προσηύδα. — ἔπεα: 1012. — πτερόεντα: 523.

202. αἰγιόχοιο: the aegis of Zeus was a shield, adorned with the head of the Gorgon, a snaky-headed monster, which petrified with chilly fear all who looked upon it. Athena was the best beloved of the children of Zeus, since she had sprung, as goddess of wisdom, full grown and fully armed from his head. As his favorite child she often bore his aegis. Achilles seems displeased at Athena's interference, and is greatly vexed that he should be prevented from killing Agamemnon. — αὖτε does not of necessity refer to an earlier appearance of Athena, but may merely denote Achilles' impatience that one trouble after another seems to have befallen him; and so he says, "And have you come too" (as an addition to all my other vexations)? — εἰλήλουθας, 1168.

203. ἴδη = ἴδηαι: 584–585. Achilles answers his own question (vs. 202) by a second rhetorical one. — ὕβριν ϝίδη, 526; 1067, 2.

204. τό: subject of τελέεσθαι, 971. — ὅτω: ironical, as usual in Homer.

205. Achilles broadly hints at his intention of killing Agamemnon for his arrogance. — ἧς (ὅς, ἥ, ὅν). — ὑπεροπλίησι: 1005. — ὀλέσσῃ: 1101.

206. γλαυκῶπις: supplements vss. 199–200, and shows why Achilles so quickly recognized the goddess. Originally it seems to have meant *owl-eyed*. Its origin was lost sight of before the time of Homer, to whom she was *gleaming-eyed*, *flashing-eyed*, etc., but it represents the earlier idea, according to which the goddess was thought of in the form of an owl, just as Jehovah was worshipped by the Israelites for a long time in the form of a bull-god, as Apollo Smintheus was once the mouse-god, etc.

207. παύσουσα: 1109, 5. — πίθηαι: Athena is not quite sure that Achilles will obey, but hopes so.

210. ἔριδος: 987. — ἕλκεο: *continue to draw*. — χειρί: 1005. — λῆγ'(ε): imperative.

211. *I.e.* abuse him roundly; only do not strike him. The goddess counsels a word-war, instead of a resort to arms, and thus there is a reversion to the situation previous to Achilles' attempt to draw his sword. — ὡς ἔσεταί περ: "tell him how it shall be," *i.e.* "tell him what shall take place."

300. Translate :

1. We lifted up our voices (*part.*) and addressed the flashing-eyed goddess (with) winged words. 2. Why, O darling daughter of aegis-bearing Zeus, have you returned to the swift black ships of the Achaeans? 3. Is it that you may see the insolence of the Zeus-nourished kings? 4. But we shall speak out to you, and we think that this will be accomplished, that they will soon lose their souls by their own arrogance. 5. Athena, the flashing-eyed, came from heaven to check the anger of Achilles, if perchance he would obey her. 6. If Achilles will cease from strife nor draw his great sword with his heavy hand, he may revile Agamemnon with harsh words as the opportunity may offer (ὡς ἔσεταί περ).

LESSON XLVI

FIRST AND SECOND PERFECT SYSTEM OF -μι VERBS

ILIAD, 212–222

301. Learn the conjugation of all the perfect and pluperfect forms of ἵστημι and of *εἴδω, 924, 966.

302. *Optional :*

303.   VOCABULARY

ἀ-πιθέ-ω*, ἀπιθήσω, ἠπίθησα, *with dat.*, 996, disobey, fail to obey, distrust.

δαίμων, ονος, ὁ, ἡ divinity, god (dess).

δῶρον, ον, τό gift, present.

ε(ἴ)ρῦμαι (ϝερῦ-), ε(ἴ)ρύσ(σ)ομαι, ε(ἴ)ρυσ(σ)άμην save, preserve, observe, protect, guard, retain.

ἐξ-είρω (ϝερ-, ϝρη-, ϝεπ-), ἐξερέω, ἐξεῖπον, ἐξείρηκα*, ἐξείρημαι, ἐξειρήθην speak out, declare.

ἐπι-πείθω (πειθ-, πιθ-, ποιθ), ἐπιπείσω, ἐπέπεισα (ἐπιπέπιθον), ἐπιπέποιθα, ἐπιπέπεισμαι*, ἐπεπείσθην* persuade, trust; *mid.* obey.

ἠμί (ἠγ-), *imperf.*, ἦν speak, say.

ἴ-σχω (ἰσχ- = σι-σ(ε)χ-), *another form of* ἔχω, have, hold, restrain, check.

κουλεόν = κολεόν, 571, 1168.

κώπη, ης, ἡ hilt, handle.

πάρ-ειμι, (ἐσ-), παρέσ(σ)ομαι be pres-

109

ent, be at hand, be near, be
beside.

σφωίτερος, η, ον of you two, belong-
ing to you two.

τρίς thrice, three times.

χρή (χρείω, χρέω), ἡ need, necessity,
fate, destiny, due, duty.

ὠθέω (ϝωθ-, ϝωθε-), ὤσω, ἔωσα,
ἔωσμαι*, ἐώσθην* shove, push,
thrust, drive, strike.

Derivatives : demon-iac, -o-logy, -o-cracy, -o-latry, pan-
demonium; Dora, Doro-thea, -thy, Theo-dore; am ;
t(h)rice.

304. Translate :

1. πάντα γὰρ τάδε τελέσσουσι θεοὶ 'Ολύμπια δώματ'
ἔχοντες, ὡς ἐγώ σοι ἐξερέω. 2. καί ποτε τρὶς τόσσα δῶρ'
ἀγλάα ἕξει 'Αχιλλεὺς εἵνεκα τῆσδ' ὕβριος 'Αγαμέμνονος 'Ατρεΐ-
δαο. 3. 'Αχιλλεὺς ἴσχεται, πείθεται δὲ θεῆιν "Ηρῃ λευκωλένῳ
'Αθηναίῃ τε γλαυκώπιδι. 4. χρή ἐστιν 'Αχιλλῆα, καὶ μάλα
περ θυμῷ κεχολωμένον, ἔπος εἰρύσασθαι θεῆιν κᾱλῆιν, ὣς γάρ
ἐστιν ἄμεινον. 5. θεοὶ μάλ' ἔκλυον 'Αχιλλῆος, οὕνεκα τοῖσιν
ἐπιπείθεται. 6. 'Αχαιοὶ ἔσχεθον χεῖρας βαρείᾱς ἐπὶ κώπης
ἀργυρέῃσι ξιφέων μεγάλων. 7. 'Αχιλλεὺς ἔωσε μέγα ξίφος
ἂψ ἐς κουλεόν. 8. 'Αχαιοὶ κακοὶ ἠπίθησαν μύθοισιν 'Αθη-
ναίης. 9. θεὰ γλαυκῶπις 'Αθήνη ἐβεβήκειν Οὐλυμπόνδε ἐς
δώματα Διός.

305. Read and translate :

Iliad, 212–222

ὧδε γὰρ ἐξερέω, τὸ δὲ καὶ τετελεσμένον ἔσται ·
καί ποτέ τοι τρὶς τόσσα παρέσσεται ἀγλαὰ δῶρα
ὕβριος εἵνεκα τῆσδε · σὺ δ' ἴσχεο, πείθεο δ' ἡμῖν."

τὴν δ' ἀπαμειβόμενος προσέφη πόδας ὠκὺς 'Αχιλλεύς ·   215
" χρὴ μὲν σφωίτερόν γε, θεά, ἔπος εἰρύσσασθαι,
καὶ μάλα περ θυμῷ κεχολωμένον · ὣς γὰρ ἄμεινον ·
ὅς κε θεοῖς ἐπιπείθηται, μάλα τ' ἔκλυον αὐτοῦ."

ἦ καὶ ἐπ' ἀργυρέῃ κώπῃ σχέθε χεῖρα βαρεῖαν,
ἂψ δ' ἐς κουλεὸν ὦσε μέγα ξίφος, οὐδ' ἀπίθησεν   220
μύθῳ 'Αθηναίης · ἡ δ' Οὐλυμπόνδε βεβήκειν
δώματ' ἐς αἰγιόχοιο Διὸς μετὰ δαίμονας ἄλλους.

LESSON XLVII   [306–309

306. 212. καί : *also.*

213. τοι : 1004 or 999. — παρέσσεται : 973, 1.

214. ἡμῖν = Ἀθηναίη καὶ ʽΗρῃ: 996. — ἴσχεο : reflexive, 1067, 1.

216. χρή (ἐστιν). — σφωίτερον is made emphatic by the following γε, whereby Achilles contrasts his attitude of respectful obedience toward the goddesses with that of stubborn defiance toward Agamemnon, whom he no longer intends to obey. — ϝέπος ϝείρυσ-, 526.

217. κεχολωμένον : 1109, 6. — καί : *even though.* — ἄμεινον (ἐστίν).

218. θεοῖς : 996. — ἔκλυον αὐτοῦ : 984, 1082.

219. ἦ: *he spoke.* — σχέθε = ἔσχεθε [ἔχω], 901.

220. οὐδ' ἀπίθησεν: litotes; cf. " not at all bad." — κουλεὸν ϝῶσε, 526.

221. μύθῳ : 996.

307. Translate :

1. I shall declare the will of the gods to you, and this also (καί) shall be accomplished. 2. At some time you shall have twice as many splendid gifts on account of this arrogance of Agamemnon, if you will restrain yourself and obey us. 3. We must obey the gods, even though (we be) greatly enraged in our hearts ; for it is better thus. 4. The gods give especial heed to (the prayer of) those who obey them. 5. Upon their silver hilts they hold their heavy hands, and thus disobey the commands of the two goddesses. 6. When Athena departs to Olympus, among the other divinities, we shall thrust our mighty swords into their scabbards.

LESSON XLVII

THE MIDDLE AND PASSIVE OF -μι VERBS

ILIAD, 223–232

308. Take a thorough review of all the -μι verbs, both regular and irregular, active, middle, and passive, all voices, modes, and tenses, 924, 949–965, 967.

309. *Optional :*

310.　　VOCABULARY

ἀντίος, η, ον in opposition, opposing, facing, meeting, to meet.
ἀριστεύς, ῆος, ὁ chief, leader.
ἀταρτηρός, ή, όν harsh, bitter.
δημο-βόρος, η, ον devouring the (goods of the) people.
ἔλαφος, ου, ὁ, ἡ deer, stag, hind.
ἐξ-αῦτις again, anew, then.
θωρήσσω (θωρηκ-), θωρήξομαι, ἐθώρηξα, ἐθωρήχθην arm, don the breastplate.
κήρ, κηρός, ἡ death, fate.
κραδίη (καρδίη, 597–598), ης, ἡ heart.
λόχος, ου, ὁ ambush, ambuscade.

λωβά-ομαι*, λωβήσομαι*, ἐλωβησάμην, insult, revile, act arrogantly, outrage, ruin, wrong.
οἰνο-βαρής, ές drunken, wine-heavy, sot.
ὄμμα, ατος, τό eye; plur., face.
οὐ-τιδανός, ή, όν worthless, of no account, cowardly, feeble.
*τλάω (τλα-, τλη-, ταλα-), τλήσομαι, ἔτλην (ἐτάλασσα), τέτληκα have the heart, have courage, endure, dare, suffer.
ὕστατος, η, ον (superl. of ὕστερος, η, ον) latest, last, uppermost, hindmost.

Derivatives: anti-dote, -pathy, -podes, anti- in compounds, as anti-American; aristo-cracy; dem-agogue, demo-cracy, epi-demic; thorax; cardi(ac-al), -algia, peri-cardium.

311.　Translate:

1. ἔπεα πτερόεντ' Ἀχιλῆος ἦεν ἀταρτηρά. 2. προσεειπὼν Ἀτρείδην Ἀχιλλεὺς ἔληγε χόλοιο. 3. Ἀγαμέμνων οὔκ ἐστιν οἰνοβαρής, οὐδ' ἔχει ὄμματα κυνὸς κραδίην δ' ἐλάφοιο, ἀλλ' ἔτλη θυμῷ θωρηχθῆναι ἅμα λαῷ ἐς πόλεμον, ἰέναι δ' ἐς λόχον σὺν ἀριστήεσσιν Ἀχαιῶν. 4. τὸ δὲ εἴδεται εἶναι κὴρ ἄλλοισιν ἀνδράσιν. 5. ἦ πολὺ λώιόν ἐστιν ἀποαιρέεσθαι δῶρα πάντων οἵ τινες εἴπωσιν ἀντίον σέθεν. 6. Ἀγαμέμνων ἐστὶ δημοβόρος βασιλεύς, ἐπεὶ ἀνάσσει οὐτιδανοῖσιν ἀνθρώποισιν· ἦ γὰρ ἂν νῦν ὕστατα λωβήσαιτο, τάχ' ἂν δὲ θυμὸν ὀλέσσαιτο.

312.　Read and translate:

ILIAD, 223–232

Πηλείδης δ' ἐξαῦτις ἀταρτηροῖς ἐπέεσσιν
Ἀτρείδην προσέειπε, καὶ οὔ πω λῆγε χόλοιο·
"οἰνοβαρές, κυνὸς ὄμματ' ἔχων, κραδίην δ' ἐλάφοιο.　　225

οὔτε ποτ' ἐς πόλεμον ἅμα λαῷ θωρηχθῆναι
οὔτε λόχονδ' ἰέναι σὺν ἀριστήεσσιν Ἀχαιῶν
τέτληκας θυμῷ· τὸ δέ τοι κῆρ εἴδεται εἶναι.
ἦ πολὺ λώιόν ἐστι κατὰ στρατὸν εὐρὺν Ἀχαιῶν
δῶρ' ἀποαιρεῖσθαι, ὅς τις σέθεν ἀντίον εἴπῃ·   230
δημοβόρος βασιλεύς, ἐπεὶ οὐτιδανοῖσιν ἀνάσσεις·
ἦ γὰρ ἄν, Ἀτρεΐδη, νῦν ὕστατα λωβήσαιο.

313. 223. ἐπέεσσιν: 1005.
224. χόλοιο: 987.
226. λᾶῷ: 1007. — πόλεμον ἅμα: 1168.
227. λόχονδ'(ε): 788, 4.
228. θυμῷ: 1009. — εἴδεται [ϝειδ-, ϝοιδ-, ϝιδ-, 966] middle: seem, appear, resemble.
230. ἀποαιρεῖσθαι: 584–585. — δῶρ' (ἀνδρός). — ἀντίον ϝείπῃ: 526.
231. δημοβόρος βασιλεύς: 978, 3. — οὐτιδανοῖσιν: 997, 1001.
232. ὕστατα: 780–781, 784.

314. Translate:

1. All the well-greaved Achaeans addressed the gods with bitter words, nor ceased they ever from their hot wrath. 2. The drunken Agamemnon has the face of a dog and the heart of a deer, nor did he ever dare in his soul to arm himself with the breastplate together with his people for war, nor to go into ambush with the leaders of the Achaeans; for this seemed to be death to his soul. 3. He thinks it much better throughout the broad camp of the Achaeans to take away the prizes of honor of all who dare to speak against him. 4. This king is a devourer of the goods of the people and he rules over worthless men. 5. The son of Atreus has now insulted for the last time, for he has lost his soul.

LESSON XLVIII

REVIEW OF NOUNS

ILIAD, 233–239

315. 1) Review all three declensions of nouns, memorizing thoroughly the meaning and forms of each word given in the paradigms, and review the rules for the inflection and gender of nouns, 626–716.

316. *Optional:*

317. VOCABULARY

ἀνα-θηλέ-ω, ἀναθηλήσω, ἀνεθήλησα† sprout, bloom (forth), (anew), bud (again).

δικασ-πόλος, ου, ὁ judge, arbiter.

θέμις, ιστος, ἡ custom, law, decree, justice, oracle, rule.

λείπω (λειπ-, λοιπ-, λιπ-), λείψω, ἔλιπον, λέλοιπα, λέλειμμαι, ἐλείφθην* LEAVE, forsake, abandon, desert.

λέπω* (λεπ-, λαπ-), λέψω, ἔλεψα, λέλαμμαι*, ἐλάπην* strip, peel, scale, hull.

ναί yea, yes, verily.

ὄζος, ου, ὁ branch, shoot, limb.

ὄρος (οὖρος, 571), εος, τό mountain.

ὅρκος, ου, ὁ oath, that by which one swears (as witness).

παλάμη, ης, ἡ PALM, hand, fist.

περί adv., and prep. with gen., dat., and acc., around, about, concerning, for, exceedingly, over, above, more than, superior; adv., around, about, beyond, over, exceedingly; with gen., around, about, concerning, beyond; with dat., around, about, concerning, for; with acc., around, about, concerning.

τομή, ῆς, ἡ cut(ting), stump.

φλοιός, οῦ, ὁ bark, peel, rind, shell.

φορέ-ω, φορήσω*, ἐφόρησα, bear, carry, bring.

φύλλον, ου, τό leaf, FOLIAGE.

φύ-ω, φύσω, ἔφῦσα (ἔφῦν), πέφῦκα bear, produce, bring forth, cause to grow.

χαλκός, οῦ, ὁ bronze, implement of bronze (axe, spear, etc.).

Derivatives: peri-anth, -cardium, -carp, -cranium, -meter, -od, -phery, -phrasis; phos-phorus; phys-ic(al), -i-o-gnomy, -i-o-logy.

318. Translate:

1. Ἀχιλλεὺς ἐξεῖπεν ἀταρτηρὰ ἔπεα τοῖσιν Ἀχαιοῖσι καὶ ὤμοσεν ὅρκον μέγαν. 2. ναὶ μὰ τόδε σκῆπτρον ὄμνυμι, τό τοι

ἔσσεται μέγας ὅρκος. 3. τόδε σκῆπτρον οὔ ποτε φύσει φύλλα
καὶ ὄζους, οὐδ᾽ ἀναθηλήσει, περὶ γάρ ῥά ἑ φύλλα τε καὶ φλοιὸν
ἐλέψαμεν χαλκῷ. 4. τὸ σκῆπτρον Ἀχιλῆος λέλοιπε τομὴν ἐν
ὄρεσσιν. 5. νῦν δ᾽ αὖθ᾽ υἷες Ἀχαιῶν, δικασπόλοι, οἱ εἰρύαται
θέμιστας πρὸς Διός, φορέουσι τὸ σκῆπτρον ἐν παλάμῃσιν.

319. Read and translate :

Iliad, 233-239

ἀλλ᾽ ἐκ τοι ἐρέω καὶ ἐπὶ μέγαν ὅρκον ὀμοῦμαι·
ναὶ μὰ τόδε σκῆπτρον · τὸ μὲν οὔ ποτε φύλλα καὶ ὄζους
φύσει, ἐπεὶ δὴ πρῶτα τομὴν ἐν ὄρεσσι λέλοιπεν,   235
οὐδ᾽ ἀναθηλήσει · περὶ γάρ ῥά ἑ χαλκὸς ἔλεψεν
φύλλα τε καὶ φλοιόν · νῦν αὐτέ μιν υἷες Ἀχαιῶν
ἐν παλάμῃς φορέουσι δικασπόλοι, οἵ τε θέμιστας
πρὸς Διὸς εἰρύαται · ὁ δέ τοι μέγας ἔσσεται ὅρκος·   239

320. 233. ἐκ, ἐπί: 1048-1049. — ὀμοῦμαι = ὀμό(σ)ομαι = ὀμοῦμαι
[ὄμνυμι]: 603, 584-585.

234. μὰ τόδε σκῆπτρον : when a speaker wished to address the assem-
bly, a herald placed a sceptre in his hands, as a sign that he " had the
floor."

235. πρῶτα : 780-781.

236. περί: 1048-1049. — χαλκός : bronze was the common metal for
implements, before the introduction of iron. Here "bronze" means
some tool of bronze, as an axe.

236-237. ἑ . . . φύλλα, φλοιόν : 1020, 1 ; 1021 and note.

234-239. τὸ μὲν οὔ . . . εἰρύαται forms a parenthesis, describing the
sceptre. There is a return to the main idea in the following words, and
this is taken up and completed in the next lesson, vss. 240-244.

239. εἰρύαται : 3d plur. = εἰρύνται, 597-598. — ὁ : masculine, where the
neuter would be expected. It takes the gender of the following predi-
cate (ὅρκος), by what is known as "attraction." — πρὸς Διός : under
the supervision of Zeus, or else the laws from (i.e. given by) Zeus.

321. Translate :

1. We shall declare and also swear a great oath. 2. By
this sceptre, ye shall not return safely home, but ye shall all

115

perish here. 3. Our sceptres will never produce leaves and branches, nor will they sprout forth, since they have left their stumps in the mountains. 4. The sons of the Achaeans with bronze peeled the sceptres round about of their leaves and branches, and now the kings, dispensers of justice, who preserve the laws given to them by Zeus, bear them in their hands.

LESSON XLIX

REVIEW OF ADJECTIVES, REGULAR AND IRREGULAR

ILIAD, 240–244

322. Review all the adjectives, both regular and irregular, learning thoroughly the meanings and forms of each as given in the paradigms, 717–734.

323. *Optional:*

324.

VOCABULARY

ἀμύσσω (ἀμυχ-), ἀμύξω, ἤμυξα gnaw, tear, bite, scratch.

ἀνδρο-φόνος, η, ον man-slaying, murderous.

δύνα-μαι, δυνήσομαι, ἐδυνησάμην, δεδύνημαι*, ἐδυνάσθην be able, can, have power.

Ἕκτωρ, ορος, ὁ Hector, *son of Priam, and leader of the Trojans.*

ἔν-δοθι within, inside, at home.

εὗτε, when, as.

οὐδ-είς, οὐδε-μία, οὐδ-έν no one, not any, none, nothing.

πί-πτω (πετ-, πτ-, πτη-), πεσέομαι,

ἔπεσον, πέπτη(κ)α fall, drop, die, perish, sink.

ποθή, ῆς, ἡ yearning, longing, regret.

τῑ-ω, τίσω, ἔτῑσα, τέτῑμαι honor, esteem.

ὑπό (ὑπαί) adv., and prep. with gen., dat., and acc., under, beneath, by, at the hands of, by means of; adv., under, secretly, behind, beneath, by, gradually; with gen., (from) under, by; with dat., (down) under; with acc., (down) under, during, toward.

Derivatives: dynam-ic, -ite, -o, dynasty; hector; hypotenuse, -thesis.

116

325. Translate:

1. ποθὴ Ἀχιλλῆος (979, 3) ἵξεται σύμπαντας υἶας Ἀχαιῶν, τότε δ' Ἀγαμέμνων ἀχνύμενός περ οὐ δυνήσεται χραισμέειν λαῷ, εὖτ' ἂν πολλοὶ ἄνδρες θνήσκοντες ὑπ' ἀνδροφόνοιο Ἕκτορος πίπτωσιν. 2. ἀμύξει δὲ θυμὸν ἔνδοθι Ἀγαμέμνων χωόμενος οὕνεκα οὐδὲν ἔτισεν Ἀχιλῆα ἄριστον Ἀχαιῶν. 3. σκῆπτρόν ἐστι τετίμένον, χρύσεον γάρ ἐστι, Ἀχιλλεὺς δὲ τὸ ἔβαλε ἐπὶ χθονί, ἕζετο δ' αὐτός. 4. Ἕκτωρ ἀπολέσει πολλοὺς Ἀχαιῶν ἐν μάχῃ, Ἀχιλλῆος οὐ παρεόντος (994).

326. Read and translate:[1]

Iliad, 240-244

ἦ ποτ' Ἀχιλλῆος ποθὴ ἵξεται υἶας Ἀχαιῶν 240
σύμπαντας· τότε δ' οὔ τι δυνήσεαι ἀχνύμενός περ
χραισμεῖν, εὖτ' ἂν πολλοὶ ὑφ' Ἕκτορος ἀνδροφόνοιο
θνήσκοντες πίπτωσι· σὺ δ' ἔνδοθι θυμὸν ἀμύξεις
χωόμενος, ὅ τ' ἄριστον Ἀχαιῶν οὐδὲν ἔτισας." 244

327. 240. Ἀχιλλῆος : 979, 3, spoken with a proud self-consciousness.
— υἶας : 1019. The thought of this and the preceding lesson is " so surely as this sceptre will never bear leaves and branches, so surely shall yearning for Achilles come upon every one of the sons of the Achaeans."
241. σύμπαντας (emphatic by position) : modifies υἶας. — τι : 780-781.
— ἀχνύμενος : 1109, 6, *although vexed.*
242. χραισμεῖν = χραισμέειν 584-585 (Ἀχαιοῖσιν).
243. ἀμύξεις : cf. Eng. " gnaw one's heart, eat out one's heart."
244. ὅ τ' (ε) : *because, in that.* — (Ἀχιλῆα) ἄριστον Ἀχαιῶν. — οὐδέν : adverbial, 780-781, 1014 *not at all ;* lit. *in respect to nothing, in no wise.*

328. Translate:

1. A great yearning for the divine son of Peleus came upon all the sons of the Achaeans, and Agamemnon, son of Atreus, was not at all able to help them, though grieved in

[1] Review the preceding lesson for the connection of thought.

his soul, when many of the brave men fell at the hands of the man-slaying Hector, son of Priam. 2. Then did Agamemnon gnaw his heart within, enraged that he in no wise did honor to Achilles, the bravest of the Achaeans.

LESSON L

REVIEW OF PRONOUNS

ILIAD, 245–249

329. Learn the meanings and memorize all the forms of the pronouns as given in the paradigms 760–779.

330. *Optional:*

331. VOCABULARY

ἀγορητής, αο, ὁ orator.

ἀν-ορού-ω*, ἀνώρουσα jump up, spring up, start up.

αὐδή, ῆς, ἡ voice, speech, discourse, language, sound, cry.

γαῖα, ης, ἡ earth, land, country.

γλυκύς, εῖα, ὑ sweet.

γλῶσσα, ης, ἡ tongue, language, speech.

ἑτέρωθεν from the other side.

ἡδυ-επής, ές SWEET-speaking, sweet-toned.

ἧλος, ου, ὁ nail, rivet, stud.

λιγύς, εῖα, ὑ shrill, clear-toned.

μέλι, ιτος, τό honey.

μηνί-ω, μηνίσω, ἐμήνῑσα rage, fume, be furious.

Νέστωρ, ορος, ὁ Nestor, *one of the Greek chieftains.*

πείρω (περ-, παρ-), —, ἔπειρα, πέπαρμαι, ἐπάρην† pierce, stud, rivet.

Πύλιος, η, ον Pylian, of Pylus.

ῥέω (ῥευ-, ῥεϝ-, ῥυ-, ῥυε- = σρευ etc. 603–604), ῥεύσομαι, ἔρρευσα*, ἐρ-ρύηκα*, ἐρρύην run, flow, stream, pour.

Derivatives: geo-graphy, -logy, -metry; glyc-erine, -ol; gloss-ary, poly-glot, epi-glottis; hetero-dox, -geneous; melli-fluous; rhetoric.

332. Translate:

1. δῖος Ἀχιλλεὺς ἕζετο χωόμενος, Ἀγαμέμνων δ᾽ ἑτέρωθεν ἐμήνιε. 2. τοῖσι δ᾽ Ἀχαιοῖσι Νέστωρ λιγὺς ἀγορητὴς Πυλίων

ἀνώρουσεν. 3. ἀπὸ γλώσσης Νέστορος αὐδὴ ἔρρεεν γλυκίων μέλιτος (993). 4. τὸ σκῆπτρόν ἐστιν πεπαρμένον χρυσείοισιν ἥλοισιν, Ἀχιλλεὺς δὲ τὸ ἔβαλε ποτὶ γαίῃ, ἔζετο δ' αὐτός

333. Read and translate :

Iliad, 245-249

ὣς φάτο Πηλεΐδης, ποτὶ δὲ σκῆπτρον βάλε γαίῃ   245
χρυσείοις ἥλοισι πεπαρμένον, ἕζετο δ' αὐτός ·
Ἀτρεΐδης δ' ἑτέρωθεν ἐμήνιε. τοῖσι δὲ Νέστωρ
ἡδυεπὴς ἀνόρουσε, λιγὺς Πυλίων ἀγορητής,
τοῦ καὶ ἀπὸ γλώσσης μέλιτος γλυκίων ῥέεν αὐδή.   249

334. 245. ποτί (with γαίῃ 1009) .

246. ἥλοισι : 1005.

248. ἀνόρουσε = ἀνώρουσε.

249. τοῦ : dem. pron., referring to Nestor. — (ἔ)ῥεεν : the imperfect of customary or repeated action. — μέλιτος : 993, honey was used by the ancients in the place of sugar, and was the sweetest thing known to the taste. Hence it was a favorite figure in comparisons where a high degree of sweetness was involved.

335. Translate :

1. When the son of Peleus had spoken all these bitter words, he hurled the sceptre to the ground and sat down in anger. 2. Many sceptres of the sons of the Achaeans were studded with golden nails. 3. The son of Atreus kept raging at the divine son of Peleus ; but Nestor, who was kindly disposed toward all the Achaeans, sprang up and addressed them (with) winged words, which were much sweeter than honey. 4. The sweet-speaking Nestor, the clear-toned orator of the Pylians, harangued all the Achaeans with many words. 5. Words sweeter than honey flow from the tongue of the aged warrior.

LESSON LI

REVIEW OF PARTICIPLES AND INFINITIVES

ILIAD, 250–259

336. Learn the meanings of all the participles and infinitives of λύω, and memorize all the forms declined, 908–909, 914–915, 920–921, 735–746.

337. *Optional:*

338.   VOCABULARY

ἄνθρωπος, ου, ὁ (mere) man, ordinary man; *cf.* ἀνήρ, real man, hero.
'Αχαιΐς, ιδος, *f.* Achaean.
γενεή, ῆς, ἡ generation, family.
γηθέω (γηθ-, γηθε-), γηθήσω, ἐγήθησα, γέγηθα rejoice.
ἠγά-θεος, η, ον very sacred, holy.
ἤδη already, at this time.
ἰκ-άν-ω come (upon), go.
μάρνα-μαι strive, fight, contend.
μέροψ, οπος, ὁ mortal, man.
νέος, η, ον (νέϝος) NEW, young, recent, late, youthful.
πένθος (πνθ-, παθ-, 597–598) εος, τό woe, grief, sadness.

πεύθομαι (πυνθάνομαι) (πυθ-, πευθ-), πεύσομαι, ἐπυθόμην (πεπυθόμην), πέπυσμαι learn (by inquiry).
πόποι alas! ah me! O dear! good gracious!
πρόσθε(ν) before, formerly, sooner.
Πύλος, ου, ἡ Pylus.
τρέφω (θρεφ-, θροφ-, θραφ-), θρέψω*, ἔθρεψα (ἔτραφον), τέτροφα, τέθραμμαι*, ἐτράφην nurture, feed, breed, grow up, nourish (619).
τρίτατος, η, ον third.
φθί-νω, φθίσω, ἔφθῖσα, ἔφθιμαι, ἐφθίθην perish, die, waste away.

Derivatives : anthropo-logy, -id, phil-, mis-anthropy ; genea-logy, genesis, hetero-, homo-geneous; neo- *in composition*, *as* Neo-Platonism, neo-phyte, -logism ; Ne-penthe, pathos (π̥θος, 597–598), a-, sym-, anti-pathy, patho-logy ; phthis-is, -ic.

339. Translate :

1. δύο γενεαὶ μερόπων ἀνθρώπων ἤδη ἐφθίατο Νέστορι.
2. αἱ γενεαὶ μερόπων ἀνθρώπων πρόσθεν ἐτράφησαν καὶ ἐγέ-

120

νοντο ἅμα Νέστορι ἐν ἠγαθέῃ Πύλῳ, μετὰ δὲ τριτάτῃ γενεῇ
ἤνασσε τότε ὁ γέρων. 3. πολλὰ καὶ μεγάλα πένθεα ἵξεται ἐπὶ
γαῖαν Ἀχαιίδα. 4. Πρίαμος παῖδές τε Πριάμου γηθησαίατο,
ἄλλοι τε Τρῶες μέγα κεν κεχαροίατο θυμῷ, εἰ πυθοίατο πάντα
τάδ᾽ Ἀχιλλῆός τε καὶ Ἀγαμέμνονος μαρναμένοιιν, τὼ γὰρ περὶ
μέν ἐστον Δαναῶν ἄλλων βουλήν, περὶ δ᾽ ἐστὸν μάχην.
5. Ἀχιλλεὺς καὶ Ἀγαμέμνων ἤστην νεωτέρω Νέστορος, ἀλλ᾽
νὐδ᾽ ὣς ἐπείθοντο γέροντι.

340. Read and translate :

Iliad, 250–259

τῷ δ᾽ ἤδη δύο μὲν γενεαὶ μερόπων ἀνθρώπων   250
ἐφθίαθ᾽, οἵ οἱ πρόσθεν ἅμα τράφεν ἠδὲ γένοντο
ἐν Πύλῳ ἠγαθέῃ, μετὰ δὲ τριτάτοισιν ἄνασσεν.
ὃ σφιν ἐὺ φρονέων ἀγορήσατο καὶ μετέειπεν ·
" ὦ πόποι, ἦ μέγα πένθος Ἀχαιίδα γαῖαν ἱκάνει ·
ἦ κεν γηθήσαι Πρίαμος Πριάμοιό τε παῖδες,   255
ἄλλοι τε Τρῶες μέγα κεν κεχαροίατο θυμῷ,
εἰ σφῶιν τάδε πάντα πυθοίατο μαρναμένοιιν,
οἳ περὶ μὲν βουλὴν Δαναῶν, περὶ δ᾽ ἐστὲ μάχεσθαι.
ἀλλὰ πίθεσθ᾽ · ἄμφω δὲ νεωτέρω ἐστὸν ἐμεῖο.

341. 250. τῷ: 998.
251. ἐφθίαθ᾽ = ἐφθίατο, 3d plur., = ἐφθίγτο, 597–598. — οἵ οἱ : the first
of these is the rel. pron., nom. plur. masc., referring to ἀνθρώπων, vs. 250 ;
the second is an enclitic (554, 760), as will be seen from the accent of
the first, and is spelled ῾ϝοι, as may be observed from the meter. Here
it is the dative of accompaniment with ἅμα. — τράφεν (= ἐτράφησαν) ἠδὲ
γένοντο, *hysteron proteron, i.e.* the time represented by ἐγένοντο comes
before that of τράφεν, although τράφεν here precedes ἐγένοντο. This
is a permissible device, as it indicates *priority of interest,* instead of the
usual one of time. Compare Shakespere's " I was bred and born."
The main idea is contained in the first expression, while the second is
added as an after-thought, for the sake of greater fullness and accuracy.
252. τριτάτοισιν is masc., referring to the general idea of *men,* as
implied in the word γενεαί, vs. 250. — ἠγα-θέῃ (ἀγα-: 1168, 571).
254. Ἀχαιίδα γαῖαν : 1019, *i.e.* " our homes."

255. γηθήσαι : 973, 2, optat. sing., *i.e.* your quarrel would be a source of rejoicing to our enemies, since it would hinder the successful prosecution of the war.

256. μέγα : 780–781. — θυμῷ : 1009.

258. βουλήν, μάχεσθαι : acc. and infinitive of specification, 1014; the two prime characteristics essential to a successful leader. — Δαναῶν : gen., because of the idea of comparison contained in the adverb περί taken with the verb ἐστέ [εἰμι], meaning *surpass, be superior,* 988. Observe how judiciously the old man mingles praise with censure.

259. ἐμεῖο : 993; cf. Shak., *Jul. Caes.,* " Love and be friends, as two such men should be; for I have seen more years, I'm sure, than ye."

342. Translate :

1. Two generations of mortal men, who were born and bred with him in the very sacred Pylus, have passed away, and he is now ruling among (those of) the third. 2. A great woe will come upon all the lands of the Achaeans, because Achilles and Agamemnon are contending. 3. Priam and the sons of Priam and all the other Trojans will greatly rejoice in their souls when they learn all these things about Achilles and Agamemnon contending, for they are better than the other Achaeans both in council and battle. 4. They are much younger than Nestor, but they will not obey him.

LESSON LII

REVIEW OF VERBS IN THE ACTIVE VOICE

ILIAD, 260–268

343. 1) Review thoroughly all the active forms of λύω, and of all the -μι verbs, paying careful attention to the meaning of each form, 904–909, 924, 949–956.

2) Make three copies of the tables of personal endings of verbs in the active, 819–825.

344. *Optional :*

345.   VOCABULARY

ἀ-θάνατος, η, ον deathless, immortal, imperishable (1168).

ἀ-θερίζω (θεριδ-), *with gen.*, 984 slight, disregard, despise.

Αἰγεΐδης, āο, ὁ son of Aegeus.

ἀντί-θεος, η, ον godlike, equal to the gods, a match for the gods.

ἀρείων, ον (*compar. of* ἀγαθός, 754, 1), better, mightier, braver.

Δρύᾱς, αντος, ὁ Dryas.

ἐκ-πάγλως terribly, horribly, awfully, dreadfully, frightfully.

Ἐξάδιος, ου, ὁ Exadius.

ἐπι-είκελος, ον like, resembling.

ἐπι-χθόνιος, ον earthly, of the earth, earth-born, upon the earth.

Θησεύς, ῆος (έος, 572), ὁ Theseus.

Καινεύς, ῆος (έος, 572), ὁ Caeneus.

κάρτιστος (= κράτιστος, 597-598), η, ον, *superl. of* καρτερός, ή, όν, mightiest, strongest, bravest, most excellent.

οἷος, η, ον such (as), of what sort, what.

ὁμῑλέ-ω, ὁμῑλήσω*, ὡμίλησα associate with, collect.

ὀρέσ-κῳος, η, ον living in mountain dens, lying in mountain lairs.

Πειρί-θοος, ου, ὁ Pirithous (1168).

ποιμήν, μένος, ὁ shepherd, guardian, protector.

Πολύ-φημος, ου, ὁ Polyphemus.

τοῖος, η, ον such (as) of the sort that, of the kind that.

φήρ, φηρός, ὁ, ἡ wild animal, (savage) beast, brute.

Derivatives : homil-y, -etics ; ferocious, fierce.

346. Translate :

1. Νέστωρ ὡμίλησεν ἀνδράσιν ἀρείοσιν Ἀγαμέμνονος Ἀχιλλῆός τε, οἱ δ᾽ οὔ ποτε τόν γ᾽ ἠθέριζον. 2. οὔ τίς πω εἶδε τοίους ἄνδρας, ο᾽ιδὲ ἴδηται, οἷον Πειρίθοόν τε Δρύαντά τε ποιμένα λᾱῶν. ὀ. κεῖνοι φῆρες ἦσαν κάρτιστοι πάντων φηρῶν ὀρεσκῴων, ἀλλ᾽ οἴδε ἥρωες ἐτράφησαν κάρτιστοι πάντων ἐπιχθονίων ἀνδρῶν, ἐμάχοντο δὲ φηρσὶν καὶ ἀπώλεσαν τοὺς ἐκπάγλως.

347. Read and translate :

Iliad, 260-268

ἤδη γάρ ποτ᾽ ἐγὼ καὶ ἀρείοσιν ἠέ περ ὑμῖν   260
ἀνδράσιν ὡμίλησα, καὶ οὔ ποτέ μ᾽ οἵ γ᾽ ἀθέριζον.
οὐ γάρ πω τοίους ἴδον ἀνέρας οὐδὲ ἴδωμαι,
οἷον Πειρίθοόν τε Δρύαντά τε ποιμένα λᾱῶν

Καινέα τ᾽ Ἐξάδιόν τε καὶ ἀντίθεον Πολύφημον
[Θησέα τ᾽ Αἰγεΐδην, ἐπιείκελον ἀθανάτοισιν].   265
κάρτιστοι δὴ κεῖνοι ἐπιχθονίων τράφεν ἀνδρῶν·
κάρτιστοι μὲν ἔσαν καὶ καρτίστοις ἐμάχοντο,
φηρσὶν ὀρεσκῴοισι, καὶ ἐκπάγλως ἀπόλεσσαν.

348. 260. **καί:** *even.* — ἀρείοσιν: 1007, an argument, " a fortiore," *i.e.*
if better men than Agamemnon and Achilles had taken his advice, so
much the more should they. — ὑμῖν: some would substitute ἡμῖν for this,
thus saving Nestor's politeness, but at the cost of his point. His whole
argument depends upon his assertion that better men even than they
had taken his advice.

262. ἴδωμαι : the subjunctive middle, with the idea of yearning for
something past and gone. ἀνέρας, 1168, 571.

265. ἀθανάτοισιν: 1003.—Brackets enclose lines supposed to be spurious.

268. φηρσὶν ὀρεσκῴοισι (in apposition with καρτίστοις of the preceding
verse) doubtless refers to the centaurs, creatures with the bodies of
horses and the heads and shoulders of men.

This passage refers to the famous battle of the Lapiths and Centaurs,
so well known in Greek legend, and a favorite subject for Greek art.

349. Translate :

1. Nestor associated with better men than the chiefs of
the Achaeans, and no one ever despised him and his good
plans.   2. We never saw such men, nor may we see them,
for they are all dead (have died).   3. Those were the
mightiest of mortal men upon the earth, and they fought
with the wild beasts living in mountain dens, and they
utterly destroyed them.

LESSON LIII

REVIEW OF THE VERB IN THE MIDDLE VOICE

ILIAD, 269-289

350. 1) Review thoroughly all the middle forms of λύω and of the -μι verbs, paying careful attention to the meaning of each form, 910-915, 957-962.

2) Make three copies of the tables of the personal endings of verbs in the middle voice, 821, and read 826-829.

351. *Optional :*

352. VOCABULARY

ἀντι-βίην with opposing might, antagonistically.

ἄπιος, η, ον (*cf.* ἀπό) far, distant.

βροτός, οῦ, ὁ mortal, man.

γείνομαι (γεν-), —, ἐγεινάμην beget, bear, produce, be born.

ἐάω (σεϝα-), ἐάσω, εἴασα, εἴακα*, εἴᾱμαι*, εἰάθην* allow, permit, leave.

ἕρκος, εος, τό hedge, fence, defence, bulwark, barrier.

κῦδος, εος, τό glory, honor, renown.

μεθ-ί-ημι (ση-, σε- = ἡ-, ἑ-, 603-604), μεθήσω, μεθῆκα (μεθέηκα), μεθεῖκα*, μεθεῖμαι*, μεθείθην let go, give up, forego, dismiss.

μεθ-ομιλέ-ω, μεθωμίλησα associate

with, consort with.

μείρομαι (σμερ-, σμορ-, σμαρ-), ἔμμορα, divide, (receive as) share, receive as lot; εἵμαρται, it is fated.

μή-τε and not, neither, nor ; μήτε . . . μήτε neither . . . nor.

μήτηρ, τέρος (τρός), ἡ mother, dam.

ὅμοῖος, η, ον equal, similar.

μοῖρα, ης, ἡ lot, portion, fate, suitability.

πέλω (πελ-, πλ-), ἔπελον, ἐπελόμην ; 2d aor. ἔπλε, ἔπλετο ; turn, move; *mid.* be, become.

σημαίνω (σημαν-), σημανέω, ἐσήμηνα, order, point out, command.

σκηπτ-οῦχος, ον sceptre-bearing.

τηλόθε(ν) far, from afar.

Derivatives : gen-, 338 ; metro-polis, -nymic, matri- (621), arch(al) ; sema-phore, semasi-ology, seman-tics, semato-logy ; tele-, 113.

353. Translate :

1. Νέστωρ δὲ μεθωμίλεεν τοῖσιν ἀνδράσιν, αὐτοὶ γὰρ τὸν

125

ἐκαλέσαντο ἐκ Πύλου, ἐξ ἀπίης γαίης. 2. Νέστωρ δὲ κατ᾽
αὐτὸν ἐμάχετο φηρσίν. 3. πάντων τῶν οἳ νῦν βροτοί εἰσιν ἐπι-
χθόνιοι, οὔ τις μαχέοιτο κείνοισι φηρσὶ κακοῖσιν. 4. κεῖνοι
δ᾽ ἄνδρες ξυνέηκαν βουλάων Νέστορος καὶ ἐπείθοντο μύθῳ.
5. ἄμεινόν ἐστιν πείθεσθαι, ἀλλ᾽ οὐκ ᾽Ατρεΐδῃ ᾽Αγαμέμνονι
ἥνδανε θῡμῷ, ἀλλ᾽ ἀγαθός περ ἐὼν ἀφεῖλε τὴν κούρην ᾽Αχιλλῆα,
οὐδ᾽ εἴασε τὸν ἔχειν τήν, ὡς υἶες ᾽Αχαιῶν ἔδοσαν τήν οἱ γέρας
πρῶτα. 6. ᾽Αχιλλεὺς δ᾽ ἤθελεν ἐρίζειν βασιλῆι ἀντιβίην.
7. οὔ ποτέ τις ἄλλος σκηπτοῦχος βασιλεύς, ᾧ Ζεὺς ἔδωκε
κῦδος, ἔμμορε τῑμῆς ὁμοίης τῑμῇ ᾽Αγαμέμνονος.

354. Read and translate:

Iliad, 269–289

καὶ μὲν τοῖσιν ἐγὼ μεθομίλεον ἐκ Πύλου ἐλθών,
τηλόθεν ἐξ ἀπίης γαίης · καλέσαντο γὰρ αὐτοί ·   270
καὶ μαχόμην κατ᾽ ἔμ᾽ αὐτὸν ἐγώ · κείνοισι δ᾽ ἂν οὔ τις
τῶν, οἳ νῦν βροτοί εἰσιν ἐπιχθόνιοι, μαχέοιτο.
καὶ μέν μευ βουλέων ξύνιεν πείθοντό τε μύθῳ.
ἀλλὰ πίθεσθε καὶ ὔμμες, ἐπεὶ πείθεσθαι ἄμεινον.
μήτε σὺ τόνδ᾽ ἀγαθός περ ἐὼν ἀποαίρεο κούρην,   275
ἀλλ᾽ ἔα, ὥς οἱ πρῶτα δόσαν γέρας υἶες ᾽Αχαιῶν ·
μήτε σύ, Πηλεΐδη, θέλ᾽ ἐριζέμεναι βασιλῆι
ἀντιβίην, ἐπεὶ οὔ ποθ᾽ ὁμοίης ἔμμορε τιμῆς
σκηπτοῦχος βασιλεύς, ᾧ τε Ζεὺς κῦδος ἔδωκεν.
εἰ δὲ σὺ καρτερός ἐσσι, θεὰ δέ σε γείνατο μήτηρ,   280
ἀλλ᾽ ὅδε φέρτερός ἐστιν, ἐπεὶ πλεόνεσσιν ἀνάσσει.
᾽Ατρεΐδη, σὺ δὲ παῦε τεὸν μένος · αὐτὰρ ἐγώ γε
λίσσομ᾽ ᾽Αχιλλῆι μεθέμεν χόλον, ὃς μέγα πᾶσιν
ἕρκος ᾽Αχαιοῖσιν πέλεται πολέμοιο κακοῖο."
τὸν δ᾽ ἀπαμειβόμενος προσέφη κρείων ᾽Αγαμέμνων ·   285
" ναὶ δὴ ταῦτά γε πάντα, γέρον, κατὰ μοῖραν ἔειπες
ἀλλ᾽ ὅδ᾽ ἀνὴρ ἐθέλει περὶ πάντων ἔμμεναι ἄλλων,
πάντων μὲν κρατέειν ἐθέλει, πάντεσσι δ᾽ ἀνάσσειν,
πᾶσι δὲ σημαίνειν, ἅ τιν᾽ οὐ πείσεσθαι ὀίω.

355. 269. τοῖσιν: 1006-1007, with such men as these, referring to the Lapithae. — ἐγώ is emphatic (761), said with a proud self-consciousness, and the effect is further heightened by the use of the middle καλέσαντο in the next verse. — αὐτοί : "*they themselves*, and no less personages, great as they were, called me, even though I lived far away; for they were willing to go to extra trouble to obtain the services of such a good warrior, passing over many brave men who lived between."

270. καλέσαντο: observe the force of the middle, "for their own sake," which denotes the special interest of the subject in the action, 1068, 1067, 3.

271. κατ' ἔμ αὐτόν: *by myself alone.*

272. Observe the repetition of the ἐγώ. — μαχέοιτο: 1105.

273. βουλέων = βουλάων, 984. — μῦθῳ: 996. — ξύνιεν [ξυνίημι], imperfect, 3d plural.

274. καί: *also.* — ἐπεὶ πείθεσθαι ἄμεινον (ἐστίν).

275. τόνδ', κούρην: 1020, 1. — ἐών : 1109, 6.

276. ἔᾱ = ἔαε (584-585) 'Αχιλλῆα ἔχειν κούρην.

275-277. Observe how impartial and undiscriminating Nestor is, in using exactly the same expression of prohibition in addressing the two contestants (μήτε σύ . . . μήτε σύ). The first of these refers of course to Agamemnon, the second to Achilles.

278. ἀντιβίην is emphatic by position. — τῑμῆς : 982.

278-279. *Never has* (any other) *sceptre-bearing king obtained honor equal* (to that of Agamemnon). That is, according to the Homeric tradition, as placed in the mouth of Nestor, Agamemnon was the mightiest ruler of his time; therefore Achilles should yield precedence to him.

280. εἰ: concessive, *even if.*

281. πλεόνεσσιν: dat., with a verb of ruling. — ὅδε: Agamemnon, of course.

282. "Nay, it is *I*, even Nestor, who entreat thee." Nestor makes a strong personal appeal to the king. The emphatic ἐγώ (761) is further stressed by being placed at the end of the verse, and by being followed by γε.

283. Νέστωρ λίσσεται 'Αγαμέμνονα μεθέμεναι χόλον 'Αχιλλῆι (997).

284. 'Αχαιοῖσιν: 997, 999. — πολέμοιο : 979, 3.

286. κατὰ μοῖραν : *fittingly.*

287. ὅδ' ἀνήρ is said by Agamemnon with supreme contempt, as he does not even deign to mention the hated name of his opponent: "this fellow." — πάντων: 988.

288. πάντων: 985. — πάντεσσι : 1001.

289. ἅ: 1014. — τιν' (ἁ) : 971, perhaps refers to Agamemnon. If so, it is superlatively ironical and sarcastic. If it merely means "many a one," as often, it still has a considerable amount of the ironical element in it.

356. *NOTE: If further practice in the translation of prose, either Greek-English or English-Greek, is desired, the instructor may make out as much of this as he wishes for his purposes. Most will find the foregoing more than adequate for the work of the first year.*

LESSON LIV

REVIEW OF THE VERB IN THE PASSIVE VOICE

ILIAD, 290–303

357. 1) Review thoroughly all the passive forms of λύω, paying special attention to the meaning of each form, 916–921.

2) Make three copies of the tables of personal endings of verbs, 821.

358. *Optional:*

359.   VOCABULARY

ἀ-έκων, ουσα, ον unwilling.

αἰέν (= αἰεί) always, EVER, forever.

αἷμα, ατος, τό blood, gore.

αἶψα quickly, immediately.

ἀν-αιρέω (αἰρε-, ἑλ-) ἀναιρήσω, ἀνέελον (ἀνεῖλον 584–585), ἀνῄρηκα*, ἀνῄρημαι*, ἀνῃρέθην* take (up), seize.

δειλός, ή, όν cowardly, cringing, miserable, pitiable.

δόρυ, δουρός (δούρατος), τό spear, beam, timber.

εἰ (*interj.*) up! come! go to!

ἐπι-τέλλω (τελ-, ταλ-) ἐπέτειλα, ἐπιτέταλμαι command, accomplish.

ἐρωέω, ἐρωήσω, ἠρώησα flow, dash, spurt.

κελαινός, ή, όν black, dark, dusky.

μήν (*cf.* μέν, μά) truly, indeed, to be sure.

ὄνειδος, εος, τό abuse, reviling, insult.

πειρά-ω, πειρήσω, ἐπείρησα* (ἐπειρησάμην), πεπείρηκα*, πεπείρημαι, ἐπειρήθην try, attempt.

προ-τί-θημι (θη-, θε-) προθήσω, προέθηκα add, grant (in addition).

ὑπ-είκ-ω, ὑπείξω* (ὑπείξομαι), ὕπειξα yield, submit, WEAKEN.

ὑπο-βλήδην interrupting, breaking in.

Derivatives : hemat-ic, -in, -ite, -o-logy, hemo-rrhage, an-aem-ic, -ia ; em-pir-ic-al, pir-ate, -acy ; pro-thet-ic.

360. Read and translate :

Iliad, 290–303

εἰ δέ μιν αἰχμητὴν ἔθεσαν θεοὶ αἰὲν ἐόντες,   290
τούνεκά οἱ προθέουσιν ὀνείδεα μυθήσασθαι ; "
τὸν δ᾽ ἄρ᾽ ὑποβλήδην ἠμείβετο δῖος Ἀχιλλεύς·
" ἦ γάρ κεν δειλός τε καὶ οὐτιδανὸς καλεοίμην,
εἰ δὴ σοὶ πᾶν ἔργον ὑπείξομαι, ὅττι κεν εἴπῃς·
ἄλλοισιν δὴ ταῦτ᾽ ἐπιτέλλεο, μὴ γὰρ ἐμοί γε   295
[σήμαιν᾽· οὐ γὰρ ἐγώ γ᾽ ἔτι σοι πείσεσθαι ὀίω.]
ἄλλο δέ τοι ἐρέω, σὺ δ᾽ ἐνὶ φρεσὶ βάλλεο σῇσιν·
χερσὶ μὲν οὔ τοι ἐγώ γε μαχήσομαι εἵνεκα κούρης
οὔτε σοὶ οὔτε τῳ ἄλλῳ, ἐπεί μ᾽ ἀφέλεσθέ γε δόντες·
τῶν δ᾽ ἄλλων, ἅ μοι ἔστι θοῇ παρὰ νηὶ μελαίνῃ,   300
τῶν οὐκ ἄν τι φέροις ἀνελὼν ἀέκοντος ἐμεῖο.
εἰ δ᾽ ἄγε μὴν πείρησαι, ἵνα γνώωσι καὶ οἵδε.
αἶψά τοι αἷμα κελαινὸν ἐρωήσει περὶ δουρί."   303

361. **290.** **αἰχμητήν** : an intentional weakening of Nestor's words in vs. 284, § 354.

294. **πᾶν ἔργον** : 1013–1014.

295. **ἐμοί γε** : as emphatic as possible.

296. **σοι** : 996. This verse is a sneering parody of vs. 289 ; some scholars consider it spurious. — **ὀίω** : is ironical, as usual.

298. **χερσί** : 1005. — **τοι** : 760.

299. **τῳ** [τὶς, τὶ 769] .

300. **μοι** : 999. — **ἔστι** : 973, 1.

301. **τῶν** resumes the **τῶν ἄλλων** of vs. 300, with added emphasis. — **ἀέκοντος ἐμεῖο** : 1111.

302. **πείρησαι** is issued in the form of a challenge : "just try it!" "I dare you to try it."

303. **δουρί** (ἐμῷ).

LESSON LV

REVIEW OF THE IRREGULAR VERBS OF THE -μι CONJUGATION

Iliad, 304–314

362. Review thoroughly all the irregular -μι verbs, and all other verb-forms not taken in the review of the last three lessons, 964–969, 922–948.

363. *Optional:*

364.   VOCABULARY

ἀντί-βιος, η, ον opposing, hostile.
ἀνώγ-ω, ἀνώξω, ἤνωξα, ἄνωγα (*for* ἤνωγα?) command, order, bid.
ἀπο-λῡμαίνομαι (λῦμαν-), purify (oneself), clean(se).
ἐείκοσι (εἴκοσι) twenty.
ἴση, [ἴσος] equal, equivalent, symmetrical, well-balanced.
ἐπι-πλέω (πλευ-, πλεϝ-, πλυ-), ἐπι-πλεύσομαι, ἐπέπλευσα*, ἐπιπέπλευκα*, ἐπιπέπλευσμαι*, sail (upon, over), navigate.
κέλευθος, ου, ἡ (*plur.* κέλευθα, ων, τά) road, way, path, journey, route.

κρίνω (κριν-, κρι-), κρινέω, ἔκρῑνα, κέκρικα**, κέκριμαι, ἐκρί(ν)θην pick out, select, choose, discern, decide, judge.
λῦμα, ατος, τό offscouring, filth.
Μενοιτιάδης, ᾱο, ὁ son of Menoetius, *Patroclus.*
πολύ-μητις, ιος wily, rich in counsel.
προ-ερύω (ϝερυ-, ϝρυ-), προερύω, προ-είρυσ(σ)α, προείρυ(σ)μαι draw forward, drag forward, launch.
ὑγρός, ή, όν wet, moist, damp, watery.

Derivatives : cris-is, crit-ic(al, -ism, -ise), -ique, -erion, hyper-crit-ical; hygro-meter, -scope.

365. Read and translate :

Iliad, 304–314

ὣς τώ γ᾽ ἀντιβίοισι μαχησαμένω ἐπέεσσιν
ἀνστήτην, λῦσαν δ᾽ ἀγορὴν παρὰ νηυσὶν Ἀχαιῶν.   305
Πηλεΐδης μὲν ἐπὶ κλισίας καὶ νῆας ἐΐσας
ἤϊε σύν τε Μενοιτιάδῃ καὶ οἷς ἑτάροισιν,
Ἀτρεΐδης δ᾽ ἄρα νῆα θοὴν ἅλαδε προέρυσσεν,

130

ἐς δ' ἐρέτας ἔκρινεν ἐείκοσιν, ἐς δ' ἑκατόμβην
βῆσε θεῷ, ἀνὰ δὲ Χρυσηΐδα καλλιπάρηον   310
εἷσεν ἄγων· ἐν δ' ἀρχὸς ἔβη πολύμητις 'Οδυσσεύς.
οἱ μὲν ἔπειτ' ἀναβάντες ἐπέπλεον ὑγρὰ κέλευθα,
λαοὺς δ' 'Ατρεΐδης ἀπολυμαίνεσθαι ἄνωγεν.
οἱ δ' ἀπελυμαίνοντο καὶ εἰς ἅλα λύματ' ἔβαλλον,   314

366. 304. ἐπέεσσιν : 1005.

305. ἀνστήτην = ἀνεστήτην.

307. Μενοιτιάδῃ : Patroclus. Like Agamemnon (vs. 7) Patroclus is first introduced by his patronymic, because he was such a well-known figure of the legend that it was not necessary to be more specific. He and Achilles were fast friends, and he stood by Achilles through all this period of trial. It is only his death in battle which furnishes a motive sufficiently powerful to induce Achilles to take a further part in the fighting. His introduction at this point is very skillfully done, as it is clearly indicated where he stands in relation to the hero.

308. προέρυσσεν : 1069, 837.

309. ἐς, ἐς : 1048–1049.

310. βῆσε : 1069. — ἀνά : 1048–1049.

311. εἷσεν : 1069. — ἄγων : 1108, Note 2.

312. κέλευθα : 1012. Cf. πόντος, sea, literally, path.

LESSON LVI

ILIAD, 315–333

367. *Optional:*

368. VOCABULARY

αἴδο-μαι (= αἰδέ-ομαι) reverence.

ἀτρύγετος, ον barren (?), restless (?).

ἐλίσσω (ϝελικ-), ἐλίξω*, εἴλιξα, εἴλιγμαι, ἐλίχθην (ει = εε, 584–585) twirl, twist, curl, turn, roll.

ἐπ-απειλέ-ω, ἐπαπειλήσω, ἐπηπείλησα threaten (against), boast.

ἔρδω (*from* ϝεργω : ϝεργ-, ϝοργ-), ἔρξω, ἔρξα, ἔοργα do, perform, make, sacrifice, WORK, accomplish.

εὑρίσκω (εὑρ-, εὑρε-), εὑρήσω*, εὗρον, εὕρηκα**, εὕρημαι*, εὑρέθην* find, come upon, hit upon.

Εὐρυ-βάτης, āo, ὁ Eurybates.

θεράπων, οντος, ὁ attendant, squire, comrade.

ἵκ-ω, ἶξον come, go.

καπνός, οὗ, ὁ smoke, vapor, mist, fume.

κῆρυξ, ῡκος, ὁ herald.

ὀτρηρός, ή, όν ready, eager, nimble, swift.

πέν-ομαι work, be busy, labor, do.

ῥῑγίων, ον worse, more horrible.

Ταλθύ-βιος, ου, ὁ Talthybius.

τελήεις, εσσα, εν complete, perfect, finished, unblemished.

προσ-φωνέ-ω, προσφωνήσω*, προσεφώνησα address, accost, speak to.

ταρβέ-ω, ταρβήσω*, ἐτάρβησα fear, be in terror, be frightened.

Derivatives: "Eureka"; therap-eutic(s, -al), psychotherapy; tel-, 4; phon-, 296.

369. Read and translate :

Iliad, 315–333

ἔρδον δ' Ἀπόλλωνι τεληέσσας ἑκατόμβας   315
ταύρων ἠδ' αἰγῶν παρὰ θῖν' ἁλὸς ἀτρυγέτοιο·
κνίση δ' οὐρανὸν ἷκεν ἑλισσομένη περὶ καπνῷ.
ὣς οἱ μὲν τὰ πένοντο κατὰ στρατόν· οὐδ' Ἀγαμέμνων
λῆγ' ἔριδος, τὴν πρῶτον ἐπηπείλησ' Ἀχιλῆι,
ἀλλ' ὅ γε Ταλθύβιόν τε καὶ Εὐρυβάτην προσέειπεν,   320
τώ οἱ ἔσαν κήρυκε καὶ ὀτρηρὼ θεράποντε·
"ἔρχεσθον κλισίην Πηληιάδεω Ἀχιλῆος·
χειρὸς ἑλόντ' ἀγέμεν Βρισηίδα καλλιπάρηον·
εἰ δέ κε μὴ δώῃσιν, ἐγὼ δέ κεν αὐτὸς ἕλωμαι
ἐλθὼν σὺν πλεόνεσσι· τό οἱ καὶ ῥίγιον ἔσται."   325
ὣς εἰπὼν προΐει, κρατερὸν δ' ἐπὶ μῦθον ἔτελλεν.
τὼ δ' ἀέκοντε βάτην παρὰ θῖν' ἁλὸς ἀτρυγέτοιο,
Μυρμιδόνων δ' ἐπί τε κλισίας καὶ νῆας ἱκέσθην.
τὸν δ' εὗρον παρά τε κλισίῃ καὶ νηὶ μελαίνῃ
ἥμενον· οὐδ' ἄρα τώ γε ἰδὼν γήθησεν Ἀχιλλεύς.   330
τὼ μὲν ταρβήσαντε καὶ αἰδομένω βασιλῆα
στήτην, οὐδέ τί μιν προσεφώνεον οὐδ' ἐρέοντο·
αὐτὰρ ὁ ἔγνω ᾗσιν ἐνὶ φρεσὶ φώνησέν τε·

370. 316. **περὶ καπνῷ**: round about *in* the smoke.

318. τά : 1012.

319. ἔριδος : 987.

321. οἱ : 999.

322. ἔρχεσθον : imperative. —κλισίην : 1019.

323. χειρός : 983. — ἀγέμεν : 1107, 11.

329. τόν : there is no need to mention his name, as it is uppermost now in the minds of all; and it is much more effective to say " *him* they found."

330 (latter part) : litotes.

331. Observe the difference in tense of the two participles : the first denotes the confusion into which they were thrown (1081) at the sight of Achilles; the other indicates their customary feeling of reverence toward him. — βασιλῆα ('Αχιλλῆα) : through no fault of their own the heralds are in a very delicate situation, as they have no desire to offend either Agamemnon or Achilles.

333. ὁ, here again, without the name of Achilles, is more poetic than to give his name. Achilles shows fine tact and a human feeling for the heralds in their embarrassment.

LESSON LVII

ILIAD, 334–347

371. *Optional :*

372.   VOCABULARY

ἄγγελος, ου, ὁ messenger, courier.

ἀπηνής, ές harsh, cruel, rude.

ἆσσον nearer, closer (*compar. of* ἄγχι).

δῑο-γενής, ές Zeus-born; Zeus-descended (1168).

ἐξ-άγ-ω, ἐξάξω, ἐξήγαγον, ἐξῆχα**, ἐξ-ῆγμαι*, ἐξήχθην* lead out, lead forth, bring forth.

ἐπ-αίτιος, η, ον blameworthy, blamable, to blame, accountable, responsible.

ἑταῖρος (ἔταρος, 571), ου, ὁ companion, comrade, follower, friend.

θνητός, ή, όν mortal, human.

θύ-ω, ἔθυσα dash, rush (headlong), be rash, rage, be insane.

μάκαρ, αρος blessed, happy, fortunate, lucky.

μάρτυρος, ου, ὁ witness.

νοέ-ω, νοήσω, ἐνόησα, νενόηκα*, νε-νόημαι*, ἐνοήθην* perceive, think, consider, plan.

ὀλο(ι)ός, ή, όν accursed, baneful, destructive (1168, 571).

ὀπίσσω back(ward), behind.

Πάτροκλος, ου, ὁ Patroclus.

πρόσσω forward, in front.

χρειώ (χρεώ, χρή) need, necessity.

133

Derivatives : angel-ic, -ology, arch-angel, ev-angel-ist, -ism ; gen- ; aetio-logy ; martyr-o-logy, -dom.

373. Read and translate :

Iliad, 334-347

"χαίρετε, κήρυκες, Διὸς ἄγγελοι ἠδὲ καὶ ἀνδρῶν ·
ἆσσον ἴτ᾽ · οὔ τί μοι ὕμμες ἐπαίτιοι, ἀλλ᾽ Ἀγαμέμνων, 335
ὃ σφῶϊ προΐει Βρισηΐδος εἵνεκα κούρης.
ἀλλ᾽ ἄγε, διογενὲς Πατρόκλεις, ἔξαγε κούρην
καί σφωιν δὸς ἄγειν. τὼ δ᾽ αὐτὼ μάρτυροι ἔστων
πρός τε θεῶν μακάρων πρός τε θνητῶν ἀνθρώπων
καὶ πρὸς τοῦ βασιλῆος ἀπηνέος, εἴ ποτε δὴ αὖτε 340
χρειὼ ἐμεῖο γένηται ἀεικέα λοιγὸν ἀμῦναι
τοῖς ἄλλοις. ἦ γὰρ ὅ γ᾽ ὀλοιῇσι φρεσὶ θύει,
οὐδέ τι οἶδε νοῆσαι ἅμα πρόσσω καὶ ὀπίσσω,
ὅππως οἱ παρὰ νηυσὶ σόοι μαχεοίατ᾽ Ἀχαιοί."
ὣς φάτο, Πάτροκλος δὲ φίλῳ ἐπεπείθεθ᾽ ἑταίρῳ, 345
ἐκ δ᾽ ἄγαγε κλισίης Βρισηΐδα καλλιπάρηον,
δῶκε δ᾽ ἄγειν. τὼ δ᾽ αὖτις ἴτην παρὰ νῆας Ἀχαιῶν,

374. 334. Διὸς ἄγγελοι: officials in antiquity regularly obtained their authority from on high, and were the earthly representatives of divine power.

337. **Πατρόκλεις**: voc., irregular.

338. **ἔστων** [εἰμί]: imperat., 964.

340. **δὴ αὖτε**, 586, does not mean "again," to denote repetition, but denotes a situation opposed to the present, as in vs. 237.

341. **ἐμεῖο**: 979, 3.

342. **τοῖς ἄλλοις**: 997, contemptuously, and with emphatic position, perhaps with a curt gesture. — **γάρ, ὀλοιῇσι**: 1168, 571.

343. *I.e.* to consider carefully and wisely. Achilles at last begins to realize that it is not merely malice on the part of Agamemnon, but a blind infatuation (ἄτη) which is leading him on to ruin.

344. **οἱ**: 997. — **μαχεοίατ᾽** (ο): opt., 3d plur.

345. **ἑταίρῳ**: 996.

LESSON LVIII

ILIAD, 348–358

375. *Optional :*

376. VOCABULARY

ἀ-πείρων, ον boundless, limitless.
ἀπ-αυράω (ϝρᾱ-), *imperf.* ἀπηύρων
with aor. sense, ἀπουρήσω*, *aor.*
part. ἀπούρᾱς (= ἀπο-ϝρᾱς) take
away, deprive, snatch away.
ἄφαρ immediately, forthwith.
βένθος, εος, τό depth.
γυνή, γυναικός, ἡ woman, wife.
δακρύ-ω*, δακρύσω*, ἐδάκρυσα, δεδά-
κρῦμαι weep, shed tears.
ἐγγυαλίζω, ἐγγυαλίξω, ἠγγυάλιξα
grant, present with.
λιάζομαι (λιαδ-), ἐλίασσα, ἐλιάσθην
bend, turn aside, sink, fall.
μινυνθάδιος, η, ον short(lived),
ephemeral, brief.
νόσφι(ν) apart, away, separate.
ὀρέγ-ω (ὀρέγ-νῡμι), ὀρέξω, ὤρεξα, ὀρώ-
ρεγμαι, ὠρέχθην* reach forth,

stretch out, extend.
ὀφείλω (ὀφέλλω) (ὀφελ-, ὀφειλε-),
ὀφειλήσω*, ὤφελον, ὠφείληκα**,
ὠφειλήθην* owe, ought, be obli-
gated ; *aor. in wishes,* would that!
πάροιθε(ν) before, formerly.
πολιός, ή, όν gray, hoary.
πόντος, ου, ὁ sea, *literally*, path.
πότνια, ης, ἡ revered, honored
(lady, queen).
τυτθός, ή, όν small, little, young,
brief.
ὑψι-βρεμέτης, ες thundering, growl-
ing (grumbling, roaring, rum-
bling, bellowing) on high, *or*
high-growling, *etc.*
χέω (χευ-, χεϝ-, χυ-), χεύω, ἔχε(υ)α,
κέχυκα*, κέχυμαι, ἐχύθην pour
(out, forth), shed (tears).

Derivatives : gyn-archy, poly-, miso-gyny, andro-gynous,
gynaeco-logy, -cracy ; bathos, batho-meter, 597–598.

377. Read and translate :

Iliad, 348–358

ἡ δ' ἀέκουσ' ἅμα τοῖσι γυνὴ κίεν.   αὐτὰρ Ἀχιλλεὺς
δακρύσας ἑτάρων ἄφαρ ἕζετο νόσφι λιασθεὶς
θῖν' ἐφ' ἁλὸς πολιῆς, ὁρόων ἐπ' ἀπείρονα πόντον ·   350
πολλὰ δὲ μητρὶ φίλῃ ἠρήσατο χεῖρας ὀρεγνύς ·
"μῆτερ, ἐπεί μ' ἔτεκές γε μινυνθάδιόν περ ἐόντα,
τιμήν πέρ μοι ὄφελλεν Ὀλύμπιος ἐγγυαλίξαι

135

Ζεὺς ὑψιβρεμέτης · νῦν δ' οὐδέ με τυτθὸν ἔτισεν.
ἦ γάρ μ' ᾿Ατρεΐδης εὐρὺ κρείων ᾿Αγαμέμνων   355
ἠτίμησεν · ἑλὼν γὰρ ἔχει γέρας, αὐτὸς ἀπούρας."
   ὣς φάτο δάκρυ χέων, τοῦ δ' ἔκλυε πότνια μήτηρ
ἡμένη ἐν βένθεσσιν ἁλὸς παρὰ πατρὶ γέροντι.

378. 348. ἀέκουσ'(α).
349. δακρύσᾱς, 1081.
350. ἐφ' (= ἔπι): 1050, 1. — ὁρόων: an " assimilated," or " distracted "
form (= ὁράων), 945–948.
351. μητρί: her name is Thetis, but is not yet mentioned, as it was
well known to the hearers of the bard. She had been wooed by Zeus
and Poseidon, but when Zeus learned that she was fated to bear a son
mightier than his father, he forced her against her will, goddess though
she was, to marry Peleus, by whom she bore Achilles.

χεῖρας ὀρεγνύς: when the ancients prayed they regularly stretched out
their hands in the direction of the divinity whom they entreated. If
this were a god of heaven, they lifted up their hands toward the sky; if
a god of the sea, they stretched out their hands as Achilles does here;
if a god of the lower world, they might even sit down and beat upon
the ground to attract his attention.

352. μινυνθάδιον: Achilles had the choice of a long and inglorious
life, or one short and full of renown. He had chosen the latter, and
now that he has made this choice, his situation is one of deep pathos.

353. τῑμήν: emphatic by position, showing how keenly the old Greek
heroes thirsted for glory, and how bitterly they resented any affront to
their honor.

356. ἠτίμησεν by position in the verse is strongly contrasted with τῑμήν
of vs. 353. — αὐτός: of his own arbitrary free will.

357. τοῦ: 984.

358. πατρὶ γέροντι: Nereus, who is too well known to the audience to
require an introduction. Homer usually calls him merely "the Old Man
of the Sea." — γέρων is here employed as an adjective, aged, old.

LESSON LIX

ILIAD, 359-379

379. *Optional :*

380. VOCABULARY

ἀνα-δύ-ω, ἀναδύσω, ἀνέδῦσα (ἀνέδῦν),
ἀναδέδυκα, ἀναδέδυμαι*, ἀνεδύθην*
rise, emerge, "dive up," plunge
up.

δια-πέρθω (περθ-, πραθ-), διαπέρσω,
διέπερσα (διέπραθον) sack (utterly),
sack thoroughly, pillage,
plunder, devastate.

ἑκατη-βόλος (= ἑκηβόλος), ου, ὁ freeshooter,
sharp-shooter, freeshooting,
sharp-shooting, shooting
according to will, sure
shooting, a dead shot.

ἐξ-αυδά-ω, ἐξαυδήσω*, ἐξηύδησα speak
out, tell, say, declare.

Ἠετίων, ωνος, ὁ Eëtion, *father of
Andromache*.

ἠύτε as, just as, like.

Θήβη, ης, ἡ Thebe, *a city in Asia
Minor*.

καθ-έζομαι (σεδ- = ἑδ-, 603-604), καθέσσομαι,
καθεῖσα, καθεεσσάμην sit
down.

καρπαλίμως quickly, suddenly,

swiftly.

κατα-ρέζω (ϝρεγ-), καταρέξω, κατέ(ρ)ρεξα,
κατερέχθην caress, stroke,
fondle.

κεύθω (κευθ-, κυθ-), κεύσω, ἔκευσα,
(ἔκυθον, κέκυθον), κέκευθα hide,
conceal, enclose.

κλαίω (κλαυ-, κλαϝ-, κλαι-, κλαιε-),
κλαύσομαι, ἔκλαυσα, κέκλαυ-
(σ)μαι* cry, weep.

ὁμίχλη, ης, ἡ mist, fog, cloud,
vapor.

ὀνομάζω (ὀνομat-), ὀνομάσω*, ὠνόμασα,
ὠνόμακα**, ὠνόμασμαι*,
ὠνομάσθην* address, call (by
name).

πάροιθε(ν) (*with gen.* 992) in front
of, before.

στενάχ-ω groan, sob, sigh.

τέκνον, ου, τό child, young, offspring.

χαλκο-χίτων, ωνος with bronze tunics.

Derivatives : onomato-poeïa, -logy.

381. Read and translate :

Iliad, 359-379

καρπαλίμως δ' ἀνέδυ πολιῆς ἁλὸς ἠύτ' ὁμίχλη,
καί ῥα πάροιθ' αὐτοῖο καθέζετο δάκρυ χέοντος,   360
χειρί τέ μιν κατέρεξεν, ἔπος τ' ἔφατ' ἔκ τ' ὀνόμαζεν·

137

" τέκνον, τί κλαίεις ; τί δέ σε φρένας ἵκετο πένθος ;
ἐξαύδα, μὴ κεῦθε νόῳ, ἵνα εἴδομεν ἄμφω."
　　τὴν δὲ βαρὺ στενάχων προσέφη πόδας ὠκὺς Ἀχιλλεύς·
" οἶσθα· τί ἦ τοι ταῦτα ἰδυίῃ πάντ' ἀγορεύω ;　　　　365
ᾠχόμεθ' ἐς Θήβην, ἱερὴν πόλιν Ἠετίωνος,
τὴν δὲ διεπράθομέν τε καὶ ἤγομεν ἐνθάδε πάντα.
καὶ τὰ μὲν εὖ δάσσαντο μετὰ σφίσιν υἷες Ἀχαιῶν,
ἐκ δ' ἕλον Ἀτρεΐδῃ Χρυσηΐδα καλλιπάρῃον.
Χρύσης δ' αὖθ' ἱερεὺς ἑκατηβόλου Ἀπόλλωνος　　　370
ἦλθε θοὰς ἐπὶ νῆας Ἀχαιῶν χαλκοχιτώνων
λυσόμενός τε θύγατρα φέρων τ' ἀπερείσι' ἄποινα,
στέμματ' ἔχων ἐν χερσὶν ἑκηβόλου Ἀπόλλωνος
χρυσέῳ ἀνὰ σκήπτρῳ, καὶ ἐλίσσετο πάντας Ἀχαιούς,
Ἀτρεΐδα δὲ μάλιστα δύω, κοσμήτορε λαῶν.　　　　375
ἔνθ' ἄλλοι μὲν πάντες ἐπευφήμησαν Ἀχαιοὶ
αἰδεῖσθαί θ' ἱερῆα καὶ ἀγλαὰ δέχθαι ἄποινα.
ἀλλ' οὐκ Ἀτρεΐδῃ Ἀγαμέμνονι ἥνδανε θυμῷ,
ἀλλὰ κακῶς ἀφίει, κρατερὸν δ' ἐπὶ μῦθον ἔτελλεν.

382. 359. ἠύτ' ὀμίχλη: the comparison is particularly appropriate
for a sea divinity, who rises easily, quietly, and mysteriously from the
water, "like a mist," and in shadowy form would resemble the "Erl-
könig."—ἁλός: 987.
　360. αὐτοῖο: 992.
　361. χειρί: 1005.
　362. σε φρένας: 1021.
　363. νόῳ: 1009. — εἴδομεν: 800. — ἵνα ϝείδομεν: 580.
　364. βαρύ: 780–781.
　365. τί: why? — ταῦτα: object of ἀγορεύω. — πάντ'(α): object of
ἰδυίῃ. — ταῦτα ϝιδυίῃ: 580.
　367. διεπράθομεν: the first person brings out prominently the fact that
Achilles had a share in the expedition and in procuring Chryseïs for
Agamemnon. — ἐνθάδε: hither.
　369. ἐκ: 1048–1049.
　370–373. ἑκατηβόλου, ἑκηβόλου: observe how this word is brought into
prominence by repetition.

LESSON LX

ILIAD, 380-400

383. *Optional :*

384. VOCABULARY

ἀκού-ω, ἀκούσομαι, ἤκουσα, ἀκήκοα*,
ἤκουσμαι*, ἠκούσθην* hear(ken).
'Ἀτρεΐων, ωνος, ὁ son of Atreus.
Βρῑσεύς, ῆος, ὁ Briseus, *father of
Briseïs.*
ἕκατος, ου, ὁ free-shooter, sharp-
shooter.
ἐπ-ασσύτερος, η, ον thick, in quick
succession.
ἐΰς, ἐῆος mighty, valiant.
κελαινεφής, ές wrapped in black
clouds.
Κρονίων, ωνος, ὁ son of Cronus.
λαμβάνω* (λαβ-, ληβ-), λήψομαι*,
(λάψομαι†), ἔλαβον, λελάβηκα†,
λέλαμμαι, ἐλήφθην*, (ἐλάμφθην†)
take, seize, lay hold of, accept.

μέγαρον, ου, τό great hall (*plu.* pal
ace).
ξυν-δέ-ω = συνδέ-ω, ξυνδήσω, ξυνέδησα,
ξυνδέδεκα*, ξυνδέδεμαι, ξυνεδέθην*
bind (hand and foot), " hog-tie."
ὀνίνημι (ὀνη-, ὀνα-), ὀνήσω, ὤνησα,
ὠνήθην* help, benefit, assist,
profit, be useful.
πάντῃ everywhere, throughout.
περι-έχω (σεχ-, σχ-, σχε-), περιέξω
(περισχήσω), περίεσχον protect,
defend, encompass, embrace.
πολλάκι(s) often, many times.
Ποσειδάων, ωνος, ὁ Poseidon, *god
of the sea, brother of Zeus, and
one of the mightiest of the Greek
divinities.*

Derivatives : acoustic(s) ; astro-labe ; syl-lable, -labus ;
panto-graph, -mime ; patri-arch, -otic, -mony.

385. Read and translate :

Iliad, 380-400

χωόμενος δ' ὁ γέρων πάλιν ᾤχετο · τοῖο δ' Ἀπόλλων   380
εὐξαμένου ἤκουσεν, ἐπεὶ μάλα οἱ φίλος ἦεν,
ἧκε δ' ἐπ' Ἀργείοισι κακὸν βέλος · οἱ δέ νυ λαοὶ
θνῆσκον ἐπασσύτεροι, τὰ δ' ἐπῴχετο κῆλα θεοῖο
πάντῃ ἀνὰ στρατὸν εὐρὺν Ἀχαιῶν. ἄμμι δὲ μάντις
εὖ εἰδὼς ἀγόρευε θεοπροπίας ἑκάτοιο.   385
αὐτίκ' ἐγὼ πρῶτος κελόμην θεὸν ἱλάσκεσθαι ·
'Ἀτρεΐωνα δ' ἔπειτα χόλος λάβεν, αἶψα δ' ἀναστὰς
ἠπείλησεν μῦθον, ὃ δὴ τετελεσμένος ἐστίν.

139

τὴν μὲν γὰρ σὺν νηὶ θοῇ ἑλίκωπες Ἀχαιοὶ
ἐς Χρύσην πέμπουσιν, ἄγουσι δὲ δῶρα ἄνακτι ·			390
τὴν δὲ νέον κλισίηθεν ἔβαν κήρυκες ἄγοντες
κούρην Βρισῆος, τήν μοι δόσαν υἷες Ἀχαιῶν.
ἀλλὰ σύ, εἰ δύνασαί γε, περίσχεο παιδὸς ἑῆος ·
ἐλθοῦσ᾽ Οὐλυμπόνδε Δία λίσαι, εἴ ποτε δή τι
ἢ ἔπει ὤνησας κραδίην Διὸς ἠὲ καὶ ἔργῳ.			395
πολλάκι γάρ σεο πατρὸς ἐνὶ μεγάροισιν ἄκουσα
εὐχομένης, ὅτ᾽ ἔφησθα κελαινεφέϊ Κρονίωνι
οἴη ἐν ἀθανάτοισιν ἀεικέα λοιγὸν ἀμῦναι,
ὁππότε μιν ξυνδῆσαι Ὀλύμπιοι ἤθελον ἄλλοι,
Ἥρη τ᾽ ἠδὲ Ποσειδάων καὶ Παλλὰς Ἀθήνη.			400

386. 380. τοῖο : 984. — ὁ serves to make γέρων emphatic, as important for the situation.

381. ἐπεὶ μάλα οἱ φίλος ἦεν : compare the note on vs. 218, § 306.

382. βέλος is used collectively.

383. ἐπώχετο κῆλα : 973, 1. — τά serves to emphasize and visualize the arrows of the god, as ὁ does the old priest in vs. 380.

389–391. τὴν μὲν . . . τὴν δέ : *the one* (Chryseïs) . . . *the other* (Briseïs), 1029–1030. — νέον : 780-781.

390. ἄνακτι : *king, lord*, referring to Apollo.

393. περίσχεο : *hold about, protect*, involves the same figure as "about me are his everlasting arms." — παιδός : 989.

394. Δία λίσαι : 525. — λίσαι : imperat.

395. ἔπει (ἔπος), ἔργῳ : 1005.

396. σεο : 984. — πατρὸς (ἐμοῦ) : 979, 1. — ἐνὶ μεγάροισιν : 525.

397. ἔφησθα : observe the imperfect. Evidently Thetis was quite proud of her achievement, and so she *kept* telling about it, as might have been expected. — κελαινεφέϊ Κρονίωνι : 997.

LESSON LXI

ILIAD, 401-412

387. *Optional:*

388. VOCABULARY

Αἰγαίων, ωνος, ὁ Aegaeon.
ἀμφί *adv., and prep. with gen., dat., and acc., about, around; adv.,* around, about, on both sides; *with gen.,* around, about, concerning, for (the sake of); *with dat.,* around, about, because of, concerning, at, by; *with acc.,* around, about.
ἄτη, ης, ἡ blind infatuation, folly, ruin, misfortune, hurt.
Βριάρεως (Βριάρηος, 573, 586), ω, ὁ Briareüs.
βίη, ης, ἡ strength, might, violence.
γαίω (γαϝ-) rejoice, exult, glory.
γόνυ, γουνός (γούνατος), τό knee.
δεσμός, οὗ, ὁ (cf. δέω) bond, band, fetter.
δέ-ω, δήσω, ἔδησα, δέδεκα*, δέδεμαι, ἐδέθην* bind, tie.
*εἴλω (εἴλομαι) (ϝελ-), ἔελσα, ἔελμαι, ἐάλην crowd, drive.
ἐκατόγ-χειρος, η, ον hundred-handed, hundred-armed.

ἐπ-αυρίσκω (ἐπαυρέω) (αὐρ-, αὐρε-), ἐπαυρήσομαι, ἐπαῦρον enjoy, reap the benefit of (*with gen.,* 982).
κτείνω (κτεν-, κτον-, κτα-ν-), κτενέω, ἔκτεινα (ἔκταν(ον)), ἔκτονα*, ἐκτάθην kill, slay, murder.
μακρός, ή, όν long, high, lofty, large, distant.
μι-μνήσκω (μνα-) μνήσω, ἔμνησα, μέμνημαι, ἐμνήσθην remind, call to mind, remember
παρ-έζομαι (σεδ- = ἑδ-, 603-604) sit beside, sit near.
πρύμνη, ης, ἡ stern of a ship.
ὑπο-δείδω (δϝι-, δϝει-, δϝοι-), ὑποδείσομαι, ὑπέδεισα, ὑποδείδοικα (ὑποδείδια) fear, shrink before, cringe before.
ὑπο-λύ-ω, ὑπολύσω, ὑπέλυσα, ὑπολέλυκα*, ὑπολέλυμαι, ὑπελύθην loose (from beneath, by stealth).
ὦκα (ὠκύς, 780-781), quickly, swiftly, suddenly.

Derivatives: amphi-theater, -bious; dia-gon-al, deca-, hepta-, hexa-, octa-, poly-gon(al), tri-gono-metry; heca-tom(b); macro-cosm; a-mnesty, mnemonic(al).

389. Read and translate:

Iliad, 401-412

ἀλλὰ σὺ τόν γ᾽ ἐλθοῦσα, θεά, ὑπελύσαο δεσμῶν.   401
ὦχ᾽ ἑκατόγχειρον καλέσασ᾽ ἐς μακρὸν Ὄλυμπον,

141

ὃν Βριάρεων καλέουσι θεοί, ἄνδρες δέ τε πάντες
Αἰγαίων᾽ · ὁ γὰρ αὖτε βίη οὗ πατρὸς ἀμείνων ·
ὅς ῥα παρὰ Κρονίωνι καθέζετο κύδεϊ γαίων ·   405
τὸν καὶ ὑπέδεισαν μάκαρες θεοὶ οὐδέ τ᾽ ἔδησαν.
τῶν νῦν μιν μνήσασα παρέζεο καὶ λαβὲ γούνων,
αἴ κέν πως ἐθέλῃσιν ἐπὶ Τρώεσσιν ἀρῆξαι,
τοὺς δὲ κατὰ πρύμνας τε καὶ ἀμφ᾽ ἅλα ἔλσαι Ἀχαιοὺς
κτεινομένους, ἵνα πάντες ἐπαύρωνται βασιλῆος,   410
γνῷ δὲ καὶ Ἀτρεΐδης εὐρὺ κρείων Ἀγαμέμνων
ἣν ἄτην, ὅ τ᾽ ἄριστον Ἀχαιῶν οὐδὲν ἔτισεν."

390. 401. δεσμῶν: 987.— **θεά** may be nominative (otherwise voca-
tive), "in thy power as goddess." In any case it is employed to indicate
her ability as more than mortal.
   403. Gods and men do not seem to have had the same language at
all times. This may be a reminiscence of an earlier stage of the
Homeric poems or of their models, when their form and language were
different from what they are at present. The older words would belong
to the language of the gods, while their later equivalent would be of the
language of men.— **Βριάρεων** = Βριάρηον, 573, 586.
   404. αὖτε: *on the other side, for his side*, as the others were previously
stronger on theirs. See the note on vs. 202.— **οὗ πατρός**: 993, Poseidon.
— **βίη**: 1010.
   405. κύδεϊ: 1005.
   406. Observe how the ὑπέδϝεισαν is echoed by οὐδέ τ᾽ ἔδησαν, a pun.
   407. τῶν: 984.— **γούνων**: 983.— **μιν**: object of μνήσασα.— **λαβὲ γούνων**:
this was the regular custom of a suppliant among the ancient Greeks.
   408. ἐπί: 1048–1049.— **Τρώεσσιν**: 996. The prayer of Achilles is
granted by Zeus, at the request of Thetis, but it is directly responsible
for the death of his dearest friend Patroclus.
   409. τούς: 971.— **κατὰ πρύμνᾶς**: because the ships were drawn up on
the shore with their sterns toward the land. Up to this time, while
Achilles had taken part in the war, the Trojans had not ventured far
from the gates of their city. Now Achilles prays that they may drive
back the Achaeans to their ships, and give them a taste of defeat under
the most dangerous conditions. For if they lose their ships, all is lost.
   Achilles disdainfully sets the names of the Achaeans at the very end
of the verse. — **τούς** — the Trojans.
   410. κτεινομένους by its position in the verse probably modifies τούς,

LESSON LXII [391-393

v. 409, as middle, but may modify Ἀχαιούς, as passive. — βασιλῆος : 982. — ἐπαύρωνται, with bitter irony : *that all may reap the benefit of their king.* The only benefit from such a king is death and woe.

411. καί : *even* the son of Atreus (dummy though he be) may realize his own folly. — ἄτην : henceforth an important word. Agamemnon later confesses his blind infatuation (ἄτη) in this matter.

LESSON LXII

ILIAD, 413-424

391. *Optional :*

392. VOCABULARY

ἀγάν-νιφος, ον snow-clad, very snowy.
ἀ-δάκρῠτος, η, ον tearless.
αἴθε (*used to introduce a wish*).
Αἰθιοπεύς, ῆος, ὁ Ethiopian.
αἰνός, ή, όν dread, terrible, awful, painful, sorrowful.
αἶσα, ης, ἡ fate, lot, portion.
ἀ-πήμων, ον unharmed, painless.
ἀπο-παύ-ω, ἀποπαύσω, ἀπέπαυσα, ἀποπέπαυκα*, ἀποπέπαυμαι, ἀπεπαύθην* cease (from), refrain (from), stop (from), restrain.
δήν long, for a long time.
Θέτις, ιδος, ἡ Thetis, *a sea goddess, wife of Peleus, mother of Achilles.*

μίνυνθα for a short time.
πάμ-παν completely, altogether.
ὀϊζῡρός, ή, όν piteous, woeful, miserable.
πάρ-ημαι (ἡσ-) sit beside.
τερπι-κέραυνος, η, ον hurling the thunderbolt; *or more probably* rejoicing in the thunderbolt.
τῶ therefore, for this (reason).
χθιζός, ή, όν yesterday(s).
Ὠκεανός, οῦ, ὁ ocean, Oceanus.
ὠκύ-μορος, η, ον swift-fated.
ὠκύ-πορος, ον swift-sailing, swift going, crossing quickly.

393. Read and translate:

Iliad, 413-424

τὸν δ᾽ ἠμείβετ᾽ ἔπειτα Θέτις κατὰ δάκρυ χέουσα ·
" ὤ μοι, τέκνον ἐμόν, τί νύ σ᾽ ἔτρεφον αἰνὰ τεκοῦσα;
αἴθ᾽ ὄφελες παρὰ νηυσὶν ἀδάκρυτος καὶ ἀπήμων   415
ἧσθαι, ἐπεί νύ τοι αἶσα μίνυνθά περ, οὔ τι μάλα δήν ·

143

νῦν δ' ἅμα τ' ὠκύμορος καὶ ὀϊζυρὸς περὶ πάντων
ἔπλεο · τῶ σε κακῇ αἴσῃ τέκον ἐν μεγάροισιν.
τοῦτο δέ τοι ἐρέουσα ἔπος Διὶ τερπικεραύνῳ
εἶμ' αὐτὴ πρὸς Ὄλυμπον ἀγάννιφον, αἴ κε πίθηται.　　420
ἀλλὰ σὺ μὲν νῦν νηυσὶ παρήμενος ὠκυπόροισιν
μήνι' Ἀχαιοῖσιν, πολέμου δ' ἀποπαύεο πάμπαν ·
Ζεὺς γὰρ ἐς Ὠκεανὸν μετ' ἀμύμονας Αἰθιοπῆας
χθιζὸς ἔβη κατὰ δαῖτα, θεοὶ δ' ἅμα πάντες ἕποντο ·

394. 414. τί, αἰνά : 780–781. — αἰνὰ τέκουσα : having borne thee to a
dreadful (sorrowful) lot.
416. τοι : 999. — μίνυνθά περ (ἐστίν). — δϝήν.
418. αἴσῃ : 1005.
419. τοι : 997. — ἐρέουσα : 1109, 5.
421. νηυσί : 1004.
422. Ἀχαιοῖσιν : 996. — πολέμου : 987.
423–4. This is to explain why his request cannot be granted immedi-
ately. It also motivates the inactivity of Achilles for this period, thus
throwing into strong relief his abiding anger.

LESSON LXIII

ILIAD, 425–435

395. *Optional :*

396.　　　　VOCABULARY

ἀπο-βαίνω (βαν-, βα-), ἀποβήσω
(ἀποβήσομαι), ἀπέβησα (ἀπέβην).
ἀποβέβηκα depart, go away.
αὐτοῦ there, at that place.
γουνάζομαι (*cf.* γόνυ), γουνάσομαι
embrace the knees, entreat, im-
plore.
δῶ (*neut. indecl.*) house, home.
δ(υ)ω-δέκατος, η, ον twelfth.

ἐντός *with gen.*, 992, within, inside.
ἐρετμόν, οῦ, τό oar.
ἐύ-ζωνος, ον well-girded, beautiful-
waisted.
ἱστίον, ου, τό sail.
ἱστο-δόκη, ης, ἡ mast-receiver.
λιμήν, ένος, ὁ harbor, anchoring
place.
ὅρμος, ου, ὁ anchorage.

144

πελάζω(πέλας), πελάσω*, ἐπέλασ(σ)α,
πέπλημαι, ἐπελάσθην (ἐπλήμην)
bring near, draw near, approach.

πολυ-βενθής, ές very deep.

προ-ερέσσω (ἐρετ-), προήρεσ(σ)α row
forward.

πρό-τονος, ου, ὁ fore-stay, cordage.

στέλλω (στελ-, σταλ-), στελέω,

ἔστειλα, ἔσταλκα**, ἔσταλμαι*,
ἐστάλην* put, place, arrange,
furl.

ὑφ-ί-ημι (ση-, σε- = ἡ-, ἑ, 603–604)
ὑφήσω, ὑφῆκα (ὑφέηκα), ὑφεῖκα*,
ὑφεῖμαι*, ὑφείθην let down, lower.

χαλκο-βατής, ές with bronze threshold, with bronze pavement.

397. Read and translate :

Iliad, 425–435

δωδεκάτῃ δέ τοι αὖτις ἐλεύσεται Οὐλυμπόνδε,   425
καὶ τότ᾽ ἔπειτά τοι εἶμι Διὸς ποτὶ χαλκοβατὲς δῶ,
καί μιν γουνάσομαι, καί μιν πείσεσθαι ὀΐω."
ὣς ἄρα φωνήσασ᾽ ἀπεβήσετο, τὸν δὲ λίπ᾽ αὐτοῦ
χωόμενον κατὰ θυμὸν ἐυζώνοιο γυναικός,
τήν ῥα βίῃ ἀέκοντος ἀπηύρων. αὐτὰρ Ὀδυσσεὺς   430
ἐς Χρύσην ἵκανεν ἄγων ἱερὴν ἑκατόμβην.
οἱ δ᾽ ὅτε δὴ λιμένος πολυβενθέος ἐντὸς ἵκοντο,
ἱστία μὲν στεῖλαντο, θέσαν δ᾽ ἐν νηὶ μελαίνῃ,
ἱστὸν δ᾽ ἱστοδόκῃ πέλασαν προτόνοισιν ὑφέντες
καρπαλίμως, τὴν δ᾽ εἰς ὅρμον προέρεσσαν ἐρετμοῖς.   435

398. 425. **δωδεκάτῃ** (ἡμέρῃ) : 1009. The Ethiopians live so far away that the gods make a rather lengthy stay, to compensate for the trouble of going on such a long trip. This twelve days' sojourn is well introduced by the poet, to make more impressive Achilles' inactivity, and to indicate how deeply his resentment had taken hold of his whole being.

426. **τοι** : 997.

427. **ὀΐω** does not imply any doubt on the part of Thetis, but is to be looked upon rather as an expression of her confidence in the outcome.

428. **ἀπεβήσετο** : 865, note 1, a "mixed" aorist, 842.

429. **γυναικός** : 979, 6.

430. **βίῃ** : 1005. — **ἀπ-ηύρων** [ἀπαυράω] : imperf., as aor. — **ἀέκοντος** : 987 or 994 (referring to Achilles).

430–487. The scene in Chrysa intervenes between the promise of Thetis and its fulfillment, and thus makes an exceptionally suitable episode to help occupy the intervening time of twelve days.

145

432. λιμένος : 992. — ἱστία : plur. (the Homeric ship had but *one* sail), to visualize its different parts; cf. the note on τόξ (a), vs. 45. § 138.

434. ἱστοδόκη : 1009. — προτόνοισιν : 1005.

435. ἐρετμοῖς : 1005.

LESSON LXIV

ILIAD, 436–449

399. *Optional:*

400.   VOCABULARY

βωμός, οὗ, ὁ (*cf.* βαίνω), altar, base, foundation.

ἑξείης in order, in turn.

ἐύ-δμητος, η, ον well-built.

εὐνή, ῆς, ἡ bed, sleeper, anchor-stone, lair, den.

κῆδος, εος, τό woe, grief, suffering.

οὐλο-χύτη, ης, ἡ poured-out barley-corn.

πολύ-στονος, η, ον causing many a groan, rich in groans.

ποντο-πόρος, ον sea-going, sea-traversing, crossing the sea.

πρυμνήσιον, ου, τό stern-cable, stern-hawser.

ῥηγμίν, ῖνος, ἡ (*cf.* ῥήγνῡμι break), beach, strand, shore.

ὑπέρ, ὑπείρ, *adv.*, *and prep. with gen. and acc.*, over, beyond, in behalf of, concerning, above; *adv.*, above; *with gen.* (from) over, for (the sake); *with acc.*, over, beyond.

*χερνίπτω (νιβ-) (χερνίπτομαι), χερνίψω, ἐχέρνιψα, ἐχερνίφθην wash the hands, pour lustral water, purify with lustral water.

401. Read and translate :

Iliad, 436–449

ἐκ δ' εὐνὰς ἔβαλον, κατὰ δὲ πρυμνήσι' ἔδησαν ·   436

ἐκ δὲ καὶ αὐτοὶ βαῖνον ἐπὶ ῥηγμῖνι θαλάσσης,

ἐκ δ' ἑκατόμβην βῆσαν ἑκηβόλῳ Ἀπόλλωνι ·

ἐκ δὲ Χρυσηὶς νηὸς βῆ ποντοπόροιο.

τὴν μὲν ἔπειτ' ἐπὶ βωμὸν ἄγων πολύμητις Ὀδυσσεὺς   440

πατρὶ φίλῳ ἐν χερσὶ τίθει, καί μιν προσέειπεν ·

"ὦ Χρύση, πρό μ' ἔπεμψεν ἄναξ ἀνδρῶν Ἀγαμέμνων

παῖδά τε σοὶ ἀγέμεν, Φοίβῳ θ' ἱερὴν ἑκατόμβην

ῥέξαι ὑπὲρ Δαναῶν, ὄφρ' ἱλασόμεσθα ἄνακτα,
ὃς νῦν Ἀργείοισι πολύστονα κήδε' ἐφῆκεν." 445
ὣς εἰπὼν ἐν χερσὶ τίθει, ὁ δὲ δέξατο χαίρων
παῖδα φίλην. τοὶ δ' ὦκα θεῷ ἱερὴν ἑκατόμβην
ἑξείης ἔστησαν ἐΰδμητον περὶ βωμόν,
χερνίψαντο δ' ἔπειτα καὶ οὐλοχύτας ἀνέλοντο. 449

402. 436. As the Greeks are not to make a long stay, they merely anchor their ship, and do not draw it out of the water upon the land, as they would otherwise. **κατὰ δὲ πρυμνῆσι' ἔδησαν**, *i.e.* the ship was rowed in close to land, and then turned around so that the stern pointed landward. The stern was then made fast to shore by means of the stern-cables (πρυμνήσια), while the prow was prevented from swinging by means of the anchor-stones (εὐναί), attached to cables and thrown out on either side of the ship well forward.   437. **ἐπὶ ϝρηγμῖνι**.

438. **βῆσαν**: causative, 1069. - - **βῆσαν ϝεκηβόλῳ** : 526.

439. **νηός** : 987.

440. **ἐπὶ βωμὸν ἄγων** : to make the god a witness of the transaction ; cf. "before the face of Jehovah," in the O. T: — **ἄγων**, 1108, note 2.

441. **ἐν χερσὶ τίθει** may mean no more than "gave into the charge of "; as in another situation the poet says ἦ (*he spoke*) ῥα καὶ ἵππον ἄγων μεγαθύμου Νέστορος υἱὸς ἐν χείρεσσι τίθει Μενελάου. (Be sure to translate this sentence !)

443. **ἀγέμεν** : inf. to denote purpose, 1107, 10.

444. **ῥέξαι** : inf. to denote purpose, 1107, 10. — **ἱλασόμεσθα** : 800.

447. **τοί** [ὁ, ἡ, τό] : nom. plur. masc.

LESSON LXV

ILIAD, 450-461

403. *Optional :*

404.   VOCABULARY

ἀν-έχω (σεχ-, σχ-), ἀνέξω (ἀνασχή-σω), ἀνέσχον (ἀνέσχεθον), ἀνό-χωκα, ἀνέσχημαι* hold up, raise, endure, suffer.

αὐερύω (= ἀν-ϝερυω = ἀϝ-ϝερυω: ϝε-ρυ-, ϝρῡ-), αὐέρυσα (= ἀνεϝερυσα, 837) draw up (the head).

δέρω (δερ-, δαρ-), δερέω*, ἔδειρα, δέδαρμαι*, ἐδάρην* skin, flay.

δί-πτυξ, υχος double, twofold.

ἐκ-τάμ-νω, ἐξέταμον cut out.

ἐπι-κραιαίνω (κραν-), ἐπεκρήηνα accomplish, perform, fulfill (in addition).

ἠμέν correl. with ἠδέ, surely, truly, on the one hand.

ἴπ-τομαι*, ἴψομαι, ἰψάμην crush, overwhelm, punish, afflict.

καλύπτω (καλυβ-), καλύψω, ἐκάλυψα, κεκάλυμμαι, ἐκαλύφθην cover, conceal, hide, envelop.

πάρος formerly, of old, before this.

ποιέ-ω, ποιήσω, ἐποίησα, πεποίηκα*, πεποίημαι, ἐποιήθην* do, make, perform, execute, cause, effect, fashion, build, produce.

προ-βάλλω (βαλ-, βλη-), προβαλέω, προέβαλον, προβέβληκα, προβέβλημαι, προεβλήθην* cast, throw forward.

σφάζω (σφαγ-), σφάξω*, ἔσφαξα, ἔσφαγμαι, ἐσφάχθην† cut the throat, slaughter, slay.

ὠμο-θετέ-ω, ὠμοθέτησα place raw meat upon.

Derivatives: epi-dermis, pachy-derm, taxi-dermist, dermato-logy; di-ptych; eu-calyptus, apo-calypse, -calyptic; poet.

405. Read and translate:

Iliad, 450–461

τοῖσιν δὲ Χρύσης μεγάλ' εὔχετο χεῖρας ἀνασχών·   450
" κλῦθί μευ ἀργυρότοξ', ὃς Χρύσην ἀμφιβέβηκας
Κίλλαν τε ζαθέην, Τενέδοιό τε ἶφι ἀνάσσεις·
ἠμὲν δή ποτ' ἐμεῦ πάρος ἔκλυες εὐξαμένοιο,
τίμησας μὲν ἐμέ, μέγα δ' ἴψαο λαὸν Ἀχαιῶν·
ἠδ' ἔτι καὶ νῦν μοι τόδ' ἐπικρήηνον ἐέλδωρ·   455
ἤδη νῦν Δαναοῖσιν ἀεικέα λοιγὸν ἄμυνον."

ὣς ἔφατ' εὐχόμενος, τοῦ δ' ἔκλυε Φοῖβος Ἀπόλλων.
αὐτὰρ ἐπεί ῥ' εὔξαντο καὶ οὐλοχύτας προβάλοντο,
αὐέρυσαν μὲν πρῶτα καὶ ἔσφαξαν καὶ ἔδειραν,
μηρούς τ' ἐξέταμον κατά τε κνίσῃ ἐκάλυψαν   460
δίπτυχα ποιήσαντες, ἐπ' αὐτῶν δ' ὠμοθέτησαν.

406.   450. ἀνασχών: see the note on vs. 351.— τοῖσιν: 997. — μεγάλ' (α): 780–781.

451. μευ: 984.

452. Τενέδοιο: 985.

148

453. ἐμεῦ : 984.
454. ἐμέ : 525, 1167-1168. — μέγα : 780-781.
455. μοι : 997.
456. Δαναοῖσιν : 997.
457. τοῦ : 984.
460. δίπτυχα (κνίσην). — αὐτῶν (μηρῶν).

LESSON LXVI

ILIAD, 462-470

407. *Optional :*

408. VOCABULARY

αἴθ-οψ, οπος bright, shining.
δαί-νῡμι, δαίσω, ἔδαισα* (ἐδαισάμην),
ἐδαίσθην* (cf. δαίς) feast, banquet, entertain.
ἐδητύς, ύος, ἡ food, feed, eating.
ἐπι-στέφ-ω, ἐπιστέψω*, ἐπέστεψα*
(ἐπεστεψάμην), ἐπέστεμμαι*, ἐπεστέφθην* surround, encircle, fill
brimming full.
ἔρος, ου, ὁ love, desire, passion.
κοῦρος, ου, ὁ young man, noble.
κρητήρ, ῆρος, ὁ mixing bowl, punch
bowl.
λείβω, ἔλειψα pour a libation.
μῆρον, ου, τό thigh-piece, thighbone.

μιστύλ-λω slice, cut into bits.
ὀβελός, οῦ, ὁ spit.
οἶνος, ου, ὁ (ϝοῖνος) WINE.
ὀπτά-ω, ὤπτησα, ὠπτήθην cook,
roast, bake.
πατέομαι* (πατ-, πατε-), ἐπασ(σ)ά-
μην, πέπασμαι eat, feed.
πεμπ-ώβολον, ου, τό five-pronged
fork.
περι-φραδέως carefully.
πόνος, ου, ὁ work, labor, toil,
trouble.
πόσις, ιος, ἡ drink(ing).
ποτόν, οῦ, τό drink(ing).
σπλάγχνον, ου, τό vitals, haslets.
σχίζη, ης, ἡ split wood.

Derivatives : edi-ble ; Stephen ; Eros, erotic ; crater 621 ;
geo-ponic(s, al) ; sym-posium, potion, potable(s) ; spleen.

409. Read and translate :

Iliad, 462-470

καῖε δ᾽ ἐπὶ σχίζῃς ὁ γέρων, ἐπὶ δ᾽ αἴθοπα οἶνον
λεῖβε· νέοι δὲ παρ᾽ αὐτὸν ἔχον πεμπώβολα χερσίν.

αὐτὰρ ἐπεὶ κατὰ μῆρα κάη καὶ σπλάγχνα πάσαντο,
μίστυλλόν τ᾽ ἄρα τἆλλα καὶ ἀμφ᾽ ὀβελοῖσιν ἔπειραν,   465
ὤπτησάν τε περιφραδέως, ἐρύσαντό τε πάντα.
αὐτὰρ ἐπεὶ παύσαντο πόνου τετύκοντό τε δαῖτα
δαίνυντ᾽, οὐδέ τι θυμὸς ἐδεύετο δαιτὸς ἐΐσης.
αὐτὰρ ἐπεὶ πόσιος καὶ ἐδητύος ἐξ ἔρον ἔντο,
κοῦροι μὲν κρητῆρας ἐπεστέψαντο ποτοῖο,   470

A CRETAN CUPBEARER
Museum of Candia, Crete
A fresco-painting from the
palace of Gnossus. The youth
carries a silver cup ornamented
with gold. His waist is tightly
drawn in by a girdle, his hair is
dark and curly ; his profile is al-
most classically Greek.

410. 462. αἴθοπα ϝοῖνον. — ἐπί : 1048-
1049.
463. χερσίν : 1005, 1009.
464. κατὰ μῆρα κάη : *were consumed* ;
since they were for the gods, while the wor-
shipers tasted of the various parts in order
to have a share in the sacrifice. See note
to vs. 471, § 414. — κατά : 1048–1049.
465. τἆλλα : crasis, 587.
467. πόνου : 987.
468. δαιτός : 986.
469. πόσιος, ἐδητύος : 979, 3.
470. ποτοῖο : 986. The wine was mixed
with water, just as is the custom among
the peasants of modern Greece. " For as it
is hurtful to drink wine or water alone ;
and as wine mingled with water is pleasant
and delighteth the taste : even so speech
finely framed delighteth the ears of them
that read the story." The Greeks usually
mixed them in the proportion of three
parts of wine to two of water ; but the
poet Hesiod recommends one part of wine
to three of water. The later Greeks, who
lacked the stern simplicity of the rustic poet,
claimed that this would be more suitable as
a drink for fishes than for men.

[411-413]

LESSON LXVII

Iliad, 471–479

411. *Optional :*

412. VOCABULARY

ἀν-άγ-ω, ἀνάξω, ἀνήγαγον, ἀνῆχα**, ἀνῆγμαι*, ἀνήχθην* lead forth, set out, go forth, drive, carry.

δέπας, αος, τό cup, goblet.

ἐπ-άρχ-ω, ἐπάρξω, ἐπῆρξα, ἐπῆργμαι*, ἐπήρχθην* begin, perform the initiatory rites.

ἠέλιος, ου, ὁ sun.

ἦμος when.

ἠρι-γένειος, α, ον early-born.

Ἠώς, Ἠόος, ἡ Eos, goddess of dawn, dawn.

ἵκμενος, η, ον favorable, welcome.

κατα-δύ-ω, καταδύσω, κατέδῦσα, (κατέδῦν), καταδέδῡκα, καταδέδυμαι*, κατεδύθην* go down, sink, set, dive.

κνέφας, αος, τό darkness, night, gloom.

κοιμά-ω (cf. κεῖμαι), κοιμήσω*, ἐκοίμησα, ἐκοιμήθην (lull to) sleep, slumber, lie down.

μέλπ-ω, μέλψω*, ἔμελψα* sing, dance, hymn, chant.

μολπή, ῆς, ἡ dance, song, singing, hymn(ing), dancing.

νωμά-ω, νωμήσω*, ἐνώμησα distribute, apportion, handle easily, brandish.

οὖρος, ου, ὁ breeze, wind.

παιήων, ονος, ὁ paean, song of praise.

παν-ημέριος, η, ον all day long.

ῥοδο-δάκτυλος, ον rosy-fingered.

τέρπω (τερπ-, ταρπ-, τραπ-), τέρψω* (τέρψομαι), ἔτερψα* (ἐτερψάμην), ἐτέρφθην (ἐτάρφθην, ἐτάρπην) please, delight, satisfy, sate, charm, rejoice.

Derivatives : cemetery ; rhodo-dendron ; dactyl(ic), ptero-dactyl ; terpsi-chorean.

413. Read and translate.

Iliad, 471–479

νώμησαν δ᾽ ἄρα πᾶσιν ἐπαρξάμενοι δεπάεσσιν,   471
οἱ δὲ πανημέριοι μολπῇ θεὸν ἱλάσκοντο,
καλὸν ἀείδοντες παιήονα, κοῦροι Ἀχαιῶν,
μέλποντες ἑκάεργον· ὁ δὲ φρένα τέρπετ᾽ ἀκούων.
ἦμος δ᾽ ἠέλιος κατέδυ καὶ ἐπὶ κνέφας ἦλθεν,   475
δὴ τότε κοιμήσαντο παρὰ πρυμνήσια νηός.

151

ἦμος δ᾽ ἠριγένεια φάνη ῥοδοδάκτυλος Ἠώς,
καὶ τότ᾽ ἔπειτ᾽ ἀνάγοντο μετὰ στρατὸν εὐρὺν Ἀχαιῶν·
τοῖσιν δ᾽ ἴκμενον οὖρον ἵει ἑκάεργος Ἀπόλλων.

414. 471. πᾶσιν : 995. — δεπάεσσιν : 1005. — ἐπαρξάμενοι refers to the beginning of their religious ceremony, which was performed in this case by each of those present pouring a few drops of wine from his cup as a libation before the drinking began.

472. μολπῇ : 1005, *with song and dance.*

473. παιήονα : 1012 (παίω, *strike*) : originally an epithet of Apollo, the "striker," "beater," "rapper," who heals by his magic stroke. Then the song having this word as a refrain ; cf. "Te Deum," a hymn of thanksgiving, which is a type of song so named from its opening words : "Te Deum laudamus."

474. μέλποντες ϝεκάϝεργον : *praising the free-worker with song and dance,* that is, singing a song of which Apollo was the theme, praising Apollo in song and dance, the most important part being the dance. The god can hear the song and see the dance, although he is far away in the land of the Ethiopians (vs. 424). — φρένα : 1014.

477. ῥοδοδάκτυλος : the old Greeks had observed the long streamers of the light of early dawn, and their never failing fancy had pictured them as the rosy fingers of a beautiful goddess.

LESSON LXVIII

ILIAD, 480–489

415. *Optional :*

416. VOCABULARY

ἄνεμος, ου, ὁ wind, breeze.

δια-πρήσσω (πραγ.), διαπρήξω, διέπρηξα, διαπέπρηγα†, διαπέπρηγμαι†, διεπρήχθην† go across, pass through, traverse, accomplish, pass over.

ἕρμα, ατος, τό beam, prop, support.

ἤπειρος, ου, ἡ (main)land, continent.

θέω (θευ-, θεϝ-), θεύσομαι run, speed.

ἰάχω (ϝιϝαχ-, ϝιϝαχε-), ἴαχα shout, howl, roar.

κῦμα, ατος, τό wave, billow.

λευκός, ή, όν white, shining.

μέσος, η, ον middle, midst, medium.

πετάννῡμι* (πετα-, πτα-), πετάσω*, ἐπέτασ(σ)α, πέπταμαι, ἐπετάσθην stretch, spread (out), unfurl, expand.

Πηλεύς, ῆος, ὁ Peleus.

152

πορ-φύρεος, η, ον dark, PURPLE, violet, glistening.

πρήθ-ω, πρήσω, ἔπρησα blow, burn, inflate.

σκίδ-ναμαι scatter, disperse.

στεῖρα, ης, ἡ cut-water, stem.

τα-νύ-ω (*for* τγ-νυ-ω, 597–598), τανύσω, ἐτάνυσ(σ)α, τετάνυσμαι, ἐτανύσθην stretch, place along.

ὑψοῦ high.

ψάμαθος, ου, ἡ sand (of the beach), dune.

Derivatives: anemone; porphyry.

417. Read and translate :

Iliad, 480–489

οἱ δ᾽ ἱστὸν στῆσαντ᾽ ἀνά θ᾽ ἱστία λευκὰ πέτασσαν ·　480
ἐν δ᾽ ἄνεμος πρῆσεν μέσον ἱστίον, ἀμφὶ δὲ κῦμα
στείρῃ πορφύρεον μεγάλ᾽ ἴαχε νηὸς ἰούσης ·
ἡ δ᾽ ἔθεεν κατὰ κῦμα διαπρήσσουσα κέλευθον.
αὐτὰρ ἐπεί ῥ᾽ ἵκοντο κατὰ στρατὸν εὐρὺν Ἀχαιῶν,
νῆα μὲν οἵ γε μέλαιναν ἐπ᾽ ἠπείροιο ἔρυσσαν　485
ὑψοῦ ἐπὶ ψαμάθοις, ὑπὸ δ᾽ ἔρματα μακρὰ τάνυσσαν,
αὐτοὶ δ᾽ ἐσκίδναντο κατὰ κλισίας τε νέας τε.
αὐτὰρ ὁ μήνιε νηυσὶ παρήμενος ὠκυπόροισιν
διογενὴς Πηλῆος υἱός, πόδας ὠκὺς Ἀχιλλεύς.　489

418. 484. κατά : *over against, off.*

480. ἀνά: 1048–1049.

481. μέσον ἱστίον : *the middle of the sail.* The Homeric ship had but one. — ἐν, ἀμφί : 1048–1049.

482. στείρῃ : 1009. — νηὸς ἰούσης : 979 : 1; 994, in the transitional stage between the dependent genitive (in this case the genitive of possession) and the genitive absolute.

483. κέλευθον : 1012.

486. ὑπό : 1048–1049.

489. υἱός : 1173, note. This verse is merely explanatory and descriptive of the ὁ in vs. 488. The poet brings us back for a moment and lets us catch another glimpse of Achilles in his sullen wrath, before leaving him for a long period.

LESSON LXIX

ILIAD, 490–499

419. *Optional:*

420. VOCABULARY

ἄκρος, η, ον sharp, high, utter.
ἄρχ-ω, ἄρξω, ἦρξα, ἦργμαι*, ἤρχθην*
begin, lead, rule, be first.
ἄτερ, *with gen.* 992, apart, away
from, without.
αὖθι here, there, in the same
place.
ἀϋτή, ῆς, ἡ battle-cry, war-whoop.
εὐρύ-οψ, οπος far-thundering, *cf.*
ὑψιβρεμέτης; (far-seeing?).
ἐφετμή, ῆς, ἡ command, behest, request, prescription.
ἠέριος, η, ον early (in the morning),
(clad in mist?).
κορυφή, ῆς, ἡ peak, summit, crest.

Κρονίδης, ᾱο, ὁ son of Cronus,
Zeus.
κῡδι-άνειρα *fem. adj.*, man-ennobling, bringing glory to men.
λήθ-ω, *with gen.*, 984, escape the
notice, be hidden; *mid.* forget.
ποθέ-ω, ποθήσω*, ἐπόθεσα (ἐπόθησα*),
yearn, long for (what is lacking), desire, lack, miss.
πολυ-δειράς, άδος many-ridged, with
many cliffs.
πωλέ-ομαι, πωλήσομαι, go, attend,
frequent, come, return.
φθι-νύθ-ω destroy, waste away, pine,
perish.

Derivatives: acro-polis, -bat(ic), -carpous, -spore, -megaly;
coryphaeus; Lethé, leth-al, -argy.

421. Read and translate :

Iliad, 490–499

οὔτε ποτ᾽ εἰς ἀγορὴν πωλέσκετο κυδιάνειραν   490
οὔτε ποτ᾽ ἐς πόλεμον, ἀλλὰ φθινύθεσκε φίλον κῆρ
αὖθι μένων, ποθέεσκε δ᾽ ἀυτήν τε πτόλεμόν τε.
ἀλλ᾽ ὅτε δή ῥ᾽ ἐκ τοῖο δυωδεκάτη γένετ᾽ ἠώς,
καὶ τότε δὴ πρὸς Ὄλυμπον ἴσαν θεοὶ αἰὲν ἐόντες
πάντες ἅμα, Ζεὺς δ᾽ ἦρχε. Θέτις δ᾽ οὐ λήθετ᾽ ἐφετμέων   495
παιδὸς ἑοῦ, ἀλλ᾽ ἥ γ᾽ ἀνεδύσετο κῦμα θαλάσσης,
ἠερίη δ᾽ ἀνέβη μέγαν οὐρανὸν Οὔλυμπόν τε.
εὗρεν δ᾽ εὐρύοπα Κρονίδην ἄτερ ἥμενον ἄλλων
ἀκροτάτῃ κορυφῇ πολυδειράδος Οὐλύμποιο.   499

422. 490. —πωλέσκετο : iterative, 900.

492. αὐτήν : always of three syllables (as may be seen from the breathing), and must not be confounded with αὐτήν [αὐτός, ή, ό] her(self).

491–492. φθινύθεσκε, ποθέεσκε : iterative, 900.

493. ἐκ τοῖο : "from *that* most important (point of time)," viz., the time when Achilles withdrew from the conflict and entreated his mother to obtain satisfaction for him from Zeus, referring to the beginning of the wrath, the day of the quarrel, so important for the action of the entire *Iliad*.

495. ἐφετμέων : 984.

497. οὐρανὸν Οὔλυμπόν τε : 1019.

498. ἄλλων : 992.

499. κορυφῇ : 1009.

LESSON LXX

ILIAD, 500–516

423. *Optional :*

424.   VOCABULARY

ἀνθερεών, ῶνος, ὁ beard, chin.

ἀπο-εῖπον speak out, deny, refuse.

ἅπτω (ἀφ-), ἅψω* (ἅψομαι), ἦψα, ἦμμαι, ἥφθην* *with gen.* 983, touch, lay hold of, attack, attach.

δεξιτερός, ή, όν right (hand), lucky.

δέος, δέος (δείους), τό fear, dread, timidity.

δεύτερος, η, ον second, succeeding, later.

εἴρομαι (= ἐρέω) (εἰρ-, εἰρε-), εἰρήσομαι, ask, inquire, question, seek.

ἐμ-φύ-ω, ἐμφύσω, ἐνέφῡσα (ἐνέφῡν) ἐμπέφυκα grow into, cling very closely.

κατα-νεύ-ω, κατανεύσω, κατένευσα, κατανένευκα* nod (down, assent).

κράτος, εος, τό power, might, rule, victory, strength, dominion.

νεφελ-ηγερέτα, ᾱο, ὁ cloud-gatherer, wrapped in clouds.

νημερτής, ές unerring, true, truthful, reliable, infallible, certain.

ὀφέλ-λω increase, magnify, exalt, swell.

σκαιός, ή, όν left (hand), unlucky.

τόφρα so long, meanwhile.

ὑπ-ίσχομαι (ἐχ-, σχ-, σχε-, *cf.* ἔχω) ὑποσχήσομαι, ὑπεσχόμην, ὑπέσχημαι* undertake, promise, assure.

Derivatives : dexter-ous; deutero-nomy, -gamy ; aristo-, auto-, demo-, demono-, gyneo-, pluto-, theo-cracy.

425. Read and translate :

Iliad, 500-516

καί ῥα πάροιθ' αὐτοῖο καθέζετο καὶ λάβε γούνων   500
σκαιῇ, δεξιτερῇ δ' ἄρ' ὑπ' ἀνθερεῶνος ἑλοῦσα
λισσομένη προσέειπε Δία Κρονίωνα ἄνακτα ·
" Ζεῦ πάτερ, εἴ ποτε δή σε μετ' ἀθανάτοισιν ὄνησα
ἢ ἔπει ἢ ἔργῳ, τόδε μοι κρήηνον ἐέλδωρ ·
τίμησόν μοι υἱόν, ὃς ὠκυμορώτατος ἄλλων   505
ἔπλετ' · ἀτάρ μιν νῦν γε ἄναξ ἀνδρῶν Ἀγαμέμνων
ἠτίμησεν · ἑλὼν γὰρ ἔχει γέρας, αὐτὸς ἀπούρας.
ἀλλὰ σύ πέρ μιν τῖσον, Ὀλύμπιε μητίετα Ζεῦ ·
τόφρα δ' ἐπὶ Τρώεσσι τίθει κράτος, ὄφρ' ἂν Ἀχαιοὶ
υἱὸν ἐμὸν τίσωσιν, ὀφέλλωσίν τέ ἑ τιμῇ."   510
ὣς φάτο · τὴν δ' οὔ τι προσέφη νεφεληγερέτα Ζεύς,
ἀλλ' ἀκέων δὴν ἧστο. Θέτις δ' ὡς ἥψατο γούνων,
ὣς ἔχετ' ἐμπεφυυῖα, καὶ εἴρετο δεύτερον αὖτις ·
" νημερτὲς μὲν δή μοι ὑπόσχεο καὶ κατάνευσον,
ἢ ἀπόειπ', ἐπεὶ οὔ τοι ἔπι δέος, ὄφρ' ἐὺ εἰδῶ,   515
ὅσσον ἐγὼ μετὰ πᾶσιν ἀτιμοτάτη θεός εἰμι."

426. 500. αὐτοῖο : 992. — γούνων : 983.
501. σκαιῇ (χειρί), δεξιτερῇ (χειρί) : 1005.
505. ἄλλων : ablatival genitive.
505-507. τίμησον, ἠτίμησεν are both emphatic, and in strong opposition and contrast.
509. τίθει : imperative, *grant.*
510. τῑμῇ : 1005.
512. γούνων : 983.
512-513. ὡς . . . ὡς : *as . . . so.* She demands a strict *yes* or *no.*
514. κατανεῦσον : negation was indicated by the ancient Greeks (and the custom still prevails among the modern Greeks) by an upward motion of the head, while affirmation was denoted by a downward nod.
515. ἔπι = ἔπεστι : 1048-1050, 2. — ἔπι δϝέος .

156

LESSON LXXI

427. Optional :

Iliad, 517-527

428.

VOCABULARY

ἀπατηλός, ή, όν deceitful, false.
ἀπο-στείχω (στειχ-, στιχ-), ἀπέστι-
χον depart, step off, march away.
ἀ-τελεύτητος, η, ον unaccomplished.
ἐρέθ-ω vex, enrage, tease, torment.
ἐχθο-δοπέ-ω, ἠχθοδόπησα engage in
hostility with, be hateful.
κεφαλή, ῆς, ἡ head.
λοίγιος, η, ον dreadful, accursed,
horrible, nasty, deadly.
μέλω (μελ-, μελε-), μελήσω, μέμηλα,

μεμέλημαι* (μέμβλεμαι), ἐμελήθην*
be a concern, be a care.
νεικέω (νεικεσ-), νεικέσ(σ)ω, ἐνεί-
κεσ(σ)α struggle, contend, revile,
quarrel, fight.
ὀχθέ-ω, ὤχθησα be vexed, be dis-
pleased, be worried.
παλιν-άγρετος, η, ον revocable, to be
taken back.
τέκμωρ neut. indecl., surety, pledge
sign, goal, limit.

Derivatives : a-cephalic, cephal-algi(a, c), cephalo-pod,
Bu-cephalus, mega-cephalous.

429. Read and translate :

Iliad, 517-527

τὴν δὲ μέγ᾽ ὀχθήσας προσέφη νεφεληγερέτα Ζεύς ·
" ἦ δὴ λοίγια ἔργ᾽, ὅτε μ᾽ ἐχθοδοπῆσαι ἐφήσεις
Ἥρῃ, ὅτ᾽ ἄν μ᾽ ἐρέθῃσιν ὀνειδείοις ἐπέεσσιν.
ἡ δὲ καὶ αὕτως μ᾽ αἰὲν ἐν ἀθανάτοισι θεοῖσιν   520
νεικεῖ, καί τέ μέ φησι μάχῃ Τρώεσσιν ἀρήγειν.
ἀλλὰ σὺ μὲν νῦν αὖτις ἀπόστιχε, μή τι νοήσῃ
Ἥρη · ἐμοὶ δέ κε ταῦτα μελήσεται, ὄφρα τελέσσω.
εἰ δ᾽ ἄγε τοι κεφαλῇ κατανεύσομαι, ὄφρα πεποίθῃς ·
τοῦτο γὰρ ἐξ ἐμέθεν γε μετ᾽ ἀθανάτοισι μέγιστον   525
τέκμωρ · οὐ γὰρ ἐμὸν παλινάγρετον οὐδ᾽ ἀπατηλὸν
οὐδ᾽ ἀτελεύτητον, ὅ τι κεν κεφαλῇ κατανεύσω."

430. 518. λοίγια ἔργα (τάδ᾽ ἔσσεται) : " a nasty mess."

519. Ἥρῃ : 1007. — ἐπέεσσιν : 1005. Hera's name occupies the most important position in the verse, and in the word order, as again in vs. 523.

520. καὶ αὔτως: *even as it is* (without any further provocation).

521. με : 971. — μάχῃ: 1005 (1009). — Τρώεσσιν : 996.

523. μελήσεται : 973, 1.

524. κεφαλῇ : 1005.

526. τέκμωρ (ἐστίν). — παλινάγρετον (ἐστίν).

527. κατανεύσω: aorist subjunctive.

LESSON LXXII

431. *Optional :*

ILIAD, 528–535

432.   VOCABULARY

αἰγλήεις, εσσα, εν bright, shining, gleaming.

ἄλ-λομαι, ἀλέομαι*, ἄλμην jump, leap.

ἀ-μβρόσιος, η, ον ambrosial, immortal, divine, deathless, heavenly.

ἅ-πᾱς, ἅ-πᾱσα, ἅ-παν all, entire, whole, all together.

βαθύς, εἶα, ύ deep, profound.

βουλεύ-ω, βουλεύσω, ἐβούλευσα, βεβούλευκα*, βεβούλευμαι*, ἐβουλεύθην* plan, counsel, advise, deliberate.

δια-τμήγω (τμηγ-, τμαγ-), διατμήξω*, διέτμηξα (διέτμαγον), διετμάγην separate, part, divide, cut apart, split.

ἕδος, εος, τό SEAT, abode, habitation, home.

ἐλ-ελίζω* (ἐλικ-), ἐλέλιξα, ἐλελίχθην shake, twirl, twist, coil, make tremble, brandish.

ἐν-αντίος, η, ον opposite, facing, before, to meet.

ἐπ-έρχομαι (ἐρχ-, ἐλθ-, ἐλευθ-, ἐλυθ-), ἐπελεύσομαι, ἐπῆλθον (ἐπήλυθον), ἐπελήλυθα (ἐπειλήλουθα) come (upon, to, toward), attack.

ἐπι-ρρώ-ομαι, ἐπερρωσάμην flow down, fall down.

κάρη, κρᾱτός (κάρητος), τό head, peak, summit.

κυάνεος, η, ον dark (blue), black, dusky (1168).

νεύ-ω, νεύσω, ἔνευσα, νένευκα* nod.

ὀφρῦς, ύος, ἡ (eye)brow.

σφός, ή, όν one's own, their (own).

χαίτη, ης, ἡ hair, locks, tresses, mane.

Derivatives : salient, 600, 603–604; bathy-bius, -metry; cyan-ide.

433. Read and translate:

Iliad, 528–535

ἦ καὶ κυανέῃσιν ἐπ᾽ ὀφρύσι νεῦσε Κρονίων·
ἀμβρόσιαι δ᾽ ἄρα χαῖται ἐπερρώσαντο ἄνακτος
κρατὸς ἀπ᾽ ἀθανάτοιο, μέγαν δ᾽ ἐλέλιξεν Ὄλυμπον. 530
τώ γ᾽ ὣς βουλεύσαντε διέτμαγεν· ἡ μὲν ἔπειτα
εἰς ἅλα ἆλτο βαθεῖαν ἀπ᾽ αἰγλήεντος Ὀλύμπου,
Ζεὺς δὲ ἐὸν πρὸς δῶμα. θεοὶ δ᾽ ἅμα πάντες ἀνέσταν
ἐξ ἑδέων, σφοῦ πατρὸς ἐναντίον· οὐδέ τις ἔτλη
μεῖναι ἐπερχόμενον, ἀλλ᾽ ἀντίοι ἔσταν ἅπαντες. 535

434. 528. ἦ [ἠμί]: *he spoke.* — ὀφρύσι: 1005. — νεῦσε Κρονίων 524; 571, 1168.

According to ancient tradition, Phidias, the greatest of Greek sculptors, based on vss. 528–530 his conception of Zeus which found its embodiment in the greatest and most famous work of art of the ancient world, his statue of the Olympian Zeus, made of gold and ivory, of colossal size, and reckoned as one of the seven wonders of the ancient world.

531. διέτμαγεν = διετμάγησαν. — ἡ μὲν ... Ζεὺς δὲ ... : zeugma.

534. πατρός: 992.

LESSON LXXIII

ILIAD, 536–550

435. *Optional:*

436. VOCABULARY

ἀ-γνο(ι)έ-ω, ἠγνοίησα, fail to notice, be ignorant of, fail to observe.

ἅλιος, η, ον of the sea, marine.

ἀπο-νόσφι(ν) apart, away (from).

ἀργυρό-πεζος, α, ον silvery footed.

αὖ anew, again, a second time, but now. δὴ αὖ, 586.

δι-είρομαι (εἰρ-, εἰρε-), διειρήσομαι inquire into, ask about item by item.

δικάζω (δικαδ-), δικάσω*, ἐδίκασ(σ)α, δεδίκασμαι*, ἐδικάσθην* judge, decide.

δολο-μήτης, āο, ὁ deceiver, craftyminded.

ἕκαστος, η, ον each, every.

ἐπι-εικής, ές suitable, fitting, proper,
　becoming, decent.

ἐπι-έλπω (ϝελπ-, ϝολπ-), ἐπέολπα
　perf., hope (for), wish (for), de-
　sire, expect.

θρόνος, ου, ὁ throne, seat, armchair.

κερτόμιος, η, ον biting, cutting,
　sharp, bitter, contemptuous.

κρυπτάδιος, η, ον hidden, secret.

μετ-αλλά-ω, μεταλλήσω*, μετάλλησα
　inquire after, seek to know,

search after.

μη-δέ and not, neither, nor.

πρότερος, η, ον former, sooner, older,
　before.

συμ-φράζομαι (φραδ-), συμφράσ(σ)ο-
　μαι, συνεφρασ(σ)άμην, συμπέφρα-
　σμαι*, συνεφράσθην devise plans
　with, counsel together.

χαλεπός, ή, όν hard, harsh, severe,
　stern, cruel, difficult.

Derivatives : metal-l-ic, -urgy ; hysteron proteron.

437. Read and translate :

Iliad, 536–550

ὣς ὁ μὲν ἔνθα καθέζετ᾽ ἐπὶ θρόνου· οὐδέ μιν Ἥρη　　536
ἠγνοίησεν ἰδοῦσ᾽, ὅτι οἱ συμφράσσατο βουλὰς
ἀργυρόπεζα Θέτις, θυγάτηρ ἁλίοιο γέροντος.
αὐτίκα κερτομίοισι Δία Κρονίωνα προσηύδα·
" τίς δὴ αὖ τοι, δολομῆτα, θεῶν συμφράσσατο βουλάς ;　540
αἰεί τοι φίλον ἐστὶν, ἐμεῦ ἀπονόσφιν ἐόντα
κρυπτάδια φρονέοντα δικαζέμεν· οὐδέ τί πώ μοι
πρόφρων τέτληκας εἰπεῖν ἔπος, ὅττι νοήσῃς."
　τὴν δ᾽ ἠμείβετ᾽ ἔπειτα πατὴρ ἀνδρῶν τε θεῶν τε·
"Ἥρη, μὴ δὴ πάντας ἐμοὺς ἐπιέλπεο μύθους　　545
εἰδήσειν· χαλεποί τοι ἔσοντ᾽ ἀλόχῳ περ ἐούσῃ.
ἀλλ᾽ ὃν μέν κ᾽ ἐπιεικὲς ἀκουέμεν, οὔ τις ἔπειτα
οὔτε θεῶν πρότερος τόν γ᾽ εἴσεται οὔτ᾽ ἀνθρώπων·
ὃν δέ κ᾽ ἐγὼν ἀπάνευθε θεῶν ἐθέλωμι νοῆσαι,
μή τι σὺ ταῦτα ἔκαστα διείρεο μηδὲ μετάλλα."　　550

438. 537. οἱ : 1004. — ἠγνοίησεν = ἠγνόησεν : 1168, 571.

538. The "Old Man of the Sea" was Nereus.

539. κερτομίοισι (μύθοισιν) : 1005.

540. τοι : 1004.

541. ἐμεῦ : 992. — ἐόντα : accusative to agree with the implied subject
of δικαζέμεν, rather than the dative to agree with τοί its antecedent.

543. **πρόφρων** receives emphasis from its position.

546. **ἐούση** : 1109, 6. — **χαλεποί** : 1023.

549. **θεῶν** : 992. — **ἐθέλω(μι)** : subjunctive.

LESSON LXXIV

ILIAD, 551–572

439. *Optional :*

440.   VOCABULARY

ἄαπτος, ον untouchable, invincible.

αἰνῶς terribly, dreadfully, awfully.

βο-ῶπις, ιδος calm-eyed, large-eyed, ox-eyed.

δαιμόνιος, η, ον possessed by a dæmon, good friend ; crazy, foolish, wretch.

ἔμ-πης nevertheless, for all that, by all means, absolutely, completely.

ἐπι-γνάμπ-τω, ἐπιγνάμψω*, ἐπέγναμ-ψα, ἐπεγνάμφθην bend, curb, subdue, win over.

ἐτ-ήτυμος, η, ον true, unfailing, sure, real, actual.

εὔκηλος, η, ον undisturbed, in peace, in calm, quiet.

ἦρα *indecl. neut. plur.* favor, benefit, pleasure, kindness, protection.

Ἥφαιστος, ου, ὁ Hephaestus, *the*

lame god of fire.

καθ-ῆμαι (ἡσ-) sit down, be seated.

κλυτο-τέχνης, ες renowned for skill in handicraft, of renowned skill.

λίην exceedingly, very, especially.

μᾶλλον [μάλα] more, rather, preferably.

μέλλω (μελλ-, μελλε-), μελλήσω*, ἐμέλλησα* be about, be destined.

Οὐρανίων, ωνος, ὁ, ἡ dweller of heaven, divinity, god(dess).

παρ-εῖπον *2d aor.,* persuade, cajole, win over, urge, outwit, delude, beguile, talk over.

ποῖος, η, ον what (sort) ? what kind ?

πρήσσω (πρᾱγ-), πρήξω, ἔπρηξα, πέ-πρηγα†, πέπρηγμαι†, ἐπρήχθην† carry through, do, accomplish, act, perform.

Derivatives : etymo-logy ; poly-, pyro-technic(al), technique ; practice, pragmati(sm, c, st), 621,

441. Read and translate :

161

Iliad, 551–572

τὸν δ᾽ ἠμείβετ᾽ ἔπειτα βοῶπις πότνια Ἥρη ·   551
" αἰνότατε Κρονίδη, ποῖον τὸν μῦθον ἔειπες.
καὶ λίην σε πάρος γ᾽ οὔτ᾽ εἴρομαι οὔτε μεταλλῶ,
ἀλλὰ μάλ᾽ εὔκηλος τὰ φράζεαι, ἄσσ᾽ ἐθέλῃσθα ·
νῦν δ᾽ αἰνῶς δείδοικα κατὰ φρένα, μή σε παρείπῃ   555
ἀργυρόπεζα Θέτις, θυγάτηρ ἁλίοιο γέροντος ·
ἠερίη γὰρ σοί γε παρέζετο καὶ λάβε γούνων ·
τῇ σ᾽ ὀΐω κατανεῦσαι ἐτήτυμον, ὡς Ἀχιλῆα
τιμήσεις, ὀλέσεις δὲ πολέας ἐπὶ νηυσὶν Ἀχαιῶν."
τὴν δ᾽ ἀπαμειβόμενος προσέφη νεφεληγερέτα Ζεύς ·   560
" δαιμονίη, αἰεὶ μὲν ὀίεαι, οὐδέ σε λήθω,
πρῆξαι δ᾽ ἔμπης οὔ τι δυνήσεαι, ἀλλ᾽ ἀπὸ θυμοῦ
μᾶλλον ἐμοὶ ἔσεαι · τὸ δέ τοι καὶ ῥίγιον ἔσται.
εἰ δ᾽ οὕτω τοῦτ᾽ ἐστίν, ἐμοὶ μέλλει φίλον εἶναι.
ἀλλ᾽ ἀκέουσα κάθησο, ἐμῷ δ᾽ ἐπιπείθεο μύθῳ,   565
μή νύ τοι οὐ χραίσμωσιν, ὅσοι θεοί εἰσ᾽ ἐν Ὀλύμπῳ,
ἆσσον ἰόνθ᾽, ὅτε κέν τοι ἀάπτους χεῖρας ἐφείω."
ὣς ἔφατ᾽, ἔδεισεν δὲ βοῶπις πότνια Ἥρη,
καί ῥ᾽ ἀκέουσα καθῆστο, ἐπιγνάμψασα φίλον κῆρ ·
ὤχθησαν δ᾽ ἀνὰ δῶμα Διὸς θεοὶ Οὐρανίωνες ·   570
τοῖσιν δ᾽ Ἥφαιστος κλυτοτέχνης ἦρχ᾽ ἀγορεύειν,
μητρὶ φίλῃ ἐπὶ ἦρα φέρων, λευκωλένῳ Ἥρῃ ·

442. 552. Not a question, but an indignant exclamation.
557. σοί : 1004. — γούνων : 983.
562. ἀπὸ θῡμοῦ : *further from my heart, i.e.* you will lose my affections.
565. ἀκέουσα : translate by another imperative, " But shut up and sit down." — μύθῳ : 996.
567. ἐφείω must be understood of blows as violent as Zeus had the power to deliver them. — ἰόνθ᾽ (ἰόντα) (με).

LESSON LXXV

ILIAD, 573-589

443. Optional ·

444. VOCABULARY

ἀμφι-κύπελλον, ου, τό double cup (goblet) ; *it may be turned upside down, the bottom forming another receptacle.*

ἀν-ἀίσσω (Ϝαι-Ϝικ-), ἀνάιξω, ἀνήιξα, ἀνηίχθην start up, dart up, spring up.

ἀν-εκτός, ή, όν endurable, tolerable, bearable. (ἀνέχω : 829, note.)

ἀντι-φέρω (φερ-, οἰ-, ἐνεκ-), ἀντοίσω bear against, oppose.

ἀργαλέος, η, ον horrible, terrible, awful, cruel, difficult.

ἀστεροπητής, ᾶο, ὁ hurler of lightning.

ἐλα-ύν-ω (*cf.* ἐλάω) drive, carry on, strike, push, press.

ἐριδαίνω (ἐριδαν-) quarrel, bicker.

ἦδος, εος, τό use, utility, advantage, superiority.

θείνω (θεν-), θενέω*, ἔθεινα strike, hit, beat.

ἵλᾶος, η, ον propitious, kindly, gentle, favorable.

καθ-άπτω (ἁφ-), καθάψω* (καθάψομαι), καθῆψα, καθῆμμαι, καθήφθην* attack, lay hold, accost, address.

κολῳός, οῦ, ὁ brawl, wrangling, quarrel.

μαλακός, ή, όν soft, gentle, tender, mild.

νῑκά-ω, νῑκήσω, ἐνίκησα, νενίκηκα*, νενίκημαι*, ἐνῑκήθην conquer, prevail, surpass.

ὀφθαλμός, οῦ, ὁ eye, sight.

παρά-φημι (φη-, φα-), παραφήσω, παρέφησα* advise, counsel, urge, persuade.

στυφελίζω (στυφελιγ-), ἐστυφέλιξα strike, thrust, hurl.

ταράσσω* (ταραχ-), ταράξω*, ἐτάραξα, τετρηχα, τετάραγμαι*, ἐταράχθην* disturb violently, throw into confusion ; *perf.*, be disturbed.

Derivatives : Niké ; ophthalm-ic, -ia, -o-logy.

445. Read and translate:

ILIAD, 573-589

"ἦ δὴ λοίγια ἔργα τάδ᾽ ἔσσεται οὐδ᾽ ἔτ᾽ ἀνεκτά,
εἰ δὴ σφὼ ἕνεκα θνητῶν ἐριδαίνετον ὧδε,
ἐν δὲ θεοῖσι κολῳὸν ἐλαύνετον · οὐδέ τι δαιτὸς   575
ἐσθλῆς ἔσσεται ἦδος, ἐπεὶ τὰ χερείονα νικᾷ.
μητρὶ δ᾽ ἐγὼ παράφημι, καὶ αὐτῇ περ νοεούσῃ,
πατρὶ φίλῳ ἐπὶ ἦρα φέρειν Διί, ὄφρα μὴ αὖτε

163

νεικείῃσι πατήρ, σὺν δ᾽ ἡμῖν δαῖτα ταράξῃ.
εἴ περ γάρ κ᾽ ἐθέλῃσιν Ὀλύμπιος ἀστεροπητὴς   580
ἐξ ἑδέων στυφελίξαι · ὁ γὰρ πολὺ φέρτατός ἐστιν.
ἀλλὰ σὺ τόν γ᾽ ἐπέεσσι καθάπτεσθαι μαλακοῖσιν ·
αὐτίκ᾽ ἔπειθ᾽ ἵλαος Ὀλύμπιος ἔσσεται ἡμῖν."
ὣς ἄρ᾽ ἔφη, καὶ ἀναΐξας δέπας ἀμφικύπελλον
μητρὶ φίλῃ ἐν χειρὶ τίθει, καί μιν προσέειπεν ·   585
" τέτλαθι, μῆτερ ἐμή, καὶ ἀνάσχεο, κηδομένη περ,
μή σε φίλην περ ἐοῦσαν ἐν ὀφθαλμοῖσιν ἴδωμαι
θεινομένην · τότε δ᾽ οὔ τι δυνήσομαι ἀχνύμενός περ
χραισμεῖν · ἀργαλέος γὰρ Ὀλύμπιος ἀντιφέρεσθαι.   589

446. 573. τάδ᾽(ε) ἔσσεται : 973, 1.

574–575. ἕνεκα θνητῶν, contemptuously, contrasted with ἐν θεοῖσι. Hephaestus essays the role of mediator, as Nestor did between Agamemnon and Achilles, but with infinitely better success.

575. δαιτός : 979, 3.

576. τά, said with a deprecating gesture. — νῑκᾷ (νῑκάει) : 584-585, 973, 1.

577. μητρί : 1004. — νοεούσῃ : 1109, 6.

578. ἐπί (1048-1049). — ἦρα φέρειν : show kindness toward.

579. νεικείῃσι, ταράξῃ : 1115. — σύν : 1048-1049.

580. ἐθέλῃσιν : 1135. — 580-581 : a good example of the figure known as aposiopesis, i.e. instead of completing his sentence, the god breaks off abruptly, and leaves to the imagination, as being beyond the power of adequate expression in words, just what Zeus might do to them all, if he should take the notion.

581. πολύ : 780-781.

582. ἐπέεσσιν : 1005. — καθάπτεσθαι : 1107, 11.

587. ἴδωμαι : 1115.

588. τι : 780-781.

589. Ὀλύμπιος (ἐστι) ; the Olympian (1027) = Zeus.

LESSON LXXVI

447. *Optional :*

ILIAD, 590–598

448. VOCABULARY

ἀλέξω (ἀλεξ-, ἀλεξε-, ἀλεκ-, ἀλκ-), ἀλεξήσω, ἠλέξησα (ἄλαλκον) ward off, defend, protect.

ἄλλο-τε at another time.

βηλός, οῦ, ὁ threshold.

ἐν-δέξιος, η, ον, to(ward) the right.

ἔν-ειμι (ἐσ-), ἐνέσ(σ)ομαι be in.

ἦμαρ, ἤματος, τό day.

θε-σπέσιος, η, ον divine, marvelous, divinely sounding.

κατα-πίπτω (πετ-, πτε-, πτη-), καταπεσέομαι, κατέπεσον, καταπέπτη(κ)α fall, drop.

κομίζω (κομιδ-), κομιῶ, ἐκόμισ(σ)α, κεκόμικα*, κεκόμισμαι*, ἐκομίσθην* bear, care for, attend, accompany.

κύπελλον, ου, τό cup, goblet.

Λῆμνος, ου, ἡ Lemnos, *an island in the Aegean near Troy.*

*μειδά-ω, ἐμείδησα smile, laugh.

μέ-μονα (μεν-, μον-, μα-) *perf. only,* be eager, desire greatly, strive zealously, intend, plan.

νέκταρ, αρος, τό NECTAR, *drink of the gods.*

οἰνο-χοέ-ω, οἰνοχοήσω*, ᾠνοχόησα pour wine, pour drink(s).

ῥίπ-τω, ῥίψω, ἔρρῑψα, ἔρρῑφα**, ἔρρῑμαι*, ἐρρίφ(θ)ην* hurl, dash, throw with a twirl, brandish.

Σίντιες, ων, οἱ Sintians.

τε-ταγ-ών (*2d aor. part. only*) touch, lay hold· of, seize.

Derivatives : Alex-ander.

449. Read and translate:

Iliad, 590–598

ἤδη γάρ με καὶ ἄλλοτ᾽ ἀλεξέμεναι μεμαῶτα   590
ῥῖψε ποδὸς τεταγὼν ἀπὸ βηλοῦ θεσπεσίοιο.
πᾶν δ᾽ ἦμαρ φερόμην, ἅμα δ᾽ ἠελίῳ καταδύντι
κάππεσον ἐν Λήμνῳ, ὀλίγος δ᾽ ἔτι θυμὸς ἐνῆεν·
ἔνθα με Σίντιες ἄνδρες ἄφαρ κομίσαντο πεσόντα."
ὣς φάτο, μείδησεν δὲ θεά, λευκώλενος Ἥρη,   595
μειδήσασα δὲ παιδὸς ἐδέξατο χειρὶ κύπελλον.
αὐτὰρ ὁ τοῖς ἄλλοισι θεοῖς ἐνδέξια πᾶσιν
οἰνοχόει γλυκὺ νέκταρ, ἀπὸ κρητῆρος ἀφύσσων.

450. 590. μεμαῶτα [μέμονα] : modifies με, object of ῥῦψε, vs. 591.

591. ποδός : 983.

592. ἦμαρ : 1015.

593. κάππεσον = κατα-πεσον = κατ-πεσον, 608–609. — ἐν Λήμνῳ : Lemnos was considered the island of Hephaestus, the god of fire, because of the volcano, Mosychulus, situated there. — θῡμός : *breath, soul, life.*

594. Σίντιες : literally "brigands," a piratical folk.

595–596. μείδησεν, μειδήσασα : the repetition to show that there is no doubt but that Hera is in good spirits once more.

596. παιδός : 987. — χειρί : 1005.

597. θεοῖς : 997, *or* 1009.

598. οἰνοχόει : strictly "to pour wine," but the meaning of the first part of the compound soon became weakened, so that it came to mean to pour anything good to drink, such as the nectar of the gods. Thus in English we say that a *green black*berry is *red*, or we speak of a *steel* pen (penna = feather), a *monthly* or *weekly* journal (jour = day), a *golden* candle*stick*, etc.

LESSON LXXVII

ILIAD, 599–611

451. *Optional :*

452.   VOCABULARY

ἀμφι-γυήεις, εσσα, εν wobbly-kneed, bow-legged (*possibly* = skillful, ambidextrous).

ἄ-σβεστος, η, ον inextinguishable.

γέλος, ου, ὁ laughter.

ἐν-όρ-νῡμι, ἐνόρσω, ἐνῶρσα (ἐνώρορον), ἐνόρωρα, ἐνορώρεμαι rouse among, kindle among, excite.

ἧχι where.

καθ-εύδω (εὐδ-, εὑδε-), καθευδήσω* sleep, slumber, rest (in bed), lie (in bed).

κατα κείω desire to lie down (rest, repose, slumber).

λαμπρός, ή, όν bright, brilliant, shining, gleaming.

Μοῦσα, ης, ἡ muse.

ὄψ, ὀπός, ἡ voice, word, speech, language.

περι-καλλής, ές very beautiful, charming.

περι-κλυτός, ή, όν famous, very renowned.

ποι-πνύ-ω, ἐποίπνῡσα bustle, hurry, puff, pant.

πραπίς, ίδος, ἡ heart, mind, soul, diaphragm.

πρό-πᾱς, ᾶσα, αν all, entire, whole.

ὕπνος, ου, ὁ sleep, slumber.

φάος, εος, τό light, gleam, luminary.

φόρμιγξ, ιγγος, ἡ lyre, harp.

χρῡσό-θρονος, ον golden-throned, *possibly* with robes embroidered with golden flowers, θρόνα.

Derivatives : a-sbestos ; muse, music, museum ; pneumonia, -atic(s), 593–596 ; hypnot(ic, ism) ; phos-phorus, photo-graph(y), -meter, 584–585.

453. Read and translate :

Iliad, 599–611

ἄσβεστος δ' ἄρ' ἐνῶρτο γέλος μακάρεσσι θεοῖσιν,
ὡς ἴδον Ἥφαιστον διὰ δώματα ποιπνύοντα.   600
ὣς τότε μὲν πρόπαν ἦμαρ ἐς ἠέλιον καταδύντα
δαίνυντ', οὐδέ τι θυμὸς ἐδεύετο δαιτὸς ἐίσης,
οὐ μὲν φόρμιγγος περικαλλέος, ἣν ἔχ' Ἀπόλλων,
Μουσάων θ', αἳ ἄειδον ἀμειβόμεναι ὀπὶ καλῇ.
αὐτὰρ ἐπεὶ κατέδυ λαμπρὸν φάος ἠελίοιο,   605
οἱ μὲν κακκείοντες ἔβαν οἰκόνδε ἕκαστος,
ἧχι ἑκάστῳ δῶμα περικλυτὸς ἀμφιγυήεις
Ἥφαιστος ποίησεν ἰδυίῃσι πραπίδεσσιν,
Ζεὺς δὲ πρὸς ὃν λέχος ἤι' Ὀλύμπιος ἀστεροπητής,
ἔνθα πάρος κοιμᾶθ', ὅτε μιν γλυκὺς ὕπνος ἱκάνοι ·   610
ἔνθα καθεῦδ' ἀναβάς, παρὰ δὲ χρυσόθρονος Ἥρη.

454. 599. The drinks were usually served in Olympus by the goddess Hebé, whose name has become a synonymn for feminine grace and maidenly beauty. In marked contrast to her is Hephaestus, rough, ungainly, and distressingly homely, who here makes his début as cupbearer to the gods, and goes through so many funny motions, like some primitive Charlie Chaplin, that all of them laugh most uproariously. — θεοῖσιν : 1004, 1009.

600. ποιπνύοντα is onomatopoetic ; we can hear the bow-legged, wobbly-kneed Hephaestus puffing as he bustles awkwardly around. Observe the heavy effect given to this verse by the spondaic ending.

602–604. δαιτός, φόρμιγγος, Μουσάων : 986. — ἀμειβόμεναι ὀπί, "antiphonally." The song was doubtless accompanied by the dance, as Homer tells us elsewhere that song and dance are the crown of the

feast; and thus the muses would be able to display their varied grace
and charms to the best advantage. The book thus begins with the
heroic and tragic figures of Achilles and Agamemnon, and ends with a
cabaret show among the gods of Olympus. — ὀπί : 1005.

606. κακκείοντες = κατακείοντες [κατακείω] : 608–609, 567.

607. ἑκάστῳ : 997.

608. πραπίδεσσιν : 1006.

609. δὲ πρός : 524. — πρὸς ϝόν, 526.

A GREEK BANQUET

From a vase painting by Duris

455. The first book of the *Iliad*, after its grim and gloomy beginning
amidst the tragedy of earthly life and its unending sorrows, closes amid
the laughter of the care-free blessed gods, feasting happily on Olympus,
" where, as they say, is the seat of the gods that standeth fast forever.
Not by winds is it shaken, nor ever wet with rain, nor doth the snow
come nigh thereto, but most clear air is spread about it cloudless, and
the white light floats over it. Therein the blessed gods are glad for all
their days." This alternate play of light and shade, of laughter and
of tears, of stern, dignified men, and frivolous, light-hearted gods, who
serve as their foil, is worked out by the poet with remarkable artistic
feeling and delicacy of touch. The scene on Olympus as contrasted
with the earlier action may best be compared to a satyr play, a kind of
burlesque show, which was regularly performed in ancient Athens at
the close of a series of tragedies, and for the same purpose, to relieve
the minds of the audience.

Calydonian boar hunt

Games at the funeral of Patroclus

Peleus, Thetis and the gods

Pursuit of Troilus by Achilles

Animal scenes, sphinxes, etc.

THE FRANÇOIS VASE

Archæological Museum, Florence

Found in an Etruscan grave in 1844. A black-figured terra cotta vase of about 600 B.C. It is nearly three feet in height and two and one half feet in diameter. The figures on the vase depict scenes from Greek mythology.

With surpassing art the poet has woven into the action and the narrative of this book the most important characters, both human and divine, of the entire poem.

"No book of Homer is so full of dramatic groups and situations as this: Apollo striding with his bow and ringing quiver; Thetis caressing the grieving and angry Achilles; Thetis before Zeus, clasping his knees and extending her right hand toward his chin; Zeus with his dark brows and ambrosial locks nodding a confirmation to his promise; Chryses with his filleted scepter and his gifts, before the two sons of Atreus; Odysseus at the altar of Apollo with the maiden whom he is restoring to her aged father, — with his companions and the hecatomb; Achilles in his rage drawing his sword from its sheath, calmed by Athena, who takes him by his long locks, — with Agamemnon before him and the other chiefs around him; the heralds of Agamemnon at the tent of Achilles, as Patroclus leads forth the fair Briseïs; Zeus and Hera on Olympus, with Hephaestus playing the part of Hebé; the assembly of the gods, Apollo playing the lyre, and the singing muses."

169

INTRODUCTION TO ATTIC GREEK

456. Dialects. — The Greek language was divided into a number of dialects, the most important groups of which were the Aeolic, Ionic (Ionic-Attic), and Doric.

457. Very closely related to Ionic is Attic, and both are usually grouped together as Ionic-Attic. In the great mass of their forms they are fundamentally alike, and differ only in minor details.

458. The Homeric poems are composed in what is known as the Homeric dialect, a mixture of Aeolic and Ionic, the bulk of the forms being Ionic (620).

459. Contraction. — Attic carries the contraction of vowels to a further extent than does any other of the Greek dialects, two or more vowels coming together and admitting of contraction practically never remaining uncontracted.

460. Hence one of the most important things for the student to do in passing from Homeric to Attic Greek is to memorize thoroughly the table of contractions (584–585).

461. In general vowels are contracted in Attic as in Homer (584–585), the only exceptions being that $\epsilon + o$ and $\epsilon + ov = ov$ in Attic instead of ϵv in Homer.

462. Treatment of ā in Attic. — After ϵ, ι, ρ, the η of Homer, when representing an earlier $\bar{a}$ (621), becomes $\bar{a}$ in Attic, except that $\rho \digamma \eta = \rho \eta$, as κόρη for κόρ $\digamma \eta$ = Homeric κούρη *maiden* and $\rho \sigma \eta = \rho \rho \eta$, as κόρρη for κόρση *one of the temples.*

463. If $\rho \eta$ is the product of the contraction of $\rho \epsilon a$ (584–585) it remained unchanged, as ὄρη = ὄρεα *mountains.*

170

464. Use of Vau. — Vau had gone entirely out of use in Attic before Attic literature begins, and it had no influence on Attic verse.

465. Consonantal change. — 1) σσ of Homer becomes ττ in Attic, as θάλασσα, πρήσσω of Homer become θάλαττα, πράττω in Attic; except that two sigmas brought together by inflection become σ, as ποσί for ποσσί (ποδσι), ἔπεσι for ἔπεσ-σι, τελέσαι for τελέσ-σαι.

2) ρσ of Homer becomes ρρ in Attic.

466. Inflection. — In the inflection of words, the chief differences between the Homeric and Attic forms are due to the greater extent to which the Attic dialect carries either contraction (584–585), or to which it carries metathesis of quantity (573).

467. Thus Homeric θαλασσάων, ἥρωι, ἥρωα, ἔπεος, ἔπεα, γέραος, γέραα, πόληος, βασιλῆος, βασιλῆα, βασιλήων, βασιλῆας, νηός, νηῶν regularly become in Attic θαλαττῶν, ἥρῳ, ἥρω, ἔπους, ἔπη, γέρως, γέρᾱ, πόλεως, βασιλέως, βασιλέᾱ, βασιλέων, βασιλέᾱς, νεώς, νεῶν.

THE DISCUS THROWER
(DISCOBOLUS)

Lancelotti Palace, Rome

Marble copy of the bronze original by Myron, a fifth century sculptor

468. Nouns and adjectives. — Attic had the following case endings, either not found or else very uncommon in Homer:

1) Dual, gen. and dat. end in -ιν instead of -ιιν.

2) Dual of the first decl., gen. and dat. ends in -αιν.

3) The dative plural of all three declensions regularly has the shorter forms : in the first declension -αις, in the second declension -οις, in the third declension -σι.

4) The gen. sing. masc. of the first declension ends in -ου.

5) The gen. sing. of nouns and adjectives with stems in ηυ, ι, υ is regularly -εως.

6) The acc. plur. of masc. and fem. nouns and adjectives with stems in ηυ, ι, υ, ες regularly ends in -εις.

7) Comparatives with stems in -ον, as ἀμείνων, may end in : ω in the acc. sing., masc. and fem., and in the nom., acc., and voc. plur. neuter; and may end in -ους in the nom., acc., and voc. plur. masc. and fem.

469. For the irregular "Attic Second Declension," and the declension of adjectives as ἵλεως, ων, of ναῦς, and of γραῦς see any good Greek grammar.

470. Pronouns. — For the declension of the personal, interrogative, indefinite, and reflexive pronouns, see any good Greek grammar.

471. Verbs. — Attic Greek has the future optative and future passive, entirely regular in formation, which may be easily learned from any good Greek grammar.

472. The middle optative, third plural, regularly ends in -ντο instead of in -ατο as in Homer; and -ατο is very rare as the ending of the third plural of Attic verbs.

473. For the Attic forms of regular -μι verbs, see any good Greek grammar.

474. For the Attic forms of the irregular verbs, εἰμί, εἶμι, φημί, ἦμαι, κεῖμαι, and οἶδα, see any good Greek grammar.

475. The first perfect active of verbs, as λέλυκα (904), is common and is the regular form in Attic Greek for verbs with *all* classes of stems.

476. In many second perfects with stems in π, β, κ, γ, the final mute of the stem is *aspirated* (619), π and β becoming φ, while κ and γ become χ. Thus πέπομφα [πέμπω], τέτριφα [τρίβω], ἦχα [ἄγω], δεδίωχα [διώκω].

477. Contracted nouns, adjectives, and verbs. — For the inflection of contract nouns, adjectives, and verbs, see any good Greek grammar.

478. The following table for Attic forms, corresponding to the table in 649 for Homeric forms, indicates the resultant endings produced by the fusion of the case endings with the stem of nouns and adjectives.

479. Table of Case Endings

FIRST DECLENSION		SECOND DECLENSION		THIRD DECLENSION	
MASC.	FEM.	M. & F.	NEUT.	M. & F.	NEUT.
ης, ᾱς	η, ᾰ, ᾱ	ος, (ους), ως[8]	ον, (ουν), ων[8]	ς (none)	—
ου, [εω[1]]	ης, ᾱς	ου,	ου, ω[8]	ος, ως[12], (ους)	ς, (φ[15])
ῃ, ᾳ	ῃ, ᾳ	ῳ,	ῳ	ι, [φ[13], η[14]]	ι, [φ[13], η[14]]
ην, ᾱν	ην, αν, ᾱν	ον, (ουν), ων[8]	ον, (ουν), ων[8]	α, ν, ω[16], ᾱ[17], (η[18])	—
η, ᾰ, ᾱ	η, ᾰ, ᾱ	ε, (ου), ς[8], [εω[9]]	ον, (ουν), ων[8]	ς none	—
ᾱ	ᾱ	ω	ω	ε, (ει, η[19], [ῡ[20]])	ε, (ει, ᾱ[21], [η[22]])
αιν	αιν	οιν, (ῳν[8])	οιν, (ῳν[8])	οιν, [(φν[23])]	οιν, [(φν[24])]
αι, [αισι[3], ᾱσι[4], ᾳσι[5], ησι[6], ᾱσι[7]]	ὡν, [εων[2]]	οι, (ῳ[8])	α, (ᾱ[10]), ω[8]	ες, ους[25], εις, [ς[26], ης[27]]	α, ω[28], (ᾱ[29], η[30])
	αι	ων	ων	ων	ων
	αι	οις, [οισι[11]], (ῳς[8])	α, (ᾱ[10]), ω[8]	σι	σι, [σσι[31]]
	ᾱς	ους, (ως[8])	α, (ᾱ[10]), ω[8]	ας, ᾱς[32], [33], ς, ους[25], εις, [ης[34] ως[35]]	α, ω[28], (ᾱ[29], η[30])

Forms in parentheses ( ) are contracted; those in square brackets [ ] are rare and need not be memorized.

1 Some proper names in Plat., Xen., Thuc., etc.
2 Ἀθηνέων Aristophanes and Plutarch.
3 Often in the poets and in inscr.; sometimes in Plato.
4 Occasionally in the poets, and in inscr.
5 In inscr.
6-7 In inscr. commonly, and in local adverbs, as θύρασι, ὥρασι, Ἀθήνησι, Θεσπιᾶσι, Πλαταιᾶσι, Ὀλυμπίασι, κτλ.
8 Attic 2d declension, several examples of which occur in the *Anab-asis*: adjectives as ἵλεως. The acc. sing. may end in ω, as ἕω.
9 Rare, as θεός, κτλ.
10 Irregularly contracted (η).
11 Very common in the drama; inscr. to 444; occasionally in Plato.
13 πόλεως, ἄστεως, βασιλέως, κτλ.

13 ἡδίῳ, κτλ.; also from contraction.
14 πόλῃ, κτλ. in inscrr. regularly 410–335.
16 ἡδίω, κτλ.; also from contraction.
18 ἀσφαλῆ, κτλ.
21 κέρᾳ, κτλ.
25 ἡδίους, κτλ.; also from contraction.
27 βασιλῆς, κτλ., regularly in inscrr. till 350 (always till 375), in Plato, and Thucydides, and should probably be restored in the works of all Attic authors written before 350.
28 ἡδίω, κτλ.; also from contractions.
30 ἄστη, κτλ.
33 ναῦς, βοῦς, ἰχθῦς, κτλ.

15 κέρᾳ, κτλ.
17 βασιλέᾱ, κτλ.
20 ἰχθῦ, κτλ.
23 ἤρων, κτλ. 24 κέρφν, κτλ.
22 ἄστη, κτλ.
26 ἤρων, ἄρκυς, ἰχθῦς, κτλ.
29 κέρᾱ, κτλ. 30 βασιλέᾱς, κτλ.
31 ἔτεσσι (inscr.).
34 βασιλῆς (Soph.). 35 ἤρως, κτλ.

SYNTAX

480. The differences in Homeric and Attic syntax can best be learned by the careful study of some good work on Attic prose composition.

481. The article. — In Attic Greek ὁ, ἡ, τό is regularly employed as the definite article (*the*), its absence ordinarily marking a noun as indefinite, as ὁ πόλεμος *the war*, πόλεμος *war*.

482. At times the article may be omitted, especially in poetry without marking the noun as indefinite.

483. At times it may represent the unemphatic possessive pronoun, as Κῦρος καταπεδήσᾱς ἀπὸ τοῦ ἅρματος τὸν θώρηκα ἐνέδῡ καὶ ἀναβὰς ἐπὶ τὸν ἵππον τὰ πάλτα εἰς τὰς χεῖρας ἔλαβε *Cyrus, having leaped down from his chariot, put on his breastplate, and having mounted his horse took his javelins in his hands.*

484. It may be employed, especially with adjectives and participles, in a generic sense, denoting a class, as ὁ ἄνθρωπος *man(kind)*, οἱ ἀγαθοί *the good*, ὁ βουλόμενος *anyone who wishes*, οἱ γέροντες *the aged.*

485. It may be used with proper names in familiar style, as ὁ Σωκράτης *Socrates.*

486. It is used in a variety of ways to form substantives :

1) With adjectives and participles, as οἱ πλούσιοι *the rich*, οἱ παρόντες *those present.*

2) With possessive pronouns, as οἱ σοί *your people*, τὰ ἡμέτερα *our possessions, our affairs.*

3) With genitives, as Θουκῡδίδης ὁ Ὀλόρου *Thucydides, son of Olorus.*

4) With locatives, as οἱ Μαραθῶνι καὶ Σαλαμῖνι *those (who fought) at Marathon and Salamis*, τὰ οἴκοι *affairs, things at home.*

5) With adverbs, as οἱ νῦν *the people of to-day*, οἱ τότε *those of that time*, οἱ ἐκεῖ *those over there.*

6) With prepositional phrases, as οἱ ἐν τῷ ἄστει *those in the city*, τὰ πρὸς τὸν πόλεμον *the things (needful) for the war.*

7) The neuter article is prefixed to any word or part of speech when considered merely as an expression, as τὸ λέγει the word "λέγει," τὸ γνῶθι σεαυτόν the (saying) "know thyself."

8) The neuter article in the singular, all cases, is used with the infinitive (articular infinitive), when emphasizing the substantive character of the infinitive. In this usage it is commonly translated by the English verbal noun in -ing, as τὸ καλῶς μάχεσθαι (the act of) fighting bravely, to fight bravely, τὸ γράφειν (nom.) writing, τοῦ γράφειν of writing, τῷ γράφειν to, or for writing, τὸ γράφειν (acc.) writing. NOTE. — The article is always thus used with the infinitive when the infinitive is construed with a preposition.

487. Verbal adjectives. — In addition to verbal adjectives in -τός, as found in Homer and denoting *possibility*, or merely as the equivalent of the perfect passive participle, Attic Greek has a verbal adjective in -τέος, similarly formed, and used with εἰμί (often omitted), expressing *necessity* or *duty*, and admitting of two constructions :

1) *Personal* (passive) construction. Only verbal nouns from transitive verbs can be thus employed, the verbal agreeing in gender and number with the subject. The agent is in the dative, as ὠφελητέα σοι ἡ πόλις ἐστί the state *must be benefited by you*, οὐ πρό γε τῆς ἀληθείας τιμητέος ἀνήρ a man *must not be honored before the truth*.

2) *Impersonal* (active) construction. In this construction, which is more frequent, the verbal is active in meaning and stands in the neuter nominative, usually singular, while its object is in the case which the finite verb would govern. The agent, if expressed, is usually in the dative, but is sometimes in the accusative as if dependent upon δεῖ, which has a meaning similar to that contained in these verbals, *one must*. Thus ἀσκητέον σοι τὴν ἀρετήν *you must cultivate virtue*, τοὺς φίλους εὐεργετητέον, τὴν πόλιν ὠφελητέον, τῶν βοσκημάτων ἐπιμελητέον *one must do favors for one's friends, benefit one's state, and care for one's cattle*, τὸν βουλόμενον εὐδαίμονα εἶναι σωφροσύνην διωκτέον καὶ ἀσκητέον *he who desires to be happy must pursue and cultivate temperance.*

175

488. ἄν in Attic. — Attic, which does not employ κέ(ν), has the following unhomeric uses of ἄν:

1) With past tenses, apparently as present conditional, as πολλοῦ ἂν ἄξιον ἦν τὸ πλουτεῖν εἰ καὶ τὸ χαίρειν αὐτῷ συνῆν *it would be worth a great deal to be wealthy if joy were associated with it.*

2) With past tenses it takes the place of the iteratives in -σκον, which are not found in Attic Greek, as ἔτρεπεν ἄν = τρέπεσκεν, ἔτρεψεν ἄν = τρέψασκεν.

3) The subjunctive with ἄν is found in general statements which are valid also for the future, where English employs the indicative present, as μαινόμεθα πάντες ὁπότ᾽ ἂν ὀργιζώμεθα, *we are all mad when we are angry.*

489–500. These sections, which are omitted from this book for the sake of brevity, refer to the standard Greek grammars. Those wishing to learn Attic Greek should now read some good Attic author, with a few sections from the grammar each day till the most important fundamentals of Attic Greek become thoroughly familiar. *Bon voyage!*

GRAMMAR

I. PHONOLOGY

501. The Greek alphabet has twenty-six letters :

FORM	SOUND	NAME	
A α	*a* as in father (when short as in *a*ha)	ἄλφα	alpha
B β	*b* as in *b*ite	βῆτα	beta
Γ γ	*g* as in *g*et (*never* soft as in obli*g*e)	γάμμα	gamma
Δ δ	*d* as in *d*eal	δέλτα	delta
E ε	*e* as in red	εἰ, ἒ (ἒ ψιλόν)	epsilon
Ϝ¹ ϝ	*w* as in *w*ine	ϝαῦ ¹ (δίγαμμα)	vau (digamma)
Z ζ	*zd* as in Ahura Mazda	ζῆτα	zeta
H η	*ê* as in Fr. fête (open *e*)	ἦτα	eta
Θ θ	*th* as in *th*ick (originally *t*+*h*)	θῆτα	theta
I ι	*i* as in mach*i*ne (when short as *i* in h*i*t)	ἰῶτα	iota
K κ	*k* as in *k*ill	κάππα	kappa
Λ λ	*l* as in English, but with a trill	λάμβδα	lambda
M μ	*m* as in *m*et	μῦ	mu
N ν	*n* as in *n*et	νῦ	nu
Ξ ξ	*x* as in wa*x*	ξεῖ (ξῖ)	xi
O o	*o* as in rose (Fr.), (closed *o*)	οὖ, ὄ (ὂ μῑκρόν)	omicron
Π π	*p* as in *p*ie	πεῖ (πῖ)	pi
Ϙ¹ ϙ	*k* as in *k*ale	ϙόππα¹	koppa
P ρ	Fr. or Ger. trilled *r*	ῥῶ	rho
Σ σ ς²	*s* as in *s*it	σίγμα	sigma
T τ	*t* as in *t*ie	ταῦ	tau
Υ υ³	*u* as in pr*u*ne (better as Fr. *ou*, *sou*)	ὖ (ὒ ψιλόν)	upsilon
Φ φ	*ph* as in so*ph*omore (originally *p*+*h*)	φεῖ (φῖ)	phi
X χ	*ch* as in lo*ch* or do*ch* (originally *c*+*h*)	χεῖ (χῖ)	chi
Ψ ψ	*ps* as in li*ps*	ψεῖ (ψῖ)	psi
Ω ω	*o* as in Fr. *o*r (open *o*)	ὦ (ὢ μέγα)	omega

1, 2, 3 : see next page for footnotes.

502. Only the capitals were used in antiquity, the small letters being introduced by mediæval copyists of Greek manuscripts.

503. The vowels are : α, ε, η, ο, ω, *pure vowels*, and
ι, υ, ϝ, *semi-vowels*.

504. The diphthongs are :

αι pronounced as *ai* in *ai*sle.

αυ   "   " *ou* in h*ou*se (or rather as *au* in Ger. H*au*s).

ει   "   " *ei* in fr*ei*ght (or better still, pronounce both vowels, ε + ι, but fuse them into a single syllable *ĕi*, with the accent on the first part).

ευ   "   " *eh* + *oo* in sp*oo*n, but fused into one syllable, somewhat as *eu* in Fr. fl*eu*r.

ηυ   "   " *ê* + *ou* in s*ou*, but fused into one syllable.

οι   "   " *o* + *ι*   "   "   "   "   "

ου   "   " *o* + *υ*   "   "   "   "   "

υι   "   " *we* in *we* (or rather as *oui* in Fr. L*oui*se).

ωυ   "   " *ō* + *ou* in s*ou*, but fused into one syllable.

505. The *improper* diphthongs are ᾳ, ῃ, ῳ. These consist of a long vowel (ā, η, ω) with an iota (ι), called *iota subscript*, written beneath, unless the first of these vowels is a capital, in which case the iota is written in the line, as ᾤχετο = Ὤιχετο = ΩΙΧΕΤΟ *went*.

NOTE. — Whenever by inflection (626) or otherwise an iota follows immediately after ā, η, or ω, it regularly becomes iota subscript (505), thus producing an improper diphthong.

506. These diphthongs are usually pronounced the same as ā, η, and ω respectively, although in Homeric times the iota was probably sounded to some extent.

---

[1] ϝ and ϙ are not ordinarily printed in Greek texts to-day, but both were common in the earlier period of the language ; and a knowledge of the use of vau (or digamma, as it is sometimes called) is necessary in order to understand the metre of Homer, as well as to explain many irregular forms.

[2] ς at the end of a word ; elsewhere σ, as σαώσεις *you will save*.

[3] As French *u* or German *ü* in later, classical Greek. For this sound, round the lips as though pronouncing the *oo* in *spoon*, and with the lips in this position pronounce the long *e* in *me*.

507. θ, ϕ, and χ may be pronounced as indicated above. In Homeric times they were pronounced somewhat as *t-h* in *fat-head*, *p-h* in *sap-head*, and *ck-h* in *thick-head*, respectively, but without the break noticeable in English between the two syllables.

508. The remaining consonants may be pronounced as specified in the list, but γ before μ, ν, γ, χ, κ, ξ is called *gamma-nasal*, and is pronounced as *n* in *song*, as κλαγγή *uproar*, pronounced clahngáy.

509. Mutes. — The letters π, β, ϕ; κ, γ, χ; τ, δ, θ are called *mutes* or *stops*.

510. They are divided into three *classes*, according to the part of the mouth most occupied in producing them :

Labial (lip) mutes (π, β, ϕ), called π-mutes.

Dental (teeth) mutes (τ, δ, θ), called τ-mutes (called also lingual (tongue) mutes.

Palatal (palate) mutes (κ, γ, χ) called κ-mutes (called also guttural (throat) mutes).

511. Mutes of the same class are called *cognate*, as being pronounced by the *same* organs of speech ; lips (labials), tongue and teeth (linguals, dentals), or palate and throat (palatals, gutturals).

512. The mutes are also grouped in three *orders*, according to the relative amount of expiratory force employed in making them :

Smooth mutes (π, τ, κ), called *tenues*.

Middle mutes (β, δ, γ), called *medials*.

Rough mutes (ϕ, θ, χ), called *aspirates*.

513. Mutes of the same order are said to be *coördinate*.

514. Nasals. — The nasals are μ, ν, and γ-nasal (508).

515. They may also be divided into three classes, corresponding to the three classes of mutes :

μ a labial.

ν a dental (lingual).

γ-nasal a palatal (guttural).

516. Liquids. — The liquids are λ and ρ, to which are sometimes added the nasals, μ and ν.

517. Spirants. — The spirants are σ and ζ.

518. Double Consonants. — The double consonants are ζ (= zd), ξ (= κσ, γσ, χσ), and ψ (= πσ, βσ, φσ).

519. Quantity. — The vowels η and ω are always long; ε and ο are always short, while α, ι, and υ are sometimes long and sometimes short, and hence are called *doubtful* vowels.

520. When the doubtful vowels are long in this text, it will be indicated (except in the direct quotations from Homer) by their having the mark (‾) placed over them, as θεά *goddess*. This mark will not be placed over vowels having the circumflex accent (534), as they are always long (537).

521. Diphthongs, including improper diphthongs (505), are always long.

522. A *syllable* is long *by nature* when it contains a long vowel or a diphthong. It is long *by position* when its vowel is followed by two or more consonants, or by a double consonant (518).

523. One or both of the consonants which make a syllable long by position may come in the following word.

524. If a mute (509), followed by a liquid (516), or by the nasals μ or ν, comes after a short vowel, and the mute and liquid (or nasal) come within the same word or the same part of a compound, the syllable is *common*, that is, it may be either long or short, according to the requirements of the verse.

525. Sometimes, under the verse ictus (1183), a short vowel followed by λ, μ, ν or ρ (occasionally σ or ϝ) forms a syllable long by position, in which case these consonants seem to have been doubled in pronunciation, and are sometimes so written.

526. If ϝ and another consonant come after a short vowel, the syllable is *common*, *i.e.* either long or short (524). Such syllables are regularly long only under the verse ictus (1183, 1171, 1168); otherwise, usually short.

527. Breathings. — Every vowel at the beginning of a word must have either the *smooth breathing* (᾿) or the *rough breathing* (῾), written over it if it is a small letter, and before it if it is an initial capital followed by small letters. If the entire word is written in capitals, the breathing is omitted.

528. The rough breathing, called *aspiration*, shows that *h* was sounded before the vowel, as ἱστός *loom, mast* (pronounced *histŏs*).

529. Initial ρ always has the rough breathing; initial υ usually has it.

530. The smooth breathing denotes that the vowel was sounded without the *h*, as ἐμός *my, mine* (pronounced *emŏs*).

531. A diphthong, except an improper one (505) at the beginning of a word takes the breathing over its second vowel, as Αὐτός (αὐτός) *self* (pronounced *owtŏs*), Υἱός (υἱός) *son* (pronounced *hwĕŏs*).

532. Improper diphthongs take the breathing over the first vowel when it is a small letter, and before it when it is an initial capital followed by small letters (505).

533. In compounds no word is written with a breathing unless it be initial, even though it originally had it, as ξυνίημι (ξύν + ἵημι) *bring together, hearken to.* In such cases the rough breathing should be pronounced.

534. Accents. — There are three accents, the acute (ʹ), the grave (ˋ), and the circumflex (ˆ), as βουλή *a plan*, βουλὴ κᾱλή *a good plan*, μῆνις *wrath*.

535. These accents are all ordinarily pronounced alike, by stressing the accented syllable, as in English. In ancient Greek they seem to have represented a difference of pitch.

536. The acute accent can stand on one of the last three syllables only of a word, the circumflex on one of the last two only, and the grave on the last only.

537. The circumflex accent can stand only over a long vowel or a diphthong.

538. If diphthongs (except improper ones, 505) have either the accent or breathing, or both, these must come over the second vowel, as αὐτούς *themselves*, οὕνεκα *because*, οὗτος (Οὗτος) *this.*

539. For improper diphthongs, these come over the first vʋwel if it is written in small letters, and before it if it is an initial capital followed by small letters (505).

540. If a vowel or a diphthong has both the accent and breathing, the acute and grave *follow* the breathing, while the circumflex is placed *over* the breathing, as ἄναξ *king, protecting lord,* ὕστερον *afterward(s),* ὣς ἔφατο *thus he spoke,* ἷφι *mightily, with might.*

541. If the accented vowel is initial, the accent as well as the breathing stands over it if it is a small letter and before it if it is a capital followed by small letters, as Ἄιδι *to Hades,* Ὄλυμπος *Olympus,* ἄλγος *grief, pain, woe.*

542. If the entire word is written in capitals, both breathing and accent are omitted.

543. The last syllable of a word is called the *ultima,* the last but one the *penult,* and the last but two the *antepenult.*

544. The antepenult when accented must have the acute, but it cannot have the accent if the last syllable is long by nature (522), or ends in either of the double consonants ξ or ψ, as ἐλώριον *booty,* but ἐλωρίον (gen.) *of booty.*

545. An accented penult has the circumflex if it is long by nature (522), while the ultima is short by nature, as σκῆπτρον *sceptre.*

546. An accented ultima may have the acute when short, as κᾱλός *good,* the acute or circumflex when long, as ψῡχή *soul,* ψῡχῆς (gen.) *of a soul.*

547. Final αι and οι are counted short when determining the accent, except in the optative and in οἴκοι (loc.) *at home,* as μῦθοι (545) *words,* θάλασσαι (544) *seas.* These diphthongs are regularly long in metrical quantity, and must be so treated when reading the verse, although considered short when determining the accent.

548. Verbs regularly have the *recessive* accent, that is, their accent is thrown as far back to the left as the rules of accent will allow. For exceptions see 902.

549. A word with the acute on the last syllable is called *oxytone* (sharp-toned).

550. Oxytones change the acute to the grave before other words, not separated by punctuation marks, in the same sentence, except before enclitics (553), elided syllables (575), or the interrogative pronoun τίς, τί *who ? which ? what ?* as ἀνά *up, up through,* but ἀνὰ στρατόν *up through the camp.*

551. Proclitics. — Some monosyllables have no accent of their own and are closely attached to the following word, as ἐν χερσίν *in his hands,* where ἐν has no accent of its own, just as in the ordinary use of the (unemphatic) definite and indefinite article in English. These words in Greek are called *proclitics,* and are accented only —

1) when followed by an enclitic (553) ;

2) at the end of a sentence ;

3) εἰς (ἐς) *into, to,* ἐκ (ἐξ) *out of, from,* ἐν *in,* and ὡς *as,* when they follow the words they modify.

552. The proclitics are :

1) The forms ὁ, ἡ, οἱ, αἱ of the pronoun (usually called the "article," from its use in later Greek, 765, 481).

2) The prepositions εἰς (ἐς) *into, to,* ἐκ (ἐξ) *out of, from,* and ἐν *in,* except when they follow the word they modify.

3) The conjunctions εἰ *if,* and ὡς *as, that* (also a preposition *to*), except when it means *thus,* or when it follows its noun.

4) The adverb οὐ (οὐκ, οὐχ) *not,* except at the end of a sentence.

553. Enclitics. — An *enclitic* is a word which regularly loses its own accent, and is pronounced as if it were a part of the preceding word, as οἰωνοῖσί τε *and for the birds,* where τε (τέ) has lost its accent, which has become attached to the last syllable of the preceding word.

554. The enclitics are :

1) The personal pronouns μεῦ, μοί, μέ, σεῦ (σέο), σοί (τοί), σέ, ἑο (εὗ), ἕθεν, οἷ, ἕ, σφί(σι), σφίν, σφέ, σφάς (σφᾶς), σφέα(ς), σφῶίν, σφωέ, σφέων, μίν.

2) The indefinite pronoun τὶς, τὶ *some (one), any (one), something, anything,* in all its forms (but not ἄσσα = τινά).

183

3) The indefinite adverbs πού (ποθί), πή, ποί, ποθέν, ποτέ, πώ, πώς

NOTE. — When used as interrogatives, the pronouns τίς, τί *who?* *which? what?* and the adverbs ποῦ (πόθι), πῆ, ποῖ, πόθεν, πότε, πῶ, πῶς. have the accent here given, which they never lose.

4) The present indicative of εἰμί *be*, and of φημί *say* (except ἔασι, the 3d pl. of εἰμί and possibly the second singular φής of φημί).

5) The particles γέ, τέ, τοί, πέρ, νύ(ν), κέ(ν), θήν, ῥά.

6) The pronominal suffix -δε, the local suffix (" preposition ") -δε, and the adverbial suffix -θε (as εἶθε, αἶθε).

555. An enclitic does not lose its accent in the following cases:
1) When it is dissyllabic and follows a word which has the acute on the penult.
2) When the preceding vowel is elided (575).
3) When there is no preceding word.
4) When there is an emphasis on the enclitic.

556. ἐστί(ν) is written with an accent on the first syllable (ἔστι) when:
1) It comes at the beginning of a sentence or of a verse of poetry :
2) It denotes *possibility* or *existence.*
3) It is preceded by οὐκ, εἰ, καί, ὡς, μή, ἀλλ', or τοῦτ'.

557. When an enclitic is followed by one or more enclitics in the same sentence, each except the last receives the acute accent on its final syllable from the enclitic following.

558. When a word is compounded with an enclitic, it is accented as though they were separate, as οὔτε (οὐ + τέ), ἤδε (ἤ + δε), οἴδε (οἴ + δε), etc.

559. In the following cases the word before an enclitic keeps its own accent, and never changes the acute to the grave :
1) If it has an acute on the antepenult (543), or the circumflex on the penult (543), it adds an acute on the ultima (543) as a second accent.
2) If it has the acute on the penult (543), or the circumflex on the ultima (543), no change is made.

NOTE. — *Remember that two acute accents cannot stand on successive syllables.*

3. If it is a proclitic or an enclitic, it takes the acute on the ultima (543).

560. Syllables. — A Greek word has as many syllables as it has vowels and diphthongs. In dividing a word into syllables, single consonants, combinations of consonants which can begin a word, and a mute (509) followed by μ or ν are usually placed at the beginning of the syllable. Other combinations of consonants are divided, as ἄν-θρω-πος *man*, φα-ρέ-τρη *quiver*, μά-χε-σθαι *to fight*, ἔ-χω *I have*, θά-λασ-σα *sea*, Ἀγ-α-μέ-μνων *Agamemnon*. Compound words are divided according to their original parts, as ξυν-έ-ηκε *brought together* (a compound of ξύν and ἕηκε, from ξυνίημι = ξύν + ἵημι = ξυν-ί-η-μι).

561. Movable Consonants. — The following words are sometimes spelled with and sometimes without a final ν, called *ν-movable:*

1) All words (except ἐσσί), ending in -σι, including -ξι and -ψι.

2) All verbs of the third person singular ending in -ε.

3) The third singular of the pluperfect ending in -ει (originally -εε, 584, 2 ; 585).

4) The verb ἐστί, and the particles κέ and νύ, all of which are enclitics (553, 554).

5) The dative plural of the personal pronouns ἄμμι, ὔμμι, σφί, σφίσι.

6) The endings φι and θε, mostly adverbial.

7) The pronoun ἐγώ *I*.

562. This nu-movable comes regularly in all these words at the end of a line of poetry and at the end of a sentence, and always when the end of a verse coincides with the end of a sentence. Elsewhere the word may be spelled with or without it, according to the pleasure of the writer or the requirements of the verse.

563. Similarly some adverbs had a movable sigma at the end, as πολλάκι(ς) *often*, and others ending in -κι(ς), μεσ(σ)ηγύ(ς), ἀτρέμα(ς), ἀντικρύ(ς), ἰθύ(ς), μέχρι(ς), ἄχρι(ς), ἀμφί(ς), οὔτω(ς), πώ(ς), ἐκ (ἐξ).

185

564. Variant Spellings. — The following words were spelled at times with a single sigma, and at times the sigma was doubled :

1) The future and aorists of verbs with stems (630) ending in a short vowel, or in a short vowel followed by a consonant.

2) The ending of the dative plural of the third declension.

3) The words ὅσ(σ)ος, ὅποσ(σ)ος, ὁσ(σ)άκι, τόσ(σ)ος, τοσ(σ)άκι, τόσ(σ)οσδε, τοσ(σ)οῦτος, μέσ(σ)ος, πρόσ(σ)ω, πρόσ(σ)οθε(ν), ὀπίσ(σ)ω, νεμεσ(σ)άω, νεμεσ(σ)ητός, νέμεσ(σ)ις, and ᾽Οδυσ(σ)εύς in all its cases.

565. In the same way, other words were spelled with a single or a double consonant, as ὅπ(π)ως, ὅπ(π)ῃ, ᾽Αχιλ(λ)εύς, ὅ(τ)τι.

566. Many words beginning with λ, μ, ν, ρ, and σ are often spelled with these letters doubled when they are brought before a short vowel by composition or inflection, as ἐπέσσυται (ἐπί, σεύομαι), ἔμμορε (μείρομαι), ἔλλαβε (λαμβάνω), ἔρρεε (ῥέω), ἀπεν(ν)ίζοντο (ἀπό, νίζω) (525).

Note. — These letters were sometimes doubled in pronunciation, although it was not represented graphically (525, 526).

567. A few words were spelled with or without a final vowel :

1) -ι ; ἐν(ί), οὐκ(ί), π(ρ)οτί = πρός ; 2) -α ; ἀν(ά), κατ(ά), παρ(ά)

568. The following words were spelled with and without τ or θ : π(τ)όλις, π(τ)όλεμος, μαλ(θ)ακός, διχ(θ)ά, τριχ(θ)ά.

569. The following words were spelled with or without initial σ : (σ)κεδάννῦμι, (σ)μῑκρός, σῦς (ὗς), συφορβός (ὑφορβός), Σελλοί (῾Ελλοί). See 603–604.

570. Some double forms are : μία (ἴα) one; γαῖα (γῆ) earth, land, country; λείβω (εἴβω) drip, drop, pour; ἐρί(γ)δουπος loud-roaring, resounding; ξύν, σύν together, with.

571. Variations in Quantity. — Some words have a syllable which may be either long or short (sometimes, but not always, represented by a difference in spelling), according to metrical convenience (525, 1168), as Ὄλυμπος (Οὔλυμπος), ὄνομα (οὔνομα), κολεόν (κουλεόν), ὄρος (οὖρος), ἀνήρ (ἀνήρ), ᾽Απόλλων (᾽Απόλλων), εἰλήλουθα (ἐλήλυθα), εἵνεκα (ἕνεκα), μήν (μέν), ἕταρος (ἑταῖρος), ἀτάρ (αὐτάρ), πολύς (πουλύς).

572. A diphthong or a long vowel, which precedes another vowel in the same word, is often shortened in pronunciation, as υἱός *son* (A, 499), where the meter requires the first syllable to be pronounced short.   In the following examples the difference in pronunciation is indicated by the spelling also :

Θησῆα	becomes	Θησέα
ἑστηότος	"	ἑσταότος
Ἄρηος	"	Ἄρεος
νηός, νῆα, νῆες, νηῶν, νήεσσι, νῆας	"	νεός, νέα, νέες, νεῶν, νέεσσι, νέας
ἠΰς	"	ἐΰς
ἧαται	"	ἕαται
κείαται	"	κέαται
*βασιλῆυς,*Ζηυς, etc. (nouns in -*ηυς)	"	βασιλεύς, Ζεύς, etc. (nouns in -εύς)

573. Metathesis of Quantity. — āo and ηo often become εω by an exchange (metathesis) of quantity ; that is, the long vowel (ā, η) becomes short (ε), while the short vowel (o) becomes long (ω).

574. The accent is not affected by metathesis of quantity, but remains as it was before the metathesis took place.   Thus Πηληιάδāο becomes Πηληιάδεω, Βριάρηος becomes Βριάρεως, etc.

575. Elision. — A *short* final vowel (very rarely the diphthongs αι and οι also) is regularly dropped when the next word begins with a vowel or a diphthong.   This is called *elision.*   An apostrophe (') marks the omission, as στέμματ' ἔχων (for στέμματα ἔχων) *having fillets,* οἴκαδ' ἱκέσθαι (οἴκαδε ἱκέσθαι) *to arrive home,* ἐπ' ὤμων (ἐπὶ ὤμων) *on his shoulders.*

576. NOTE. — When a final short vowel, preceded by one or more vowels in the same word, is elided, only the last vowel is lost, and the other vowels remain unchanged, as μῦρί' Ἀχαιοῖς.

577. The most frequent occurrences of elision are in :
1) Words of one syllable ending in -ε, as γέ, δέ, κέ, τέ.
2) Prepositions and conjunctions of two syllables, as ἀλλά, ἀμφί, ἐπί, παρά.
3) Some common adverbs, as μάλα, τάχα, ἅμα, ἔτι, ἔπειτα, εἶτα.

578. In the following words elision does not usually take place :
1) ἄχρι, μέχρι, περί, πρό, ὅτι, τί and its compounds.

187

2) Monosyllables (except those ending in -ε, and a very few others, as σά, ῥά, and (rarely) σοί, τοί, μοί).

3) Words ending in -υ.

579. Elision occurs also in the formation of compound words, but then without the apostrophe to mark it, as ἐπευφήμησαν (ἐπὶ εὐφήμησαν) *they shouted assent.*

580. When the following word begins with a vowel, preceded by ϝ, elision does not ordinarily take place, as ἐνὶ οἴκῳ = ἐνὶ ϝοίκῳ *in (our) home;* but ἐὺ δ᾽ ϝοίκαδε *happily home(ward).*

581. ϝ, a semi-vowel corresponding to Eng. *w,* thus varied between its consonantal and vocalic value (cf. 526).

582. A smooth mute (512) brought before a rough breathing (527) by elision (575) is changed to the *cognate* rough mute (511-512). Thus κ before a rough breathing becomes χ, τ becomes θ, and π becomes φ, as αἰδεῖσθαί θ᾽ ἱερῆα *and to reverence the priest,* for αἰδεῖσθαί τε ἱερῆα; ὦχ᾽ ἑκατόγχειρον καλέσασ᾽ ἐς μάκρον Ὄλυμπον *quickly having summoned the hundred-handed (giant) into lofty Olympus,* for ὦκα ἑκατόγχειρον, etc.; ἀφίει *he sent (him) away,* for ἀπο-ίει.

583. If an accented final syllable of a *preposition* or a *conjunction* is elided (575), the accent of the word is lost with the elided syllable. Other words so accented throw the accent back on the preceding syllable, but do not change the acute to the grave (534, 550).

584. Contraction. — When one vowel follows another vowel in the same word, contraction sometimes (but not usually) takes place. When vowels are thus contracted, the following are the rules:

1) Vowels which regularly form diphthongs do so, as α + ι = αι. ο + ι = οι, etc.

NOTE. — Observe that the long vowels ᾱ, η, ω, when followed by ι regularly form the improper diphthongs ᾳ, ῃ, ῳ (505).

2) Two *like* sounds unite in the common long sound, that is, two a-sounds (α), two e-sounds (ε, η), two i-sounds (ι), two

o-sounds (o, ω), or two u-sounds (υ), unite to form the common long (ᾱ, η, ῑ, ω, ῡ) sounds, *except εε becomes ει, and οο becomes ου.*

3) An o-sound absorbs an a-sound or an e-sound and becomes long o (ω), *except εο gives ευ, while οε becomes ου.*

4) If an a-sound comes together with an e-sound, the one which comes first absorbs the other and becomes long (ᾱ, η).

5) A vowel coming before a diphthong beginning with the same vowel may be absorbed, and ε may be absorbed before οι. In other cases a vowel before a diphthong may be contracted with the first vowel of the diphthong, a following iota becoming iota subscript (505), and a following υ disappearing.

585.   TABLE OF CONTRACTIONS

α + α = ᾱ	ε + ᾱ = η	η + ε = η	ο + η = οι
ᾱ + α = ᾱ	ε + αι = ῃ	η + ει = ῃ	(rarely ῳ)
α + ᾱ = ᾱ	(rarely αι)	(rarely η)	ο + ι = οι
α + αι = αι	ε + ε = ει	η + η = η	ο + ο = ου
α + ᾳ = ᾳ	ε + ει = ει	η + ῃ = ῃ	ο + οι = οι
α + ε = ᾱ	ε + η = η	η + ι = ῃ	ο + ου = ου
α + ει = ᾳ	ε + ῃ = ῃ	η + οι = ῳ	ο + υ = ου
(rarely = ᾱ)	ε + ι = ει	ι + ε = ῑ	ο + ω = ω
α + η = ᾱ	ε + ο = ευ	ι + ι = ῑ	ο + ῳ = ῳ
α + ῃ = ᾳ	ε + οι = οι	ο + α = ω	υ + ι = ῡ
ᾰ + ι = αι	ε + ου = ευ	(rarely ᾱ)	υ + υ = ῡ
ᾱ + ι = ᾳ	ε + υ = ευ	ο + αι = αι	ω + α = ω
α + ο = ω	ε + ω = ω	ο + ε = ου	ω + ε = ω
α + οι = ῳ	ε + ῳ = ῳ	ο + ει = οι	ω + ι = ῳ
α + ου = ω	η + α = η	(rarely ου)	ω + ο = ω
α + ω = ω	η + αι = ῃ	ο + η = ω	ω + ω = ω
ε + α = η			

586. Somewhat akin to contraction is *synizesis,* which takes place when two successive vowels which do not form a diphthong are pronounced as one syllable for the sake of the meter, as Πηληϊάδεω *of the son of Peleus,* where -δεω must be pronounced as one syllable; θεοὶ δοῖεν *may the gods grant,* where θεοὶ is also pronounced as one syllable.   Or the two syllables forming synizesis may come in separate words, as δὴ οὕτως *thus,* pronounced as two syllables, or as δὴ αὖ *again,* pronounced as one syllable.

189

587. Crasis. — A vowel or a diphthong which ends a word may be contracted and combined into a single syllable with the vowel which begins the word following. This is very rare in Homer. A *coronis* (') is usually placed over the syllable contracted, as τἆλλα *the other* (*parts*), for τὰ ἄλλα.

588. In crasis the first word loses its accent, while the accent of the second remains, which may change however from the acute to the circumflex, if the rules of accent require it, because of the long syllable which arises from it.

589. When two or more syllables are contracted into one, if either had an accent before contraction, the contracted syllable has one.

590. In the case of the contracted penult (543) or antepenult (543), the accent follows the regular rules.

591. A contracted ultima (543) takes the acute accent if it had the acute before contraction. If the penult (543) had the acute and is contracted with the ultima, the ultima takes the circumflex.

592. Syncope is the suppression of a short vowel within a word, as τίπτε; *why in the world ?* for τί ποτε.

593. Ablaut. —In many words which are closely related occurs a change (sometimes disappearance) of the vowel, as in Eng. *sing, sang, song, sung.* This is known as *Ablaut* (*Vowel Gradation*).

594. Ablaut has *strong grades* and a *weak grade*, in the latter of which the vowel (sometimes) does not appear (*disappearing grade*).

595. The most important grades are :

STRONG	WEAK
1) ε, ο	—, or α
2) ᾱ (usually η in Homer), ω	α
3) η, ω	ε, α
4) ω	ο
5) ει, οι	ι
6) ευ, ου	υ

NOTE. — (5) and (6) are really part of (1), being the short vowels ε, ο combined with ι and υ, forming the diphthongs ει, οι.

596. EXAMPLES. — 1) βέλ-ος *missile*, ἐκη-βόλ-ος *free-shooter*, ὑπο-βλή-δην *breaking in, shooting in*, βάλ-λω *shoot, hurl ;* φέρ-ω *bear*, βουλη-φόρ-ος *counsel-bearing*, δί-φρ-ος *chariot (bearer, carrier)*, φαρ-έτρη *quiver (arrow-carrier)*. 2) φη-μί (originally φā-μί, 621) *I speak*, φω-νέω *I lift up the voice, speak*, ἔ-φα-το *he spoke*. 3) τί-θη-μι *I put, place*, θω-ή *fine (penalty placed upon one)*, τί-θε-μεν *we place ;* ῥήγ-νῦμι *I break*, ἔρ-ρωγ-α *I broke*, ἐρ-ράγ-η *it was broken*. 4) δῶ-ρον *gift*, δό-σις *gift*. 5) λείπ-ω *I leave*, λέ-λοιπ-α *I have left*, ἔ-λιπ-ον *I left*. 6) ἐ-λεύ-σομαι *I shall come*, εἰλή-λουθ-α *I have come*, ἤ-λυθ-ον *I came*.

597. Sonant Consonants. — In an earlier stage of the language, the liquids (λ, ρ) and μ, ν of the nasals were often vocalic (sonant) ; that is, they were used as vowels in certain combinations. In this case they are ordinarily written with a small circle underneath, to distinguish them from the consonantal λ, ρ, μ, ν.

598. In Greek as we know the language :

1) Vocalic λ (λ̥), becomes consonantal (λ) and a strengthening vowel is developed either before or after, as ἔσταλμαι *I am sent*, for an earlier ἐστλ̥μαι ; πίμπλαντο *were filled*, for an earlier πι(μ)-πλ̥ντο ; πολύς *much*, for an earlier πλ̥υς.

2) Similarly vocalic ρ (ρ̥) becomes consonantal (ρ), and a strengthening vowel is developed either before or after it, as καρδίη, κραδίη (= καρδίā, κραδίā, 621) *heart*, for an earlier κρ̥διā, καρτερός, κρατερός *strong, harsh*, for an earlier κρ̥τερος.

3) Vocalic μ (μ̥) becomes short a, as in δέκα *ten*, for an earlier δεκμ̥, ἔλυσα *I loosed*, for an earlier ἐλυσμ̥.

4) Vocalic ν (ν̥) also becomes short a, as in the ending -α of the accusative singular, and the ending -ας of the accusative plural, masculine and feminine, of the third declension, for an earlier -ν̥ and -ν̥ς. Compare πόδα (acc. sing.) *foot* with Lat. pedem, which is for an earlier ποδν̥ (pedm). It occurs commonly elsewhere, as εἰρύαται *they protect*, for εἰρυνται, βαθύς *deep*, ἔπαθον *I suffered*, for earlier βν̥θυς, ἐπν̥θον.

NOTE. — Occasionally the vocalic nasals μ, ν (μ̥, ν̥) became consonantal (μ, ν), with or without the development of a strengthening vowel, as βένθος *depth*, πένθος *woe*, for earlier βν̥θος, πν̥θος.

599. In the case of the development of a short strengthening vowel, two spellings of the same word often arose, or else different forms of the same stem were used, as κρατερός, καρτερός *strong, harsh;* καρδίη, κραδίη *heart;* ἔβαλον *I hurled,* ἐβλήθην *I was hurled.*

600. Consonantal ι. — Many Greek words earlier had a consonantal (semi-vocalic) ι, sounded as *i* in *onion,* and written ι̯. Its loss when following the final consonant of the stem of a word caused the following changes in spelling:

λι̯ = λλ; κι̯, χι̯ = σσ; τι̯, θι̯ = σσ (sometimes σ); δι̯ = ζ between vowels; γι̯ = ζ after a vowel; γι̯ = δ after a consonant; ανι̯, αρι̯, ονι̯, ορι̯ = αιν, αιρ, οιν, οιρ; ενι̯, ερι̯, ινι̯, ιρι̯, υνι̯, υρι̯ = ειν, ειρ, ῑν, ῑρ, ῡν, ῡρ.

601. Compensative Lengthening. — The loss of one or more consonants in a word usually occasions the lengthening of the preceding vowel. This is called *compensative lengthening.* When it takes place, α, ι, υ = ᾱ, ῑ, ῡ; ε = ει; ο = ου.

602. Consonantal v. — ϝ (vau, digamma) was simply a consonantal (semi-vocalic) *v* (just as *w* in English usually represents a consonantal *u*), and one often becomes the other in Greek, as may be seen from the declension of such forms as βασιλεύς (*βασιληυς) *king,* νηῦς *ship,* and βοῦς (*βωυς) *ox, cow,* of which the genitives are βασιλῆος, νηός, βοός (for an earlier βασιληϝος, νηϝος, βωϝος) (572). The final υ of the stem (630) of these words thus first became ϝ and was then lost.

NOTE. — In a few words ϝ became υ and remained, as ἀπούρᾱς *having taken away* (= ἀποϝρᾱς), αὐέρυσαν *they drew up* (the heads of the victims) (= ἀϝερυσαν = ἀϝϝερυσαν = ἀνϝερυσαν).

603. Loss of Sigma. — The rough breathing (527) in Greek often represents a lost sigma. A sigma between two vowels usually became the rough breathing (compare the change of intervocalic *s* to *r* in early Latin) and was then lost.

604. Compare

GREEK	ὑπέρ *over*	ἅλς *the (salt) sea*	ἵστημι *stand*
LATIN	super	sal	sisto
GREEK	ἡμι *half*	ἕξ *six*	ἑπτά (ἑπτμ 597,598,3)*seven*
LATIN	semi-	sex	septem
GREEK	ἕδος *seat*	ἕ *self*	ἠώς (ἀϝ-ώς) *dawn*
LATIN	sedes	se	aurora (ausosa)
GREEK	ὁμός *similar*	ἅλλομαι (ἁλι̯-) *leap*	ὕπνος *sleep*
LATIN	simi-lis	salio	somnus (sopnos, cf. sopor)
GREEK	ὅς, ἥ, ὅν (ϝος, ϝη, ϝον) *one's own*		γένεος *of a race* (γενε-ός)
LATIN	suus, sua, suum (svas, sva, svom)		generis (genesis)
GREEK	genitive plural ending, feminine, 1st decl. ᾱων (ᾱ-ών)		
LATIN	" " " " " " ārum (āsum)		

605. Final Consonants. — The only consonants which can stand at the end of a word are ν, ρ, and ς (including ξ and ψ). Other consonants coming at the end of a word are dropped, as δῶμα *house* (for δωματ); ὑπόδρα *askance, scowlingly* (for ὑποδρακ); ἔλυε for ἔλυετ. Cf. amat, amabat, etc.

606. ἐκ (ἐξ) *out of, from,* and οὐκ (οὐχ) *not,* are apparent exceptions, but as proclitics (551) they are attached closely to the following word.

607. οὐ, οὐκ, οὐχ *not* are the variant spellings for this word according as it comes before a consonant, a smooth breathing, or a rough breathing, respectively. At the end of a sentence, clause, or verse, the form οὐκί is sometimes found.

608. Consonant Change. — There are certain changes which some of the consonants undergo, mostly in the nature of assimilation, that is, a consonant becomes similar to, or the same as the consonant following (*partial*, or *complete* assimilation).

609. Thus κάππεσον (κατπεσον) *I fell* has complete assimilation of the τ to the following π, while in ἐπέμφθην (ἐπεμπθην) *I was conducted, sent,* there is only partial assimilation.

610. The most important of these changes are:
1) A labial (π, β, φ), or a palatal (κ, γ, χ) mute before a dental (τ, δ, θ) mute must be of the same order (512).

193

2) A dental (τ, δ, θ) mute before another dental mute becomes σ.

3) Before μ a labial mute (π, β, ϕ) becomes μ, while the palatal mutes κ and χ regularly become gamma-nasal (508), and a dental mute (τ, δ, θ) regularly becomes σ.

4) Before σ: a labial mute (π, β, ϕ) combines and becomes ψ.

a palatal mute (κ, γ, χ) combines and becomes ξ.

a dental mute (τ, δ, θ) is usually assimilated (608), becoming σ, and one σ is often dropped, as $\pi o\sigma(\sigma)\iota = \pi o\delta\sigma\iota$ *with his feet.*

5) μ before a labial mute (π, β, ϕ) remains unchanged.

6) ν before a labial mute (π, β, ϕ) becomes μ.

ν before a palatal mute (κ, γ, χ) becomes gamma-nasal (508).

ν before λ, ρ is assimilated (608), becoming λ, or ρ respectively.

7) A smooth mute (512) before θ becomes a rough mute of the same class (510).

8) $\beta + \nu$ becomes $\mu\nu$; δ or $\tau + \pi$ becomes $\pi\pi$; $\delta + \lambda = \lambda\lambda$; $\lambda + \nu = \lambda\lambda$; $\nu + \mu = \mu\mu$.

9) $\tau + \iota$ (when ι is final, or medial followed by another vowel) usually $= \sigma\iota$, $\pi\lambda o\acute{\upsilon}\sigma\iota o\varsigma$ ($\pi\lambda o\hat{\upsilon}\tau o\varsigma$).

NOTE. — $\nu\tau$ before final ι becomes $\nu\varsigma$; the ν is then dropped and the preceding vowel lengthened by compensation, 601, 613.

611. Thus, with the exception of $\dot{\epsilon}\kappa$ (*out of, from*) in composition, the only combinations of mutes which can occur are $\pi\tau$, $\kappa\tau$, $\beta\delta$, $\gamma\delta$, $\phi\theta$, $\chi\theta$, $\pi\phi$, $\kappa\chi$, and $\tau\theta$.

NOTE. — γ before κ, γ, χ, ξ is a nasal (508, 515) and not a mute.

612. When ν is brought before ρ by inflection (626) or composition, a δ is developed to assist the pronunciation. Similarly, when a μ is brought before ρ (or λ) a β is developed, as $\dot{\alpha}\nu\acute{\eta}\rho$, $\dot{\alpha}\nu\delta\rho\acute{o}\varsigma$ ($\dot{\alpha}\nu\rho o\varsigma$) *a man, of a man,* $\ddot{\alpha}\mu\beta\rho o\tau o\varsigma$ ($\dot{\alpha}$-$\mu\rho\tau o\varsigma$, 597), *immortal,* $\mu\acute{\epsilon}\mu\beta\lambda\epsilon\tau\alpha\iota$ ($\mu\epsilon\mu\lambda\epsilon\tau\alpha\iota$) *is a concern.* For a similar development in English compare *tender* (Lat. tenerum), *cinder* (Lat. cinerem), *number* (Lat. numerum), *humble* (Lat. humilem).

613. μ, ν, $\nu\tau$, $\nu\delta$, $\nu\theta$, ρ, λ before σ, and σ before ν are regularly dropped and the preceding vowel is lengthened by compensation (601).

614. In prepositional compounds, ἐν before λ, ρ, or σ remains unchanged, while σύν (ξύν) before σ becomes συσ-, and before σ + a consonant or before ζ becomes συ-.

615. μ before σ is dropped and the preceding vowel lengthened, or else the μ is doubled, as εἰμί (ἐσμι) *I am*, ἔμμεναι (ἐσμεναι) *to be*.

616. Words spelled with an initial ρ have this letter regularly doubled when by composition or inflection it comes to stand after a vowel (not a diphthong).

617. λ, μ, ν, and σ are often doubled under similar conditions (525, 566).

618. σ between consonants, except in compounds, is dropped.

619. If a syllable begins with an *aspiration* (a rough breathing, or a rough mute φ, θ, χ), the preceding syllable may not ordinarily have an aspiration, but becomes smooth, as τίθημι (θιθημι) *I put, place*, τρέφω (θρεφω) *I nurture*, πέφηνα (φεφηνα) *I shone*, ἔχω (ἐχω) *I have*. This is known as *dissimilation*.

NOTE. — This rule is not always observed in the formation of the aorist passive, where two rough mutes may begin successive syllables.

620. Dialects. — The Homeric poems are a mixture of two Greek dialects, Aeolic and Ionic, the bulk of the forms being Ionic. Certain apparent irregularities are due to the Aeolic element in them.

621. The long alpha (ᾱ) of the earlier language and found in most of the other Greek dialects regularly becomes η in Ionic Greek, as βουλή *desire, plan* (βουλά). Long alpha in the Homeric poems is regularly due to contraction (584–585), to compensative lengthening (601), or else is an Aeolic form.

622. Punctuation. — Greek punctuation differs from English in having the semicolon and the colon represented by a single dot above the line (·), while the interrogation mark has the same form as the English semicolon (;).

623. Transliteration. — So many Greek words have come into English through the medium of the Latin that the system of transliteration usually employed by the old Romans is the one commonly used for the mass of Greek words in our tongue.

This in general represented the Greek letters by their corresponding English equivalents. Those which differ at all were regularly transliterated as follows:

ζ = z, as ζῶον *animal* (zoölogy, zoön, epizoötic).

κ = c, as δέκα *ten* (decalogue, decagon, decade).

υ = y,[1] as πῦρ *fire* (pyre, pyrotechnic(al), pyrography, pyrolatry).

αι = (a)e, as παῖς (stem παιδ) *child* (pedagogue, paedobaptism, paedogenesis).

ει = e, i, ei, as χείρ *hand* (chirography), εἰδῶλον (idol), εἰδός *appearance*(kaleidoscope), μουσεῖον *dwelling of the muses* (museum).

οι = (o)e, as οἶκος *house*, *home* (economy, ecology), ὅμοῖος *like* (hom(o)eopathy, homoeomorphous).

ου = u, as βοῦς *ox*, *cow* (bucolic, Bucephalus, bucentaur, bucranium).

ευ = eu,[2] as εὖ *well* (euphony, eulogy, euphemism).

ῥ = rh, as ῥέω *flow* (rhetoric, rheum(atism), catarrh).

γ-nasal (508) = n, as ἄγγελος *messenger* (angel(ic, -ology), evangel).

Iota-subscript (505) was usually omitted, as ᾠδή *ode*, Θρῄκη *Thrace*. η in Homeric Greek, when representing an ᾱ in later (Attic) Greek (621), was often transliterated by a, as Ἥρη *Hera*, Ἀθήνη *Athena*. This rule applies especially to η when following ε, ι, ρ (462), or when final.

624. The following special rules apply to final endings:

οι = i, as Ἀχαιοί *Achaei*, Δαναοί *Danai*.

η = a (sometimes e) (621): Σπάρτη *Sparta*, Ἰθάκη *Ithaca*, Ἑκάτη *Hecaté*.

ος = us (sometimes os): Πάτροκλος *Patroclus*, Ὄλυμπος *Olympus;* but Λῆμνος *Lemnos*, Δῆλος *Delos*, etc.

ον = um, as Σούνιον *Sunium*, Παλλάδιον *Palladium*.

τια, τιη = cy: δημοκρατίη *democracy*.

ιη, ια = y, as Ἀρκαδίη *Arcadia*, *Arcady*, φιλοσοφίη (φιλέω *love*, σοφίη *skill*, *wisdom*), *philosophy*, literally = *love of wisdom*.

---

[1] Only when standing alone; never when part of a diphthong.

[2] Occasionally = ev in compounds, as εὐάγγελος *messenger of good* (news) (evangel, evangelist(ic), evangelic(al)).

625. Greek proper names are transliterated according to the foregoing rules. They are put into the nominative (639), and are pronounced by ignoring the Greek accent and by accenting the penult (543) of the word if it is long (522) in Greek, otherwise the antepenult (543), as Λητώ *Léto*, Ὄλυμπος *Olýmpus.*

II. MORPHOLOGY

INFLECTION

626. Inflection, including declension (nouns, adjectives, pronouns), comparison (adjectives, adverbs), and conjugation, is the fusion of a so-called stem (630), and certain elements which express relationship to other words.

627. A root is the essential part of a word which remains after it has been analyzed into its various parts, and all prefixes, suffixes, and formative elements have been removed.

628. A stem often has more than one form, its different forms usually standing in ablaut (593-595) relation to each other. It is ordinarily derived from a root, by the addition of various formative elements, prefixes, and suffixes.

629. Some roots are also stems, and are combined directly with inflectional elements.

630. An inflected word is in general made up of two parts :
1) The fundamental part, or stem.
2) The inflectional element (usually an ending, commonly called a *suffix;* sometimes a prefix, as in the case of the augment, 830), which combines with the stem to form case, number, tense, person, etc.

631. The last letter of the stem is called the *stem characteristic,* and from this last letter stems are classified as *vowel stems, mute* (509) *stems, liquid* (516) *stems,* etc.

DECLENSION

Nouns

632. Nouns, pronouns, and adjectives are declined.

633. Number. — There are three numbers in Greek, the *singular* denoting one, the *dual* denoting two (usually referring to a pair or objects closely associated, or belonging together by nature and forming a closely related, unified group, as χεῖρε, ὀφθαλμώ, ἵππω *the two hands, eyes, horses.* Compare *yoke, team, pair* in English), and the *plural* denoting more than two.

Note. — The plural is often used interchangeably with the dual to denote only two.

634. Gender. — There are three genders, the masculine, feminine, and neuter.

635. The gender must usually be learned by observation, but in general :

1) The names of males are masculine.

2) The names of females are feminine.

3) The names of rivers, winds, and months are usually masculine.

4) The names of countries, towns, trees, and islands are usually feminine.

5) Most nouns denoting qualities and conditions are feminine.

636. A few nouns are used either as masculine or feminine, as παῖς *child,* which may be of either gender, and may mean either *boy* or *girl,* as may be required by occasion. Such words are said to be of *common gender.*

637. The demonstrative (often relative, or personal) pronoun most extensively used in the Homeric poems is ὁ, ἡ, τό, the first form being masculine, the second feminine, and the third neuter.

638. The form of the noun which appears in the vocabulary is the nominative singular, unless otherwise indicated. This is followed by the ending of the genitive singular, which denotes to which declension the noun belongs. After the ending of the genitive singular is placed the appropriate form of this pronoun, to indicate the gender. Thus θεός, οὗ, ὁ *god* is second declension masculine; βουλή, ῆς, ἡ *wish, will, plan* is first declension feminine, and ἄλγος, εος, τό *pain, woe* is third declension neuter.

639. Cases. — There are five cases in Greek, the nominative, genitive, dative, accusative, and vocative, together with remnants of three lost cases, the locative, instrumental, and ablative (657).

640. All these cases except the nominative and vocative are called *oblique* cases.

641. Accent of Nouns. — The accent of a noun usually remains in all the forms on the same syllable as in the nominative singular, or at least as near that syllable as the general rules of accent will allow. Thus ἥρως *hero* (nominative singular), but ἡρώων *of heroes* (genitive plural). See 544 ff.

642. Words monosyllabic in the nominative singular, when becoming dissyllabic by declension, regularly have the accent on the final syllable in all the dissyllabic forms of the genitive and dative of all numbers, and on the penult of the dual (trisyllabic), but keep the accent on the first syllable in all other cases.

643. An accented ultima in general takes the acute, but in the genitive and dative of all numbers a long ultima, if accented, takes the circumflex, as ψῡχή *soul* (nom. sing.), but ψῡχῆς *of a soul* (gen. sing.), ψῡχῇ *to, for a soul* (dat. sing.), etc.

644. Declensions. — Nouns are declined in two general ways:

1) The *vowel* declension, for stems (630) ending in the pure vowels, ᾱ, ο.

2) The *consonant* declension, for stems ending in a consonant, or the semi-vowels, ι, υ.

645. The vowel declension has two forms, according as the noun stem ends in ᾱ or ο. Hence we have:

1) The *a* declension, commonly called the *first declension;*

2) The *o* declension, commonly called the *second declension.*

646. The consonant declension, for stems ending in a semi-vowel (ι, υ, which were at times semi-consonantal) or a consonant, is commonly called the *third declension.*

647. Words of the first declension have stems ending in ᾱ, which either becomes shortened in the nominative singular to ᾰ, or else becomes η (621), except in the one word θεά *goddess*, and a very few proper names. Nouns of the first declension are either masculine or feminine.

648. Case Endings. — To form the various cases, numbers, and genders, the following case endings were fused with the stems of substantives and adjectives:

199

	VOWEL DECLENSION				CONSONANT DECLENSION	
	First		**Second**			
	MASC.	FEM.	M. AND F.	NEUT.	M. AND F.	NEUT.

SINGULAR

	MASC.	FEM.	M. AND F.	NEUT.	M. AND F.	NEUT.
Nom.	ς (none)	none	ς	ν	ς (none)	none
Gen.	ο (ιο ?)	ς	ο (ιο)	ο (ιο)	ος	ος
Dat.	ι	ι	ι	ι	ι	ι
Acc.	ν	ν	ν	ν	ν, α (ν)[1]	none
Voc.	none	none	none [2]	ν	ς (none)	none

DUAL

N. A. V.	none	none	none	none	ε	ε
G. D.	ιιν	ιιν	ιιν	ιιν	οιιν	οιιν

PLURAL

N. V.	ι	ι	ι	ᾰ	ες	ᾰ
Gen.	ων	ων	ων	ων	ων	ων
[3] Dat.	(ι)σι, ις	(ι)σι, ις	(ι)σι, ις	(ι)σι, ις	σ(σ)ι, εσ(σ)ι [4]	σ(σ)ι, εσ(σ)ι [4]
Acc.	νς [5]	νς [5]	νς [5]	ᾰ	νς,[5] ᾰς [1]	ᾰ

649. When these suffixes combined with the stem of a word, the following endings were produced:

FIRST DECLENSION		SECOND DECLENSION	

SINGULAR

	MASC.	FEM.	MASC. AND FEM.	NEUT.
N.	ης, [α, ᾱς] [6]	η, α, ᾱ	ος, [(ως, ους)[6]]	ον
G.	ᾱο, [εω, ω] [7]	ης, ᾱς	οιο, ου, [οο, ωο (ω)]	
D.	ῃ, [ᾳ]	ῃ, ᾳ	ῳ	ῳ
A.	ην, [ᾱν]	ην, αν, ᾱν	ον, [(ων)]	ον
V.	η, α, [ᾱ]	η, α, ᾱ	ε [ος]	ον

---

[1] 597; 598, 4.

[2] But with ablaut of the final vowel of the stem ο : ε (595).

[3] Usually ισι; rarely the shorter form ις.

[4] -εσι unusually rare.   [5] 613.

[6] Forms in square brackets [ ] are rare and need not be memorized; those in parentheses ( ) are contracted.

[7] -εω, -εων regularly pronounced as one syllable by synizesis, 586; -εω usually contracted to -ω after a vowel.

		DUAL		
N. A. V.	ᾱ	ᾱ	ω	ω
G. D.	[ᾱιν]	[ᾱιν]	οιιν	οιιν

		PLURAL		
N. V.	αι	αι	οι, [(φ)]	α
G.	ᾱων, [ἑων,[1] (ῶν)]	ᾱων, [ἑων, ῶν]	ων	ων
D.	ῃσι, ῃς	ῃσι, ῃς [αις]	οισι, οις	οισι, οις
A.	ᾱς	ᾱς	ους, [(ως)]	α

Third (Consonant) Declension

SINGULAR

	MASC. AND FEM.	NEUT.
N.	s (none)	———
G.	ος, [(ευς, ους, ως)]	ος [(ευς, ους, ως)]
D.	ι, [(ῑ, φ)]	ι, [(ῑ)]
A.	α, ν [(η, ω)]	———
V.	(s none)	———

DUAL

N. A. V.	ε	ε
G. D.	οιιν	οιιν

PLURAL

N. V.	ες, [(εις, ους)]	α, [(η, ω)]
G.	ων	ων
D.	σι, εσσι, [εσι]	σι, εσσι, [εσι]
A.	s, ας, [(ῑς, ῡς, εις)]	α, [(η)]

650. Observe that the dative singular of all declensions ends in ι, which always becomes iota subscript (505) after long vowels (584, 1, note).

651. The dative plural regularly ends in σι, to which may be added nu-movable (561, 1).

652. -ῃσι and -οισι are the regular forms for the ending of the dative plural in the first two declensions. Occasionally the shorter forms, -ῃς, -οις, are found, but this is almost always before vowels, and it is possible that in that case they should be treated as examples of elision (575) and written -ῃσ' and -οισ'.

653. The genitive plural of all forms ends in -ων.

---

[1] See footnote 7 on preceding page.

654. There are but two forms of the dual in each declension, one (masc. only) for the nominative, accusative, and vocative; the other for the genitive and dative.

Note. — The form of the gen. and dat. dual of the first declension is uncertain. Instead of -ηιν, some read -αιν (-αιν)

655. As in Latin, the vocative singular is often like the nominative, and the vocative plural of all forms is always like the nominative plural.

656. *The nominative, accusative, and vocative of all neuters are alike, and in the plural end in short -α.*

657. In an earlier stage of the language there were three other cases : the *instrumental*, denoting instrument, means, manner, etc., the *locative*, denoting the place where, and the *ablative*, denoting separation, source, etc. There are only remnants of these left in Greek, as the dative became fused with the instrumental and locative, taking over most of their uses, while the genitive absorbed most of the functions of the ablative.

658. In addition to the endings given in the tables (648–649), two other suffixes, -φι(ν) and -θεν, were sometimes used. For their uses, see 712, 715.

PARADIGMS

Nouns

First Declension Feminine

659. βουλή, ῆς, ἡ (a, the) desire, will, plan, counsel, council.
(βουλᾱ-) [1]

SINGULAR

N. βουλή (a, the) plan (*as subject*).
G. βουλῆς of; off, from (a, the) plan.
D. βουλῇ to, for; with, by; in, at, on (a, the) plan.
A. βουλήν (a, the) plan (*as object*).
V. βουλή O plan!

---

[1] In the paradigms the stem of the word will be indicated each time in parentheses ; it will not be accented, and will be followed by a dash, as (βουλᾱ-) above.

DUAL

N. A. V. βουλά (the) two plans (*as subject, or object*); O two plans!
G. D. βουλῇιν of; off, from; to, for; with, by; in, at, on (the) two plans.

PLURAL

N. V. βουλαί (the) plans (*as subject*); O plans!
G. βουλάων [ἑων, -ῶν] of; off, from (the) plans.
D. βουλῇσι, ῇς to, for; with, by; in, at, on (the) plans.
A. βουλάς (the) plans (*as object*).

660. Use of Article. — Observe that there are no words used regularly in Homeric Greek with the meaning of the English article, either definite (*the*) or indefinite (*a, an*). One decides from the context whether or not the English article is to be employed in translation.

661. Meanings of Cases. — The variety of meaning found in the genitive and dative is due to the fact that each represents the fusion of two or more earlier cases (657). An attempt is made to represent this above by the use of semicolons to separate meanings which once belonged to different cases.

662. καλὴ βουλή (a, the) good plan.
    (κᾱλᾱ- βουλᾱ-)

SINGULAR

N. κᾱλὴ βουλή (a, the) good plan (*as subject*).
G. κᾱλῆς βουλῆς of; off, from (a, the) good plan.
D. κᾱλῇ βουλῇ to, for; with, by; in, at, on (a, the) good plan.
A. κᾱλὴν βουλήν (a, the) good plan (*as object*).
V. κᾱλὴ βουλή O good plan!

DUAL

N. A. V. κᾱλὰ βουλά (the) two good plans (*as subject, or object*); O two good plans!
G. D. κᾱλῇιν βουλῇιν of; off, from; to, for; with, by; in, at, on (the) two good plans.

PLURAL

N. V. κᾱλαὶ βουλαί (the) good plans (*as subject*); O good plans!
G. κᾱλάων βουλάων [ἑων, ῶν] of; off, from (the) good plans.
D. κᾱλῇσι βουλῇσι, ῇς to, for; with, by; in, at, on (the) good plans.
A. κᾱλὰς βουλάς (the) good plans (*as object*).

663. θεά, âs, ἡ   θάλασσα, ης, ἡ   γαῖα, ης, ἡ
      (θεᾱ-)   (θαλασσᾱ-)   (γαιᾱ-)
      goddess   sea   land, country, earth

SINGULAR

N. V.	θεά	θάλασσα	γαῖα
G.	θεᾱς	θαλάσσης	γαίης
D.	θεᾳ	θαλάσσῃ	γαίῃ
A.	θεάν	θάλασσαν	γαῖαν

DUAL

N. A. V.	θεά	θαλάσσᾱ	γαίᾱ
G. D.	θεῆιν	θαλάσσῃιν	γαίῃιν

PLURAL

N. V.	θεαί	θάλασσαι	γαῖαι
G.	θεάων [ῶν]	θαλασσάων [έων, ῶν]	γαιάων [έων, ῶν]
D.	θεῆσι, ῆς [θεαῖς]	θαλάσσῃσι, ης	γαίῃσι, ης
A.	θεάς	θαλάσσᾱς	γαίᾱς

FIRST DECLENSION MASCULINE

664. Ἀτρείδης, ᾱο, ὁ   Αἰνείᾱς, ᾱο, ὁ   αἰχμητής, ᾱο, ὁ
     (Ἀτρεϝιδᾱ-)   (Αἰνειᾱ-)   (αἰχμητᾱ-)
     son of Atreus   Aeneas   spearman, warrior

SINGULAR

N.	Ἀτρείδης	Αἰνείᾱς	αἰχμητής [αἰχμητά]
G.	Ἀτρείδᾱο [εω]	Αἰνείᾱο [ω]	αἰχμητᾱο [έω]
D.	Ἀτρείδῃ	Αἰνείᾳ	αἰχμητῇ
A.	Ἀτρείδην	Αἰνείᾱν	αἰχμητήν
V.	Ἀτρείδη	Αἰνείᾱ	αἰχμητά

DUAL

N. A. V.	Ἀτρείδᾱ	αἰχμητά
G. D.	Ἀτρείδῃιν	αἰχμητῇιν

PLURAL

N. V.	Ἀτρείδαι	αἰχμηταί
G.	Ἀτρεϊδάων [έων, ῶν]	αἰχμητάων [έων, ῶν]
D.	Ἀτρείδῃσι, ης	αἰχμητῇσι, ῆς
A.	Ἀτρείδᾱς	αἰχμητάς

665. Observe that the original ā of the stem of first declension nouns commonly becomes η throughout the singular (621). It rarely remains ā (in θεά *goddess*, and a few proper names).

666. In some feminines the $\bar{a}$ of the stem becomes $\breve{a}$ in the nominative, which is found also in the accusative and vocative, but in the genitive and dative singular the $\bar{a}$ of the stem becomes η, just as in nouns ending in η in the nominative singular.

667. The masculines usually take the case-ending -ς in the nominative singular; the feminines do not.

668. The nominative singular of a few masculines ends in -$\breve{a}$; a very few end in -$\bar{a}$ς, but most end in -ης. Those ending in -$\breve{a}$, excepting those with variant forms in -ης, regularly have the recessive accent (548), and all are adjectival except the proper name Θυέστα *Thyestes*.

669. Masculines and feminines of the first declension are all declined alike in the dual and plural.

670. Masculines ending in -ης and -$\bar{a}$ς in the nominative singular retain this η or $\bar{a}$ throughout the singular, with the exception that the genitive singular always has either the ending -$\bar{a}$ο (regular) or -εω (rare).

671. Those ending in -$\breve{a}$ in the nominative have the same form also in the vocative singular, but otherwise are declined like those ending in -ης.

672. Feminines ending in -η or -$\bar{a}$ in the nominative singular retain this throughout the singular.

673. Those ending in -$\breve{a}$ retain this only in the nominative, accusative, and vocative: the genitive and dative are declined the same as those ending in -η.

674. *Masculines are declined like feminines except in the nominative and genitive singular, and occasionally in the vocative singular.*

675. Masculines ending in -δης have -η in the vocative singular; those ending in -της [-τα], compound nouns, and names of nationalities have -$\breve{a}$; those ending in -$\bar{a}$ς have -$\bar{a}$.

THE SECOND DECLENSION

676. Nouns of the second declension have stems ending in -ο (-ε in the voc. sing. m. and f., which stands in ablaut relation (593–595) to the -ο). They are chiefly masculine and neuter, with a

205

very few feminines. The masculines and feminines end in -ς in the nominative singular, the neuters in -ν. These when combined with -ο of the stem give the endings -ος for the masculines and feminines and -ον for neuters.

677. The masculines and feminines are declined alike; the neuters differ from them in two respects:

1) The nominative, accusative, and vocative singular all end in -ν (*i.e.* -ον).

2) The nominative, accusative, and vocative plural end in -ă.

678. θῡμός, οῦ, ὁ spirit, life, soul.　　κακὸς πόλεμος, ου, ὁ evil war.
　　　(θῡμο-)　　　　　　　　　　　　　　(κακο- πολεμο-)

SINGULAR

N.	θῡμός	κακὸς πόλεμος
G.	θῡμοῦ, οῖο [όο]	κακοῦ πολέμου, οῖο, οιο [όο, οο]
D.	θῡμῷ	κακῷ πολέμῳ
A.	θῡμόν	κακὸν πόλεμον
V.	θῡμέ	κακὲ πόλεμε

DUAL

N. A. V.	θῡμώ	κακὼ πολέμω
G. D.	θῡμοῖιν	κακοῖιν πολέμοιιν

PLURAL

N. V.	θῡμοί	κακοὶ πόλεμοι
G.	θῡμῶν	κακῶν πολέμων
D.	θῡμοῖσι, οῖς	κακοῖσι πολέμοισι, οῖς οις
A.	θῡμούς	κακοὺς πολέμους

679. κᾱλὸν ἔργον, ου, τό noble deed.　　κακὴ νοῦσος, ου, ἡ destructive
　　　(κᾱλο- ϝεργο-)　　　　　　　　　　(κακᾱ- νουσο-)　　　　plague.

SINGULAR

N.	κᾱλὸν ἔργον	κακὴ νοῦσος
G.	κᾱλοῦ ἔργου, οῖο, οιο [όο, οο]	κακῆς νούσου, οιο [οο]
D.	κᾱλῷ ἔργῳ	κακῇ νούσῳ
A.	κᾱλὸν ἔργον	κακὴν νοῦσον
V.	κᾱλὸν ἔργον	κακὴ νοῦσε

DUAL

N. A. V.	κᾱλὼ ἔργω	κακὰ νούσω
G. D.	κᾱλοῖιν ἔργοιιν	κακῇιν νούσοιιν

PLURAL

N. V.	κᾱλὰ ἔργα	κακαὶ νοῦσοι
G.	κᾱλῶν ἔργων	κακάων [ἐων, ῶν] νούσων
D.	κᾱλοῖσι ἔργοισι, οἷς, οις	κακῇσι νούσοισι, ῇς οις
A.	κᾱλὰ ἔργα	κακὰς νούσους

THE THIRD DECLENSION

680. Nouns of the third declension are masculine, feminine, and neuter.

681. There are many forms of the nominative of third declension nouns, which must be learned partly by practice, but in general :

1) Masculine and feminine stems, except those ending in ν, ρ, and σ, add σ to the stem and make the usual euphonic changes (613).

2) Masculine and feminine stems ending in ρ, σ and most of those ending in ν make no change except to lengthen the last vowel if it is short, ε becoming η and ο becoming ω.

3) Stems ending in ν(τ) either make no change except to lengthen the last vowel if it is short, dropping final τ wherever it occurs, or else they add σ to the stem and make the usual euphonic changes (613), loss of ν(τ) and lengthening of the preceding vowel. Thus the stems : δαιμον-, θῑν-, μελαν-, γεροντ- give the nominatives δαίμων *divinity*, θίς *shore, beach*, μέλᾱς *black* and γέρων *old man*, respectively.

682. In neuters the nominative singular is usually the stem, with the exception of those with stems ending in τ which is dropped wherever it occurs (605).

683. As a rule the stem of third declension nouns may be found by dropping the case ending (-ος) of the genitive singular.

684. The dative singular regularly ends in ι, but occasionally in ῑ.

685. The accusative singular of masculine and feminine nouns is regularly formed by adding ν to stems ending in vowels and by adding γ (597) to consonantal stems. γ of course regularly becomes -ᾰ (598, 4), thus making the case ending of accusatives sin-

207

gular masculine and feminine regularly -ν for vowel stems and -ǎ for consonantal stems.

686. The dative plural is formed in two ways :
1) By adding -εσσι (rarely -εσι) to the stem.
2) By adding -σι (rarely -σσι) to the stem.

687. Note. — When -σι [-σσι] is added, the preceding consonants are assimilated, or dropped, according to the rules (613 ff.). Thus πούς, ποδός, ὁ *foot* gives ποσ-σί (from ποδ-σι), which may be further simplified to ποσί; νύξ, νυκτός, ἡ *night* gives νυξί (from νυκτ-σι) ; γέρων, γέροντος, ὁ *old man*, gives γέρουσι (from γεροντ-σι), etc. The longer forms of the datives of these nouns are πόδεσσι, νύκτεσσι, γερόντεσσι.

688. The accusative plural of masculines and feminines originally ended in -γς (-νς), which gives the ending -ας (598, 4) for consonant stems, and -ῑς, -ῡς (613 ff.) as the regular ending for the vowel stems.

689. Note. — A few vowel stems seem to have had -ας in the accusative plural, formed by analogy from the consonantal stems.

690. Words ending in -ις and -υς in the nominative singular, but with dental mute (τ, δ, θ) stems very rarely drop the mute and take the accusative singular ending (-ν) of vowel stems.

691. The vocative singular is either the same as the nominative, or else the same as the stem, final consonants except ν, ρ, ς (605) being dropped whenever they occur.

692. Compensative lengthening (601) regularly takes place in the formation of the dative plural when ντ is thus dropped, but does not take place when only one letter, as τ, δ, θ, σ, ν, is dropped ; as πᾶσι (παντ-σι), γέρουσι (γεροντ-σι), δαίμοσι (δαιμον-σι).

693. Dental Mute Stems

ἄναξ, ἄνακτος, ὁ (ϝανακτ-) king, lord	νύξ, νυκτός, ἡ (νυκτ-) night	παῖς, παιδός, ὁ, ἡ (παϝιδ-) child	γέρων, γέροντος, ὁ (γεροντ-) old man

SINGULAR

N.	ἄναξ	νύξ	παῖς	γέρων
G.	ἄνακτος	νυκτός	παιδός	γέροντος

D.	ἄνακτι	νυκτί	παιδί	γέροντι
A.	ἄνακτα	νύκτα	παῖδα	γέροντα
V.	ἄναξ [ἄνα]	νύξ	παῖ	γέρον

DUAL

N. A. V.	ἄνακτε	νύκτε	παῖδε	γέροντε
G. D.	ἀνάκτοιιν	νυκτοῖιν	παίδοιιν	γερόντοιιν

PLURAL

N. V.	ἄνακτες	νύκτες	παῖδες	γέροντες
G.	ἀνάκτων	νυκτῶν	παίδων	γερόντων
D.	ἀνάκτεσσι [εσι] ἄναξι	νύκτεσσι [εσι] νυξί	παίδεσσι [εσι] παισί	γερόντεσσι [εσι] γέρουσι
A.	ἄνακτας	νύκτας	παῖδας	γέροντας

694. Observe the irregular accent of παίδων (642), genitive plural of παῖς. This word is somewhat irregular, owing to the fact that it was earlier dissyllabic (πάϝις). It has the following variants of accent: nom. sing. πάις, παῖς ; voc. sing. πάι, παῖ.

695.   LABIAL AND PALATAL STEMS

αἴξ, αἰγός, ὁ, ἡ	κῆρυξ, ῦκος, ὁ	Αἰθίοψ, οπος, ὁ
(αἰγ-)	(κηρῦκ-)	(Αἰθιοπ-)
goat	herald	Ethiopian

SINGULAR

N.	αἴξ	κῆρυξ	Αἰθίοψ
G.	αἰγός	κήρῡκος	Αἰθίοπος
D.	αἰγί	κήρῡκι	Αἰθίοπι
A.	αἴγα	κήρῡκα	Αἰθίοπα
V.	αἴξ	κῆρυξ	Αἰθίοψ

DUAL

N. A. V.	αἴγε	κήρῡκε	Αἰθίοπε
G. D.	αἰγοῖιν	κηρύκοιιν	Αἰθιόποιιν

PLURAL

N. V.	αἴγες	κήρῡκες	Αἰθίοπες
G.	αἰγῶν	κηρύκων	Αἰθιόπων
D.	αἴγεσσι [εσι] αἰξί	κηρύκεσσι [εσι] κήρυξι	Αἰθιόπεσσι [εσι] Αἰθίοψι
A.	αἴγας	κήρῡκας	Αἰθίοπας

209

696.   Liquid and Nasal Stems

δαίμων, ονος, ὁ	φρήν, φρενός, ἡ	χείρ, ος, ἡ
(δαιμον-)	(φρεν-)	(χειρ-)
divinity	diaphragm, heart, mind	hand, arm

SINGULAR

N.	δαίμων	φρήν	χείρ
G.	δαίμονος	φρενός	χειρός
D.	δαίμονι	φρενί	χε(ι)ρί
A.	δαίμονα	φρένα	χεῖρα
V.	δαῖμον	φρήν	χείρ

DUAL

N. A. V.	δαίμονε	φρένε	χεῖρε
G. D.	δαιμόνοιιν	φρενοῖιν	χειροῖιν

PLURAL

N. V.	δαίμονες	φρένες	χεῖρες
G.	δαιμόνων	φρενῶν	χειρῶν
D.	{ δαιμόνεσσι [εσι] δαίμοσι	{ φρένεσσι [εσι] φρεσί	{ χείρεσσι [εσι] χερσί
A.	δαίμονας	φρένας	χεῖρας

Liquid Stems

697. Several words ending in -ηρ in the nominative singular have three different grades of ablaut (593–595), -ηρ, -ερ, -ρ in the stem.   The vocative singular regularly has recessive accent (548).

SINGULAR

πατήρ, τέρος, τρός, ὁ father	μήτηρ, τέρος, τρός, ἡ mother
(πατερ-, -ηρ, -ρ)	(μᾱτηρ-, -ερ, -ρ)

N.	πατήρ	μήτηρ
G.	πατέρος, τρός	μητέρος, τρός
D.	πατέρι, τρί	μητέρι, τρί
A.	πατέρα	μητέρα
V.	πάτερ	μῆτερ

DUAL

N. A. V.	πατέρε	μητέρε
G. D.	πατέροιιν	μητέροιιν

PLURAL

N. V.	πατέρες	μητέρες
G.	πατέρων, τρῶν	μητέρων

D. πατράσι   μητράσι
A. πατέρας   μητέρας

θυγάτηρ, τέρος, τρός, ἡ daughter	ἀνήρ, έρος, δρός, ὁ man
(θυγατηρ-, -ερ, -ρ)	(ἀνηρ-, -ερ, -ρ)
SINGULAR	
N. θυγάτηρ	ἀνήρ
G. θυγατέρος, τρός	ἀνέρος, ἀνδρός
D. θυγατέρι, τρί	ἀνέρι, ἀνδρί
A. θυγατέρα, θύγατρα	ἀνέρα, ἄνδρα
V. θύγατερ	ᾶνερ
DUAL	
N. A. V. θυγατέρε	ἀνέρε, ἄνδρε
G. D. θυγατέροιιν	ἀνέροιιν, ἀνδροῖιν
PLURAL	
N. V. θυγατέρες, θύγατρες	ἀνέρες, ἄνδρες
G. θυγατέρων, θυγατρῶν	ἀνέρων, ἀνδρῶν
D. θυγατράσι, τέρεσσι	ἀνδράσι, ἄνδρεσσι
A. θυγατέρας, θύγατρας	ἀνέρας, ἄνδρας

698. Observe that a δ is developed in the forms of ἀνήρ between ν and ρ whenever they would otherwise come together (612). The initial ἀ is often long, 571, 1168.

699. In the genitive and dative singular of ἀνήρ, μήτηρ, and θυγάτηρ, the shorter forms have the accent, after the analogy of πάτηρ, πατρός, πατρί, which was originally monosyllabic (πατρ), and follows the regular rules for the accentuation of monosyllabic nouns (642).

700. The ρά in the dative plural, and these forms in general are explained in 597–598.

701. STEMS IN ηυ (ευ), ου, AND ωϝ

βασιλεύς, ῆος, ὁ	βοῦς, βοός, ὁ, ἡ	νηῦς, νηός (νεός), ἡ	ἥρως, ωος, ὁ
(βασιληυ-, -ευ-, -ηϝ-)	(βου-, βωϝ-, βοϝ-)	(νᾱυ-, νᾱϝ- 621)	(ἡρωϝ-)
king	ox, cow	ship, bark	hero, mighty warrior
SINGULAR			
N. βασιλεύς	βοῦς	νηῦς	ἥρως
G. βασιλῆος [-έος]	βοός	νηός [νεός]	ἥρωος
D. βασιλῆι [-έι]	βοΐ	νηΐ	ἥρωι
A. βασιλῆα [-έα]	βοῦν [βῶν]	νῆα [νέα]	ἥρωα
V. βασιλεῦ	βοῦ	νηῦ	ἥρως

DUAL

| N. A. V. | βασιλῆε | βόε | νῆε | ἥρωε |
| G. D. | βασιλήοιιν | βοοῖιν | νηοῖιν | ἡρώοιιν |

PLURAL

N. V.	βασιλῆες	βόες	νῆες	ἥρωες
G.	βασιλήων	βοῶν	νηῶν [νεῶν]	ἡρώων
D.	βασιλήεσσι βασιλεῦσι	βόεσσι βουσί	νήεσσι [νέεσσι] νηυσί	ἡρώεσσι ἥρωσι
A.	βασιλῆας	βόας (βοῦς)	νῆας (νέας)	ἥρωας

702. The shortening of a vowel before a following vowel in such forms as βασιλεύς (*βασιληυς), νηός (νεός) is explained in 572.

703. Observe that the υ of the stem of these words became ϝ in many cases and was then lost (602).

704. STEMS IN ι (ει, ει), AND υ (ευ, εϝ)

| πόλις, ιος, ἡ
(πολι-, -ει-)
city | πῆχυς, εος, ὁ
(πηχυ-, -εϝ-)
forearm | ἄστυ, εος, τό
(ϝαστυ-, εϝ-)
city, town | νέκῡς, υος, ὁ
(νεκῡ-)
corpse | δάκρυ, υος, τό
(δακρυ-)
tear |

SINGULAR

N.	πόλις	πῆχυς	ἄστυ	νέκῡς	δάκρυ
G.	πόλιος, -ηος	πήχεος	ἄστεος	νέκυος	δάκρυος
D.	πόλιι, -ῑ, -ηι, -ει	πήχεϊ	ἄστεϊ	νέκυϊ	δάκρυϊ
A.	πόλιν	πῆχυν	ἄστυ	νέκῡν	δάκρυ
V.	πόλι	πῆχυ	ἄστυ	νέκῡ	δάκρυ

DUAL

| N. A. V. | πόλιε | πήχεε | ἄστεε | νέκυε | δάκρυε |
| G. D. | πολίοιιν | πηχέοιιν | ἀστέοιιν | νεκύοιιν | δακρύοιιν |

PLURAL

N. V.	πόλιες, -ηες	πήχεες	ἄστεα	νέκυες	δάκρυα
G.	πολίων	πηχέων	ἀστέων	νεκύων	δακρύων
D.	πολίεσσι πόλεσι, -ισι	πηχέεσσι πήχεσι	ἀστέεσι ἄστεσι	νεκύεσσι νέκῡσ(σ)ι	δακρύεσσι δάκρυσι
A.	πόλιας, -ηας -ῑς, (-εις?)	πήχεας	ἄστεα	νέκυας [-ῦς]	δάκρυα

705. Forms as πόλις, πῆχυς, ἄστυ show different grades of ablaut (593–595): ι, ει, and υ, ευ (εϝ).

706. Observe the loss of the υ and ι in such words as πῆχυς, εος, ἄστυ, εος, and πόλις. They first become ϝ, or ι̯ of course (602, 600).

707. Nouns with Stems in -ς (-εσ, -ασ- -οσ) and in τ

ἔπος, εος, τό	γέρας, αος, τό	ἠώς, ἠόος, ἡ	δῶμα	ἦμαρ, ἥματος, τό
(ϝεπεσ-)	(γερασ-)	(ἀϝσοσ-)	(δωματ-)	(ἦμαρ-, ἦματ-)
word, speech	prize (of honor)	Eos, dawn	house, home	day

SINGULAR

N.	ἔπος	γέρας	ἠώς	δῶμα	ἦμαρ
G.	ἔπεος	γέραος	ἠόος	δώματος	ἥματος
D.	ἔπεϊ	γέραϊ	ἠόι	δώματι	ἥματι
A.	ἔπος	γέρας	ἠόα	δῶμα	ἦμαρ
V.	ἔπος	γέρας	ἠώς	δῶμα	ἦμαρ

DUAL

N. A. V.	ἔπεε	γέραε		δώματε	ἥματε
G. D.	ἐπέοιιν	γεράοιιν		δωμάτοιιν	ἡμάτοιιν

PLURAL

N. V.	ἔπεα	γέρα(α)		δώματα	ἥματα
G.	ἐπέων	γεράων		δωμάτων	ἡμάτων
D.	{ ἐπέεσσι ἔπε(σ)σι	{ γεράεσσι γέρα(σ)σι		{ δωμάτεσσι δώμασι	{ ἡμάτεσσι ἥμασι
A.	ἔπεα	γέρα(α)		δώματα	ἥματα

708. Observe that stems ending in σ lose this σ when it comes between two vowels (603). Thus these words were formerly declined:

SINGULAR

N.	ἔπος	γέρας	ἠϝώς	= ἀϝσως (621)	= αυσως (602)
G.	ἐπεσος	γερασος	ἠϝοσος = ἀϝσοσος		= αυσοσος
D.	ἐπεσι	γερασι	ἠϝοσι = ἀϝσοσι		= αυσοσι

and thus throughout the whole declension, all numbers. The loss of intervocalic σ (603–604), and of ϝ also from ἠώς (602), gave the forms found above, 707.

709. *Observe that all nouns ending in -ος in the nominative singular are masculine or feminine (almost always masculine) if of the second declension, and that they are neuter if of the third declension.*

710. Nouns ending in -μα, in the nominative singular, and all others with genitives in -ατος are neuter.

711. The old ending -θι may be added to the stem of a noun or a pronoun to indicate *place where.*

712. The ending -θεν may be added to the stem of a noun or a pronoun to indicate *source* or *separation,* or to express various other relations of the genitive, as οὐρανόθεν *from heaven,* σέθεν *of you.*

713. -δε, a postpositive (15, 3) enclitic (553; 554, 6), with the force of a preposition (εἰς, ἐς, ἐπί), may be added to the accusative to denote *place to which,* or *limit of motion,* as ἀγορήνδε *to the assembly.*

714. The ending -ι may be added to the stem of a noun to denote *place where,* or *in which* (the locative, 657), as οἴκοι *at home.*

715. The ending -φι(ν), added to the stem of a noun or pronoun, is used to express various relations, both singular and plural, of both genitive and dative (especially when used in the instrumental sense).

716. Irregular Nouns. — There are various types of irregularity in the formation and declension of nouns; the gender in the plural may be different from that in the singular; words may be declined from two separate stems (heteroclites), but have the same nominative singular; they may have cases formed from another stem than the nominative singular (metaplastic forms); or they may be used in only one case, or part of the cases (defectives). Irregular nouns can best be learned from the lexicon, as one meets them in reading and has occasion to use them. Most of them are very rare.

Adjectives

717. Adjectives have three declensions, as nouns, and follow the same general rules.

718. With respect to form they may be divided into four classes :

1) Adjectives of the first and second (vowel) declensions.

2) Adjectives of the second declension (mostly compounds).

214

3) Adjectives of the first and third declensions.

4) Adjectives of the third (consonant) declension.

719. The form of the adjective which appears in the vocabulary is the nominative singular of all genders (except in the case of a very few of only one gender, in which case the nominative and genitive singular are given).

720. Adjectives of the first and second declensions have three endings (ος, η, ον) in the nominative singular, for the three genders, masculine, feminine, and neuter, respectively.

ADJECTIVES OF THE FIRST AND SECOND DECLENSIONS

721. κᾱλός, ή, όν beautiful, noble

(κᾱλο-, κᾱλᾱ-, κᾱλο-)

SINGULAR

	MASC.	FEM.	NEUT.
N.	κᾱλός	κᾱλή	κᾱλόν
G.	κᾱλοῦ, οἶο [όο]	κᾱλῆς	κᾱλοῦ, οἶο [όο]
D.	κᾱλῷ	κᾱλῇ	κᾱλῷ
A.	κᾱλόν	κᾱλήν	κᾱλόν
V.	κᾱλέ	κᾱλή	κᾱλόν

DUAL

	MASC.	FEM.	NEUT.
N. A. V.	κᾱλώ	κᾱλά	κᾱλώ
G. D.	κᾱλοῖιν	κᾱλῇιν	κᾱλοῖιν

PLURAL

	MASC.	FEM.	NEUT.
N. V.	κᾱλοί	κᾱλαί	κᾱλά
G.	κᾱλῶν	κᾱλάων [έων, ῶν]	κᾱλῶν
D.	κᾱλοῖσι, οῖς	κᾱλῇσι, ῇς	κᾱλοῖσι, οῖς
A.	κᾱλούς	κᾱλάς	κᾱλά

φίλος, η, ον dear, lovely, beloved

(φιλο-, φιλᾱ-, φιλο-)

SINGULAR

	MASC.	FEM.	NEUT.
N.	φίλος	φίλη	φίλον
G.	φίλου, οιο [οο]	φίλης	φίλου, οιο [οο]
D.	φίλῳ	φίλῃ	φίλῳ
A.	φίλον	φίλην	φίλον
V.	φίλε	φίλη	φίλον

215

DUAL

N. A. V.	φίλω	φίλᾱ	φίλω
G. D.	φίλοιιν	φίλῃιν	φίλοιιν

PLURAL

N. V.	φίλοι	φίλαι	φίλα
G.	φίλων	φιλάων [έων, ῶν]	φίλων
D.	φίλοισι, οις	φίλῃσι, ῃς	φίλοισι, οις
A.	φίλους	φίλᾱς	φίλα

NOTE. — Superlatives (as ἄριστος, η, ον), participles in ος, η, ον and all words that have these three endings in the nominative singular are similarly declined.

722. The feminine of adjectives of the first and second declen· sions regularly ends in -η, and is declined as above ; a few end in the -α, as δῖος, α, ον, and are declined as θάλασσα (663).

723. Adjectives of the second declension have only two endings (ος, ον), of which the first is both masculine and feminine, the second neuter. Most of these adjectives are compounds.

724. The masculine form of many adjectives is often used for both masculine and feminine, even in the case of those which have separate forms for the feminine.

725. Adjectives of the first and third declensions have a sepa· rate form for the feminine, which is declined like a noun in -α (θάλασσα, 663) of the first declension.

726. The masculine and neuter of adjectives with stems in -υ-, -εϝ- are declined like πῆχυς and ἄστυ respectively (704).

727.   πτερόεις, εσσα, εν wingéd

(πτεροϝεντ-, ϝετϳα-, ϝεντ-)

SINGULAR

N.	πτερόεις	πτερόεσσα	πτερόεν
G.	πτερόεντος	πτεροέσσης	πτερόεντος
D.	πτερόεντι	πτεροέσσῃ	πτερόεντι
A.	πτερόεντα	πτερόεσσαν	πτερόεν
V.	πτερόεν	πτερόεσσα	πτερόεν

DUAL

N. A. V.	πτερόεντε	πτεροέσσᾱ	πτερόεντε
G. D.	πτεροέντοιιν	πτεροέσσῃιν	πτεροέντοιιν

PLURAL

N. V.	πτερόεντες	πτερόεσσαι	πτερόεντα
G.	πτεροέντων	πτεροεσσάων [έων, ῶν]	πτεροέντων
D.	{ πτεροέντεσ(σ)ι πτερόεσ(σ)ι	{ πτεροέσσησι πτεροέσσης	{ πτεροέντεσ(σ)ι πτερόε(σ)σι
A.	πτερόεντας	πτεροέσσᾱς	πτερόεντα

εὐρύς, εἶα, ύ broad, wide
(εὐρυ-, εϝ-; εϝια-; υ-, εϝ-)

SINGULAR

N.	εὐρύς	εὐρεῖα	εὐρύ
G.	εὐρέος	εὐρείης	εὐρέος
D.	εὐρέι	εὐρείῃ	εὐρέι
A.	εὐρύν [έα]	εὐρεῖαν	εὐρύ
V.	εὐρύ(ς)	εὐρεῖα	εὐρύ

DUAL

N. A. V.	εὐρέε	εὐρείᾱ	εὐρέε
G. D.	εὐρέοιιν	εὐρείῃιν	εὐρέοιιν

PLURAL

N. V.	εὐρέες	εὐρεῖαι	εὐρέα
G.	εὐρέων	εὐρειάων [έων, ῶν]	εὐρέων
D.	εὐρέ(ε)σ(σ)ι	εὐρείῃσι	εὐρέ(ε)σ(σ)ι
A.	εὐρέας	εὐρείᾱς	εὐρέα

728. Observe that πτεροϝετια gives πτερόεσσα (600), while εὐρεϝος gives εὐρέος, etc. 602.

729. Adjectives of the third declension have only two endings, one for the masculine and feminine, the other for the neuter. Most of them have stems in -ον (nominatives in -ων, -ον), and in -ες (nominative in -ης, -ες).

730. A very few defectives have stems in -ωπ (nominative in -ωψ, -ωπις).

731.   ἀμείνων, ον better, braver   ἀεικής, ές unseemly
      (ἀμεινον-)   (-ἀ-ϝεικεσ-)

SINGULAR

MASC. AND FEM.	NEUT.	MASC. AND FEM.	NEUT.
N. ἀμείνων	ἄμεινον	ἀεικής	ἀεικές
G. ἀμείνονος	ἀμείνονος	ἀεικέος	ἀεικέος

217

D.	ἀμείνονι	ἀμείνονι	ἀεικέι	ἀεικέι
A.	ἀμείνονα	ἄμεινον	ἀεικέα	ἀεικές
V.	ἄμεινον	ἄμεινον	ἀεικές	ἀεικές

DUAL

N. A. V.	ἀμείνονε	ἀμείνονε	ἀεικέε	ἀεικέε
G. D.	ἀμεινόνοιιν	ἀμεινόνοιιν	ἀεικέοιιν	ἀεικέοιιν

PLURAL

N. V.	ἀμείνονες [ους]	ἀμείνονα	ἀεικέες	ἀεικέα
G.	ἀμεινόνων	ἀμεινόνων	ἀεικέων	ἀεικέων
D.	{ ἀμεινόνεσ(σ)ι ἀμείνοσι	{ ἀμεινόνεσ(σ)ι ἀμείνοσι	ἀεικέ(ε)σ(σ)ι	ἀεικέ(ε)σ(σ)ι
A.	ἀμείνονας [ους]	ἀμείνονα	ἀεικέας	ἀεικέα

732.   STEMS IN ντ AND IN ν

πᾶς, πᾶσα, πᾶν all, every
(παντ-, παντια-, παντ-)

SINGULAR

N.	πᾶς	πᾶσα	πᾶν
G.	παντός	πάσης	παντός
D.	παντί	πάσῃ	παιτί
A.	πάντα	πᾶσαν	πᾶν
V.	πᾶς	πᾶσα	πᾶν

DUAL
(None)

PLURAL

N. V.	πάντες	πᾶσαι	πάντα
G.	πάντων	πᾱσἄων [έων, ῶν]	πάντων
D.	{ πάντεσ(σ)ι πᾶσι	{ πάσῃσι πάσῃς	{ πάντεσ(σ)ι πᾶσι
A.	πάντας	πάσᾱς	πάντα

μέλᾱς, μέλαινα, μέλαν black, dark
(μελαν-, μελανια-, μελαν-)

SINGULAR

N.	μέλᾱς	μέλαινα	μέλαν
G.	μέλανος	μελαίνης	μέλανος
D.	μέλανι	μελαίνῃ	μέλανι
A.	μέλανα	μέλαιναν	μέλαν
V.	μέλαν	μέλαινα	μέλαν

DUAL

| N. A. V. | μέλανε | μελαίνᾱ | μέλανε |
| G. D. | μελάνοιιν | μελαίνῃιν | μελάνοιιν |

PLURAL

N. V.	μέλανες	μέλαιναι	μέλανα
G.	μελάνων	μελαινᾱων [έων, ῶν]	μελάνων
D.	{ μελάνεσ(σ)ι / μέλασι	{ μελαίνῃσι / μελαίνῃς	{ μελάνεσ(σ)ι / μέλασι
A.	μέλανας	μελαίνᾱς	μέλανα

Irregular Adjectives

733. μέγας, μεγάλη, μέγα great, large
(μεγα-, μεγαλο-, μεγαλᾱ-, μεγαλο-)

SINGULAR

N.	μέγας	μεγάλη	μέγα
G.	μεγάλου, οιο	μεγάλης	μεγάλου, οιο
D.	μεγάλῳ	μεγάλῃ	μεγάλῳ
A.	μέγαν	μεγάλην	μέγα
V.	μέγα(s)	μεγάλη	μέγα

DUAL

| N. A. V. | μεγάλω | μεγάλᾱ | μεγάλω |
| G. D. | μεγάλοιιν | μεγάλῃιν | μεγάλοιιν |

PLURAL

N. V.	μεγάλοι	μεγάλαι	μεγάλα
G.	μεγάλων	μεγαλᾱων [έων, ῶν]	μεγάλων
D.	μεγάλοισι, οις	μεγάλῃσι, ῃς	μεγάλοισι, οις
A.	μεγάλους	μεγάλᾱς	μεγάλα

πολύς, πολλή, πολύ much, many
(πολυ-, πολεϝ-; πολϝᾱ-; πολυ-, πολεϝ-)

SINGULAR

N.	πολύς [πουλύς]	πολλή	πολύ [πουλύ]
G.	πολέος	πολλῆς	πολέος
D.	πολέι	πολλῇ	πολέι
A.	πολύν [πουλύν]	πολλήν	πολύ [πουλύ]
V.	πολύ(s)	πολλή	πολύ

DUAL

(none)

219

PLURAL

N. V.	πολέες	πολλαί	πολέα
G.	πολέων	πολλάων [έων, ῶν]	πολέων
D.	πολέ(ε)σ(σ)ι	πολλῆσι, ῆς	πολέ(ε)σ(σ)ι
A.	πολέας [πολῦς]	πολλάς	πολέα

734. In addition to the irregular form πολύς, πολλή, πολύ, there is another form (πολλός, ή, όν) of this adjective which is regular and declined like κᾱλός, ή, όν (721).

Declension of Participles

735. All middle and passive participles, except those of the first and second aorist passive, are declined like κᾱλός, ή, όν (721).

736. All active participles (except the perfect, 744) and both first and second aorist passive participles have stems in -ντ. The masculine and neuter are of the third declension, the feminine of the first.

737. The vocative of participles has the same form as the nominative.

738. Participles with stems in οντ usually have the nominative singular masculine in -ων, as γέρων 693.

739. But the present and second aorist of -μι verbs (διδούς, δούς), and all stems ending in αντ, εντ, υντ, add ς, lose ντ (613), and lengthen the preceding vowel (giving ους, ᾱς, εις, ῡς 601). The dative plural of these stems is similarly formed.

740. Participles with stems in οντ, ending in -ων, ουσα, ον in the nominative singular:

λύων, ουσα, ον loosing, freeing
(λυοντ-, λυοντια-, λυοντ-)

SINGULAR

N. V.	λύων	λύουσα	λύον
G.	λύοντος	λυούσης	λύοντος
D.	λύοντι	λυούσῃ	λύοντι
A.	λύοντα	λύουσαν	λύον

DUAL

N. A. V.	λύοντε	λυούσᾱ	λύοντε
G. D.	λυόντοιιν	λυούσῃιν	λυόντοιιν

PLURAL

N. V. λύοντες	λύουσαι	λύοντα
G. λυόντων	λυουσᾶων [ἑων, ῶν]	λυόντων
D. λύοντεσ(σ)ι, λύουσι	λυούσῃσι, λυούσῃς	λυόντεσ(σ)ι, λύουσι
A. λύοντας	λυούσᾱς	λύοντα

741. Participles with stems in οντ, αντ, εντ, υντ, ending in ς in the nominative singular masculine:

PRESENT PARTICIPLE : διδούς, οὖσα, όν giving
(διδοντ-, διδοντι̯α-, διδοντ-)

SINGULAR

	MASC.	FEM.	NEUT.
N. V.	διδούς	διδοῦσα	διδόν
G.	διδόντος	διδούσης	διδόντος
D.	διδόντι	διδούσῃ	διδόντι
A.	διδόντα	διδοῦσαν	διδόν

DUAL

N. A. V.	διδόντε	διδούσᾱ	διδόντε
G. D.	διδόντοιιν	διδούσῃιν	διδόντοιιν

PLURAL

	MASC.	FEM.	NEUT.
N. V.	διδόντες	διδοῦσαι	διδόντα
G.	διδόντων	διδουσάων [ἑων, ῶν]	διδόντων
D.	{ διδόντεσ(σ)ι / διδοῦσι	{ διδούσῃσι / διδούσῃς	{ διδόντεσ(σ)ι / διδοῦσι
A.	διδόντας	διδούσᾱς	διδόντα

AORIST PARTICIPLE : λύσᾱς, ᾱσα, αν having loosed
(λῡσαντ-, λῡσαντι̯α-, λῡσαντ-)

SINGULAR

	MASC.	FEM.	NEUT.
N. V.	λύσᾱς	λύσᾱσα	λῦσαν
G.	λύσαντος	λῡσάσης	λύσαντος
D.	λύσαντι	λῡσάσῃ	λύσαντι
A.	λύσαντα	λύσᾱσαν	λῦσαν

DUAL

N. A. V.	λύσαντε	λῡσάσᾱ	λύσαντε
G. D.	λῡσάντοιιν	λῡσάσῃιν	λῡσάντοιιν

221

PLURAL

N V.	λύσαντες	λύσᾱσαι	λύσαντα
G.	λῡσάντων	λῡσᾱσάων [έων, ῶν]	λῡσάντων
D.	{ λῡσάντεσ(σ)ι { λύσᾱσι	{ λῡσάσῃσι { λῡσάσῃς	{ λῡσάντεσ(σ)ι { λύσᾱσι
A.	λύσαντας	λῡσάσᾱς	λύσαντα

742.   AORIST PASSIVE PARTICIPLE

λυθείς, εῖσα, έν (having been) loosed
(λυθεντ-, λυθεντι̯α-, λυθεντ-)

SINGULAR

	MASC.	FEM.	NEUT.
N. V.	λυθείς	λυθεῖσα	λυθέν
G.	λυθέντος	λυθείσης	λυθέντος
D.	λυθέντι	λυθείσῃ	λυθέντι
A.	λυθέντα	λυθεῖσαν	λυθέν

DUAL

N. A. V.	λυθέντε	λυθείσᾱ	λυθέντε
G. D.	λυθέντοιιν	λυθείσῃιν	λυθέντοιιν

PLURAL

N. V.	λυθέντες	λυθεῖσαι	λυθέντα
G.	λυθέντων	λυθεισάων [έων, ῶν]	λυθέντων
D.	{ λυθέντεσ(σ)ι { λυθεῖσι	{ λυθείσῃσι { λυθείσῃς	{ λυθέντεσ(σ)ι { λυθεῖσι
A.	λυθέντας	λυθείσᾱς	λυθέντα

743.   SECOND AORIST ACTIVE PARTICIPLE

δύς, δῦσα, δύν having entered
(δυντ-, δυντι̯α-, δυντ-)

SINGULAR

	MASC.	FEM.	NEUT.
N. V.	δύς	δῦσα	δύν
G.	δύντος	δύσης	δύντος
D.	δύντι	δύσῃ	δύντι
A.	δύντα	δῦσαν	δύν

DUAL

N. A. V.	δύντε	δύσᾱ	δύντε
G. D.	δύντοιιν	δύσῃιν	δύντοιιν

222

PLURAL

N. V.	δύντες	δῦσαι	δύντα
G.	δύντων	δυσᾶων [έων, ῶν]	δύντων
D.	δύντεσ(σ)ι / δῦσι	δύσησι / δύσης	δύντεσ(σ)ι / δῦσι
A.	δύντας	δύσᾱς	δύντα

Perfect Active Participles

744. Perfect active participles have stems in (κ)οτ. Those which have κ are called first perfects, those without κ second perfects.

λελυκώς, υῖα, ός having loosed
(λελυκοτ-, λελυκυσι̯α-, λελυκοτ-)

SINGULAR

	MASC.	FEM.	NEUT.
N. V.	λελυκώς	λελυκυῖα	λελυκός
G.	λελυκότος	λελυκυίης	λελυκότος
D.	λελυκότι	λελυκυίη	λελυκότι
A.	λελυκότα	λελυκυῖαν	λελυκός

DUAL

	MASC.	FEM.	NEUT.
N. A. V.	λελυκότε	λελυκυίᾱ	λελυκότε
G. D.	λελυκότοιιν	λελυκυίῃιν	λελυκότοιιν

PLURAL

	MASC.	FEM.	NEUT.
N. V.	λελυκότες	λελυκυῖαι	λελυκότα
G.	λελυκότων	λελυκυιάων [έων, ῶν]	λελυκότων
D.	λελυκότεσ(σ)ι / λελυκόσι	λελυκυίῃσι / λελυκυίῃς	λελυκότεσ(σ)ι / λελυκόσι
A.	λελυκότας	λελυκυίᾱς	λελυκότα

εἰδώς, (ε)ιδυῖα, εἰδός knowing
(ϝειδϝοτ-, ϝ(ε)ιδϝυσι̯α-, ϝειδϝοτ-)

SINGULAR

	MASC.	FEM.	NEUT.
N. V.	εἰδώς	(ε)ιδυῖα	εἰδός
G.	εἰδότος	(ε)ιδυίης	εἰδότος
D.	εἰδότι	(ε)ιδυίη	εἰδότι
A.	εἰδότα	(ε)ιδυῖαν	εἰδός

223

DUAL

N. A. V.	εἰδότε	(ε)ἰδυΐᾱ	εἰδότε
G. D.	εἰδότοιιν	(ε)ἰδυΐηιν	εἰδότοιιν

PLURAL

N. V.	εἰδότες	(ε)ἰδυῖαι	εἰδότα
G.	εἰδότων	(ε)ἰδυιάων [έων, ῶν]	εἰδότων
D. {	εἰδότεσ(σ)ι	{ (ε)ἰδυίῃσι	{ εἰδότεσ(σ)ι
{	εἰδόσι	{ (ε)ἰδυίῃς	{ εἰδόσι
A.	εἰδότας	(ε)ἰδυΐᾱς	εἰδότα

NOTE 1. — λελυκώς, υἶα, ός does not occur in Homer, and there are very few first perfects in Homeric Greek. The forms of the first perfect participle, as given above are common in later Greek.

NOTE 2. — Perfect participles are often declined with ω instead of o throughout; and at times end in -ων, -ουσα, -ον and are inflected with the same endings as the present participle.

745. Participles of contract verbs, 936–944 (usually left uncontracted) are declined in their contracted forms as follows:

τῑμῶν, οὖσα, ῶν (τῑμάων, άουσα, άον) honoring
(τῑμαοντ-, τῑμαοντια-, τῑμαοντ-)

SINGULAR

	MASC.	FEM.	NEUT.
N. V.	τῑμῶν	τῑμῶσα	τῑμῶν
G.	τῑμῶντος	τῑμώσης	τῑμῶντος
D.	τῑμῶντι	τῑμώσῃ	τῑμῶντι
A.	τῑμῶντα	τῑμῶσαν	τῑμῶν

DUAL

N. A. V.	τῑμῶντε	τῑμώσᾱ	τῑμῶντε
G. D.	τῑμώντοιιν	τῑμώσῃιν	τῑμώντοιιν

PLURAL

N. V.	τῑμῶντες	τῑμῶσαι	τῑμῶντα
G.	τῑμώντων	τῑμωσάων [έων, ῶν]	τῑμώντων
D. {	τῑμῶντεσ(σ)ι	{ τῑμώσῃσι	{ τῑμῶντεσ(σ)ι
{	τῑμῶσι	{ τῑμώσῃς	{ τῑμῶσι
A.	τῑμῶντας	τῑμώσᾱς	τῑμῶντα

ποιῶν, εὖσα, εὖν (έων, έουσα, ίον)
(ποιεοντ-, ποιεοντμα-, ποιεοντ-)

SINGULAR

	MASC.	FEM.	NEUT.
N. V.	ποιῶν	ποιεῦσα	ποιεῦν
G.	ποιεῦντος	ποιεύσης	ποιεῦντος
D.	ποιεῦντι	ποιεύσῃ	ποιεῦντι
A.	ποιεῦντα	ποιεῦσαν	ποιεῦν

DUAL

	MASC.	FEM.	NEUT.
N. A. V.	ποιεῦντε	ποιεύσᾱ	ποιεῦντε
G. D.	ποιεύντοιιν	ποιεύσῃιν	ποιεύντοιιν

PLURAL

	MASC.	FEM.	NEUT.
N. V.	ποιεῦντες	ποιεῦσαι	ποιεῦντα
G.	ποιεύντων	ποιευσάων [έων, ῶν]	ποιεύντων
D.	ποιεύντεσ(σ)ι / ποιεῦσι	ποιεύσῃσι / ποιεύσῃς	ποιεύντεσ(σ)ι / ποιεῦσι
A.	ποιεῦντας	ποιεύσᾱς	ποιεῦντα

746. The participles of -οω contract verbs (as χολόω *anger*) end in -ῶν, οὖσα, οὖν (as χολῶν, χολοῦσά, χολοῦν) in the nominative singular, and are quite regular in their declension, the genitive being χολοῦντος, χολούσης, χολοῦντος; the dative being χολοῦντι, χολούσῃ, χολοῦντι, etc.

Comparison of Adjectives

747. Most adjectives form their comparatives by adding -τερος, η, ον, and their superlatives by adding -τατος, η, ον to the stem of the masculine positive.

748. If the penult of the stem is long by nature or position (522), the stem for the comparative and superlative remains unchanged. If it is short, it is regularly lengthened, ο becoming ω.

749. EXAMPLES

Positive	Comparative	Superlative
πιστός (πιστο-) faithful, trustworthy	πιστότερος	πιστότατος
μαλακός (μαλακο-) soft, gentle	μαλακώτερος	μαλακώτατος

750. The declension of comparatives and superlatives is usually the regular vowel declension of adjectives, as κᾱλός, ή, όν (721).

225

751. Some adjectives, mainly those in -υς and -ρος, form the comparative and superlative by changing these endings to -ιων, -ιον for the comparative, and to -ιστος, η, ον for the superlative.

752.   EXAMPLES

Positive	Comparative	Superlative
ἡδύς sweet	ἡδίων, ἥδιον sweeter	ἥδιστος, η, ον sweetest
αἰσχρός shameful	αἰσχίων, ιον more shameful	αἴσχιστος, η, ον most shameful

753. The comparative of these adjectives is declined like ἀμείνων, ον (731), and the superlative like κᾱλός, ή, όν (721).

754. The most important cases of irregular comparison are:

Positive	Comparative	Superlative
1) ἀγαθός good, brave, noble	ἀρείων, ον ἀμείνων, ον βέλτερος, η, ον λωίων, ον (λωίτερος, η, ον)	ἄριστος, η, ον
2) κρατύς (κραταιός, ή, όν) powerful	κρείσσων, ον	κράτιστος (κάρτιστος)
κρατερός, ή, όν (καρτερός) powerful	φέρτερος	φέρτατος (φέριστος)
3) κακός, ή, όν bad, cowardly	κακίων, ον (κακώτερος) ἥσσων, ον χείρων, ον (χειρότερος) (χερείων, ον)	κάκιστος, η, ον ἥκιστος, η, ον
4) κᾱλός, ή, όν beautiful, noble	καλλίων, ον	κάλλιστος, η, ον
5) μέγας large, mighty	μείζων, ον (μέζων, ον?)	μέγιστος, η, ον
6) μῑκρός small, tiny	μείων, ον	
7) ἐλαχύς small, tiny	ἐλάσσων, ον	ἐλάχιστος, η, ον
8) ὀλίγος small, few	ὀλείζων, ον (ὀλίζων, ον)	ὀλίγιστος, η, ον
9) πολύς much, many	πλείων, ον (πλέων, ον)	πλεῖστος, η, ον
10) φίλος dear, lovely	φίλτερος, η, ον (φιλίων, ον)	φίλτατος, η, ον

755. Some adjectives do not occur in the positive. Their comparatives and superlatives are formed from prepositions, adverbs, verbs, nouns, and pronouns.

226

756. The comparative and superlative may express merely a high degree of the quality, without any idea of comparison being involved, and at times may indicate simply characteristic or possession.

Numerals

757. The Greek numerals were as follows:

	CARDINALS	ORDINALS	ADVERBS
1	εἷς, μία (ἴα), ἕν	πρῶτος, η, ον	ἅπαξ
2	δύο (δύω)	δεύτερος, η, ον	δίς
3	τρεῖς, τρία	τρί(τα)τος, η, ον	τρίς
4	τέσσαρες (πίσυρες), τέσσαρα	τέταρτος (τέτρατος), η, ον	τετράκις
5	πέντε	πέμπτος, η, ον	πεντάκις*
6	ἕξ	ἕκτος, η, ον	ἑξάκις*
7	ἑπτά	ἕβδομος (ἑβδόματος), η, ον	ἑπτάκις*
8	ὀκτώ	ὄγδοος (ὀγδόατος), η, ον	ὀκτάκις*
9	ἐννέα	ἔνατος (εἴνατος), η, ον	ἐνάκις
10	δέκα	δέκατος, η, ον	δεκάκις
11	ἕνδεκα	ἑνδέκατος, η, ον	ἑνδεκάκις*
12	δ(υ)ώδεκα, δύο καὶ δέκα	δ(υ)ωδέκατος, η, ον	δ(υ)ωδεκάκις*
13	τρεισκαίδεκα (τρεῖς καὶ δέκα)	τρεισκαιδέκατος, η, ον	τρεισκαιδεκάκις*
14	τεσσαρεσκαίδεκα	τέταρτος (τέτρατος) καὶ δέκατος, η. ον	τεσσαρεσκαιδεκάκις*
15	πεντεκαίδεκα	πέμπτος καὶ δέκατος, η, ον	πεντεκαιδεκάκις*
16	ἑκκαίδεκα	ἕκτος καὶ δέκατος, η, ον	ἑκκαιδεκάκις*
17	ἑπτακαίδεκα	ἕβδομος καὶ δέκατος, η, ον	ἑπτακαιδεκάκις*
18	ὀκτωκαίδεκα	ὄγδοος καὶ δέκατος, η, ον	ὀκτωκαιδεκάκις*
19	ἐννεακαίδεκα	ἔνατος καὶ δέκατος, η, ον	ἐννεακαιδεκάκις*
20	εἴκοσι (ἐείκοσι)	εἰκοστός (ἐεικοστός), ή, όν	εἰκοσάκις
21	εἷς καὶ εἴκοσι (εἴκοσι καὶ εἷς, εἴκοσιν εἷς)	πρῶτος καὶ εἰκοστός	εἰκοσάκις ἅπαξ
30	τριήκοντα	τριηκοστός,* ή, όν	τριηκοντάκις*
40	τεσσαράκοντα	τεσσαρακοστός,* ή, όν	τεσσαρακοντάκις*
50	πεντήκοντα	πεντηκοστός,* ή, όν	πεντηκοντάκις*
60	ἑξήκοντα	ἑξηκοστός,* ή, όν	ἑξηκοντάκις*
70	ἑβδομήκοντα*	ἑβδομηκοστός,* ή, όν	ἑβδομηκοντάκις*
80	ὀγδώκοντα	ὀγδωκοστός,* ή, όν	ὀγδωκοντάκις*
90	ἐνενήκοντα (ἐννήκοντα)	ἐνενηκοστός,* ή, όν	ἐνενηκοντάκις*

100	ἑκατόν	ἑκατοστός,* ἡ, όν	ἑκατοντάκις*
200	διηκόσιοι, αι, α	διηκοσιοστός,* ἡ, όν	διηκοσιάκις*
300	τριηκόσιοι, αι, α	τριηκοσιοστός,* ἡ, όν	τριηκοσιάκις*
400	τετρακόσιοι,* αι, α	τετρακοσιοστός,* ἡ, όν	τετρακοσιάκις*
500	πεντηκόσιοι, αι, α	πεντακοσιοστός,* ἡ, όν	πεντακοσιάκις*
600	ἑξακόσιοι,* αι, α	ἑξακοσιοστός,* ἡ, όν	ἑξακοσιάκις*
700	ἑπτακόσιοι,* αι, α	ἑπτακοσιοστός,* ἡ, όν	ἑπτακοσιάκις*
800	ὀκτακόσιοι,* αι, α	ὀκτακοσιοστός,* ἡ, όν	ὀκτακοσιάκις*
900	ἐνακόσιοι,* αι, α	ἐν(ν)ακοσιοστός,* ἡ, όν	ἐνακοσιάκις*
1000	χίλιοι, αι, α	χιλιοστός,* ἡ,* όν	χῑλιάκις*
2000	δισχίλιοι, αι, α	δισχῑλιοστός,* ἡ, όν	δισχῑλιάκις*
3000	τρισχίλιοι, αι, α	τρισχῑλιοστός,* ἡ, όν	τρισχῑλιάκις*
10,000	μύριοι,* αι, α (δεκά-χῑλοι, αι, α)	μῡριοστός,* ἡ, όν	μῡριάκις*
20,000	δισμύριοι,* αι, α	δισμῡριοστός,* ἡ, όν	δισμῡριάκις*
100,000	δεκακισμύριοι,* αι, α	δεκακισμῡριοστός,* ἡ, όν	δεκακισμῡριάκις*

758.   Declension of the First Four Cardinals

εἷς, μία, ἕν one	δύω (δύο)	τρεῖς [1], τρία	τέσσαρες, τέσσαρα
(ἐν-, μιᾱ-, ἑν-)	(δυω-, ο-)	(τρε-, τρι-)	(τεσσαρ-)
εἷς μία ἕν	δύω indecl.	τρεῖς [1] τρία	τέσσαρες τέσσαρα
ἑνός μιῆς ἑνός		τριῶν τριῶν	τεσσάρων τεσσάρων
ἑνί μιῇ ἑνί		τρισί τρισί	τέσσαρσι τέσσαρσι
ἕνα μίαν ἕν		τρεῖς τρία	τέσσαρας τέσσαρα

759. In addition to the above forms there occur at times for μία, ἴα (ἰῆς, ἰῇ, ἴαν); for ἑνί, ἰῷ; for τέσσαρες, πίσυρες.

Personal Pronouns

760. The personal pronouns are declined as follows:

SINGULAR

N. V.	ἐγώ(ν) I	σύ [τύνη] you	—— he, she, it
G.	ἐμεῖο, μευ (ἐμέο, ἐμεῦ, ἐμέθεν)	σεῖο, σεο (σέο, σεῦ, σευ, σέθεν)	εἷο, ἑο, (ἕο, εὗ, εὐ, ἕθεν, ἔθεν)
D.	ἐμοί, μοι	σοί, τοι [τεΐν]	ἑοῖ, οἱ (οἱ)
A.	ἐμέ, με	σέ, σε	ἑέ, ἑ (ἕ, μιν)

[1] = τρέες, 584, 2.

DUAL

| N. A. V. | νώϊ, νώ | σφῶϊ, σφώ | σφωε |
| G. D. | νῶϊν | σφῶϊν (σφῷν) | σφωϊν |

PLURAL

N. V.	ἡμεῖς (ἄμμες)	ὑμεῖς (ὔμμες)	
G.	ἡμείων (ἡμέων)	ὑμείων (ὑμέων)	σφείων, σφεων
			(σφέων, σφῶν)
D.	{ ἡμῖν (ἄμμι(ν),	{ ὑμῖν (ὔμμι(ν),	{ σφίσι, σφισι
	ἡμῖν, ἡμιν)	ὔμῖν)	(σφι(ν))
A.	{ ἡμέας (ἡμας,	ὑμέας (ὔμμε)	{ σφέας, σφε(ας),
	ἡμεας, ἄμμε)		σφάς

761. The nominative singular of the personal pronouns is used only for the sake of emphasis and contrast, being omitted under other conditions.

762. The oblique cases of these pronouns are enclitic (553), but if the pronoun is emphatic these cases keep their accent, and the longer forms of the first person are then used. This happens as a rule after prepositions. The forms without accent in the above table are enclitic.

763. The pronoun of the third person is sometimes used as a reflexive, that is, it refers to the subject of the leading verb of the sentence.

764. The possessive pronouns are formed from the stems of the personal pronouns and are declined like adjectives of the vowel declension, *i.e.* like κᾱλός, ή, όν (721).

Possessive Pronouns

SING. ἐμός, ή, όν my, mine. σός, σή, σόν (τεός, τεή, τεόν) your(s).
ἑός, ἑή, ἑόν (ὅς, ἥ, ὅν) his, her(s), its (own), [my, your own].

DUAL. νωίτερος, η, ον our(s). σφωίτερος, η, ον your(s).

PLURAL. ἡμέτερος, η, ον our(s). ἁμός, ή, όν our(s).
ὑμέτερος, η, ον your(s). ὑμός, ή, όν your(s).
σφέτερος, η, ον their(s). σφός, σφή, σφόν their(s).

765. The most common pronoun, ὁ, ἡ, τό, used regularly as the definite article in later Greek, is usually employed as the demonstrative, but sometimes as a personal or as a relative pronoun in Homer. It is declined as follows:

ὁ, ἡ, τό this, that; he, she, it; who, which, what

SINGULAR

	MASC.	FEM.	NEUT.
N.	ὁ	ἡ	τό
G.	τοῦ, τοῖο	τῆς	τοῦ, τοῖο
D.	τῷ	τῇ	τῷ
A.	τόν	τήν	τό

DUAL

	MASC.	FEM.	NEUT.
N. A.	τώ	(τώ)	τώ
G. D.	τοῖιν	(τοῖιν)	τοῖιν

PLURAL

	MASC.	FEM.	NEUT.
N.	οἱ (τοί)	αἱ (ταί)	τά
G.	τῶν	τάων [τῶν]	τῶν
D.	τοῖσι, τοῖς	τῇσι, τῇς	τοῖσι, τοῖς
A.	τούς	τάς	τά

766. The intensive pronoun is declined as follows:

αὐτός, ἡ, ὁ self, same

SINGULAR

	MASC.	FEM.	NEUT.
N.	αὐτός	αὐτή	αὐτό
G.	αὐτοῦ, εἶο	αὐτῆς	αὐτοῦ, οἷο
D.	αὐτῷ	αὐτῇ	αὐτῷ
A.	αὐτόν	αὐτήν	αὐτό

DUAL

	MASC.	FEM.	NEUT.
N. A.	αὐτώ	(αὐτώ)	αὐτώ
G. D.	αὐτοῖιν	(αὐτοῖιν)	αὐτοῖιν

PLURAL

	MASC.	FEM.	NEUT.
N.	αὐτοί	αὐταί	αὐτά
G.	αὐτῶν	αὐτάων [έων, ῶν]	αὐτῶν
D.	αὐτοῖσι, οἷς	αὐτῇσι, ῇς	αὐτοῖσι, οἷς
A.	αὐτούς	αὐτάς	αὐτά

767. The most important interrogative pronoun, τίς, τί who? which? what? has the acute accent always on the first syllable, and never changes the acute to the grave, even when followed by other words.

768. The indefinite τὶς, τὶ *some (one), any (one), something, anything, a(n)* is spelled and declined the same as the interrogative, but differs from it in accent, the indefinite pronoun being always an enclitic, 553 ff.

769. Indefinite and Interrogative Pronouns

τὶς, τὶ some (one), any (one), something   τίς, τί, who? which? what?

SINGULAR

MASC. AND FEM.	NEUT.	MASC. AND FEM.	NEUT.
N. τὶς	τὶ	τίς	τί
G. τέο (τεῦ)		τέο (τεῦ)	
D. τέῳ (τῷ, τινί)		τέῳ (τῷ, τίνι)	
A. τινά	τὶ	τίνα	τί

DUAL

N. A. τινέ	τινέ	τίνε	τίνε
G. D. τινοῖιν	τινοῖιν	τίνοιιν	τίνοιιν

PLURAL

N. τινές	τινά (ἄσσα)	τίνες	τίνα
G. τεῶν	τεῶν	τέων	τέων
D. τεοῖσι	τεοῖσι	τέοισι	τέοισι
A. τινάς	τινά (ἄσσα)	τίνας	τίνα

770. The relative pronouns are ὅς, ἥ, ὅ, and ὁ, ἡ, τό *who, which, what* (765), together with the indefinite relative pronoun ὅστις; ἥτις, ὅτι (ὅς τις, ἥ τις, ὅ τι) *whoever, whichever, whatever,* 776.

771. The most important demonstrative pronouns are οὗτος, αὕτη, τοῦτο *this,* (ἐ)κεῖνος, η, ο *that,* ὁ, ἡ, τό (used also as a relative and as a personal pronoun, 765) *this, that,* with its compounds, as ὅδε, ἥδε, τόδε ; ὅγε, ἥγε, τόγε (ὁ γε, ἥ γε, τό γε), etc.

772. These pronouns are declined in the main like adjectives of the vowel declension (καλός, ή, όν, 721) with the exception that the neuter nominative and accusative singular ends in -ο instead of in -ον.

231

773.   Relative Pronoun

ὅς (ὅ), ἥ, ὅ who, which, what

SINGULAR

	MASC.	FEM.	NEUT,
N.	ὅς (ὅ)	ἥ	ὅ
G.	οὗ [ὅου, ὅο]	ἧς [ἕης]	οὗ [ὅου, ὅο]
D.	ᾧ	ᾗ	ᾧ
A.	ὅν	ἥν	ὅ

DUAL

N. A.	ὥ	(ὥ)	ὥ
G. D.	οἷιν	(οἷιν)	οἷιν

PLURAL

N.	οἵ	αἵ	ἅ
G.	ὧν	ὧν	ὧν
D.	οἷσι, οἷς	ᾗσι, ᾗς	οἷσι, οἷς
A.	οὕς	ἅς	ἅ

774.   Demonstrative Pronouns

(ἐ)κεῖνος, η, ο that

SINGULAR

	MASC.	FEM.	NEUT.
N.	(ἐ)κεῖνος	(ἐ)κείνη	(ἐ)κεῖνο
G.	(ἐ)κείνου, οιο	(ἐ)κείνης	(ἐ)κείνου, οιο
D.	(ἐ)κείνῳ	(ἐ)κείνῃ	(ἐ)κείνῳ
A.	(ἐ)κεῖνον	(ἐ)κείνην	(ἐ)κεῖνο

DUAL

N. A.	(ἐ)κείνω	((ἐ)κείνω)	(ἐ)κείνω
G. D.	(ἐ)κείνοιιν	((ἐ)κείνοιιν)	(ἐ)κείνοιιν

PLURAL

N.	(ἐ)κεῖνοι	(ἐ)κεῖναι	(ἐ)κεῖνα
G.	(ἐ)κείνων	(ἐ)κεινάων [έων, ῶν]	(ἐ)κείνων
D.	(ἐ)κείνοισι, οις	(ἐ)κείνῃσι, ῃς	(ἐ)κείνοισι, οις
A.	(ἐ)κείνους	(ἐ)κείνᾱς	(ἐ)κεῖνα

ὅδε, ἥδε, τόδε this

SINGULAR

N.	ὅδε	ἥδε	τόδε
G.	τοῦδε, τοῖοδε	τῆσδε	τοῦδε, τοῖοδε

232

D.	τῷδε	τῇδε	τῷδε
A.	τόνδε	τήνδε	τόδε

DUAL

N. A.	τώδε	(τώδε)	τώδε
G. D.	τοῖνδε	(τοῖνδε)	τοῖνδε

PLURAL

N.	οἵδε (τοίδε)	αἵδε (ταίδε)	τάδε
G.	τῶνδε	τᾶωνδε [τῶνδε]	τῶνδε
D.	τοῖσ(ι)δε	τῇσ(ι)δε	τοῖσ(ι)δε
A.	τούσδε	τάσδε	τάδε

οὗτος, αὕτη, τοῦτο this

SINGULAR

	MASC.	FEM.	NEUT.
N.	οὗτος	αὕτη	τοῦτο
G.	τούτου, οιο	ταύτης	τούτου, οιο
D.	τούτῳ	ταύτῃ	τούτῳ
A.	τοῦτον	ταύτην	τοῦτο

DUAL

N. A.	τούτω	(τούτω)	τούτω
G. D.	τούτοιν	(τούτοιν)	τούτοιν

PLURAL

N.	οὗτοι	αὗται	ταῦτα
G.	τούτων	ταυτάων [έων, ῶν]	τούτων
D.	τούτοισι, οις	ταύτῃσι, ῃς	τούτοισι, οις
A.	τούτους	ταύτᾱς	ταῦτα

NOTE. — The dative plural of ὅδε, ἥδε, τόδε at times has τοίσδεσ(σ)ι instead of τοῖσ(ι)δε.

775. Compounds of ὁ, ἡ, τό (as ὅδε, ἥδε, τόδε; ὅγε, ἥγε, τόγε) are declined the same as the simple form (ὁ, ἡ, τό) with the additional part (-γε, -δε, etc.) attached. As these are compounds, formed of the simple pronouns and the enclitics, they are accented the same as the simple forms without the enclitics (553, 558).

776. The indefinite relative pronoun (ὅστις, ἥτις, ὅ τι) *whoever, whichever, whatever*, is a compound of the simple relative (ὅς, ἥ, ὅ) and the indefinite τὶς, τὶ, each part of which is declined separately (or sometimes only the latter part).

233

777. ὅ τι, the neuter of the indefinite relative pronoun, is thus printed in most texts, that it may not be confused with the conjunction, ὅτι *that, because, why.*

778. The Reciprocal Pronoun

ἀλλήλοιιν, ῃιν, οιιν (of) one another

DUAL

MASC.	FEM.	NEUT.
G. ἀλλήλοιιν	ἀλλήλῃιν	ἀλλήλοιιν
D. ἀλλήλοιιν	ἀλλήλῃιν	ἀλλήλοιιν
A. ἀλλήλω	ἀλλήλᾱ	ἀλλήλω

PLURAL

G. ἀλλήλων	ἀλληλάων [έων, ῶν]	ἀλλήλων
D. ἀλλήλοις(ι)	ἀλλήλῃς(ι)	ἀλλήλοις(ι)
A. ἀλλήλους	ἀλλήλᾱς	ἄλληλα

779. This pronoun is used only in the genitive, dative, and accusative.

Adverbs

780. Most Greek adverbs are of twofold origin :

1) Isolated case-forms of nouns, pronouns, and adjectives, which became crystallized and used in an adverbial connection.

2) Adverbs formed by means of various suffixes (630), of which the origin is unknown.

781. The most common occurrence of the use of various cases of the noun, pronoun, and adjective adverbially is the employment of the neuter accusative of the adjective, singular or plural, with or without the pronoun τό, τά, as an adverb. The neuter of nouns and pronouns is sometimes, but less commonly, used in the same way.

782. A great number of adverbs end either in -ω or in -ως.

783. Those ending in -ως are adverbs of manner, and are formed from adjectives and pronouns. They have the accent of the genitive plural neuter of the word from which they are formed.

784. For the comparative of these abverbs, the neuter accusative singular of the comparative of the adjective is used, and for the superlative the neuter accusative plural of the superlative of the adjective.

785. Adverbs of place which end in -ω (and a few others) form the comparative by adding -τέρω, and the superlative by adding -τάτω to the stem (630).

786. The prepositions were originally adverbs, and most of them are still so used in Homer.

787.　　　　　　　Examples of Formation

ADJECTIVE	STEM	GENITIVE PLURAL	ADVERB
κᾱλός, ή, όν	κᾱλο-	κᾱλῶν	κᾱλῶς
κακός, ή, όν	κακο-	κακῶν	κακῶς
ἄλλος, η, ο	ἀλλο-	ἄλλων	ἄλλως

788. The most important suffixes (630) used in the formation of adverbs (780, 2) are:

1) -ι, -σι, -θι, -ου, denoting *place where.*

2) -θι, -θε(ν), denoting *place where.*

3) -θεν, denoting *place whence.*

4) -δε (originally an enclitic preposition = English *to*), denoting *whither.*

5) -σε, denoting *whither.*

6) -τε, denoting *time.*

7) -τος, denoting *where.*

8) -κα (origin unknown), as in αὐτί-κα.

9) -κας (origin unknown), as in ἐ-κάς.

10) -κις (with generalizing, indefinite meaning; akin to τὶς, τὶ), as πολλά-κις *many a time, often.*

11) Some other endings are -α, -δην, -δον, -τι, -στι.

Verbs

789. Verbs, as well as all other inflected (626–630) forms, consist of two principal elements:

1) the *stem;*

2) the *ending,* or *suffix.*

235

790. Often more than one suffix is fused with a verb stem, to indicate its various relations of *mode, tense, voice, person, number,* etc., as λύ-ο-μεν, λύ-ε-τε (from λύ-ω *loose*), where the primary stem of the verb is λυ-, to which the suffixes are attached.

791. The forms of a Greek verb fall into two main classes :
1) *Finite* (indicative, subjunctive, optative, and imperative).
2) *Infinite* (infinitive and participle).

792. The *characteristics* of the finite forms are the *personal endings, augment, reduplication, voice, mode,* and *tense signs,* etc.

793. The participle is a verbal adjective, and is used as other adjectives.

794. The infinitive is a verbal noun, formerly used in several cases, but restricted in Greek to old case-forms of the dative and locative.

795. Thematic and Athematic forms. — With respect to form Greek verbs fall into two main classes :
1) -ω verbs, *i.e.* those ending in -ω in the first person singular, present active indicative, sometimes called *thematic* verbs (796).
2) -μι verbs, *i.e.* those ending in -μι in the first person singular, present active indicative, sometimes called *athematic* verbs (797).

796. The thematic verbs are so named because in a majority of their forms the personal ending (819–821) is preceded by % (o before μ or ν, or in the optative mode, otherwise ε), which is called the *thematic* vowel. Thus, λυ% (λύω) is called the *theme,* to which the personal endings (819–821) are attached.

797. *Athematic* verbs do not have this connecting vowel, but the personal endings are attached directly to the stem of the verb.

798. Many verbs which are regularly thematic may have athematic forms, as δέχθαι, δέκτο (δέχομαι) ; λύμην, λύτο (λύω) ; ἆλτο (ἅλλομαι), etc.

799. In the subjunctive these thematic vowels, %, are regularly long, being ω/η respectively.

800. In some cases the thematic vowel is short in the subjunctive, particularly in the dual and plural of the present and second

236

aorist of -μι verbs, the first aorist and second perfect of all verbs, and the second aorist of all verbs having athematic second aorists in the indicative.

801. Strictly speaking no Greek verb is thematic or athematic throughout; but certain of their forms are inflected thematically and others athematically.

802. Those inflected thematically are: all futures; all presents and imperfects of -ω verbs (thematic presents); all second aorists having the thematic vowel (ending in -ον in the first person singular, active indicative, 865); all subjunctives.

803. The athematic forms are: the presents and imperfects in all voices of -μι (athematic) verbs; all aorists passive (except the subjunctive forms); all middle and passive perfects and pluperfects; all second aorists whose tense stem does not end in the thematic vowel (796); a few verbs (as ἵστημι) in the second perfect and pluperfect, active; all first aorists, active and middle. The perfects and pluperfects active are primarily athematic in their inflection.

804. In the thematic inflection the tense stem varies, %, as indicated above.

805. In the athematic inflection the final vowel of the tense stem is usually long (lengthened grade) in the singular, and commonly (but not always) is short (standing in ablaut relation (593-595), weakened or disappearing grade) in the dual and plural. This is particularly true of athematic presents and imperfects, second aorists, perfects, and pluperfects active.

806. Voices and Modes. — The Greek verb has three voices: active, middle, and passive. Each voice has six modes: the indicative, subjunctive, optative, imperative, infinitive, and participial.

807. Tense systems. — The Greek verb has the following nine systems of tenses:

1) *present*, consisting of the present and imperfect.

2) *future*, consisting of the future, active and middle.

3) *first aorist*, consisting of the first aorist, active and middle.

4) *second aorist*, consisting of the second aorist, active and middle.

237

5) *first perfect*, consisting of the first perfect and pluperfect active.

6) *second perfect*, consisting of the second perfect and pluperfect active.

7) *perfect middle*, consisting of the perfect, pluperfect, and future perfect middle (passive).

8) *first passive*, consisting of the first aorist passive.

9) *second passive*, consisting of the second aorist passive.

808. Each of these systems has a stem, called the *tense stem*, to which are added certain endings to denote person and number.

809. Tense Suffixes. — The suffixes (630) by which the various tense stems are formed from the verb stem are as follows:

1) *present*: *a*) thematic %⁄ (o before μ or ν, or in the optative, otherwise ε), as λύ-ο-μεν, λύ-ε-τε; *b*) athematic none, as φά-μεν, φά-τε.

2) *future*: *a*) σ(σ)%⁄ (same rule as the present for %⁄; σ after long vowels or diphthongs; either σ or σσ after short vowels), as λύ-σο-μεν, καλέσ-σο-μεν.

b) εσ%⁄ in liquid and nasal stems (514–516), and σ regularly dropped (603), as βαλ-έ-ω, φαν-έ-ω; exceptions κέλ-σω, κύρ-σω, ὄρ-σω.

3) *first aorist* σ(σ)α (σ after long vowels or diphthongs; either σ or σσ after short vowels).

b) σ%⁄ in a few cases.

c) σ is usually lost in liquid and nasal verbs, and the preceding vowel lengthened by compensation (601), as ἔ-μειν-α, ἔ-φην-α, for ἐμενσα, ἐφανσα.

Exceptions to *c*): ἔ-κελ-σα, ἔ-κυρ-σα, ὦρ-σα.

4) *second aorist*: *a*) thematic %⁄, as ἐ-λίπ-ο-μεν, ἐ-λίπ-ε-τε.

b) athematic none, as ἔ-βη-ν, ἔ-στη-ν, ἔ-δῦ-τε, ἔ-γνω-ν.

5) *first perfect* κα, pluperfect κε, as βέ-βη-κα, ἐ-βε-βή-κε-α (-η).

6) *second perfect* α, pluperfect ε, as πέ-ποιθ-α, ἐ-πε-ποίθ-ε-α (-η), or none, as ἔ-στα-μεν, ἔ-στα-τε.

7) *perfect middle* none, as λέ-λυ-μαι; future perfect σ(σ)%⁄.

8) *first passive* θη/ε, as ἐ-λύ-θη-μεν, ἔ-λυ-θε-ν.

9) *second passive* η/ε, as ἐ-δάμ-η-μεν, ἔ-δαμ-ε-ν.

810. Principal Parts. — The principal parts of a verb are the first person singular of each tense system found in it.

811. No verb has all the tense systems entire. Most verbs have no more than six: the present, future, first aorist, first (or second) perfect active, perfect middle (passive), and the first or second aorist passive. If the verb does not have a future active, the future middle (passive) is given. If the verb has a second aorist, it is added.

812. Of deponent verbs (897) the principal parts are: the present, future, perfect, and aorist. This includes both first and second aorists, middle and passive, if they occur.

813. Mode Suffix. — Observe that the optative has also the mode suffix $i/\iota\eta$, which contracts with the final vowel of the tense stem, as λύοιμι for λυ-ο-ῐ-μι, ἱσταίην for ἱ-στα-ιη-ν.

814. Tenses. — Of the tenses, seven are found in the indicative mode: the present, imperfect, aorist, future, perfect, pluperfect, and future perfect.

815. The other modes have the present, aorist, and perfect tenses; the infinitive and participle have in addition the future tense.

816. The tenses of the indicative are distinguished as:

1) *principal* (*primary*) tenses: the present, future, perfect, and future perfect.

2) *past* (*secondary*) tenses: imperfect, aorist, and pluperfect (*historical* tenses).

817. The passive has a distinct form only in the aorist;[1] in the other tenses the middle form has both the middle and passive meaning.

818. Number and Person. — There are three numbers (singular, dual, plural) of the Greek verb, as in nouns, and three persons (first, second, third).

819. Endings. — Certain suffixes, called personal endings, are attached to the tense stems of the various finite (791) modes, and

---

[1] Two second future forms (δαήσεαι, μιγήσεσθαι) are found.

other endings are attached to the infinitives and participles, to make the complete verbal forms.

820. Some of these personal endings have undergone considerable changes.

821. In their earlier form they were as follows:

ACTIVE		MIDDLE	
Indicative primary tenses, and Subjunctive	*Indicative secondary tenses, and Optative*	*Indicative primary tenses, and Subjunctive*	*Indicative secondary tenses, and Optative*
		SINGULAR	
1 -μι, -ω	-ν, -ν̥ = -α	-μαι	-μην
2 -σι, -ς, -(σ)θα	-ς, -σθα	-σαι	-σο
3 -τι = -σι	-(τ)	-ται	-το
		DUAL	
1 ———	———	-μεθον	[-μεθον]
2 -τον	-τον	-σθον	-σθον
3 -τον	-την	-σθον	-σθην
		PLURAL	
1 -μεν	-μεν	-μεθα (-μεσθα)	-μεθα (-μεσθα)
2 -τε	-τε	-σθε	-σθε
3 -ντι = -νσι	-ν(τ), -σαν	-νται (-αται = -γται, 597–598)	-ντο (-ατο = -ν̥το 597–598)

Imperative

ACTIVE	MIDDLE
	SINGULAR
2 —, -θι, -ς	-σο
3 -τω	-σθω
	DUAL
2 -τον	-σθον
3 -των	-σθων
	PLURAL
2 -τε	-σθε
3 -ντων	-σθων

822. Observe that the subjunctive has the same endings throughout as the primary tenses of the indicative, while the optative (except at times in the first singular, when it ends in -μι), has the same endings as the secondary tenses of the indicative.

823. The first and second aorists passive have the same endings as the secondary tenses of the active voice.

824. PRIMARY ENDINGS OF THE ACTIVE VOICE (INDICATIVE AND SUBJUNCTIVE)

1 sing.: -μι is found in the present indicative of all -μι verbs, and in a few subjunctives of -ω verbs. -ω is found in the present indicative of all -ω verbs, in all futures, and in the subjunctive. In the perfect indicative there is no personal ending, -α taking the place of the thematic vowel.

2 sing.: -σι is found only in ἐσσί *you are;* elsewhere -ς has taken its place. -θα (-σθα) is used at times in the perfect, imperfect and pluperfect of the indicative, and occasionally in the subjunctive and optative.

3 sing.: -τι is found only in ἐστί *he is.* It becomes -σι in the other -μι verbs, and -σι is occasionally found in the subjunctive of -ω verbs. -ω verbs have another ending, -ει, of which the origin is uncertain. The perfect, -ε, has no personal ending.

3 plur.: -ντι regularly becomes -νσι, and ν is then lost, with lengthening of the preceding vowel (613). Many -μι verbs seem to have ended in -αντι, which first became -ανσι, and then -ᾱσι (613). The perfect of consonant stems ended in -ντι (-νσι) which became -ντι (-νσι) and then -ασι (597-8). Generally -ασι in both present and perfect has been replaced by -ᾱσι.

825. SECONDARY ENDINGS OF THE ACTIVE (INDICATIVE AND OPTATIVE)

1 sing.: -ν after vowels remained unchanged; after consonants it became -ν, and then -α (597-8). Pluperfect -εα is usually contracted to -η. The optative has -ν when the mode suffix is -ιη- (813); otherwise it has -μι.

3 sing.: -τ is always dropped (605); ἔλυε from ἐλυετ; cf. *amat,* ἔλῡσε has no personal ending; it takes its -ε from the perfect.

2 dual: -την sometimes occurs instead of -τον.

3 dual: -τον sometimes occurs instead of -την.

241

3 plur.: -ν is for an earlier -ντ, τ being lost (605), the vowel before it being regularly short. -σαν, from the first aorist ending, is used in the imperfect, and often in the second aorist of -μι verbs, at times in the aorist passive, in the pluperfect active, and in the optative when it has the mode suffix -ιη-.

826. Middle Endings, Primary and Secondary (Indicative, Subjunctive, and Optative)

2 sing.: -σαι drops its σ between vowels (603), except in the perfect, and in the present indicative of -μι verbs.

2 sing. (secondary): -σο regularly drops its σ between vowels (603), except in the pluperfect, and in the imperfect of -μι verbs. In a few cases σ is dropped in the pluperfect.

Dual: the first dual -μεθον is rare; -σθον occurs once instead of -σθην.

3 plur.: -νται, -ντο regularly become -αται, -ατο (-͜νται, -͜ντο) in the perfect and pluperfect of verbs with consonant stems, stems ending in -ι, occasionally in vowel stems, and always in the optative. Elsewhere occasionally -νται, -ντο become -αται, -ατο (597–8).

827. Endings of the Imperative

2 sing. active: -ε of the second sing. is the thematic vowel, and forms like λύε, ἄειδε have no personal ending.

-θι is common, with both an active and passive meaning. In the first aorist passive -θι becomes -τι after -θη- of the passive stem (619).

-ς occurs in a few cases. The endings of the aorist, -σον (active) and -σαι (middle) are obscure.

2 sing. middle: -σο loses its σ between vowels (603), except in the perfect of all verbs and the pres. of -μι verbs.

Endings of the Infinitives, Participles, and Verbal Adjectives

828. Infinitives have the following endings:

1) dative (794): -αι (-ναι, -μεναι, -εναι, -σαι active; and -σθαι, -θαι middle and passive).

2) locative (794): -εν, -μεν (following the thematic vowel ε, ε-εν regularly contracts to -ειν, 584–5).

829. Participles have the following endings added to the tense stem:

1) -ντ- for all active tenses, except the perfect (usually), and the first and second aorists passive.

2) -οτ- (-ϝοτ-), occasionally -οντ- in the perfect active.

3) -μενο- (feminine -μενᾱ-) in the middle; and in the passive, except the aorist passive.

NOTE. — Verbal adjectives end in -τός, and are usually equivalent to passive (sometimes active) participles in meaning, or else denote possibility, as γνωτός [γιγνώσκω] *known*, ποιητός [ποιέω] *made*, τυκτός [τεύχω] *made*. They are formed by adding the ending τός to the verb stem, usually as it appears in the first or second aorist passive.

830. Augment. — Greek verbs prefix an *augment* (increase) at the beginning of the secondary (816) tenses of the indicative, to denote past time.

831. This augment is of two kinds:

1) *syllabic* augment, which prefixes ἐ- to verbs beginning with a consonant, as λύω *I loose*, imperfect ἔλυον *I was loosing*.

2) *temporal* augment, which lengthens the first syllable of words beginning with a vowel or a diphthong, as ἀκούω *I hear*, ἤκουον *I was hearing*.

832. When augmented α, ε regularly become η; ι, ο, υ become ῑ, ω, ῡ respectively; αι and ᾳ become ῃ; while οι becomes ῳ.

833. Of course η, ῃ, ῑ, ῡ, ω, and ῳ do not undergo any change when augmented.

834. Verbs beginning with ρ regularly double it after the augment. Those beginning with λ, μ, ν, or σ sometimes double the initial consonant after the augment.

835. Verbs beginning with a vowel formerly preceded by a lost consonant (usually ϝ, or σ), may take the syllabic instead of the temporal augment, as ἐάνδανον, imperfect of ἀνδάνω (σϝανδανω) *please*.

836. When initial σ has thus been lost, the augment always

contracts with the first vowel of the stem, according to the rules
(584–5); when initial ϝ has been lost, contraction may or may not
take place. Thus ἔχω (σεχω), imperfect εἶχον (ἐσεχον, ἐεχον);
ἕπομαι (σεπομαι), imperfect εἰπόμην (ἐσεπομην, ἐεπομην); εἶδον
(ἐϝιδον), second aorist of ὁράω (ϝοραω); ἄγνῡμι (ϝαγνῡμι, aorist ἔαξα
(ἐϝαξα).

837. *The augment, both syllabic and temporal, is often omitted.*

838. Compound Verbs. — Some prepositions (originally adverbs)
are prefixed to verbs, the whole forming a compound. If the
preposition ends with a vowel and the verb begins with one, the
vowel of the preposition is usually elided (575), as διίστημι
(διά-ἵστημι), ἀφαιρέω (ἀπό-αιρέω (582)).

839. The augment of compound verbs comes between the
preposition and the verb. If two vowels are thus brought
together, the first is usually elided, as ἀπολύω *loose, free;* imperfect
ἀπέλυον (ἀπό-ἔλυον); aorist ἀπέλῡσα (ἀπό-ἔλῡσα).

840. Imperfect. — The imperfect (a secondary tense (816)) is
formed by adding the secondary endings (821) to the *augmented*
stem of the present, as λύω *I loose,* imperfect ἔλυον *I was loosing;*
τίθημι *I place,* imperfect ἐτίθην.

841. First Aorist. — The first aorist of vowel and mute verbs
(849) (a secondary tense, 816) is regularly formed by adding
-σ(σ)α to the augmented verb stem, followed by the personal
endings of the secondary tenses. If the verb stem ends in a
long vowel or a consonant only one σ is ever added; if it ends
in a short vowel, either one or two sigmas may be used.

842. "Mixed" Aorists. — A few aorists (sometimes called
"mixed aorists") are formed by adding -σ‰, followed by the per-
sonal endings of the secondary tenses, to the augmented verb stem.

843. ἵημι *throw, send;* δίδωμι *give, grant;* and τίθημι *put, place,*
have -κα in the aorist instead of -σα.

844. Future. — The future (a primary tense) of vowel and
mute verbs (849) is regularly formed by adding the tense suffix
-σ(σ)‰ to the verb stem, followed by the personal endings of
the primary tenses.

845. If the verb stem ends in a long vowel, the stem is not affected by the addition of -σ% and -σα in the formation of the future and aorist.

846. If the verb stem ends in a short vowel, all tenses except the present and imperfect regularly lengthen this, α and ε becoming η; o becoming ω; as ποιέω, ποιήσω, ἐποίησα; χολόω, χολώσω, ἐχόλωσα. Exception: ἐάω gives ἐάσω, εἴασα.

847. Some verbs do not lengthen the short vowel according to the rule in 846.

848. These, and a few others, usually have σ before the personal ending of the perfect middle and the aorist passive.

849. Classes of Verbs. — Verbs are called *vowel verbs, liquid verbs, nasal verbs,* and *mute verbs,* according as their stem ends in a vowel, a liquid, a nasal, or a mute (509–516).

850. Mute Verbs. — If the verb stem ends in a mute, the following euphonic changes take place:

1) a labial mute (π, β, φ) unites with the sigma following and forms ψ, as πέμπω, πέμψω (πεμπσω), ἔπεμψα (ἐπεμπσα) *send, escort:* ἀμείβω, ἀμείψω, ἤμειψα (ἀμειβσω, ἠμειβσα) (*ex*)*change;*

2) a palatal mute (κ, γ, χ) unites with the sigma following and forms ξ, as ἀρήγω, ἀρήξω (ἀρηγσω), ἤρηξα (ἤρηγσα) *help, assist;* τεύχω, τεύξω (τευχσω), ἔτευξα (ἐτευχσα) *make, fashion, cause.*

3) a lingual mute (τ, δ, θ) before the σ is assimilated (610, 4), as πείθω, πείσω, ἔπεισα *persuade;* ἀείδω, ἀείσω, ἤεισα *sing.*

851. Liquid and Nasal Verbs. — If a verb stem ends in a liquid (λ, ρ) or a nasal (μ, ν), the future is regularly formed by adding -εσ%, with the loss of σ between vowels (603), to the verb stem, to which are attached the primary personal endings, as βάλλω, βαλέω (from βαλεσω) *throw, shoot.*

852. In a few cases the first ε is omitted, and σ is retained in verbs of this kind, as ὄρνῡμι, ὄρσω *arouse, stir up.*

853. A few verbs in addition to those with liquid and nasal stems have lost σ in the future, as καλέω, καλέω *call, summon.* In general these verbs have a liquid or nasal before the final vowel of the stem, and imitate the forms of the futures of liquid and nasal verbs.

854. Those formations in which σ is dropped after a or ε are sometimes called "Attic futures."

855. A few verbs have active forms in the present, but middle forms in the future, as ἀκούω, ἀκούσομαι *hear*.

856. Verbs with liquid and nasal stems regularly form their aorists by dropping the σ and lengthening the stem vowel by compensation (601), a becoming η, ε becoming ει, ι becoming ῑ, and υ becoming ῡ, as φαίνω (φαν-), φανέω (φανεσω), ἔφηνα (ἐφανσα) *show;* μένω, μενέω (μενεσω), ἔμεινα (ἐμενσα) *remain, await.*

857. In some cases the σ is retained in formations of this kind, as ὄρνῡμι, ὦρσα *stir up, arouse;* κέλλω, ἔκελσα *land;* κύρω, κύρσω *meet.*

858. The present of most liquid and nasal verbs regularly lengthens the last syllable of the stem by compensation (601) as the original form of the stem of these verbs ended in consonantal ι (600).

859. Presents in -λλω are from an earlier form in -λιω. Thus ἀγγέλλω, βάλλω, στέλλω, τέλλω, etc., were originally ἀγγελιω, βαλιω, στελιω, τελιω, etc. In these cases the last syllable of the stem is lengthened by doubling the final λ.

860. Verbs with presents in -αινω, -αιρω, -εινω, -ειρω, -ῑνω, -ῑρω, ῑνω, ῡρω originally had the endings -ανιω, -αριω, -ενιω, -εριω, -ινιω, -ιριω -υνιω, -υριω (consonantal ι, 600) respectively.

861. The quantity of the last vowel of the stem of many verbs often varies, as λύω, λύσω, ἔλῡσα, λέλυκα*, λέλυμαι, ἐλύθην.

862. Ablaut (vowel gradation, 593–595) is seen in the various tense systems of many verbs, particularly in what are known as "second" (863) tenses. The second aorist and second passive systems commonly have the weak (594–595) grades ι, υ, α. The other systems usually have the corresponding strong grades ει (οι), ευ (ου), η (ω); οι, ου, ω in the second perfect. When ε is preceded or followed by a liquid or a nasal its weak grade is α.

863. Second Tenses. — Many verbs have what are called *second* tenses, as second aorists (active, middle, and passive), and second perfects and pluperfects (active). These second tenses are irregular in formation, and are thus named to distinguish them from the more common, regularly formed tenses, which are called *first* tenses.

864. The meaning of these *second* tenses ordinarily corresponds to that of the *first* tenses, except in the comparatively few cases when a verb has both forms. Then the first and second tenses may differ slightly in meaning, usually by the first being transitive (sometimes causative), the second intransitive. Compare the Americanism *shine, shined, shined,* used transitively, as in the expression " he shined my shoes," with the more common forms of the verb, *shine, shone, shone,* used intransitively, as " the sun shone." " Shined " may be compared in form and meaning to a first aorist, while " shone " would correspond in form and meaning to a second aorist. Thus in Greek, ἔβην (2d aor.) signifies *I went, walked* (intransitive), while ἔβησα (1st aor.) signifies *I caused to go, walked* (transitive), as in English *I walked my horse* (ἔβησα ἵππον) *i.e.* I caused my horse to walk.

865. Second aorists are formed in various ways:

1) A common method is for them to have the secondary (816) endings, following the thematic vowel %, thus being conjugated like the imperfect, as ἔχω, ἕξω, ἔσχον *to have,* where ἔσχον the second aorist is conjugated like ἔλυον, the imperfect of λύω *to loose.*

2) Many have the secondary endings attached directly to the tense stem, and thus are conjugated like the aorist passive, but without the θ of the passive stem. Thus ἔβην (βαίνω), ἔδῡν (δύω), ἔγνων (γιγνώσκω), etc. These are athematic (797) of course.

3) Others end in -α and are conjugated with the same endings as the first (regular) aorists, but without the σ, as εἶπα, ἔκηα.

4) Many are reduplicated (867), as ἤγαγον [ἄγω], κεχαρόμην [χαίρω].

NOTE. — The stem of the second aorist usually differs from the present, regularly standing in ablaut (593-5) relation to it, as βαίνω; ἔβην; λείπω, ἔλιπον.

866. The stem of the singular of athematic (797, 865, 2) second aorists regularly stands in ablaut (593–5) relation to the stem found in the dual and plural.

867. Reduplication. — The perfect and pluperfect (with a few presents, second aorists and futures) in all modes have *reduplication* (doubling), which regularly denotes completed (sometimes intensified) action, a state, or a condition.

868. Verbs beginning with a single consonant, except ρ, prefix this consonant, followed by the letter ε, as δύω, δέδυκα *go in.* Often the stem stands in ablaut (593–5) relation to the stem of the present, as βαίνω (βαν-, βα-), βέβηκα *come, go.*

869. Verbs beginning with a double consonant (518), with two consonants (except a mute followed by a liquid or nasal (509, 516), those beginning with ρ, and some beginning with μ, instead of being reduplicated, simply add ε, the reduplication in these cases having the same form as the syllabic augment (830–1).

870. A rough mute when reduplicated is changed to its *cognate* smooth (510–511), as φύω, πέφυκα; θνήσκω, τέθνηκα. This is *deaspiration* (dissimilation) (619).

871. In verbs beginning with a vowel or diphthong the reduplication has the form of the *temporal* (831) augment, as οἴχομαι, ᾤχωκα.

872. Verbs beginning with a vowel which was formerly preceded by a lost consonant may take the reduplication in the form of the syllabic augment (830–1).

873. Some verbs beginning with α, ε, or ο, followed by a consonant, reduplicate by repeating this vowel and the consonant and by lengthening the vowel, α and ε becoming η, and ο becoming ω, as ἔδω, ἐδηδώς; ἀραρίσκω, ἄρηρα; ὄλλῡμι, ὄλωλα. This is sometimes called " Attic reduplication."

874. A few verbs reduplicate the present by prefixing the first consonant of the stem followed by ι, as ἵστημι (σιστημι 603–4), τίθημι, δίδωμι, ἵημι (σιτημι 603–4), πίμπλημι, γίγνομαι, γιγνώσκω, μιμνήσκω.

875. When the reduplicated perfect begins with a consonant, the pluperfect prefixes the syllabic augment (ἐ) to the reduplication, as βέβηκα (perfect), ἐβεβήκεα (pluperfect).

876. In other cases the pluperfect usually retains the temporal (831) augment of the perfect unchanged.

877. Perfect. — The first (regular) perfect adds -κα, the pluperfect -κε, to the reduplicated theme to form the singular. The dual and plural regularly have the endings of the second perfect, except at times in the third plural, which often has the endings of the first perfect.

878. The stem is not affected by the addition of -κα, -κε, except that a final short vowel is usually lengthened (846).

879. This form of the perfect (first or regular perfect) is found only in verbs with vowel stems and in only about twenty verbs in the whole of the Homeric poems.

880. Second Perfect. — The stem of the second (irregular) perfect is formed by adding -α to the reduplicated theme, and the pluperfect by adding -ε.

881. The second perfects are the earlier and are much more common in the Homeric poems than are the first or κ-perfects. They are found regularly in verbs with consonantal and sometimes in those with vowel stems.

882. The singular of the first and second perfect and pluperfect active regularly stands in ablaut (593-5) relation to the dual and plural, the dual and plural having the weak (disappearing) grade (594-5), while the singular has the strong grade.

883. Both perfect and pluperfect are rare in Homer, the latter occurring in only about twenty verbs.

884. The reduplication is occasionally omitted.

885. Verbs compounded with a preposition (838) regularly have the augment and the reduplication between the preposition and the verb, as ἀμφιβέβηκα, προβέβουλα (ἀμφιβαίνω, προβούλομαι).

886. When futures and second aorists are reduplicated it is usually after the manner of the reduplication of perfects; presents are reduplicated in various ways, but chiefly with ι (874).

887. Middle Voice. — The endings of the middle are different from those of the active. See the table, 821.

888. Passive. — The aorist passive has active endings; the other forms of the passive have middle endings.

889. Since only the aorist[1] of the passive differs in form from the middle, all the other tenses having the same forms in both voices, the context must determine in these other tenses which voice is intended.

890. The aorist middle, especially the athematic (797) aorist, is often used instead of the aorist passive. On the other hand the aorist passive is often used with a middle meaning.

891. The perfect and pluperfect, middle and passive are athematic (797), *i.e.* the personal endings are attached directly to the reduplicated verb stem.

892. The future perfect passive stem is formed by adding $-\sigma^\epsilon_o$ to the perfect middle (passive) stem. A vowel which precedes this $-\sigma^\epsilon_o$ is lengthened, even though it be short in the perfect middle.

893. The first aorist passive stem is formed by adding θ^ϵ/η to the verb stem.

894. Sometimes a sigma also is added to the verb stem before the θ^ϵ/η.

895. Before the theta of the passive stem, π and β become ϕ; κ and γ become χ; τ, δ, and θ regularly become σ (610, 1, 2).

896. Many verbs have a second aorist passive, which does not have the θ, but otherwise has the same endings as the first aorist passive.

897. Deponent Verbs. — There are many verbs which have no active forms, but the middle, or the middle and passive are used with an active meaning. These are called *deponent* verbs.

898. Defective Verbs. — Many verbs do not have all the principal parts, that is, they are *defective*. When any parts are omitted

---

[1] But see 817, note, for two exceptions.

from the vocabularies of this book, it indicates that these forms do not occur either in Homer or in later classical Greek.

899. Periphrastic Forms. — There are some forms of the verb in Greek which are expressed at times by a compound of the verb *to be* (εἰμί) with a participle of the verb. These are called *periphrastic* forms. The most important are :

1) The perfect and pluperfect, represented at times by the perfect participle with the present and imperfect respectively of εἰμί.

2) The future perfect, both active and passive, represented by the future of εἰμί with the perfect active and middle (passive) participle.

900. Iterative Forms. — Many verbs have what are called *iterative* forms in the *imperfect and aorist*, active and middle. These have no augment and add σκ followed by the personal endings to the verb stem. Some have a connecting vowel (usually ε, sometimes α), others do not. Thus from ποθέω comes ποθέεσκον, from φθινύθω comes φθινύθεσκον, etc.

901. A few verbs have special forms in the present and second aorist made by adding θ to the tense stem, as ἔσχεθον from ἔχω (2d aor. ἔσχον), φθινύθω from φθίνω.

Accent of Verbs

902. Verbs, both simple and compound (838), usually have the *recessive* accent (548), except in the following cases :

1) A few second aorists imperative, 2d singular, have the acute on the ultima, as εἰπέ, ἐλθέ, εὑρέ, λαβέ. When compounded these verbs have the recessive accent.

2) The following forms accent the penult : the first aorist active infinitive, the second aorist active infinitive (usually contracted with the ultima), the second aorist middle infinitive (except πρίασθαι, ὄνασθαι), the perfect middle (passive) infinitives and participles, and all infinitives in -ναι or -μεν, except those in -μεναι.

3) The following participles have the acute on the ultima for the masculine and neuter, and the circumflex on the penult of the feminine: the second aorist active, all those of the third declension (except the first aorist active) ending in -ς in the nominative

singular masculine, and the present participles of εἰμί, εἶμι and κίω (ἐών, ἰών, κιών)

4) For the variations in the enclitic forms of εἰμί, φημί, see the paradigms 964, 967, and 554–556.

5) The accent of athematic optatives never goes further to the left than the diphthong containing the ι of the mode sign.

6) In unaugmented compound verbs the accent cannot go further to the left than the last syllable of the preposition with which the verb is compounded.

7) Unaugmented monosyllabic second aorists have the circumflex when containing a long vowel, as βῆ (= ἔβη).

8) In augmented and reduplicated compound forms the accent cannot go further back than the augment or reduplication.

9) Middle imperatives in -εο have the acute on the penult when compounded with monosyllabic prepositions.

10) The exceptions are only apparent in the accent of contracted forms 936–944, including the aorist passive subjunctive, λυθέω = λυθῶ, and optative, λυθέ-ῑ-μεν = λυθεῖμεν, the future of liquid and nasal verbs, and the present and second aorist active and middle subjunctive of most -μι verbs. See 951–952.

903. Final -αι and -οι of the optative, and the final -οι of the locative οἴκοι *at home,* are always considered long when determining the accent; otherwise final -αι, -οι are considered short for purposes of accent (547).

904.   Conjugation of **λύ-ω** [1] *I loose*

Active

Indicative

PRESENT	IMPERFECT
S. 1 **λύω** I loose, am loosing, do loose	**ἔλυον** I was loosing, I loosed, did loose
2 **λύεις** you loose, are loosing, do loose	**ἔλυες** you were loosing, you loosed, did loose
3 **λύει** he looses, is loosing, does loose	**ἔλυε** he was loosing, he loosed, did loose

---

[1] Observe that the υ of λύω is long only when followed by σ; otherwise it is short.

Du. 2 λύετον you two loose, *etc.*   ἐλύετον you two were loosing, *etc.*
   3 λυέτον they two loose, *etc.*   ἐλυέτην they two were loosing, *etc.*

Pl. 1 λύομεν we loose, *etc.*   ἐλύομεν we were loosing, *etc.*
   2 λύετε you loose, *etc.*   ἐλύετε you were loosing, *etc.*
   3 λύουσι they loose, *etc.*   ἔλυον they were loosing, *etc.*

FUTURE	AORIST

S. 1 λύσω I shall (will) loose   ἔλυσα I loosed, did loose
  2 λύσεις you will (shall) loose   ἔλυσας you loosed, did loose
  3 λύσει he will (shall) loose   ἔλυσε he loosed, did loose

Du. 2 λύσετον you two will (shall)   ἐλύσατον you two loosed, did loose
      loose
   3 λύσετον they two will (shall)   ἐλυσάτην they two loosed, did loose
      loose

Pl. 1 λύσομεν we shall (will) loose   ἐλύσαμεν we loosed, did loose
   2 λύσετε you will (shall) loose   ἐλύσατε you loosed, did loose
   3 λύσουσι they will (shall)   ἔλυσαν they loosed, did loose
      loose

PERFECT [1]	PLUPERFECT [1]

S. 1 λέλυκα I have loosed   ἐλελύκη (-εα) I had loosed
  2 λέλυκας you have loosed   ἐλελύκης (-εας) you had loosed
  3 λέλυκε he has loosed   ἐλελύκει (-εε) he had loosed

Du. 2 λελύκατον you two have   ἐλελύκετον you two had loosed
      loosed
   3 λελύκατον they two have   ἐλελυκέτην they two had loosed
      loosed

Pl. 1 λελύκαμεν we have loosed   ἐλελύκεμεν we had loosed
   2 λελύκατε you have loosed   ἐλελύκετε you had loosed
   3 λελύκᾱσι they have loosed   ἐλελύκεσαν they had loosed

905.   The Subjunctive

PRESENT [2]	AORIST [2]

S. 1 λύω(μι) I may loose [3]   λύσω(μι) I may loose [3]
  2 λύῃς(θα) you may loose   λύσῃς(θα) you may loose
  3 λύῃ(σι) he may loose   λύσῃ(σι) he may loose

---

[1] The perfect of λύω is not found in Homer, but these are the ordinary forms in Attic Greek. For the Homeric perfect system see 922–924, 966.
[2] See footnote 1 on next page.   [3] See footnote 2 on next page.

Du. 2 λύητον you two may loose   λύσητον you two may loose
   3 λύητον they two may loose   λύσητον they two may loose
Pl. 1 λύωμεν we may loose   λύσωμεν we may loose
   2 λύητε you may loose   λύσητε you may loose
   3 λύωσι they may loose   λύσωσι they may loose

PERFECT [1], [3]

S. 1 λελύκω I may loose [2]   Pl. λελύκωμεν we may loose [2]
   2 λελύκῃς(θα) you may loose   λελύκητε you may loose
   3 λελύκῃ(σι) he may loose   λελύκωσι they may loose

Du. 2 λελύκητον you two may   Du. 3 λελύκητον they two may
     loose   loose

906.   OPTATIVE
               PRESENT [1]

S. 1 λύοιμι may I loose [4]   Du. 1
   2 λύοις(θα) may you loose   2 λύοιτον may you two loose
   3 λύοι may he loose   3 λυοίτην may they two loose

PLURAL

λύοιμεν may we loose
λύοιτε may you loose
λύοιεν may they loose

AORIST [1]   PERFECT [1, 3]

S. 1 λύσαιμι may I loose [5]   λελύκοιμι may I loose [5]
   2 λύσαις(θα) (λύσειας) may you loose   λελύκοις(θα) may you loose
   3 λύσαι (λύσειε) may he loose   λελύκοι may he loose

---

[1] The different tenses of the subjunctive, optative, imperative, and infinitive, do not of themselves represent distinctions of time. The present of these tenses denotes *continuance* of action, as λύειν (pres. infin.) *to be loosing* (at any time).

The aorist denotes simply the *occurrence* of an action, its time being exactly the same as the present, as λῦσαι (aor. inf.) *to loose* (at any time).

The perfect denotes completion of an action, as λελυκέμεν (perf. inf.) *to have loosed* (at any time).

[2] Also *let me loose*, and various other meanings which must be learned from the syntax.

[3] Not found in Homer; see footnote 1 on preceding page. The subjunctive and optative perfect are very rare in Homer.

[4] Also, *I may, might, could, would, should loose*, with various other meanings which must be learned from the syntax. Read the notes to 905.

[5] Read the notes at the end of 905.

Du. 2 λύσαιτον may you two loose   λελύκοιτον may you two loose
    3 λυσαίτην may they two loose   λελυκοίτην may they two loose
Pl. 1 λύσαιμεν may we loose   λελύκοιμεν may we loose
    2 λύσαιτε may you loose.   λελύκοιτε may you loose
    3 λύσαιεν (λύσειαν) may they   λελύκοιεν may they loose
      loose

907.   IMPERATIVE

          PRESENT [1]   AORIST [1]

S. 2 λύε loose (continue to loose)   λῦσον loose
  3 λυέτω let him loose (con-   λῡσάτω let him loose
    tinue to loose)

Du. 2 λύετον loose (you two), con-   λύσατον loose (you two)
     tinue to loose
   3 λυέτων let those (two) loose   λῡσάτων let those (two) loose.
     (continue to loose)

Pl. 2 λύετε loose (continue to   λύσατε loose
     loose)
   3 λυόντων let them loose (con-   λῡσάντων let them loose
     tinue to loose)

908.   INFINITIVE [1]

PRES.   λύειν (λύμεν, λύμεναι, λυέμεν, λυέμεναι) to loose, to be loosing
FUT.   λύσειν (λῡσέμεν, λῡσέμεναι) to loose, to be about to loose, to be
       loosing
AOR.   λῦσαι (λῡσάμεν, λῡσάμεναι) to loose, to have loosed.
PERF. [2] λελυκέμεν, λελυκέ(με)ναι to loose, to have loosed.

909.   PARTICIPLE

PRES.   λύων, ουσα, ον (740) loosing
FUT.   λύσων, σουσα, σον (being) about to loose, desiring to loose
AOR.   λῡσᾱς, σᾱσα, σαν (741) having loosed
PERF.[2] λελυκώς, κυῖα, κός (744) having loosed

---

[1] Read the notes at the end of 905.
[2] Not found in Homer ; see note 3, 905.

Middle Voice of λύω *loose*

910. INDICATIVE

PRESENT

S. 1 λύομαι I loose (for) myself, I am loosed [1]
2 λύεαι [(λύῃ)] you loose (for) yourself, are loosed
3 λύεται he looses (for) himself, is loosed

Du. 2 λύεσθον you two loose (for) yourselves, are loosed
3 λύεσθον they two loose (for) themselves, are loosed

Pl. 1 λυόμε(σ)θα we loose (for) ourselves, are loosed
2 λύεσθε you loose (for) yourselves, are loosed
3 λύονται they loose (for) themselves, are loosed

IMPERFECT

S. 1 ἐλυόμην I was loosing (for) myself, was being loosed [1]
2 ἐλύεο [(ἐλύευ)] you were loosing (for) yourself, were being loosed
3 ἐλύετο he was loosing (for) himself, was being loosed

Du. 2 ἐλύεσθον you two were loosing (for) yourselves, were being loosed
3 ἐλυέσθην they two were loosing (for) themselves, were being loosed

Pl. 1 ἐλυόμε(σ)θα we were loosing (for) ourselves, were being loosed
2 ἐλύεσθε you were loosing (for) yourselves, were being loosed
3 ἐλύοντο they were loosing (for) themselves, were being loosed

FUTURE

S. 1 λύσομαι I shall loose (for) myself, shall be loosed
2 λύσεαι [(λύσῃ)] you will loose (for) yourself, will be loosed
3 λύσεται he will loose (for) himself, will be loosed

Du. 2 λύσεσθον you two will loose (for) yourselves, will be loosed
3 λύσεσθον they two will loose (for) themselves, will be loosed

Pl. 1 λυσόμε(σ)θα we will loose (for) ourselves, will be loosed
2 λύσεσθε you will loose (for) yourselves, will be loosed
3 λύσονται they will loose (for) themselves, will be loosed

---

[1] The most common meanings are *I loose for myself, I am loosed; I was loosing for myself, I was being loosed*, etc. The context must determine which of these is most suitable. When it has an active meaning, *I loose*, it is with the strict implication of loosing *one's own*, or something in which the subject has an active personal interest, hence : *to ransom, redeem, deliver,* etc.

AORIST

S. 1 ἐλῡσάμην I loosed (for) myself, was loosed   ¹ ἐλύμην
   2 ἐλύσαο [(ἐλύσω)] you loosed (for) yourself, were loosed ἔλυ(σ)ο
   3 ἐλύσατο he loosed (for) himself, was loosed   ἔλυτο

Du. 2 ἐλύσασθον you two loosed (for) yourselves, were loosed ἔλυσθον
   3 ἐλῡσάσθην they two loosed (for) themselves, were ἐλύσθην
      loosed

Pl. 1 ἐλῡσάμε(σ)θα we loosed (for) ourselves, were loosed ἐλύμε(σ)θα
   2 ἐλύσασθε you loosed (for) yourselves, were loosed   ἔλυσθε
   3 ἐλύσαντο they loosed (for) themselves, were loosed   ἔλυντο

PERFECT

S. 1 λέλυμαι I have loosed (for) myself, have been loosed
   2 λέλυσαι you have loosed (for) yourself, have been loosed
   3 λέλυται he has loosed (for) himself, has been loosed

Du. 2 λέλυσθον you two have loosed (for) yourselves, have been loosed
   3 λέλυσθον they two have loosed (for) themselves, have been loosed

Pl. 1 λελύμε(σ)θα we have loosed (for) ourselves, have been loosed
   2 λέλυσθε you have loosed (for) yourselves, have been loosed
   3 λέλυνται (λελύαται) ² they have loosed (for) themselves, have been
      loosed

PLUPERFECT

S. 1 ἐλελύμην I had loosed (for) myself, had been loosed
   2 ἐλέλυσο you had loosed (for) yourself, had been loosed
   3 ἐλέλυτο he had loosed (for) himself, had been loosed

Du. 2 ἐλέλυσθον you two had loosed (for) yourselves, had been loosed
   3 ἐλελύσθην they two had loosed (for) themselves, had been loosed

Pl. 1 ἐλελύμε(σ)θα we had loosed (for) ourselves, had been loosed
   2 ἐλέλυσθε you had loosed (for) yourselves, had been loosed
   3 ἐλέλυντο (ἐλελύατο) ² they had loosed (for) themselves, had been
      loosed

FUTURE PERFECT

S. 1 λελύσομαι I shall have loosed (for) myself, shall have been loosed
   2 λελύσεαι [(-ῃ)] you will have loosed (for) yourself, will have been
      loosed
   3 λελύσεται he will have loosed (for) himself, will have been loosed

---

¹ Less common, athematic (797–798) 2d aorist forms, 863–865, 2.

² -αται, -ατο (= -̥νται, -̥ντο, 597–598) regularly in verbs with consonantal
stems, and stems ending in ι; sometimes in stems ending in other vowels.

Du. 2 λελύσεσθον you two will have loosed (for) yourselves, will have been loosed

   3 λελύσεσθον they two will have loosed (for) themselves, will have been loosed

Pl. 1 λελῡσόμε(σ)θα we shall have loosed (for) ourselves, shall have been loosed

   2 λελύσεσθε you will have loosed (for) yourselves, will have been loosed

   3 λελύσονται they will have loosed (for) themselves, will have been loosed

911.   Subjunctive

PRESENT [1]

S. 1 λύωμαι I may loose (for) myself, may be loosed [1]

   2 λύηαι [(λύῃ)] you may loose (for) yourself, may be loosed

   3 λύηται he may loose (for) himself, may be loosed

Du. 2 λύησθον you two may loose (for) yourselves, may be loosed

   3 λύησθον they two may loose (for) themselves, may be loosed

Pl. 1 λυώμε(σ)θα we may loose (for) ourselves, may be loosed

   2 λύησθε you may loose (for) yourselves, may be loosed

   3 λύωνται they may loose (for) themselves, may be loosed

AORIST [1]

S. 1 λύσωμαι I may loose (for) myself, be loosed [1]

   2 λύσηαι [(λύσῃ)] you may loose (for) yourself, be loosed

   3 λύσηται he may loose (for) himself, be loosed

Du. 2 λύσησθον you two may loose (for) yourselves, be loosed

   3 λύσησθον they two may loose (for) themselves, be loosed

Pl. 1 λῡσώμε(σ)θα we may loose (for) ourselves, be loosed

   2 λύσησθε you may loose (for) yourselves, be loosed

   3 λύσωνται they may loose (for) themselves, may be loosed

PERFECT [1]

S. 1 λελυμένος ἔω I may loose (for) myself, may be loosed

   2 λελυμένος ἔῃς you may loose (for) yourself, may be loosed

   3 λελυμένος ἔῃ he may loose (for) himself, be loosed

Du. 2 λελυμένω ἔητον you two may loose (for) yourselves), may be loosed

   3 λελυμένω ἔητον they two may loose (for) themselves, may be loosed

---

[1] Read the note at the end of 905.

Pl. 1 λελυμένοι ὦμεν we may loose (for) ourselves, may be loosed
    2 λελυμένοι ἦτε you may loose (for) yourselves, may be loosed
    3 λελυμένοι ὦσι they may loose (for) themselves, may be loosed

912.   OPTATIVE

PRESENT[1]

S. 1 λυοίμην may I loose (for) myself, may I be loosed[2]
   2 λύοιο may you loose (for) yourself, may you be loosed
   3 λύοιτο may he loose (for) himself, may he be loosed

Du. 2 λύοισθον may you two loose (for) yourselves, may you two be
        loosed
    3 λυοίσθην may they two loose (for) themselves, may they two be
        loosed

Pl. 1 λυοίμε(σ)θα may we loose (for) ourselves, may we be loosed
    2 λύοισθε may you loose (for) yourselves, may you be loosed
    3 λύοιατο may they loose (for) themselves, may they be loosed

AORIST[1]

S. 1 λῡσαίμην may I loose (for) myself, may I be loosed[2]
   2 λύσαιο may you loose (for) yourself, may you be loosed
   3 λύσαιτο may he loose (for) himself, may he be loosed

Du. 2 λύσαισθον may you two loose (for) yourselves, may you two be
        loosed
    3 λῡσαίσθην may they two loose (for) themselves, may they two be
        loosed

Pl. 1 λῡσαίμε(σ)θα may we loose (for) ourselves, may we be loosed
    2 λύσαισθε may you loose (for) yourselves, may you be loosed
    3 λῡσαίατο may they loose (for) themselves, may they be loosed

PERFECT[1]

S. 1 λελυμένος εἴην may I loose (for) myself, may I be loosed[2]
   2 λελυμένος εἴης may you loose (for) yourself, may you be loosed
   3 λελυμένος εἴη[3] may he loose (for) himself, may he be loosed

Du. 2 λελυμένω εἴτον may you two loose (for) yourselves, may you two
        be loosed
    3 λελυμένω εἴτην may they two loose (for) themselves, may they two
        be loosed

---

[1] Read the note at the end of 905.
[2] Read the note on 906.
[3] Also λελῦτο (= λελυ-ῖ-το).

PL. 1 λελυμένοι εἶμεν may we loose (for) ourselves, may we be loosed
2 λελυμένοι εἶτε may you loose (for) yourselves, may you be loosed
3 λελυμένοι εἶεν may they loose (for) themselves, may they be loosed

913. IMPERATIVE

PRESENT [1]

S. 2 λύεο [(λύευ)] loose (for) yourself, be loosed
3 λυέσθω let him loose (for) himself, let him be loosed

DU. 2 λύεσθον loose (for) your two selves, be loosed
3 λυέσθων let those two loose (for) themselves, let them be loosed

PL. 2 λύεσθε loose (for) yourselves, be loosed
3 λυέσθων let them loose (for) themselves, let them be loosed

AORIST [1]

S. 2 λῦσαι loose (for) yourself, be loosed
3 λῡσάσθω let him loose (for) himself, let him be loosed

DU. 2 λύσασθον loose (for) your two selves, be loosed
3 λῡσάσθων let these two loose (for) themselves, let them be loosed

PL. 2 λύσασθε loose (for) yourselves, be loosed
3 λῡσάσθων let them loose (for) themselves, let them be loosed

PERFECT [1]

S. 2 λέλυσο loose (for) yourself, be loosed
3 λελύσθω let him loose (for) himself, let him be loosed

DU. 2 λέλυσθον loose (for) yourselves, be loosed
3 λελύσθων let them loose (for) themselves, let them be loosed

PL. 2 λέλυσθε loose (for) yourselves, be loosed
3 λελύσθων let them loose (for) themselves, let them be loosed

914. INFINITIVE [1]

PRES. λύεσθαι to loose (for) one's self, to be loosed
FUT. λύσεσθαι to loose (for) one's self, to be loosed, to be about to
be loosed
AOR. λύσασθαι to loose (for) one's self, to be loosed, to have loosed
PERF. λελύσθαι to loose (for) one's self, to be loosed, to have loosed
F. PERF. λελύσεσθαι to loose (for) one's self, to be loosed

---

[1] Read the note on 905.

915.   PARTICIPLE

PRES. λυόμενος, η, ον loosing (for) one's self, being loosed.

FUT. λῡσόμενος, η, ον being about to loose (for) one's self, being about to be loosed, desiring to loose, . . . etc.

AOR. λῡσάμενος, η, ον having loosed (for) one's self, having been loosed

PERF. λελυμένος, η, ον having loosed (for) one's self, having been loosed.

FUT. PERF. λελῡσόμενος, η, ον being about to have loosed (for) one's self, being about to have been loosed

PASSIVE[1] VOICE

Aorist only

916.   INDICATIVE

S. 1 ἐλύθην I was loosed
   2 ἐλύθης you were loosed
   3 ἐλύθη he was loosed

DU. 2 ἐλύθητον you two were loosed

    3 ἐλυθήτην they two were loosed

PL. 1 ἐλύθημεν we were loosed

    2 ἐλύθητε you were loosed
    3 ἐλύθησαν (ἔλυθεν) they were loosed

917.   SUBJUNCTIVE [2]

λυθῶ (λυθέω)[3] I may be loosed [4]
λυθῇς (λυθέῃς) you may be loosed
λυθῇ (λυθέῃ) he may be loosed

λυθῆτον (λυθέητον) you two may be loosed
λυθῆτον (λυθέητον) they two may be loosed

λυθῶμεν (λυθέωμεν) we may be loosed
λυθῆτε (λυθέητε) you may be loosed
λυθῶσι (λυθέωσι) they may be loosed

918.   OPTATIVE [2]

S. 1 λυθείην may I be loosed [4]
   2 λυθείης may you be loosed
   3 λυθείη may he be loosed

DU. 2 λυθεῖτον (λυθείητον) may you two be loosed
    3 λυθείτην (λυθειήτην) may they two be loosed

919.   IMPERATIVE [2]

λυθῆτι be loosed
λυθήτω let him be loosed

λύθητον be loosed

λυθήτων let them be loosed

---

[1] Occasionally with a middle meaning.   [3] Read 951–952.
[2] Read the note on 905.   [4] Read the note on 906.

261

OPTATIVE (*continued*)　　　　IMPERATIVE (*continued*)

PL. 1 λυθεῖμεν (λυθείημεν) may we
　　　be loosed
　　2 λυθεῖτε (λυθείητε) may you be　　λύθητε be loosed
　　　loosed
　　3 λυθεῖεν (λυθείησαν) may they　　λυθέντων let them be loosed
　　　be loosed

920.　　　　　　INFINITIVE

　　λυθῆναι (λυθήμεναι) to be loosed, to have been loosed

921.　　　　　　PARTICIPLE

　　λυθείς, εῖσα, έν (742) having been loosed

922.　PERFECT SYSTEM OF βαίνω (βαν-, βα-), *come, go, walk*

INDICATIVE	SUBJUNCTIVE[1]	OPTATIVE	IMPERATIVE	INFINITIVE
S. 1 βέβηκα	βεβήκω	βεβήκοιμι		βεβάμεν(αι)
2 βέβηκας	βεβήκῃς(θα)	βεβήκοις	βέβαθι	
3 βέβηκε	βεβήκῃ(σι)	βεβήκοι	βεβάτω	PARTICIPLE
Du. 2 βέβατον	βεβήκετον	βεβήκοιτον	βέβατον	βεβαώς, υῖα,
3 βέβατον	βεβήκετον	βεβηκοίτην	βεβάτων	ός
PL. 1 βέβαμεν	βεβήκομεν	βεβήκοιμεν		
2 βέβατε	βεβήκετε	βεβήκοιτε	βέβατε	
3 βεβάᾱσι	βεβήκωσι	βεβήκοιεν	βεβάντων	
βεβήκᾱσι				

PLUPERFECT

S. 1 ἐβεβήκεα (-η 585)	Du.	PL. ἐβέβαμεν
2 ἐβεβήκεας (-ης 585)	ἐβέβατον	ἐβέβατε
3 ἐβεβήκεε (-ει 585)	ἐβεβάτην	ἐβέβασαν

923.　SECOND PERFECT SYSTEM OF πείθω (πειθ-, ποιθ-, πιθ-),
　　　　　　　　　　　persuade

INDICATIVE	SUBJUNCTIVE[1]	PARTICIPLE	PLUPERFECT
S. 1 πέποιθα	πεποίθω	πεποιθώς, πεπι-	ἐπεποίθεα (-η 585)
2 πέποιθας	πεποίθῃς(θα)	θυῖα, πεποιθός	ἐπεποίθεας (-ης 585)
3 πέποιθε	πεποίθῃ(σι)		ἐπεποίθεε (-ει 585)
Du. 2 *πέπιστον	πεποίθετον		*ἐπέπιστον
3 *πέπιστον	πεποίθετον		*ἐπεπίστην

[1] Very rare ; the dual and plural forms are uncertain.

PL. 1 πέπιθμεν   πεποίθομεν   ἐπέπιθμεν
2 *πέπιστε   πεποίθετε   *ἐπέπιστε
3 πεποίθᾱσι   πεποίθωσι   ἐπεποίθεσαν
   *πεπίθᾱσι   (*ἐπέπισαν)

924. SECOND PERFECT SYSTEM OF ἵστημι (στη-, στα-), *stand*

PERFECT

INDICATIVE	SUBJUNCTIVE [1]	OPTATIVE	IMPERATIVE	INFINITIVE
S. 1 ἕστηκα	ἑστήκω	ἑσταίην		ἑστάμεν (αι)
2 ἕστηκας	ἑστήκῃς(θα)	ἑσταίης	ἕσταθι	
3 ἕστηκε	ἑστήκῃ(σι)	ἑσταίη	ἑστάτω	PARTICIPLE
DU. 2 ἕστατον	ἑστήκετον	ἑσταῖτον	ἕστατον	ἑσταώς, υῖα,
3 ἕστατον	ἑστήκετον	ἑσταίτην	ἑστάτων	ός
PL. 1 ἕσταμεν	ἑστήκομεν	ἑσταῖμεν		
2 ἕστατε	ἑστήκετε	ἑσταῖτε	ἕστατε	
3 ἑστᾶσι	ἑστήκωσι	ἑσταῖεν	ἑστάντων	
ἑστήκᾱσι				

PLUPERFECT

S. 1 ἑστήκεα (-η 585)	DU.	PL. ἕσταμεν
2 ἑστήκεας (-ης 585)	ἕστατον	ἕστατε
3 ἑστήκεε (-ει 585)	ἑστάτην	ἕστασαν

925. PERFECT MIDDLE SYSTEM OF LABIAL VERBS: τρέπω (τρεπ-, τραπ-) *turn*, OF PALATAL VERBS: τεύχω (τευχ-, τυχ-, τυκ-) *fashion, make*, AND OF DENTAL VERBS: πεύθομαι (πευθ-, πυθ-) *learn*

INDICATIVE

S. 1 τέτραμμαι (τετραπμαι)   τέτυγμαι (τετυχμαι)   πέπυσμαι (πεπυθμαι)
2 τέτραψαι (τετραπσαι)   τέτυξαι (τετυχσαι)   πέπυσαι (πεπυθσαι)
3 τέτραπται (τετραπται)   τέτυκται (τετυχται)   πέπυσται (πεπυθται)
DU. 2 τέτραφθον (τετραπσθον) τέτυχθον (τετυχσθον) πέπυσθον (πεπυθσθον)
3 τέτραφθον (τετραπσθον) τέτυχθον (τετυχσθον) πέπυσθον (πεπυθσθον)
PL. 1 τετράμμε(σ)θα (τε-   τετύγμε(σ)θα (τετυχ- πεπύσμε(σ)θα (πεπυθ-
    τραπμε(σ)θα)   με(σ)θα)   με(σ)θα)
2 τέτραφθε (τετραπσθε)   τέτυχθε (τετυχσθε)   πέπυσθε (πεπυθσθε)
3 τετράφαται (τετραπν-   τετύχαται (τετυχν- πεπύθαται (πεπυθνται)
    ται)   ται) (τετεύχαται)

---

[1] Very rare ; the dual and plural forms are uncertain.

263

PLUPERFECT INDICATIVE

SINGULAR

1 ἐτετράμμην (ἐτετραπμην)	ἐτετύγμην (ἐτετυχμην)	ἐπεπύσμην (ἐπεπυθμην)
2 ἐτέτραψο (ἐτετραπσο)	ἐτέτυξο (ἐτετυχσο)	ἐπέπυσο (ἐπεπυθσο)
3 ἐτέτραπτο (ἐτετραπτο)	ἐτέτυκτο (ἐτετυχτο)	ἐπέπυστο (ἐπεπυθτο)

DUAL

2 ἐτέτραφθον (ἐτετραπσθον)	ἐτέτυχθον (ἐτετυχσθον)	ἐπέπυσθον (ἐπεπυθσθον)
3 ἐτετράφθην (ἐτετραπσθην)	ἐτετύχθην (ἐτετυχσθην)	ἐπεπύσθην (ἐπεπυθσθην)

PLURAL

1 ἐτετράμμε(σ)θα (ἐτετραπμε(σ)θα)	ἐτετύγμε(σ)θα (ἐτετυχμε(σ)θα)	ἐπεπύσμε(σ)θα (ἐπεπυθμε(σ)θα)
2 ἐτέτραφθε (ἐτετραπσθε)	ἐτέτυχθε (ἐτετυχσθε)	ἐπέπυσθε (ἐπεπυθσθε)
3 ἐτετράφατο (ἐτερταπγτο)	ἐτετύχατο (ἐτετυχγτο) (ἐτετεύχατο)	ἐπεπύθατο (ἐπεπυθγτο)

PERFECT SUBJUNCTIVE

1 τετραμμένος ἔω (τετραπμενος) etc.	τετυγμένος ἔω (τετυχμενος)	πεπυσμένος ἔω (πεπυθμενος)

PERFECT OPTATIVE

1 τετραμμένος εἴην etc.	τετυγμένος εἴην	πεπυσμένος εἴην

PERFECT IMPERATIVE

SINGULAR

2 τέτραψο (τετραπσο)	τέτυξο (τετυχσο)	πέπυσο (πεπυθσο)
3 τετράφθω (τετραπσθω)	τετύχθω (τετυχσθω)	πεπύσθω (πεπυθσθω)

DUAL

2 τέτραφθον (τετραπσθον)	τέτυχθον (τετυχσθον)	πέπυσθον (πεπυθσθον)
3 τετράφθων (τετραπσθων)	τετύχθων (τετυχσθων)	πεπύσθων (πεπυθσθων)

PLURAL

2 τέτραφθε (τετραπσθε)	τέτυχθε (τετυχσθε)	πέπυσθε (πεπυθσθε)
3 τετράφθων (τετραπσθων)	τετύχθων (τετυχσθων)	πεπύσθων (πεπυθσθων)

PERFECT INFINITIVE AND PARTICIPLE

τετράφθαι (τετραπσθαι)	τετύχθαι (τετυχσθαι)	πεπύσθαι (πεπυθσθαι)
τετραμμένος, η, ον (τετραπμενος)	τετυγμένος, η, ον (τετυχμενος)	πεπυσμένος, η, ον (πεπυθμενος)

926. For the change in the vowel of the stem between the singular and the dual and plural of the perfect active, see 882.

927. For the euphonic changes found in the perfect middle, by means of which the regular forms are derived from the forms in parentheses, see 608 ff.

928. -νται, -ντο (-γται, -γτο) of the third plural middle and passive become -αται, -ατο after a consonant, of course (597–598).

929. π-mutes and κ-mutes (510) are *aspirated* (619) before the endings -αται, -ατο of the third plural, π and β becoming φ, and κ and γ becoming χ.

930. SECOND AORIST SYSTEM OF βαίνω (βαν-, βα-) *come, go*,
γιγνώσκω (γνω-, γνο-) *know*, AND OF δύ-ω *enter, sink*.

INDICATIVE

S. 1 ἔβην	ἔγνων	ἔδῡν
2 ἔβης	ἔγνως	ἔδῡς
3 ἔβη	ἔγνω	ἔδῡ
Du. 2 ἔβητον (ἔβατον)	ἔγνωτον	ἔδῡτον
3 ἐβήτην (ἐβάτην)	ἐγνώτην	ἐδύτην
Pl. 1 ἔβημεν (ἔβαμεν)	ἔγνωμεν	ἔδῡμεν
2 ἔβητε (ἔβατε)	ἔγνωτε	ἔδῡτε
3 ἔβησαν (ἔβασαν, ἔβαν)	ἔγνωσαν (ἔγνον)	(ἔδῡσαν) ἔδυν

SUBJUNCTIVE

S. 1 βήω etc.   γνώω (γνῶ 585), etc.   δύω etc.

OPTATIVE

S. 1 βαίην etc.   γνοίην etc.   δύην (= δυίην) etc.

IMPERATIVE

S. 2 βῆθι etc.   γνῶθι etc.   δῦθι etc.

INFINITIVES AND PARTICIPLES

βάς, βᾶσα, βάν   γνούς, γνοῦσα, γνόν   δύς, δῦσα, δύν
βῆναι (βήμεναι)   γνῶναι (γνώμεναι)   δῦναι (δύμεναι)

265

FIRST AORIST SYSTEM OF LIQUID VERBS

φαίνω (STEM φαν-) *show*

931. FIRST AORIST ACTIVE

	INDICATIVE	SUBJUNCTIVE	OPTATIVE	IMPERATIVE	INFINITIVE
S. 1	ἔφηνα	φήνω(μι)	φήναιμι		φῆναι
2	ἔφηνας	φήνῃς(θα)	φήναις(θα)	φῆνον	
3	ἔφηνε	φήνῃ(σι)	φήναι (φή- νειε)	φηνάτω	PARTICIPLE
					φήνᾱς, ᾱσα, αν
Du. 2	ἐφήνατον	φήνητον	φήναιτον	φήνατον	
3	ἐφηνάτην	φήνητον	φηναίτην	φηνάτων	
Pl. 1	ἐφήναμεν	φήνωμεν	φήναιμεν		
2	ἐφήνατε	φήνητε	φήναιτε	φήνατε	
3	ἔφηναν	φήνωσι	φήναιεν (φή- νειαν)	φηνάντων	

932. FIRST AORIST MIDDLE

	INDICATIVE	SUBJUNCTIVE	OPTATIVE	IMPERATIVE	INFINITIVE
S. 1	ἐφηνάμην	φήνωμαι	φηναίμην		φήνασθαι
2	ἐφήναο	φήνηαι	φήναιο	φῆναι	
3	ἐφήνατο	φήνηται	φήναιτο	φηνάσθω	PARTICIPLE
Du. 2	ἐφήνασθον	φήνησθον	φήναισθον	φήνασθον	φηνάμενος, η, ον
3	ἐφηνάσθην	φήνησθον	φηναίσθην	φηνάσθων	2D AOR. PASS.
Pl. 1	ἐφηνάμε(σ)θα	φηνώμε(σ)θα	φηναίμε(σ)θα		ἐφάνην
2	ἐφήνασθε	φήνησθε	φήναισθε	φήνασθε	ἐφάνης
3	ἐφήναντο	φήνωνται	φήναιατο	φηνάσθων	ἐφάνη, etc.

SECOND AORIST SYSTEM OF λείπω (λειπ-, λοιπ-, λιπ-) *leave*

933. SECOND AORIST ACTIVE

	INDICATIVE	SUBJUNCTIVE	OPTATIVE	IMPERATIVE	INFINITIVE
S. 1	ἔλιπον	λίπω	λίποιμι		λιπεῖν (λιπέεν),
2	ἔλιπες	λίπῃς(θα)	λίποις(θα)	λίπε	λιπέμεν(αι)
3	ἔλιπε	λίπῃ(σι)	λίποι	λιπέτω	
Du. 2	ἐλίπετον	λίπητον	λίποιτον	λίπετον	PARTICIPLE
3	ἐλιπέτην	λίπητον	λιποίτην	λιπέτων	λιπών, οῦσα, όν
Pl. 1	ἐλίπομεν	λίπωμεν	λίποιμεν		
2	ἐλίπετε	λίπητε	λίποιτε	λίπετε	
3	ἔλιπον	λίπωσι	λίποιεν	λιπόντων	

934. SECOND AORIST MIDDLE

	INDICATIVE	SUBJUNCTIVE	OPTATIVE	IMPERATIVE	INFINITIVE
S. 1	ἐλιπόμην	λίπωμαι	λιποίμην		λιπέσθαι
2	ἐλίπεο	λίπηαι	λίποιο	λιπέο	
3	ἐλίπετο	λίπηται	λίποιτο	λιπέσθω	PARTICIPLE
DU. 2	ἐλίπεσθον	λίπησθον	λίποισθον	λίπεσθον	λιπόμενος, η, ον
3	ἐλιπέσθην	λίπησθον	λιποίσθην	λιπέσθων	
PL. 1	ἐλιπόμε(σ)θα	λιπώμε(σ)θα	λιποίμε(σ)θα		
2	ἐλίπεσθε	λίπησθε	λίποισθε	λίπεσθε	
3	ἐλίποντο	λίπωνται	λιποίατο	λιπέσθων	

935. SECOND AORIST PASSIVE SYSTEM OF τρέφω (τρεφ-, τροφ-, τραφ-, FOR θρεφ-, ETC. 619) *nourish*

	INDICATIVE	SUBJUNCTIVE	OPTATIVE	IMPERATIVE
S. 1	ἐτράφην	τραφῶ	τραφείην	
2	ἐτράφης	τραφῇς	τραφείης	τράφητι
3	ἐτράφη	τραφῇ	τραφείη	τραφήτω
DU. 2	ἐτράφητον	τραφῆτον	τραφεῖτον (τραφείητον)	τράφητον
3	ἐτραφήτην	τραφῆτον	τραφείτην (τραφειήτην)	τραφήτων
PL. 1	ἐτράφημεν	τραφῶμεν	τραφεῖμεν (τραφείημεν)	
2	ἐτράφητε	τραφῆτε	τραφεῖτε (τραφείητε)	τράφητε
3	ἐτράφησαν	τραφῶσι	τραφεῖεν (τραφείησαν)	τραφέντων
	(ἔτραφεν)			

INFINITIVE τραφῆναι (τραφήμεναι)   PARTICIPLE τραφείς, εῖσα, έν

Contract Verbs

936. Verbs which end in -αω, -εω, -οω ; -αομαι, -εομαι, -οομαι (including the futures of liquids and nasals) in the first person singular are contracted in the present and imperfect at times. For the laws of contraction see 584-585.

937. Verbs in -οω, -οομαι, are usually contracted ; those in -αω, -αομαι, -εω, -εομαι, may be, but are usually left uncontracted.

938. PRESENT SYSTEM OF τῑμάω *honor*

PRESENT

	INDICATIVE	SUBJUNCTIVE	OPTATIVE
S. 1	(τῑμάω) τῑμῶ	(τῑμάω) τῑμῶ	(τῑμάοιμι) τῑμῷμι
2	(τῑμάεις) τῑμᾷς	(τῑμάῃς) τῑμᾷς	(τῑμάοις) τῑμῷς
3	(τῑμάει) τῑμᾷ	(τῑμάῃ) τῑμᾷ	(τῑμάοι) τῑμῷ

267

Ancient Greece
and the Aegean
Scale of Miles
0 10 20 30 40 50   100   150

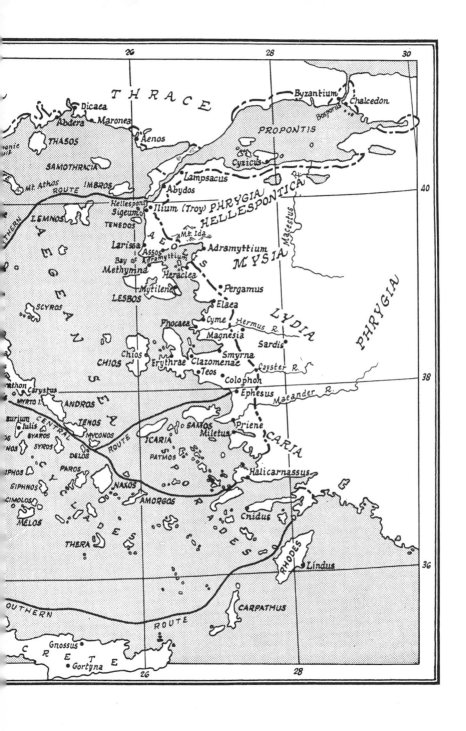

Du. 2 (τῑμάετον) τῑμᾶτον　(τῑμάητον) τῑμᾶτον　(τῑμάοιτον) τῑμῷτον
　　3 (τῑμάετον) τῑμᾶτον　(τῑμάητον) τῑμᾶτον　(τῑμαοίτην) τῑμῴτην

Pl. 1 (τῑμάομεν) τῑμῶμεν　(τῑμάωμεν) τῑμῶμεν　(τῑμάοιμεν) τῑμῷμεν
　　2 (τῑμάετε) τῑμᾶτε　(τῑμάητε) τῑμᾶτε　(τῑμάοιτε) τῑμῷτε
　　3 (τῑμάουσι) τῑμῶσι　(τῑμάωσι) τῑμῶσι　(τῑμάοιεν) τῑμῷεν

	IMPERATIVE	IMPERFECT INDICATIVE
S. 1		(ἐτίμαον) ἐτίμων
2	(τίμαε) τίμᾱ	(ἐτίμαες) ἐτίμᾱς
3	(τῑμαέτω) τῑμάτω	(ἐτίμαε) ἐτίμᾱ
Du. 2	(τῑμάετον) τῑμᾶτον	(ἐτῑμάετον) ἐτῑμᾶτον
3	(τῑμαέτων) τῑμάτων	(ἐτῑμαέτην) ἐτῑμάτην
Pl. 1		(ἐτῑμάομεν) ἐτῑμῶμεν
2	(τῑμάετε) τῑμᾶτε	(ἐτῑμάετε) ἐτῑμᾶτε
3	(τῑμαόντων) τῑμώντων	(ἐτίμαον) ἐτίμων

PART. (τῑμάων, ουσα, ον) τῑμῶν, ῶσα,　INFIN. (τῑμάειν = τῑμαεεν) τῑμᾶν,
ῶν, 745.　　　　　　　　　　　　　　　(τῑμήμεναι)

939　　　MIDDLE AND PASSIVE

PRESENT

INDICATIVE	SUBJUNCTIVE	OPTATIVE
S. 1 (τῑμάομαι) τῑμῶμαι	(τῑμάωμαι) τῑμῶμαι	(τῑμαοίμην) τῑμῴμην
2 (τῑμάεαι) τῑμᾷ	(τῑμάηαι) τῑμᾷ	(τῑμάοιο) τῑμῷο
3 (τῑμάεται) τῑμᾶται	(τῑμάηται) τῑμᾶται	(τῑμάοιτο) τῑμῷτο
Du. 2 (τῑμάεσθον) τῑμᾶσθον	(τῑμάησθον) τῑμᾶσθον	(τῑμάοισθον) τῑμῷσθον
3 (τῑμάεσθον) τῑμᾶσθον	(τῑμάησθον) τῑμᾶσθον	(τῑμαοίσθην) τῑμῴσθην
Pl. 1 (τῑμαόμε(σ)θα) τῑμώμε(σ)θα	(τῑμαώμε(σ)θα) τῑμώμε(σ)θα	(τῑμαοίμε(σ)θα) τῑμῴμε(σ)θα
2 (τῑμάεσθε) τῑμᾶσθε	(τῑμάησθε) τῑμᾶσθε	(τῑμάοισθε) τῑμῷσθε
3 (τῑμάονται) τῑμῶνται	(τῑμάωνται) τῑμῶνται	(τῑμαοίατο) τῑμῷατο

IMPERFECT INDICATIVE	PRESENT IMPERATIVE	INFINITIVE
S. 1 (ἐτῑμαόμην) ἐτῑμώμην		(τῑμάεσθαι) τῑμᾶσθαι
2 (ἐτῑμάεο) ἐτῑμῶ	(τῑμάεο) τῑμῶ	
3 (ἐτῑμάετο) ἐτῑμᾶτο	(τῑμαέσθω) τῑμάσθω	

Du. 2 (ἐτῑμάεσθον)   ἐτῑ- (τῑμάεσθον) τῑμᾶσθον   PARTICIPLE
         μᾶσθον
      3 (ἐτῑμαέσθην)   ἐτῑ- (τῑμαέσθων) τῑμάσθων   (τῑμαόμενος, η, ον) τῑ-
         μάσθην   μώμενος, η, ον

Pl. 1 (ἐτῑμαόμε(σ)θα)
         ἐτῑμώμε(σ)θα
      2 (ἐτῑμάεσθε)   ἐτῑ- (τῑμάεσθε) τῑμᾶσθε
         μᾶσθε
      3 (ἐτῑμάοντο)   ἐτῑ- (τῑμαέσθων) τῑμάσθων
         μῶντο

Present System of ποιέω do, make

940.   Active

PRESENT INDICATIVE   IMPERFECT   PRESENT SUBJUNCTiVE¹

S. 1 (ποιέω) ποιῶ   (ἐποίεον) ἐποίευν   (ποιέω) ποιῶ
   2 (ποιέεις) ποιεῖς   (ἐποίεες) ἐποίεις   (ποιέῃς) ποιῇς
   3 (ποιέει) ποιεῖ   (ἐποίεε) ἐποίει   (ποιέῃ) ποιῇ

Du. 2 (ποιέετον) ποιεῖτον   (ἐποιέετον) ἐποιεῖτον   (ποιέητον) ποιῆτον
    3 (ποιέετον) ποιεῖτον   (ἐποιεέτην) ἐποιείτην   (ποιέητον) ποιῆτον

Pl. 1 (ποιέομεν) ποιεῦμεν   (ἐποιέομεν) ἐποιεῦμεν   (ποιέωμεν) ποιῶμεν
   2 (ποιέετε) ποιεῖτε   (ἐποιέετε) ἐποιεῖτε   (ποιέητε) ποιῆτε
   3 (ποιέουσι) ποιεῦσι   (ἐποίεον) ἐποίευν   (ποιέωσι) ποιῶσι

OPTATIVE¹   PRESENT   IMPERATIVE

S. 1 (ποιέοιμι) ποιοῖμι or (ποιεοίην) ποιοίην
   2 (ποιέοις) ποιοῖς   (ποιεοίης) ποιοίης   (ποίεε) ποίει
   3 (ποιέοι) ποιοῖ   (ποιεοίη) ποιοίη   (ποιεέτω) ποιείτω

Du. 2 (ποιέοιτον) ποιοῖτον   (ποιέετον) ποείτον
    3 (ποιεοίτην) ποιοίτην   INFINITIVE   (ποιεέτων) ποιείτων

Pl. 1 (ποιέοιμεν) ποιοῖμεν   (ποιέειν) ποιεῖν, (ποιή-
   2 (ποιέοιτε) ποιοῖτε   μεναι, ποιῆναι)   (ποιέετε) ποιεῖτε
   3 (ποιέοιεν) ποιοῖεν   (ποιεόντων) ποιεύντων

PARTICIPLE

(ποιέων, ουσα, ον) ποιῶν, εῦσα, εῦν, 745

---

¹ Attic forms ; not contracted in Homer.

941.　　　　MIDDLE AND PASSIVE

INDICATIVE

PRESENT	IMPERFECT
S. 1 (ποιέομαι) ποιεῦμαι	(ἐποιεόμην) ἐποιεύμην
2 (ποιέεαι) ποιεῖαι, -έαι	(ἐποιέεο) ἐποιεῖο, -έο
3 (ποιέεται) ποιεῖται	(ἐποιέετο) ἐποιεῖτο
Du. 2 (ποιέεσθον) ποιεῖσθον	(ἐποιέεσθον) ἐποιεῖσθον
3 (ποιέεσθον) ποιεῖσθον	(ἐποιέεσθην) ἐποιείσθην
Pl. 1 (ποιεόμε(σ)θα) ποιεύμε(σ)θα	(ἐποιεόμε(σ)θα) ἐποιεύμε(σ)θα
2 (ποιέεσθε) ποιεῖσθε	(ἐποιέεσθε) ἐποιεῖσθε
3 (ποιέονται) ποιεῦνται	(ἐποιέοντο) ἐποιεῦντο

PRESENT

SUBJUNCTIVE	OPTATIVE
S. 1 (ποιέωμαι) ποιῶμαι	(ποιεοίμην) ποιοίμην
2 (ποιέηαι) ποιῇ	(ποιέοιο) ποιοῖο
3 (ποιέηται) ποιῆται	(ποιέοιτο) ποιοῖτο
Du. 2 (ποιέησθον) ποιῆσθον	(ποιέοισθον) ποιοῖσθον
3 (ποιέησθον) ποιῆσθον	(ποιεοίσθην) ποιοίσθην
Pl. 1 (ποιεώμε(σ)θα) ποιώμε(σ)θα	(ποιεοίμε(σ)θα) ποιοίμε(σ)θα
2 (ποιέησθε) ποιῆσθε	(ποιέοισθε) ποιοῖσθε
3 (ποιέωνται) ποιῶνται	(ποιεοίατο) ποιοίατο

PRESENT IMPERATIVE

S. 2 (ποιέο) ποιεῦ	Du. 2 (ποιέεσθον) ποι-εῖσθον	Pl. 2 (ποιέεσθε) ποι-εῖσθε
3 (ποιεέσθω) ποιείσθω	3 (ποιεέσθων) ποι-είσθων	3 (ποιεέσθων) ποι-είσθων

INFIN. (ποιέεσθαι) ποιεῖσθαι　　　PART. (ποιεόμενος, η, ον) ποιεύμενος, η, ον

PRESENT SYSTEM OF χολόω *anger, vex*

942.　　　　ACTIVE

PRESENT INDICATIVE	IMPERFECT	PRESENT SUBJUNCTIVE
S. 1 (χολόω) χολῶ	(ἐχόλοον) ἐχόλουν	(χολόω) χολῶ
2 (χολόεις) χολοῖς	(ἐχόλοες) ἐχόλους	(χολόῃς) χολοῖς
3 (χολόει) χολοῖ	(ἐχόλοε) ἐχόλου	(χολόῃ) χολοῖ
Du. 2 (χολόετον) χολοῦτον	(ἐχολόετον) ἐχολοῦτον	(χολόητον) χολῶτον
3 (χολόετον) χολοῦτον	(ἐχολοέτην) ἐχολούτην	(χολόητον) χολῶτον

PL. 1 (χολόομεν) χολοῦμεν (ἐχολόομεν) ἐχολοῦμεν (χολόωμεν) χολῶμεν
2 (χολόετε) χολοῦτε (ἐχολόετε) ἐχολοῦτε (χολόητε) χολῶτε
3 (χολόουσι) χολοῦσι (ἐχόλοον) ἐχόλουν (χολόωσι) χολῶσι

PRESENT

OPTATIVE	IMPERATIVE

S. 1 (χολόοιμι) χολοῖμι
2 (χολόοις) χολοῖς (χόλοε) χόλου
3 (χολόοι) χολοῖ (χολοέτω) χολούτω
Du. 2 (χολόοιτον) χολοῖτον (χολόετον) χολοῦτον
3 (χολοοίτην) χολοίτην (χολοέτων) χολούτων
PL. 1 (χολόοιμεν) χολοῖμεν
2 (χολόοιτε) χολοῖτε (χολόετε) χολοῦτε
3 (χολόοιεν) χολοῖεν (χολοόντων) χολούντων

PART. (χολόων, ουσα, ον) χολῶν, οὖσα, οὖν, 746   INF. (χολόειν) χολοῦν

943.   MIDDLE AND PASSIVE

PRESENT INDICATIVE	IMPERFECT	PRESENT SUBJUNCTIVE
S. 1 (χολόομαι) χολοῦμαι	(ἐχολοόμην) ἐχολούμην	(χολόωμαι) χολῶμαι
2 (χολόεαι) χολοῖ	(ἐχολόεο) ἐχολοῦ	(χολόηαι) χολοῖ
3 (χολόεται) χολοῦται	(ἐχολόετο) ἐχολοῦτο	(χολόηται) χολῶται
Du. 2 (χολόεσθον) χολοῦσθον	(ἐχολόεσθον) ἐχολοῦσθον	(χολόησθον) χολῶσθον
3 (χολόεσθον) χολοῦσθον	(ἐχολοέσθην) ἐχολούσθην	(χολόησθον) χολῶσθον
PL. 1 (χολοόμε(σ)θα) χολούμε(σ)θα	(ἐχολοόμε(σ)θα) ἐχολούμε(σ)θα	(χολοώμε(σ)θα) χολώμε(σ)θα
2 (χολόεσθε) χολοῦσθε	(ἐχολόεσθε) ἐχολοῦσθε	(χολόησθε) χολῶσθε
3 (χολόονται) χολοῦνται	(ἐχολόοντο) ἐχολοῦντο	(χολόωνται) χολῶνται

PRESENT OPTATIVE	IMPERATIVE	INFINITIVE
S. 1 (χολοοίμην) χολοίμην		(χολόεσθαι) χολοῦσθαι
2 (χολόοιο) χολοῖο	(χολόεο) χολοῦ	
3 (χολόοιτο) χολοῖτο	(χολοέσθω) χολούσθω	
Du. 2 (χολόοισθον) χολοῖσθον	(χολόεσθον) χολοῦσθον	PARTICIPLE
		(χολοόμενος, η, ον)
3 (χολοοίσθην) χολοίσθην	(χολοέσθων) χολούσθων	χολούμενος, η, ον

271

PRESENT OPTATIVE   IMPERATIVE

Pl. 1 (χολοοίμε(σ)θα) χολοίμε(σ)θα
     2 (χολόοισθε) χολοῖσθε   (χολόεσθε) χολοῦσθε
     3 (χολοοίατο) χολοίατο   (χολοέσθων) χολούσθων

944. These verbs may be contracted as indicated above, and are regularly so contracted in later classical Greek.

945. The manuscripts of the Homeric poems often show a series of forms for verbs ending in -αω (as τιμάω) and in -οω (as χολόω), which are known as "assimilated" (sometimes called "distracted") forms. In these cases αε, αει, αη, αη give a double a sound, by the a assimilating the e sound; but αο, αω, αοι, αου give a double o sound, by the o assimilating the a sound. Usually one of the vowels is lengthened, sometimes both.

αε = 1) αα   αω = 1) οω   οο = 1) οω
     2) ᾱα   2) ωω   2) ωο
αει = 1) αᾳ   αοι = 1) οῳ   οοι = οῳ
     2) ᾱᾳ   2) ωοι   οου = οω
αη = 1) αᾳ   αου = 1) οω
     2) ᾱᾳ   2) ωω
αο = 1) οω
     2) ωο

946. These forms are used also in futures in -αω from -ασω (603).

947. They are found only when the second syllable in the original form is long by nature or by position (522).

948. The following forms of ὁράω (ϝορα-) *see*, may serve as examples of assimilation of an -αω verb:

INDICATIVE

		CONTRACTED	ASSIMILATED
S.	1 ὁράω	ὁρῶ	ὁρόω
	2 ὁράεις	ὁρᾷς	ὁράᾳς
	3 ὁράει	ὁρᾷ	ὁράᾳ
Du.	2 ὁράετον	ὁρᾶτον	———
	3 ὁράετον	ὁρᾶτον	———
Pl.	1 ὁράομεν	ὁρῶμεν	———
	2 ὁράετε	ὁρᾶτε	———
	3 ὁράουσι	ὁρῶσι	ὁρόωσι

	SUBJUNCTIVE			OPTATIVE	
	CONTR.	ASSIM.		CONTR.	ASSIM.
ὁράῃς	ὁρᾷς	ὁράᾳς	ὁράοιμι	ὁρῷμι	ὁρόῳμι

		PARTICIPLE			INFINTIVE	
	CONTR.	ASSIM.			CONTR.	ASSIM.
MASC. ὁράων	ὁρῶν	ὁρόων	ὁράεσθαι		ὁρᾶσθαι	ὁράασθαι
GEN. ὁράοντος	ὁρῶντος	ὁρόωντος	ὁράειν		ὁρᾶν	ὁράαν
FEM. ὁράουσα	ὁρῶσα	ὁρόωσα				

REGULAR VERBS IN -μι

ἵστημι (στη-, στα-), (make) stand; τίθημι (θη-, θε-), put; ἵημι (ἡ-, ἑ-) send; δίδωμι (δω-, δο-), give, grant

Active Voice

949. INDICATIVE

PRESENT

S. 1	ἵστημι	τίθημι	ἵημι	δίδωμι
2	ἵστης	τίθης(θα)	ἵης, ἱεῖς	διδοῖς(θα)
3	ἵστησι	τίθησι, τιθεῖ	ἵησι, ἱεῖ	δίδωσι (διδοῖ)
DU. 2	ἵστατον	τίθετον	ἵετον	δίδοτον
3	ἵστατον	τίθετον	ἵετον	δίδοτον
PL. 1	ἵσταμεν	τίθεμεν	ἵεμεν	δίδομεν
2	ἵστατε	τίθετε	ἵετε	δίδοτε
3	ἱστᾶσι	τιθεῖσι (θέουσι)	ἱεῖσι	διδοῦσι

IMPERFECT

S. 1	ἵστην	ἐτίθην	ἵειν	ἐδίδουν
2	ἵστης	ἐτίθεις	ἵεις	ἐδίδους
3	ἵστη	ἐτίθει	ἵει	ἐδίδου
DU. 2	ἵστατον	ἐτίθετον	ἵετον	ἐδίδοτον
3	ἱστάτην	ἐτιθέτην	ἱέτην	ἐδιδότην
PL. 1	ἵσταμεν	ἐτίθεμεν	ἵεμεν	ἐδίδομεν
2	ἵστατε	ἐτίθετε	ἵετε	ἐδίδοτε
3	ἵστασαν	ἐτίθεσαν	ἵεσαν, ἵεν	ἐδίδοσαν

FUTURE

S. 1	στήσω	θήσω	ἥσω	δώσω
2	στήσεις	θήσεις	ἥσεις	δώσεις
3	στήσει	θήσει	ἥσει (ἕσει)	δώσει

Du. 2 στήσετον   θήσετον   ἥσετον   δώσετον
    3 στήσετον   θήσετον   ἥσετον   δώσετον

Pl. 1 στήσομεν   θήσομεν   ἥσομεν   δώσομεν
    2 στήσετε   θήσετε   ἥσετε   δώσετε
    3 στήσουσι   θήσουσι   ἥσουσι   δώσουσι

FIRST AORIST

S. 1 ἔστησα   ἔθηκα   ἕηκα   ἔδωκα
   2 ἔστησας   ἔθηκας   ἕηκας   ἔδωκας
   3 ἔστησε   ἔθηκε   ἕηκε   ἔδωκε

Du. 2 ἐστήσατον   *ἐθήκατον   *ἑήκατον   *ἐδώκατον
    3 ἐστησάτην   *ἐθηκάτην   *ἑηκάτην   *ἐδωκάτην

Pl. 1 ἐστήσαμεν   *ἐθήκαμεν   ἑήκαμεν   *ἐδώκαμεν
    2 ἐστήσατε   *ἐθήκατε   *ἑήκατε   *ἐδώκατε
    3 ἔστησαν (ἔστασαν) ἔθηκαν   ἕηκαν   ἔδωκαν

SECOND AORIST

S. 1 ἔστην
   2 ἔστης
   3 ἔστη

Du. 2 ἐστήτον   ἔθετον   εἷτον   ἔδοτον
    3 ἐστήτην   ἐθέτην   εἵτην   ἐδότην

Pl. 1 ἔστημεν   ἔθεμεν   εἷμεν   ἔδομεν
    2 ἔστητε   ἔθετε   εἷτε   ἔδοτε
    3 ἔστησαν (ἔσταν) ἔθεσαν   εἷσαν   ἔδοσαν

950.   SUBJUNCTIVE

PRESENT

S. 1 ἱστῶ(μι)   τιθῶ(μι)   ἱῶ(μι)   διδῶ(μι)
   2 ἱστῇς(θα)   τιθῇς(θα)   ἱῇς(θα)   διδῷς(θα)
   3 ἱστῇ(σι)   τιθῇ(σι)   ἱῇ(σι)   διδῷ(σι)

Du. 2 ἱστῆτον   τιθῆτον   ἱῆτον   διδῶτον
    3 ἱστῆτον   τιθῆτον   ἱῆτον   διδῶτον

Pl. 1 ἱστῶμεν   τιθῶμεν   ἱῶμεν   διδῶμεν
    2 ἱστῆτε   τιθῆτε   ἱῆτε   διδῶτε
    3 ἱστῶσι   τιθῶσι   ἱῶσι   διδῶσι

SECOND AORIST

S. 1 στῶ(μι)   θῶ(μι)   ὦ(μι)   δῶ(μι)
   2 στῇς(θα)   θῇς(θα)   ᾖς(θα)   δῷς(θα)
   3 στῇ(σι)   θῇ(σι)   ᾖ(σι)   δῷ(σι)

Du. 2	στῆτον	θῆτον	ἦτον	δῶτον
3	στῆτον	θῆτον	ἦτον	δῶτον
Pl. 1	στῶμεν	θῶμεν	ὦμεν	δῶμεν
2	στῆτε	θῆτε	ἦτε	δῶτε
3	στῶσι	θῶσι	ὦσι	δῶσι

951. The second aorist subjunctive of -μι verbs (949 ff.) seems to have had a double form of inflection:

1) With a short thematic (796) vowel, as θήω, θήεις, θήει, θήετον, θηέτην, θήομεν, θήετε, θήουσι (τίθημι *put, place*).

2) With a long thematic (796) vowel, as θήω, θήῃς, θήῃ, θήητον, θήητον, θήωμεν, θήητε, θήωσι.

The vowel of the stem is then shortened (572), producing —

3) θέω, θέῃς, θέῃ, θέητον, θέητον, θέωμεν, θέητε, θέωσι.

This form then undergoes contraction (584–585), giving —

4) θῶ, θῇς, θῇ, θῆτον, θῆτον, θῶμεν, θῆτε, θῶσι.

952. The subjunctives of athematic (797; 865, 2) second aorists and the subjunctives passive of both first and second aorists are similarly formed. Thus, λυθῶ, λυθῇς, λυθῇ, etc., contracted from λυθέω, λυθέῃς, λυθέῃ, etc.; τραφῶ, τραφῇς, τραφῇ, etc., contracted from τραφέω, τραφέῃς, τραφέῃ, etc.

953.   Optative

                           PRESENT

S. 1	ἱσταίην	τιθείην	ἱείην	διδοίην
2	ἱσταίης	τιθείης	ἱείης	διδοίης
3	ἱσταίη	τιθείη	ἱείη	διδοίη
Du. 2	ἱσταῖτον	τιθεῖτον	ἱεῖτον	διδοῖτον
3	ἱσταίτην	τιθείτην	ἱείτην	διδοίτην
Pl. 1	ἱσταῖμεν	τιθεῖμεν	ἱεῖμεν	διδοῖμεν
2	ἱσταῖτε	τιθεῖτε	ἱεῖτε	διδοῖτε
3	ἱσταῖεν	τιθεῖεν	ἱεῖεν	διδοῖεν

                           SECOND AORIST

S. 1	σταίην	θείην	εἵην	δοίην
2	σταίης	θείης	εἵης	δοίης
3	σταίη	θείη	εἵη	δοίη
Du. 2	σταῖτον	θεῖτον	εἷτον	δοῖτον
3	σταίτην	θείτην	εἵτην	δοίτην

Pl. 1 σταῖμεν　　θεῖμεν　　εἷμεν　　δοῖμεν
　　2 σταῖτε　　θεῖτε　　εἷτε　　δοῖτε
　　3 σταῖεν, σταίησαν　θεῖεν　εἷεν　δοῖεν

954.　　　IMPERATIVE

PRESENT

S. 2 ἵστη (-ā)　τίθει (= -εε)　ἵει (= ἵεε)　δίδου (δίδωθι)
　3 ἱστάτω　τιθέτω　ἱέτω　διδότω

Du 2 ἵστατον　τίθετον　ἵετον　δίδοτον
　3 ἱστάτων　τιθέτων　ἱέτων　διδότων

Pl. 2 ἵστατε　τίθετε　ἵετε　δίδοτε
　3 ἱστάντων　τιθέντων　ἱέντων　διδόντων

SECOND AORIST

S. 2 στῆθι　θές　ἕς　δός
　3 στήτω　θέτω　ἕτω　δότω

Du. 2 στῆτον　θέτον　ἕτον　δότον
　3 στήτων　θέτων　ἕτων　δότων

Pl. 2 στῆτε　θέτε　ἕτε　δότε
　3 στάντων　θέντων　ἕντων　δόντων

955.　　　INFINITIVE

PRESENT

ἱστάμεν(αι)　τιθέμεν(αι) (1168)　ἱέμεν(αι)　διδόμεν(αι) (διδοῦναι)

SECOND AORIST

στῆναι (στήμεναι)　θεῖναι (θέμεν[αι])　εἷναι (ἕμεν[αι])　δοῦναι (δόμεν[αι])

956.　　　PARTICIPLE

PRES. ἱστάς, ἱστᾶσα, ἱστάν　τιθείς, εἷσα, έν　ἱείς, εἷσα, έν　διδούς, οὖσα, όν
2 AOR. στάς, στᾶσα, στάν　θείς, θεῖσα, θέν　εἵς, εἷσα, ἕν　δούς, δοῦσα, δόν

NOTE 1. — For the second perfect system of ἵστημι, see 924.
NOTE 2. — δίδωμι may have (very rarely) διδώσω instead of δώσω in the future.

Middle Voice

957.　　　INDICATIVE

PRESENT

S. 1 ἵσταμαι　τίθεμαι　ἵεμαι　δίδομαι
　2 ἵστασαι　τίθεσαι　ἵεσαι　δίδοσαι
　3 ἵσταται　τίθεται　ἵεται　δίδοται

Du. 2	ἵστασθον	τίθεσθον	ἵεσθον	δίδοσθον
3	ἵστασθον	τίθεσθον	ἵεσθον	δίδοσθον
Pl. 1	ἱστάμε(σ)θα	τιθέμε(σ)θα	ἱέμε(σ)θα	διδόμε(σ)θα
2	ἵστασθε	τίθεσθε	ἵεσθε	δίδοσθε
3	ἵστανται	τίθενται	ἵενται	δίδονται

IMPERFECT

S. 1	ἱστάμην	ἐτιθέμην	ἱέμην	ἐδιδόμην
2	ἵστασο	ἐτίθεσο	ἵεσο	ἐδίδοσο
3	ἵστατο	ἐτίθετο	ἵετο	ἐδίδοτο
Du. 2	ἵστασθον	ἐτίθεσθον	ἵεσθον	ἐδίδοσθον
3	ἱστάσθην	ἐτιθέσθην	ἱέσθην	ἐδιδόσθην
Pl. 1	ἱστάμε(σ)θα	ἐτιθέμε(σ)θα	ἱέμε(σ)θα	ἐδιδόμε(σ)θα
2	ἵστασθε	ἐτίθεσθε	ἵεσθε	ἐδίδοσθε
3	ἵσταντο	ἐτίθεντο	ἵεντο	ἐδίδοντο

FUTURE

S. 1	στήσομαι	θήσομαι	ἥσομαι	δώσομαι
2	στήσεαι	θήσεαι	ἥσεαι	δώσεαι
3	στήσεται	θήσεται	ἥσεται	δώσεται
Du. 2	στήσεσθον	θήσεσθον	ἥσεσθον	δώσεσθον
3	στήσεσθον	θήσεσθον	ἥσεσθον	δώσεσθον
Pl. 1	στησόμε(σ)θα	θησόμε(σ)θα	ἡσόμε(σ)θα	δωσόμε(σ)θα
2	στήσεσθε	θήσεσθε	ἥσεσθε	δώσεσθε
3	στήσονται	θήσονται	ἥσονται	δώσονται

FIRST AORIST

S. 1	ἐστησάμην	——	——	——
2	ἐστήσαο	——	——	——
3	ἐστήσατο	ἐθήκατο	——	——
Du. 2	ἐστήσασθον	——	——	——
3	ἐστησάσθην	——	——	——
Pl. 1	ἐστησάμε(σ)θα	——	——	——
2	ἐστήσασθε	——	——	——
3	ἐστήσαντο	——	——	——

SECOND AORIST

S. 1	——	ἐθέμην	εἵμην	ἐδόμην
2	——	ἔθεο	εἷο	ἔδοεο (ου)
3	——	ἔθετο	εἷτο	ἔδοτο
Du. 2	——	ἔθεσθον	εἷσθον	ἔδοσθον
3	——	ἐθέσθην	εἵσθην	ἐδόσθην

277

HOMERIC GREEK

PL. 1	——	ἐθέμε(σ)θα	εἵμε(σ)θα	ἐδόμε(σ)θα
2	——	ἔθεσθε	εἷσθε	ἔδοσθε
3	——	ἔθεντο	εἷντο	ἔδοντο

958. SUBJUNCTIVE

PRESENT

S. 1	ἱστῶμαι	τιθῶμαι	ἱῶμαι	διδῶμαι
2	ἱστῆαι	τιθῆαι	ἱῆαι	διδῶαι
3	ἱστῆται	τιθῆται	ἱῆται	διδῶται
DU. 2	ἱστῆσθον	τιθῆσθον	ἱῆσθον	διδῶσθον
3	ἱστῆσθον	τιθῆσθον	ἱῆσθον	διδῶσθον
PL. 1	ἱστώμε(σ)θα	τιθώμε(σ)θα	ἱώμε(σ)θα	διδώμε(σ)θα
2	ἱστῆσθε	τιθῆσθε	ἱῆσθε	διδῶσθε
3	ἱστῶνται	τιθῶνται	ἱῶνται	διδῶνται

SECOND AORIST

S. 1	——	θῶμαι	ὧμαι	δῶμαι
2	——	θῆαι	ἧαι	δῶαι
3	——	θῆται	ἧται	δῶται
DU. 2	——	θῆσθον	ἧσθον	δῶσθον
3	——	θῆσθον	ἧσθον	δῶσθον
PL. 1	——	θώμε(σ)θα	ὥμε(σ)θα	δώμε(σ)θα
2	——	θῆσθε	ἧσθε	δῶσθε
3	——	θῶνται	ὧνται	δῶνται

959. OPTATIVE

PRESENT

S. 1	ἱσταίμην	τιθείμην	ἱείμην	διδοίμην
2	ἱσταῖο	τιθεῖο	ἱεῖο	διδοῖο
3	ἱσταῖτο	τιθεῖτο	ἱεῖτο	διδοῖτο
DU. 2	ἱσταῖσθον	τιθεῖσθον	ἱεῖσθον	διδοῖσθον
3	ἱσταίσθην	τιθείσθην	ἱείσθην	διδοίσθην
PL. 1	ἱσταίμε(σ)θα	τιθείμε(σ)θα	ἱείμε(σ)θα	διδοίμε(σ)θα
2	ἱσταῖσθε	τιθεῖσθε	ἱεῖσθε	διδοῖσθε
3	ἱσταίατο	τιθείατο	ἱείατο	διδοίατο

SECOND AORIST

S. 1	——	θείμην	εἵμην	δοίμην
2	——	θεῖο	εἷο	δοῖο
3	——	θεῖτο	εἷτο	δοῖτο

Du. 2 ——	θεῖσθον	εἷσθον	δοῖσθον
3 ——	θείσθην	εἵσθην	δοίσθην
Pl. 1 ——	θείμε(σ)θα	εἵμε(σ)θα	δοίμε(σ)θα
2 ——	θεῖσθε	εἷσθε	δοῖσθε
3 ——	θείατο	εἵατο	δοίατο

960. IMPERATIVE

PRESENT

S. 2 ἵστασο	τίθεσο	ἵεσο	δίδοσο
3 ἱστάσθω	τιθέσθω	ἱέσθω	διδόσθω
Du. 2 ἵστασθον	τίθεσθον	ἵεσθον	δίδοσθον
3 ἱστάσθων	τιθέσθων	ἱέσθων	διδόσθων
Pl. 2 ἵστασθε	τίθεσθε	ἵεσθε	δίδοσθε
3 ἱστάσθων	τιθέσθων	ἱέσθων	διδόσθων

SECOND AORIST

S. 2 ——	θέο (θεῦ)	ἕο	δόο (δοῦ)
3 ——	θέσθω	ἕσθω	δόσθω
Du. 2 ——	θέσθον	ἕσθον	δόσθον
3 ——	θέσθων	ἕσθων	δόσθων
Pl. 2 ——	θέσθε	ἕσθε	δόσθε
3 ——	θέσθων	ἕσθων	δόσθων

961. INFINITIVE

| PRESENT ἵστασθαι | τίθεσθαι | ἵεσθαι | δίδοσθαι |
| SEC. AOR. —— | θέσθαι | ἕσθαι | δόσθαι |

962. PARTICIPLE

| PRESENT ἱστάμενος, η, ον | τιθέμενος, η, ον (τιθή-, 1168) | ἱέμενος, η, ον | διδόμενος, η, ον |
| SEC. AOR. —— | θέμενος, η, ον | ἕμενος, η, ον | δόμενος, μ, ον |

963. For the second perfect system of ἵστημι see 924.

IRREGULAR VERBS IN -μι

964. εἰμί (ἐσ-) *be*

	INDICATIVE		SUBJUNCTIVE	OPTATIVE	IMPERATIVE
	PRESENT	IMPERFECT		PRESENT	
S. 1	εἰμί	ἦα (ἔα, ἔον)	ἔω	εἴην	
2	ἐσσί (εἶς)	ἦσθα (ἔησθα)	ἔῃς(θα)	εἴης (ἔοις)	ἴσθι*
3	ἐστί	ἦεν (ἤην, ἔην, ἦν)	ἔῃ(σι) (ἦσι)	εἴη (ἔοι)	ἔστω

279

Du. 2 ἐστόν   ἦστον   ἔητον   εἴτον   ἔστον
    3 ἐστόν   ἦστην   ἔητον   εἴτην   ἔστων
Pl. 1 εἰμέν   ἦμεν   ἔωμεν   εἴμεν
    2 ἐστέ   ἦτε   ἔητε   εἴτε   ἔστε
    3 εἰσί (ἔασι) ἦσαν (ἔσαν) ἔωσι (ὦσι) εἴεν   ἔστων

FUTURE   ἔσ(σ)ομαι, ἔσεαι, etc.   INFIN.   εἶναι, ἔμ(μ)εν(αι)
MID. IMPER.   ἔσσο   PARTIC.   ἐών, ἐοῦσα, ἐόν

965.   εἶμι (εἰ-, ἰ-) *come, go*

		INDICATIVE		PRESENT	
	PRES	IMPERF.	SUBJ.	OPT.	IMPER.
S. 1	εἶμι	ἦια (ἤιον)	ἴω(μι)	ἴοιμι	
2	εἶσ(θα)	ἤεισ(θα)	ἴῃς(θα)	ἴοις	ἴθι
3	εἶσι	ἤει (ἤιε, ἦε, ἴε)	ἴῃ(σι)	ἴοι (ἰείη)	ἴτω
Du. 2	ἴτον	ἴτον	ἴητον	ἴοιτον	ἴτον
3	ἴτον	ἴτην	ἴητον	ἰοίτην	ἴτων
Pl. 1	ἴμεν	ἤομεν	ἴωμεν	ἴοιμεν	
2	ἴτε	ἦτε	ἴητε	ἴοιτε	ἴτε
3	ἴᾱσι	ἤισαν (ἦσαν, ἤιον, ἴσαν)	ἴωσι	ἴοιεν	ἰόντων

FUT. εἴσομαι   INFIN. ἰέναι, ἴμεν(αι)   PARTIC. ἰών, οὖσα, όν

966.   *εἴδω (εἴδομαι) (ϝειδ-, ϝοιδ-, ϝιδ-), εἰδήσω, εἶδον, οἶδα *know*
                    Active

		INDICATIVE		SECOND PERFECT	
	2D PERF.	2D PLUPERF.	SUBJ.	OPT.	IMPER.
S. 1	οἶδα	ἤδεα	εἰδῶ (εἰδέω, ἰδέω)	εἰδείην	
2	οἶσθα (οἶδας)	ἤδης(θα) (ἤειδεις)	εἰδῇς(θα)	εἰδείης	ἴσθι
3	οἶδε	ἤδη (ἤδεε, ἤειδει)	εἰδῇ(σι)	εἰδείη	ἴστω
Du. 2	ἴστον	ἴστον	εἴδετον	εἰδεῖτον	ἴστον
3	ἴστον	ἴστην	εἴδετον	εἰδείτην	ἴστων
Pl. 1	ἴδμεν	ἴδμεν	εἴδομεν [1]	εἰδεῖμεν (εἰδείημεν)	

[1] The only Homeric examples of the first and second person plural subjunctive have the short mode vowel (-ομεν, -ετε, 800).

2 ἴστε	ἴστε	εἴδετε [1]	εἰδεῖτε	ἴστε
			(εἰδείητε)	
3 ἴσ(σ)ᾱσι	ἴσαν	εἰδῶσι	εἰδεῖεν	ἴστων
			(εἰδείησαν)	

FUT. εἰδήσω (εἴσομαι)   INFIN. ἴδμεν(αι)   PARTIC. εἰδώς, υἶα (ἰδυῖα), ός

967.   φημί (φη-, φα-) say, speak

Active

	INDICATIVE		PRESENT		
	PRES.	IMPERF. (2D AOR.)	SUBJ.	OPT.	IMPER.
S. 1	φημί	ἔφην	φῶ(μι)	φαίην	
2	φής, φῆσθα	ἔφης(θα)	φῇς(θα)	φαίης	φαθί
					(φάθι)
3	φησί	ἔφη	φῇ(σι)	φαίη	φάτω
DU. 2	φατόν	ἔφατον	φῆτον		φάτον
3	φατόν	ἐφάτην	φῆτον		φάτων
PL. 1	φαμέν	ἔφαμεν	φῶμεν	φαίημεν (φαῖμεν)	
2	φατέ	ἔφατε	φῆτε	φαίητε	φάτε
3	φᾱσί	ἔφασαν (ἔφαν)	φῶσι	φαίησαν (φαῖεν)	φάντων

PARTIC. φάς, φᾶσα, φάν   INFIN. φάναι, φάμεν(αι)

NOTE. — The active imperative and infinitive do not occur in Homer, who uses the middle forms, φάο, φάσθαι, etc.

968.   κεῖ-μαι lie, recline

	INDICATIVE		PRESENT		
	PRES.	IMPERF.	SUBJ.	IMPER.	INFIN.
S. 1	κεῖμαι	ἐκείμην	κεῖται (κῆται)		κεῖσθαι
2	κεῖσαι	ἔκεισο		κεῖσο	
3	κεῖται	ἔκειτο		κείσθω	
DU. 2	κεῖσθον	ἔκεισθον		κεῖσθον	PART.
3	κεῖσθον	ἐκείσθην		κείσθων	κείμενος, η, ον
PL. 1	κείμε(σ)θα	ἐκείμε(σ)θα			
2	κεῖσθε	ἔκεισθε		κεῖσθε	
3	κέαται (κέον-	ἔκειντο (ἐκείατο,		κείσθων	
	ται, κέαται)	ἐκέατο)			

FUT. κείσομαι

---

[1] See footnote on preceding page.

969.   ἧμαι (ἡσ-) *sit*

	INDICATIVE		PRESENT	
	PRES.	IMPERF.	IMPER.	INFIN.
S. 1	ἧμαι	ἥμην		ἧσθαι
2	ἧσαι	ἧσο	ἧσο	
3	ἧσται	ἧστο	ἥσθω	
Du. 2	ἧσθον	ἧσθον	ἧσθον	PART.
3	ἧσθον	ἥσθην	ἥσθων	ἥμενος, η, ον
Pl. 1	ἥμε(σ)θα	ἥμε(σ)θα		
2	ἧσθε	ἧσθε	ἧσθε	
3	ἧνται (ἥαται, ἕαται)	ἧντο (ἥατο, ἕατο)	ἥσθων	

III. SYNTAX

GENERAL

970. The subject of a finite verb is in the nominative case, as ὀλέκοντο δὲ λαοί *and the people kept perishing,* ἔδεισεν δ᾽ ὁ γέρων *and that old man feared.*

971. The subject of an infinitive is regularly in the accusative, ἄμμε ὀίω ἂψ ἀπονοστήσειν *I think we shall return home,* βούλομ᾽ ἐγὼ λαὸν σόον ἔμμεναι *I wish my people to be safe.* The subject of the infinitive is usually omitted when it is the same as the subject or object, either direct or indirect, of the main verb.

972. When the infinitive is used to express a command (1107, 11), its subject, when expressed, is in the nominative when of the second person, and in the accusative when of the third person, as σὺ τόν γ᾽ ἐπέεσσι καθάπτεσθαι μαλακοῖσιν *but do you attack him with soft words.*

973. A finite verb regularly agrees with its subject nominative in person and number, except:

1) A neuter plural subject may take its verb in the singular, as ᾤχετο κῆλα θεοῖο *the shafts of the god sped,* τὰ δέδασται *these have been distributed.*

2) With two or more subjects connected by *and,* the verb may agree with one of the subjects and be understood with the rest, as μή νύ τοι οὐ χραίσμῃ σκῆπτρον καὶ στέμμα θεοῖο *lest the sceptre and the fillet of the god avail thee naught,* εἰ δὴ ὁμοῦ πόλεμός τε δαμᾷ καὶ λοιμὸς Ἀχαιούς *if war and pestilence at the same time crush the Achaeans.*

3) When referring to *two,* the plural and dual are often interchanged or united, as δεινὼ δέ οἱ ὄσσε φάανθεν *and her eyes appeared terrible,* τώ οἱ ἔσαν κήρυκε καὶ ὀτρηρὼ θεράποντε *who were his two heralds and ready attendants,* τὼ δ᾽ αὐτὼ μάρτυροι ἔστων *and let these two be witnesses.*

974. A noun or an adjective in the predicate after verbs meaning *be, appear, become, be thought, made, named, chosen, regarded,* and the like, agrees with the subject in case, as ὁμηγερέες τε γένοντο *and they became assembled;* ὃς ἄριστος 'Αχαιῶν εὔχεται εἶναι *who boasts that he is far the mightiest of the Achaeans,* τὸ δέ τοι κῆρ εἴδεται εἶναι *but that seems (to be) even as death to you,* δειλός τε καὶ οὐτιδανὸς καλεοίμην *I should be called both coward and worthless.*

975. Apposition. — A noun used in connection with another noun to describe it, and denoting the same person or thing, agrees with it in case, and is said to be in apposition with it, as 'Ατρεΐδης ἄναξ ἀνδρῶν *the son of Atreus, king of men,* Χρύσην ἠτίμασεν ἀρητῆρα *he slighted Chryses, the priest.*

976. The verb εἰμί (especially the forms of the third person singular and plural ἐστί, εἰσί) is often omitted, when it can easily be supplied from the context.

977. Other words are at times omitted, as ναὶ μὰ τόδε σκῆπτρcν = ναὶ μὰ τόδε σκῆπτρον ὄμνυμι *yea, by this sceptre (I swear).*

NOUNS
Nominative Case

978. A noun is in the nominative:

1) When it is the subject of a finite verb (970).

2) When it is in the predicate after certain verbs (974).

3) Sometimes for the vocative, as δημοβόρος βασιλεύς *king, who devour (the goods of) the people!*

Genitive Case

The Greek genitive represents two earlier cases (657): 1) the *genitive proper,* denoting the class to which a person or thing belongs. 2) the *ablatival genitive* (formerly the ablative), usually expressing *separation, source, cause.*

979. Some of the most common uses of the genitive are:

1) Possession, as ψῡχὰς ἡρώων *souls of warriors,* Διὸς βουλή *the will of Zeus,* ἐπὶ νῆας 'Αχαιῶν *to the ships of the Achaeans:* the *possessive genitive.*

2) The *subject* of an action or feeling, as μῆνιν 'Αχιλῆος *the wrath of Achilles (i.e.* felt by Achilles): the *subjective genitive.*

3) The *object* of an action or feeling, as 'Αχιλῆος ποθή *a yearning of (i.e. for) Achilles,* πόοιως καὶ ἐδητύος ἔρον *the desire of (i.e. for) food and drink:* the *objective genitive.*

4) Material or contents, as πυραὶ νεκύων *funeral pyres of corpses,* ἑκατόμβᾱς ταύρων ἠδ' αἰγῶν *hecatombs of bulls and of goats:* genitive of *material.*

5) Measure of time, space, or value (price), as κούρης Χρῡσηΐδος ἄποινα δέξασθαι *to accept the ransoms for the maiden Chryseïs:* genitive of *price.*

6) Cause or origin, as εὐχωλῆς ἐπιμέμφεται *he finds fault on account of a vow* (unperformed), χωόμενον γυναικός *vexed for the sake of a woman:* the genitive of *cause.*

7) The whole after words denoting the part, as τίς θεῶν; *which (one) of the gods?* τὸ πλεῖον πολέμοιο *the greater part of the war:* the *partitive* genitive.

980. The partitive genitive may follow all adjectives, adverbs, nouns, and participles, which denote a part, as οἰωνοπόλων ὄχ' ἄριστος *far the best of augurs,* οἶος 'Αργείων *alone of the Argives,* τῶν δ' ἄλλων οὔ τις ὁρᾶτο *but not any one of the others saw her.*

981. A genitive in the predicate after verbs meaning *to be,* etc., and other copulative verbs, may express any of the relations of the *attributive* genitive (979, 1–7).

982. Any verb whose action affects the object in part only, or which means to *share,* or to *enjoy,* may take the genitive, as ἀρνῶν κνίσης αἰγῶν τε τελείων ἀντιάσᾱς *having partaken of the fat of unblemished lambs and goats,* ἵνα πάντες ἐπαύρωνται βασιλῆος *in order that all may reap the benefits of their king.*

983. Verbs meaning to *begin, make trial of, take hold of, touch, attain, claim, aim, hit, miss,* take the genitive, as κόμης ἕλε Πηλεΐωνα *she grabbed Achilles by the hair of his head,* λαβὲ γούνων *lay hold of his knees,* χειρὸς ἑλόντε *having taken hold of her hand,* ποδὸς τεταγών *having seized me by the foot.*

984. Verbs signifying to *taste, smell, hear, perceive, comprehend, remember, forget, desire, care for, spare, neglect, wonder at, admire, despise,* take the genitive, as κλῦθί μευ *hear me!* σέθεν δ' ἐγὼ οὐκ ἀλεγίζω οὐδ' ὄθομαι κοτέοντος *I reck not of thee, nor am I concerned at thine anger,* κήδετο Δαναῶν *she grieved for the Danaans,* καὶ μέν μευ βουλέων ξύνιεν *and they hearkened to my advice,* τῶν μιν μνήσᾱσα *having reminded him of this,* Θέτις οὐ λήθετ᾽ ἐφετμέων *Thetis did not forget the behests.*

985. The genitive follows verbs signifying to *rule, lead, direct,* as ὅς Τενέδοιο ἀνάσσεις (thou) *who dost rule Tenedos,* ὃς πάντων Ἀργείων κρατέει *who rules all the Argives.*

986. Verbs signifying *fulness* and *want* take the genitive of material (979, 4). Those meaning to *fill* take the accusative of the thing filled, and the genitive of material, as μένεος φρένες πίμπλαντο *his diaphragm was filled with rage,* κοῦροι κρητῆρας ἐπεστέψαντο ποτοῖο *the young men filled the mixing bowls to the brim with drink.*

987. The genitive may denote that from which anything is *separated* or *distinguished* (genitive of separation); hence it is used after verbs meaning *remove, restrain, release, cease, fail, differ, give up,* etc., as λῆγ᾽ ἔριδος *cease from strife,* πολέμου δ᾽ ἀποπαύεο *but refrain from war.* It is used also to denote *source,* as δεινὴ κλαγγὴ γένετ᾽ ἀργυρέοιο βιοῖο *a terrifying clang arose from the silver bow.*

988. The genitive follows verbs signifying *surpass, be inferior to,* and all others which imply a comparison (993), as Κλυταιμ(ν)ήστρης προβέβουλα *I prefer (her) to Clytaem(n)estra,* περὶ πάντων ἔμμεναι ἄλλων *to be above all others,* οἳ περὶ βουλὴν Δαναῶν ἐστε (you) *who surpass the Danaans in counsel.*

989. Verbs compounded with a preposition are often followed by the genitive, as τὰ πολίων ἐξεπράθομεν *what(soever) we took as spoil from the cities,* περίσχεο παιδός *protect your son.*

990. The genitive may denote time within which anything takes place.

991. Many adjectives kindred in meaning or derivation to verbs which take the genitive are followed by the genitive (objective).

992. Many adverbs, chiefly those of place, and those derived from adjectives which take the genitive, are construed with the genitive, as τηλόθι πάτρης *far from her native land,* πάροιθ᾽ αὐτοῖο *in front of him,* λιμένος ἐντός *within the harbor.*

993. Adjectives and adverbs of the comparative degree take the genitive (988), unless followed by ἤ (ἠέ) *than,* as οὔ ἑθέν ἐστι χερείων

286

she is not inferior to her (literally *not worse than*), φέρτερός εἰμι σέθεν *I am mightier than you*, γλυκίων μέλιτος *sweeter than honey.*

994. A noun and a participle not closely connected grammatically with the rest of the sentence may stand by themselves in the genitive. This construction is called the *genitive absolute.* Examples: αὐτοῦ κινηθέντος *as the god moved*, ἐμεῦ ζῶντος καὶ ἐπὶ χθονὶ δερκομένοιο *while I live and look out upon the earth.*

Dative Case

The Greek dative represents three earlier cases (657): 1) the *dative proper*, denoting *to* or *for* which something is or is done. 2) the *instrumental (dative)*, denoting *instrument, means, manner, cause, accompaniment.* 3) the *locative (dative)*, denoting *place where* and *time when.*

995. The indirect object of a transitive verb is in the dative, as τήν οἱ πόρε Φοῖβος Ἀπόλλων *which Phoebus Apollo granted to him*, πῶς τοι δώσουσι γέρας *how shall they give you a prize of honor?*

996. Many verbs which in English are transitive are intransitive in Greek and take the dative. The verbs of this class are mainly those meaning *serve, benefit, defend, assist, please, obey, trust, satisfy, advise, exhort*, and their opposites; also those signifying *abuse, anger, blame, envy, friendliness, hostility, reproach, threats, etc.*, as βασιλῆι χολωθείς *incensed at the king*, οὐκ Ἀτρεΐδη ἤνδανε θυμῷ *it was not pleasing to the son of Atreus in his soul*, μή νύ τοι οὐ χραίσμη σκῆπτρον καὶ στέμμα θεοῖο *lest the sceptre and the fillet of the god avail thee not*, ἐπείθετο μύθῳ *he obeyed the command*, μοὶ ἀρήξειν *to defend me*, ὅτε χώσεται ἀνδρὶ χέρηι *when he becomes enraged at an inferior*, ἀπειλήσω δέ τοι ὧδε *and I shall threaten you as follows*, μήνι Ἀχαιοῖσιν *continue to rage against the Achaeans.*

997. A person or thing for whose advantage or disadvantage a thing exists or is done is put in the dative, as αὐτοὺς δὲ ἑλώρια τεῦχε κύνεσσιν οἰωνοῖσί τε δαῖτα *and it made themselves a booty for the dogs and a banquet for the birds*, παῖδα δ᾽ ἐμοὶ λῦσαι *but free for me my child*, τόδε μοι κρήηνον ἐέλδωρ *accomplish for me this desire*, ἡμῖν ἀπὸ λοιγὸν ἀμῦναι *to ward off destruction for (from) us*, καὶ δή μοι γέρας αὐτὸς ἀφαιρήσεσθαι ἀπειλεῖς *and you threaten to take away for (from)* *me my prize of honor,* Ἀχιλλῆι μεθέμεν χόλον *to forego (your) anger for Achilles,* σὺν δ᾽ ἡμῖν δαῖτα ταράξῃ *and he should throw the banquet into confusion for us.*

998. The dative of interest or reference denotes the person to whose case a statement is limited.

999. The dative with εἰμί, γίγνομαι, and verbs of similar meaning, may denote the possessor, as τῶν δ᾽ ἄλλων ἅ μοι ἔστι παρὰ νηί *but of all else which are mine beside my ship,* τώ οἱ ἔσαν κήρῦκε *who were his two heralds.*

1000. The dative of the personal pronouns often denotes the possessor, without such verbs as εἰμί, γίγνομαι, etc., as ὄσσε δέ οἱ πυρὶ ἐίκτην *and his two eyes were like fire,* ὅ μοι γέρας ἔρχεται ἄλλῃ *my prize of honor is going elsewhere,* δεινὼ δέ οἱ ὄσσε φάανθεν *and her eyes gleamed terribly.*

1001. The dative is used after verbs meaning to *give commands,* and to *lead the way for,* as νήεσσ᾽ ἡγήσατ᾽ Ἀχαιῶν Ἴλιον εἴσω *and he led the way for the ships of the Achaeans into Troy,* Μυρμιδόνεσσι ἄνασσε *rule the Myrmidons.*

1002. The dative follows some verbal nouns and many adjectives and adverbs of kindred meaning with verbs which take the dative, as τὰ κάκ᾽ ἐστὶ φίλα φρεσί *evil is dear to your heart,* οὔ τί μοι αἴτιοί εἰσιν *they are in no wise blamable toward me,* ἔχθιστός μοί ἐσσι *you are most hateful to me,* ἐπεὶ μάλα οἱ φίλος ἦεν *since he was exceeding dear to him,* χαλεποί τοι ἔσονται *they will be (too) hard for you,* ἴλᾱος ἔσσεται ἡμῖν *he will be propitious toward us.*

1003. The dative is used after all words signifying *likeness,* or *unlikeness, agreement, disagreement, union,* or *approach,* as νυκτὶ ἐοικώς *like unto night,* ὄσσε δέ οἱ πυρὶ ἐίκτην *and his eyes were like unto fire,* οὐ σοί ποτε ἶσον ἔχω γέρας *never have I a prize of honor equal to you(rs),* ἐπιείκελον ἀθανάτοισιν *like unto the immortals.*

1004. The dative follows many verbs compounded with ἐν, σύν, and ἐπί, and some compounded with πρός, παρά, περί, and ὑπό, as αὐτοῖσι βέλος ἐφιείς *hurling a dart upon them,* ὃς Ἀργείοισι κήδε᾽ ἐφῆκεν *who brought sorrows upon the Argives,* νηυσὶ παρήμενος *sitting beside the ships,* σοί γε παρέζετο *she sat down beside you,* οἱ συμφράσσατο βουλὰς Θέτις *Thetis devised plans with him,* μητρὶ δ' ἐγὼ παράφημι *but I advise my mother,* ἐνῶρτο γέλος θεοῖσιν *laughter arose among the gods.*

1005. The dative is used to denote *cause, manner, means, instrument,* and *agency,* as τίσειαν Δαναοὶ ἐμὰ δάκρυα σοῖσι βέλεσσιν *may the Danaans atone for my tears with thy darts,* ἔπεσιν καὶ χερσὶν ἀρήξειν *to assist with words and hands,* ὑπεροπλί σι τάχ' ἄν ποτε θῦμὸν ὀλέσσῃ *by his deeds of arrogance he will soon lose his life,* μηδὲ ξίφος ἕλκεο χειρί *and do not continue to draw your sword with your hand,* ἔπεσιν ὀνείδισον *revile him with words,* χερσὶ οὐ μαχήσομαι *I will not fight with my hands,* κύδεϊ γαίων *rejoicing in his glory,* τῶ σὲ κακῇ αἴσῃ τέκον *therefore I bore you to an evil lot,* τὴν βίῃ ἀέκοντος ἀπηύρων *whom they took away by violence against his will,* μολπῇ θεὸν ἱλάσκοντο *they appeased the god with music and dancing,* λάβε γούνων σκαιῇ *she seized his knees with her left (hand),* τοὶ κεφαλῇ κατανεύσομαι *I shall nod assent to you with my head.*

1006. The dative is used to denote the circumstance, or that by which a thing or person is accompanied. The dative of circumstance is most common with abstract or semi-abstract words, and is often used to express the reason or occasion. σοὶ ἅμ' ἑσπόμεθα *we accompany you,* οἵ οἱ ἅμα τράφεν ἠδὲ γένοντο *who were bred and born with him,* ἑκάστῳ δῶμα Ἥφαιστος ποίησεν ἰδυίῃσιν πραπίδεσσιν *Hephaestus made a home for each with cunning mind,* τίς σφωε ἔριδι ξυνέηκε; *who brought these two together in strife?*

1007. The dative is used with verbs signifying to *be with, follow, join, agree, be like, fight, strive, trust, be pleased,* and occasionally with those meaning to *buy* and to *abound,* as οὐκ Ἀτρείδῃ ἥνδανε *it was not pleasing to the son of Atreus,* καί οἱ πείθονται Ἀχαιοί *and the Achaeans trust in him,* ἀνδράσιν μάχεσθαι *to fight with men,* καρτίστοις ἐμάχοντο *they fought with the mightiest,* ἐριζέμεναι βασιλῆι *to strive with the king,* οὔ τοι μαχήσομαι *I will not fight with you.*

1008. The dative is used to denote the agent, after the past tenses, particularly the perfect and pluperfect of the passive.

1009. The dative with or without a preposition is used to denote the place where an action takes place. It is used of towns and countries, the great divisions of the world, the chief spheres of

action, of the parts of a thing, or of the human body, after some
verbs that imply locality or time, and after some verbs of motion
where we should expect the accusative with a preposition, as οὐχ
ἥνδανε θυμῷ *it was not pleasing in his soul,* τόξ᾽ ὤμοισιν ἔχων *having
his bow on his shoulders,* τοῖσι δ᾽ ἀνέστη Κάλχᾱς *and Calchas arose
among them,* μὴ κλέπτε νόῳ *do not play the thief in your heart,* ἄμφω
θῡμῷ φιλέουσα *loving both (of them) in her heart,* φρεσὶ θύει *he rages
in his mind,* ἥμενον κορυφῇ *seated upon the summit,* μάχῃ Τρώεσσιν
ἀρήγειν *to assist the Trojans in battle,* δεκάτῃ δ᾽ ἀγορήνδε καλέσσατο
λᾱὸν Ἀχιλλεύς *but on the tenth (day) Achilles summoned the people
to an assembly,* δωδεκάτῃ δ᾽ ἐλεύσεται Οὐλυμπόνδε *but on the twelfth
(day) he will come to Olympus,* πολλὰς δὲ ψῡχὰς Ἄιδι προΐαψεν *and
sent many souls to Hades,* σὺ δ᾽ ἐνὶ φρεσὶ βάλλεο σῇσιν *and do you
place it in your heart,* ἄγουσι δὲ δῶρα ἄνακτι *and they are taking pres-
ents to the lord,* κάππεσον ἐν Λήμνῳ *I fell into Lemnos.*

1010. The dative is used to denote in what particular point or
respect something is true, as ὁ γὰρ βίῃ οὗ πατρὸς ἀμείνων *for he is
better in strength than his own father.* Cf. 1014.

Accusative Case

1011. The direct object of a transitive verb is in the accusative
case, as νοῦσον ὦρσε *he roused a plague,* Χρύσην ἠτίμασεν *he dishon-
ored Chryses,* λῡσόμενος θύγατρα *to ransom his own daughter,* φέρων
ἄποινα *bearing ransoms,* στέμματ᾽ ἔχων *having fillets,* ἐλίσσετο Ἀχαιούς
he kept entreating the Achaeans.

1012. Any verb whose meaning permits may take an accusative
of cognate form, or equivalent meaning. This is called the *cog-
nate* accusative, and may follow intransitive as well as transitive
verbs, as εἶπας ἔπος *you have spoken a word,* ὁδὸν ἐλθέμεναι *to go (on)
a journey,* ἔπος τ᾽ ἔφατο *and she spoke a word.*

1013. The words ἔπος, μῦθος, and ἔργον with pronouns or adjec-
tives are at times practically equivalent to the neuter of the pro-
noun or adjective without these words, as εἴ σοι πᾶν ἔργον ὑπείξομαι
if I shall yield to you in every matter.

1014. An accusative restricting the force of the verb to a part,
character, quality, or attribute of the subject may follow many

verbs that are intransitive or reflexive in meaning. This is the *accusative of the part affected*, or *accusative of specification*, and may also accompany a noun, an adjective, or even a whole sentence, as πόδας ὠκὺς Ἀχιλλεύς *swift-footed Achilles* (literally *Achilles swift with respect to his feet*), χωόμενος κῆρ *enraged in heart*, οὔ ἑθέν ἐστι χερείων, οὐ δέμας οὐδὲ φυήν οὔτ᾽ ἄρ φρένας οὐδέ τι ἔργα *she is not inferior to her, neither in build nor beauty nor disposition, nor yet in accomplishments.*

1015. The accusative is used to denote extent of time or space, as πᾶν δ᾽ ἦμαρ φερόμην *and all day long I fell*, πρόπαν ἦμαρ δαίνυντο *the whole day through they feasted*, ἀκέων δὴν ἦστο *he sat silent a long time.*

1016. The accusative dependent upon an omitted verb follows the adverbs of swearing νή, and μά, as μὰ Ἀπόλλωνα *by Apollo!* ναὶ μὰ τόδε σκῆπτρον *yea, by this sceptre!* (977)

1017. The verbs εἶπον and αὐδάω, and more often their compounds, may take an accusative of the person addressed, as Κάλχαντα προσέειπεν *he addressed Calchas*, οὐδέ τί μιν προσεφώνεον *nor did they say anything to him.*

1018. The accusative may be used of the person about whom a thing is *told, known, thought,* or *provided:*
1) The person or thing is treated as the thing said or known, and not merely as spoken or known about, as οὐδ᾽ ἤν Ἀγαμέμνονα εἴπῃς *not even if you should say Agamemnon.*
2) The real object of the verb is a fact expressed by a limiting clause or word.

1019. Words denoting the goal are in the accusative after verbs of motion, as ὅν κεν ἵκωμαι *upon whom(soever) I may come*, κνίση δ᾽ οὐρανὸν ἵκεν *and the savor went to heaven*, ἔρχεσθον κλισίην Ἀχιλῆος *go to the barrack(s) of Achilles.*

1020. The following classes of verbs may be construed with two accusatives:
1) Verbs of *asking, teaching, reminding, demanding, clothing, unclothing, depriving,* and *taking away,* as ἔμ᾽ ἀφαιρεῖται Χρυσηίδα Φοῖβος Ἀπόλλων *Phoebus Apollo is depriving me of Chryseïs*, μήτε σὺ τόνδ᾽ ἀποαίρεο κούρην *nor do you deprive him of the maiden.*

2) Verbs of *naming, choosing, appointing, making, thinking, regarding,* and the like, as αὐτοὺς δὲ ἑλώρια τεῦχε κύνεσσιν οἰωνοῖσί τε δαῖτα *and made themselves a booty for the dogs and a banquet for the birds,* ὃν Βριάρεων καλέουσι θεοί, ἄνδρες δέ τε πάντες Αἰγαίωνα *whom the gods call Briareüs, but all men (call) Aegaeon.*

3) Verbs meaning *to do anything to* or *say anything of a person.*

1021. The accusative may denote an object which is affected by an action, and a second accusative of the particular part affected may be added (*accusative of the whole and part*), as τί δέ σε φρένας ἵκετο πένθος; *but what grief has come upon you in your heart?* περὶ γάρ ῥά ἑ χαλκὸς ἔλεψεν φύλλα τε καὶ φλοιόν *the bronze has stripped it of leaves and bark round about.* NOTE. — Some would classify the accusative of this last sentence under 1020 above.

Vocative Case

1022. The vocative, with or without ὦ, is used in addressing a person or thing, as θεά *goddess!* ὦ ᾿Αχιλεῦ *O Achilles!* ᾿Ατρεῖδαι *sons of Atreus!* NOTE. — The nominative is often used for the vocative, 978, 3.

ADJECTIVES

1023. The positive of an adjective may imply that the quality indicated is not in the proper proportion for the purpose under consideration, as μὴ δὴ πάντας ἐμοὺς ἐπιέλπεο μύθους εἰδήσειν · χαλεποί τοι ἔσονται *do not hope to know all my plans; they will be too hard for you* (to understand).

1024. The comparative and superlative endings of adjectives are often employed merely to denote an unusually high degree of the quality signified, without any idea of comparison being involved.

1025. An adjective agrees with its noun in gender, number, and case, but not always in form, since they may belong to different declensions, as νοῦσος κακή *an evil plague,* where νοῦσος, although feminine, is of the second declension and ends in -ος. This rule applies also to adjective pronouns and participles, as μυρί᾿ ἄλγεα *countless woes,* πολλὰς δ᾿ ἰφθίμους ψυχὰς ῎Αιδι προΐαψεν *and sent many valiant souls to Hades,* διαστήτην ἐρίσαντε *these two separated after* *they had quarreled,* δῖος Ἀχιλλεύς *godlike Achilles,* ἦλθε θοὰς ἐπὶ νῆας *he came to the swift ships,* θεοὶ Ὀλύμπια δώματ᾽ ἔχοντες *the gods who have Olympian homes.*

1026. When referring to *two*, the plural and the dual are freely interchanged (973, 3), as δύο γενεαί *two generations,* τὼ δ᾽ αὐτὼ μάρτυροι ἔστων *and these two themselves be witnesses.*

1027. An adjective or a participle, usually with the pronoun ὁ, ἡ, τό, may be used substantively as a noun, as τά τ᾽ ἐόντα τά τ᾽ ἐσσόμενα πρό τ᾽ ἐόντα *both what is, what will be, and what has been before,* τὰ κακά *these calamities, such calamities* (1034).

PRONOUNS

1028. The Pronoun ὁ, ἡ, τό. — There are three chief uses of the pronoun, ὁ, ἡ, τό:

1) As an independent demonstrative (and third personal) pronoun, meaning *this, that, he, she, it.* This is its original use, and the one most commonly met with in Homer, as ὁ νοῦσον ὦρσε *he roused a plague,* τὸν Χρύσην ἠτίμασεν ἀρητῆρα Ἀτρεΐδης *the son of Atreus dishonored that (well-known) Chryses, the priest,* τὴν δ᾽ ἐγὼ οὐ λύσω *but I will not free her,* ἔδεισεν δ᾽ ὁ γέρων *and that old man feared.*

2) As an article properly speaking ("the"), that is, modifying and making definite a noun, but not having any particular demonstrative force. This is its ordinary use in Greek after Homer.

3) As a relative pronoun, as τὸν τέκε Λητώ *whom Leto bore,* τώ οἱ ἔσαν κήρυκε *who were his two heralds,* τήν μοι δόσαν υἷες Ἀχαιῶν *whom the sons of the Achaeans gave unto me.*

Note. — Many expressions in Homer which are translated into English by the relative pronoun in a subordinate clause seem to have been coördinate originally. Thus the pronoun (ὁ, ἡ, τό) in these last three sentences may well have been thought of as demonstrative with asyndeton rather than as relative, 1113–1114.

1029. As an independent pronoun it has two main uses:

1) It is "resumptive," that is, it refers to something already mentioned, Χρύσην ἠτίμασεν, ὁ γὰρ ἦλθε θοὰς ἐπὶ νῆας *he dishonored Chryses, for he came to the swift ships.*

2) It makes a contrast, usually in combinations, such as ὁ μὲν
. . . ὁ δέ, and other words which help to give this effect.

1030. ὁ μὲν . . . ὁ δέ and οἱ μὲν . . . οἱ δέ are frequently used
to contrast both definite and indefinite persons and things.

1031. Its use with an adversative particle generally, but not
always, marks a change of subject, as ὁ δέ *but the other.*

1032. The use of ὁ, ἡ, τό as an article has evidently arisen from
its employment as an independent pronoun, followed by a noun
in apposition, as ἡ δ' ἀέκουσα ἅμα τοῖσι γυνὴ κίεν *but she went with
them against her will,* i.e. *the woman,* where γυνή is added as an
afterthought for the sake of greater definiteness.

1033. So also it may serve to introduce a new person, in this
case anticipating the noun, as αὐτὰρ ὁ μήνιε νηυσὶ παρήμενος διογενὴς
Πηλῆος υἱὸς πόδας ὠκὺς Ἀχιλλεύς *but he kept raging as he sat beside
the ships, did the Zeus-born son of Peleus, the swift-footed Achilles.*

1034. With the adjective or participle it is often used as a
substantive, as τὸ πλεῖον *the greater part,* τὰ κακά *these calamities,
such calamities* (1027).

1035. It is also used with the neuter accusative, singular or
plural, of the adjective as an adverb, as τὰ πρῶτα *at first* (780–781).

1036. On the other hand, the masculine or feminine with an
adverb may be used substantively.

1037. Nouns with a possessive pronoun take the article only
when they refer to a definite individual, as τὸ σὸν μένος *this anger
of yours.*

1038. It usually has a demonstrative force, and its absence
does not mark a noun as indefinite, as μῆνιν ἄειδε, θεά, Πηληιάδεω
Ἀχιλῆος *sing, goddess, the wrath of the son of Peleus, Achilles.*

1039. The Personal Pronouns. — The nominative of the personal
pronouns is used mainly for emphasis and contrast, as σὺ δὲ σύνθεο
but do you consider. If the subject is unemphatic, the pronoun
is usually omitted, as ὣς ἔφατο *thus he spoke* (761).

1040. The oblique cases of the third personal pronoun are
anaphoric, that is, they have an antecedent previously expressed

to which they refer, when unaccented; but when they are accented they have their original reflexive use, as ἀπὸ ἕο κάββαλεν υἱόν *she hurled her son from her*, καί οἱ πείθονται Ἀχαιοί *and the Achaeans trust in him*.

1041. Demonstrative Pronouns. — The demonstrative pronouns are thus distinguished:

1) (ἐ)κεῖνος, η, ο is used of something remote from the speaker.

2) ὁ, ἡ, τό differs from οὗτος, (ἐ)κεῖνος, ὅδε, etc., in that it usually marks a contrast in objects, but does not distinguish them as near and far, present and absent, etc.

3) The compounds of ὁ, ἡ, τό are used of something near the speaker, or of something associated with him.

4) οὗτος is used of something which has been mentioned already, or else of something of particular interest or concern to the second person.

5) ὁ, ἡ, τό in addition to being employed as a relative and as a personal pronoun is used to mark a contrast.

6) αὐτός in all its cases regularly means *self*, but at times may mean *same;* it is regularly intensive and is used especially to contrast a man or an object with other less important details, as clothing, weapons, and appurtenances of various kinds.

1042. Possessive Pronouns. — The possessive pronouns are as a rule equivalent to the possessive genitive of the personal pronoun, as παῖς ἐμός = παῖς ἐμοῦ *my child.*

1043. The Interrogative Pronouns. — The interrogative τίς, τί *who? which? what?* may be either substantive or adjective, and may be used in either direct or indirect questions.

1044. The Indefinite Pronoun. — The indefinite τὶς, τὶ *some (one), something, any (one), anything* may be either substantive or adjective, but is sometimes almost the equivalent of the English indefinite article, *a(n)*, as τινὰ μάντιν ἐρείομεν *let us ask a seer.*

1045. Relative Pronouns. — A relative agrees with its antecedent in gender and number, but its case depends upon the construction of the clause in which it stands, as μῆνιν ἄειδε, ἣ ἄλγε ἔθηκεν *sing the wrath which caused woes.*

1046. The antecedent of the relative may be omitted when it can easily be supplied from the context, especially when it is indefinite, as λώϊόν ἐστι δῶρ' ἀποαιρεῖσθαι, ὅστις σέθεν ἀντίον εἴπῃ *it is better to take away the gifts (of that man) whoever speaks against you.*

1047. The antecedent is sometimes attracted into the relative clause. It then agrees in case with the relati· e.

PREPOSITIONS

1048. Most prepositions were originally adverbs (chiefly local), and are often so employed in Homer (without case), as ἐν δέ *but therein,* ὑπό *below,* παρά *by his side.*

1049. They are used both with nouns and verbs, but are often separated from the words they modify, sometimes following them. This separation in the case of verbs has been incorrectly named *tmesis* (τμῆσις *cutting*), as κρατερὸν ἐπὶ μῦθον ἔτελλεν *and he enjoined a stern command (upon him),* where ἐπί is to be taken with ἔτελλεν as part of the verbal idea, καὶ ἐπὶ κνέφας ἦλθεν *and darkness came on,* where ἐπί must be joined with ἦλθεν.

1050. Dissyllabic prepositions regularly have the accent on the ultima, but in two cases they take the accent on the penult:

1) When they follow the word modified (with the exception of ἀμφίς, ἀνά, ἀντί, διά), as ᾧ ἔπι πολλὰ μόγησα *for which I underwent great toil,* θῖν' ἐφ' ἁλός *upon the shore of the sea.*

2) When a preposition stands for itself compounded with a verb, as ἔνι, ἔπι, μέτα, πάρα, πέρι (all compounded with εἰμί), and ἄνα for the imperative of ἀνίστημι *stand up! up!*

1051. Prepositions are used with the genitive, dative, and accusative cases; some are used with all three cases, some with only two, and some with only one.

1052. They are used to emphasize or to define more clearly certain case relations. Of course the prepositions do not " govern " these cases, but the cases take the prepositions.

1053. The genitive with prepositions primarily denotes that *from* which something proceeds, the dative that *in* or *by* which something is or is done, the accusative that *toward, over, along*, or *upon* which motion occurs.

1054. The primary relations expressed by prepositions are those of *place* and *time*, but they may express *cause, origin, agency, condition, purpose*, and various other relations.

1055. Prepositions are used in forming compound verbs, many of which, particularly those compounded with ἐν, ἐπί, and σύν, are construed with the dative.

1056. With the genitive alone are used the following:

ἀντί instead of
ἀπό off, from, away from

ἐκ (ἐξ) out of, from
πρό before

1057. And the following, known as *improper* prepositions:

ἄγχι near, close
ἄνευ without
ἄντα, ἀντίον opposite, facing
ἀντικρύ straight to
ἄψ behind
ἕνεκα (εἵνεκα) on account of
ἕκητι by will of
ἐκτός without
ἐντός within

μεσσηγύς between
μέσφα until
νόσφι(ν) apart from
ὄπισθε(ν) (from) behind
πάλιν back from
πάροιθε(ν) before, in front of
πρόσθε(ν) before
τῆλε far (from)
τηλόθι far (from)

together with several others not so common.

1058. With the dative alone are used: ἐν(ί), εἰν *in*, and σύν (ξύν) *with*.

1059. With the accusative alone are used εἰς (ἐς) *into, to*, -δε *to*.

1060. With the genitive and accusative are used: διά *through on account of*, ὑπέρ *over, on behalf of*, and κατά *down (through)*.

1061. The following are used with the genitive, dative, and accusative:

ἀμφί around, about, on both sides.
ἀνά (up)on, up through, along.
ἐπί (up)on, to, toward, against.
μετά with, after.

παρά beside, to the side of, from beside.
περί around, concerning.
πρός toward, with reference to.
ὑπό under, by means of.

297

SYNTAX OF THE VERB

1062. A transitive verb is one whose action *passes over* to an object in the accusative, as μῆνιν ἄειδε *sing the wrath,* ἐλίσσετο Ἀχαιούς *he kept entreating the Achaeans.*

1063. An intransitive verb is one whose action does not pass over to an object, as ἦλθε *he came.*

1064. In verbs with both first and second tenses (first aorist, second aorist, first perfect, second perfect, etc.), the first tense is usually transitive (often causative, 1069), the second intransitive.

1065. The active voice denotes the subject as acting, as νοῦσον ἀνὰ στρατὸν ὦρσε *he kindled a plague up through the camp.*

1066. The passive voice denotes the subject as being acted upon, as Διὸς δ' ἐτελείετο βουλή *but the will of Zeus was being accomplished.*

1067. The middle voice denotes the subject as acting reflexively:

1) *upon itself,* as πείθομαι *I persuade myself (obey),* φαίνομαι *I show myself (appear).*

2) *for itself,* as καλέομαι *I call for myself, summon.*

3) *upon something belonging to itself, or in which it has a special interest,* as λύομαι *I loose my own, ransom.*

1068. It is often difficult to distinguish in translation between the active and middle, but the action of the middle always has some reference, either direct or indirect, to the subject, and the subject has an interest in, or is affected by the action.

1069. Some verbs are used at times in a *causative* sense, that is, the subject causes something to be done by another, as ἂν δ' αὐτὴν Χρυσηίδα βήσομεν *let us cause Chryseïs to go on board* (864).

1070. Sometimes the present tense indicates that an action is only attempted; this is called the *conative* present, as ἀρνύμενος *striving to win.*

1071. When an active verb which takes two accusatives (1020) becomes passive, the accusative of the *thing* is retained, while the accusative of the *person* becomes the subject, as ἀναιδείην ἐπιειμένε *O thou clothed in shamelessness!*

1072. The tenses denote *time* of action and *kind* of action.

1073. The time of action is indicated by the tenses only in the indicative.

1074. The present is denoted by the present tense, and by the perfect.

1075. The past is denoted by the imperfect, aorist, and pluperfect. The future is denoted by the future and the future perfect.

1076. Continued or repeated action is denoted by the present, the imperfect, and (occasionally) the future.

1077. Completed action denoting a permanent state is indicated by the perfect, pluperfect, and future perfect.

1078. Action that simply takes place is indicated by the aorist and (sometimes) the future.

1079. The imperfect denotes the continuance of action in past time, customary or repeated action, as ἔλυον, *I loosed, was loosing, kept loosing, was accustomed to loose.*

1080. The aorist indicative denotes the simple occurrence of an action in past time, as ἔλῦσα *I loosed, did loose.*

1081. *Inceptive aorist :* The aorist of verbs denoting a state or a condition, or continued action, usually denotes the entrance into the state, or the beginning of the action, as ἐδάκρῦσε *he fell to weeping.*

1082. The aorist is often used to express a general truth. It is then called a *gnomic* aorist, and is considered a primary tense, as ὅς κε θεοῖς ἐπιπείθηται, μάλα τ᾽ ἔκλυον αὐτοῦ *whoever obeys the gods, him they especially hear.*

1083. The future ordinarily denotes that an action will take place later ; but may express desire or a command.

1084. The perfect regularly denotes a state or a condition (usually as the result of completed action), and should be translated by the present, as προβέβουλα *I prefer,* ἀμφιβέβηκας *(who) dost protect.*

Moods

1085. The adverbs ἄν and κέ(ν) are often used to qualify the meaning of the moods ; they are used in two ways :

1) In independent clauses they are used with the subjunctive, the optative, and with the past and future tenses of the indicative; and also with the participle and infinitive, when they represent the independent indicative and optative.

2) In dependent clauses, usually with the subjunctive.

1086. These adverbs usually give a touch of indefiniteness to the clause in which they stand. They have no exact equivalent in English. When they appear in the conclusion of conditional sentences, they are usually translated by *could*, or *would*, in English.

1087. The subjunctive with these adverbs is used almost the same as the future indicative, or the potential optative (1105).

1088. They are used in simple sentences and in the apodosis (conclusion) of complex sentences to express limitation by circumstances or conditions.

1089. They are regularly found in final clauses referring to the future.

1090. They are usually found in conditional clauses in the optative and in the subjunctive, when the governing verb is future, or in a mood which implies futurity.

1091. They are not ordinarily used in conditional, relative, and temporal clauses with the subjunctive in comparisons and similes, or when they refer to events which occur repeatedly or at an indefinite time, or when they refer to sayings which have a general application.

The Moods in Simple Sentences

THE INDEPENDENT INDICATIVE WITHOUT ἄν OR κέ(ν)

1092. Without ἄν or κέ(ν) the indicative mood simply states a fact, either positively or negatively, asks a question, or makes an exclamation.

1093. An unattainable wish which refers to the present or to the past is expressed by a past tense of the indicative with αἴθε (εἴθε), or εἰ γάρ ; the negative is μή.

1094. To express an unattainable wish, ὤφελον *ought* is used with the present infinitive to denote present time and continued past action, or with the aorist infinitive to denote past time.

THE INDEPENDENT INDICATIVE WITH ἄν OR κέ(ν)

1095. The aorist (and sometimes the imperfect) indicative is used with ἄν or κέ(ν) to denote past possibility, probability, necessity, or a cautious statement.

1096. The past tenses of the indicative may be used with ἄν or κέ(ν) to denote unreality.

1097. ἄν or κέ(ν) may be used with the future indicative with a conditional or limiting meaning.

THE INDEPENDENT SUBJUNCTIVE WITHOUT ἄν OR κέ(ν)

1098. The subjunctive without ἄν or κέ(ν) is used in the first person, present and aorist, to express a desire or a request (hortatory subjunctive), as τινὰ μάντιν ἐρείομεν *let us ask some seer.*

1099. The aorist subjunctive is used in the second and third persons (and sometimes in the first) with μή in prohibitions, as μή σε κιχήω *let me not come upon you.*

1100. The present and aorist subjunctive are used in the first person (rarely in the third) in deliberative questions as to what may be done advantageously or with propriety.

1101. The subjunctive is frequently used as nearly the equivalent of the future indicative, and refers to some future event. It is usually qualified by ἄν or κέ(ν), and the negative is οὐ.

THE INDEPENDENT OPTATIVE WITHOUT ἄν OR κέ(ν)

1102. The independent optative without ἄν or κέ(ν) is used to express a wish that something may happen, as ὑμῖν θεοὶ δοῖεν *may the gods grant to you.*

1103 The potential optative (1105), which regularly takes ἄν or κέ(ν), is occasionally found without either.

1104. The optative is employed at times to express a command, a request, or an exhortation, being practically equivalent to the imperative.

1105. With ἄν or κέ(ν) the optative is used to express a future action as dependent upon circumstances or conditions. This is called the *potential* optative, and is usually to be translated by *might, could, would,* etc.

The Imperative

1106. The imperative expresses a command, or a request; the negative is μή.

The Infinitive

1107. 1) The only tenses which occur in the infinitive are the present, future, aorist, perfect, and future perfect. The middle and passive differ in form in the aorist only.

2) In the subjunctive, optative, imperative, and infinitive, the tenses do not of themselves indicate time.

3) The present in these moods denotes an action simply as continued.

4) The aorist denotes an action simply as brought to pass.

5) The perfect denotes an action simply as completed.

6) The subject of an infinitive is usually in the accusative, but may be omitted when it is the subject of the leading verb, or its direct or indirect object.

7) The infinitive may be the subject of a verb, especially an impersonal one, or ἐστί(ν).

8) It may be the object of a verb, especially verbs indicating *wish, command, advice, consent, attempt,* and the like.

9) The infinitive may depend upon adjectives or substantives, especially those denoting *ability, fitness, willingness,* or have a similar meaning to verbs which take the infinitive (1107, 7).

10) The infinitive also may express purpose; the negative is μή.

11) The infinitive is used also to express a command with the nominative of the second person, or with the accusative of the third person for the subject if expressed; the subject may be omitted. In this usage it is the equivalent of the imperative.

The Participle

1108. The participle has only the present, future, aorist, perfect, and future perfect tenses. It is used attributively as an adjective to modify a noun, or the noun may be omitted and the participle (usually with the pronoun, ὁ, ἡ, τό) may be used as a substantive. Such participles usually indicate time present, past, or future relatively to the time of the main verb.

NOTE 1. — The aorist participle may denote time contemporaneous with the action of the main verb, as μειδήσᾱσα ἐδέξατο κύπελλον *she took the cup with a smile.*

NOTE 2. — On the other hand, the present participle may express time previous to the action of the main verb, as Χρῡσηΐδα εἶσεν ἄγων *leading Chryseïs on board he seated her.*

1109. The participle may express :

1) Time, as τοῖσι δ᾽ ἀνιστάμενος μετέφη Ἀχιλλεύς *when he had risen among them Achilles addressed them.*

2) Cause, as ἄμφω φιλέουσα *because she loved them both.*

3) Manner or means.

4) Condition.

5) Purpose or desire (usually the future participle), as λῡσόμενος θύγατρα *(desiring) to ransom his own daughter;* μαχησόμενος *(desiring) to fight, for the purpose of fighting.*

6) Concession, as ἀλόχῳ περ ἐούσῃ *even though you are my wife.*

7) Attendant circumstance.

1110. The Greek often employs a participle where we should use a relative clause, as θεοὶ Ὀλύμπια δώματ᾽ ἔχοντες *the gods who have Olympian homes.*

1111. A noun and a participle, not closely connected grammatically with the rest of the sentence, may stand by themselves in the genitive in the construction known as the *genitive absolute.* See 994.

1112. This construction arose from the use of the genitive modified by a participle, where the genitive was dependent upon some word in the main construction of the sentence, and many cases are on the border line between the absolute and the dependent constructions.

COMPOUND SENTENCES

1113. Asyndeton, or the omission of conjunctions between independent elements of a sentence, is often used to mark lively and rapid descriptions.

1114. Parataxis, or coördination, was often employed where one would expect a subordinate construction. 1028, note.

SUBORDINATE CONSTRUCTIONS

Purpose Clauses

1115. Clauses which denote purpose or final clauses are introduced by the final particles ὡς, ὅπ(π)ως, ἵνα, ὄφρα, ἕως; the negative is μή.

1116. Purpose clauses take the subjunctive after primary (816) tenses, the optative (occasionally the subjunctive) after secondary tenses.

1117. The subjunctive sometimes takes ἄν or κέ(ν), especially with ὡς, ὅπ(π)ως, and ὄφρα.

Object Clauses

1118. The two main types of object clauses are:

1) Object clauses with verbs of effort.

2) Object clauses with verbs of fear.

1119. ὅπ(π)ως (sometimes ὡς and ἵνα) is used to introduce object clauses with verbs of effort. These clauses take the future indicative after both primary and secondary tenses (816). The negative is μή.

1120. With verbs of effort object clauses may take the construction of purpose clauses, with ὅπ(π)ως and the subjunctive or optative.

1121. With verbs of caution negative object clauses take the construction of clauses with verbs of effort or with verbs of fear.

1122. With verbs of effort, object clauses may take the subjunctive with ἄν after ὅπ(π)ως, and sometimes after ὡς.

1123. With verbs meaning *to consider, plan, try,* the subjunctive with or without κέ(ν), or the optative is used. These object clauses do not take the future indicative.

1124. The subjunctive, optative, or the future indicative, with ὅπ(π)ως (ὅπ(π)ως μή in the negative) may follow verbs of will or desire, instead of the infinitive which is the usual construction after these verbs.

Object Clauses after Verbs of Fear

1125. With verbs of fear, which refer to the future, object clauses have the subjunctive after primary tenses, and the optative (sometimes the subjunctive) after secondary tenses (816).

1126. With μή or ὅπ(π)ως μή, the subjunctive or optative may be used to indicate a possible object of fear. The aorist subjunctive may refer to past time, as δέδοικα μή σε παρείπῃ *I fear lest she has beguiled you*.

1127. The indicative with μή (μὴ οὐ in the negative) is used to express fear which refers to the present or past time. The aorist is employed in this construction.

Causal Clauses

1128. Causal clauses are introduced by ὅτι, ἐπεί, ἐπειδή, ὅτε, ὅ, ὅ τε, ὁπ(π)ότε, οὕνεκα, ὡς, and εὖτε.

1129. Causal clauses which denote a fact regularly have the indicative after both primary and secondary tenses.

1130. Causal clauses which denote an alleged or a supposed reason have the optative after secondary tenses.

Result Clauses (Consecutive Clauses)

1131. Clauses of result are introduced by various words, some of the most common being ὥστε, ὡς, οἷος, ὅσ(σ)ος.

1132. These clauses may employ either the infinitive or the finite verb:

1) The infinitive is used to indicate an anticipated, natural, or possible result; the negative is μή.

2) When the finite verb is used, any form of the simple sentence may be employed. The indicative (especially in the aorist) is the form most commonly used, denoting the actual result of the action of the principal verb; the negative is οὐ.

Conditional Clauses

1133. A conditional sentence regularly consists of two principal elements:

1) The condition, denoting a supposed or assumed (*if*) case, called the *protasis*.

305

2) The conclusion, denoting what follows if the condition is realized, called the *apodosis*.

1134. εἰ and αἰ are used to introduce conditional clauses, in the indicative and optative.

1135. εἰ ἄν, εἰ (αἰ) κε(ν), ἤν are used to introduce conditional clauses in the subjunctive.

1136. In the conclusion ἄν or κέ(ν) is employed with the optative to indicate possibility, and with the past tenses of the indicative to indicate the unfulfillment of the condition, or repetition.

1137. The negative of the condition is μή; of the conclusion it is οὐ when the conclusion is considered a fact if the condition be true.

1138. Present unreal conditional sentences have εἰ with the optative in the condition, and ἄν with the optative in the conclusion.

1139. Past unreal conditional sentences have the aorist or imperfect indicative in the condition, and in the conclusion either the aorist or imperfect indicative with ἄν or κέ(ν), or the present or aorist optative with ἄν or κέ(ν). The imperfect of unreal conditions represents past time.

1140. More vivid future conditions have:

1) εἰ ἄν, ἤν with the subjunctive in the condition, and in the conclusion either the future indicative or some other form referring to future time.

2) The subjunctive with κέ(ν) in both condition and conclusion.

3) (Rarely) εἰ (αἰ), κε(ν) with the future in the condition.

1141. Less vivid future conditions have εἰ κε(ν), εἰ ἄν, with the optative in the condition, and in the conclusion may have the present indicative, the simple future indicative, the future indicative with κέ(ν), the hortatory subjunctive, the subjunctive with ἄν or κέ(ν), or the optative, with the same force as the optative with ἄν or κέ(ν).

1142. Present general conditions have ἄν (ἤν) with the subjunctive in the condition, and the present indicative or its equivalent in the conclusion.

306

1143. Past general conditions have εἰ with the optative in the condition, and the imperfect indicative or its equivalent in the conclusion.

1144. Ordinary relative clauses, which define more closely a definite antecedent, have the constructions of other simple sentences, except κέ(ν) or ἄν may be used with the future.

1145. Relative clauses of purpose have the subjunctive (usually with κέ(ν)) after primary tenses, and the optative after secondary tenses, although the future indicative may be used.

1146. More vivid future conditional relative clauses have the subjunctive, usually with ἄν or κέ(ν), and sometimes the future with ἄν or κέ(ν).

1147. Less vivid future conditional relative clauses have the optative with ἄν or κέ(ν) in the main clause, and sometimes have ἄν or κέ(ν) with the optative in the relative clause.

1148. Present generalizing relative clauses usually have ἄν or κέ(ν) with the subjunctive in the relative clause, or the present indicative or an equivalent in the main clause.

1149. Past generalizing relative clauses have the optative in the relative clause, and the imperfect indicative or its equivalent in the main clause.

Temporal Clauses

1150. Temporal clauses are introduced by the temporal conjunctions ὅτε, ὁπ(π)ότε, ἕως, εὖτε, ἦμος, ὅπ(π)ως, ὄφρα; ἐπεί, ἐπειδή, ἐξ (ἀφ᾽) οὗ; εἰς ὅτε (κέ(ν)), εἰς ὅ (κέ(ν)).

1151. Temporal clauses which refer to the future or to indefinite present time have the subjunctive with ἄν or κέ(ν).

1152. Temporal clauses which refer to future time have ἄν or κέ(ν) with the optative in the temporal clause, and may have the future indicative, or the subjunctive with ἄν or κέ(ν) in the main clause.

Indirect Questions

1153. Indirect questions keep the mood and tense of direct questions, after primary tenses (the indicative, the past indicative with ἄν, the deliberative subjunctive, or the potential optative with

307

ἄν or κέ(ν)). After secondary tenses they may keep the mood and tense of direct questions, but generally change to the optative.

Indirect Discourse

1154. The kind of the leading verb or expression in a sentence involving indirect discourse determines the construction :

1) Verbs of saying have either the infinitive or a ὅτι (ὡς) clause.

2) Verbs of thinking and believing usually take the infinitive.

3) Verbs of knowing, learning, perceiving, hearing, showing, and the like, usually have the participle, but may have a ὅτι (ὡς) clause.

1155. Clauses in indirect discourse introduced by ὅτι or ὡς, after primary tenses keep the mood and tense of the direct form unchanged.

1156. Indicatives and subjunctives without ἄν or κέ(ν) usually become optative after secondary tenses, but may remain unchanged.

1157. Subordinate verbs after primary tenses keep their original mood and tense.

1158. The optative is not employed in indirect discourse except in indirect questions (1153). After both primary and secondary tenses in principal clauses, the same past tense is used that would have been employed in an independent clause, from the speaker's point of view. After the secondary tenses the future is generally represented by ἔμελλον with the infinitive.

IV. PROSODY

Rules of Quantity, the Hexameter

1159. Every vowel which has the circumflex accent is long (537).

1160. The vowel of the ultima in every word having the circumflex on the penult is short (545).

1161. If a long penult has the acute accent, then the ultima must be long also.

1162. If the ultima is short and the penult has the acute accent, then the penult must be short also.

1163. If the antepenult has the accent, the vowel of the ultima must be short (544).

1164. Exceptions to these rules are to be found only in the cases of the diphthongs αι and οι, when final, which are then considered short (except in the optative and οἴκοι) for the purpose of accent but must be counted long when marking the feet of the verse (547).

1165. Apparent exceptions to these rules are to be found in the case of certain classes of compounds, as οὔτε, μήτε, οὔτις, μήτις, ἥδε, οἶδε, αἶδε, τούσδε, τάσδε, etc., where the primary form is accented without considering the following enclitic as an integral part of the word.

1166. Most exceptions to the rules of quantity are only apparent.

1167. If an apparently short final syllable stands where a long one is expected, it is probable that:

1) The pause of the caesura (1185) or diaeresis (1188) fills out the time required for the foot, allowing the same freedom as at the end of a verse, or

2) The following word has lost an initial ϝ, making the preceding syllable long by position. For various forms of *metrical lengthening*, see 525, 566, 571, 1168.

1168. Metrical Lengthening. — Syllables containing a short vowel, followed by a single consonant, or by another vowel, are lengthened under the verse ictus (1183). Compare 525, 566, 571, 1167.

Special Rules for Determining the Length of Syllables by their Position in Hexameter

1169. If a long syllable is followed by a short, then the next syllable must be short also.

1170. If a short syllable is followed by a long, then the preceding syllable must be short also.

1171. The first syllable of each foot must be long, and is to be given slightly more stress than the other half of the foot (1183).

1172. When a word ends in a short vowel (and sometimes the diphthongs αι and οι), and the next word begins with a vowel, the final vowel of the first word is regularly elided (575).

1173. When a word ends in a long vowel or a diphthong and the next word begins with a vowel, the long final vowel or diphthong is regularly shortened.

NOTE. — Sometimes a long vowel or diphthong is shortened when followed by a vowel within the same word.

1174. If a word ends in a short vowel and the next word originally began with vau (ϝ), elision ordinarily does not take place (580), but may, as ἐὺ δ᾽ οἴκαδε = ἐὺ δ᾽ ϝοίκαδε.

1175. If a word ends in a long vowel or a diphthong and the next word originally began with a vau (ϝ), the long final vowel or diphthong ordinarily remains long.

1176. If a word ends in a long vowel or a diphthong and has the verse-accent on it, the long vowel or diphthong may remain long, even though the next word begins with a vowel. Cf. 1168.

1177. When a word ending in a vowel is followed by a word beginning with a vowel, the result is *hiatus*. Hiatus is ordinarily avoided in poetry either 1) by elision; 2) by the use of movable consonants, 561-563; 3) by the shortening of a final long vowel or diphthong, 1173; 4) by crasis or synizesis, 586-587.

1178. Hiatus may be allowed 1) when there is a distinct pause in sense (diaeresis or caesura 1185–1189) between the vowels which produce it; 2) when the verse-accent (ictus) falls on the long vowel or diphthong which is followed by another vowel; 3) when elision has already taken place; 4) after *ι* or *υ*; 5) when a long vowel or diphthong is shortened (weak or improper hiatus).

1179. The metre of the Homeric poems is the *dactylic* (sometimes called the *heroic*) hexameter, the most common of all Greek verse.

1180. There are six feet to the verse, the first five being either *dactyls* (that is, one long followed by two shorts — ∪ ∪), or its equivalent, the *spondee* (that is, two longs — —). The sixth foot is always a spondee.

1181. In dactylic hexameter the ictus (verse accent) is always on the first syllable of each foot (1183).

1182. The fifth foot is usually a dactyl, only about one verse in twenty having a spondee in this place, which gives the verse a movement slower than usual. It is then called a *spondaic* verse.

1183. In each foot one part is distinguished from the other by a slight stress of voice, called the *ictus* (1171, 1181).

1184. The final syllable of a verse may be either long or short, but as there is a slight pause here, the final syllable in hexameter is always considered long, making the last foot of the verse always a spondee, 1180.

1185. Whenever a word ends within a foot, it is called *caesura*. If this coincides with a pause in the verse, it is called the caesura of the verse. The caesura is employed with great skill in the Homeric poems to make the verse more melodious and to aid in its recital.

1186. There is almost always a caesura in the third foot. It occurs either after the first syllable of the foot, or else between the two short syllables.

1187. The pause after the first syllable is called the *masculine* caesura, that after the second the *feminine*.

1188. Whenever the end of a word coincides with the end of a foot, it is called *diaeresis*. When this falls with a pause, it is called the diaeresis of the verse.

311

1189. The most important diaeresis is the one which comes at the end of the fourth foot. From its common employment in pastoral poetry it is called the *bucolic* diaeresis.

1190. For metrical purposes all vowels and syllables of Greek words may be divided into long and short.

1191. The rhythm of Greek verse is based upon the regular succession of long and short syllables.

1192. To obtain facility in reading the verse, a considerable quantity of it should be memorized, special attention being paid to the quantity (that is, twice as much time should be given to each long syllable as to a short), and the pauses should be carefully observed. Although English verse is primarily accentual rather than quantitative, still the memorizing of a few lines of English dactylic hexameter (Longfellow's "Evangeline,"[1] for example, mediocre though it be) will materially aid in getting the swing and the movement of the Greek hexameter.

---

[1] This is the forest primaeval, the murmuring pines and the hemlocks,
Bearded with moss, and in garments green, indistinct in the twilight,
Stand like Druids of eld, with voices sad and prophetic,
Stand like harpers hoar, with beards that rest on their bosoms.

GREEK–ENGLISH VOCABULARY

NOTE. — Words preceded by an asterisk (*) are assumed forms; those followed by an asterisk are Attic, analogous to known Homeric forms, but not found in Homer; those followed by a double asterisk (**) are Attic not analogous to Homeric forms; those followed by a dagger (†) are not Epic, or Attic, but are Ionic, or Lyric; those followed by a hyphen (-) are stems (626–630).

A

ἀ-, ἀ-, "*alpha copulative,*" *an inseparable prefix, denoting likeness, union, association with, intensification.*

ἀ(ν), "*alpha privative*"; *see* ἀν-.

ἄ (ὅs, ἥ, ὅ).

ἄαπτος, ον untouchable, invincible.

ἄγαγε (ἄγω) = ἤγαγε (837).

ἀγαθός, ή, όν good, noble, brave, useful, advantageous.

Ἀγαμέμνων, ονος, ὁ Agamemnon, *king of Mycenae, brother of Helen's husband, Menelaus, and commander in chief of the allied Greek military expedition against Troy.*

ἀγάν-νιφος, η, ον snow-clad, very snowy.

ἄγγελος, ον, ὁ messenger, courier.

ἄγε, ἄγετε (ἄγω), *pres. act. imperat., used as interject.,* up! come! go! go to!

ἀγείρομεν (ἀγείρω), *vs. 142* = ἀγείρω-μεν (800), *aor. subjunct.*

ἀγείρω (ἀγερ-), ἤγειρα, ἀγήγερμαι, ἠγέρθην collect, assemble, gather.

ἀγέμεν(αι) (ἄγω) = ἄγειν, *pres. act. inf.*

ἀ-γέραστος, η, ον without a prize of honor, γέρας.

ἀγλαός, ή, όν bright, shining, splendid, glorious.

ἀ-γνο(ι)έ-ω, ἠγνοίησα fail to notice (observe), be ignorant of (1168).

ἄγοντες (ἄγω), *pres. act. particip.*

ἀγορά-ομαι, ἠγορησάμην harangue, address an assembly.

ἀγόρευε (ἀγορεύω), *vs. 385* = ἠγόρευε (837), *imperf.*

ἀγορ-εύ-ω, ἀγορεύσω, ἠγόρευσα speak, say, tell, harangue, address an assembly.

ἀγορή, ῆς, ἡ assemblage, assembly, meeting (place), gathering, harangue.

ἀγορήνδε (ἀγορήν, -δε, 788, 4) to the assembly.

ἀγορήσατο (ἀγοράομαι) = ἠγορήσατο (837).

ἀγορητής, ᾶο, ὁ orator, addresser of an assembly.

ἄγχι near, close (by), at hand.

ἄγ-ω, ἄξω, ἤγαγον, ἦχα**, ἦγμαι*, ἤχθην* lead, drive, conduct, bring.

ἀ-δάκρῡτος, η, ον tearless.

ἀεί see αἰεί.

ἄειδε (ἀείδω), *imperat.*

ἄειδον (ἀείδω) = ἤειδον (837), *imperf.*

ἀείδ-ω, ἀείσω, ἤεισα sing (of), hymn, chant.

313

ἀ-εικής, ές unseemly, grievous, shameful, unfitting.

ἀ-έκων, ουσα, ον unwilling.

ἄζομαι (ἁγ-) reverence.

ἀζόμενοι (ἄζομαι), particip.

ἀ-θάνατος, η, ον deathless, immortal, imperishable (1168).

ἀθέριζον (ἀ-θερίζω) = ἠθέριζον (837), imperf.

ἀ-θερίζω (θεριδ-) slight, disregard, despise.

Ἀθηναίη, ης, ἡ = Ἀθήνη.

Ἀθήνη, ης, ἡ Athena, goddess of war, wisdom, and the arts.

αἱ (ὁ, ἡ, τό).

αἵ (ὅς, ἥ, ὅ).

αἱ = εἰ if, whether.

Αἴᾱς, αντος, ὁ Ajax, after Achilles, the mightiest of the Greek warriors.

Αἰγαίων, ωνος, ὁ Aegaeon, a sea-divinity.

Αἰγείδης, ᾱο, ὁ son of Aegeus, Theseus.

αἰγί-οχος, η, ον aegis-bearing, aegis-holding.

αἰγλήεις, εσσα, εν bright, shining, gleaming.

αἰγῶν (αἴξ, αἰγός, ὁ, ἡ).

αἰδέομαι (αιδεσ-), αἰδέσ(σ)ομαι, ᾐδεσ(σ)άμην, ᾔδεσμαι*, ᾐδέσθην reverence.

Ἄιδι (*Ἄις, Ἄιδος, ὁ).

αἴδο-μαι = αἰδέομαι reverence.

αἰδομένω (αἴδομαι), dual particip.

αἰεί (αἰέν, ἀεί) (= αἰϝεί) always, EVER, continually, eternally.

αἰέν = αἰεί.

αἴθε, used to introduce a wish.

Αἰθιοπεύς, ῆος, ὁ Ethiopian.

αἰθ-οψ, οπος bright, shining, gleaming.

αἷμα, αἵματος, τό blood, gore.

αἰνός, ή, όν dread(ful), terrible, awful, painful, sorrowful.

αἰνότατος, η, ον (αἰνός, ή, όν), superl.

αἰνῶς terribly, dreadfully, awfully.

αἴξ, αἰγός, ὁ, ἡ goat.

αἱρέω (αιρε-, ἑλ-), αἱρήσω, ἕλον (εἷλον, 584–585), ᾕρηκα*, ᾕρημαι*, ᾑρέθην* take, seize, deprive ; mid., choose, take for oneself.

*Ἄις, Ἄιδος, ὁ Hades, god of the lower world.

αἶσα, ης, ἡ fate, lot, portion.

αἴτιος, η, ον blamable, to blame, guilty, accountable, responsible.

αἰχμητής, ᾱο, ὁ spearman, warrior.

αἶψα immediately, straightway, quickly.

ἀκέων, ουσα, ον silent, in silence, being silent, quiet.

ἀκουέμεν(αι) (ἀκούω), infin.

ἄκουσα (ἀκούω) = ἤκουσα (837).

ἀκού-ω, ἀκούσομαι, ἤκουσα, ἀκήκοα*, ἤκουσμαι*, ἠκούσθην* hear(ken).

ἄκρος, η, ον sharp, high, utter.

ἀκρότατος, η, ον (ἄκρος, η, ον), superl.

ἄλα (ἅλς, ἁλός, ὁ, ἡ), acc.

ἄλαδε = ἅλα-δε (788, 4) to the sea.

ἄλγος, εος, τό grief, pain, woe, trouble.

ἀλεγίζω (ἀλεγιδ-) care, reck, consider, regard, worry.

ἀλεξέμεν(αι) (ἀλέξω), infin.

ἀλέξω (ἀλεξ-, ἀλεξε-, ἀλεκ-, ἀλκ-), ἀλεξήσω, ἠλέξησα (ἄλαλκον) ward off, defend, protect.

ἅλιος, η, ον of the sea, briny, salty, marine.

ἀλλά but, moreover.

ἄλλη elsewhere.

ἄλλομαι (σαλ-, = ἁλ-, 603–604), ἁλό-μαι*, ἡλάμην (ἅλμην) jump, leap, bound.

ἄλλος, η, ο other, another.

ἄλλο-τε at another time.

ἁλός (ἅλς, ἁλός, ὁ, ἡ).

ἄ-λοχος (cf. λέχος), ου, ἡ wife, spouse.

ἅλς, ἁλός, ὁ, ἡ sea, brine.

ἆλτο (ἅλλομαι), 2d aor. (798).

ἅμα at the same time, together with.

ἀ-μβρόσιος, η, ον ambrosial, deathless, immortal, divine, heavenly.

ἀμειβόμεναι (ἀμείβω), fem. plur. particip.

ἀμείβ-ω, ἀμείψω, ἤμειψα, ἠμείφθην* (ex)change; mid., reply, answer.

ἀμείνων, ον (ἀγαθός, ή, όν), comparat., better, braver, superior, preferable.

ἄμμε (ἐγώ), acc. plur.

ἄμμι(ν) (ἐγώ), dat. plur.

ἀ-μύμων, ον blameless, noble.

ἀμῦναι (ἀμύνω), aor. act. infin.

ἄμῦνον (ἀμύνω), aor. act. imperat.

ἀμύνω (ἀμυν-), ἀμυνέω*, ἤμῡνα ward off, defend, protect, avert.

ἀμύξεις (ἀμύσσω).

ἀμύσσω (ἀμυχ-), ἀμύξω, ἤμυξα* (ἠμυξάμην) gnaw, tear, bite, scratch.

ἀμφ-ηρεφής, ές covered at both ends.

ἀμφί, adv., and prep. with gen., dat., and acc., about, around; with gen., around, about, on both sides; with gen., around, about, concerning, for (the sake of); with dat., around, about, because of, concerning, at, by; with acc., around, about.

ἀμφι-βαίνω (βαν-, βα-), ἀμφιβήσω (ἀμφιβήσομαι), ἀμφέβησα (ἀμφέβην), ἀμφιβέβηκα, ἀμφιβέβαμαι*, ἀμφεβάθην* surround, go (a)round, protect.

ἀμφιβέβηκας (ἀμφιβαίνω), perf.

ἀμφι-γυήεις, εσσα, εν wobbly-kneed, bow-legged, bandy-legged; possibly skillful, ambidexterous.

ἀμφι-κύπελλον, ου, τό double cup,

goblet; it may be turned upside down, the bottom forming another receptacle.

ἀμφι-μέλᾱς, αινα, αν black all round, very black.

ἄμφω, οιιν, dual, both.

ἄν = κέ(ν) (1085–1091).

ἄν, vs. 143, = ἀνά.

ἀν- (ἀ- before consonants), "alpha privative," an inseparable adverb and preposition, not, un-, dis-, -less, without.

ἀνά (ἄν), adv., and prep. with gen., dat., and acc., (up)on, along, up through, thereon, high on; adv., (up)on, thereon; with dat., (up)on, along; with acc., through(out), up through.

ἀνα-βαίνω (βαν-, βα-), ἀναβήσω (ἀναβήσομαι), ἀνέβησα (ἀνέβην), ἀναβέβηκα, ἀναβέβαμαι*, ἀνεβάθην* go up, ascend.

ἀναβάντες, ἀναβάς (ἀναβαίνω), aor. act. participp.

ἀνάγοντο (ἀνάγω) = ἀνήγοντο (837), imperf.

ἀν-άγ-ω, ἀνάξω, ἀνήγαγον, ἀνῆξα**, ἀνῆγμαι*, ἀνήχθην* lead forth, set out, go forth, drive, carry.

ἀνα-δύ-ω, ἀναδύσω, ἀνέδῡσα (ἀνέδῡν), ἀναδέδυκα, ἀναδέδυμαι*, ἀνεδύθην* rise, emerge, "dive up," plunge up.

ἀνα-θηλέ-ω, ἀναθηλήσω, ἀνεθήλησα† sprout, bloom (forth, anew), bud (again), blossom.

ἀν-αιδείη, ης, ἡ shamelessness.

ἀν-αιδής, ές shameless, unfeeling.

ἀναΐξᾱς (ἀναΐσσω), aor. act. particip.

ἀν-αιρέ-ω (αἱρε-, ἑλ-), ἀναιρήσω, ἀνέελον (ἀνεῖλον, 584–585), ἀνῄρηκα*, ἀνῄρημαι*, ἀνῃρέθην* take up, snatch up, seize.

ἀν-αΐσσω (ϝαι-ϝικ-), ἀναΐξω, ἀνήϊξα,

ἀνηίχθην start up, dart up, spring up.

ἄναξ, ἄνακτος, ὁ king, lord, protector, chief(tain).

ἀν-ά-ποινος, ον unransomed, without a ransom paid.

ἄνασσε, vs. 180 (ἀνάσσω), imperat.

ἄνασσε(ν), vs. 252, (ἀνάσσω) = ἤνασσε(ν) (837), imperf.

ἀνάσσω (ϝανακ-), ἀνάξω, ἤναξα rule (over), guard, protect.

ἀναστάς (ἀνίστημι), 2d aor. act. particip.

ἀναστήσειε(ν) (ἀνίστημι), aor. act. optat., caus., 1069.

ἀνάσχεο (ἀνέχω), 2d aor. mid. imperat.

ἀνασχών (ἀνέχω), 2d aor. act. particip.

ἀνα-φαίνω (φαν-), ἀναφανέω, ἀνέφηνα, ἀναπέφηνα*, ἀναπέφασμαι, ἀνεφάνην reveal, show (up), manifest.

ἀνδάνω (σϝαδ-, σϝαδε-), ἀδήσω†, εὔαδον (= ἔϝαδον), ἕᾱδα please, delight, charm.

ἄνδρα, ἀνδράσι(ν), ἄνδρες, ἀνδρί, ἀνδρῶν (ἀνήρ).

ἀνδρο-φόνος, ον man-slaying, murderous.

ἀνέβη (ἀναβαίνω).

ἀνέδῡ, ἀνεδύσετο (ἀναδύω).

ἀν-εκτός, ή, όν endurable, bearable, tolerable.

ἀνέλοντο (ἀναιρέω), 2d aor. mid.

ἀνελών (ἀναιρέω), 2d aor. particip.

ἄνεμος, ου, ὁ wind, breeze.

ἀνέρας (ἀνήρ) (1168, 571).

ἀνέσταν (ἀνίστημι), 2d aor. act. indic., 3d plur.

ἀνέστη (ἀνίστημι), 2d aor. act.

ἀν-έχω (σεχ-, σχ-), ἀνέξω (ἀνασχήσω), ἀνέσχον (ἀνέσχεθον), ἀνόχωκα, ἀνέσχημαι* hold up, raise, endure.

ἀνήρ, ἀνδρός, ὁ (real) man, warrior,

hero, as distinguished from ἄνθρωπος (mere) man (1168, 571).

ἀνθερεών, ῶνος, ὁ chin, beard.

ἄνθρωπος, ου, ὁ (mere) man, as distinguished from ἀνήρ (real) man, warrior, hero.

ἀνιστάμενος (ἀνίστημι), present particip.

ἀν-ί-στημι (στη-, στα-), ἀναστήσω, ἀνέστησα (ἀνέστην), ἀνέστηκα, ἀνέσταμαι*, ἀνεστάθην* stand (up), set up, raise, (a)rise.

ἀν-ορού-ω*, ἀνώρουσα jump up, spring up, start up.

ἀνστήτην (ἀνίστημι) = ἀνεστήτην (837), 2d aor. dual.

ἀντ-άξιος, η, ον equivalent, of equal value.

ἄντην openly, before the face.

ἀντιά-ω, ἀντιάσω (ἀντιάω, ἀντιόω, 603–604, 945–948), ἠντίασα approach, prepare, share, partake, go (come) to meet.

ἀντι-βίην with opposing might, in opposition, antagonistically.

ἀντί-βιος, η, ον opposing, hostile.

ἀντί-θεος, η, ον godlike, equal to the gods, a match for the gods.

ἀντίος, η, ον in opposition, opposing, hostile, facing, meeting, to meet.

ἀντιόωσαν (ἀντιάω) = ἀντιάουσαν (945–948), pres. particip., fem.

ἀντι-φέρω (φερ-, οἰ-, ἐνεκ-), ἀντοίσω bear against, oppose.

ἀνώγ-ω, ἀνώξω, ἤνωξα, ἄνωγα (for ἤνωγα? 884) command, order, bid.

ἄξω (ἄγω).

ἀπ᾽ = ἀπό (575).

ἀπ-αμείβ-ω, ἀπαμείψω, ἀπήμειψα, ἀπημείφθην* (ex)change; mid., reply, answer, respond.

ἀπ-άνευθε(ν) apart, away.

ἄ-πᾱς, ἄ-πᾶσα, ἄ-παν all, entire, whole, all together.

ἀπατηλός, ή, όν deceitful, false.

ἀπ-αυράω = ἀπαϝράω (ϝρᾱ-); imperf., with aor. meaning ἀπηύρων; ἀπουρήσω; aor. particip. ἀπούρᾱς (= ἀπόϝρᾱς) take away, deprive, snatch away.

ἀπεβήσετο (ἀποβαίνω) (842).

ἀπεδέξατο (ἀποδέχομαι).

ἀπειλέ-ω, ἀπειλήσω, ἠπείλησα threaten, boast, menace.

ἀπεῖπον = ἀποεῖπον.

ἀ-πείρων, ον boundless, limitless.

ἀπελῡμαίνοντο (ἀπολῡμαίνομαι).

ἀπέλῡσε (ἀπολύω).

ἀ-περείσιος, ον boundless, limitless, countless, immeasurable (1168).

ἀπ-έχω (σεχ-, σχ-), ἀφέξω (ἀποσχήσω), ἀπέσχον (ἀπέσχεθον) hold from.

ἀ-πήμων, ον unharmed, painless, without hurt (damage, pain, sorrow).

ἀπηνής, ές harsh, cruel, rude.

ἀπηύρων (ἀπαυράω).

ἀ-πιθέ-ω*, ἀπιθήσω, ἠπίθησα disobey, fail to obey, distrust.

ἄπιος, η, ον (cf. ἀπό) far, distant.

ἀπό adv., and prep. with gen., off, from, away, back.

ἀποαίρεο (ἀφαιρέω), imperat.

ἀποαιρεῖσθαι (ἀφαιρέω), infin.

ἀπο-αιρέω = ἀφαιρεω.

ἀπο-βαίνω (βαν-, βα-), ἀποβήσω (ἀποβήσομαι), ἀπέβησα (ἀπέβην), ἀποβέβηκα, ἀποβέβαμαι*, ἀπεβάθην* depart, go away.

ἀπο-δέχ-ομαι, ἀποδέξομαι, ἀπεδεξάμην (ἀπεδέγμην), ἀποδέδεγμαι, ἀπεδέχθην* receive (from), accept (from).

ἀπο-δί-δωμι (δω-, δο-), ἀποδώσω, ἀπέδωκα, ἀποδέδωκα,* ἀποδέδομαι,

ἀπεδόθην give back, restore, return, give away, pay.

ἀποδοῦναι (ἀποδίδωμι), aor. act. infin.

ἀπο-εῖπον (ϝεπ-), 2d aor., speak out, deny, refuse.

ἄ-ποινα, ων, τά ransom(s).

ἀπολέσθαι (ἀπόλλῡμι), aor. infin.

ἀπόλεσ(σ)αν (ἀπόλλῡμι) = ἀπώλεσ(σ)αν (837).

ἀπ-όλλῡμι (ὀλ-, ὀλε-, ὀλο-), ἀπολέσ(σ)ω, ἀπώλεσ(σ)α, ἀπόλωλα destroy, kill, ruin; mid., perish, die.

Ἀπόλλων, ωνος, ὁ Apollo, god of light, and patron of music, poetry, and healing (1168, 571).

ἀπο-λῡμαίνομαι (λῡμαν-) purify (oneself), clean(se).

ἀπο-λύ-ω, ἀπολύσω, ἀπέλῡσα, ἀπολέλυκα*, ἀπολέλυμαι, ἀπελύθην loose, set free.

ἀπο-νοστέ-ω*, ἀπονοστήσω, ἀπενόστησα return (home), go (home), come.

ἀπο-νόσφι(ν) apart, away (from).

ἀποπαύεο (ἀποπαύω), imperat.

ἀπο-παύ-ω, ἀποπαύσω, ἀπέπαυσα, ἀποπέπαυκα*, ἀποπέπαυμαι, ἀπεπαύθην* cease (from), refrain (from), stop (from), desist, restrain.

ἀπο-στείχω (στειχ-, στιχ-), ἀπέστιχον depart, step off, march away.

ἀπόστιχε (ἀποστείχω), aor. imperat.

ἀπο-τίνω (τει-, τι-, τινϝ-), ἀποτίσω, ἀπέτῑσα, ἀποτέτῑκα*, ἀποτέτῑσμαι*, ἀπετίσθην* repay, requite, recompense, atone for.

ἀποτίσομεν (ἀποτίνω).

ἀπούρᾱς (ἀπαυράω).

ἀ-πρίατος, η, ον unbought, without price, free.

ἅπτω (ἀφ-), ἅψω* (ἅψομαι), ἧψα,

ἦμμαι, ἤφθην* touch, lay hold of, attach, attack.

ἀπ-ωθέω (ϝωθ-, ϝωθε-), ἀπώσω, ἀπέωσα, ἀπέωσμαι*, ἀπεώσθην shove away, push off, drive away.

ἀπώσει (ἀπωθέω).

ἄρ, ἄρα, ῥα naturally, of course, as you know, as you might expect, that is, in effect. It is not always translatable into English, which has for it no exact equivalent.

ἀρά-ομαι, ἀρήσομαι, ἠρησάμην, ἤραμαι* pray, curse, invoke.

ἀρ-αρ-ίσκω (ἀρ-), ἦρσα (ἤραρον), ἄρηρα, ἤρθην suit, adapt, adjust.

ἀργαλέος, η, ον horrible, terrible, awful, cruel, difficult.

Ἀργεῖος, ου, ὁ Argive, Greek.

Ἄργος, εος, τό Argos, a country and city in Greece.

ἀργός, ή, όν bright, shining, swift, flashing.

ἀργύρεος, η, ον silver(y), of silver.

ἀργυρό-πεζος, α, ον silvery-footed.

ἀργυρό-τοξος, ον of a silver bow, equipped with a silver bow, silver-bowed (one), Apollo.

ἀρείοσι(ν) (ἀρείων, ον).

ἀρείων, ον (ἀγαθός, ή, όν) comparat. (754, 1), better, mightier, braver.

ἀρήγ-ω, ἀρήξω, ἤρηξα help, assist, succor.

ἀρήν, ἀρνός, ὁ, ἡ lamb.

ἀρῆξαι (ἀρήγω), aor. infin.

ἀρήξειν (ἀρήγω), fut. infin.

ἀρητήρ, ῆρος, ὁ priest, pray-er.

ἀριστεύς, ῆος, ὁ chief, nobleman, leader.

ἄριστος, η, ον (ἀγαθός, ή, όν) superl., best, noblest, bravest, fairest.

ἄρ-νυ-μαι, ἀρέομαι*, ἠρόμην (ἠράμην) acquire, win, save, preserve.

ἀρνῶν (ἀρήν, ἀρνός, ὁ, ἡ).

ἄρσαντες (ἀραρίσκω), aor. particip.

ἀρχός, οῦ, ὁ leader, commander, ruler, chief, guide, pilot.

ἄρχ-ω, ἄρξω, ἦρξα, ἦρχα*, ἦργμαι*, ἤρχθην* begin, be first, lead, rule.

ἄ-σβεστος, η, ον inextinguishable.

ἄσσα (ὅστις, ἥτις, ὅ τι), nom. and acc. plur. neut.

ἆσσον (ἄγχι) comparat., nearer, closer.

ἀστεροπητής, ᾶο, ὁ hurler of lightning.

ἀτάρ = αὐτάρ (571) but, moreover, on the other hand.

ἀταρτηρός, ή, όν harsh, bitter.

ἀ-τελεύτητος, ον unaccomplished.

ἄτερ apart, away (from), without.

ἄτη, ης, ἡ blind infatuation, folly, ruin, misfortune, hurt.

ἀ-τῑμάζω (τῑμαδ-), ἀτῑμάσω*, ἠτίμασα dishonor, insult, slight, despise.

ἀ-τῑμά-ω, ἀτῑμήσω, ἠτίμησα, dishonor, insult, slight, despise.

ἄ-τῑμος, ον dishonored, unhonored, despised.

ἀτῑμότατος, η, ον (ἄτῑμος, ον), superlat.

Ἀτρεΐδης, ᾱο, ὁ son of Atreus, usually refers to Agamemnon.

Ἀτρεΐων, ωνος, ὁ son of Atreus, usually refers to Agamemnon.

ἀτρύγετος, ον barren? restless? a word of uncertain meaning.

αὖ anew, again, a second time, but now.

αὐδά-ω, αὐδήσω*, ηὔδησα speak, say, declare, shout, cry out.

αὐδή, ῆς, ἡ voice, speech, discourse, language, sound, cry.

ἀυερύω (= ἀν-ϝερυω = ἀϝ-ϝερυω: ϝερυ-, ϝρυ-), ἀυέρυσα draw up (the head).

αὖθ', vs. 370 = αὖτε (575, 582).

αὖθ' = αὖθι

αὖθι here, there, in this (that) place.

αὐτάρ (ἀτάρ, 571) but, moreover, on the other hand.

αὖτε anew, again, a second time, but now.

ἀῦτή, ῆς, ἡ battle-cry, war-whoop.

αὐτ-ῆμαρ (on) the (self)same day.

αὐτίκα on the spot, immediately, forthwith.

αὖτις back again, anew.

αὐτίχ' = αὐτίκα (575, 582).

αὐτός, ή, ό self, him(self), her(self), it(self), same.

αὐτοῦ there, at that place.

αὖτως in the same way, thus, so, as matters now are.

ἀφ-αιρέω (αἱρε-, ἑλ-), ἀφαιρήσω, ἀφέελον (ἀφεῖλον, 584–585), ἀφήρηκα*, ἀφήρημαι*, ἀφηρέθην* take away, rob, deprive.

ἄφαρ immediately, forthwith.

ἀφέλεσθε (ἀφαιρέω), 2d aor. mid.

ἄφενος, εος, τό wealth, riches.

ἀφέξει (ἀπέχω), fut.

ἀφίει (ἀφίημι), imperf.

ἀφ-(-ημι (ση-, σε- = ἡ-, ἑ-, 603–604) ἀφήσω, ἀφέηκα (ἀφῆκα), ἀφεῖκα*, ἀφεῖμαι,* ἀφείθην send away, dismiss, hurl, drive (off).

ἀφύξειν (ἀφύσσω).

ἀφύσσω (ἀφυγ-), ἀφύξω dip up, draw (out), collect, heap up.

'Αχαιίς, ίδος fem., Achaean.

'Αχαιός, οῦ, ὁ Achaean, Greek.

'Αχιλ(λ)εύς, ῆος, ὁ Achilles.

ἄχ-νυ-μαι be grieved, be vexed, be enraged.

ἄχος, εος, τό woe, pain, grief.

ἄψ back (again), backward(s).

B

βαθύς, εῖα, ύ deep, profound.

βαίνω (βαν-, βα-), βήσω (βήσομαι), ἔβησα (ἔβην), βέβηκα, βέβαμαι*, ἐβάθην* come, go, walk.

βάλλεο (βάλλω), imperat. mid.

βάλλω (βαλ-, βλη-), βαλέω, ἔβαλον, βέβληκα, βέβλημαι, ἐβλήθην* throw, hurl, shoot, dash.

βαρύς, εῖα, ύ heavy, weighty, violent, severe, grave, serious, important.

βασιλεύς, ῆος, ὁ king, ruler, chief-(tain).

βάτην (βαίνω) = ἐβάτην (837), 2d aor., dual.

βεβήκει(ν) (βαίνω) = ἐβεβήκει(ν) (837), pluperf.

βέλος, εος, τό (cf. βάλλω) dart, arrow, shaft, missile.

βένθος, εος, τό depth.

βῆ (βαίνω) = ἔβη (837), 2d aor.

βηλός, οῦ, ὁ threshold.

βῆσαν, βῆσε (βαίνω), aorr. (837), causat. (1069, 864).

βήσομεν (βαίνω), vs. 144 = βήσωμεν (800), aor. act. subjunct., causat. (1069, 864).

βίη, ης, ἡ strength, might, violence.

βιός, οῦ, ὁ bow.

βουλεύσαντε (βουλεύω), aor. act. particip., dual.

βουλεύ-ω, βουλεύσω, ἐβούλευσα, βεβούλευκα*, βεβούλευμαι*, ἐβουλεύθην* plan, counsel, advise, deliberate.

βουλή, ῆς, ἡ plan, will, wish, purpose, counsel, council.

βουλη-φόρος, ον counsel-bearing, full of counsel, discreet.

βούλ-ομαι (βουλ-, βουλε-), βουλήσομαι*, βέβουλα, βεβούλημαι*, ἐβουλήθην* wish, desire, be willing, prefer.

βοῦς, βοός, ὁ, ἡ bull, ox, cow.

βοῦς (βοῦς, βοός, ὁ, ἡ), vs. 154 = βόας, acc. plur.

βο-ῶπις, ιδος *fem.*, calm-eyed, large-eyed, ox-eyed.

Βριάρεως (= Βριάρηος, ου, ὁ, 573, 586), ω, ὁ Briareüs, *a sea-divinity.*

Βρῑσεύς, ῆος, ὁ Briseus, *father of Briseïs.*

Βρῑσηίς, ίδος, ἡ Briseïs, *daughter of Briseus.*

βροτός, οῦ, ὁ mortal, man.

βωμός, οῦ, ὁ (*cf.* βαίνω) foundation, base, altar.

βωτι-άνειρα *fem.*, man-nourishing, nurturing heroes; *as substant.*, nurse of heroes.

Γ

γ᾽ = γέ (*575*).

γαῖα, ης, ἡ earth, land, country.

γαίω (γαϜ-) rejoice, exult, glory.

γάρ *postpos. conj.*, for, in fact.

γέ *postpos. enclit. emphasizing the preceding word or clause*, indeed, at least, at any rate.

γείνομαι (γεν-), ἐγεινάμην beget, produce, bear, be born.

γέλος, ου, ὁ laughter, merriment, hilarity.

γενεή, ῆς, ἡ generation, family, stock.

γένετο (γίγνομαι) = ἐγένετο (*837*), *2d aor.*

γένηται (γίγνομαι), *2d aor. subjunct.*

γένοντο (γίγνομαι) = ἐγένοντο (*837*), *2d aor.*

γεραιός, ή, όν old, aged, ancient; *masc. as substant.*, old man.

γέρας, αος, τό prize (of honor).

γέρων, οντος, ὁ old man.

γηθέω (γηθ-, γηθε-), γηθήσω, ἐγήθησα, γέγηθα rejoice, be glad, exult.

γηθῆσαι (γηθέω), *aor. optat.*

γῆρας, αος, τό old age, eld.

γί-γνομαι (γεν-, γενε-, γον-), γενήσομαι*, ἐγενόμην, γέγονα, γεγένημαι*,

ἐγενήθην† become, be, arise, be born.

γι-γνώσκω (γνω-, γνο-), γνώσομαι, ἔγνων, ἔγνωκα*, ἔγνωσμαι*, ἐγνώσθην* KNOW, recognize, learn, perceive.

γλαυκ-ῶπις, ιδος *fem.*, gleaming-eyed, flashing-eyed, "owl-eyed."

γλυκίων, ον (γλυκύς, εῖα, ύ) *comparat.*, sweeter.

γλυκύς, εῖα, ύ sweet.

γλῶσσα, ης, ἡ tongue, speech, language.

γνῶ, γνώωσι (γιγνώσκω), *2d aorr., act. subjunct.*

γόνυ, γουνός (γούνατος) τό KNEE.

γουνάζομαι (*cf.* γόνυ), γουνάσομαι embrace the knees, entreat, implore.

γούνων (γόνυ, γουνός, τό).

γυνή, γυναικός, ἡ woman, wife.

Δ

δ᾽ = δέ (*575*).

δαιμόνιος, η, ον possessed (by a daemon); good friend; crazy, foolish, wretch.

δαίμων, ονος, ὁ, ἡ divinity, god, goddess.

δαί-νῡ-μι (*cf.* δαίς), δαίσω, ἔδαισα* (ἐδαισάμην) entertain, feast, banquet.

δαίς, δαιτός, ἡ portion, feast, banquet.

δάκρυ, υος, τό tear.

δακρύ-ω*, δακρύσω*, ἐδάκρυσα, δεδάκρυμαι weep, shed tears.

δαμᾷ (δαμάζω) = δαμάει (*584–585*), = δαμασει (*603–604*) *fut.*

δαμάζω* (δαμαδ-), δαμά(σ)ω, ἐδάμασ-(σ)α, ἐδαμάσθην subdue, overcome, crush, DOMINATE.

Δαναός, οῦ, ὁ Danaan, *Greek.*

δασμός, οῦ, ὁ division (of spoil).

δάσ(σ)αντο (δατέομαι) = ἐδάσ(σ)αντο (837), aor.

δατέομαι (δατ-, δατε-), δάσ(σ)ομαι, ἐδασ(σ)άμην, δέδασμαι divide, distribute, allot.

δέ, postpos. conjunct., and, but, for, so.

-δε, with acc., (788, 4) to, up to.

δέδασται (δατέομαι), perf.

δείδοικα (δείδω).

δείδω (δϝει-, δϝοι-, δϝι-), δείσομαι, ἔδεισα, δείδοικα (δείδια) fear, be afraid.

δειλός, ή, όν fearful, cowardly, cringing, miserable, pitiable.

δεινός, ή, όν dread(ful), awful, terrible, fearful.

δέκατος, η, ον tenth.

δέμας, αος, τό build, stature, size, form, body, structure.

δέξασθαι, δέξατο (δέχομαι).

δεξιτερός, ή, όν right (hand), lucky.

δέος, δέος (δείους), τό fear, dread, timidity.

δέπας, αος, τό cup, goblet.

δέρκομαι (δερκ-, δορκ-, δρακ-), ἔδρακον, δέδορκα, ἐδέρχθην* (ἐδράκην*) see, look, behold.

δέρω (δερ-, δαρ-), δερέω*, ἔδειρα, δέδαρμαι*, ἐδάρην* skin, flay.

δεσμός, οῦ, ὁ (cf. δέω) bond, band, fetter.

δεύομαι (δευ-, δευε-), δευήσομαι, ἐδεύησα lack, need, be in want.

δεῦρο hither, to this place, here.

δεύτερος, η, ον second, succeeding, later.

δέχθαι (δέχομαι), aor. infin.

δέχ-ομαι, δέξομαι, ἐδεξάμην (ἐδέγμην), δέδεγμαι, ἐδέχθην* receive, accept.

δέ-ω, δήσω, ἔδησα, δέδεκα*, δέδεμαι, ἐδέθην* bind, tie.

δή indeed, truly, forsooth, now.

δηθύν-ω loiter, tarry, delay.

δηλέ-ομαι*, δηλήσομαι, ἐδηλησάμην, δεδήλημαι harm, hurt, destroy, damage, wrong, ruin.

δημο-βόρος, ον devouring (the goods of) the people.

δήν = δϝήν, an old accusative, for a long time, long.

διά, adv., and prep. with gen. and acc., through, by means of, on account of; adv., between, among; with gen., through; with acc., through, by means of, on account of, during.

Δία (Ζεύς, Διός, ὁ), acc.

δι-άν-διχα in two ways, differently.

δια-πέρθω (περθ-, παθ-), διαπέρσω, διέπερσα (διέπραθον) sack (utterly, thoroughly), plunder, pillage, devastate.

δια-πρήσσω (πρᾱγ-), διαπρήξω, διέπρηξα, διαπέπρηγα†, διαπέπρηγμαι†, διεπρήχθην† go across, pass through, traverse, pass over, accomplish.

διαστήτην (δίστημι) = διεστήτην (837), 2d aor. dual.

δια-τμήγω (τμηγ-, τμαγ-), διατμήξω*, διέτμηξα (διέτμαγον), διετμάγην separate, divide, part, cut apart, split.

δί-δωμι (δω-, δο-), (δι)δώσω, ἔδωκα, δέδωκα*, δέδομαι, ἐδόθην give, grant, bestow.

διείρεο (διείρομαι), imperat.

δι-είρομαι (είρ-, είρε-), διειρήσομαι inquire into, ask about item by item.

διεπράθομεν (διαπέρθω).

δι-έπω (σεπ-, σπ-), διέψω, διέσπον accomplish, perform, go through, be engaged in.

διέτμαγεν (διατμήγω), aor. 3d plur.

Διί (Ζεύς, Διός, ὁ), dat.

δι-ί-στημι (στη-, στα-), διαστήσω, διέστησα (διέστην), διέστηκα, διέσταμαι*, διεστάθην stand apart, separate, divide.

διί-φιλος, η, ον dear to Zeus, beloved of Zeus (1168).

δικαζέμεν(αι) (δικάζω), infin.

δικάζω (δικαδ-), δικάσω*, ἐδίκασ(σ)α, δεδίκακα**, δεδίκασμαι*, ἐδικάσθην* judge, decide, pronounce judgment.

δικασ-πόλος, ου, ὁ judge, arbiter, dispenser of justice.

δῖο-γενής, ἐς born of Zeus, Zeus-descended (1168).

Διός (Ζεύς, Διός, ὁ).

δῖος, α, ον divine, godlike, glorious, heavenly.

δῖο-τρεφής, ἐς Zeus-nourished, under the protection of Zeus.

δί-πτυξ, υχος double, two-fold.

δοῖεν (δίδωμι), 2d aor. optat.

δολο-μήτης, αο, ὁ deceiver, crafty-minded.

δόμεν(αι) (δίδωμι), 2d aor. infin.

δόντες (δίδωμι), 2d aor. particip.

δόρυ, δουρός (δούρατος), τό beam, timber, spear.

δός (δίδωμι), 2d aor. act. imper.

δόσαν (δίδωμι) = ἔδοσαν (837), 2d aor.

δουρί (δόρυ, δουρός, τό).

Δρύας, αντος, ὁ Dryas.

δύνα-μαι, δυνήσομαι, ἐδυνησάμην, δεδύνημαι*, ἐδυνάσθην be able, can.

δύο (δύω) two.

δ(υ)ω-δέκατος, η, ον twelfth.

δῶ, indecl., τό house, home.

δω-δέκατος, η, ον (δυωδέκατος, η, ον) twelfth.

δώῃ(σι) (δίδωμι), 2d aor. act. subjunct., 3d sing.

δῶκε (δίδωμι) = ἔδωκε (837), aor.

δῶμα, ατος, τό house, home, building.

δῶρον, ου, τό gift, present.

δώσει (δίδωμι).

δῷ(σι) (δίδωμι), 2d aor. act. subjunct., 3d sing.

δώσουσι (δίδωμι).

δώωσι (δίδωμι), 2d aor. subjunct.

E

ἕ (εἶο, ἕο), acc. sing.

ἕα (ἔάω) = ἔαε (584-585), imperat.

ἐάω (σεϝα-), ἐάσω, εἴασα, εἴακα*, εἴαμαι*, εἰάθην* permit, allow, leave.

ἔβαν (βαίνω) = ἔβησαν 2d aor.

ἔβη (βαίνω), 2d aor.

ἐγγυαλίζω (ἐγγυαλιγ-), ἐγγυαλίξω, ἠγγυάλιξα grant, present with.

ἔγνω (γιγνώσκω), 2d aor., 3d sing.

ἐγώ(ν), ἐμεῖο I.

ἔδειραν (δέρω).

ἔδεισε(ν) (δείδω).

ἐδέξατο (δέχομαι).

ἔδησαν (δέω).

ἐδητύς, ύος, ἡ food, feed.

ἕδος, εος, τό SEAT, abode, habitation.

ἔδωκε(ν) (δίδωμι).

ἐείκοσι = εἴκοσι twenty.

ἔειπες = εἶπες (εἴρω).

ἐέλδωρ indecl., τό desire, wish.

ἕζομαι (σεδ-, = ἑδ-, 603-604), ἕσσομαι, εἷσα, ἑ(ε)σσάμην SIT down, seat.

ἧκε (ἵημι).

ἑῆος (ἐύς).

(ἐ)θέλω (ἐθελ-, ἐθελε-), ἐθελήσω, ἠθέλησα, ἠθέληκα* wish, desire, be willing.

ἔθεν, ἐθέν (εἶο, ἕο).

ἔθεσαν, ἔθηκε (τίθημι), aorr.

1) εἰ, interj., up! come! go to!

2) εἰ (αἰ) if, whether.

*εἴδω (εἴδομαι) (ϝειδ-, ϝοιδ-, ϝιδ-), εἰδήσω (εἴσομαι), εἶδον, οἶδα, pluperf. ᾔδεα; in act.: aor. see; fut. and perf. know; mid. seem, appear.

εἰδώς (*εἴδω) perf. act. particip.

εἴθ᾽ = εἴτε (575, 582).

εἴκοσι = ἐείκοσι twenty.

ἐίκτην (*εἴκω), pluperf. dual.

εἴκω (ϝεικ-, ϝοικ-, ϝικ-), εἴξω, ἔοικα be like, resemble, be fitting, seem (likely), appear (suitable).

εἰλήλουθας (ἔρχομαι).

*εἴλω (εἴλομαι) (ϝελ-), ἔελσα, ἔελμαι, ἐάλην crowd, drive.

εἶμι (εἰ-, ἰ-), εἴσομαι come, go ; pres. often with fut. meaning, shall (will) come, go.

εἰμί (ἐσ-), ἔσ(σ)ομαι be, exist. εἶναι (εἰμί), infin.

εἵνεκα = ἕνεκα (571) on account of, because of, for the sake of.

εἷο (ἕο) of him, her, it (760).

εἷος = ἧος while, until.

εἶπας, εἶπε, εἰπέ, εἰπεῖν, εἶπες, εἴπῃ, εἴπῃς, εἴποι, εἶπον, εἰπών (εἴρω), 2d aorr.

εἴρομαι (= ἐρέω) (εἰρ-, ἐρε-), εἰρήσομαι ask, inquire, question, seek.

ἐ(ἰ)ρῦμαι (ϝερῡ-), ἐ(ἰ)ρύσ(σ)ομαι, ἐ(ἰ)ρυσ(σ)άμην save, preserve, observe, protect, guard, retain.

εἴρω (ϝερ-, ϝρη-, ϝεπ-), ἐρέω, εἶπον (ἔειπον), εἴρηκα*, εἴρημαι, ἐρρήθην speak, say, tell.

εἰς, ἐς, adv. and prep. with acc., into, to, until, therein.

εἷς, μία, ἕν one, only, sole.

ἐίσᾱς, ἐίσης (ἴσος, η (ἐίση), ον).

εἶσε(ν) (ἕζομαι) aor., causat., (1069).

εἴσεται (*εἴδω).

εἰσί(ν) (εἰμί), 3d plur.

εἴσω into, within, often with acc.

εἴτε . . . εἴτε whether . . . or.

ἐκ (ἐξ), adv., and prep. with gen., out of, (away) from.

ἑκά-εργος (ϝεκάϝεργος), ου, ὁ free-worker, working his will, Apollo.

ἑκάη (καίω).

ἕκαστος, η, ον each, every.

ἑκατη-βελέτης, āο, ὁ free-shooter, free-shooting, sharp-shooter, a dead shot, epithet of Apollo.

ἑκατη-βόλος, ου, ὁ free-shooter, sharp-shooter, free-shooting, sharp-shooting, shooting according to will, sure-shooting, a dead shot.

ἑκατόγ-χειρος, ον hundred-handed, hundred-armed.

ἑκατόμ-βη, ης, ἡ HECATOMB, sacrifice, a number of animals, originally one hundred cattle, offered in sacrifice.

ἕκατος, ου. ὁ free-shooter, sharp-shooter, a dead shot.

ἐκεῖνος, η. ο (κεῖνος, η, ο) that (one); he, she, it

ἔκηα (καίω).

ἑκη-βόλος, ου, ὁ free-shooter, sharp-shooter, epithet of Apollo, originally an adjective, shooting according to will (desire, inclination, pleasure) ; as substant., free-shooter, sure-shooter, sharp-shooter, a dead shot.

ἔκλαγξαν (κλάζω).

ἔκλυε, ἔκλυες, ἔκλυον (*κλεύω).

ἐκ-παγλος, ον terrible, dreadful, awful, frightful, fearful.

ἐκπαγλότατος, η, ον (ἔκπαγλος, ον), superl.

ἐκ-πάγλως terribly, horribly, awfully, dreadfully, frightfully.

ἐκ-πέρθω (περθ-, πραθ-), ἐκπέρσω, ἐξέπερσα (ἐξέπραθον) sack (utterly), plunder, pillage, devastate.

ἐκ-τάμ-νω, ἐξέταμον cut out.

Ἕκτωρ, ορος, ὁ Hector, son of Priam, and leader of the Trojans.

ἐλα-ύν-ω (cf. ἐλάω) drive, carry on, strike, push, press.

323

ἔλαφος, ου, ὁ, ἡ deer, stag, hind, doe.

ἐλά-ω, ἐλά(σ)(σ)ω, ἤλασ(σ)α, ἐλή-λακα*, ἐλήλαμαι, ἠλάθην* drive, carry on, strike, push, press.

ἕλε (αἱρέω) = ἕελε (837), 2d aor.

ἐλελίζω* (ἑλικ-), ἐλέλιξα, ἐλελίχθην shake, twirl, twist, coil, make tremble, brandish.

ἐλεύσεται (ἔρχομαι).

ἔλεψε (λέπω).

ἐλθέμεν(αι), ἐλθοῦσα, ἐλθών (ἔρχομαι), 2d aor., infinitives and partt.

ἐλίκ-ωψ, ωπος, masc.; ἑλικ-ῶπις, ιδος, fem., bright-eyed, flashing-eyed.

ἔλιπε (λείπω).

ἑλίσσω (ϝελικ-), ἑλίξω*, ἑέλιξα, ἑέλιγμαι, ἑελίχθην (ἑε = ει, 584–585) twirl, twist, curl, turn, roll.

ἕλκεο (ἕλκω), mid. imperat.

ἕλκω (σελκ-, = ἑλκ-, 603–604) draw, drag, pull, tug.

ἕλον (αἱρέω) = ἕελον (837).

ἑλόντε, ἑλοῦσα (αἱρέω), 2d aor. partt.

ἕλσαι (εἴλω).

ἕλωμαι, ἑλών (αἱρέω), 2d aor. forms.

ἐλώριον, ου, τό booty, spoil(s), prey.

ἔμ' = ἐμέ, ἐμέθεν, ἐμεῖο, ἐμεῦ (ἐγώ).

ἔμεν(αι), ἔμμεν(αι) = εἶναι (εἰμί).

ἔμμορε (μείρομαι).

ἐμοί (ἐγώ).

ἐμός, ή, όν my, mine.

ἐμπεφυυῖα (ἐμφύω), perf. particip., fem.

ἔμ-πης nevertheless, for all that, by all means, absolutely, completely.

ἐμ-φύ-ω, ἐμφύσω, ἐνέφυσα (ἐνέφυν), ἐμπέφυκα grow in(to), cling very closely.

ἐν(ί), εἰν, adv., and prep. with dat., in, at, among, on, there(in, on).

ἐν-αντίος, η, ον opposite, facing, before, to meet.

ἐναρίζω (ἐναριγ-), ἐναρίξω, ἠνάριξα strip of armor, spoil, slay.

ἐν-δέξιος, η, ον to(ward) the right, from left to right.

ἔν-δοθι within, inside, at home.

ἔν-ειμι (ἐσ-), ἐνέσ(σ)ομαι be in.

ἕνεκα = εἵνεκα (571), with gen., usually postpos., on account of.

ἐνῆεν (ἔνειμι), imperf.

ἔνθα then, thereupon.

ἐνθά-δε here, there; hither, thither.

ἐνί = ἐν.

ἐνν-ῆμαρ (for) nine days.

ἐν-όρ-νῡ-μι, ἐνόρσω, ἐνῶρσα (ἐνώρορον), ἐνόρωρα, ἐνορώρεμαι rouse among, kindle among, excite.

ἔντο (ἵημι), 2d aor. mid.

ἐντός within, inside.

ἐνῶρτο (ἐνόρνῡμι), 2d aor. mid.

ἐξ = ἐκ.

ἔξαγε (ἐξάγω), imperat.

ἐξ-άγ-ω, ἐξάξω, ἐξήγαγον, ἐξῆχα**, ἐξῆγμαι*, ἐξήχθην* lead out, lead forth, bring forth.

Ἐξάδιος, ου, ὁ Exadius.

ἐξ-αλαπάζω (ἀλαπαγ-), ἐξαλαπάξω, ἐξηλάπαξα sack utterly, destroy utterly.

ἐξαύδα (ἐξαυδάω) = ἐξαύδαε (584–585), imperat.

ἐξ-αυδά-ω, ἐξαυδήσω*, ἐξηύδησα speak out, tell, say, declare.

ἐξ-αῦτις again, anew, then.

ἐξείης one after another, in turn, in order.

ἐξ-είρω (ϝερ-, ϝρη-, ϝεπ-), ἐξερέω, ἐξεῖπον, ἐξείρηκα*, ἐξείρημαι, ἐξερρήθην speak out, tell, say, declare.

ἐξεπράθομεν (ἐκπέρθω).

ἐξερέω (ἐξείρω).

ἐξέταμον (ἐκτάμνω).

ἕο, εἷο (760) of him, her, it.

ἔοικε (*εἴκω), perf.

ἐοικώς (*εἴκω), perf. act. particip.

ἐόντα, ἐόντες (εἰμί), participles.

ἑός, ἑή, ἑόν = ὅς, ἥ, ὅν his, her(s), its (own).

ἑοῦσαν, ἑούσῃ (εἰμί), fem. participles.

ἐπ᾽ = ἐπί (575).

ἐπ-αγείρω (ἀγερ-), ἐπήγειρα, ἐπαγήγερμαι, ἐπηγέρθην collect, gather (together).

ἐπ-αίτιος, ον blameworthy, responsible, blamable, accountable.

ἐπ-απειλέ-ω, ἐπαπειλήσω, ἐπηπείλησα threaten (against), boast.

ἐπ-άρχ-ω, ἐπάρξω, ἐπῆρξα, ἐπῆργμαι*, ἐπήρχθην* begin, perform the initiatory rites.

ἐπάσαντο (πατέομαι).

ἐπ-ασσύτερος, η, ον thick, close, in quick succession, crowded.

ἐπ-αυρίσκω* (ἐπαυρέω*) (ἐπαυρίσκομαι) (αὐρ-, αὐρε-), ἐπαυρήσομαι, ἐπαῦρον enjoy, reap the benefit of.

ἔπεα, ἐπέεσι (ἔπος, εος, τό).

ἐπεί when, since, for.

ἔπει = ἐπεΐ (ἔπος, εος, τό) (584–585).

ἐπειδή when, since, for, indeed.

ἔπειθ᾽ (vs. 583) = ἔπειτα (575, 582).

*ἐπ-είκω (ϝεικ-, ϝοικ-, ϝικ-), ἐπέοικα perf. as pres., be seemly, be fitting either (in addition, also).

ἔπ-ειμι (εἰ-, ἰ-), ἐπείσομαι come (upon, on), approach.

ἔπεισι(ν) (ἔπειμι), 3d sing.

ἔπειτα then, thereupon.

ἐπ-έοικα (ϝεικ-, ϝοικ-, ϝικ-), perf. only, be fitting (either, also).

ἐπεπείθεθ᾽ (ἐπιπείθομαι) = ἐπεπείθετο (575, 582).

ἐπέπλεον (ἐπιπλέω).

ἐπερρώσαντο (ἐπιρρώομαι).

ἐπ-έρχομαι (ἐρχ-, ἐλθ-, ἐλευθ-, ἐλυθ-), ἐπελεύσομαι, ἐπῆλθον (ἐπήλυθον), ἐπελήλυθα (ἐπειλήλουθα) come upon (to, toward), attack.

ἔπεσ(σ)ι (ἔπος, εος, τό).

ἐπέσσυται (ἐπισσεύω).

ἐπεστέψαντο (ἐπιστέφω).

ἐπ-ευ-φημέ-ω*, ἐπευφημήσω, ἐπευφήμησα shout assent, approve.

ἐπηπείλησε (ἐπαπειλέω).

ἐπί, adv., and prep. with gen., dat., and acc., to (up)on, against, by; adv., (up)on, thereon; with gen., (up)on, over, during; with dat., (up)on, in, for, about, against, at, beside, by; with acc., (up)on, up to, over, against.

ἔπι (ἔπειμι) = ἔπεστι, vs. 515.

ἐπι-γνάμπ-τω, ἐπιγνάμψω*, ἐπέγναμψα, ἐπεγνάμφθην bend, curb, subdue, win over.

ἐπι-είκελος, ον like, resembling.

ἐπι-εικής, ές suitable, fitting, proper, becoming, decent.

ἐπιειμένε (ἐπιέννῡμι, ἐφέννῡμι), perf. particip., voc.

ἐπιέλπεο (ἐπιέλπω), imperat. mid.

ἐπι-έλπω (ϝελπ-, ϝολπ-), ἐπέολπα cause to hope, make hope; mid., hope (for), wish for, desire, expect.

ἐπι-έννῡμι* (ἐφ-έννῡμι*) (ἐφέννυμαι) (ϝεσ-), ἐφέσ(σ)ω, ἐφέσσα, ἐφεῖμαι (ἐφέσμαι), both with and without elision of the prep., clothe, invest.

ἐπι-κρ(αι)αίνω (κραν-), ἐπεκρήηνα accomplish, perform, fulfill (also, in addition).

ἐπικρήηνον (ἐπικραιαίνω), aor. imperat.

ἐπι-μέμφ-ομαι, ἐπιμέμψομαι*, ἐπεμεμψάμην*, ἐπεμέμφθην* blame, find fault (with), reproach.

ἐπιπείθεο (ἐπιπείθω), mid. imperat.

ἐπι-πείθω (πειθ-, ποιθ-, πιθ-), ἐπιπείσω, ἐπέπεισα (ἐπιπέπιθον), ἐπιπέποιθα, ἐπιπέπεισμαι, ἐπεπείσθην* persuade; mid., trust (in), believe, obey.

ἐπι-πλέω (πλευ-, πλεϝ-, πλυ-), ἐπι-
πλεύσομαι, ἐπέπλευσα*, ἐπιπέ-
πλευκα*, ἐπιπέπλευσμαι* sail (up-
on, over), navigate.

ἐπι-ρρώ-ομαι, ἐπερρωσάμην flow down
(upon), fall upon.

ἐπι-σ(σ)εύω (σευ-, συ-), ἐπέσ(σ)ευα,
ἐπέσσυμαι, ἐπεσ(σ)ύθην drive on,
hurry on, urge.

ἐπι-στέφ-ω, ἐπιστέψω*, ἐπέστεψα*
(ἐπεστεψάμην), ἐπέστεμμαι*, ἐπε-
στέφθην* surround, encircle, fill
brimming full.

ἐπιτέλλεο (ἐπιτέλλω), mid. imperat.

ἐπι-τέλλω (τελ-, ταλ-), ἐπέτειλα, ἐπι-
τέταλμαι command, accomplish.

ἐπι-τηδές sufficiently, in sufficient
numbers, appropriately, suitably.

ἐπι-φέρω (φερ-, οἰ-, ἐνεκ-), ἐποίσω,
ἐπήνεικα (ἐπήνεικον), ἐπενήνοχα**,
ἐπενήνεγμαι*, ἐπηνέχθην* bear upon,
bear against.

ἐπι-χθόνιος, ον upon the earth,
earthly, earth-born, of the earth.

ἔπλεο, ἔπλετο (πέλω), 2d aor.

ἐποίσει (ἐπιφέρω).

ἐπ-οίχομαι (οἰχ-, οἰχε-, οἰχο-), ἐποι-
χήσομαι*, ἐπῴχωκα go to, go
against, attack, ply.

ἔπος, εος, τό word, saying, command,
speech.

ἕπω (σεπ-, σπ-), ἕψω, ἔσπον be busy,
perform; mid., follow, accompany,
attend.

ἐπῴχετο (ἐποίχομαι).

ἔργον (ϝέργον), ου, τό work, deed,
accomplishment, feat.

ἔρδω (from ϝερζω: ϝεργ-, ϝοργ-),
ἔρξω, ἔρξα, ἔοργα do, perform, make,
sacrifice, work, accomplish.

ἐρέθιζε (ἐρεθίζω), imperat.

ἐρεθίζω, ἐρεθίσω, ἠρέθισα vex.

ἐρέθ-ω vex, enrage, torment, tease.

ἐρείομεν, vs. 62 (ἐρέω) = ἐρείωμεν (800),
subjunct.

ἐρέοντο (εἴρομαι).

ἐρέουσα (εἴρω), fut. particip., fem.

ἐρέτης, αο, ὁ oarsman, rower, sailor.

ἐρετμόν, οῦ, τό oar.

ἐρέφ-ω*, ἐρέψω*, ἤρεψα roof (over),
cover, build.

ἔρεψα (ἐρέφω) = ἤρεψα (837).

1) ἐρέω (ἐρεϝ-) ask, inquire, seek; 2)
ἐρέω (εἴρω).

ἐρητύ-ω, ἠρήτυσα, ἠρητύθην check,
restrain, control, contain, curb.

ἐρι-βῶλαξ, ακος rich-clodded, heavy-
clodded, fertile.

ἐριδαίνω (ἐριδαν-), ἠριδησάμην quar-
rel, bicker, strive, fight.

ἔριδι, ἔριδος (ἔρις, ἔριδος, ἡ).

ἐρίζω (ἐριδ-), ἤρισ(σ)α, ἐρήρισμαι*
quarrel, strive, fight.

ἔρις, ιδος, ἡ strife, quarrel, fight.

ἐρίσαντε (ἐρίζω), aor. particip.

ἕρκος, εος, τό hedge, fence, defense,
bulwark, barrier.

ἕρμα, ατος, τό beam, prop, support,
stay.

ἔρος, ου, ὁ love, desire, passion.

ἐρύσ(σ)ομεν, vs. 141 (ἐρύω) = aor.
subjunct. (800).

ἐρύω (ϝερυ-, ϝρυ-), ἐρύω, εἴρυσ(σ)α,
εἴρῦ(σ)μαι draw, drag, launch.

ἔρχομαι (ἐρχ-, ἐλθ-, ἐλευθ-, ἐλυθ-),
ἐλεύσομαι, ἦλθον (ἤλυθον), ἐλήλυθα
(εἰλήλουθα) come, go.

ἐρωέ-ω, ἐρωήσω, ἠρώησα flow, spout,
spurt, dash.

ἐς = εἰς.

ἔσαν (εἰμί) = ἦσαν (837), imperf.

ἔσεαι, ἔσ(σ)εται (εἰμί).

ἐσθλός, ή, όν good, noble, brave, true,
helpful, kind(ly), virile.

ἔσονται (εἰμί).

ἐσπόμεθα (ἕπω).

ἔσ(σ)εται, ἐσσί, ἐσσόμενα, ἔσται (εἰμί).

ἔσταν (ἵστημι), 2d aor.

ἐστέ (εἰμί).

ἔστησαν (ἵστημι).

ἐστί(ν), ἐστόν, ἔστω, ἔστων (εἰμί).

ἔσφαξαν (σφάζω).

ἔτ᾽ = ἔτι (575).

ἑταῖρος (ἕταρος, 571), ου, ὁ comrade, companion, follower, friend.

ἔτεκες (τίκτω).

ἐτέλεσ(σ)as (τελείω).

ἑτέρωθεν from the other side.

ἐτ-ήτυμος, ον true, unfailing, sure, real, actual.

ἔτι still, in addition, further(more).

ἔτῑσας, ἔτῑσε (τίνω).

ἔτλη (*τλάω).

ἑτοιμάζω* (ἑτοιμαδ-), ἑτοιμάσω*, ἡτοίμασ(σ)α prepare, make ready.

ἐτράπετο (τρέπω).

ἐύ, εὖ well, successfully, happily, prosperously, favorably, luckily.

ἐύ-δμητος, ον well-built.

ἐύ-ζωνος, ον well-girded, beautiful-waisted.

εὔκηλος, ον undisturbed, in peace, (in) calm, quiet.

ἐυ-κνήμῑς, ῖδος well-greaved.

εὐνή, ῆς, ἡ bed, sleeper, anchor-stone, lair, den.

εὐξαμένοιο, εὐξαμένου, εὔξαντο (εὔχομαι).

εὑρίσκω (εὑρ-, εὑρε-), εὑρήσω*, εὗρον, εὕρηκα*, εὕρημαι*, εὑρέθην* find, come upon, hit upon.

Εὐρυ-βάτης, āο, ὁ Eurybates.

εὐρύ-οψ, οπος far-thundering (cf. ὑψι-βρεμέτης); possibly far-seeing.

εὐρύς, εῖα, ύ wide, broad, large.

ἐύς, ἐῆος mighty, valiant, good(ly).

εὖτε when, as.

ἐυ-τείχεος, ον well-walled.

εὔχ-ομαι, εὔξομαι, ηὐξάμην, ηὔγμαι* pray, talk loud, boast, exult.

εὐχωλή, ῆς, ἡ vow, boast, prayer.

ἐφ᾽ = ἔπι = ἐπί.

ἔφατο (φημί).

ἐφείω (ἐφίημι), 2d aor. subjunct.

ἐφέννῡμι (ἐπιέννῡμι).

ἐφετμή, ῆς, ἡ command, request, behest, prescription.

ἔφη (φημί).

ἐφῆκε(ν), ἐφήσεις (ἐφίημι).

ἔφησ(θα) (φημί).

ἐφθίαθ᾽ (φθίνω) = ἐφθίατο (575, 582), 3d plur., pluperf.

ἐφιείς (ἐφίημι), particip.

ἐφ-ί-ημι (ση-, σε-, = ἡ-, ἑ-, 603–604), ἐφήσω, ἐφέηκα (ἐφῆκα), ἐφεῖκα*, ἐφεῖμαι*, ἐφείθην shoot against, hurl upon, send upon.

ἔχ᾽ (ἔχω) = ἔεχε = εἶχε (837, 584–585).

ἐχε-πευκής, ές sharp, biting.

ἔχετο (ἔχω) = ἐέχετο = εἴχετο (837, 584–585).

ἔχθιστος, η, ον (ἐχθρός, ή, όν), superlat.

*ἐχθο-δοπέ-ω, ἠχθοδόπησα engage in hostility with, be hateful.

ἐχθρός, ή, όν hateful, hated, enemy, odious, hostile.

ἔχον (ἔχω) = ἔεχον = εἶχον (837, 584–585).

ἔχω (σεχ-, σχ-, σχε-), ἕξω (σχήσω), ἔσχον (ἔσχεθον), ὄχωκα, ἔσχημαι* (-ώγμαι) have, hold, keep.

ἔω, ἐών (εἰμί).

Z

ζά-θεος, η, ον very sacred, holy, sacrosanct.

Ζεύς, Διός, ὁ Zeus, father and king of gods and men.

ζώ-ω live.

H

ἤ (ἠέ) or, than, whether; ἤ . . . ἤ either . . . or, whether . . . or.

1) ἦ surely, indeed, truly, for a fact, certainly.

2) ἦ (ἠμί), imperf. 3d sing.

ἡ (ὁ, ἡ, τό).

ἥ (ὅς, ἥ, ὅ).

ἠγά-θεος, η, ον very sacred, holy, sacrosanct (ἀγα-, 1168, 571).

ἥ γε (ὅ γε, ἥ γε, τό γε).

ἡγέ-ομαι, ἡγήσομαι, ἡγησάμην, ἥγημαι* lead (the way), guide, command, rule.

ἥγερθεν (ἀγείρω), aor. pass. 3d plur.

ἡγήσατο (ἡγέομαι).

ἠγνοίησε (ἀγνοιέω).

ἥγομεν (ἄγω).

ἠδέ and, also, on the other hand.

1) ἤδη already, now, at this time.

2) ὕδη (*εἴδω), pluperf.

ἦδος, εος, τό use, utility, advantage, superiority.

ἡδυ-επής, ές sweet-toned, sweet-speaking.

ἡδύς, εῖα, ύ sweet.

ἠέ, ἦέ = ἤ.

ἠέλιος, ου, ὁ sun.

ἦεν (εἰμί).

ἠέριος, η, ον early in the morning; possibly clad in mist.

Ἠετίων, ωνος, ὁ Eëtion, father of Andromache.

ἤθελον (ἐθέλω).

ἥιε (εἶμι).

ἧκε (ἵημι).

ἤκουσαν (ἀκούω).

ἤλασαν (ἐλάω).

ἦλθε, ἦλθον (ἔρχομαι).

ἧλος, ου, ὁ nail, rivet, stud.

ἤλυθον (ἔρχομαι).

ἧμαι (ἦσ-) sit, be seated.

ἦμαρ, ατος, τό day.

ἠμείβετο (ἀμείβω).

ἠ-μέν surely, indeed, truly, on the one hand ; correl. with ἠδέ.

ἠμένη, ἥμενον (ἧμαι).

ἡμέτερος, η, ον our(s).

ἠμί (ἠγ-), imperf. ἦν, speak, say, tell.

ἡμῖν (ἐγώ).

ἦμος when.

ἦν = ἄν if.

ἦν : 1) (ὅς, ἥ, ὅ) ; 2) (ὅς, ἥ, ὅν).

ἥνδανε (ἀνδάνω).

ἧος while, until.

ἠπείλησε (ἀπειλέω).

ἤπειρος, ου, ἡ main(land), continent.

ἦρα, indecl., τά favor, benefit, pleasure, kindness, protection.

ἠρᾶθ᾽ (ἀράομαι) = ἠρᾶτο = ἠράετο (584–585, 575, 582).

Ἥρη, ης, ἡ Hera, consort of Zeus and queen of the gods.

ἠρήσατο (ἀράομαι).

ἠρι-γένειος, α, ον early-born, born early in the morning.

ἦρχε (ἄρχω).

ἥρως, ωος, ὁ hero, mighty warrior, protector, savior.

ἧς : 1) (ὅς, ἥ, ὅ) ; 2) (ὅς, ἥ, ὅν).

ἦσθαι (ἧμαι).

ἧσι, vv. 205, 333 (ὅς, ἥ, ὅν).

ἧστο (ἧμαι).

ἠτίμασε(ν) (ἀτῑμάζω).

ἠτίμησε (ἀτῑμάω).

ἦ τοι surely, indeed, truly, for a fact, certainly.

ἦτορ, ορος, τό heart, soul, spirit.

ηὔδᾱ (αὐδάω) = ηὔδαε (584–585).

ἠΰ-κομος, ον fair-haired, well-haired, beautiful-tressed, well-tressed, having a rich harvest of long, flowing hair (= ἐΰ-κομος, 1168, 571).

ἠΰτε just as, like.

Ἥφαιστος, ου, ὁ Hephaestus, the lame god of fire.

ἠχήεις, εσσα, εν (onomatopoetic) (re)echoing, roaring, (re)sounding, thundering.

ἧχι where.

ἥψατο (ἅπτω).

Ἠώς, Ἠόος, ἡ goddess of the dawn, dawn.

ἠώς, ἠόος, ἡ dawn.

Θ

θ᾽ = τέ (575, 582).

θάλασσα, ης, ἡ sea.

θαμβέ-ω, θαμβήσω*, ἐθάμβησα wonder, be amazed, be frightened, stand aghast.

θαμέες, ειαί, έα thick, crowded.

θάνατος, ου, ὁ death.

θαρσέ-ω, θαρσήσω*, ἐθάρσησα, τεθάρσηκα take heart, take courage, be bold, dare, be resolute.

θεά, ᾶς, ἡ goddess, divinity.

θείνω (θεν-), θενέω*, ἔθεινα strike, hit, beat.

θέλε (ἐθέλω) = ἔθελε, imperat.

θέμις, ιστος, ἡ custom, law, decree, justice, oracle, rule.

-θεν (gen. ending, 712), from.

θεο-είκελος, ον godlike.

θεο-προπέ-ω prophesy, inquire of a god, declare an oracle, interpret the divine will.

θεο-προπίη, ης, ἡ oracle, prophecy.

θεο-πρόπιον, ου, τό oracle, prophecy.

θεός, οῦ, ὁ god, divinity.

θεράπων, οντος, ὁ attendant, squire, comrade.

θέσαν (τίθημι) = ἔθεσαν (837), 2d aor.

θε-σπέσιος, η, ον divine, marvelous, divinely sounding.

Θεστορίδης, āο, ὁ son of Thestor, Calchas.

Θέτις, ιδος, ἡ Thetis, a sea-goddess, wife of Peleus, and mother of Achilles.

θέω (θευ-, θεϜ-), θεύσομαι run, speed.

Θήβη, ης, ἡ Thebe, a city in Asia Minor.

θῆκε(ν) (τίθημι) = ἔθηκε(ν) (837).

θήομεν (τίθημι) = θήωμεν (800), 2d aor., subjunct.

Θησέα (Θησεύς, ῆος, ὁ) = Θησῆα (572).

Θησεύς, ῆος, ὁ Theseus.

θίς, θῑνός, ἡ beach, shore, strand.

θνήσκω (θνη-, θαν-), θανέομαι, ἔθανον, τέθνηκα die, be killed.

θνητός, ή, όν mortal, human.

θοός, ή, όν swift, speedy, quick.

θρόνος, ου, ὁ THRONE, seat, arm-chair.

θυγάτηρ, τέρος, τρός, ἡ DAUGHTER.

θῡμός, οῦ, ὁ heart, soul, spirit, courage, passion.

θΰ-ω, ἔθῡσα rush (headlong), dash, be rash, rage, be insane.

θωρήσσω* (θωρήσσομαι) (θωρηκ-), θωρήξομαι, ἐθώρηξα, ἐθωρήχθην arm, don the cuirass, put on the breastplate.

Ι

ἰάχω (ϜιϜαχ-, ϜιϜαχε-), ἴαχα shout, howl, roar.

ἴδῃ (*εἴδω), 2d aor. subjunct.

ἴδμεν (*εἴδω), perf.

Ἰδομενεύς, ῆος, ὁ Idomeneus, leader of the Cretans.

ἴδον, ἰδοῦσα (*εἴδω), 2d aorr.

ἰδυίη (*εἴδω), perf. particip., fem.

ἴδωμαι, ἰδών (*εἴδω), 2d aorr.

ἵει (ἵημι).

ἰέναι (εἶμι).

ἱερεύς, ῆος, ὁ priest, holy man.

ἱερόν, οῦ, τό sacrifice, sacred rite, victim for sacrifice (1168).

ἱερός, ή, όν sacred, holy.

ἵ-ημι (= σισημι, ση-, σε-, = ἡ-, ἑ-, 603-604), ἥσω, ἕηκα (ἧκα), εἷκα*, εἷμαι*, εἵθην throw, hurl, shoot, send.

ἴθι (εἶμι), imperat.

ἱκ-ἄν-ω come (upon), go.

ἵκμενος, η, ον (cf. ἵκω) favorable, prospering, welcome.

ἱκ-νέ-ομαι, ἵξομαι, ἱκόμην, ἷγμαι come, arrive, reach (one's destination).

ἵκ-ω, ἵξον come, go.

ἵλᾱος, η, ον propitious, kind(ly), gentle, favorable.

ἱλά-σκομαι, ἱλάσ(σ)ομαι, ἱλασ(σ)άμην, ἱλάσθην* propitiate, appease.

Ἴλιος, ου, ἡ Ilium, Troy, the Troad, i.e. the region around Troy.

ἵμεν(αι) (εἶμι) (infin., 965).

ἵνα in order that, (so) that, where.

ἵξεται (ἱκνέομαι).

ἰόνθ' (εἶμι) = ἰόντα (vs. 567) (575, 582), particip.

ἰός, οῦ, ὁ arrow.

ἰούσης (εἶμι), fem. particip.

ἵππος, ου, ὁ, ἡ horse, mare.

ἵπ-τομαι*, ἵψομαι, ἱψάμην crush, overwhelm. punish, afflict.

ἵς, ἵνός, ἡ (instrumental ἷφι) power, might, strength, violence.

ἴσαν (εἶμι), imperf., 965.

ἴσος, η (ἴση), ον equal, equivalent, well-balanced, symmetrical.

ἵ-στημι (σιστημι : στη-, στα-, 603–604), στήσω, ἔστησα (ἔστην), ἔστηκα, ἵσταμαι*, ἐστάθην set up, stand, make stand, take one's stand, station.

ἱστίον, ου, τό sail.

ἱστο-δόκη, ης, ἡ mast-receiver.

ἱστός, οῦ, ὁ loom, mast.

ἵσχεο (ἴσχω), imperat.

ἴσχω (ἰσχ- = σι-σ(ε)χ-) another form of ἔχω have, hold, keep.

ἴτε, ἴτην (εἶμι) (965).

ἴφθῑμος, (η), ον mighty, valiant, stout-hearted, brave, 723–724.

ἷφι (ἵς, ἵνός, ἡ), instrumental, mightily, with might.

ἴψαο (ἵπτομαι).

ἰών (εἶμι) (particip. 965).

K

κ' = κέ(ν) (575).

καθ-άπτω (ἀφ-), καθάψω* (καθάψομαι), καθῆψα, καθῆμμαι, καθήφθην* lay hold, attach, attack, accost, address.

καθ-έζομαι (σεδ-, = ἑδ-, 603–604), καθέσσομαι, καθεῖσα, καθε(ε)σσάμην sit down, seat.

καθ-εύδω (εὐδ-, εὐδε-), καθευδήσω* sleep, slumber, rest (in bed), lie (in bed).

κάθ-ημαι (ἡσ-), sit down, be seated.

κάθησο (κάθημαι), imperat.

καθῆστο (κάθημαι), imperf.

καί and, also, even, furthermore ; καί . . . καί both . . . and, not only . . . but also.

Καινεύς, ῆος (έος, 572), ὁ Caeneus.

καίω (καυ-, καϝ-, και-), καύσω*, ἔκηα, κέκαυκα*, κέκαυμαι*, ἐκάην burn, consume.

κακκείοντες (κατακείω) = κατ(α)κείοντες, pres. particip.

κακός, ή, όν bad, poor, ugly, mean, cowardly, wicked, evil.

κακῶς evilly, wickedly, harshly, cowardly.

καλέω (καλε-, κλη-), καλέω, ἐκάλεσ-(σ)α, κέκληκα*, κέκλημαι, ἐκλήθην* call, summon, convoke.

καλλι-πάρῃος, ον beautiful-cheeked, fair-cheeked.

κᾱλός, ή, όν good(ly), noble, brave, fair, righteous, beautiful, handsome.

καλύπτω (καλυβ-), καλύψω, ἐκάλυψα, κεκάλυμμαι, ἐκαλύφθην cover, conceal, hide, envelop.

Κάλχᾱς, αντος, ὁ Calchas.

κάμνω (καμ-, κμη-), καμέομαι, ἔκαμον, κέκμηκα do, make, toil, be weary, suffer, accomplish with pain.
κάμω (κάμνω), 2d aor. subjunct.
καπνός, οῦ, ὁ smoke, mist, vapor, fume.
κάππεσον (καταπίπτω) = καππεσον = κατέπεσον (837, 608, 609).
καρδίη (κραδίη, 597–598), ης, ἡ heart.
κάρη, κρᾱτός (κάρητος), τό head, peak, summit.
κάρηνον, ου, τό peak, summit, headland, citadel.
καρπαλίμως quickly, suddenly, swiftly.
καρπός, οῦ, ὁ fruit, crop, produce, harvest.
καρτερός, ή, όν (κρατερός, ή, όν, 597–598), strong, mighty, severe, harsh, stern.
κάρτιστος (κράτιστος, 597–598), η, ον, superl. of καρτερός, ή, όν mightiest, strongest, bravest, most excellent, harshest, sternest.
κατά, adv., and prep. with gen. and acc., down (from, over, through); adv., down, below; with gen., down (over, from, below); with acc., down (along, through), according to, on.
κατα-δύ-ω, καταδύσω, κατέδῡσα (κατέδῡν), καταδέδῡκα, καταδέδυμαι*, κατεδύθην* go down, sink, set, dive.
κατα-καίω (καυ-, καϝ-, και-), κατακαύσω*, κατέκηα, κατακέκαυκα*, κατακέκαυμαι*, κατεκάην burn down, consume.
κατα-κεί-ω desire to lie down (rest, slumber, repose).
κατάνευσον (κατανεύω), aor. imperat.
κατα-νεύ-ω, κατανεύσω, κατένευσα, κατανένευκα* nod (down, assent).
κατα-πέσσω (πεκ-, πεπ-), καταπέψω*,

κατέπεψα, καταπέπεμμαι*, κατεπέφθην* digest, repress, cook.
καταπέψῃ (καταπέσσω), aor. subjunct.
κατα-πίπτω (πετ-, πτε-, πτη-), καταπεσέομαι, κατέπεσον (κάππεσον), καταπέπτη(κ)α fall down, drop.
κατα-ρέζω (ϝρεγ-), καταρέξω, κατέρ(ρ)εξα, κατερέχθην caress, stroke, fondle.
κατέδῡ (καταδύω).
κατέρ(ρ)εξε(ν) (καταρέζω).
κέ(ν) = ἄν, 1085–1091.
κεῖ-μαι, κείσομαι lie, recline, repose.
κεῖνος, η, ο = ἐκεῖνος, η, ο that (one), he, she, it.
κελαι-νεφής, ές black-clouded, wrapped in dark clouds.
κελαινός, ή, όν black, dark, dusky.
κέλευθος, ου, ἡ (plur. κέλευθοι and κέλευθα), road, way, path, journey, route.
κέλομαι (κελ-, κελε-, κλ-) κελήσομαι, ἐκελησάμην* (ἐκεκλόμην) urge, command, bid, request.
κέ(ν) = ἄν (1085–1091), haply, perchance, perhaps.
κερδαλεό-φρων, ον crafty-minded, cunning (-minded), sly, mindful of gain.
κερτόμιος, ον biting, cutting, sharp, bitter, contemptuous, reviling.
κεῦθε (κεύθω), imperat.
κεύθω (κευθ-, κυθ-), κεύσω, ἔκευσα (ἔκυθον, κέκυθον), κέκευθα hide, conceal, enclose.
κεφαλή, ῆς, ἡ head.
κεχαροίατο (χαίρω), 2d aor. optat.
κεχολωμένον, κεχολώσεται (χολόω).
κῆδος, εος, τό woe, grief, care, sorrow, concern, suffering.
κήδω (κηδ-, κηδε-, καδ-), κηδήσω, ἐκήδησα*, κέκηδα* grieve, distress, hurt, afflict.

κῆλον, ου, τό arrow, dart, shaft.

κήρ, κηρός, ἡ death, fate.

κῆρ, κῆρος, τό heart, soul.

κῆρυξ, ῦκος, ὁ herald.

κίε(ν) (κίω) = ἔκιεν (837).

Κίλλα, ης, ἡ Cilla, a town in the Troad.

κῑνέ-ω*, κῑνήσω*, ἐκίνησα, κεκίνημαι*, ἐκῑνήθην move, stir; mid. and pass., move (self), bestir, go, come.

κῑνηθέντος (κῑνέω), aor. pass. particip.

κιχᾰνω (κιχ-, κιχε-), κιχήσομαι, ἐκιχησάμην (ἔκιχον, ἐκίχην) come upon, overtake, arrive at.

κιχήω (κιχάνω), aor. subjunct.

κίω come, go, depart.

κιών (κίω), particip.

κλαγγή, ῆς, ἡ CLANG, noise, shriek (up)roar.

κλάζω (κλαγγ-), κλάγξω*, ἔκλαγξα, κέκληγα CLANG, roar, shriek, resound.

κλαίω (κλαυ-, κλαϝ-, κλαι-, κλαιε-), κλαύσομαι, ἔκλαυσα, κέκλαυ(σ)μαι* cry, weep.

κλέπτε (κλέπτω), imperat.

κλέπτω (κλεπ-, κλοπ-, κλαπ-), κλέψω*, ἔκλεψα, κέκλοφα**, κέκλεμμαι*, ἐκλέφθην† (ἐκλάπην*) steal, be stealthy, deceive, hide.

κλεύω (κλευ-, κλεϝ-, κλυ-), ἔκλυον (κέκλυον), κέκλυκα hear, hearken to.

κλισίη, ης, ἡ hut, barrack, tent.

κλισίηθεν, gen. ablat. sing., from the barrack (hut, tent).

κλισίηνδε (788, 4) to the hut (barrack, tent).

κλῦθι (*κλεύω), aor. imperat.

Κλυται-μ(ν)ήστρη, ης, ἡ Clytaem-(n)estra, wife of Agamemnon.

κλυτο-τέχνης, ες renowned for skill in handicraft, of renowned skill.

κνέφας, αος, τό darkness, night, gloom.

κνίση, ης, ἡ fat, savor, odor of roast meat.

κοῖλος (κόιλος), η, ον hollow.

κοιμᾶθ' (κοιμάω) = ἐκοιμᾶτο = ἐκοιμάετο (575, 582, 584-585, 837).

κοιμά-ω (cf. κεῖμαι), κοιμήσω*, ἐκοίμησα, ἐκοιμήθην (lull to) sleep, slumber, lie down.

κο(υ)λεόν (571), οῦ, τό sheath, scabbard (1168).

κολῳός, οῦ, ὁ brawl, wrangle, quarrel.

κόμη, ης, ἡ hair, locks, tresses.

κομίζω (κομιδ-), κομιῶ, ἐκόμισ(σ)α, κεκόμικα**, κεκόμισμαι*, ἐκομίσθην* care for, attend, accompany, bear (off).

κομίσαντο (κομίζω) = ἐκομίσαντο (837)

κορυφή, ῆς, ἡ peak, summit, crest.

κορωνίς, ίδος curved, bent.

κοσμήτωρ, ορος, ὁ marshal(ler), commander.

κοτέ-ω, ἐκότεσ(σ)α, (-άμην), κεκότη(κ)α hold a grudge, be vindictive, be angry.

κότος, ου, ὁ grudge, rancor, hate.

κουλεόν (κολεόν, 571), οῦ, τό sheath, scabbard (1168).

κούρη, ης, ἡ girl, maid(en), young woman.

κουρίδιος, η, ον lawfully wedded, legally married, married in youth.

κοῦρος, ου, ὁ young man, noble, page.

κραδίη, ης, ἡ = καρδίη, ης, ἡ (597-598).

κρ(αι)αίνω (κραν-), ἐκρήηνα accomplish, perform, fulfill.

κρατερός, ή, όν = καρτερός, ή, όν (597-598).

κρατέω (κρατεσ-) rule, bear sway.

κρᾱτός (κάρη, κρᾱτός, τό).

332

κράτος, εος, τό power, might, sway, rule, victory, strength, dominion.

κρείσσων, ον (cf. κράτος power) comparat., mightier, more powerful, better.

κρείων, ουσα, ον ruling, prince(ss), ruler.

κρήγυος, ον good, helpful, favorable, honest, true, truthful, useful.

κρήηνον (κραιαίνω) aor. imperat.

κρητήρ, ῆρος, ὁ mixing-bowl, punch-bowl.

κρίνω (κριν-, κρι-), κρινέω, ἔκρῖνα, κέκρικα**, κέκριμαι, ἐκρί(ν)θην pick out, select, choose, discern, decide, judge.

Κρονίδης, āο, ὁ son of Cronus, Zeus.

Κρονίων, ωνος, ὁ son of Cronus, Zeus.

κρυπτάδιος, η, ον hidden, secret.

κτείνω (κτεν-, κτον-, κτα-ν-), κτενέω, ἔκτεινα (ἔκταν, ἔκτανον), ἔκτονα*, ἐκτάθην kill, slay, murder.

κῡάνεος, η, ον dark (blue), black, dusky (1168).

κῡδι-άνειρα fem., man-ennobling, bringing glory to men.

κῡδιστος, η, ον (cf. κῦδος) superl., most glorious.

κῦδος, εος, τό glory, honor, renown.

κῦμα, ατος, τό swelling wave, billow.

κύνας, κύνεσσι(ν), κυνός (κύων, κυνός, ὁ, ἡ).

κυν-ώπης (voc. κυνῶπα) dog-faced, dog-eyed, shameless.

κύπελλον, ου, τό cup, goblet.

κύων, κυνός, ὁ, ἡ dog.

κώπη, ης, ἡ hilt, handle.

Λ

λάβε (λαμβάνω) = ἔλαβε (837).

λαβέ (λαμβάνω), 2d aor. imperat. (902, 1).

λαμβάνω* (λαβ-, ληβ-), λάψομαι†,

ἔλαβον, λελάβηκα†, λέλαμμαι. ἐλάμφθην† (ἐλήφθην*) take, seize, lay hold of, accept.

λαμπ-ετά-ω shine, gleam, blaze, flame.

λαμπετόωντι (λαμπετάω), particip. (945-948).

λαμπρός, ή, όν bright, brilliant, shining, gleaming.

λᾱός, οῦ, ὁ people, host, soldiery.

λάσιος, η, ον hairy, shaggy, rough, bushy.

λείβ-ω, ἔλειψα pour a libation.

λείπω (λειπ-, λοιπ-, λιπ-), λείψω, ἔλιπον, λέλοιπα, λέλειμμαι, ἐλείφθην* leave, forsake, abandon, desert.

λέλοιπε(ν) (λείπω).

λέπω* (λεπ-, λαπ-), λέψω, ἔλεψα, λέλαμμαι*, ἐλάπην* strip, peel, scale, hull.

λευκός, ή, όν white, shining.

λευκ-ώλενος, ον white-armed.

λεύσσω (λευκ-) see, behold, observe, LOOK.

λέχος, εος, τό bed, couch.

λῆγ᾽ (λήγω) = 1) λῆγε (575), imperat.; 2) ἔληγε (575, 837), imperf.

λήγ-ω, λήξω, ἔληξα cease (from), refrain, SLACKEN, weaken.

λήθ-ω escape the notice, be hidden ; mid., forget, lose sight of.

Λῆμνος, ου, ἡ Lemnos, an island in the Aegean near Troy.

Λητοῦς (Λητώ, όος, ἡ) = Λητόος (584-585).

Λητώ, όος, ἡ Leto, mother of Apollo.

λιάζομαι (λιαδ-), ἐλίασσα, ἐλιάσθην bend, turn aside, sink, fall.

λιγύς, εῖα, ύ shrill, clear-toned.

λίην exceedingly, very, especially.

λιμήν, ένος, ὁ harbor, anchoring-place.

λίσαι (λίσσομαι), aor. imperat.

λίσσομαι (λιτ-), ἐλ(λ)ισάμην (ἐλιτό-μην) beg, entreat.

λοίγιος, η, ον dreadful, destructive, accursed, horrible, nasty, deadly.

λοιγός, οῦ, ὁ destruction, ruin, curse, death.

λοιμός, οῦ, ὁ pest(ilence), plague.

λόχονδε (λόχον, -δε) (788, 4) to an ambush.

λόχος, ου, ὁ ambush, ambuscade.

λῦμα, ατος, τό offscouring, filth.

λῦσαι (λύω), aor. infin.

λύσαιτε (λύω), aor. optat.

λῦσαν (λύω) = ἔλῦσαν, 837.

λύ-ω, λύσω, ἔλῦσα, λέλυκα*, λέλυμαι, ἐλύθην loose, free, break up, destroy.

λωβά-ομαι*, λωβήσομαι*, ἐλωβησάμην insult, revile, act arrogantly, ruin, wrong.

λωβήσαιο (λωβάομαι), aor. optat.

λωίων, ον, comparat. of ἀγαθός, ή, όν better, superior, preferable.

M

μ' (ἐγώ) = με (575), acc.

μά (cf. μέν, μήν), adv. used in swearing, surely, verily.

μάκαρ, αρος blessed, happy, fortunate, lucky.

μακρός, ή, όν long, high, lofty, large, distant.

μάλα very, exceedingly, even, by all means, much, enough.

μαλακός, ή, όν soft, gentle, tender, mild.

μάλιστα, superl. of μάλα, most, especially, by all means.

μᾶλλον, comparat. of μάλα, more, rather, preferably.

μαντεύ-ομαι, μαντεύσομαι, ἐμαντευσάμην predict, prophesy, act as seer, divine.

μάντις, ιος, ὁ seer, prophet, soothsayer.

μαντοσύνη, ης, η gift of prophecy.

μάρνα-μαι strive, fight, contend.

μάρτυρος, ου, ὁ witness.

μαχέ-ομαι (= μάχ-ομαι), μαχήσομαι (-έσσομαι?) (μαχέομαι), ἐμαχεσ-(σ)άμην, μεμάχημαι* fight, battle.

μάχη, ης, ἡ battle, fight, fray.

μάχ-ομαι fight, battle.

με (ἐγώ).

μεγά-θῡμος, ον great-souled.

μέγαρον, ου, τό great hall; plur. palace.

μέγας, μεγάλη, μέγα large, great, mighty, tall.

μέγιστος, η, ον, superl. of μέγας, μεγάλη, μέγα.

μεθέμεν(αι) (μεθίημι), 2d aor. infin.

μεθ-ί-ημι (ση-, -σε = ἥ-, ἕ-, 603-604), μεθήσω, μεθέηκα (μεθῆκα), μεθείκα*, μεθεῖμαι*, μεθείθην let go, give up, forego, dismiss.

μεθ-ομῑλέ-ω, μεθωμῑλησα associate with, consort with.

μειδά-ω. ἐμείδησα smile, laugh.

μείζων, ον, comparat. of μέγας, larger, greater, mightier, taller.

μεῖναι (μένω), aor. infin.

μείρομαι (σμερ-, σμορ-, σμαρ-), ἔμμορα divide, (receive as) share, receive (as lot); εἵμαρται, perf. mid., it is fated.

μελᾱς, μέλαινα, μέλαν, black, dark, dusky

μελήσεται (μέλω).

μέλι, ιτος, τό honey.

μέλλω (μελλ-, μελλε-), μελλήσω*, ἐμέλλησα* be about, be destined.

μέλπ-ω, μέλψω*, ἔμελψα* sing, dance, hymn, chant.

μέλω (μελ-, μελε-), μελήσω, ἐμέλησα*, μέμηλα, μέμβλεμαι (μεμέλημαι*), ἐμελήθην* be a concern, be a care.

μεμαῶτα (μέμονα), particip.

μέ-μονα (μεν-, μον-, μα-) *perf. only,* be eager, desire greatly, strive zealously, intend, plan.

μέν (*cf.* μήν, μά), *correl. with* δέ, on the one hand, truly ; μὲν . . . δέ on the one hand . . . on the other, partly . . . partly, the one(s) . . . the other(s).

Μενέ-λαος, ου, ὁ Menelaus, *king of Sparta, brother of Agamemnon, and husband of Helen.*

Μενοιτιάδης, āo, ὁ son of Menoetius, *Patroclus.*

μένος, εος, τό rage, anger, might, courage, fury, power, spirit.

μένω (μεν-, μενε-), μενέω, ἔμεινα, μεμένηκα**, remain, await.

μερ-μηρίζω (μηριγ-), ἐμερμήριξα ponder, consider.

μέροψ, οπος mortal, human, man.

μέσ(σ)ος, η, ον middle, midst, medium.

μετά *adv., and prep. with gen., dat., and acc.,* with, in, among, amid, into the midst of, after, next to ; *adv.,* among, after(ward), around, about, in the direction, in pursuit ; *with gen.,* with ; *with dat.,* among, in the midst of ; *with acc.,* among, into the midst of, after, in pursuit of, to.

μετάλλᾱ (μεταλλάω) = μετάλλαε (*584–585*), *imperat.*

μετ-αλλά-ω, μεταλλήσω*, ἐμετάλλησα inquire after, seek to know, search after.

μεταλλῶ = μεταλλάω (*584–585*).

μεταξύ between, intervening.

μετατρέπῃ (μετατρέπω) = μετατρέπεαι (*584–585*), *2d sing.*

μετα-τρέπω (τρεπ-, τροπ-, τραπ-), μετατρέψω, μετέτρεψα (μετέτραπον), μετατέτροφα**, μετατέτραμμαι, μετ-

ετράφθην turn around ; *mid.,* turn oneself toward, heed.

μετά-φημι (φη-, φα-), μεταφήσω, μετέφησα*, *imperf.* μετέφην, μετεφάμην speak among, address, converse with.

μετα-φράζω (φραδ-), μεταφράσω* (μεταφράσ(σ)ομαι), μετέφρασα (μετεπέφραδον), μεταπέφρακα**, μεταπέφρασμαι*, μετεφράσθην tell, point out, declare (later, hereafter, among) ; *mid.,* consider later, plan hereafter, reflect on later.

μετέειπε(ν) (μετεῖπον).

μετ-εῖπον (ϝεπ-), *2d aor.* spoke among, addressed.

μετέφη (μετάφημι).

μετ-όπισθε(ν) afterward(s), later, (here)after.

μεῦ, μευ (ἐγώ).

μή not, lest, that not.

μη-δέ and not, but not, nor, not even ; μηδὲ . . . μηδέ neither . . . nor.

μήν (*cf.* μέν, μά), truly, indeed, surely, verily.

μῆνις, ιος, ἡ wrath, fury, madness, rage.

μηνί-ω, μηνίσω, ἐμήνῑσα rage, fume, be furious, be mad.

μηρίον, ου, τό thigh-bone, thigh-piece.

μῆρον, ου, τό thigh-piece, thigh-bone, thigh.

μηρός, οῦ, ὁ thigh.

μή-τε and not, neither, nor ; μήτε . . . μήτε neither . . . nor.

μήτηρ, τέρος (τρός), ἡ MOTHER, dam.

μητίετα, āo, ὁ counsellor, (prudent) adviser.

μι-μνήσκω (μνα-), μνήσω, ἔμνησα, μέμνημαι, ἐμνήσθην remind, recall, call to mind, remember

μίν, *acc. sing.,* all genders, him, her, it.

μίνυνθα short(ly), for a short time.

μινυνθάδιος, η, ον short-lived, ephemeral, brief.

μίστυλλον = ἐμίστυλλον (837).

μιστύλ-λω slice, cut into bits.

μνήσᾱσα (μιμνήσκω), aor. act. particip., fem.

μογέ-ω, ἐμόγησα toil, struggle, endure hardship.

(ἐ)μοί (ἐγώ).

μοῖρα, ης, ἡ lot, fate, portion, suitability.

μολπή, ῆς, ἡ dance, song, dancing, singing, hymn(ing).

Μοῦσα, ης, ἡ Muse. *The Muses were daughters of Zeus, and were patronesses of music, dancing, poetry, and song.*

μῡθέ-ομαι, μῡθήσομαι, ἐμῡθησάμην speak, tell, declare.

μῦθος, ου, ὁ word, command, story.

μῡρίοι, αι, α countless, innumerable.

Μυρμιδών, όνος, ὁ Myrmidon, *Greek.*

N

ναί yea, yes, verily.

ναίω (νασ-), ἔνασσα, ἐνάσθην dwell, inhabit; *mid.,* be situated.

νέας (νηῦς, νηός, ἡ) = νῆας (572).

νέηαι (νέομαι), *2d sing. subjunct.*

νεικέω (νεικεσ-), νεικέσ(σ)ω, ἐνείκεσ(σ)α struggle, contend, revile, quarrel, fight.

νέκταρ, αρος, τό nectar, drink of the gods.

νέκῡς, υος, ὁ dead body, corpse.

νέομαι (νεσ-), *usually in fut. sense,* come, go, return.

νέος (= νέϝος), η, ον NEW, young, youthful, recent, late.

Νέστωρ, ορος, ὁ Nestor, *the oldest of the Greek chieftains.*

νεύ-ω, νεύσω, ἔνευσα, νένευκα* nod.

νεφελ-ηγερέτα, āο, ὁ cloud-gatherer, wrapped in clouds.

νεῶν (νηῦς, νηός, ἡ) = νηῶν (572).

νεώτερος, η, ον (νέος, η, ον), *comparative.*

νῆα, νῆας, νήεσσι, νηί (νηῦς, νηός, ἡ).

νημερτής, ές unerring, true, truthful, reliable, faithful, infallible, certain.

1) **νηός, οῦ, ὁ** temple, shrine, fane.

2) **νηός, νηυσί (νηῦς, νηός, ἡ).**

νηῦς, νηός, ἡ ship.

νῑκά-ω, νῑκήσω, ἐνίκησα, νενίκηκα*, νενίκημαι*, ἐνῑκήθην conquer, prevail, surpass.

νοεούσῃ (νοέω), *fem. particip.*

νοέ-ω, νοήσω, ἐνόησα, νενόηκα*, νενόημαι*, ἐνοήθην* perceive, think, consider, plan.

νόος, ου, ὁ mind, plan, purpose.

νόσφι(ν) apart, away, aside, separate.

νοῦσος, ου, ἡ plague, pestilence, disease, sickness.

νύ, *encl.,* now, indeed, to be sure, surely, then.

νῦν now, at this time, as matters now are, as it is; *commonly implies a contrast.*

νύξ, νυκτός, ἡ night, darkness.

νωμά-ω, νωμήσω*, ἐνώμησα distribute, apportion, handle easily, brandish.

Ξ

ξανθός, ή, όν tawny, yellow, blond.

ξίφος, εος, τό sword.

ξύν = σύν.

ξυν-δέ-ω (= συν-), ξυνδήσω, ξυνέδησα, ξυνδέδεκα*, ξυνδέδεμαι, ξυνεδέθην* bind (hand and foot), "hog-tie."

ξυνέηκε (ξυνίημι).

ξῡνήιος, η, ον common (stock, possessions).

ξύνιεν (ξυνίημι), *imperf., 3d plur.*

ξυν-ί-ημι (ση-, σε-,= ἡ-, ἱ-, 603–604), ξυνήσω, ξυνέηκα (ξυνῆκα), ξυνεῖκα*, ξυνεῖμαι*, ξυνείθην bring together, throw together, hearken, heed.

Ο

ὁ, ἡ, τό this, that ; he, she, it ; who, which, what.

ὅ (ὅς, ἥ, ὅ).

ὀβελός, οῦ, ὁ spit.

ὅ γε, ἥ γε, τό γε this, that ; he, she, it.

ὅ-δε, ἥ-δε, τό-δε this (here).

ὁδός, οῦ, ἡ road, way, path, journey, expedition.

'Οδυσ(σ)εύς, ῆος, ὁ Odysseus (Ulysses).

ὄζος, ου, ὁ branch, shoot, limb.

ὄθ-ομαι care, consider, reck, regard, worry.

οἱ (ὁ, ἡ, τό).

οἵ (ὅς, ἥ, ὅ).

οἱ (εἷο, ἑο).

οἶδε (*εἴδω).

ὁίεαι (ὀίω), 2d sing.

ὀιζυρός, ή, όν piteous, woeful, miserable.

οἴκαδε (cf. οἶκος -δε, 788, 4) homeward, to home.

οἴκοι (οἶκος), locative, at home.

οἴκόνδε (οἶκος, 788, 4), home(ward), to home.

οἶκος, ου, ὁ house, home.

οἰνο-βαρής, ές WINE-heavy, sot(tish).

οἴνοπα (οἶνοψ, οπος).

οἶνος (Ϝοῖνος), ου, ὁ WINE.

οἰνο-χοέ-ω, ᾠνοχόησα pour WINE, pour drink(s).

οἶν-οψ, οπος WINE-colored, WINE-faced.

οἶος, η, ον alone, sole, only.

οἷος, η, ον such (as), of what sort, what.

οἷς (ὅς, ἥ, ὅν), dat. plur.

οἶσθα (*εἴδω), perf., 2d sing.

ὀιστός, οῦ, ὁ arrow, shaft.

οἴχομαι (οἰχ-, οἰχε-, οἰχο-), οἰχήσομαι*, ᾤχωκα come, go, depart.

ὀίω (ὀίω) (οἰ-, οἰε-), οἰήσομαι*, ᾠισά-μην, ὠίσθην think, suppose, imagine, believe, expect.

οἰωνο-πόλος, ου, ὁ bird-interpreter, augur, soothsayer.

οἰωνός, οῦ, ὁ bird (of prey), vulture, omen.

ὀλέκω kill, destroy, ruin.

ὀλέσ(σ)εις, ὀλέσ(σ)ῃς, ὀλέσ(σ)ῃ (ὀλ-λῦμι).

ὀλίγος, η, ον little, few, small, of slight value, cheap.

ὄλλῦμι (ὀλ-, ὀλε-, ὀλο-), ὀλέσ(σ)ω, ὤλεσ(σ)α, ὄλωλα destroy, kill, ruin, lose ; mid., perish, die.

ὀλο(ι)ός, ή, όν (cf. ὄλλῦμι) accursed, baneful, destructive (571, 1168).

'Ολύμπιος, η, ον Olympian.

"Ολυμπος (Οὔλυμπος, 571), ου, ὁ Olympus, a tall mountain in northern Greece, the home of the gods.

ὀμ-ηγερής, ές collected, gathered, assembled.

ὁμῖλέ-ω, ὁμῑλήσω*, ὡμίλησα associate with, collect.

ὁμίχλη, ης, ἡ mist, fog, cloud, vapor.

ὄμμα, ατος, τό eye ; plur., face.

ὄμνῦμι (ὀμ-, ὀμε-, ὀμο-), ὀμοῦμαι (= ὀμό(σ)ομαι = ὀμόομαι, 603–604, 584–585), ὤμοσ(σ)α, ὀμώμοκα*, ὀμώμο(σ)μαι*, ὠμό(σ)θην* pledge with an oath, swear (by, to).

ὁμοῖος, η, ον equal, similar.

ὁμοιό-ω*, ὁμοιώσω*, ὡμοιώθην liken, make like, compare, make equal.

ὄμοσ(σ)ον (ὄμνῦμι), aor. imperat.

ὁμοῦ together, at the same time.

ὀμοῦμαι (ὄμνῦμι), fut.

ὁμῶς equally, alike, together, at the same time.

ὅν (ὅς, ἥ, ὅ), (ὅς, ἥ, ὅν).

ὄναρ, indecl., τό dream.

ὀνείδειος, ον reviling, abusive, slanderous.

ὀνειδίζω (cf. ὄνειδος), ὠνείδισα revile, slander, reproach, abuse.

ὀνείδισον (ὀνειδίζω), aor. imperat.

ὄνειδος, εος, τό abuse, slander, reviling, insult.

ὀνειρο-πόλος, ου, ὁ dream-interpreter, dreamer of dreams.

ὄνησα (ὀνίνημι) = ὤνησα (837).

ὀνίνημι (ὀνη-, ὀνα-), ὀνήσω, ὤνησα, ὠνήθην* help, benefit, favor, assist, profit, be useful.

ὀνομάζω (cf. ὄνομα name), ὀνομάσω*, ὠνόμοσα, ὠνόμακα**, ὠνόμασμαι*, ὠνομάσθην* address, call (by name).

ὀξύς, εῖα, ύ sharp, biting, keen, cutting, acid.

ὀπί (ὄψ, ὀπός, ἡ).

ὄπι(σ)θε(ν) behind, from behind, later, latter.

ὀπίσ(σ)ω back(ward), behind, later.

ὁ(π)-πότε when(ever).

ὅ(π)-πως that, in order that, how that.

ὀπτά-ω, ὤπτησα, ὠπτήθην cook, roast, bake.

ὅ(π)πως see above.

ὁρᾶτο (ὁράω) = ὡράετο (837, 584–585).

ὁράω (Ϝορ-, Ϝιδ-, ὀπ-), ὄψομαι, εἶδον ὄπωπα, ὦμμαι* (ἑώρᾱμαι)*, ὤφθην* see, behold, look, observe.

ὀρέγ-νῡμι (= ὀρέγω) reach forth, stretch out, extend.

ὀρεγνύς (ὀρέγνῡμι), particip.

ὀρέγ-ω (cf. ὀρέγνῡμι), ὀρέξω, ὤρεξα, ὀρώρεγμαι, ὠρέχθην* reach forth, stretch out, extend.

ὀρέσ-κῳος, ον living in mountain dens, lying in mountain lairs.

ὅρκος, ου, ὁ oath, that by which one swears (as witness).

ὁρμαίνω (ὁρμαν-), ὥρμηνα toss about, turn over (in mind), turn about, consider, plan, ponder.

ὅρμος, ου, ὁ anchorage.

ὄρ-νῡμι, ὄρσω, ὦρσα (ὤρορον), ὄρωρα, ὀρώρεμαι stir up, kindle, incite, excite, arouse.

ὄρος (οὖρος, 571), εος, τό mountain.

ὀρόων (ὁράω) = ὁράων (945–948), pres particip.

ὅς, ἥ, ὅ who, which, what.

ὅς, ἥ, ὅν his, her(s), its (own).

ὅσ(σ)ος, η, ον how much, how many, how large, how great, how long.

ὄσσε, ὄσσοιιν, τώ eyes.

ὄσσομαι (ὀκ-) eye, look (upon), glare at.

ὅσ(σ)ος, η, ον how much, how many, how large, how great, how long.

ὅ(σ)-τις, ἥ-τις, ὅ(τ)-τι who(so)-(ever), which(ever), what(ever).

ὅτ’ = ὅτε (575), when(ever), that.

ὅ(σ)-τε, ἥ-τε, ὅ-τε who, which, what.

ὅ(τ)-τι that, because.

ὅ(τ) τι (ὅστις, ἥτις, ὅ τι).

ὀτρηρός, ή, όν ready, eager, nimble, swift.

ὅ(τ) τι (= ὅ τι).

οὐ, οὐκ, οὐχ not, no.

οὗ (ὅς, ἥ, ὅ).

οὐ-δέ and not, not even, nor, but not.

οὐδ-είς, οὐδε-μία, οὐδ-έν no one, not one, not any, none, nobody, nothing.

οὔθ’ = οὔτε (575, 582).

οὐκ (οὐ).

οὐλόμενος, η, ον (cf. ὄλλῡμι) accursed, destructive, deadly, baneful (1168).

οὐλο-χύτη, ης, ἡ poured-out barley corn.

Οὔλυμπος ("Ολυμπος, ου, ὁ, *571*, 1168).

οὖν therefore, hence, now, then, in fact.

οὔνεκα (= οὗ ἕνεκα) because.

οὔ-ποθ' = οὔ-ποτε (575, 582), not ever, never.

οὔ-πω not ever, never.

Οὐρανίων, ωνος, ὁ, ἡ dweller of heaven, divinity, god(dess).

οὐρανόθεν (*gen. ablat.*), from heaven.

οὐρανός, οῦ, ὁ heaven, sky.

οὐρεύς, ῆος, ὁ mule (ὀρεύς, 1168).

1) οὖρος. ου. ὁ breeze. wind.

2) οὖρος (ὄρος, εος. τό, 571), mountain (1168).

οὔ-τε and not, nor; οὔτε . . . οὔτε neither . . . nor.

οὐ-τιδανός, ή, όν worthless, of no account, cowardly, feeble.

οὗτος, αὕτη, τοῦτο that (one).

οὕτω(s) thus, so, in this way.

ὀφείλω (ὀφελ-, ὀφειλε-), ὀφειλήσω*, ὤφελον, ὠφείληκα**, ὠφειλήθην* owe, ought, be obligated ; *aor. in wishes*, would that !

ὄφελες (ὀφείλω) = ὤφελες (*837*).

ὄφελλε(ν) (ὀφέλλω) = ὤφελλε(ν) (*837*).

1) ὀφέλλω = ὀφείλω.

2) ὀφέλ-λω increase, magnify, swell.

ὀφθαλμός, οῦ, ὁ eye, sight.

ὄφρα until, in order that, while.

ὀφρύς, ύος, ἡ (eye)brow.

ὄχα far, by far.

ὀχθέ-ω*, ὤχθησα be vexed, be displeased, be worried.

ὄψ, ὀπός, ἡ voice, word, speech, language.

Π

παῖδα, παῖδες, παιδός (παῖς, παιδός, ὁ, ἡ).

παιήων, ονος, ὁ PAEAN, song of praise.

παῖς, παιδός, ὁ, ἡ child, son, daughter.

παλάμη, ης, ἡ PALM, hand, fist.

παλίλ-λογος, ον gathered together again, re-collected, re-assembled.

πάλιν back, backward(s), again, anew.

παλιν-άγρετος, ον revocable, to be taken back.

Παλλάς, άδος, ἡ Pallas (Athena).

πάμ-παν completely, altogether, entirely.

πᾶν (πᾶς, πᾶσα, πᾶν).

παν-ημέριος, η, ον all day long, enduring the whole day through.

πάντα, πάντας, πάντες, πάντεσσι (πᾶς, πᾶσα, πᾶν).

πάντη everywhere, throughout.

πάντων (πᾶς, πᾶσα, πᾶν).

παρά (πάρ) adv., and prep., with gen., dat., and acc., from the side of, by the side of, to the side of, beside, along ; adv., beside, near by ; with gen., from (the side of, beside) ; with dat., by (the side of), near, beside ; with acc., to the side of, along (by).

πάρα = παρῆν (πάρειμι).

παρά-φημι (φη-, φα-), παραφήσω, παρέφησα* ; imperf., παρέφην, παρεφάμην advise, counsel, urge, persuade, win over.

παρέξεο (παρέξομαι), imperat.

παρ-έζομαι (σεδ-, = έδ-, 603–604) sit beside, sit near.

πάρ-ειμι (ἐσ-), παρέσ(σ)ομαι be present (at hand, near, beside).

παρ-εῖπον (ϝειπ-) *2d aor.*, persuade, cajole, win over, urge, outwit, delude, beguile, talk over.

παρελεύσεαι (παρέρχομαι).

παρ-έρχομαι (ἐρχ-, ἐλθ-, ἐλευθ-, ἐλυθ-), παρελεύσομαι, παρῆλθον (παρήλυθον), παρελήλυθα (παρειλήλουθα)

339

evade, pass by, outwit, delude,
elude, circumvent.

παρέσσεται (πάρειμι).

πάρ-ημαι (ἡσ-) sit beside.

πάροιθε(ν) before, formerly, in front
of.

πάρος formerly, of old, before this.

πᾶς, πᾶσα, πᾶν all, every, (the)
whole.

πάσαντο (πατέομαι) = ἐπάσαντο (837).

πᾶσι(ν) (πᾶς, πᾶσα, πᾶν).

πατέομαι* (πατ-, πατε-), ἐπασ(σ)ά-
μην, πέπασμαι eat, feed.

πατήρ, πατρός (πατέρος), ὁ FATHER,
sire.

πάτρη, ης, ἡ FATHERland, native
land.

πατρί (πατήρ, πατρός, ὁ).

Πάτροκλος (-έης), ου (-ῆος), ὁ Patro-
clus, chum of Achilles.

πατρός (πατήρ, τρός, ὁ).

παῦε (παύω), imperat.

παύσαντο (παύω) = ἐπαύσαντο (837).

παύσειεν, παύσουσα (παύω).

παύω, παύσω, ἔπαυσα, πέπαυκα*, πέ-
παυμαι, ἐπαύθην* cease, stop,
pause, check, restrain, hold off.

πεῖθεο (πείθω), imperat.

πείθω (πειθ-, ποιθ-, πιθ-), πείσω,
ἔπεισα (πέπιθον), πέποιθα, πέπει-
σμαι*, ἐπείσθην* persuade, win
over, mislead ; mid., trust in, be-
lieve, obey.

πειρά-ω, πειρήσω, ἐπείρησα* (ἐπειρη-
σάμην), πεπείρηκα†, πεπείρημαι,
ἐπειρήθην try, attempt, make trial.

πείρησαι (πειράω), mid. imperat.

Πειρί-θοος, ου, ὁ Pirithous (1168).

πείρω (περ-, παρ-), ἔπειρα, πέπαρμαι,
ἐπάρην† pierce, stud, rivet.

πείσεις, πείσεσθαι (πείθω).

πελάζω (cf. πέλας near), πελάσω,
ἐπέλασ(σ)α, πέπλημαι, ἐπελάσθην

(ἐπλήμην) bring near, draw near,
approach.

πέλω (πελ-, πλ-), ἔπελον, ἐπελόμην ;
2d aor., ἔπλε, ἔπλετο turn, move ;
mid., be, become.

πέμπω (πεμπ-, πομπ-), πέμψω, ἔπεμψα,
πέπομφα**, πέπεμμαι*, ἐπέμφθην*
send, escort, conduct.

πεμπ-ώβολον, ου, τό five-pronged fork.

πέμψω (πέμπω).

πένθος, εος, τό woe, grief, sadness.

πέν-ομαι work, be busy, labor, do.

πεπαρμένον (πείρω), perf. mid. particip.

πεπίθοιμεν, πεποίθης (πείθω).

πέρ encl., exceedingly, very, even
(if), although.

περί adv., and prep, with gen., dat.,
and acc., around, about, concern-
ing, for, exceedingly, above, over,
more than, superior ; adv., around,
about, beyond, over, exceedingly ;
with gen., around, about, concern-
ing, beyond ; with dat., around,
about, concerning, for ; with acc.,
around, about, concerning.

περι-έχω (σεχ-, σχ-, σχε-), περιέξω
(περισχήσω), περιέσχον encompass,
embrace, protect, defend.

περι-καλλής, ές very beautiful,
charming.

περι-κλυτός, ή, όν, famous, very re-
nowned.

περίσχεο (περιέχω), 2d aor. mid.
imperat.

περι-φραδέως very carefully.

πεσόντα (πίπτω), 2d aor. particip.

πετάννυμι* (πετα-, πτα-), πετάσω*,
ἐπέτασ(σ)α, πεπέτακα*, πέπταμαι,
ἐπετάσθην stretch, spread out, un-
furl.

πέτασσαν (πετάννυμι) = ἐπέτασ(σ)αν,
(837).

πεύθομαι (πυνθάνομαι) (πευθ-, πυθ-),

340

πεύσομαι, ἐπυθόμην (πεπυθόμην), πέπυσμαι learn (by inquiry).

Πηλεΐδης, āo, ὁ son of Peleus, Achilles.

Πηλεΐων, ωνος, ὁ son of Peleus, Achilles.

Πηλέος (Πηλεύς, ῆος, ὁ) = Πηλῆος (572).

Πηλεύς, ῆος, ὁ Peleus, husband of Thetis, and father of Achilles.

Πηληιάδης, āo, ὁ son of Peleus, Achilles.

πίθεσθε (πείθω), 2d aor. imperat.

πίθηαι, πίθηται (πείθω).

πίμπλαντο (πίμπλημι) = ἐπίμπλαντο (837).

πίμ-πλημι (πλη-, πλα-), πλήσω, ἔπλησα (ἐπλήμην), πέπληκα*, πέπλησμαι*, ἐπλήσθην fill, sate, stuff.

πίονα (πίων, ειρα, πῖον).

πί-πτω (πετ-, πτ-, πτη-), πεσέομαι, ἔπεσον, πέπτη(κ)α fall (down), drop, perish, die, sink.

πίων, πίειρα, πῖον fat, rich, fertile.

πλογχθέντας (πλάζω), aor. pass. particip.

πλάζω (πλαγγ), πλάγξομαι, ἔπλαγξα, ἐπλάγχθην beat (back), baffle, (cause to) wander.

πλείων, ον (πολύς, πολλή, πολύ), comparat.

πλεόνεσσι (πλέων, ον = πλείων, ον, 571).

πλέων, ον = πλείων, ον, 571.

πλοῦτος, ου, ὁ wealth, riches, abundance.

ποδ-άρκης, ες swift-footed, able-footed.

πόδας, ποδός (πούς, ποδός, ὁ).

ποθέεσκε (ποθέω), iterative (900).

ποθέ-ω, ποθήσω*, ἐπόθεσα (ἐπόθησα*) yearn, long for (what is lacking), desire, lack, miss.

ποθή, ῆς, ἡ yearning, longing, desire, lack, regret.

ποθί encl., ever, at any time.

ποιέ-ω, ποιήσω, ἐποίησα, πεποίηκα*, πεποίημαι, ἐποιήθην* do, make, perform, execute, cause, effect, fashion, build, produce.

ποιμήν, ένος, ὁ shepherd, guardian, protector.

ποῖος, η, ον what (sort)? what kind ?

ποι-πνύ-ω, ἐποίπνῡσα bustle, hurry, puff, pant.

πολέας (πολύς, πολλή, πολύ).

π(τ)ολεμίζω (cf. π(τ)όλεμος), π(τ)ο λεμίξω war, battle, fight.

πόλεμος (πτόλεμος), ου, ὁ war, battle, fight, fray.

πολιός, ή, όν gray, hoary.

πόλις (πτόλις), ιος, ἡ city, community, state.

πολλάκις often, many times.

πολλός, ή, όν = πολύς, πολλή, πολύ much, many, numerous.

πολυ-άϊξ, ῑκος impetuous, onrushing.

πολυ-βενθής, ές very deep.

πολυ-δειράς, άδος many ridged, with many cliffs.

πολύ-μητις, ιος wily, shrewd, rich in counsel.

πολύς, πολλή, πολύ = πολλός, ή, όν much, many, numerous.

πολύ-στονος, ον causing many groans, rich in groans.

Πολύ-φημος, ου, ὁ Polyphemus.

πολύ-φλοισβος, ον much-roaring, loud-roaring, heavy-thundering.

πόνος, ου, ὁ work, labor, toil, trouble.

ποντο-πόρος, ον crossing the sea, sea-traversing, sea-going.

πόντος, ου, ὁ sea.

πόποι alas ! ah me ! oh dear ! good gracious !

πόρον (πορ-, πρω-) 2d aor., = ἔπορον (837) give, grant, bestow, furnish ; perf., πέπρωται it is fated.

πορ-φύρεος, η, ον dark PURPLE, violet, glistening.

Ποσειδάων, ωνος, ὁ Poseidon, *god of the sea, brother of Zeus, and one of the mightiest of the Greek divinities.*

πόσις, ιος, ἡ drink(ing).

ποτέ *encl.*, ever, at any (some) time, once.

ποτί = προτί (πρός).

πότνια, ης, ἡ revered, honored (lady, queen).

ποτόν, οῦ, τό drink(ing).

πού *encl.*, any(where, way), some (where, way, how), perhaps.

πούς, ποδός, ὁ foot.

πραπίς, ίδος, ἡ heart, mind, soul, diaphragm.

πρήθ-ω, πρήσω, ἔπρησα burn, blow, inflate.

πρῆξαι (πρήσσω).

πρῆσε(ν) (πρήθω) = ἔπρησε(ν) (*837*).

πρήσσω (πρᾱγ-), πρήξω, ἔπρηξα, πέπρηγα†, πέπρηγμαι†, ἐπρήχθην† carry through, accomplish, perform, do, act.

Πρίαμος, ου, ὁ Priam, *the aged king of Troy.*

πρίν sooner, until, before, formerly.

πρό, *adv., and prep. with gen.*, before, in front, forth, forward.

προ-βάλλω (βαλ-, βλη-), προβαλέω, προέβαλον, προβέβληκα, προβέβλημαι, προεβλήθην* cast forward, throw forward, cast forth.

προβέβουλα (προβούλομαι).

προ-βούλομαι (βουλ-, βουλε-), προβουλήσομαι*, προβέβουλα, προβεβούλημαι*, προεβουλήθην* prefer, wish rather, desire rather.

προ-ερέσσω (ἐρετ-), προήρεσ(σ)α row forward.

προ-ερύω (Ϝερυ-, Ϝρυ-), προερύω,

προείρυσ(σ)α, προείρυ(σ)μαι draw forward, drag forward, launch.

πρόες (προίημι), *2d aor. imperat.*

προθέουσι(ν) (προτίθημι), *3d plur.*

προ-ϊάπ-τω, προϊάψω, προΐαψα hurl forward, send forth.

προΐαψε(ν) (προϊάπτω).

προΐει (προίημι).

προ-ΐ-ημι (ση-, σε-, = ἡ-, ἑ-, *603–604*), προήσω, προέηκα (προῆκα), προείκα*, προείμαι*, προείθην send forward, send forth, give up.

πρό-πᾱς, πρό-πᾱσα, πρό-παν all, entire, whole.

πρός, π(ρ)οτί, *adv., and prep. with gen., dat., and acc.*, to, toward, also, at, on, from, on behalf of; *with gen.*, from before, at the bidding, in the sight; *with dat.*, on, at, by; *with acc.*, to, toward, (up)on, against.

προσ-αυδά-ω, προσαυδήσω*, προσηύδησα address, speak to, say to, accost.

προσ-εῖπον (προσέειπον) (Ϝεπ-), *2d aor.*, spoke to, addressed.

προσέφη (πρόσφημι).

προσεφώνεον (προσφωνέω).

προσηύδα (προσαυδάω).

πρόσθε(ν) before, formerly, sooner.

πρόσ(σ)ω forward, in front, forth.

πρόσ-φημι (φη-, φα-), προσφήσω, προσέφησα*; *imperf.* προσέφην, προσεφάμην speak to, address, accost.

προσ-φωνέ-ω, προσφωνήσω*, προσεφώνησα speak to, address, accost.

πρόσω = πρόσ(σ)ω.

πρότερος, η, ον former, sooner, older, before.

π(ρ)οτί = πρός.

προ-τί-θημι (θη-, θε-), προθήσω, προέθηκα, προτέθεικα*, προτέθειμαι*, προετέθην add, grant in addition, place upon also.

πρό-τονος, ου, ὁ fore-stay, cordage.

πρό-φρων, ον eager, glad, zealous, joyful, kind(ly).

πρύμνη, ης, ἡ stern of a ship.

πρυμνήσιον, ου, τό stern-cable, stern-hawser.

πρώτιστος, η, ον (πρῶτος, η, ον), superl.

πρῶτος, η, ον first, foremost, chief.

πτερόεις, εσσα, εν winged, flying.

πτόλεμος = πόλεμος, ου, ὁ.

πτολίεθρον (cf. π(τ)όλις), ου, τό city.

πτόλις = πόλις, ιος, ἡ.

πυθοίατο (πεύθομαι, πυνθάνομαι), optat.

Πύλιος, η, ον Pylian, of Pylus.

Πύλος, ου, ἡ Pylus, a city and district on the west coast of the Peloponnesus.

πῦρ, πυρός, τό fire.

πυρή, ῆς, ἡ (funeral) pyre.

πώ, encl., in some way, in any way, ever, yet, at some time, at any time.

πωλέομαι, πωλήσομαι come, go, attend, frequent, return.

πωλέσκετο (πωλέω), iterative (900).

πώ-ποτε ever yet, at any time.

πώς, encl., (in) some way, somehow, (in) any way, perhaps.

πῶς how? in what way?

P

ῥά (ἄρα, ἄρ).

ῥέζω (Ϝρεγ-), ῥέξω, ἔρ(ρ)εξα, ἐρέχθην work, accomplish, do, perform, make, sacrifice.

ῥέξαι, ῥέξᾱς (ῥέζω).

ῥέω (σρευ-, σρεϜ-, σρυ-, σρυε- = ῥευ-, 603-604), ῥεύσομαι, ἔρρευσα*, ἐρ-ρύηκα*, ἐρρύην run, flow, stream, pour.

ῥηγμίν, ῖνος, ἡ (cf. ῥήγνῡμι break) beach, strand, shore.

ῥίγιων, ον (cf. ῥῖγος cold) worse, more horrible.

ῥίπ-τω, ῥίψω, ἔρρῑψα, ἔρρῑφα**, ἔρρῑμαι*, ἐρρίφ(θ)ην* hurl, dash, throw with a twirl, brandish.

ῥῖψε(ν) (ῥίπτω) = ἔρρῑψε(ν) (837).

ῥοδο-δάκτυλος, ον rosy-fingered.

Σ

σ' = 1) σε, 2) σοί (575).

σαό-ω, σαώσω, ἐσάωσα, ἐσαώθην save, protect, rescue, preserve.

σαώτερος, η, ον (σάος, η, ον), comparat.

σάος, η, ον = σόος, η, ον.

σέ, σέθεν, σέο (σύ).

σημαίνω (σημαν-), σημανέω, ἐσήμηνα, σεσήμασμαι*, ἐσημάνθην* point out, order, command.

σῆσ(ι) (σός, σή, σόν).

Σίντιες, ων, οἱ Sintians, early inhabitants of Lemnos.

σκαιός, ή, όν left (hand), unlucky.

σκηπτ-οῦχος, η, ον SCEPTRE-holding, sceptre-bearing.

σκῆπτρον, ου, τό SCEPTRE, staff.

σκίδ-νημι scatter, disperse.

σκιόεις, εσσα, εν shady, shadowy.

Σμινθεύς, ῆος, ὁ Smintheus, mouse god, epithet of Apollo.

σοί (σύ).

σοῖσι, σόν (σός, σή, σόν).

σόος, η, ον (= σωος = σάϜος) safe, sound, unhurt, unharmed, well.

σός, σή, σόν your(s).

σπλάγχνον, ου, τό vitals, haslets.

στείλαντο (στέλλω) = ἐστείλαντο (837).

στεῖρα, ης, ἡ cut-water, stem.

στέλλω (στελ-, σταλ-), στελέω, ἔστειλα, ἔσταλκα**, ἔσταλμαι*, ἐστάλην* put, place, arrange, furl.

στέμμα, ατος, τό fillet, wreath.

στενάχ-ω groan, sob, sigh.

στῆ (ἴστημι) = ἔστη (837).

στῆθος, εος, τό breast, chest.

στήσαντο, στήτην (ἴστημι) = ἐστήσαντο, ἐστήτην (837).

στρατός, οῦ, ὁ army, encampment, camp, host.

στυγέω (στυγ-, στυγε-), ἔστυξα (ἔστυγον), ἐστυγήθην† hate, loathe, dislike, make hateful, hold in horror, fear.

στυφελίζω (στυφελιγ-), ἐστυφέλιξα strike, thrust, hurl.

σύ, σέο you.

σύμ-πᾶς, σύμ-πᾶσα, σύμ-παν all (together).

συμ-φράζομαι (φραδ-), συμφράσ(σ)ομαι, συνεφρασ(σ)άμην, συμπέφρασμαι devise plans with, counsel together.

σύν, adv., and prep. with dat., with, together (with), along with.

σύνθεο (συντίθημι), 2d aor. imperat.

συν-τί-θημι (θη-, θε-), συνθήσω, συνέθηκα, συντέθεικα*, συντέθειμαι*, συνετέθην put together, unite, perceive, comprehend, heed, consider.

σφάζω (σφαγ-), σφάξω*, ἔσφαξα, ἔσφαγμαι, ἐσφάχθην† slaughter.

σφί(ν), σφίσι(ν) (εἷο, ἑο).

σφός, σφή, σφόν one's own, their own.

σφώ (σύ), σφῶε (εἷο, ἑο), σφῶι (σύ), σφωίν (εἷο, ἑο).

σφωίτερος, η, ον of you two, belonging to you two.

σχέθε (ἔχω) = ἔσχεθε (837).

σχίζη, ης, ἡ split wood.

T

τ' = τέ (575).

τά (ὁ, ἡ, τό).

τάδε (ὅδε, ἥδε, τόδε).

Ταλθύ-βιος, ου, ὁ Talthybius.

τᾶλλα = τὰ ἄλλα (587).

τάνυσ(σ)αν (τανύω) = ἐτάνυσ(σ)αν (837).

τα-νύ-ω (for τγ-νυ-ω, 597–598), τανύ(σ)ω, ἐτάνυσ(σ)α, τετάνυσμαι, ἐτανύσθην stretch, place along.

ταράξῃ (ταράσσω).

ταράσσω* (ταραχ-), ταράξω*, ἐτάραξα, τέτρηχα, τετάραγμαι*, ἐταράχθην* disturb violently, throw into confusion; perf. be disturbed.

ταρβέ-ω, ταρβήσω*, ἐτάρβησα fear, be in terror, be frightened.

ταῦθ' (οὗτος, αὕτη, τοῦτο) = ταῦτα (575, 582).

ταῦρος, ου, ὁ bull.

ταῦτα (οὗτος, αὕτη, τοῦτο).

τάχα (cf. ταχύς, 781) quickly, swiftly, soon.

τέ, postpos. encl., and, also; τέ . . . τέ, or τέ . . . καί both . . . and, not only . . . but also.

τέκε (τίκτω) = ἔτεκε (837).

τέκμωρ, indecl., τό surety, pledge, sign, goal, limit.

τέκνον, ου, τό child, young, offspring, descendant.

τέκον (τίκτω) = ἔτεκον (837).

τέκος, εος, τό child, young, offspring, descendant.

τεκοῦσα (τίκτω), 2d aor. fem. particip.

τέλειος, η, ον complete, finished, full-grown, unblemished, perfect.

τελείω (τελέω) (τελεσ-), τελέ(σ)(σ)ω, ἐτέλεσ(σ)α, τετέλεκα**, τετέλεσμαι, ἐτελέσθην fulfill, accomplish, perform, complete.

τελέσ(σ)ῃ, τελέσ(σ)ω (τελείω).

τελέω = τελείω.

τελήεις, εσσα, εν complete, finished, perfect, full-grown, unblemished.

τέλλω (τελ-, ταλ-), ἔτειλα, τέταλμαι raise. rise, command, enjoin upon.

Τένεδος, ου, ἡ Tenedos, *a small island in the Aegean near Troy.*

τεός, ή, όν thy, thine, your(s).

τερπι-κέραυνος, ον rejoicing in the thunderbolt; *possibly* hurling the thunderbolt.

τέρπω (τερπ-, ταρπ-, τραπ-), **τέρψω*** (τέρψομαι), **ἔτερψα*** (ἐτερψάμην, ἐταρπόμην, τεταρπόμην), **ἐτέρφθην** (ἐτάρφθην, ἐτάρπην), please, delight, sate, satisfy, charm, rejoice.

τε-ταγ-ών, *2d aor. act. particip. only,* touch, lay hold of, seize.

τετελεσμένον, τετελεσμένος (τελείω).

τέτλαθι (*τλάω), *2d perf. imperat.*

τέτληκας (*τλάω).

τετρα-πλῇ fourfold, four-ply, quadruply.

τετύκοντο (τεύχω).

τεύχω (τευχ-, τυχ-, τυκ-), **τεύξω, ἔτευξα** (τέτυκον), **τέτευχα, τέτυγμαι, ἐτύχθην** do, make, perform, prepare, fashion, cause.

τῇ (ὁ, ἡ, τό).

τηλόθε(ν) far, from afar.

τηλόθι far (from, away), at a distance.

τήν (ὁ, ἡ, τό).

τήνδε, τῆσδε (ὅδε, ἥδε, τόδε).

τί (τίς, τί); **τί** (τὶς, τὶ).

τίθει (τίθημι) = 1) ἐτίθει (*837*), 2) *imperat.*

τί-θημι (θη-, θε-), **θήσω, ἔθηκα, τέθεικα*, τέθειμαι*, ἐτέθην** put, place, cause.

τίκτω (= τι-τεκω : τεκ-, τοκ-), **τέξω, ἔτεκον, τέτοκα*** bear, produce, give birth to, beget.

τῖμά-ω, τῑμήσω, ἐτίμησα, τετίμηκα*, τετίμημαι, ἐτιμήθην* honor, gain honor, bestow honor; *mid.,* avenge, exact recompense.

τῖμή, ῆς, ἡ honor, satisfaction, recompense, retribution, value.

τίμησον (τῖμάω), *aor. imperat.*

τινά (τὶς, τὶ), **τίνα** (τίς, τί).

τίνω (τει-, τι-, τινϝ-), **τίσω, ἔτῑσα, τέτῑκα*, τέτῑσμαι*, ἐτίσθην*** requite, atone for, pay the penalty for.

τίπτε (= τί ποτε, 592) why (in the world)?

τὶς, τὶ *encl.,* *indef.,* some (one, thing), any (one, thing); **τὶ** *as adverb* (780–781), at all.

τίς, τί *interrog.,* who? which? what? **τί** *as adverb* (780–781), why?

τίσειαν (τίνω), *optat.*

τῖσον (τίνω), *imperat.,* (τῖω), *imperat.*

τίσωσι(ν) (τῖω) (τίνω).

τῖ-ω, τίσω, ἔτῑσα, τέτῑμαι honor, esteem, bestow honor upon.

***τλάω** (τλα-, τλη-, ταλα-), **τλήσομαι, ἐτάλασ(σ)α** (ἔτλην), **τέτληκα** have the heart, have courage, endure, dare, suffer.

τλῆναι (*τλάω).

τό (ὁ, ἡ, τό).

τόδε (ὅδε, ἥδε, τόδε).

τοί: *1)* (σύ), *2)* (ὁ, ἡ, τό), *3)* surely.

τοῖο (ὁ, ἡ, τό).

τοῖος, η, ον such (as), of the sort that, of the kind that.

τοῖσ(ι) (ὁ, ἡ, τό).

τομή, ῆς, ἡ cut(ting), stump.

τόν (ὁ, ἡ, τό).

τόνδε (ὅδε, ἥδε, τόδε).

τόξον, ου, τό bow.

τόσ(σ)ος, η, ον so much, so great, so large, so many, so long.

τότε then, at that time.

τοῦ (ὁ, ἡ, τό).

τοῦδε (ὅδε, ἥδε, τόδε).

τούνεκα (= τοῦ ἕνεκα, 587) on account of this, for this reason, therefore, consequently.

τούς (ὁ, ἡ, τό).

τοῦτο (οὗτος, αὕτη, τοῦτο).

τόφρα so long, meanwhile.

τράπετο (τρέπω) = ἐτράπετο (837).

τράφεν (τρέφω) = ἔτραφεν, 2d aor., 3d plur.

τρέπω (τρεπ-, τροπ-, τραπ-), τρέψω, ἔτρεψα (ἔτραπον), τέτροφα**, τέτραμμαι, ἐτράφθην turn (around), put to flight; mid., turn oneself, flee.

τρέφω (τρεφ-, τροφ-, τραφ- = θρεφ-, θροφ-, θραφ-, 619), θρέψω*, ἔθρεψα (ἔτραφον), τέτροφα, τέθραμμαι*, ἐτράφην nurture, nourish, feed, breed, grow up.

τρι-πλῇ threefold, three-ply, triply.

τρίς thrice, three times.

τρί(τα)τος, η, ον third.

Τροίη, ης, ἡ Troy, the city, a famous ancient city in Asia Minor, commanding the Hellespont (Dardanelles). According to the legend it was sacked and burned, after a siege of ten years, by the Greeks under the leadership of Agamemnon.

Τρῶες, ων, οἱ Trojans, inhabitants of Troy.

τυτθός, ή, όν small, little, young, brief.

τῶ (cf. ὁ, ἡ, τό) therefore.

τώ, τῷ (ὁ, ἡ, τό).

τῳ (τὶς, τὶ).

τῶν (ὁ, ἡ, τό).

Υ

ὕβρις, ιος, ἡ insolence, wantonness, frowardness, hybris.

ὑγρός, ή, όν wet, moist, damp, watery.

υἱός, οῦ (ἑος, ος), ὁ son, descendant, offspring.

ὑμεῖς, ὑμῖν, ὕμμες, ὕμμι(ν) (ἐγώ).

ὑπέδεισαν (ὑποδείδω) = ὑπέδϝεισαν.

ὑπ-είκω (ὑπο-είκω) (Ϝεικ-), ὑπείξω (ὑπείξομαι, ὑποείξομαι), ὑπεῖξα (ὑποείξα) yield, submit, WEAKEN.

ὑπελύσαο (ὑπολύω).

ὑπέρ, ὑπείρ adv., and prep. with gen. and acc., over, beyond, in behalf of, concerning, above; adv., above; with gen., above, (from) over, for the sake; with acc., over, beyond.

ὑπερ-οπλίη, ης, ἡ arrogance, insulting conduct, deed of insolence (1168).

ὕπνος, ου, ὁ sleep, slumber.

ὑπό (ὑπαί), adv., and prep. with gen., dat., and acc., under, beneath, by, at the hands of, by means of; adv., under(neath), secretly, behind, beneath, by, gradually; with gen., (from) under, by; with dat., (down) under; with acc., (down) under, during, toward.

ὑπο-βλήδην (cf. βάλλω) interrupting, breaking in.

ὑπ-ίσχομαι (σι-σ-(ε)χ-, cf. ἔχω : σεχ-, σχ-, σχε-), ὑποσχήσομαι, ὑπεσχόμην, ὑπέσχημαι* undertake, promise, assure.

ὑπο-δείδω (δϝει-, δϝοι-, δϝι-), ὑποδείσομαι, ὑπέδεισα, ὑποδείδοικα (ὑποδείδια fear, shrink before, cringe before.

ὑπό-δρα scowlingly, askance, looking at (δέρκομαι) darkly, from beneath (ὑπό) the brows drawn down.

ὑπο-λύ-ω, ὑπολύσω, ὑπέλῦσα, ὑπολέλυκα*, ὑπολέλυμαι, ὑπελύθην loose (from beneath, by stealth).

ὑπόσχεο (ὑπίσχομαι), 2d aor. imperat.

ὕστατος, η, ον (superl. of ὕστερος, η, ον) latest, last, uppermost, hindmost.

ὕστερος, η, ον behind, later, further-(more), at another time.

ὑφ' = ὑπό (575, 582).

ὑφέντες (ὑφίημι), 2d aor. particip.

ὑφ-ί-ημι (ση-, σε- = ἡ-, ἑ-, 603–604), ὑφήσω, ὑφῆκα (ὑφῆκα), ὑφεῖκα*, ὑφεῖμαι*, ὑφείθην let down, lower.

ὑψι-βρεμέτης, āο, ὁ thundering, growling (grumbling, roaring, rumbling, bellowing) on high, or high thundering, etc.

ὑψοῦ (on) high, lofty, loftily.

Φ

φάανθεν (φαείνω) = ἐφάενθεν (837), 3d plur. (945–948).

φαείνω (φαεν-), ἐφαάνθην shine, gleam, glare, flash.

φαίνω (φαν-), φανέω, ἔφηνα, πέφηνα*, πέφασμαι, ἐφάν(θ*)ην show, shine ; mid. appear.

φάνη (φαίνω) = ἐφάνη (837).

φάος, εος, τό light, gleam, luminary.

φαρέτρη, ης, ἡ quiver.

φάσγανον, ον, τό sword, sabre.

φάσθαι, φάτο = ἔφατο (φημί).

φέρτατος, η, ον (φέρτερος, η, ον), superl.

φέρτερος, η, ον mightier, better, braver, stronger, more powerful, more productive, more profitable.

φέρω (φερ-, οἰ-, ἐνεκ-), οἴσω, ἤνεικα (ἤνεικον), ἐνήνοχα**, ἐνήνεγμαι*, ἠνέχθην* bear, bring, carry.

φεύγω (φευγ-, φυγ-), φεύξομαι, ἔφυγον, πέφευγα, πέφυγμαι flee, fly, escape, run (off, away, along).

φημί (φη-, φα-), φήσω, ἔφησα* ; imperf., ἔφην, ἐφάμην speak, say, tell.

φήρ, ός, ὁ, ἡ wild animal, (savage) beast, brute.

φησί(ν) (φημί).

Φθίη, ης, ἡ Phthia, a town and district in northern Greece, home of Achilles.

Φθίηνδε (788, 4), to Phthia.

φθινύθεσκε (φθινύθω), iterative.

φθι-νύ-θω destroy, waste away, pine, perish.

φθίνω (φθινϝ-), φθίσω, ἔφθῖσα, ἔφθιμαι, ἐφθίθην destroy, consume, perish, die, waste away.

φιλέ-ω, φιλήσω, ἐφίλησα, πεφίληκα*, πεφίλημαι*, ἐφιλήθην love, cherish, entertain hospitably.

φιλο-κτεανώτατος, η, ον superl., most avaricious, most greedy of gain.

φίλος, η, ον dear, darling, lovely, beloved.

φλοιός, οῦ, ὁ bark, peel, rind, hull, shell.

Φοῖβος, ου, ὁ Phoebus = clear, bright, shining ; surname of Apollo, god of light.

φορέ-ω, φορήσω*, ἐφόρησα bear, carry, bring.

φόρμιγξ, ιγγος, ἡ lyre, harp.

φράζω* (φράζομαι) (φραδ-), φράσω* (φράσ(σ)ομαι), ἔφρασ(σ)α (ἐπέφραδον), πέφρακα**, πέφρασμαι*, ἐφράσθην tell, point out, declare ; mid., consider, plan, think.

φράσαι (φράζω), aor. mid. imperat.

φρένα, φρένας, φρένες, φρεσί(ν), (φρήν, φρενός, ἡ).

φρήν, φρενός, ἡ diaphragm, heart, mind, spirit, disposition.

φρονέ-ω think, consider, plan ; ἐὺ φρονέω be well (kindly) disposed, be wise (prudent), think carefully.

φύγοιμεν (φεύγω).

φυή, ῆς, ἡ form, nature, growth, beauty, character, appearance.

φύλλον, ου, τό leaf, FOLIAGE.

φύ-ω, φύσω, ἔφῦσα (ἔφῦν), πέφῦκα bear, produce, bring forth, (cause to) grow.

φωνέ-ω, φωνήσω*, ἐφώνησα speak, lift up the voice.

Χ

χαίρω (χαρ-, χαρε-, χαιρε-), χαιρήσω, ἐχηράμην (κεχαρόμην), κεχάρη(κ)α, κεχάρ(η)μαι*, ἐχάρην rejoice, be glad, hail ! welcome !

χαίτη, ης, ἡ hair, locks, tresses, mane.

χαλεπός, ή, όν hard, harsh, severe, stern, cruel, difficult.

χαλκο-βατής, ές with bronze threshold, with bronze pavement.

χαλκός, οῦ, ὁ bronze, implement of bronze (axe, sword, spear, etc.).

χαλκο-χίτων, ωνος with bronze tunic, clad in a bronze tunic.

χαρίεις, εσσα, εν pleasing, grateful, graceful, agreeable.

χείρ, χε(ι)ρός, ἡ hand, arm.

χερείων, ον worse, inferior.

χέρης, ες worse, inferior, meaner, underling, subject.

χερ-νίπτομαι (νιβ-), χερνίψομαι, ἐχερνιψάμην wash the hands, pour lustral water, purify with lustral water.

χερσί(ν) (χείρ, χε(ι)ρός, ἡ).

χέω (χευ-, χεϜ-, χυ-), χεύω, ἔχε(υ)α, κέχυκα*, κέχυμαι, ἐχύθην pour (out, forth), shed (tears).

χθιζός, ή, όν yesterday(s), of (on) yesterday.

χθών, χθονός, ἡ earth, land, country.

χόλος, ου, ὁ hot (furious) wrath, blind anger, choler.

χολό-ω, χολώσω, ἐχόλωσα, κεχόλωμαι, ἐχολώθην anger, enrage, vex, infuriate.

*χραισμέ-ω, χραισμήσω, ἐχραίσμησα (ἔχραισμον) help, assist, benefit, avail.

χρε(ι)ώ (χρή).

χρή (χρειώ, χρεώ) need, necessity, destiny, due, duty, obligation.

χρύσε(ι)ος, η, ον gold(en), of gold.

Χρύση, ης, ἡ Chrysa, a town in the Troad.

Χρυσηίς, ίδος, ἡ Chryseïs, daughter of Chryses.

Χρύσης, āο, ὁ Chryses, a priest of Apollo, from the town Chrysa.

χρῡσό-θρονος, ον golden-throned ; possibly with robes embroidered with golden flowers, θρόνα.

χώ-ομαι, χώσομαι*, ἐχωσάμην be angry (enraged, irritated, infuriated).

Ψ

ψάμαθος, ου, ἡ sand (of the beach), dune.

ψῡχή, ῆς, ἡ soul, life, spirit, breath.

Ω

ὦ O!

ᾧ (ὅς, ἥ, ὅ).

ὦ-δε thus, so, in this way, as follows.

ὠθέω (Ϝωθ-, Ϝωθε-), ὤσω, ἔωσα, ἔωσμαι*, ἐώσθην* shove, push, thrust, drive, strike.

ὦκα (cf. ὠκύς, 780-781) quickly, swiftly, suddenly.

Ὠκεανός, οῦ, ὁ ocean, Oceanus.

ὠκύ-μορος, ον swift-fated.

ὠκυ-μορώτατος, η, ον (ὠκύμορος, η, ον), superl.

ὠκύ-πορος, ον crossing-quickly, swift-going, swift-sailing.

ὠκύς, εῖα, ύ swift, speedy, quick, sudden.

ὠμίλησα (ὁμιλέω).

ὠμο-θετέ-ω, ὠμοθέτησα place raw meat (upon).

ὤ-μοι alas ! ah me ! good gracious ! O dear !

ὦμος, ου, ὁ shoulder.

ὤνησας (ὀνίνημι).

ὦ πόποι alas ! ah me ! O dear ! good gracious !

ὤπτησαν (ὀπτάω).

ὤρμαινε (ὁρμαίνω).

ὦρσε (ὄρνῡμι).

ὡς, ὥς, ὧς how, so (tnat), in order that, since, like (as), when, thus; in this way ; ὡς . . . ὥς as . . . so.

ὦσε (ὠθέω).

ᾧτε (ὅστε, ἥτε, ὅτε).

ὥχ’ = ὦκα (575, 582).

ᾤχετο (οἴχομαι).

ὤχθησαν (ὀχθέω).

ᾠχόμεθα (οἴχομαι).

ENGLISH–GREEK VOCABULARY

A

a, an, *not ordinarily expressed in Greek; sometimes* **a, a certain** τὶς, τὶ.

able, be δύναμαι.

about ἀμφί, περί; about, lie κεῖμαι.

above ὑπέρ, περί; be above περί εἰμι.

accept δέχομαι.

accomplish τελείω (τελέω), κραιαίνω, διέπω, πρήσσω.

accomplishment ἔργον, ου, τό.

accursed οὐλόμενος, η, ον.

Achaean Ἀχαιός, οῦ, ὁ.

Achilles Ἀχι(λ)λεύς, ῆος, ὁ.

adapt ἀραρίσκω.

address ἀγοράομαι, ἀγορεύω, προσαυδάω, πρόσφημι, μετάφημι; προσεῖπον, μετεῖπον 2d aor.

aegis-bearing αἰγίοχος, η, ον.

again, back again αὖτις (αὖθι), αὖ, πάλιν.

against ἀντίος, η, ον; (adv.) ἀντίον.

Agamemnon Ἀγαμέμνων, ονος. ὁ.

aged γεραιός, ή, όν.

Ajax Αἴας, αντος, ὁ.

alas ὤμοι = ὢ μοι.

all πᾶς, πᾶσα, πᾶν; all together σύμπᾶς, ᾶσα, αν.

alone οἶος, η, ον.

along παρά (with gen., dat., and acc.).

also καί, τέ, δέ.

although *not expressed in Greek; see* 1109, 6, *and* even though.

always αἰεί, αἰέν.

amazed, be θαμβέω.

ambush λόχος, ου, ὁ; ambush, into λόχονδε (788, 4).

among μετά.

a(n) *not expressed in Greek; see* a *and* καί, τέ, δέ.

anger χόλος, ου, ὁ; μένος, εος, τό; μῆνις, ιος, ἡ; to anger ἐρεθίζω, χολόω.

angry χωόμενος, η, ον (χώομαι).

another ἄλλος, η, ο.

answer ἀμείβομαι, ἀπαμείβομαι.

any, any one, any thing τὶς, τὶ.

apart ἀπάνευθε(ν).

Apollo Ἀπόλλων, ωνος, ὁ.

appear φαίνομαι (*mid. of* φαίνω *to* show).

appease ἱλάσκομαι.

Argive Ἀργεῖος, ου, ὁ.

arise ἀνίστημι (to stand up); ἀναβαίνω (to go up, ascend); γίγνομαι (to become, be, arise).

arm with the breast-plate θωρήσσω.

army στρατός, οῦ, ὁ.

around περί.

arrogance ὑπεροπλίη, ης, ἡ (1168).

arrow ὀιστός, οῦ, ὁ; ἰός, οῦ, ὁ; κῆλον, ου, τό.

as ἧος, εἷος, εἵως, (ἕως) ὡς, ὥς; *use participle.*

as many (as) τό(σ)σος, η, ον.

as the opportunity may offer ὡς ἔσεται περ.

ascend ἀναβαίνω.

askance ὑπόδρα.

assemble ἀγείρω.

assemble(d) ὁμηγερής, ές.

assembly ἀγορή, ῆς, ἡ ; assembly, to the ἀγορήνδε (788, 4).

associate with ὁμιλέω (dat.).

at (use the dative) ; at all τί ; at home οἴκοι ; at some time ποτέ ; at the hands of ὑπό (gen.) ; at the same time ὁμοῦ.

Athena 'Αθήνη, ης, ἡ ; 'Αθηναίη, ης, ἡ.

atone for τίνω.

Atreus, son of 'Ατρεΐδης, āο, ὁ.

attack ἐποίχομαι.

attendant θεράπων, οντος, ὁ.

avail χραισμέω (dat.).

avaricious (see most avaricious).

B

back, back again ἄψ, πάλιν, αὖ(τις).

bad κακός, ή, όν.

banquet δαίς, δαιτός, ἡ.

barrack κλισίη, ης, ἡ.

battle μάχη, ης, ἡ.

be (become) εἰμί, γίγνομαι, πέλομαι.

bear φέρω, φορέω (to carry); τίκτω, γείνομαι (to bring forth).

beautiful κᾱλός, ή, όν.

beautiful-cheeked, beauteous-cheeked καλλιπάρῃος, ον.

beauty φυή, ῆς, ἡ.

because οὕνεκα, ὅτι, ἕνεκα.

become γίγνομαι.

behind ὄπι(σ)θε(ν).

beloved φίλος, η, ον.

beside παρά ; use dat.

best ἄριστος, η, ον.

better φέρτερος, η, ον ; ἀρείων, ον ; ἀμείνων, ον.

between μεταξύ, μεσσηγύ(ς).

bird οἰωνός, οῦ, ὁ.

biting ἐχεπευκής, ές.

bitter ἀταρτηρός, ή, όν.

black μέλᾱς, αινα, αν ; κελαινός, ή, όν ;

black on both sides, black all around ἀμφιμέλᾱς, αινα, αν.

blamable αἴτιος, η, ον.

blame ἐπιμέμφομαι.

blameless ἀμύμων, ον.

blaze λαμπετάω.

blood αἷμα, ατος, τό.

board, go on board ἀναβαίνω.

boast εὔχομαι.

booty ἐλώριον, ου, τό.

born, be γίγνομαι.

both ἄμφω, οιιν ; both . . . and, καί . . . καί ; καί . . . τέ ; τέ . . . τέ.

boundless ἀπερείσιος, η, ον ; μῡρίοι, αι, α.

bow τόξον, ου, τό ; βιός, οῦ, ὁ.

branch ὄζος, ου, ὁ.

brave κᾱλός, ή, όν ; ἀγαθός, ή, όν ; bravest ἄριστος, η, ον.

breast στῆθος, εος, τό.

breed τρέφω.

bright-eyed ἑλίκωψ, ωπος (mas.) ; ἑλικῶπις, ιδος (fem.).

bring φέρω, φορέω, ἄγω.

bring together ξυνίημι, ἀγείρω.

Briseïs Βρισηΐς, ίδος, ἡ.

broad εὐρύς, εῖα, ύ.

bronze χαλκός, οῦ, ὁ.

build δέμας, αος, τό.

bull ταῦρος, ου, ὁ ; βοῦς, βοός, ὁ.

bulwark ἕρκος, εος, τό.

burn καίω ; burn down κατακαίω.

but δέ, γέ, δή, αὖτε, ἀλλά, ἀλλὰ καί.

by use the dative, παρά, ἐπί with the dat., or ὑπό with the gen. ; by (means of) διά with acc. ; by all means μάλιστα.

C

Calchas Κάλχᾱς, αντος, ὁ.

call καλέω.

camp στρατός, οῦ, ὁ.

care (for) ὄθομαι (gen.), κήδομαι (gen.).

carry φέρω, φορέω.

cast βάλλω.

cattle βόες, ῶν, οἱ, αἱ.

cause τεύχω, τίθημι.

cause to go into εἰσβαίνω; cause to go up (on board) ἀναβαίνω (1069).

cease, stop παύω; cease from λήγω.

certain, a τὶς, τὶ.

check παύω, ἐρητύω.

chest στῆθος, εος, τό.

chief ἀριστεύς, ῆος, ὁ.

child παῖς, παιδός, ὁ, ἡ.

Chrysa Χρύση, ης, ἡ.

Chryseïs Χρυσηίς, ίδος, ἡ.

Chryses Χρύσης, āο, ὁ.

Cilla Κίλλα, ης, ἡ.

city π(τ)όλις, ιος, ἡ; ἄστυ, εος, τό.

clang κλαγγή, ῆς, ἡ; κλάζω.

clear-toned λιγύς, εῖα, ύ.

clothe ἐπιέννῦμι (ἐφέννῦμι).

Clytaem(n)estra Κλυταιμ(ν)ήστρη, ης, ἡ.

collect ἀγείρω, ἀφύσσω.

come βαίνω, ἔρχομαι, ἱκνέομαι, οἴχομαι, εἶμι.

come! ἄγε, ἄγετε.

come upon ἔπειμι, ἱκνέομαι, κιχάνω.

command μῦθος, ου, ὁ; command, give command τέλλω, ἐπιτέλλω, ἀνώγω.

commander ἀρχός, οῦ, ὁ.

common (stores) ξυνήιος, η, ον.

compare ὁμοιόω.

comrade ἕταρος (ἑταῖρος), ου, ὁ.

consider φράζω (mid.), ἀλεγίζω, μερμηρίζω, μετατρέπομαι.

consider afterward μεταφράζω (mid.).

contend μάρναμαι.

continue, keep doing (a thing), use imperfect (1079).

council ἀγορή, ῆς, ἡ; βουλή, ῆς, ἡ.

counsel βουλή, ῆς, ἡ.

counsel-bearing βουληφόρος, ον.

counsellor μητίετα, āο, ὁ.

countless μῦρίοι, αι, α; ἀπερείσιος, η, ον.

covered at both ends ἀμφηρεφής, ές.

cow βοῦς, βοός, ἡ.

coward(ly) δειλός, ή, όν; κακός, ή, όν.

crafty-minded κερδαλεόφρων, ον.

crop καρπός, οῦ, ὁ.

crush δαμάζω.

curb ἐρητύω, παύω.

D

Danaan Δαναός, οῦ, ὁ.

dare *τλάω.

darling φίλος, η, ον.

dart βέλος, εος, τό; κῆλον, ου, τό.

daughter θυγάτηρ, τέρος (τρός), ἡ; παῖς, παιδός, ἡ.

dead, be (have died), use perf. of θνήσκω die.

dead body νέκῦς, υος, ὁ.

dear φίλος, η, ον.

death θάνατος, ου, ὁ; κήρ, κηρός, ἡ.

declare ἐξείρω.

deed ἔργον, ου, τό.

deer ἔλαφος, ου, ὁ, ἡ.

defend ἀρήγω (dat.).

depart βαίνω, ἀποβαίνω.

desire θῡμός, οῦ, ὁ.

despise ἀθερίζω.

destroy δηλέομαι, ὀλέκω, ὄλλῦμι; destroy (utterly) ἀπόλλῡμι.

destruction λοιγός, οῦ, ὁ.

devourer of (the goods of) the people, devouring δημοβόρος, η, ον.

did, emphatic, implied in past tense of verb.

die θνήσκω.

digest καταπέσσω.

dishonor ἀτῑμά(ζ)ω.

dishonored ἄτῑμος, η, ον.

dismiss μεθίημι, λύω.

disobey ἀπιθέω (dat.).

dispenser of justice δικασπόλος, ου, ὁ.
disposed, well ἐὺ φρονέων.
distant ἄπιος, η, ον.
divide δατέομαι.
divine δῖος, α, ον ; θεοείκελος, η, ον.
divinity δαίμων, ονος, ὁ, ἡ ; θεός, οῦ, ὁ ;
θεά, ᾶς, ἡ.
division (of spoil) δασμός, οῦ, ὁ.
do ἔρδω, ποιέω, πρήσσω ; do (auxiliary
verb, emphatic, implied in present
tense of verb).
dog κύων, κυνός, ὁ, ἡ.
down (from) κατά (with gen. and
acc.).
drag ἐρύω, ἕλκω ; drag forward προ-
ερύω.
draw ἐρύω, ἕλκω.
dread(ful) δεινός, ή, όν.
drive away ἐλάω, ἐλαύνω ; drive back
πάλιν πλάζω, παλιμπλάζω.
drunken οἰνοβαρής, ές.

E

earth χθών, χθονός, ἡ ; γαῖα, ης, ἡ.
either . . . or ἤ . . . ἤ ; after nega-
tives οὔτε . . . οὔτε.
elsewhere ἄλλῃ.
encampment στρατός, οῦ, ὁ.
enjoin τέλλω, ἐπιτέλλω.
enrage χολόω ; be enraged ἄχνυμαι,
χώομαι.
entreat λίσσομαι.
equal ἴσος, η (ἐίση), ον.
equally ὁμῶς.
equivalent ἀντάξιος, η, ον.
escape φεύγω.
escort πέμπω.
especial(ly) μάλα, μάλιστα.
eternal, being forever αἰὲν ἐών, ἐοῦσα,
ἐόν.
Eurybates Εὐρυβάτης, ᾶο, ὁ.
even though καί.
ever πώ, ποτέ ; for ever αἰεί, αἰέν.

every πᾶς, πᾶσα, πᾶν ; everything (all
things) πάντα, ων, τά.
evil κακός, ή, όν.
evilly κακῶς.
expedition ὁδός, οῦ, ἡ.
eye ὄσσομαι ; ὄμμα, ατος, τό ; ὀφθαλ-
μός, οῦ, ὁ.
eyes ὄσσε (dual), ὄμματα, ων, τά.

F

face ὄμματα, ων, τά.
fair κᾱλός, ή, όν.
fair-haired ἠύκομος, ον.
fall πίπτω.
far, by far ὄχα, πολύ, πολλόν ; far
(away) τηλόθι.
fat κνίση, ης, ἡ ; πίων, πίειρα, πῖον.
father πατήρ, πατρός (πατέρος), ὁ.
fatherland πάτρη, ης, ἡ.
fear δείδω.
fertile ἐριβῶλαξ, ακος.
fight μάχομαι, μάρναμαι.
fill πίμπλημι.
fillet στέμμα, ατος, τό.
filth λῦμα, ατος, τό.
find κιχάνω.
fire πῦρ, πυρός, τό.
first πρῶτος, η, ον ; first(ly), at first
(adv.) (τό) πρῶτον, (τὰ) πρῶτα.
fitting, be ἐπέοικα, ἔοικα (*είκω).
fittingly κατὰ μοῖραν.
flashing-eyed ἑλίκωψ, ωπος, m. ;
ἑλικῶπις, ιδος, f. ; γλαυκῶπις,
ιδος, f.
flow ἐρωέω, ῥέω.
fly φεύγω.
follow ἕπομαι (with dat.).
for prep. (use dat.) ; conj. γάρ.
for this (reason) τούνεκα.
forebode ὄσσομαι.
forego μεθίημι.
fourfold τετραπλῇ.
free λύω, ἀπολύω.

353

free-shooter ἐκηβόλος, ου, ὁ; ἑκατηβε-
λέτης, ᾱο, ὁ.

free-worker ἑκάεργος, ου, ὁ.

from *use the gen.*, *or* ἐκ (ἐξ), παρά,
ἀπό (*with gen.*).

from the time when ἐξ οὗ.

fulfill τελείω.

funeral pyre πυρή, ῆς, ἡ.

G

gather (together) ἀγείρω; gather to-
gether again ἐπαγείρω; gathered
together ὁμηγερής, ές; gathered to-
gether again παλίλλογος, η, ον.

generation γενεή, ῆς, ἡ.

gift δῶρον, ου, τό; gift of honor γέ-
ρας, αος, τό; gift of prophecy μαντο-
σύνη, ης, ἡ.

girl κούρη, ης, ἡ.

give δίδωμι; ἔπορον (2d aor.).

give back ἀποδίδωμι.

give up προΐημι, ἀποδίδωμι.

gleam φαείνω.

glorious ἀγλαός, ή, όν; δῖος, α, ον.

glory κῦδος, εος, τό.

gnaw ἀμύσσω.

go βαίνω, εἶμι, ἔρχομαι, κίω; go down,
descend καταβαίνω; go on board,
go up, ascend ἀναβαίνω.

goat αἴξ, αἰγός, ὁ, ἡ.

god θεός, οῦ, ὁ.

goddess θεά, ᾶς, ἡ.

god-like δῖος, α, ον; θεοείκελος, η, ον.

gold(en), of gold χρύσεος, η, ον.

good(ly) κᾱλός, ή, όν; ἀγαθός, ή, όν;
κρήγυος, η, ον.

grant δίδωμι, ἔπορον (2d aor.).

grant in addition προτίθημι.

great μέγας, μεγάλη, μέγα; greater
μείζων, ον; greater (part) τὸ
πλεῖον.

greatly πολύ, πολλά, μάλα, μέγα.

great-souled μεγάθῡμος, η, ον.

Greek Ἀχαιός, οῦ, ὁ; Δαναός, οῦ, ὁ;
Ἀργεῖος, ου, ὁ.

grief ἄχος, εος, τό.

grieve κήδω; be grieved ἄχνυμαι, κή-
δομαι (gen.).

ground γαῖα, ης, ἡ; χθών, χθονός, ἡ.

grow weary κάμνω.

grudge κότος, ου, ὁ.

guide ἡγέομαι (dat.).

H

Hades *Ἄϊς, Ἄϊδος, ὁ.

hairy λάσιος, η, ον.

hand χείρ, χε(ι)ρός, ἡ.

hap(ly) κέ(ν), ἄν.

happily εὖ, ἐΰ.

harangue ἀγορεύω, ἀγοράομαι.

harsh ἀταρτηρός, ή, όν; κακός, ή, όν.

harshly κακῶς.

hate στυγέω.

hateful ἐχθρός, ή, όν; most hateful
ἔχθιστος, η, ον.

have ἔχω, ἴσχω.

he ὁ, ἡ, τό; αὐτός, ή, ὁ; *also implied
in the verb.*

hear *κλεύω with gen., ἀκούω.

hearken (to) συντίθημι, *κλεύω with
gen., ἀκούω.

heart κῆρ, κῆρος, τό; φρήν, φρενός, ἡ;
ἦτορ, ορος, τό; κραδίη (καρδίη), ης, ἡ.

heaven οὐρανός, οῦ, ὁ; from heaven
οὐρανόθεν.

heavy βαρύς, εῖα, ύ.

hecatomb ἑκατόμβη, ης, ἡ.

Hector Ἕκτωρ, ορος, ὁ.

heed, give heed to *κλεύω (gen.), ὄθο-
μαι (gen.).

help *χραισμέω (dat.).

her, him, it ὁ, ἡ, τό; αὐτός, ή, ὁ; μίν
(acc. only).

her (own) ὅς, ἥ, ὅν; ἑός, ἑή, ἑόν.

Hera Ἥρη, ης, ἡ.

herald κῆρυξ, ῡκος, ὁ.

here ἐνθάδε.
hero ἥρως, ωος, ὁ.
hilt κώπη, ης, ἡ.
him, her, it ὁ, ἡ, τό; αὐτός, ἡ, ὁ; μίν (acc. only).
himself, herself, itself αὐτός, ἡ, ὁ.
his, her(s), its (own) ὅς, ἥ, ὅν (ἑός, ἑή, ἑόν)
hither δεῦρο.
hold ἔχω, ἴσχω.
hold a grudge κοτέω, κότον ἔχειν.
hollow κοῖλος, η, ον.
home οἶκος, ου, ὁ; δῶμα, ατος, τό; home, at οἴκοι; home(ward) οἴκαδε, οἴκόνδε.
honey μέλι, ιτος, τό.
honor τῑμή, ῆς, ἡ; κῦδος, εος, τό; honor, do honor to τῑμάω, τίω.
horse ἵππος, ου, ὁ, ἡ.
host στρατός, οῦ, ὁ.
hot wrath χόλος, ου, ὁ.
how? πῶς.
how much ὅσ(σ)ος, η, ον.
hurl ἵημι, βάλλω; hurl upon ἐφίημι (with dat.).

I

I ἐγώ(ν), μεῦ.
Idomeneus Ἰδομενεύς, ῆος, ὁ.
if ἤν, αἰ, εἰ.
Ilium Ἴλιος, ου, ἡ.
immediately αὐτίκα, αἶψα.
impetuous πολυάϊξ, ῑκος.
implore λίσσομαι.
in ἐν(ί) (with dat.), or use simple dat.
in no wise οὐδέν (780–781).
in order that ὅπ(π)ως, ὥς, ἵνα.
in person αὐτός, ἡ, ὁ.
in single combat κατ' αὐτόν.
in sufficient numbers ἐπιτηδές.
in two ways διάνδιχα.
inferior χέρης, ες; χερείων, ον.
insolence ὕβρις, ιος, ἡ.

insult λωβάομαι, ἀτῑμά(ζ)ω.
into εἰς (ἐς) (acc.); εἴσω.
it (implied in the verb); ὁ, ἡ, τό; αὐτός, ἡ, ὁ; μίν (acc.).

J

justice θέμις, ιστος, ἡ; dispenser of justice, judge δικασπόλος, ου, ὁ.

K

keep (doing a thing), continue, use imperfect (1079).
kill ὀλέκω, ὄλλῡμι, ἀπόλλῡμι.
kindle ὀρνῡμι.
kindly disposed, be εὖ (ἐὺ) φρονέω.
king ἄναξ, ἄνακτος, ὁ; βασιλεύς, ῆος, ὁ.
know γιγνώσκω, *εἴδω.

L

lack δεύομαι (gen.).
lamb ἀρήν, ἀρνός, ὁ, ἡ.
land γαῖα, ης, ἡ.
last ὕστατος, η, ον; for the last time ὕστατα, ὕστατον (781).
later ὕστερος, η, ον.
law θέμις, ιστος, ἡ.
lawful(ly) wedded κουρίδιος, η, ον.
lay upon ἐπιφέρω (dat.).
lead, lead away ἄγω; lead the way, guide ἡγέομαι (dat.); lead upon ἀνάγω.
leader ἀριστεύς, ῆος, ὁ.
leaf φύλλον, ου, τό.
learn πυνθάνομαι, πεύθομαι.
leave λείπω.
let use subj. or imperat.; let, allow ἐάω.
Leto Λητώ, Λητόος (Λητοῦς), ἡ.
lie κεῖμαι.
lift up the voice φωνέω.
like unto, be *εἴκω (dat.).
live ζώω.

living in mountain dens (lairs) ὀρέσ-κῳος, η, ον.
locks κόμη, ης, ἡ.
loiter δηθύνω.
longer ἔτι; longer, no οὐ(κ) ἔτι.
look, look out upon δέρκομαι, ὁράω.
loom ἱστός, οὖ, ὁ.
loose λύω.
lord ἄναξ, ἄνακτος, ὁ.
lose ὄλλῡμι.
loud-roaring πολύφλοισβος, ον.
love φιλέω.
lovely φίλος, η, ον.
lying in mountain lairs ὀρέσκῳος, η, ον.

M

maiden κούρη, ης, ἡ.
make τεύχω, ποιέω.
man ἀνήρ, ἀνέρος (ἀνδρός), ὁ; ἄνθρω-πος, ου, ὁ; man, ordinary man, mere man ἄνθρωπος, ου, ὁ.
man-nourishing βωτιάνειρα (fem.).
man-slaying ἀνδροφόνος, η, ον.
many πολλός, ή, όν.
marshal(ler) κοσμήτωρ, ορος, ὁ.
may subjunct., optat.
Menelaus Μενέλᾱος, ου, ὁ.
might subjunct., optat.; μένος, εος, τό; ἴς; might, with might, mightily ἶφι.
mightier κρείσσων, ον.
mightiest κάρτιστος, η, ον.
mightily μέγα, ἶφι.
mighty μέγας, μεγάλη, μέγα.
mind φρήν, φρενός, ἡ · νόος, ου, ὁ.
more πλέων, ον; πλείων, ον.
more safe(ly) σαώτερος, η, ον.
mortal μέροψ, οπος, ὁ; βροτός, οῦ, ὁ, ἡ.
most avaricious φιλοκτεανώτατος, η, ον.
most glorious κύδιστος, η, ον.
most hateful ἔχθιστος, η, ον.

most terrible ἐκπαγλότατος, η, ον.
mother μήτηρ, μητέρος (μητρός), ἡ.
mountain ὄρος (οὖρος 571), εος, τό.
much πολλός, ή, όν; πολύς, πολλή πολύ.
mule οὐρεύς, ῆος, ὁ.
must χρή ἐστι(ν).
my ἐμός, ή, όν, used only for sake of clearness or emphasis.
Myrmidon Μυρμιδών, όνος, ὁ.

N

nail ἦλος, ου, ὁ.
native land πάτρη, ης, ἡ.
neither οὔτε; neither . . nor οὔτε . . . οὔτε; μήτε . . . μήτε.
Nestor Νέστωρ, ορος, ὁ.
never (not ever), not ever at any time οὔπω, οὔποτε.
nine days ἐννῆμαρ.
noble κᾱλός, ή, όν.
noblest ἄριστος, η, ον.
noise κλαγγή, ῆς, ἡ.
none, no one, nothing οὔτις, τι; οὐ-δείς, οὐδεμία, οὐδέν.
nor οὔτε, οὐδέ, μηδέ.
not οὐ (οὐκ, οὐχ).
now νῦν.
numbers (see in sufficient numbers).

O

O ὦ.
oarsman ἐρέτης, ᾱο, ὁ.
oath ὅρκος, ου, ὁ.
obey πείθομαι, mid. of πείθω persuade (dat.).
obtain (one's share) μείρομαι.
Odysseus Ὀδυσ(σ)εύς, ῆος, ὁ.
of (use the gen.).
offscouring λῦμα, ατος, τό.
old γεραιός, ή, όν.
old age γῆρας, αος, τό.
old man γέρων, οντος, ὁ; γεραιός, οῦ, ὁ.

Olympian Ὀλύμπιος, η, ον.
Olympus Ὄλυμπος, ου, ὁ.
on ἐπί, dat.
on account of (use gen.), εἵνεκα, ἕνεκα (gen.).
on the selfsame day αὐτῆμαρ.
once ποτέ.
one εἷς, μία, ἕν; which (one)? τίς, τί; ones . . . others οἱ μὲν . . . οἱ δέ.
openly ἄντην.
opposing ἀντίβιος, η, ον.
opposition, in ἀντιβίην.
or ἤ (ἠέ); whether . . . or εἴτε . . . εἴτε.
oracle θεοπρόπιον, ου, τό; θεοπροπίη, ης, ἡ.
orator ἀγορητής, ᾱο, ὁ.
order, give orders μῡθέομαι, κέλομαι, σημαίνω, ἐπιτέλλω, ἀνώγω.
other ἄλλος, η, ο.
our ἡμέτερος, η, ον, used only for the sake of clearness or emphasis.
ourselves ἡμεῖς, used only for the sake of clearness or emphasis.
outwit παρέρχομαι.
ox βοῦς, βοός, ὁ.

P

partake ἀντιάω.
pass away φθίνω.
peel λέπω.
people λᾱός, οῦ, ὁ.
perchance κέ(ν), πώ(ς), ἄν.
perfect τελήεις, εσσα, εν.
perform ῥέζω, τεύχω, ποιέω, ἔρδω.
perhaps κέ(ν), πού, πώς, ἄν.
perish ἀπόλλῡμι, mid.
person, in αὐτός, ή, ὁ.
persuade πείθω.
pest(ilence) λοιμός, οῦ, ὁ.
Phoebus Φοῖβος, ου, ὁ.
Phthia Φθίη, ης, ἡ.
place τίθημι; place in εἰστίθημι.

plague νοῦσος, ου, ἡ; λοιμός, οῦ, ὁ.
plan βουλή, ῆς, ἡ.
please, be pleasing ἁνδάνω (dat.).
pleasing χαρίεις, εσσα, εν.
ply ἐποίχομαι.
ponder ὁρμαίνω.
pray εὔχομαι, ἀράομαι.
prayer εὐχή, ῆς, ἡ.
prefer προβούλομαι.
prepare ἑτοιμάζω.
preserve ἐρύομαι.
Priam Πρίαμος, ου, ὁ.
priest ἀρητήρ, ῆρος, ὁ; ἱερεύς, ῆος, ὁ.
prize (of honor) γέρας, αος, τό.
produce φύω.
prophecy, gift of μαντοσύνη, ης, ἡ.
prophesy μαντεύομαι, θεοπροπέω.
prophet μάντις, ιος, ὁ.
protect ἀμφιβαίνω, ἀνάσσω.
purify (oneself) ἀπολῡμαίνομαι.
put τίθημι, βάλλω.
Pylian Πύλιος, η, ον.
Pylus Πύλος, ου, ἡ.
pyre πυρή, ῆς, ἡ.

Q

quarrel ἐρίζω; ἔρις, ιδος, ἡ.
quickly αἶψα.
quiver φαρέτρη, ης, ἡ.

R

rage μηνίω.
ransom ἄποινον, ου, τό; λύομαι.
rather than ἤ (ἠέ).
ready ὀτρηρός, ή, όν.
receive δέχομαι, ἀποδέχομαι.
recognize γιγνώσκω.
recompense τῑμή, ῆς, ἡ; ἀποτίνω τίνω.
regard ἀλεγίζω (gen.)
rejoice γηθέω, χαίρω.
release λύω, ἀπολύω.
remain μένω.

restrain ἐρητύω; ἴσχω.
return νέομαι, ἱκνέομαι; return home-
(ward) ἀπονοστέω, οἴκαδ᾽ ἱκνέομαι.
reveal ἀναφαίνω.
reverence ἅζομαι, αἰδέομαι, αἴδομαι.
revile ὀνειδίζω.
reviling ὄνειδος, εος, τό; ὀνείδειος, η, ον.
riches ἄφενος, εος, τό; πλοῦτος, ου, ὁ.
roar κλαγγή, ῆς, ἡ; ἠχή, ῆς, ἡ.
roaring ἠχήεις, εσσα, εν.
roll, curl ἑλίσσω.
roof (over) ἐρέφω.
round about περί.
rouse ἀνίστημι, ὄρνῡμι.
rule (over) ἀνάσσω (gen.), κρατέω
(gen.).
ruling κρείων, ουσα, ον.

S

sack πέρθω; sack (utterly) ἐκπέρθω,
ἐξαλαπάζω.
sacred ἱερός, ή, όν.
sacrifice ἱερόν, οῦ, τό; ἔρδω, ῥέζω.
safe(ly) σόος (σάος = σάϝος), η, ον.
safer, more safely σαώτερος, η, ον
(comp. of σάος, η, ον).
sail upon ἐπιπλέω.
sailor ἐρέτης, ᾱο, ὁ.
save σαόω.
savor κνίση, ης, ἡ.
say ἀγορεύω, φημί, εἶπον (2d aor.).
scabbard κο(υ)λεόν, οῦ, τό.
sceptre σκῆπτρον, ου, τό.
sceptre-bearing σκηπτοῦχος, η, ον.
sea θάλασσα, ης, ἡ; ἅλς, ἁλός, ὁ, ἡ; to
the sea ἅλαδε (788, 4).
seat (oneself), sit down ἕζομαι; seat
ἕδος.
see ὁράω, λεύσσω, *εἴδω.
seem εἴδομαι, *εἴκω.
seemly, be *εἴκω.
seer μάντις, ιος, ὁ; οἰωνοπόλος.
seize αἱρέω.

select κρίνω.
self αὐτός, ή, ό.
selfsame day αὐτῆμαρ.
send πέμπω, προϊάπτω, ἵημι; send
away ἀφίημι.
separate διίστημι.
shadowy σκιόεις, εσσα, εν.
shameless ἀναιδής, ές.
shamelessness ἀναιδείη, ης, ἡ.
share ἀντιάω.
sharp ὀξύς, εῖα, ύ; ἐχεπευκής, ές.
she ἡ (ὁ, ἡ, τό), αὐτή (αὐτός, ή, ό),
used only for the sake of emphasis
or clearness; implied in the ending
of the verb.
shining ἀγλαός, ή, όν.
ship νηῦς, νηός, ἡ.
shoot βάλλω.
shoulder ὦμος, ου, ὁ.
shout assent ἐπευφημέω.
silent, in silence ἀκέων, ουσα, ον.
silver, of silver ἀργύρεος, η, ον.
silver bow(ed) (of, with) ἀργυρό-
τοξος, η, ον.
since ἐπεί, ἐπειδή.
sing ἀείδω, μέλπω.
sit (down) ἧμαι, ἕζομαι, καθέζομαι.
slay ἐναρίζω.
slight ἀτῑμά(ζ)ω.
small ὀλίγος, η, ον.
Smintheus Σμινθεύς, ῆος, ὁ.
smoke καπνός, οῦ, ὁ.
so ὥς.
so great(ly) τόσ(σ)ος, η, ον.
so that ὅπ(π)ως, ὡς.
some (one) τὶς, τὶ; some . . . others
οἱ μὲν . . . οἱ δέ.
son υἱός, οῦ (ἑος, ος), ὁ; son of Atreus
Ἀτρεΐδης, ᾱο, ὁ; son of Menoetius
Μενοιτιάδης, ᾱο, ὁ; son of Peleus
Πηληιάδης, ᾱο, ὁ; son of Thestor
Θεστορίδης, ᾱο, ὁ.
soon τάχα.

soothsayer οἰωνοπόλος, ου, ὁ.
soul ψῡχή, ῆς, ἡ; θῡμός, οῦ, ὁ; φρήν, φρενός, ἡ.
speak φημί, μῡθέομαι, αὐδάω, εἴρω; εἶπον (2d aor.); speak among μετάφημι, μετέειπον (μετεῖπον) (2d aor.); speak out ἐξείρω; speak to προσεῖπον, εἶπον (2d aor.).
spear δόρυ, δουρός (δούρατος), τό.
spirit ἦτορ, ορος, τό; θῡμός, οῦ, ὁ.
splendid ἀγλαός, ή, όν.
spoke among μετεῖπον (μετέειπον).
spring up ἀνορούω.
sprout (forth) ἀναθηλέω.
stand ἵστημι.
stealthy, be κλέπτω.
stern κρατερός, ή, όν (καρτερός, ή, όν).
still ἔτι.
strand θίς, θῑνός, ἡ.
strife ἔρις, ιδος, ἡ.
strive μάρναμαι.
strong καρτερός, ή, όν (κρατερός).
stronger φέρτερος, η, ον.
struggle μογέω.
stud πείρω.
stump τομή, ῆς, ἡ.
such (as) τοῖος, η, ον.
sufficient numbers, in ἐπιτηδές.
suggest τίθημι (ἐπὶ φρεσί).
summit κάρηνον, ου, τό.
summon καλέομαι (mid. of καλέω call).
surely ἦ, δή, μέν, μήν, μά.
swear ὄμνῡμι.
sweet γλυκύς, εῖα, ύ; sweeter γλυκίων, ον.
sweet-speaking, sweet-toned ἡδυεπής, ές.
swift θοός, ή, όν; ὠκύς, εῖα, ύ.
swift-footed ποδάρκης, ες; πόδας ὠκύς, εῖα, ύ.
sword ξίφος, εος, τό; φάσγανον, ου, τό.

T

take αἱρέω; take away ἀφαιρέω; take back ἀφαιρέω; take courage θαρσέω; take up ἀναιρέω.
Talthybius Ταλθύβιος, ου, ὁ.
tarry δηθύνω.
tawny ξανθός, ή, όν.
tear δάκρυ, υος, τό.
tell μῡθέομαι, εἴρω; εἶπον (2d aor.).
temple νηός, οῦ, ὁ.
Tenedos Τένεδος, ου, ἡ.
tent κλισίη, ης, ἡ.
terrible δεινός, ή, όν; ἔκπαγλος, ον; most terrible ἐκπαγλότατος, η, ον; terribly ἐκπάγλως.
than (use gen. after comparatives) ἤ.
that (conj.) ὄφρα, ἵνα, ὅτε; (because) that ὅτε; that (pron.) κεῖνος, η, ο ((ἐ)κεῖνος, η, ο); ὁ, ἡ, τό; ὅδε, ἥδε, τόδε; ὥς.
the [ὁ, ἡ, τό] not ordinarily expressed in Homeric Greek.
their, their own; his, her, its own ἑός, ἑή, ἑόν (ὅς, ἥ, ὅν) used only for the sake of emphasis or clearness.
them plur. of ὁ, ἡ, τό; αὐτός, ή, ό.
themselves plur. of αὐτός, ή, ό.
then τότε, ἔπειτα.
there (implied in the verb); αὐτοῦ.
therefore τούνεκα.
therein ἐς, εἰς, ἐν(ί).
thereupon τότε, ἔπειτα.
these two σφωέ.
they (implied in the verb); οἱ, αἱ, τά.
thigh μηρός, οῦ, ὁ.
thigh-piece μηρίον, ου, τό.
think ὀίω (οἴω), φράζω (mid.).
third τρί(τα)τος, η, ον.
this (thing) ὁ, ἡ, τό; οὗτος, αὕτη, τοῦτο; ὅδε, ἥδε, τόδε.
though, however much πέρ.
though . . . yet δὲ . . . δέ.

threaten ἀπειλέω; threaten (against) ἐπαπειλέω.
threefold τριπλῇ.
thrice τρίς.
through διά.
throughout κατά, ἀνά.
thrust ὠθέω.
thus ὡς, οὕτω(s).
time, from the time when ἐξ οὗ.
to, toward εἰς (ἐς), ἐπί, πρός, π(ρ)οτί, εἴσω, μέχρι; or use dat.
together with ἅμα, σύν (dat.).
tongue γλῶσσα, ης, ἡ.
toward see to.
Trojan Τρωικός, ή, όν.
Trojans Τρῶες, ων, οἱ.
Troy Τροίη, ης, ἡ; Ἴλιος, ου, ἡ.
trust (in) πείθομαι (dat.).
try πειράω.
turn around μετατρέπω.
twenty (ἐ)είκοσι.
twice δίς.
two use the dual or δύο (δύω).

U

unblemished τέλειος, η, ον.
unbought ἀπρίατος, η, ον.
unransomed ἀνάποινος, η, ον.
unseemly ἀεικής, ές.
until ὄφρα.
unwilling ἀέκων, ουσα, ον.
up, up through ἀνά.
upon ἐν, ἐπί, ἀνά; use dat.
uproar κλαγγή, ῆς, ἡ.
urge ἐπισσεύω, κέλομαι.
us ἡμας (from ἐγώ).
utter μῦθέομαι.

V

valiant ἴφθῖμος, η, ον.
very πέρ, μάλα, μέγα, πολύ, πολλόν, πολλά; very mighty μέγιστος, η,

ον; κρείσσων, ον; very sacred ζάθεος, η, ον; ἠγάθεος, η, ον.
vex ἐρεθίζω, χολόω; be vexed ἄχνυμαι.
vow εὐχωλή, ῆς, ἡ.

W

war π(τ)όλεμος, ου, ὁ; π(τ)ολεμίζω.
ward off ἀμύνω, ἀπαμύνω.
warrior αἰχμητής, ᾶο, ὁ; ἥρως, ωος, ὁ.
watery ὑγρός, ή, όν.
way κέλευθος, ου, ἡ (plur. also κέλευθα, ων, τά).
we (implied in verb) ἡμεῖς.
we ourselves ἡμεῖς; αὐτοί, αἱ, ά.
wealth πλοῦτος, ου, ὁ; ἄφενος, εος, τό.
well ἐύ, εὖ.
well-balanced ἶσος, η (ἐίση), ον.
well-disposed, be ἐὺ φρονέω.
well-greaved ἐυκνήμῖς, ῖδος.
well-situated ἐὺ ναιόμενος, η, ον.
well-walled ἐυτείχεος, ον.
what ὁ, ἡ, τό; ὅς, ἥ, ὅ (rel.); what? τίς, τί (interr.).
when ὁπ(π)ότε; εὖτε; use participle.
when(ever) ὁπ(π)ότε.
which ὁ, ἡ, τό; ὅς, ἥ, ὅ (rel.); which? (one) τίς, τί (interrog.).
while ἧος (use participle).
white-armed λευκώλενος, η, ον.
who, which, what (rel.) ὅς, ἥ, ὅ; ὁ, ἡ, τό; ὅστις, ἥτις, ὅτι; ὅστε, ἥτε, ὅτε; who? which? what? (interr.) τίς, τί.
why? τί, τίπτε.
wicked κακός, ή, όν.
wife ἄλοχος, ου, ἡ.
wild beast φήρ, φηρός, ὁ, ἡ.
will βουλή, ῆς, ἡ.
willing, be ἐθέλω, βούλομαι.
wily πολύμητις, ιος.
win, strive to ἄρνυμαι.
winged πτερόεις, εσσα, εν.

wise, in no οὔτι, οὐδέν (780–781).

wish βούλομαι, ἐθέλω.

with σύν, ἅμα (dat.); use dat.

within ἐν, ἔνδοθι, εἴσω.

without a prize of honor ἀγέραστος, η, ον.

woe ἄλγος, εος, τό; πένθος, εος, τό.

word ἔπος, εος, τό.

worse ῥίγιων, ον.

worthless οὐτιδανός, ή, όν.

would use optat. or subj.

wrath μῆνις, ιος, ἡ; χόλος, ου, ὁ; μένος, εος, τό.

Y

yea ναί.

yearning ποθή, ῆς, ἡ.

yet ἔτι.

yield ὑπείκω.

you (yourself) σύ, σεῖο, used only for the sake of emphasis or clearness · otherwise implied in the verb.

young νέος, η, ον; younger νεώτερος, η, ον.

your σός, σή, σόν; ὑμέτερος, η, ον; used only for the sake of emphasis or clearness.

Z

zealous(ly) πρόφρων, ον.

Zeus Ζεύς, Διός, ὁ.

Zeus-nourished διοτρεφής, ές.